Earthly Delights

Earthly Delights

Rosalind Creasy

Illustrated by Marcie Hawthorne

Sierra Club Books

San Francisco

This book is dedicated to Robert,
with whom I have shared
the delights of this earth.

Printed and bound in the United States of America by The Kingsport Press, an Arcata Graphics company. Color photo sections printed by Dai Nippon Printing Company, Ltd., Tokyo, Japan.
10 9 8 7 6 5 4 3 2 1

A Yolla Bolly Press Book

Earthly Delights was produced in association with the publisher at The Yolla Bolly Press, Covelo, California. Editorial and design staff: James and Carolyn Robertson, Barbara Youngblood, Aaron Johnson, and Juliana Yoder.

The Sierra Club, founded in 1892 by John Muir, has devoted itself to the study and protection of the earth's scenic and ecological resources—mountains, wetlands, woodlands, wild shores and rivers, deserts and plains. Its publications are part of the nonprofit effort the club carries on as a public trust. There are more than fifty chapters coast to coast, in Canada, Hawaii, and Alaska. For information about how you may participate in the club's programs to enjoy and preserve wilderness and the quality of life, please address inquiries to Sierra Club, 730 Polk Street, San Francisco, California 94109.

Library of Congress Cataloging in Publication Data

Creasy, Rosalind.
Earthly delights.

"A Yolla Bolly Press book."
Bibliography: p. 189
Includes index.
1. Gardening. 2. Gardening—United States.
I. Title.
SB453.C775 1985   635   84-23517
ISBN 0-87156-841-1
ISBN 0-87156-840-3 (pbk.)

Grateful acknowledgment is made to the following people for permission to reprint photographs and illustrations: pages 29 (top right) and 42, photos by Kit Anderson; page 29 (bottom), photo by Robert L. Carissimi; page 30 (top), photo by Jean Halama; page 32 (bottom left), photo by John Earl; pages 36 and 155, illustrations by Aaron Johnson; page 79, photo by Dave Schaefer, courtesy of Gardens For All; page 84, photo by John Withee; page 93, photo by Ann Cooper; page 97 (top), photo by Erwin Bauer; page 97 (bottom right), photo by Keith Logan; page 99 (bottom left), photo courtesy of Rod McLellan Company; page 131, photo courtesy of Gardens For All; page 138, illustration courtesy of All-America Selections; pages 146, 168 (top left), 174, and 177, photos by Michael Thompson; page 168 (bottom right), photo by Kate Gessert; back cover and back flap, photo by Robert Creasy.

Camassia Leichtlinii

Captions for full-page photographs: page ii, herb vinegars at Caprilands in Coventry, Connecticut; page iv, Rosalind Creasy's pleasure garden in northern California; page 44, Karla Patterson of the Morton Arboretum in Lisle, Illinois; page 76, a beautiful example of Hopi blue corn, strawberry popcorn, and the result of cross-pollination between sweet corn and Hopi blue corn; page 146, Joe Gessert is looking for fish in the backyard water garden; page 158, this Park Seed Company demonstration garden shows that many flowers and vegetables can be grown in a small area; and page 174, Kate and Sarah Gessert are harvesting from their cottage garden.

Contents

Introduction 1

Part One: Ecosystem Gardens 5
The Meadow Garden 23
The Woodland Garden 35
The Prairie Garden 45
The Chaparral Garden 55

Part Two: Ark Gardens 67
The Heirloom Vegetable Garden 77
The Wildlife Garden 89
The Heritage Rose Garden 107
The Orchid Garden 117

Part Three: Pleasure Gardens 127
The Gourmet Garden 133
The Child's Garden 147
The Moneysaving Garden 159
The Cottage Garden 175

Acknowledgments 183
Bibliography 187
Index 192

Introduction

Imagine that you get out of bed one summer Saturday morning and *don't* say to yourself, "I guess I'll have to spend two hours mowing and edging the lawn, and, darn it, the roses need spraying, and the hedge needs clipping again." Instead, you wander, with a cup of tea in hand, out onto the back patio to see if the kiwi vine has set fruit or if any strawberries are ripe enough to put on your cereal. While out in back you smell the fragrant Damask rose that never needs spraying and listen to a woodpecker drumming in the background. As you putter around, you see which flowers are available for that night's party as well as share a moment with your child, watching a black and yellow caterpillar eat the dill and wondering if the swallowtail butterfly it is to become will stay in your yard or flit away to someone else's.

Sound idyllic? Maybe too much so to be convincing? Before I present my case for this livable garden, let's take a look at the bottom line: the financial and emotional toll modern landscaping fashion exacts. Today's typical yard—with its traditional, large lawn, its mandatory evergreens across the front of the house, and its few street trees—if shored up with a sit-on mower, electric trimmers, and bags of fertilizers and herbicides, or a maintenance service that brings in all that stuff, is one of the most unrewarding, resource-consuming, and expensive yards imaginable.

Locked into this vision of what a yard should be, homeowners don't realize that their landscapes are costing them thousands of dollars a year—not only in expenditures but in losses resulting from poor solar design. These barren yards "cost" us money by failing to lower air-conditioning bills by shading south walls from the summer sun and by failing to cut our heating bills with well-placed evergreens that serve as windbreaks. Further, these yards saddle us with any number of boring, repetitive chores and yield very little pleasure—not to mention their failure to produce food and flowers for the table.

Gardeners of this traditional style are more apt to spend their time trying to figure out why the lawn has dead spots or what disease afflicts the roses than enjoying a bird's song or taking pleasure in the progress of the native wildflowers they saved from the snowplow's blade last fall. In this all-too-typical scenario, our yards have become just one more set of chores, right up there with cleaning the oven and changing the oil in the car, one more source of worry, and one more drain on the pocketbook. Thus, Part One of this book encourages readers to pull back and let the natural habitat be part of the garden. Instead of continually trying to enforce an artificial man-made system, it encourages you to design your garden more in concert with nature and the habitat that existed before your garden was installed. A number of different approaches are explored. For instance, homeowners in the Midwest and parts of the Northeast and Northwest, where meadows and prairies are indigenous, can enhance a small lawn with a meadow or prairie garden, thus cutting down on maintenance and giving the family an area to enjoy the parade of seasons. In forested habitats, yards that carve out woodland gardens require less maintenance too, and the owners can watch the bustle of nest building and enjoy a cool place to sit on a steamy August day. Gardeners on the West Coast can cut down on watering by putting in a jewel-colored chaparral garden in a silvery setting.

Part Two portrays the garden as an ark. The concept is Noah's Ark, with a difference: the ship is made of soil, not wood, and the beings ensconced there against the dangers of the outside world are primarily plants and seeds, not animals. Readers will find information on how to identify both wild and domestic species in danger and how to save them, both as growing plants and as seeds. These ideas are so fundamental and simple they have formed the basis of our agricultural heritage from time immemorial, but restating them in the context of the modern world inspires excitement and new resolve. Heritage societies and seed banks are forming in many communities across the country, and they are circulating species of flowers, vegetables, and fruits that have been out of common view for a long time. Readers of this section will find many practical suggestions for turning their gardens into lush and fruitful arks.

In Part Two we look more closely at the damages already sustained by the web of life with which we share the world's resources. In the process this section addresses the gardener whose bent is to roll up the sleeves and *work*. Whereas restoring and maintaining natural ecosystems require a relative lack of intervention compared with traditional landscaping methods, actively seeking solutions to existing environmental problems takes energy and involvement.

The problem Part Two tackles is the most critical of all the environmental issues we face: the permanent extinction of more and more species of plant and animal life, resulting from pollution and the dismantling of natural ecosystems. Many forms of life are already gone forever, but countless more are in danger of being lost. Gardeners with the interest and energy—and knowledge, too, for one must be able to identify and nurture an endangered species either in the wild or in the garden in order to save it—can make a tremendous difference in this regard. Gardeners interested in coming aboard this ark can choose among gardens filled with heirloom vegetables such as 'Jacob's Cattle' bean and purple broccoli; wildlife habitats filled with plants for birds and butterflies; heritage rose gardens bursting with roses called 'Maiden's Blush', 'Austrian Copper', and 'Belinda'; and a windowsill orchid garden filled with chartreuse, crystalline yellow, and showy bronze blooms.

Part Three, Pleasure Gardens, is the bold effort to take on the Puritan work ethic. The guiding principle there is the restatement of a famous presidential quote: "Ask not what you can do for your garden, but what your garden can do for you." The idea is that gardening need not be an obligation or a chore; it can be primarily a source of relaxation, enjoyment, even therapy, if we toss out the "thou shalts" and create exactly the kinds of gardens we want. Thus, cooks can plant gourmet gardens —even further, Chinese cooks can plant Chinese gourmet gardens; Italian cooks, Italian gardens. Gardeners who want the garden to help save money can put in a moneysaving garden. Parents who long to spend some time relaxing with their small children can make children's gardens with their offspring; and those of you who long to kick off your shoes and just plain enjoy life in the garden can put in a pleasure border filled with fragrance, bright colors, succulent foods for the table, and edible flowers. Forget fashion, forget the tyranny of the lawn and shrub border. Think about what you like to do in life and plant a garden to match.

I have a dream, a dream that the American yard will be redefined. Instead of a piece of mandatory lawn stretching from sea to shining sea, choices will be made. On the one hand, homeowners who want less involvement will choose gardens that require less maintenance and yards that serve as depositories for native plants and animals. On the other hand, homeowners who glory in gardening will choose to use their energy to nurture some of the endangered wild and domestic plants. And, finally, I dream that the yard will be redefined to be an opportunity to partake of the earth's greatest treasure: the rich diversity of species, of which we are only one.

PART ONE

ECOSYSTEM GARDENS

What did the land look like before your home was built on it? Was it a meadow filled with milkweed and goldenrod? a pine forest alive with the chatter of jays? a prairie or a sage-filled chaparral? Did an elk migration path cross your front yard? Did a rare lady's-slipper grow there, or a native Franklinia tree now never found in the wild? Whatever your land looked like once upon a time, it is certain that workers showed up one day with a shovel or bulldozer and leveled part of that area to bare dirt. How much they leveled varied from lot to lot, but no matter how little earth was disturbed to situate the house, the first step had been taken toward creating a suburban, people-oriented ecosystem and permanently altering the existing natural environment.

Occasionally, after a house is built, the surrounding flora is allowed to close back in around it, but that is certainly the exception. In most cases new landscapes are designed in keeping with prevailing fashions. And for the better part of the past two centuries, those fashions have favored "immigrant" plants and human-made hybrids—varieties created by breeders—over naturally occurring species. Thus, while most American yards contain a tree or two left over from the undeveloped days, such as a maple, magnolia, or oak, the majority of plants in the American garden never would have grown there naturally. Our yards are melting-pot ecosystems: hydrangeas, rhododendrons, and chrysanthemums from the Orient; apples, irises, and daffodils from Europe; acacias and eucalyptuses from Australia; gladiolus and even so-called Kentucky bluegrass from Africa. All are immigrants.

Most of us, although surrounded by such people-created, artificial ecosystems, have never evaluated their function or questioned their long-term impact on our lives and the environment. When our population was smaller and life was less complex, when gasoline was cheaper and chemical pollution was not a problem, when numerous habitats and species weren't endangered, there were fewer reasons to question the validity of the "exotic" approach. Now, however, people of many different disciplines, philosophies, and lifestyles are questioning the appropriateness of some of our traditional landscaping techniques and styles.

In response we are developing new landscape techniques, sometimes referred to as *natural gardening* or *ecoscaping*. These developing responses cover a great range of involvement with the natural, occurring habitat. For example, some homeowners are choosing to modify a traditional yard by including a few native plants; some are choosing to enhance and modify an existing habitat, combining the natives with a small lawn and a flower border; still others are enjoying the challenge of trying to reestablish, as closely as possible, a meadow, prairie, woodland, or chaparral area, whichever habitat would have been there eons ago. Though these approaches vary in labor intensity, they all take as their theme the native ecosystem that existed prior to human development of the land.

Enhancing and modifying the existing habitat instead of putting in an artificial one have some practical advantages for the homeowner. Usually the more closely the landscaping reflects the natural landscape, the less maintenance and expense for the homeowner. Also, by eliminating many of the nagging chores, such as having to spray the roses or water the begonias and the lawn, you will have more time for a pleasurable involvement with your yard. As an added bonus, because so much of suburbia is building-coded into conformity, natural landscapes can give you a yard where the plants, and even the style, can be as different as you want from your neighbors'.

Certainly, on a day-to-day level these reasons for "going native" are convincing enough. In addition, consider the long-range values if you feel strongly about the direction things are taking on a global scale. Will our grandchildren have to take their children to nature centers to view a few of the rare remaining robins, say, or monarch butterflies? We ourselves must already depend on books to see and show our children a substantial number of plant and animal species that are gone forever. By landscaping with an eye to restoring and preserving our natural ecosystems, and by stemming the tide of bluegrass that threatens to stretch from coast to coast, we can, with appropriate alterations to create niches for ourselves, make safe corners here and there in which indigenous plants and animals can thrive. Each household's contribution may be small, indeed, but the combined effort could mean the continued existence of many habitats and the living things that depend on them.

Native Plants

There is a shopping center called The Oaks in our neighborhood. It derived its name from the magnificent native oak trees incorporated in the design. The oaks could not take the urbanized treatment and they died, so the center is now just a barren expanse of asphalt. In New England I've seen the Blueberry Farms housing development, where there's nary a blueberry bush to be seen. I've begun to think of these earthy touches by the developers in their project names as nostalgia, at best, and, at worst, as nasty jokes on the victims of their zeal. Native plants and the animals that depend on them are disappearing at the hand of

NATIVE PLANT COMMUNITIES

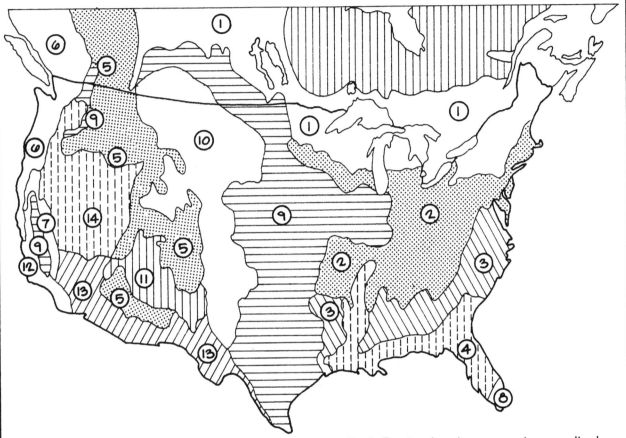

1. Northern mixed forest
2. Eastern deciduous forest
3. Southeastern mixed forest
4. Outer coastal plain forest
5. Rocky mountain forest
6. Pacific forest
7. Sierra cascade forest
8. True subtropical
9. Tall-grass prairie
10. Short-grass prairie
11. Pinon-juniper woodland
12. Coastal chaparral
13. Warm desert
14. Cold desert

To choose the native plants for your ecosystem garden, you must first determine in which kind of habitat you live. Look over this map to see which ecosystem is dominant for your area. As you can see, the primary ecosystem of the Northeast and the Northwest is a woodland. But just knowing you are in a woodland ecosystem is not enough; there are hardwood maple forests as well as coniferous forests. Also, interspersed among woodland areas are clearings we call meadows: some are boggy, others are dry.

The ecosystem of the greater part of our heartland is the prairie. Prairie ecosystems become more and more arid the farther west they are, so prairies are described as dry-land or wet-land prairies. While some of the arid West could be classified as desert—complete with cactuses and roadrunners—there, too, one finds great variation. For instance, there is scrub oak chaparral as well as a similar habitat of pinon pine and rabbitbrush. Desert areas, marshes, bayous, tropical rain forests, and beachside sand dunes represent other ecosystems in this country. For further detailed information about your own ecosystem, consult the books recommended at the ends of the chapters on ecosystem gardens and inquire at local nurseries, universities, and native plant societies.

man at an alarming rate. Every year greater numbers are added to the endangered species list. The United States already lists 1,400 endangered species.

To ponder the reasons that native plants have been ignored and underutilized is an interesting philosophical exercise. After all, European gardens are filled with California poppies, lupines, Michaelmas daisies, Monterey cypress, penstemons, columbines, Oregon grape, and Virginia creeper. It appears that on both sides of the Atlantic the status of those who could afford landscaped yards was enhanced by the inclusion of exotic imported plants.

Perhaps that's less than generous. It may well be that the early settlers who came to this country were a bit homesick and wanted to be surrounded by plants from their homeland. Or perhaps they brought with them plants they knew how to grow. For whatever reason they favored the imports, it's particularly ironic that Americans have never paid much attention to native species, since we have one of the most varied floras from which to choose.

Our great diversity of climates and geology has created an incredible array of plants: from lady's-slipper orchids, sword ferns, and blueberries, through yuccas and magnolias, to the giant redwoods. Geography is one reason for our great diversity, but another is weather. North America was less affected by the ice ages than were many other parts of the world. The advancing ice stopped short of our southern waters, enabling our plant species to survive and, after the ice retreated, reestablish their old territories. As a result, we have one of the world's most diversified floras.

Note: It is critical to choose the right plant for the climate. The zone map on page 186 will help you select plants that will grow successfully in your yard. The map, adapted from a map prepared by the U.S. Department of Agriculture, delineates hardiness zones and is used consistently by nurseries, seed companies, and almost all gardening books.

Because native plants have been undervalued for years in this country, information on growing them has been relatively sparse and suppliers have virtually ignored them. When natives were stocked, there were often problems: some are hard to germinate, nobody knew how to grow some of them, and, most important, consumers didn't buy them. Nursery people in the West had additional problems because many western natives are particularly challenging to grow in containers because they are usually drought tolerant with deep root systems that cannot withstand being confined or overwatered.

The new interest shown by home landscapers in environmental quality, resource conservation, and cost effectiveness, as well as gardeners' boredom with overdressed petunias, has kindled a nationwide interest in native plants. People concerned about maintenance costs and gardening time are attracted to native plants because, as a rule, once established, these plants can be easier to care for than many of the imported or hybridized varieties. They have evolved and adapted to native soils and climates—certainly no one visits the wild black-eyed susans or jack-in-the-pulpits with a watering can and a bag of fertilizer. In addition, such plants have struck their own balance with the indigenous insects and diseases, so they rarely need spraying. (They do, of course, have problems with introduced pests such as gypsy moths and Japanese beetles.) In fact, natives are sometimes considered hard to grow because most don't like to be fussed over, watered, and fertilized: they sometimes die from too much care.

Furthermore, an "official" expertise in natives is growing apace. Botanists, conservationists, and government officials concerned about our diminishing plant communities have become interested in preserving some of the nation's diverse habitats, be it a section of virgin prairie or a part of The Everglades. They have funneled energy and money into learning about native plants and disseminating information on them. Consequently, quite a bit of material is now available from government agencies. Help is also available from interested horticulturists, universities, native plant nurseries, and—probably of most value to the home gardener—numerous native plant societies whose plant mavens can advise home gardeners on what to grow, where to plant it, and how to take care of it. These dedicated native plant lovers will sometimes even share seeds and plants with gardeners who are sure to plant and care for them.

Working with Native Plants

From the new wealth of material, we can glean a few basic guidelines for working with native plants.

1. Even though a plant may be native to your area, it may not do well in your yard. Your soil could be quite different from that of your neighbor only a few hundred feet away, as could be the drainage and exposure to cold winds. Get to know your particular mini-climate. Compare notes with other gardeners in your area. Do the same plants grow well? Does your yard have any unusual characteristics? For instance, if your yard is situated on a hill or in a gully, if your soil seems much more acidic, sandy, or claylike than surrounding properties, have an extension agent or local university help you choose native plants for your yard.

2. You can't always determine what is native to your area by observing what is growing nearby because many species brought from other parts of the world have escaped and taken up lodging in our woods, meadows, and grasslands. The discussion of weeds in this section describes many of the introduced plants. Books about native plants for your area usually tell which plants are indigenous and sometimes describe introduced species.

3. Some native plants have very specific growing requirements and are not domesticated like some of our commonly grown garden plants. (Analogous is the situation of keeping wild and domestic animals: the koala bear eats only a specific type of eucalyptus, but domesticated cows and sheep, long selected by humans for their adaptability, eat different kinds of grasses from all over the world.) Many of our domesticated plants are adaptable to a wide range of conditions; still others have been selected to be compatible to human environments, whether it be air pollution, road salt, or lawn-water runoff. However, many native plants are very adaptable: Jerusalem artichokes, goldenrod, coreopsis, gaillardia, Douglas fir, and Lawson cypress, for example, grow over a wide range. Still, thousands aren't adaptable. Again, therefore, I emphasize that you must do your homework and find out the specifics about your garden—its soil, climate, and drainage—and get the native plants that are suited to it.

4. If you want many different native plants in your yard, you will have to seek them out. Often you will have to obtain them from friends or contact native plant nurseries for plants and seeds.

5. Do not dig up a plant in the wild unless it is being threatened in some direct way, such as by a building project or a snowplow. Do not collect seeds without permission, and never take all of the seeds: leave some for the habitat. (See the information in Ark Gardens on how to avoid purchasing plants that are illegally taken from the wild and the information in the section on how to rescue native plants.)

Unless you live in an unusually pristine area, even with the most conscientious of efforts you will not be able to exactly duplicate what was naturally there. The chances are that when your house and driveway went in, topsoil was removed or compacted; or maybe a concrete mixer was emptied into the ground, and the diluted cement changed the pH; or perhaps a marsh was drained. In addition, you or previous homeowners may have applied herbicides or planted invasive species such as honeysuckle, barberry, or Bermuda grass, all of which can make returning the site to its previous condition a formidable task.

Another important consideration is that *you* have specific requirements; your yard is for you and your family as well as for providing a habitat for other living things. Perhaps you have a nonnative wisteria or European birch that gives you great visual pleasure or shades the house in summer, a plant you would miss if you took it out. Houses surrounded by prairies, meadow grasses, or chaparral need a lush, green, fireproof buffer. Homes completely surrounded by woodlands, with trees planted up to the house, can be cold and make you feel confined. In addition, babies can't crawl in the arctostaphylos, and you can't play badminton in the wild strawberries.

Setting Your Goals

To begin your landscape project, you must set goals. Your goals could be any or all of the following: to have a low-maintenance yard, to save money, to help preserve some of the area's vanishing plants and animals, to learn about your environment, to spend more time relaxing with the children, to use fewer resources, to have a more unusual yard. Be aware when setting your goals that many of these goals are interdependent. Also, you should realize that these landscapes will need more maintenance at the beginning, before the plants fill in, than they will after they are well established. In order to save money, you may want to spend time locating seeds in the wild instead of buying them.

Another part of the planning process is to develop realistic expectations. Meadows pictured on calendars and seed packets knock your eyes out with what's called "lollipop color," great swaths of red or orange poppies, mounds of butterfly weed and coneflowers, or fields of

blue lupines. However, in real life, those spectacular shows are very unusual; to duplicate them takes more effort than to have just an average meadow. If you want to have great swaths of color in your meadow, you will have to mow it occasionally, weed out particularly invasive species, overseed it with a wildflower mix, and probably water it. (Nature generally gives her biggest flower shows only in wet years.) Meadows and wildflower gardens aren't the only landscape situations where we like pizzazz. Most of us also like natural landscapes to have a big show. Instead of purely green woodland walks, we like banks of blooming laurel or azaleas; a small waterfall is nice too. Traditionally landscaped yards, whether filled with exotics or natives, usually have more color and more plants of unusual shapes than natural ones because the plants have been chosen to stand out. Nursery catalogs offer an array of plants that have the biggest, showiest blooms and the most varied colors. Let's face it, most of us like nature with the volume turned up. Hence, one decision you will have to make is how much of a purist you want to be. Your options range from populating your yard with only indigenous species to putting a few particularly showy native shrubs and trees around your lawn.

Maintenance

Maintenance is synonymous with "putting your finger in the dike of succession." No matter what degree of involvement you choose to have with your yard, there are a few basic concepts that these more natural forms of landscaping involve. Ecosystems of all types change —they are dynamic. Homeowners try to stop the process: we put our fingers in the dike, and we call it "maintenance." We pull out the oak seedling that the squirrel planted, we prune the ivy, and we mow the grass. However, if people were removed from the earth, a hundred years from now our houses would be obliterated by ivy, oak trees, honeysuckle, and thousands of other species. When uninterrupted by humans, over the years a meadow often becomes a woodland, a young pine forest might mature to a mixed-hardwood forest, and bogs fill up to become meadows. This phenomenon is called *succession*. The implications of succession for the homeowner who wants a natural landscape are many. For instance, if you want to convert your lawn area to a woodland, you are trying to compress a long evolutionary process into a few years. You will have to make some compromises and make sure a number of soil and moisture conditions that support woodlands are available, as well as wait to put in shade-loving, understory plants until the trees have grown for a while. Those homeowners who want a wildflower meadow or prairie will have to control the encroachment of shrubs and trees. Almost all homeowners will have to contend with many herbaceous plants, most of which we refer to as weeds. Herbaceous plants can be considered the pioneers of ecological succession; they are usually the first species to grow in a cleared or disturbed area. Some are indigenous, but, increasingly, particularly in suburban areas, they are introduced species that are even more aggressive than native ones. These aggressive annual and perennial plants

Kudzu, *Pueraria lobata*, from Japan has become a "green cancer," often growing seventy-five feet in a season, smothering hundreds of native plants.

need control in any meadow, prairie, woodland, or arid-climate garden until you have established a fairly stable habitat.

Planning Your Landscape

Scan the map and determine your ecological region; then, to get your first taste of landscaping with natives, turn to the chapter in Part One that most closely corresponds to your region.

In most parts of the country, slightly modifying your existing yard by adding a few native plants takes little more effort than going to your local nursery and asking someone there to recommend a selection. A more ambitious effort, taking out some of the lawn and replacing it with a section of meadow or prairie plants or augmenting your arid hillside with some choice chaparral plants, will require some research, into both your own ecosystem and the sources for some of the more unusual plants.

However, it is this middle ground that I have outlined in detail in The Woodland Garden, The Meadow Garden, The Prairie Garden, and The Chaparral Garden.

To make much more ambitious changes in your yard, such as replacing large parts of your nonnative yard and closely approximating what was there originally or starting out with a piece of bare ground, you will need much more direction than this book can give. For help on such large-scale natural landscaping, you will need to acquaint yourself with information on plant communities, concepts of climax vegetation and succession, and basic botany. In addition, you will need information on drainage, soil types, and basic design. Armed with some basic botany and microclimate information to identify your original environment, you can examine your particular goals and landscaping needs in the context of your native ecosystem.

Use the book list at the end of this introduction to Part One to do some reading on your particular region. Don't be discouraged; helpful people and information are available.

Weed or Native Plant, Friend or Foe?

Ecoscaping is not just an excuse to let your yard "go to the dogs." Untended land, particularly in suburban areas, fills up with blown-in newspapers, sow thistles, and old tires and can become a neighborhood nuisance. Ecoscaping is an active process, and even though it is low maintenance, it requires some well-timed tasks and supervision to make your yard attractive. It is *low* maintenance, not *no* maintenance. An important maintenance task, as any gardener knows, is guarding against those intrusive species known as weeds.

Weeds, weeds, weeds. Ask people to name a weed and the odds are overwhelming that they will name the dandelion. How many hours of toil, tons of herbicides, and millions of dollars have gone toward obliterating this cheerful survivor. Herbicide advertisements and media emphasis on pristine lawns and flowerbeds have focused our attention on the dandelion and other herbaceous plants that invade lawns, flowerbeds, and waste areas. Sadly for wild plants, this media blitz has given us a very limited view of weeds.

What is a weed anyway? The usual definition is: Any plant that is out of place. But when people think of weeds, they usually think of them as "out of place" in a lawn, a garden, or an agricultural setting. Well, many of them are, but we must think of weeds in a more global way; that is, plants that are out of place in a wild ecosystem. The fact is that millions of acres of natural areas are as overrun with weeds as are the most weedy vegetable gardens or lawns. Our mindset about weeds, that is, only plants that are out of place in cultivated areas, is so strong that I've unnerved friends and relatives while driving or walking through so-called wild areas by giving a running patter of the names of all the invading species, nonnative plants that have escaped the confines of a cultivated plot. Suburbia, too, is overrun. Half the trees, it seems, that abut the famous Merritt Parkway in Connecticut are escaped ailanthus—the tree in the title *A Tree Grows in Brooklyn*, which came from China. Square miles of the Southeast are covered with what's referred to as the "green cancer," kudzu. This vine, imported from Japan, first as an ornamental, then by some well-meaning government officials who used it for erosion control, can sometimes grow seventy-five feet in one season. It climbs over and smothers whole stands of trees and obliterates habitats. There are virtually no controls, chemical or biological, and kudzu marches along "eating up" the South.

Scotch broom, Japanese honeysuckle, and lantana are plants that evoke strong emotions. For many gardeners they elicit pleasure because they bloom so effortlessly; to a member of the native plant society or to a farmer they are often a scourge. Homeowners, gardeners, nurseries, landscape architects, even park department personnel have long examined only one side of the equation—is it pretty? The other side of the equation has to be: Does the plant benefit or hurt any aspects of the environment? The ornamental gardener has no idea what mayhem some of his treasured plants cause. Just as many rural dog owners don't know that their pet dogs run in packs occasionally and kill deer and the neighbors' chickens, so home gardeners are oblivious to the damage done by some of their plants. Farmers use tons of herbicide trying to control escaped lantana in Florida and honeysuckle in the Northeast; square miles of native plants and the animals that depend on them are annihilated because gardeners are enchanted by purple loosestrife, as well as many, many more lovely but—to the native species—deadly plants. With many of the weed species it is like closing the barn door after the horse is gone; already hundreds of square miles of lantana, kudzu, and Scotch broom are out of control. The aim here is to help contain some of these species and not add to the problem. Take purple loosestrife, for example; yesterday a catalog arrived in my mail advertising wildflower seed mixes. There it was—touted as a great, easy-to-grow wildflower for meadows and landscaping use— 250,000 seeds for $10. And it was in most of the seed mixes as well. I shudder when I think of the hundreds of acres of native vegetation and the species that depend on them that will be obliterated!

Home gardens are not the only source of invasive weed species. Agriculture and the government have unwittingly done their share —maybe even our beloved Johnny Appleseed is suspect because there are thickets of wild apples crowding out their neighbors in parts of the Northeast. Everyone must share the responsibility for altering native habitat, and because there are so many millions of us now, everyone, including the home gardener, must take responsibility for halting the spread of invasive species.

When I was visiting the Citrus Arboretum in Orlando, Florida, I was told that almost half of the herbicide used in Florida citrus orchards is used to control lantana. Since lantana is such a noxious weed, you would think that it would not be sold in nurseries. Not so! In the West, native plant societies schedule weekend outings to kill rampant Scotch broom, and while members are out trying to eradicate the plant, they drive past nurseries selling it. Farmers in the East battle Japanese honeysuckle. Again, you would think honeysuckle would not be sold in nurseries, but it is!

The numbers of introduced ornamental plants that are growing out of control are legion: English ivy is climbing up into trees and covering the ground in the Northwest; Oriental bittersweet, sometimes called the "strangler of the North," marches across the Northeast; Scotch broom and pampas grass infiltrate miles of California's most scenic route, Highway 1; and in the warm climates of Florida and Hawaii, where freezing temperatures do not cut down the invading armies, the most notorious weeds, like hybrid lantana, Brazilian pepper, casuarina, and melaleuca (punk tree), go berserk. It is estimated that fully 16 percent of the plants in southern Florida are nonnative! Some of these often-attractive invaders are so ubiquitous that they have been given deceiving local names; for instance, Brazilian pepper is commonly referred to as "Florida holly."

The sad fact is that although we have been conditioned to see dandelions in the lawn, pigweed in the vegetable rows, and grass in the farmer's field as negative, we have been conditioned to see Oriental bittersweet, multiflora roses, and Scotch broom as beautiful; and almost as if to prove their value, you can go to the nursery and pay $5 for one in a container. We must not continue to compound the problem; otherwise, the habitats of this nation will lose their diversity.

Above The cajeput tree, *Melaleuca quinquenervia,* which was introduced from arid Australia many years ago now grows rampant in Florida. Often the trees are only two to three feet apart, completely obliterating square miles of native plants in the water-rich environment of The Everglades. While this problem has existed for years, only recently has the sale of the cajeput tree been prohibited in Florida.

Left In contrast, melaleuca varieties growing in arid California are welcome, well-behaved additions to the landscape. Because individual species behave differently in different ecosystems, it is imperative that you become acquainted with the plants that can become a problem in your area.

Controlling Weeds

If you are gardening with a thought to the environment, the issue of escaped plants becomes very tricky. Environmental gardening often means choosing plants that need little coddling with fertilizers, irrigation, and pesticides. (If you are gardening on a city lot, far from any natural vegetation, the problem of which plants become problems is moot; but if you are adjacent to a wild area, the problem is one that should give you cause to do some research.) The problem is that some plants that are easy to grow are *so* vigorous that they become a problem in themselves. Therefore, one of the questions you should ask yourself before you choose a plant for your yard is: Does it grow *too* well? You will have to judge at what point a vigorous grower becomes a rampant weed that crowds out native vegetation in your area. To determine that, look around and try to identify some of the introduced species you see. It is difficult to find people who are well informed and can advise you about local invasive species, although some local extension agents and university environmental studies people may be able to give you an idea. Most nurseries and seed companies, in my experience have been hair-pullingly frustrating to deal with on the subject. They are either oblivious to the problem or will say, "Hey, that's business. If I don't sell Scotch broom in California, someone else will. The public wants it."

Here are some guidelines for approaching the problem of identifying and controlling weeds.

1. *Very* carefully examine recommended plant lists that are circulated by well-meaning agencies and organizations. The water department, for example, publishes lists of drought-tolerant plants, but on the list will be plants such as Scotch broom, pampas grass, and pennisetum grass, all of which are very invasive

species. Organizations interested in birds often publish lists of species that provide shelter and food for birds. Many of the serious pest plants, while they do provide food for birds, are spread by birds and crowd out native plants that are food for butterflies, bumblebees, and small mammals. Frequently listed are such offenders as multiflora roses, blackberries, Oriental bittersweet, Brazilian pepper, and honeysuckle. In both of these examples, unfortunately, the people putting together the lists were looking only at one part of the environmental problem.

2. Beware when a garden book warns you that a particular plant may seed itself and become a pest. These plants should be used only with discretion.

3. Examine the composition of a wildflower mix before you order it. Does it contain the seeds of any problem ornamentals?

4. Look around your garden and see if you have any plants that are creating a problem.

5. Plants don't have to be exotic to become a problem. Some of this country's native plants, such as cattails and milkweed, can become invasive if they are planted in certain areas of the country or near a well-tended garden area.

6. A plant such as Brazilian pepper, which is invasive in Florida, can be well behaved in another climate, in northern California, for example.

Green Invaders

I have put together a list of some of the worst offenders for different parts of the country. It is by no means comprehensive, and many plants will respond differently from one area to another. Therefore, some of the plants on this list may be all right in your yard but not in most. Aside from avoiding the plants on this list, the most important thing you can do is to be aware that some of the lovely plants you see around you every day, when seen from a global point of view, make the lowly dandelion a pushover.

Northeast, Middle Atlantic, and Parts of the Midwest

Japanese barberry, *Berberis Thunbergii*
Japanese honeysuckle, *Lonicera japonica*
Multiflora rose, *Rosa multiflora*
Oriental bittersweet, *Celastrus orbiculatus*
Purple loosestrife, *Lythrum Salicaria*
Yellow bedstraw, *Galium verum*

Northwest

Bracken fern, *Pteridium aquilinum*
Cattail, *Typha latifolia*
English daisy, *Bellis perennis*
English ivy, *Hedera Helix*
Foxglove, *Digitalis purpurea*
Goldenrod, *Solidago canadensis*
Ground ivy, *Glechoma hederacea*
Himalayan blackberry, *Rubus procerus*
Hypericum, *Hypericum calycinum*
Oxeye daisy, *Chrysanthemum Leucanthemum*
Periwinkle, *Vinca major*
Scotch broom, *Cytisus scoparius*

Gulf States

Bermuda grass, *Cynodon Dactylon*
Brazilian pepper, *Schinus terebinthifolius*
Kudzu, *Pueraria lobata*
Lantana, *Lantana* hybrids
Punk tree (cajeput tree), *Melaleuca quinquenervia*
She-oak (ironwood), *Casuarina equisetifolia*

Southwest

Acacia, *Acacia melanoxylon,* plus many other species
Bermuda grass, *Cynodon Dactylon*
Eucalyptus, *Eucalyptus,* many species
Fountain grass, *Pennisetum setaceum*
Himalayan blackberry, *Rubus procerus*
Ivy, *Hedera,* many species
Pampas grass, *Cortaderia jubata*
Scotch broom, *Cytisus,* most species

Many Parts of the Country

Ailanthus (tree of heaven), *Ailanthus altissima*
Bamboo, running types
Chicory, *Cichorium Intybus*
Horsetail, *Equisetum hyemale*
Japanese knotweed, *Polygonum cuspidatum*
Morning-glory, *Ipomoea,* most species
Purslane, *Portulaca oleracea*
Watercress, *Nasturtium officinale*

Though attractive, foxglove has become a pest plant in the Northwest.

HOW TO RESCUE NATIVE PLANTS

Sometimes you hear about proposed demolition and/or construction in areas where native plants still thrive. A rescue effort can often save a number of the plants. The following are a few guidelines.

1. The most effective tool for saving native plants is an informal organization and a hotline. In the absence of a full-scale group effort, an individual can still be very effective.

2. Keep your eye on prime native habitats. Also, check city planning schedules for proposed development. Try to look over the site as soon as possible to determine which, if any, species are in danger. The sooner you make your assessment, the more options you have.

3. As soon as you know of a proposed development, contact the developer, express your concern, and offer to organize the plant-saving effort, or find someone to do it if you can't.

4. Once the developer's cooperation is assured, contact your local native plant societies, garden clubs, 4-H, and other interested organizations.

5. If you are experienced with rescuing native plants, you can show others how to do it; if you aren't, find someone who is. Saving plants is not just a matter of going into the woods or a meadow with a shovel. When possible, collect seeds of plants that are too large to be moved.

6. Help develop an informational flyer on digging up, transplanting, and caring for natives in your area; and seek an organization that can distribute the flyers to interested people.

Join the individuals and organizations all over the country who are providing a valuable service for the environment and future generations by saving endangered native plants and who have the bonus of enjoying these plants in their own gardens.

Trillium

Sources of Information

Books

Bruce, Hal. *How to Grow Wildflowers and Wild Shrubs and Trees in Your Own Garden.* New York: Alfred A. Knopf, 1976. Valuable cultural and source information. East Coast oriented from an environmentalist's viewpoint. This text includes an encyclopedia of wildflowers and their sources.

Diekelmann, John, and Schuster, Robert. *Natural Landscaping, Designing with Native Plant Communities.* New York: McGraw-Hill Book Co., 1982. A basic text necessary for informed natural landscaping. It covers in detail how to re-create stable plant communities. Useful primarily for the Northeast, Midwest, and Northwest.

Holm, LeRoy G. et al. *The World's Worst Weeds.* Honolulu: The University Press of Hawaii, 1977. A technical description of agricultural weed problems.

Koopowitz, Harold, and Kaye, Hilary. *Plant Extinction—A Global Crisis.* Washington, D.C.: Stone Wall Press, 1983. The best book for concerned homeowners. It gives extensive information about our endangered ecosystem and speaks extensively about invasive weed species.

Kruckeberg, Arthur R. *Gardening with Native Plants of the Pacific Northwest.* Seattle: University of Washington Press, 1982. A great resource for northwesterners, this book includes growing information for the Northwest as well as detailed information on species for the garden.

Mohlenbrock, Robert H. *Where Have All the Wildflowers Gone?* New York: Macmillan Co., 1983. An excellent discussion of the wildflower problem.

Ortho Books, William H. W. Wilson. *Landscaping with Wildflowers and Native Plants.* San Francisco: Ortho Books, Chevron Chemical Company, 1984. A most valuable and up-to-date book covering in detail most of the many ecosystems in this country. The book contains numerous lists of native plants to choose for your landscape as well as information on how to plant and maintain them.

Smyser, Carol A. *Nature's Design.* Emmaus, Pa.: Rodale Press, 1982. A very detailed primer for designing your yard around native habitats and with native plants.

Consumer Note

When is a native not a native? Like "organic" or "natural," the term "native" has sometimes been abused. Too often nurseries and, especially, mail-order firms will call a particular seed mix a native wildflower mix, for example, when often as many as half of the seeds in the mix are native to Europe, not to the United

States, much less to a particular region. Nurseries will often sell plants from another part of the country and call them natives. Theoretically they are natives, but if the reason you are growing natives is to help preserve a habitat or to provide food for indigenous species of animals, these so-called natives may not be appropriate. Plants from other ecosystems are fine, but they don't usually further the goals of habitat preservation. If you want truly indigenous species, you must research your ecosystem and determine the precise species you want.

Be aware that hybrids of native plants exist. Some of our natives have been bred for home gardens and have few of the characteristics of their hardy cousins. For example, I purchased some particularly showy mimulus for my drought-tolerant flower border one year. In our area mimulus grows wild and blooms all summer with no watering, but the mimulus I had bought continually wilted. I investigated and found out that they were mimulus hybrids and needed practically as much water as most garden flowers. So, again, natives aren't always natives.

Moist meadow lily

Aquilegia canadensis

Chapter 1
The Meadow Garden

When I was a child living in a Boston suburb, the neighborhood was filled with houses and lawns, but across the street from us we were lucky enough to have a small vacant lot. Certainly, we enjoyed tumbling on the lawns and playing croquet, but some of my fondest memories are of exploring the vacant lot. (Isn't it interesting how people-centered the word *vacant* is.) In the lot—actually a meadow—we looked for ripe milkweed pods, pulled them apart, and rubbed the silky fibers against our noses; then we blew the plumes into the wind and watched them float away. Also, we watched monarch butterflies, picked goldenrod, collected sumac pods, and made secret hideaways under the arching branches of the willow. In the evenings we caught lightning bugs and put them in a jar. That vacant lot is no more. Now there is a white house with a lawn, two yews, six junipers, one dogwood, and a maple tree.

Today there are fewer and fewer vacant lots. Driving across the country you see, mile after mile, suburban lawn abutting suburban lawn. Some of the lawns are small; others cover an acre or two. But that is changing as more people begin to question the overemphasis on lawns. Less and less are people willing to spend two or three hours a week tending their lawns; furthermore, homeowners are questioning the value of spending money on fertilizers and water, spreading questionable chemicals on the soil around their homes, and wasting resources. (Annually Americans use 3 million pounds of nitrogen fertilizer on their lawns; that's as much as all of India uses on its agriculture in a year.) And, finally, people are becoming bored with the sterility of lawns and concerned about the obliteration of the habitats of native plants, animals, and birds.

One alternative to the large lawn is the meadow. You've heard the term *meadow,* but what is it really? Botanically, a meadow is a somewhat stable plant community that is dominated by grasses. It is associated with a climate that has quite a bit of rain, as compared to a prairie that is usually found in drier parts of the country. A meadow's composition changes with soil type, climate, and available moisture. A meadow in a boggy corner of Oregon will be very different from a meadow on a dry hillside in New Jersey.

Humans, too, change the makeup of a meadow. Unmanaged meadows in many suburban areas are filled primarily with introduced weeds, brush, young trees, and, sometimes, wind-blown trash. Managed meadows in suburban areas, on the other hand, can require fairly little maintenance and still be exciting areas that are filled with black-eyed susans, poppies, sumac, columbines, milkweeds, or other indigenous species—all changing with the seasons.

If you have a fairly large piece of property or a yard in an area where all the yards aren't trimmed to military precision, you can consider converting some of your yard to a meadow. But first consider the following limitations of a meadow.

1. Some municipalities have so-called weed ordinances, which usually state that homeowners cannot let their lawns grow taller, say, than four or eight inches. These old laws were enacted before there was an awakening to the environmental ramifications of square miles of lawns. The object of these laws was to give cities controls over negligent homeowners and to prevent fire hazards. These laws are still on the books in some areas, and you might encounter them. Be aware, though, that these types of laws have been successfully overturned by concerned citizens.

2. Remember that meadow areas are usually one of the first steps in the natural succession of ecosystems. If not maintained as a meadow, unless it's in a very boggy area, the expanse will probably eventually become a woodland.

3. Once established, meadows are full-sun habitats. Trees shade out the sun-loving plants and are appropriate only on the periphery.

4. Meadow areas are not interchangeable with lawns. They are occasionally appropriate in small areas, but generally they function as a supplement to a small lawn area.

5. Meadow grasses and flowers produce more pollen than a mowed lawn and should be avoided if anyone in your family has severe allergy problems.

If your yard is sunny, if the neighborhood is

appropriate, and if allergies aren't a problem, the advantages of a meadow are numerous, as indicated by the following list.

1. Meadows planted with indigenous species of grasses and flowers attract native birds, small mammals, butterflies, and other insects.

2. Meadows change dramatically with the seasons, providing much more visual pleasure than a huge lawn does and a valuable learning experience as well.

3. Meadows require very little maintenance. They need only annual mowing to keep the woody species from taking over and occasional weed control to keep them looking neat. They also need little watering—none if nature is cooperative at seeding time and if flowers are not expected all summer long in arid climates.

4. Meadow flowers and grasses will give you a long season of flowers, both fresh and dry, to cut and to enjoy in the house.

5. Meadows that are well maintained and generously overseeded will give your yard a boost of spectacular color with very little effort.

If you live in a part of the country where the meadow is an appropriate ecosystem, particularly in the Northeast and the Northwest, creating one will be an exciting project. If you live in the Midwest, see Chapter 3 for a variation on the meadow, the prairie.

Planning and Preparation

Meadows are delightfully variable: each one is unique in some way. Even when meadows are planted with the same seed mix, different climates and soils and the germinating seeds of the species that were originally growing there will combine to give you an unpredictable show; and that's half the fun. The process of putting in your own meadow is fairly straightforward. First, choose a sunny area for your meadow; it can be as small as one hundred square feet or as large as several acres. See the accompanying plan for ideas on how you might situate your meadow. Notice that the meadow is away from the house. As a rule, this is recommended because: (1) trees are often needed near the house for protection from wind and sun, (2) meadows cannot function the way lawn does as a place to play ball or to sunbathe, (3) meadows are usually inhabited by mice and other small mammals that would not be welcome in the house, and (4) meadow grasses in dry periods can become a fire hazard. Notice also that the vegetable garden and orchard are fenced and separated somewhat from the meadow garden. The reason for that is to try to minimize visits from the meadow's inhabitants and to cut down on the damage they might inflict.

Once you have decided where you will put your meadow, ask yourself the following questions:

1. Which kinds of wildflowers and grasses are native to my area? (If you need help, refer to the resources at the end of this chapter.) Successful meadows can be created also by sowing seed mixes that are not blended especially for your area, but you will probably not attract as many indigenous insects and birds, and fewer species will reseed themselves. If you don't have the time or inclination to "fine-tune" your meadow to your area, an interesting alternative is to try the Meadow in a Can, a colorful, easily grown, premixed selection that is distributed by Clyde Robin Seed Company (the address is given in the resource section at the end of this chapter).

2. What is the drainage like? If the soil stays moist for much of the year, you must choose species that tolerate poor drainage.

3. How much seed shall I order? Measure the area to be seeded and consult a seed catalog. To give you a rough idea, Clyde Robin, the "granddaddy" of wildflower nurseries, recommends the following amounts: for an area that has some trees and shrubs, sow five pounds of seed per acre; for a clear area, eight pounds per acre; and if you want a big, lush show, try fifteen pounds per acre.

Lupinus nanus

4. Shall I look for bargains when shopping for seeds? Buy good seeds. There is no surer way of wasting money in gardening than to buy cheap seeds. Good wildflower seeds, costing $20 to $30 per pound, may seem expensive; but, relatively speaking, they're not. Seeding is the least expensive way to landscape an area; with seeds, more than with most other things in life, you get what you pay for. The reason for the expense is that many of the wildflower seeds must be collected in the wild—an expensive operation. In contrast, clover, which is often used as a cheap filler in wildflower mixes, can be field grown and picked by machine; therefore many of the inexpensive seed mixes are mostly clover seeds combined with only a few seeds of the more desirable species. In addition, many of the cheaper mixes contain more easily obtained European flower seeds, not natives. That may not be a problem if you're not a purist, but the native flowers are more likely to attract our native insects and birds, and they are more likely to reseed themselves year after year. In addition, they are less likely to become weeds that crowd out native vegetation. Weed seeds and poor germination rates can also be a problem with cheap seeds. If your budget is tight, seed more lightly and let the flowers reseed themselves. Another option, of course, is to collect your own seeds. (To do this, you must be aware of where the flowers are growing, when they bloom, and when the seeds of each species are ripe. You must beat the birds to the harvest and catch the seeds before they fall to the ground.)

5. How do I prepare the soil? If the proposed meadow area is quite weedy, it is best to till up the soil a few weeks before planting, and keep the area well watered. This procedure will germinate the weed seeds. Before you plant the flower seeds, you should plow under the newly sprouted weeds. If you have the time and patience to repeat this procedure, you will probably give your flowers a very strong start and dramatically cut your weeding chores.

How to Plant a Meadow

Steve Atwood at Clyde Robin Seed Company recommends the following procedure for planting a meadow. If possible, plant in the fall; that gives the flowers enough time to get established and set seed the next fall. If you plant in the spring, the chances are that you will have to reseed the next year.

If you have an existing lawn area, plow it under; remove as many weeds and stones as possible, then rake the area. If you are over-seeding an existing meadow area and you want a good flower show, remove a lot of the grasses. Most wildflowers have a hard time competing with grasses, particularly if the grasses are already established. (A word of caution: Don't just cast the seeds on hard, dry ground; you will just feed the birds a very expensive meal.) Rough up the soil. Use a spade if the soil is heavy or packed down. If it's sandy soil, rake it well. Before you plant, mix your seeds with coarse sand: five parts of sand to one part seed. This mixture allows you to spread the seeds more evenly. Sow the seeds, then either water very gently with a fan spray that will softly puddle the soil over the seeds or rake the area very lightly. Try not to cover the seeds with more than one-eighth inch of soil. Once the seeds are sown, you must keep the area moist for two or three weeks. Water lightly if it does not rain. (Fall plantings are often accompanied by rain, a work-saving advantage if you live in an arid climate.)

This landscaped yard provides for people as well as for some native plants and wildlife. People live snugly, protected from winter winds by evergreen shrubs and trees. A fence ensures that most of the harvest of tomatoes and lettuce and other vegetables ends up on the kitchen table, not in some bunny's mouth. The orchard is planted with dwarf trees so that netting can easily be put in place for protection from birds. A path and sitting area were added to the meadow so that sunny hours can be spent enjoying the business of living that meadows so embody. In addition, you may be able to pick black-eyed susans, tiger lilies, and goldenrod; watch birds gather seeds and nesting materials; and see butterflies sip nectar from the ever-present flowers.

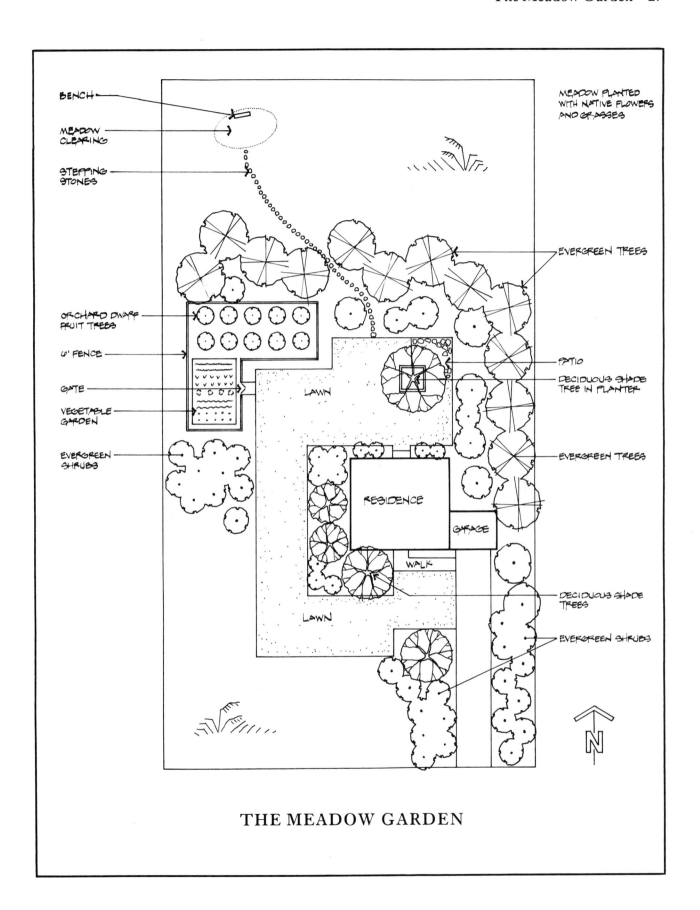

BENCH

MEADOW CLEARING

STEPPING STONES

ORCHARD DWARF FRUIT TREES

6' FENCE

GATE

VEGETABLE GARDEN

EVERGREEN SHRUBS

MEADOW PLANTED WITH NATIVE FLOWERS AND GRASSES

EVERGREEN TREES

PATIO

DECIDUOUS SHADE TREE IN PLANTER

EVERGREEN TREES

LAWN

RESIDENCE

GARAGE

WALK

LAWN

DECIDUOUS SHADE TREES

EVERGREEN SHRUBS

N

THE MEADOW GARDEN

How to Maintain a Meadow

If you live in an arid climate and want flowers well into the summer, you will have to irrigate the meadow area often enough to keep the flowers growing well. Weeds can be a problem—are they taking over or becoming an eyesore? If they are, you will have to weed by hand or turn the field over and start again *after* germinating the weed species and turning the area over once more.

Most wildflower mixes contain both annual and perennial flowers. The annuals will bloom the first year, but the perennials usually take two years to bloom. The perennials are well worth the wait because they continue to bloom year after year, and generally their show increases each year (particularly when the flowers you choose are native to the area).

A meadow is not no maintenance; it is *low* maintenance. To keep the area a meadow, you must mow it at least once a year, in the fall after the flowers have seeded themselves. Get a mower that will mow six to ten inches off the ground. Often you can rent one. This type of machine is sometimes called a *flail mower*. Because weeds in the area will start to take over, plow up the area every five years or so and resow it. To avoid being disappointed, you should keep in mind that annual flowers give the biggest color show the first year after planting. Although they will reseed year after year, usually they don't reseed as heavily as you sowed them originally. If you have chosen an all-annual selection, you may want to reseed from year to year. If you choose a mix that is mostly perennials, it will have some color the first year and gradually more color each year thereafter.

Clockwise from top left Instead of a large lawn, part of this yard has been planted with a wildflower mix. Sitting on the deck, lemonade in hand, one can enjoy up close the daily changes in a mini-meadow.

Meadow seed mixes that will create a meadow such as this one are available at many nurseries. Several reliable sources of seed mixes are given at the end of this chapter. Even though the mixes often contain many nonnative flowers, they can be an easy way to start a meadow.

One of the stars of a meadow garden is often the black-eyed susan.

Above This beautiful prairie setting is enjoyed and maintained by David Kropp and Ray Schulenberg, prairie enthusiasts. It is seen here in late spring, with pink and lavender coneflowers among the emerging grasses. Through summer and fall it will be filled with the wandlike seed heads of five species of grasses and the blooms of sixty varieties of flowering prairie plants. Kropp and Schulenberg harvest about six gallon jarfuls of prairie seeds every year and share them with others interested in prairie restoration. (Landscape design: The Kropp Company)

Left Butterfly weed, *Asclepias tuberosa,* is a spectacular inhabitant of much of this nation's prairie. It is a star performer in a border of prairie flowers and in a more natural planting of prairie grasses and flowers.

Opposite, clockwise from top left The Littauers' chaparral garden in the spring is filled with bright blue native ceanothus varieties and yellow dendromecon, as well as some drought-tolerant African species of yellow and white daisies. (Landscape design: Rosalind Creasy)

Fremontodendron is one of the showiest of the West Coast native shrubs.

Drought-tolerant chaparral gardens can be supplemented with showy water-loving annuals during the winter rainy season. Here illustrator Marcie Hawthorne enjoys the orange calendulas among the drought-tolerant permanent plantings of the purple spikes of pride of Madeira, *Echium fastuosum;* old-fashioned bearded iris; and African daisies, *Osteospermum.* (Landscape design: Rosalind Creasy)

Sources of Information

Books

Brooklyn Botanic Garden Handbooks. *Gardening with Wild Flowers*. No. 38. Brooklyn, N.Y.: Brooklyn Botanic Garden. How to incorporate wildflowers in your garden. This handbook is available for a small charge from Brooklyn Botanic Garden, 1000 Washington Avenue, Brooklyn, NY 11225.

Crockett, James Underwood, and Allen, Oliver E. *Wildflower Gardening*. Alexandria, Va.: Time-Life Books, 1977. A general view of the subject, with specific information on a number of wildflower species.

The next four entries are useful guides for identifying your own flowers or those in the wild; use these guides for pleasure and for seed collecting.

Duncan, Wilbur H., and Foote, Leonard E. *Wildflowers of the Southeastern United States*. Athens, Ga.: University of Georgia Press, 1975.

Niehaus, Theodore F., and Ripper, Charles L. *A Field Guide to Pacific States Wildflowers*. Boston: Houghton Mifflin, 1976.

Peterson, Roger Tory, and McKenny, Margaret. *A Field Guide to Wildflowers of Northeastern and North Central North America*. Boston: Houghton Mifflin, 1968.

Rickett, Harold William. *Wild Flowers of the United States*. 6 vols. New York: McGraw-Hill Book Co., 1966-70.

Nurseries

Larner Seeds
P.O. Box 60143
Palo Alto, CA 94306
Specialists in native and naturalized seeds of New England and California.

Midwest Wildflowers
Box 64
Rockton, IL 61072
Specialists in midwestern wildflowers.

Painted Meadows Seed Company
P.O. Box 1494
Charlottesville, VA 22902
Specialists in East Coast wildflowers.

Plants of the Southwest
1570 Pacheco Street
Santa Fe, NM 87501
Southwestern native flowers and Indian varieties of vegetables that are adapted to the Southwest. Catalog $1.

Clyde Robin Seed Company
P.O. Box 2366
Castro Valley, CA 94546
The granddaddy of wildflower seed companies in this country has been in business for seventy years. It carries a large collection of wildflower seeds from all over the country and will select for your area. Catalog $2.

Opposite, clockwise from top A reed fence with a Japanese-style gate adds mystery and design while daffodils add a splash of color to Robert and Joyca Cunnan's woodland garden.

The entry to the Cunnans' garden shows how a graceful path through native trees, enhanced with flowers and a small clearing, can carve an inviting setting for a home. (Landscape design: Robert and Joyca Cunnan)

Woodland anemones such as this one, *Anemone lancifolia*, brighten up a woodland garden.

Cornus florida

Chapter 2
The Woodland Garden

Woodland gardens can provide serenity, privacy, a feeling of seclusion, protection from winter winds, and a cool, dappled retreat on hot summer days. Woodland gardens also provide a never-ending drama. Paths that lead into woodland gardens invite strolling and exploration. Patios, porches, and kitchen windows that have a view of a woodland garden are never boring places to be. Busy chickadees flit to and fro, jays scold their neighbors, chipmunks dash from tree trunk to tree trunk, the days are full of meaningful activity—the business of living.

Woodlands take many different forms: hardwood forests of rock maple and ash in Vermont, loblolly pine forests in the South, ponderosa and pinon pine in the West, and bigleaf maple and hemlock in the Northwest. Woodland gardens are appropriate to a large part of this country; their native range includes most of the northern regions of this country as well as more southerly mountainous areas. In keeping with the philosophy of this book, I'm stressing woodland gardens that represent the indigenous habitat of your own property. While it may be interesting to create a woodland garden in a grassland habitat, the point here is to

restore or preserve native habitats so that indigenous species can better reproduce themselves. In addition, woodland gardens in a woodland habitat will benefit the homeowner because naturally occurring habitats usually require less maintenance.

Woodland gardens are amazingly flexible. If you live in an existing woodland area, you can carve out and enhance it to meet your needs. If the ground has been laid bare or if you are removing a large lawn, you can create a woodland area with patience and skill. The size of your property is not a limiting factor; you can create woodland gardens in an area as small as twenty feet by twenty feet or in an area as large as twenty acres. If you have a small area, you may want to follow some of the Japanese gardening concepts. Traditional Japanese gardeners have long captured the essence of woodlands in miniature gardens. In contrast, if you have a large area, you would do well to control only the area near your home and along paths leading through the woods.

Woodlands are complex systems. When mature, they usually include a canopy of tall, shading trees; understory trees, young trees and those trees that have adapted to shady conditions; a shrub understory, both tall and short shrubs; and herbaceous shade-loving plants. Another characteristic, which is important to homeowners who want to carve a garden area in a woodland, is the varied plant community that develops at the edges of woodlands and forests. Areas on the periphery of a forest, next to a meadow, for example, or in a clearing, usually have a number of sun-loving herbaceous plants, shrubs, and small trees. These plants give you, the garden designer, a wide variety of plants from which to choose when making your garden.

There are a number of elements that will influence the way you design a landscape based on a woodland habitat. If you are starting from scratch, you must analyze the existing conditions and assess what must be done to approximate the conditions you want. If you are modifying an existing woodland area, the main issues are how to make the existing area provide protection for the house from wind and sun, how to make the area suitable for your household, and how to create a lovely garden. One further consideration is how to create a garden that will benefit the plants and animals in the area. This chapter includes an example of how to design a specific woodland garden. Also, Chapter 6 includes information that may be helpful.

Planning and Preparation

The first steps for creating a woodland garden are similar no matter where you live, whether your garden is large or small or whether you are starting from scratch or altering an existing woodland. To begin, you must set and analyze your goals and make an inventory of what is on the site.

First, goal setting. What do you want from your garden? Is it mainly for viewing from the house? for entertaining? for a children's play yard? or mainly for food production? Only you know the answer. Woodland gardens are a source of year-round interest and beauty; woodland gardens offer hospitable surroundings for a patio or barbecue area. In addition, few gardens can give children such a rich area for exploring and playing. If food gardening is one of your goals, however, you must plan your garden carefully, and if you have a small yard, the combination of woodland and food production may be impossible. Woodland gardens are primarily shade gardens, and most food plants need full sun.

Next, the inventory. What do you have to work with? If you are modifying an existing garden, identify first those plants that you want to preserve. Which special features make the area unique and beautiful—maybe a rock outcropping, a gnarled old oak near the house, a marsh, or a stream? While you are taking inventory, include an analysis of the property's soil characteristics and drainage and exposure; all these factors dictate what your woodland garden will be like. Make a map of your property, locating all the features on it so you will be able to work with them later.

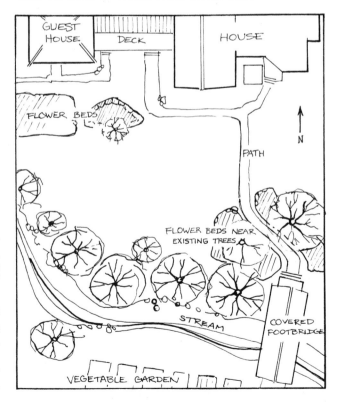

What needs to be removed? Do some of the trees block a beautiful view or obliterate what little winter sun your home receives? Are some of the trees and shrubs really invasive weeds that should come out? Has the existing landscaping outgrown its bounds? Are the yews starting to lift the roof? If providing habitat for wildlife is one of your goals, are there a number of modifications that should be made (see Chapter 6)?

How does your garden area function? Does the present wood area, or proposed one, provide a windbreak? Are there deciduous trees that shade the house in summer? If the woodland area is large enough to be managed to provide wood for the fireplace and stove, is that one of your goals? If so, you will need to choose trees that are suitable.

At this point you may need further direction. Either obtain some of the books recommended at the end of this chapter or hire a professional designer who works with native plants to help you create your garden.

Modifying Existing Gardens

If your home has been built in an existing woodland, your landscaping job will be quite different from that of someone who is starting from scratch. Yours will be a job of sculpturing and molding an area to please your eye. Here are a few guidelines.

1. Create some open spaces in the woodland area. These spaces can be created by lawn, groundcovers, paths, patios, or all four. Most homeowners prefer some of the open area to be adjacent to the house because it provides a protected sitting area. A grove of trees very near the house can give you a feeling of claustrophobia.

2. Create paths that lead both you and the viewer's eye out into the woods. Clear some of the trees and shrubs from beside the walks for flowering woodland natives that can be enjoyed by the family as they meander down the path.

3. Thin out the canopy near the open areas and remove some of the trees to allow more sun for flowering shrubs and small trees such as mountain laurel, serviceberry, dogwood, native rhododendron, and low-bush blueberry. Concentrate the flowering plants in the thinned-out areas and near places where people enjoy sitting or walking or where they can be viewed from the house.

Starting from Scratch

If you are starting a woodland garden from scratch, it is necessary to take into account many of the aesthetic considerations mentioned above. In addition, you will probably have to do some research to find out what would have grown there naturally. Instead of inventorying your yard, you must inventory the surrounding woodland vegetation to see what is indigenous. If woodlands in your area have been obliterated, you can get information from the library, the local native plant society, and the university extension service.

When you plan to create a woodland garden from scratch, it is crucial to realize that you are trying to compress into a few years what nature takes generations to achieve; therefore, you have to be aware of how you must help the process. Some general guidelines for planning a new woodland garden are given below.

1. Examine the soil and drainage because they dictate which plants you can choose.

2. Trees, shrubs, and woodland wildflowers need a soil rich in humus. If the soil in your garden has been depleted of organic matter over the years through ignorance or neglect, you will have to improve the soil with compost before you start planting, then you will have to mulch the area for the first few years.

3. A new woodland garden is produced in stages. Only after a number of years will the area be shady enough that you can plant many of the shade-loving, forest-floor dwellers. Until the trees fill in, plant sun-loving wildflowers.

Trees for Woodland Gardens

Trees for Northeastern and Midwestern Woodland Gardens

Acer species. Maples of all types give substance and grandeur to woodland gardens. The real star, however, is the sugar maple with its spectacular fall foliage that is famous throughout the world. Maples are excellent grove trees that provide not only fall color but food and shelter to woodland animals.

Amelanchier species. Most serviceberry species are colorful and provide berries for people and birds.

Betula species. Birches are graceful grove trees that provide food for birds, beautiful bark, and fall color. Few woodland gardens are as graceful as those that feature birches. To show them off to their best advantage, combine them with some of the native evergreens.

Cornus species. Dogwoods, one of our woodland favorites, provide colorful flowers and food for birds. Place them near paths and clearings so their flower show can be fully appreciated.

Diospyros virginiana. The persimmon is a handsome tree that provides food for birds and people, as well as a show of orange foliage and fruit in the fall.

Fraxinus species. Many of the native ashes are very attractive woodland trees that give vibrant fall color. When grown in woodland gardens instead of formal yards, their propensity to reseed themselves nearly ceases to be a problem.

Ilex species. Many of the native hollies are extremely attractive, and they provide food for birds. Since they are evergreen, they can give protection from the wind in the winter.

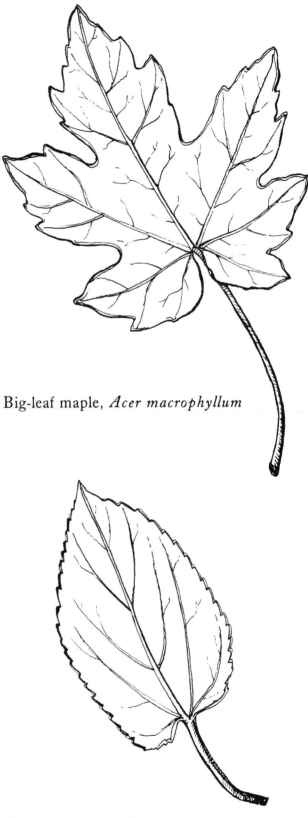

Big-leaf maple, *Acer macrophyllum*

Western catalpa, *Catalpa speciosa*

Juniperus virginiana. Attractive evergreen that attracts birds and protects homes from the wind.

Liquidambar Styraciflua. Sweet gums are stately trees that are beautiful in groves or by themselves. They give handsome fall color in the southern regions of the East Coast.

Liriodendron Tulipifera. Tulip trees are vigorous, handsome trees that are effective in groves or by themselves.

Pinus species. Many of the native pines form the basis for striking woodland gardens. Use their evergreen foliage to advantage as a windbreak for winter winds. To keep the pine-tree woodland garden from being too dense and dark, thin it near your living areas and the paths and plant the transition areas between the pines and the open areas with flowering shrubs, small trees, and deciduous plants that have showy fall foliage.

Quercus species. Most of the oaks are suitable for woodland gardens and are all-time favorites of wildlife.

Trees for Western and Northwestern Woodland Gardens

Cornus Nuttallii. Pacific dogwoods are a special treat, particularly in the Douglas-fir and hemlock woodland garden, where their white or light pink blooms are a contrast to the dark green background foliage of the conifers.

Populus tremuloides. Quaking aspens are to the West what birches are to the East, ornamental clumping grove trees of outstanding beauty. Aspens are water lovers and should not be planted near sewer lines or in small yards; give them room to spread, and feature their clumping tendencies in your woodland garden. To take full advantage of their spectacular fall foliage, combine them with some of the native evergreens.

Shagbark hickory, *Carya ovata*

Tulip, *Liriodendron Tulipifera*

Pseudotsuga Menziesii. Douglas firs are large, graceful evergreens that are suitable for large properties. Woodland gardens using these beauties can be filled with shade-loving native ferns, flowering shrubs, and perennials.

Sequoia sempervirens. Few woodland gardens on the West Coast rival the redwood forest. If redwoods are native to your area and if you have lots of room, plant groves of redwoods. They grow quickly, and within a few years you can put in the shade-loving sorrel and native sword ferns.

Tsuga heterophylla. This native hemlock has a wide range and is a handsome evergreen that needs lots of room to spread. Make it the basis for a dramatic woodland garden.

By looking at the illustration of Jean Richardson's garden, you can get a feel for how a pleasure garden can be carved out of a natural woodland.

When the Richardsons bought the lot fifteen years ago, it was covered with native woods; namely, sugar and red maples, ash, black cherry, white pine, hemlock, buckthorn, shad, beech, and canoe birch. When building, the Richardsons left as many of the trees as possible but cleared an area around the house to create a garden. Lawn areas and many different ground covers are used to form the design lines and to allow a view of the wooded areas. Jean has put in a small vegetable and herb garden that is near the house and that takes advantage of the available sunlight. Other nonnative plants around the house include azaleas, rhododendrons, coral bells, ajuga, lupines, yellow primroses, pachysandra, daylilies, hybrid lilies, foxgloves, lilies-of-the-valley, sweet woodruff, snow-on-the-mountain, and violets—all give color and variety to enhance this woodland garden.

In the natural woods, among the rock outcroppings, and in a number of areas near the house are various native ferns, including Christmas fern, sensitive fern, and ostrich fern and wildflowers such as wild ginger, trillium, Solomon's seal, columbine, lungwort, wild iris, rhododendron, viburnum, myrtle, and jack-in-the-pulpit. Some of these natives have been planted; others, such as the myrtle, have migrated in on their own. All in all, the Richardsons' garden has given great pleasure to the occupants of the house while still allowing the native wildlife, both plants and animals, to have their own habitat.

Opposite The Richardsons carved a woodland garden out of native woods. They left most of the trees and shrubs in place but included a clearing where showy natives and exotics could be featured as well as a small vegetable-growing area. The result is a garden that gives joy to the owners and provides a habitat for native plants and animals. The plants include:
1. Amelanchier (shad)
2. Sweet woodruff (ground cover)
3. *Viburnum carlcephalum*
4. Weigela
5. *Viburnum tomentosum*
6. *Euonymus alata*
7. Forsythia 'Beatrix Farrand'
8. Canoe birch
9. White pine
10. Snow-on-the-mountain
11. Wild azaleas
12. Rhododendrons
13. Daylilies
14. Lily of the valley
15. Honeysuckle
16. Bayberry
17. Azaleas
18. *Malus* 'Dorothea'

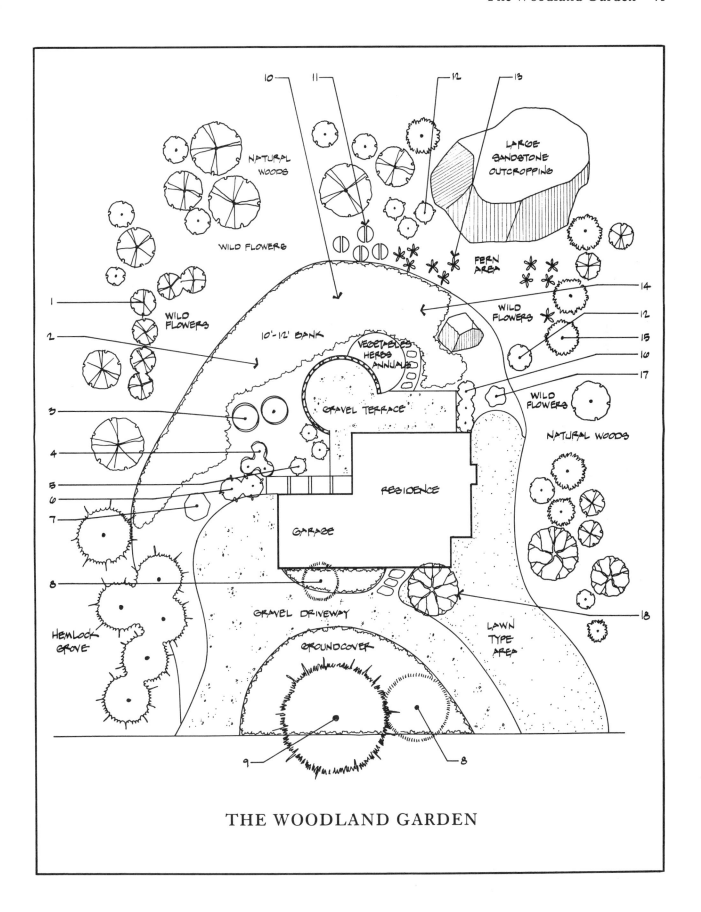

THE WOODLAND GARDEN

Jean Richardson enjoys adding vegetables and flowers to her woodland garden.

Sources of Information

Books

Bruce, Hal. *How to Grow Wildflowers and Wild Shrubs and Trees in Your Own Garden.* New York: Alfred A. Knopf, 1976. Contains good information about putting in a native garden for people on the East Coast and in the Midwest.

Du Pont, Elizabeth N. *Landscaping with Native Plants in the Middle-Atlantic Region.* Chadds Ford, Pa.: Brandywine Conservancy, 1978. A valuable resource for gardeners wanting a woodland garden on the Atlantic coast.

Kruckeberg, Arthur R. *Gardening with Native Plants of the Pacific Northwest.* Seattle: University of Washington Press, 1982. A wonderful source of information about northwestern natives, with suggestions of many plants to use in a woodland garden.

Demonstration Gardens

Garden in the Woods
Hemenway Road
Framingham, MA 01701

Ida Cason Calloway Gardens
Route 27
Pine Mountain, GA 31822

Morton Arboretum
Lisle, IL 60532

Nurseries

Forest Farm
990 Tetherow Road
Williams, OR 97544
This nursery carries native plants. Catalog $1.50.

Salter Tree Farm
Route 2, Box 1332
Madison, FL 32340
This company carries seeds of southern native trees and shrubs.

F.W. Schumacher Company
36 Spring Hill Road
Sandwich, MA 02563
This nursery carries seeds of a number of trees.

Chapter 3

The Prairie Garden

In the heartland of America lies an ecosystem that has produced an array of flowers and grasses that is more varied than that found nearly any place on earth. That ecosystem is the American prairie. A treat awaits you if you have not yet discovered the beauty of a border filled with native prairie flowers and grasses. The options range from the bright "lollipop" colors of some of the flowers to the more subdued colors and ephemeral seed heads of the mauve- and bronze-hued plume grasses. Some of these plants take care of themselves, while others are a challenge to the gardener and need tending. If you live in an area that was once a prairie habitat (nearly half the country), no matter what your gardening style or time, you owe it to yourself to enjoy a patch of prairie natives.

When Europeans first arrived on this continent, the midwestern prairies stretched for millions of square miles. Today these virgin prairie ecosystems are in such danger that most of what exists is in patches the size of a football field; and those are in jealously guarded preserves. The great expanses of bluestem and needle grass, the thunder of buffalo hooves, and the cries of prairie chickens have nearly disappeared. They have been replaced by the much-needed corn and wheat farms and cattle ranches and the less necessary bluegrass lawns. A valuable ecosystem, as well as part of our history, has been nearly obliterated.

Biologically, the definition of a prairie is a treeless expanse dominated by native grasses, some short and others many feet tall, and forbs (broad-leaved plants, usually those that flower). This definition gives little hint of the *wonders* of a prairie, however. Willa Cather defined it more poetically: the "sea of wind-blown grasses" and "the stain of crimson phlox" as far as one could see. I, a newcomer to the prairie, was most impressed with the variety of grass seed heads: some like wands, some like feathers, others like soft plumes, but all luminescent in the sunlight.

When that treeless expanse covered a great part of this country, within it different types of prairies could be discerned: the tall-grass prairies of Iowa and Nebraska, where the rainfall is heavy; the short-grass prairies of the semi-arid plains of Colorado, Kansas, and northern Texas; and the sagebrush grasslands of the cold, arid parts of Idaho and Wyoming. Right down the middle of the Midwest, where there were a number of different conditions, was a large section of mixed-grass prairie.

Homeowners interested in enjoying prairie plants or in preserving some of the endangered prairie habitat have a number of choices. For the busy homeowner who wants a small lawn or who needs grass for a play area and is looking for a low-maintenance lawn, some of the short, hardy prairie grasses such as buffalo grass and sideoats grama can be used as fairly tall, informal lawns. These lawns need mowing only three or four times a year and require little water and fertilizer. While they will never look as formal or lush as a bluegrass lawn, these "ecology" lawns are appropriate in many areas. Other low-maintenance prairie gardens are composed of borders of some of the particularly easy-to-grow prairie flowers such as coreopsis, coneflowers, and many of the grasses.

For gardeners or environmentalists who want a challenge, installing an authentic prairielike area in the yard, with all its beauty and seasonal changes, can be a consuming but highly rewarding endeavor. While prairie plantings can be fairly low maintenance when well established, the actual process of creating an authentic prairie area of half an acre or more can require much effort.

Because humans have completely obliterated the natural system, those wanting to establish and maintain an area of prairie today must contend with a number of problems. First, aggressive, introduced plants such as wild morning-glory, European oat, dandelion, and bluegrass pose a problem when you are trying to start your prairie plants. Because most prairie plants tend to put most of the first-year growth into the roots, not into top growth, their sparse leaves are often shaded or crowded out by the lush invaders. And once the prairie plants do become established, they must compete with aggressive, introduced, woody plants such as multiflora roses, Japanese honeysuckle, Siberian elm, and numerous other trees that shade the sun-loving natives.

A second problem encountered by the gardener wanting to establish a prairie is how to find out what grew naturally in the area. With so many houses, roads, and parking lots where the native habitats once were, one must do some botanical sleuthing in order to reestablish the preexisting ecosystem. In addition, the introduced exotic plants (never seen by a buffalo, of course) range from Euell Gibbons's wild asparagus to Queen Anne's lace and wild mustard.

Another challenge for the prairie restorer is dealing with local ordinances: (1) weed-abatement laws (laws that prohibit high grasses, although these laws have been overturned on many occasions by prairie enthusiasts) are a community's stubborn hold on the traditional landscaping styles that require clipped lawns and formal shrub borders; and (2) restrictions against burning. Nature maintained and protected her prairie by burning it to the ground every few years. The frequent burning killed young shrubs and trees that would have invaded and shaded out the prairie plants and helped germinate some of the prairie seeds. Burning your prairie may not be feasible because of fire regulations or because of your prairie's proximity to dwellings. If that is the case, you can compromise by mowing it every year instead and reseeding it often.

As you can see, putting in a sizable prairie and helping it become well established can be a challenge, albeit a rewarding one. Once established, prairie plantings dramatically set off every type of house, from the sod-roofed prairie house to the old Victorian mansion. In addition, instead of experiencing the boredom of a large lawn, you will enjoy day-to-day changes. Prairies offer a variety of blooms, from shooting stars and butterfly weed to tall-grass seed plumes. They invite birds, butterflies, and small mammals that are completely dependent on the prairie ecosystem.

Those who are interested in a large expanse of prairie will do well to join one of the myriad prairie preservation organizations. These dedicated people can give you information on your particular area and help you locate seeds, transplants, and even the machinery to seed large areas. Besides the "ecology lawn" and a full-fledged prairie restoration, there are two other exciting, and less ambitious, options for prairie gardening that are covered in detail in the next few pages: (1) planting a somewhat formal flowerbed with a collection of prairie grasses and forbs, and (2) seeding a flowerbed or a small section of the yard with a random mix of prairie plants from a seed packet.

Planning and Preparation

There are two types of gardens that can give you a taste of prairie gardening. They are ideal for beginners or for people with limited time. One is a prairie patch, which incorporates a small piece of mixed prairie in your yard; the other, a prairie border, is a flower border featuring individual prairie plants. Pat Armstrong, ecobiologist, longtime prairie enthusiast, and head of the Morton Arboretum Prairie Restoration Project in Illinois, has put together some basic prairie plant information on these two types of prairie gardens. The following recommendations are hers.

For both prairie gardens follow these suggestions.

1. Pick a site that gets as much sun as possible; full sun is best.

2. Most prairie plants are not too particular about soil. They will grow in rich black soil and in poor sandy soils. In addition, they can tolerate clay soil with poor drainage. Some plants are better adapted to one condition or another, however, and individual plants will have different growth habits in different soils.

3. You can obtain seeds and plants for your prairie patch in a number of ways. Get plants from friends and neighbors who can make divisions or who have extra plants. You can buy plants from some local nurseries and prairie organizations. Seeds are available at some nurseries (see the list at the end of this chapter)

and from friends, neighbors, and prairie organizations. You can collect seeds from wild areas such as those along railroad right-of-ways and public back roads. (Never take plants from an area unless you know it has been condemned for a road or a building. Native plants are best left in their native environment. In addition, never take all of the seeds of any plant, and don't remove seeds from private land or from public parks.)

4. It is best to obtain seeds and plants that have been grown near you; they will be better adapted to your local climate and soil type. Using seeds and plants purchased from a distant nursery may result in poor gardens and can introduce exotic genes into the local gene pool.

5. Plant either in the spring or in the fall. If you sow seeds in the spring, use stratified (cold-treated) seeds; otherwise, germination will not occur that spring. If you sow in the fall, you can use recently purchased or collected seeds because the seeds will stratify naturally over the winter and sprout in the spring. Seeds should be planted late enough in the fall so that weed seeds don't germinate before winter, thereby getting a head start on the prairie plants.

6. An alternative to seeding in place is buying plants of many of the species or raising plants from seeds in pots so that you can set them out exactly where you want them. This method sometimes gives the plants a head start.

7. Prairie plants have evolved in a grassland environment that is subject to brush fires every few years. (Prairie plants, as a rule, are very flammable, and for that reason should not be used directly adjacent to buildings.) Fire is a beneficial agent; the flames return the nutrients to the soil and remove the litter. For modern prairies, burning is even more valuable, especially if done in the spring, because it tends to control the exotic, nonnative weeds that usually appear earlier in the spring than the prairie plants. If you cannot burn your prairie patch,

mow it and rake it fairly clean early in the spring to allow the sun to warm up the soil. Mowing controls woody weeds and allows the emerging prairie plants to come up in full sun.

8. As a rule it is best not to fertilize prairie plants. Usually they do not need it, and fertilizer encourages weed plants.

For the prairie patch, follow these suggestions in addition to the first eight.

1. Prepare the soil ahead of time to eliminate as many weeds as possible. To do this, plow and disk it several times, giving the weeds time to germinate between diskings, or use herbicides well in advance of your prairie planting.

2. Get a mixture of seeds and plants that has been recommended by a local prairie lover, or choose from the list that appears later in this chapter.

3. Have patience. Remember that prairie plants spend their first year or two making roots. For instance, a compass plant that is seven inches high and has only one leaf usually has a tap root that is five or six feet long. Your prairie patch, therefore, is not going to look like much the first two years. (A few plants do grow from seed to flower in one season, but they are exceptions.) When most people plant a prairie, they plant a cover crop of oats or wild rye at the same time. Then, at least, they have something to look at and to keep the weeds down until the prairie plants are established.

4. Maintaining the prairie patch the first two years involves weeding and mowing. Mow the new patch when it is about three or four inches high. That will cut the flower stalks off the weeds and prevent their reseeding. It will not harm the young prairie plants because they will still be quite small when you mow. If you recognize the weeds, you can control them by hand weeding. (If you plant the prairie plants in rows, it will help you identify them and weed them.) Burning the prairie patch in the early spring also controls weeds.

For the prairie border, follow these suggestions in addition to the first eight.

1. Choose a sunny site and lay out a pleasing design. See the model drawing in this chapter. Don't make the area too wide to maintain; either make the area narrow or make a path through it, which will allow you to weed and to pick flowers.

2. Obtain the species suggested on the plan and plant them either in the spring or in the fall. Use Pat Armstrong's suggestions for placement because she has selected the individual species for their height, form, and color.

3. Keep the bed well weeded and cut off the litter in the early spring. The prairie border will probably not come into its full glory until the third summer.

Armstrong's suggestions for the prairie patch and the prairie border include only twenty-one species—there are hundreds—and are meant as a stepping-off place, not as a "forever" arrangement. She has chosen them for their ease of growing, beauty, and length of bloom, with the progression of size and bloom duplicating the show that the prairie gives. For your prairie patch, choose from the list those species that would have grown in your area naturally. You can randomly scatter the species suggested in the proportion you want. For your prairie border, follow the suggestions for species placement, making substitutions of close relatives if you cannot obtain the ones suggested. All of the plants on the list have been chosen for their wide adaptability; nevertheless, there will be some variation in their growth habits in different soils and climates. You may want to move some of them after they have grown for a few years if in your particular miniclimate they are shorter or taller than predicted.

Prairie Plants

The following plants are included in the planting diagram on page 51.

1. Big bluestem, *Andropogon Gerardii*. The tallest prairie grass, a must for any prairie gar-

den. Blooms from August to September; three to eight feet tall; colorful in the fall.

2. Indian grass, *Sorghastrum nutans.* A must for prairie gardens. Blooms from August to October; three to six feet tall; colorful in the fall.

3. Switch-grass, *Panicum virgatum.* Has large open seed heads. Blooms from August to September; three to five feet tall.

4. Blazing-star, *Liatris aspera, L. punctata, L. pycnostachya, L. spicata.* Cattaillike pink blooms appear in August; three to four feet tall.

5. White wild indigo, *Baptisia leucantha.* White, sweet-pea-like flowers. Blooms in June and July; three to four feet tall.

6. Little bluestem, *Andropogon scoparius.* Tufted, clumping, medium-size grass. Blooms in August; two to four feet tall; colorful in the fall.

7. Cream wild indigo, *Baptisia leucophaea.* Mound-producing plant. Cream yellow, sweet-pea-like flowers bloom in May; one to two feet tall.

8. Pasque flower, *Anemone patens,* var. *Wolfgangiana.* Earliest prairie plant to bloom. Lavender flowers appear in April; one foot tall.

9. New England aster, *Aster novae-angliae.* Showy prairie aster. Purple flowers bloom from September to November; four to six feet tall.

10. Yellow coneflower, *Ratibida pinnata.* Yellow blooms appear in July and August; five to six feet tall.

11. Prairie coreopsis, *Coreopsis palmata.* Prolific yellow flowers. Blooms from June to August; two feet tall.

12. Butterfly weed, *Asclepias tuberosa.* The showiest of the milkweeds. Orange flowers bloom from June to August; two feet tall.

13. Northern dropseed, *Sporobolus heterolepis.*

Little bluestem grass, *Andropogon scoparius,* and purple prairie clover, *Petalostemon purpureum,* are common inhabitants of the prairie.

Loveliest of the prairie grasses. Blooms in August or September; three feet tall.

14. Purple coneflower, *Echinacea pallida.* Flowers have drooping pink petals and rounded purple centers. Blooms in June or July; two feet tall.

15. Lead plant, *Amorpha canescens.* A prairie shrub with tiny blue green leaflets and spikes of deep purple flowers. Blooms in June or July; two feet tall.

Sideoats grama and Texas coneflower are often found together and are much more common now than the native grouse that used to inhabit much of the prairie.

16. Purple prairie clover, *Petalostemon purpureum*. Purple blooms from July to August; one foot tall.

17. Stiff goldenrod, *Solidago rigida*. Large flowering goldenrod. Blooms from August to October; three to four feet tall.

18. Prairie smoke, *Geum triflorum*. Early spring bloomer with three pink bell-like flowers that never open. Blooms from April to June; one foot tall.

19. Bird-foot violet, *Viola pedata*. Showiest of the prairie violets. Blue violet flowers bloom from May to June; five inches tall.

20. Shooting-star, *Dodecatheon Meadia*. Pink blooms appear in May or June; one to two feet tall.

21. Blue-eyed grass, *Sisyrinchium albidum, S. angustifolium, S. campestre*. Small plants with blue or white flowers. Blooms from May to June; six to eight inches tall.

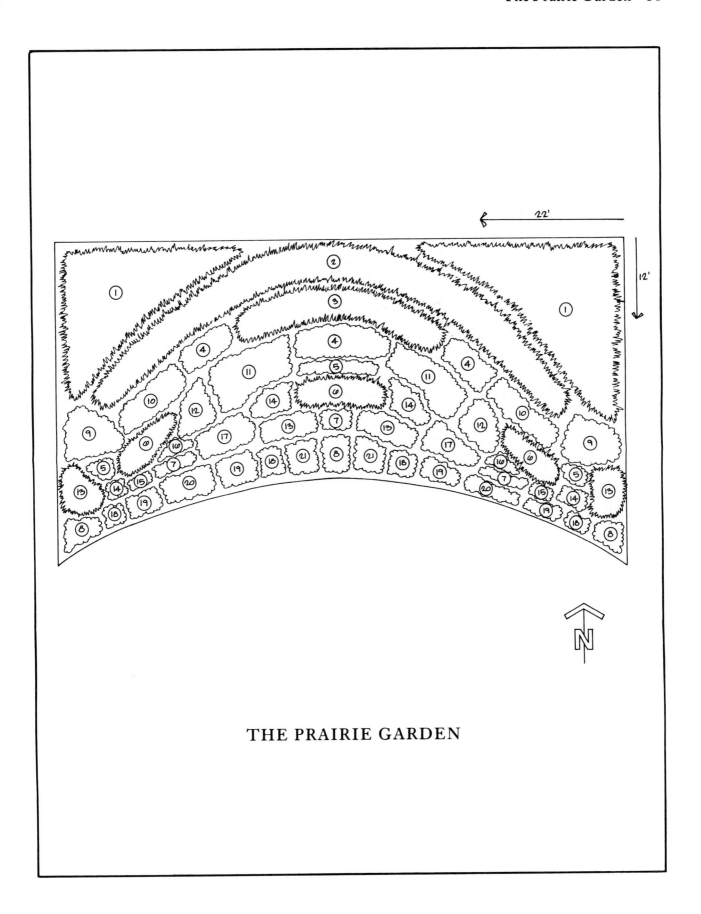

THE PRAIRIE GARDEN

Sources of Information

Books

Diekelmann, John, and Schuster, Robert. *Natural Landscaping, Designing with Native Plant Communities.* New York: McGraw-Hill Book Co., 1982. Basic information on landscaping with natural ecosystems, including prairies.

Nichols, Stan, and Entine, Lynn. *Prairie Primer.* Madison: University of Wisconsin—Extension, 1978. A marvelous little book for beginners that has all the basics.

Rock, Harold W. *Prairie Propagation Handbook.* Hales Corners, Wis.: Milwaukee County Department of Parks, 1981. This basic text is necessary for those who are interested in maintaining a prairie garden.

Smith, J. Robert, and Smith, Beatrice S. *The Prairie Garden.* Madison: University of Wisconsin Press, 1980. A useful book that describes in detail seventy native prairie plants and how to use them in your yard. In addition, it details how to collect seeds, raise your own plants, and maintain a prairie.

Demonstration Gardens

Alfred L. Boerner Botanical Gardens
Wehr Nature Center
5879 South 92nd Street
Hales Corners, WI 53130
This botanical organization has been very active in prairie restoration, has a prairie project, and can offer extensive information on prairie gardening.

Morton Arboretum
Lisle, IL 60532
The Morton Arboretum has a wonderful stand of prairie that is open to the public, as well as a very well informed staff.

Shaw Arboretum
P.O. Box 38
Gray Summit, MO 63039
A wonderful prairie to walk through. It's about a half hour's drive from St. Louis. The arboretum offers information on prairies.

Nurseries

Wildflower and Prairie Grass Seeds

Midwest Wildflowers
Box 64
Rockton, IL 61072

Prairie Restoration
P.O. Box 327
Princeton, MN 55371

Stock Seed Farms
R.R. Box 112
Murdock, NB 68407

Wehr Nature Center
5879 South 92nd Street
Hales Corners, WI 53130
Sells only mixed prairie seeds.

Windrift Prairie Nursery
Route 2
Oregon, IL 61061
Catalog 30 cents in stamps.

Native Grass Seeds

L.L. Olds Seed Company
P.O. Box 7790
Madison, WI 53707

Sharp Bros. Seed Company
Healy, KS 67850

Iris Shrevei, an inhabitant of the moist regions of the prairie.

Eschscholzia californica

Chapter 4

The Chaparral Garden

The cobalt blue ceanothus blooms, the delicate pink manzanita flowers, and the drifts of California poppies glorify spring in northern California. In southern California the lavender sages, the majestic Matilija poppies, and the cheerful California red fuchsias give a dazzling show in summer. In New Mexico the brilliant yellow rabbit brush and alders contrast with the red soil to enliven fall. Throughout the Southwest native plants enrich our environment. Newcomers to this climate, unfamiliar with native plants and bent on duplicating an eastern garden, have often overlooked many of these beauties. If you want a spectacular flowerbed, instead of choosing the usual delphiniums, dahlias, and foxgloves that need continual staking, spraying, and watering, consider the pleasure and relative low maintenance of a flower border filled with lupines, velvet purple sages, ruby red penstemons, yellow fluffy buckwheat blooms, and California poppies. Not only are these natives much easier to maintain, most of them attract native hummingbirds and butterflies.

The American Southwest is an exciting place to garden. The native flora is extremely varied because there are more extremes of climate zones in the Southwest than in most of the rest of the world. It is not an unusual year when Mount Whitney registers 30 degrees below zero and Furnace Creek, less than one hundred miles away in Death Valley, registers 120 degrees six months later. In California some northern areas get more than one hundred inches of rain a year, while desert areas sometimes go a full year without any rain at all. In some places valuable moisture is available from fog or an occasional thunderstorm, but most plants native to the Southwest must adapt to limited water conditions, and adaptation over eons to the West's arid climates has filled this part of the world with literally thousands of drought-tolerant plant species. Thus, the gardener has many native plants to choose from that don't require constant watering and pampering.

The many climate zones, as well as proximity to the ocean and great variations in soils, have created a dramatic number of dominant plant communities in the Southwest. Those in the coastal areas supplement the winter rains with fog off the ocean. Plants from these areas will not grow well in dry inland gardens unless they have occasional summer watering. Redwood forests with wood sorrel and sword ferns; plants of the coastal strands—lupines, wild strawberries, and silk-tassel—all need some supplemental watering if grown in areas away from the coast. In sharp contrast to the fog-loving redwood forests are the deserts, where yuccas, pinon pines, and creosote bushes must be able to survive extreme summer temperatures with little moisture and, often, strongly alkaline soils, caliche (deposits of sand or clay impregnated with crystalline salts that are impenetrable to roots), and drying winds as well. Most of the desert plants not only don't need much water, they often can't tolerate it and sometimes have been labeled temperamental by gardeners who plant them near a lawn or feel sorry for them during midsummer and continually water them.

There are great variations in climate in the American Southwest, more than in many other areas of the world; therefore, you must be very aware of your microclimate when you choose native plants. When a plant is labeled *native,* the question has to be: native to where? A particular California native will not necessarily be appropriate to all parts of California, just as a particular Arizona native may not be native to all parts of Arizona. Consequently, a thorough investigation of your yard's climate is the first order of business when you want to select native plants.

In addition to considerations of climate, there are other factors that you must know about the plants of the Southwest when you are going to put in a garden of indigenous plants.

1. Because most residents in the Southwest are immigrants from rainier climates, typically we have chosen plants and garden styles that revolve around constant summer irrigation.

Therefore our garden practices and expectations are not always compatible with native plants. For example, lawn watering has killed many natives.

2. Most drought-tolerant plants can't tolerate much, if any, summer watering and generally need very fast drainage. (If watered too much, often they will appear to thrive the first few summers, only to die within two or three years.)

3. The seeds of a number of native plants need special treatment before they will germinate. In their native state some will not germinate until a fire has heated them or the acid in an animal's stomach has activated them. (There are ways of duplicating these processes, so don't be discouraged when seeds you have collected won't germinate.)

4. The majority of southwestern natives look their best in the winter and spring, and that does not always fit the expectations of gardeners from other parts of the country. The California buckeye, for instance, in order to avoid water loss, sheds its large fleshy leaves in midsummer. Many desert, or arid-climate, wildflowers have a short life cycle, blooming in the rainy spring and dying soon after. If you wish to counterbalance the winter- and spring-blooming natives, you can supplement them with compatible summer- and fall-blooming plants from other parts of the world.

5. Many of the southwestern native plants are very limited in their adaptability. They are quite fussy about the kind of soil, drainage, and watering they get.

6. A number of southwestern natives can adapt to many different soils and watering schedules and are useful for "fleshing out" your indigenous native garden or for using with your exotic plants. A few choices are: many of the native pines, baccharis, some of the ceanothus hybrids, toyon, redbud, monkey flower, and Douglas iris. (For many additional suggestions, see the publication of the Santa Barbara Botanic Garden that is described on page 64.)

7. Hillsides in various parts of the West are subject to erosion and slippage. Many of the native plants have very strong root systems and are useful to retain the soil. Select manzanita, Matilija poppy, buckwheat, ceanothus species, toyon, sumac, and oak species.

8. Many chaparral plants, including some that would do well in flower borders, such as sage, native grasses, and buckwheat, are quite flammable. Because fire is a hazard in much of the Southwest, plants like these should be used sparingly and should be combined with some of the fire-retarding plants such as ice plant, Capeweed, African daisy, toyon, and rosemary to offset fire danger. As a rule, using low flower borders like the one suggested, rather than many flammable trees near the house, makes your landscaping somewhat fire resistant.

9. Western native seeds and plants are in short supply in local nurseries. For a large selection, you will probably need to have your nursery order plants from one of the wholesale nurseries listed at the end of this chapter. If you are lucky, you will find a local retail nursery that specializes in native plants, and you can choose what you want there.

Southwestern native plants are versatile landscape plants that, when established in their native range, are easier to maintain, cost less to keep up, and use fewer resources than the traditional landscape plantings. Unfortunately many of these beautiful plants are used too infrequently. Still, they are "at home" in shrub borders and are useful as ground covers, shade trees, and vines. They make stunning, drought-tolerant flower borders.

Chaparral Flower Borders

The English perennial flower border has inspired many gardeners all over the world to duplicate this beautiful array of blooming plants. Unfortunately in arid climates gardeners have been frustrated because delphinium, astilbe, phlox, dahlia, foxglove, and many

Ceanothus, also known as California lilac, is covered with bright blue clusters of blossoms in the spring.

of the other perennials that are the backbone of those bouquet borders are hard to grow in arid conditions and need regular watering. Even when well watered, they never look as lush as they do in a cool moist climate.

Fortunately there are alternative flower borders for western gardens that can help assuage the craving for vast swaths of bright and varied flowers. Borders can be filled with flowering plants that love the heat and in most cases need little watering, plants that come primarily from the American Southwest and other arid climates of the world—the Mediterranean, South Africa, and Australia.

Because I favor native plants, I use them to form the backbone of my flower borders. There are bright yellow, orange, pink, purple, fire-engine red, and cobalt blue flowers, which attract native insects and hummingbirds. This rainbow of flowers is often set off by either gray or gray green foliage, and the combination is striking, making the borders quite distinctive. While it is possible to choose native species that bloom in late summer and fall, the majority of the western natives bloom in late winter, spring, and early summer. If you want to prolong the blooming season, select carefully for the late-blooming natives and flesh them out with a number of exotics that also bloom later. Not only are the resulting borders beautiful, they are versatile. They can be put in a small, sunny, sidewalk strip in the suburbs or on a hillside. They can be designed to be low maintenance, or they can be a lifetime hobby, constantly changing and challenging the gardener.

In order to accommodate the usual garden of exotic plants and natives from other parts of the West, most books for southwestern gardeners stress the great range of garden conditions that exist in people's gardens in order to acquaint gardeners with the changes in soil and watering they must make in their gardens. I, on the other hand, stress the differences in order to underline the importance of analyzing your site and climate, so you will appreciate how carefully you must match the plants to your conditions. The point is not to alter the conditions with soil amendments and watering schedules, but to fine-tune the right plants for the area.

I am not a purist; I am in full sympathy with the gardener who wants to have a showy garden all year round. Still, I think it is best to arrange the garden habitat around the indigenous habitat, its plants, and its animals. Then choose plants from other areas (exotics) that require similar growing conditions to enrich the planting. Don't impose a completely artificial habitat on the site, supplementing it with only an occasional native plant. To get ideas for your own chaparral garden, look at the coastal California shrub and flower garden filled with natives that is included in this chapter.

Planning and Preparation

Choose a sunny part of your yard. It can be down the side of the driveway, around the patio, on the back hillside, an area visible from the kitchen window, or up the front walk—anywhere that you will enjoy the show!

Measure the area and draw it to scale on paper. Lay sheets of tracing paper over the scale drawing, and make several designs. Use your imagination and play around with beds of different shapes. Also, experiment to see if a path through the garden is interesting. Add mounds and a boulder or two, or think about whether a fence across the back would make the area more interesting. For additional inspiration, look at pictures in garden books. Here are a few design hints.

1. Paths and fences near or in the bed will help unify the area and give it strong lines.

2. Most native plants are rather informal and look best with designs incorporating relaxed, curved, or freeform lines rather than straight lines, strong geometric forms, and clipped hedges.

3. Natural-looking materials such as wood and stone generally are the most pleasing visually.

4. Flat, level areas are often made more interesting with mounds or planter boxes.

5. Native flower borders work well with a number of inexpensive or recycled building materials, such as railroad ties, driftwood, used concrete paths and walls, recycled barn timbers, and telephone poles.

6. Unify the planting bed by choosing three or four species of plants that will predominate; otherwise, the design will be too jumbled.

7. Instead of using all colors, select three or four colors of flowers to unify the design, for example, red, orange, yellow, and white; or pink, purple, yellow, and blue; or red, yellow, and blue. Try to limit yourself as much as possible to the color combinations you choose.

After you have created a pleasing design on paper, determine your garden's soil conditions. Is the soil acidic or alkaline? sandy or clayey? Is the drainage good, or is the area boggy in the winter? What are the weather conditions? Determine the winter low and the summer high temperatures as well as the predominant wind direction. Is yours a sunny warm yard or a cool shady one? For more information, contact local experts: airports often have information on weather conditions, university extension people have soil information, and local nurseries and plant societies can help you analyze your soil conditions. The books listed at the end of this chapter also contain helpful information.

Once you know your climate, soil, and weather conditions, you can start looking for plants that will grow in your garden. Make a list of native and drought-tolerant flowering plants that you've found to be appropriate for your garden. Beside the name of each plant, write its height, flower color, and blooming season. Select the flower colors you would like. Choose plants of different heights, clustering the taller ones to the rear, the shorter ones in the front. Then select some plants that bloom at different times of the year so your garden will be interesting all year round. If you are using boulders or walls, cluster around them plants that have spiky foliage or flowers such as sage, Douglas iris, lupine, echium, red-hot-poker, and fortnight lily. If you are using retaining walls or planter boxes or are planting on a hillside, try plants that cascade, such as ivy geranium, prostrate rosemary, bougainvillea, African daisy, ice plant, lantana, and the native prostrate ceanothus, manzanita, and California fuchsia.

Planting the Drought-tolerant Garden

The best time to plant West Coast natives is in the fall before the rains come so that the roots can get well established before the long hot summer. Most drought-tolerant plants have strong, deep root systems. If possible, dig large planting holes. If gophers are a problem, surround the root ball with a basket made of chicken wire. Make sure that the basket protrudes above the ground three or four inches to prevent the gophers from crawling over the top. To prevent root-rot problems, plant the natives so that the crowns (where the bark meets the root tissue) are an inch or two above the soil

line, thus preventing water from covering that area for long periods of time. To conserve water and to add organic matter to the soil, mulch (cover the soil with two or three inches of organic matter) and water the plants well.

Most of the plants recommended in this chapter need biweekly watering the first two summers. Once the plants are established, they can survive the dry summer with only three or four waterings. Actually many of the natives can go through the whole summer with no supplemental watering; however, many gardeners prefer to water them a few times in the summer so they will be more lush. The most efficient and effective way to water is to use a drip irrigation system. (If you live in an area where the fire danger is high, consider, instead, installing an overhead watering system so that if a fire occurs, you could turn it on.)

Dr. Littauer planting in a wire basket for gopher control.

Maintaining the Drought-tolerant Border

Once established, usually in two years, the drought-tolerant border requires a minimum of maintenance. The bed will need annual pruning and fertilizing, weeding a few times a year, and an occasional watering. Pruning is particularly necessary for some of the rangy natives, such as dendromecon, sage, and Matilija poppy to keep them in bounds. Keep an eye out for an occasional gopher or pest problem. (Some of the plants recommended in this section, such as the fast-growing echium, lavender, and lantana and the ceanothus and sage are either short-lived or tend to get woody with age and need to be taken out and replaced in five or six years. All are fast growers, and replacements will fill in quickly.)

A Sample Garden

A beautiful model for a native, drought-tolerant flower border is the one I put together with Ernest and Deveda Littauer for their northern California yard. The Littauers' home is situated on a hillside and is surrounded by native chaparral. They wanted a design that included their patio hillside and the new deck area around the hot tub. The design for their yard had to take into account the Littauers' gardening style: They are avid gardeners but prefer propagating and putting in new plants, picking flowers, and puttering, to watering, weeding, spraying, mowing, and clipping. They love bright colors and unusual plants and were intent on using a number of native and drought-tolerant exotic plants in their garden.

The problems the Littauers have in their yard are similar to those of many hillside gardens on the West Coast; that is, fire danger, deer, and gophers. We reduced the fire danger by selecting fire-retarding plants and by eliminating those plants that are particularly combustible. We controlled the gophers primarily by planting most plants in chicken-wire baskets. We kept the deer problem to a minimum by choosing as many deer-resistant species as possible. Those included sage, African daisy, ice plant, rosemary, and echium. We also used the 'Dark Star' ceanothus, which is reputed to be somewhat deerproof.

To give coherence and strong lines to both hillside areas, we first created paths through the areas and sculptured some of the flat areas by adding mounds. The Littauers gave me carte blanche on plant choices, and, to unify the garden, I chose some of the Littauers' favorite colors: lavender, yellow, and blue. In addition, I used a number of plants with gray green foliage to help the garden merge into primarily gray green native chaparral. For the predominant vegetation I chose a number of blue ceanothus, sage, light pink ice plant, yellow dendromecon, many colors of penstemon, prostrate blue rosemary, and, for a fast-growing ground cover, yellow Capeweed. To give more summer and fall bloom, I added lavender echium, white fortnight lily, pink New Zealand tea, and, given my penchant for edible plants, a beautiful red-flowered pomegranate.

Responding with enthusiasm to the delightful spectrum of native plants, the Littauers soon started propagating and planting many more natives, a list of which follows. The Littauers' experience yielded a few words of advice.

1. The couple visited a nursery expressly devoted to native plants and received advice as well as getting a large selection of plants.

2. They were observant gardeners and noticed that the Matilija poppy was starting to become invasive, so they took it out.

3. They started to grow many of the natives from seed so that they would have a larger selection. (Ernest stresses strongly that it is important to start your native seeds in a sterile medium such as perlite so that they don't develop fungus problems.)

4. Ernest admonishes you not to feel sorry for and water the very drought tolerant plants when they start to look parched in the summer.

5. As beginning native gardeners, they found the book *California Native Trees and Shrubs* invaluable.

6. The Littauers have a windy yard and found that a number of their plants blew over, particularly when gophers had been eating the roots. They recommend heavily pruning the taller plants that are prone to wind damage.

7. They also experienced the frustration of an exotic plant "gone crazy"—a previously planted Scotch broom became a nuisance—it spread too freely—and needed to be eradicated.

Native Plants for a Drought-tolerant Garden

Buckwheat, *Eriogonum* species, chartreuse, white, brown

Bush poppy, *Dendromecon rigida,* yellow

California fuchsia, *Zauschneria californica,* red

California lilac, *Ceanothus* species, blue, white

California poppy, *Eschscholzia californica,* orange, yellow

Douglas iris, *Iris Douglasiana,* white, purple

Evening primrose, *Oenothera Hookeri,* yellow

Fremontodendron, *Fremontodendron californicum,* yellow

Island bush snapdragon, *Galvezia speciosa,* red

Lupine, *Lupinus arboreus,* purple, yellow, white

Manzanita, *Arctostaphylos* species, pink

Monkey flower, *Mimulus* species, yellow, orange

Penstemon, *Penstemon cordifolius,* red, yellow

Redbud, *Cercis occidentalis,* magenta

Sage, *Salvia* species, purple, red, lavender

Sugarbush, *Rhus ovata,* red, cream

Toyon, *Heteromeles arbutifolia,* white, red berries

Tree anemone, *Carpenteria californica,* white

Penstemon

Nonnative, Drought-tolerant Flowering Plants

The following nonnatives combine well with California natives. They require little water and will grow in many climate zones in the West. Choose those that will grow well in your area. These perennials can be supplemented with spring-blooming wildflowers and bulbs.

African daisy, *Arctotis* species, orange, yellow
    and *Osteospermum fruticosum,* purple, white
Aloe, *Aloe* species, red, yellow
Bougainvillea, *Bougainvillea* species, rose,
    red, orange, purple
Cape honeysuckle, *Tecomaria capensis,*
    orange
Capeweed, *Arctotheca calendula,* yellow
Echium, *Echium* species, purple
Fortnight lily, *Dietes vegeta,* white
Geranium, *Pelargonium* species, red, orange,
    lavender, pink
Grevillea, *Grevillea* species (low-growing
    types), red, pink
Iris, *Iris* species (bearded types), older varieties
    are more drought tolerant
Lantana, *Lantana* species, yellow, pink, laven-
    der, white, red, salmon
Lavender, *Lavandula* species, lavender
Natal plum, *Carissa* species, white
New Zealand tea, *Leptospermum* species,
    pink, rose
Oleander, *Nerium Oleander* (dwarf types),
    salmon, pink
Pineapple guava, *Feijoa Sellowiana,* reddish
Plumbago, *Plumbago auriculata,* blue
Pomegranate, *Punica Granatum,* red
Red-hot-poker, *Kniphofia Uvaria,* red, yellow,
    white
Rock rose, *Cistus* species, white, pink
Rosemary, *Rosmarinus* species, blue
Sedum, *Sedum* species, white, pink, yellow
Senecio, *Senecio Greyi,* yellow
Statice (sea lavender), *Limonium Perezii,*
    lavender

Scrub oak

The layout of this chaparral garden emphasizes blooming plants. The Littauers' chaparral garden is ablaze with blue ceanothus, yellow Capeweed and dendromecon, pink New Zealand tea, and white African daisies. It can be viewed from both the deck and the house. To give the garden form as well as color, retaining walls and a curving path were added.

1. African daisies
2. New Zealand tea
3. Capeweed
4. Ceanothus 'Ray Hartman'
5. Rock rose
6. Ceanothus 'Dark Star'
7. Mexican bush sage
8. Dendromecon
9. Pomegranate
10. Lemon
11. Lime
12. Lion's-tail sage
13. Pink ice plant
14. Bougainvillea
15. Fremontodendron
16. Purple sage
17. Penstemon
18. Echium
19. Ceanothus 'Snow Ball'
20. Redbud
21. Rosemary
22. Fortnight lily
23. Lavender

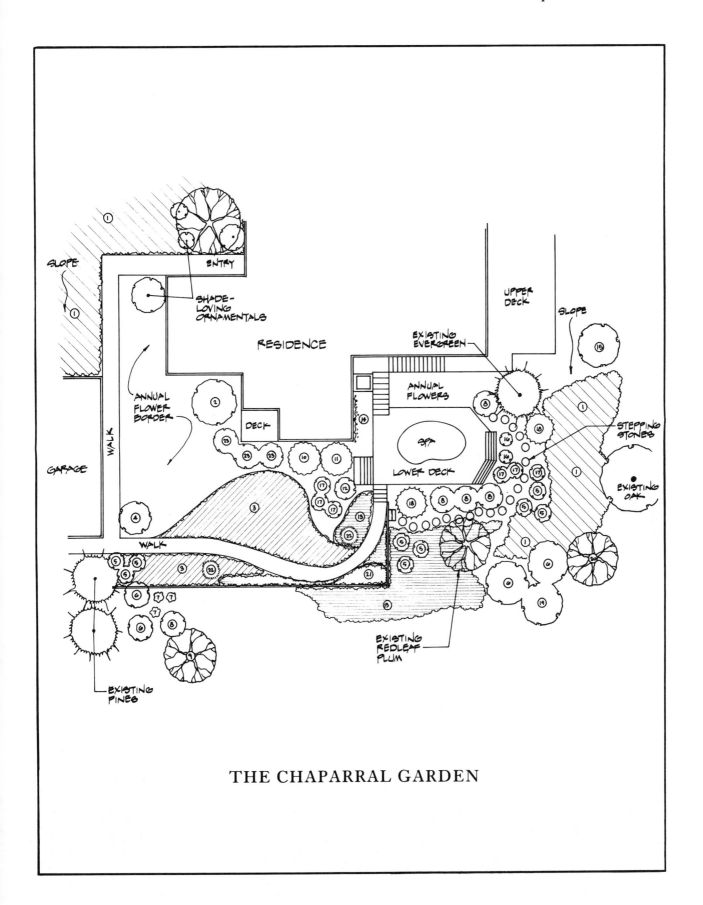

THE CHAPARRAL GARDEN

Sources of Information

Books

Lenz, Lee W., and Dourley, John. *California Native Trees and Shrubs for Garden and Environmental Use in Southern California and Adjacent Areas.* Claremont, Calif.: Rancho Santa Ana Botanic Garden, 1981. This book is excellent for the gardener who is just beginning to use native plants.

Ortho Books, Chevron Chemical Company editorial staff. *All About Perennials.* San Francisco: Ortho Books, 1981. This book is primarily about water-loving nonnative plants; however, it has valuable information about how to work with perennial flower borders and flower color.

Ortho Books, Chevron Chemical Company editorial staff. *The World of Cactuses and Succulents.* San Francisco: Ortho Books, 1977. How to grow, select, and maintain cactuses and succulents.

Perry, Bob. *Trees and Shrubs for Dry California Landscapes.* San Dimas, Calif.: Land Design Publishing, 1981. Valuable information about drought-tolerant plants; color prints.

Santa Barbara Botanic Garden. *Native Plants for Southern California Gardens.* No. 12. Santa Barbara: Santa Barbara Botanic Garden, 1969. Detailed information on California native plants and the growing conditions they prefer.

Saratoga Horticultural Foundation. *Selected California Native Plants with Commercial Sources.* 3rd ed. Saratoga, Calif.: Saratoga Horticultural Foundation, 1983. This book is particularly helpful in finding sources for the native plants you want.

Smith, Ken. *Western Home Landscaping.* Tucson, Ariz.: H.P. Books, 1978. A helpful book for home landscapers. It has quite a bit of information on drought-tolerant plants and how to put in a drip irrigation system.

Sunset Books editorial staff. *New Western Garden Book.* Menlo Park, Calif.: Lane Publishing Co., 1979. This book is a must for all western gardeners; it's considered the bible of West Coast gardening.

Additional information on native and drought-tolerant plants is available from the California State Water Resources Board and from many local water districts.

Demonstration Gardens

Rancho Santa Ana Botanic Garden
1500 North College Avenue
Claremont, CA 91711

Regional Parks Botanic Garden
Tilden Regional Park
Berkeley, CA 94708

Santa Barbara Botanic Garden
1212 Mission Canyon Road
Santa Barbara, CA 93105

Nurseries

Ask your local nursery to order from the following wholesale sources.

For northern California:

Saratoga Horticultural Foundation
20605 Verde Vista Lane
Saratoga, CA 95070

For midcoast and southern California:

Native Sons
379 West El Campo Road
Arroyo Grande, CA 93420

Tree of Life Nursery
P.O. Box 736
San Juan Capistrano, CA 92693

You can order seeds by mail from:

Clyde Robin Seed Company
P.O. Box 2366
Castro Valley, CA 94546

Consumer Note

Two hints on obtaining southwestern natives are: (1) many of the drought-tolerant natives have long taproots and don't do well in nursery containers; buy them as small as possible, or start them in place from seed; and (2) get to know and frequent local native plant nurseries, and join your native plant society; they will be your best sources of information and plants.

Yucca species

PART TWO

ARK GARDENS

Recreating and preserving ecosystems are effective ways of enabling nature to preserve itself, but setting up such environments often results in fairly stable, low-maintenance yards that for some people just don't satisfy the need to roll up the sleeves and *garden*. In seeking an outlet for an abundance of creative energy, both active gardeners and frustrated conservationists might consider adopting this chapter's guiding concept: the garden as ark, a la Noah himself. The idea here is to seek out and save plant species—both wild and domestic—that are threatened with extinction. Raise them in a garden designed especially to allow them to thrive, safe from the rigors of an advancing civilization seemingly bent on stamping them out. The challenge and excitement of rescuing and growing a rare orchid or caring for an endangered rose that was once grown in ancient Rome give zest to gardening.

When we think of Noah's Ark, we picture lions, tigers, and giraffes, not daffodils, lady's-slippers, and sacks of seeds. People think in terms of saving animals, not plants; and, hence, modern Noahs tend to be more interested in saving whales and baby seals than prairie bunch grasses and tropical orchids.

What good does it do, though, to save the giant panda and not its bamboo habitat? I don't dispute the necessity of saving animals, but if we fail to preserve plants and their ecosystems, the animals that depend on those plants will disappear no matter what.

Sometimes I feel like the child in *The Emperor's New Clothes*. Nearly every column, book, or conference on gardening is filled with news of the latest ruffled petunia or new rose color. "Look," they say, "the world is filled with new and better plants." I want to get up on a rooftop and shout, "Hold it! What about the species we're losing?" For every new petunia or begonia we create each week, we allow three species of plants in the wild to become extinct; and we doom to the scrap heap numerous "out-of-fashion" domestic plants. How can so many plant lovers be so blind? Ninety percent of the material written about plants in this country is concerned with the newest cultivated plants; it ignores the historical domestic species and the grim plight of the ever-more-vulnerable wild species. We gardeners must get involved in preserving plants. Let's hear it for the endangered *plant* species of the world!

Why should we bother to save ecosystems and rare and heritage plants? Some cite philosophical reasons, saying that such organisms and environments have as much right to existence on earth as we do. Others want to preserve them because it is fun to work with these living pieces of history. But the practical reasons should convince us of the necessity for conservation. Like the panda, *we* can't survive without plants. While it appears that this country runs on Big Macs, the real fuel is the ten pounds of hay per pound of body weight consumed by the cattle from which our Big Macs are made. Moreover, if animals disappeared from this planet, we would still eat well. As it is, plants provide food, clothing, and shelter for the majority of the people on earth. In addition to providing basic human needs, plants enrich our lives by giving us healing medicines, shade on sweltering summer days, and even the cotton for our jeans.

Herbal Medicine

Take two pieces of willow bark and call me in the morning. Because our medicines come in bottles and have unfamiliar names, few of us are aware that many of them have been derived from plants. Digitalis, which regulates the heartbeat, comes from foxglove; ipecac, which induces vomiting and is helpful in cases where poison has been ingested, comes from the roots of the cephaelis plant; and quinine, which controls malaria, comes from cinchona trees. Even the precursor to good old aspirin was first discovered in a plant: willow bark. Less well known is the fact that many of the so-called wonder drugs discovered between 1930 and 1960 were of vegetative origin: antibiotics come from molds, and reserpine comes from Indian snake root. Oral contraceptives and cortisone resulted from research done on the Mexican yam. It seems ironic, but just as medical botany is taking off, well equipped with spectrographs, electron microscopes, and computers to analyze and take advantage of newly discovered plants, many ecosystems and their plants are slipping away.

In areas other than medical botany, plant life is being explored as an important resource. In Israel, for example, certain plants are being bred to serve as indicators of pollution levels. Elsewhere, a certain wild cucumber has been discovered that can temporarily acidify human seminal fluid, thus offering a contraceptive method that could revolutionize birth control. And in the new field of genetic engineering, though the actuality is years away, scientists are developing the potential to implant a gene from a bean plant into a tomato plant to make the tomato plant capable of fixing nitrogen in the soil the way the bean plant does. Such a tomato would not need as much nitrogen fertilizer as our contemporary varieties do. In theory, then, eventually we will be able to create almost any kind of plant we want, feature by feature, so long as we maintain a large enough gene pool to draw from.

Nearly 200 species of wild plants are lost every year, and the rate of loss is accelerating. The shocking truth is that biologists estimate that by the year 2000, 25 percent, or 40,000 species, of higher plants will be extinct. Compare that estimate with the historical figures: A mere 200 species have been lost over the last 500 years.

What can we do? As I stated in Part One, saving endangered plant species begins with preserving ecosystems. And while it is of value to keep endangered species alive by growing them in an alien habitat, once plants are taken out of their natural habitats and domesticated, they, like animals, change subtly over generations, adapting to their new environments. In addition, many species, although they stay alive for a number of years, fail to reproduce in an altered environment, so only their fleeting presence is gained. In Part Two, based on the assumption that you have maintained the natural ecosystem in at least a portion of your yard, I give detailed information on active conservation measures that are meant both to satisfy your passion for gardening and to preserve nature's diversity.

What the Master Gardener Can Do

If you are one of our nation's true plant mavens, you may be skilled enough to raise and propagate, in an approximation of their original habitats, some of the endangered orchids, cactuses, succulents, or other wild species. While this is not the optimum situation, at least it may keep them alive until a suitable habitat for them can be found. In addition, some rare plants that propagate easily can be maintained in the garden as a means of educating the public about the need to conserve rare plants. (Experienced gardeners should contact Dr. Rolf Martin, Department of Chemistry, Brooklyn College, Brooklyn, NY 11210, to learn about the program of the Rare and Endangered Native Plant Exchange.) Furthermore, keeping these endangered plants alive may help future breeding programs or provide seeds for wild areas.

Adele Dawson in Vermont takes an active part in saving native plants such as this bottle gentian that she saved from the snowplow's blade. Keep an eye out for possible development areas and become involved in saving plants that would otherwise be destroyed.

Gardens with a Purpose

Domestic plants as well as wild ones need an ark. Save seeds from open-pollinated (non-hybrid) vegetables and fill your yard with endangered domestic plants, both ornamental and edible. The gardens described in Part Two —the heirloom vegetable garden, the wildlife garden, the heritage rose garden, and the orchid garden—incorporate these principles with dazzling effects.

When we think of an endangered plant species, we almost always envision a beleaguered plant out in the wild. But wild plants are not the only ones endangered. More and more botanists are becoming aware that our valuable domestic gene pool is being depleted at an ever-accelerating rate.

By *gene pool* I mean the rich heritage of flowers and edibles that people have been cultivating for centuries. Some of these plants have origins as far back as ancient Greece and Rome. Even some of the plants that our great-great-grandparents grew one hundred years ago were quite different from those that we have in our gardens today. In fact, the gardens of our great-great-grandparents had many flowers and vegetables we may never have seen: red celery, 'Howling Mob' corn, 'Maiden's Blush' roses, 'Dwarf-Giant' tomato, 'Lazy Wife's' beans, and thousands more.

What has happened to those plant species? Many simply dropped out of favor. Gardening is as susceptible to the whims of fashion as any other endeavor in our society. During the last ten to twenty years, for example, fragrant roses were out of favor and large double petunias were in. Now it looks as if fragrant roses are coming back into vogue. Also back with us are some of the old-fashioned single petunias and some of the more subtle marigolds and zinnias. Certainly there are many varieties to choose from, particularly when it comes to ornamental plants. Over the hundreds of years that people have been cultivating plants, there have been,

for example, between 17,000 and 18,000 varieties of daffodils. Not all of the thousands of varieties are of value, but many of the old-timers that have disappeared would be cherished today. Some have unusual forms; many were very fragrant; still others grew with little water. Sadly, however, when these plants go out of favor, within a generation or two they often disappear altogether—another example of our "throw-away" culture.

The sight of some of Great-Aunt Polly's and Great-Uncle Jack's fruits and vegetables would probably surprise you. Instead of a 'Granny Smith' apple tree or 'Thompson Seedless' grapes, they may have had a 'Red Astrachan' or a 'Baldwin' apple tree or 'Muscat of Alexandria' grapes. And they may have grown some particularly tasty, but odd-colored, vegetables, such as yellow beets and tomatoes, purple broccoli and cauliflower, and blue corn and potatoes. Besides varieties unfamiliar to contemporary gardeners, they may have grown types of edibles that are out of favor now; for instance, there were gooseberries, quince, Good King Henry (a spinachlike vegetable), and rampion (a white edible tuber).

Corporations and the Seed Business

Fashion and taste aren't the only reasons your edible garden differs from those of your ancestors. Our evolving understanding of breeding techniques has resulted in great improvements in disease resistance and plant adaptability and vigor. Unfortunately for home gardeners, many of the improvements developed by breeders have been aimed at the needs of the commercial grower. Years ago vegetable plants acclimated to people's own gardens and tastes because year after year gardeners collected the seeds from their best plants, those that grew best in their miniclimates and the ones whose taste they preferred. Nowadays many of the available varieties are determined

by the corporations that control the seed industry. An analogy with the clothing industry comes to my mind: Today most of us have sacrificed the style and fit of personally tailored clothes for the convenience and low cost of garments off the rack.

While some wonderful new hybrid vegetables and fruits (that is, plants created through selected crossbreeding) have been made available for home gardeners, it's their biggest customer, the farmer, whose interests increasingly dominate seed-breeding. The seed companies, to help the farmer, have bred for yield and disease resistance. While those characteristics have indisputably benefited the home grower, other characteristics; namely, uniformity in size, ability to withstand machine picking and sorting, uniform ripening, and the ability to ripen after harvest, are not in the interests of home gardeners but have been foisted upon them.

Nevertheless, those modern miracles, the cardboard tomato, the tasteless strawberry, and the juiceless peach—always available, handsome to look at, and a waste of the effort it takes to chew, much less grow—are a reality. With "progress" we are losing the delicious varieties of yesteryear.

Seed Saving

What can be done before it's too late? The solution is to grow many of the open-pollinated varieties of vegetables and to save seeds—so obvious and simple a solution to the problem that it might embarrass you, as it did me when I first started doing it. Turn now to the detailed description of a simple-to-create heirloom vegetable garden, in the following chapter, where you will find a thorough discussion of the time-honored practice of saving seeds.

PLANT RUSTLING

Rustled plants are those that are taken illegally from the wild. Plant rustlers go out into wild areas and dig up rare plants as well as some that are on the endangered species list, often illegally taking plants from private lands or national parks. The most commonly rustled plants are native orchids and cactuses. Plants from both of these families are slow growing, sometimes taking as long as five to ten years to be of salable size. Some of these plants are bought on impulse by the home-owner who just wants a few inexpensive house plants; still others are bought by collectors of rare plants. Collectors often don't realize the pressure they put on endangered plants in the wild and on the legitimate nursery people who propagate the rare plants only to compete with rustlers who sometimes sell the black-market plants out of the back of their trucks. Plant rustlers have no greenhouses to heat, no plants to water, and no expensive endangered-plant inspection permits to buy.

Ironically, while endangered-plant legislation was created to protect plants, according to the people at Grigsby's Cactus Nursery and other conscientious growers, the Endangered Species Act sometime does more harm than good. For instance, buying and selling of endangered species are controlled, and inspections are made and paid for when plants are sold across state lines. These controls increase the cost of growing plants legitimately and make the low prices charged by the black-market rustlers even more attractive. If the public stops buying from plant rustlers, fewer endangered plants will be taken illegally from the wild and legitimate growers will be encouraged to grow them in abundance.

Faith Campbell, a member of the Natural Resources Defense Council, gives the follow-ing guidelines for avoiding rustled plants. Be very cautious when buying any unusual plants. If the price seems too good to be true, it probably is. Buy only from established nurseries; never buy from roadside stands or trucks. Ask whether the plants were propagated. Notice whether the dealer has many plants of the same size and species. Notice whether cactuses and succulents look fresh, green, and symmetrical or "beat up," scarred, and skewed in shape. Most propagated cactuses will be small, symmetrical, and unscarred. Ask about care of the plants; if the seller can't tell you, he probably didn't propagate them.

There are a few plants to be particularly careful about because they are threatened by extinction. They are living-rock cactus, *Ariocarpus agavoides;* Aztec cactus, *Aztekium Ritteri;* artichoke cactus, *Obregonia Denegrii;* Amalia orchid, *Laelia jongheana;* blue vanda orchid, *Vanda coerulea;* fire orchid, *Renanthera Imschootiana;* green pitcher plant, *Sarracenia oreophila;* mountain sweet pitcher plant, *Sarracenia Jonesii;* giant pitcher plant, *Nepenthes rajah;* ghostman, *Pachypodium namaquanum;* spiral aloe, *Aloe polyphylla;* and broadleaf cycad, *Encephalartos latifrons.*

For a list of nurseries that propagate most, if not all, of their own native plants, write to The New England Wild Flower Society, Garden in the Woods, Hemenway Road, Framingham, MA 01701. The catalog is $1.50.

Cactuses and succulents that have been propagated in a nursery usually look healthier and more uniform than those that have been dug up (illegally, no doubt) in the wild. When looking for unusual native plants, frequent reputable nurseries such as Grigsby's, where a number of endangered species are propagated.

Chapter 5

The Heirloom Vegetable Garden

Just as civilization has saved "Aida," the Mona Lisa, and *Macbeth* for future generations, so should we save seeds of old-time vegetables and grafting material of heirloom fruit trees, says Carolyn Jabs in her book *The Heirloom Gardener.* They represent valuable achievements made by generations of gardeners and give a large range of choices to our descendants. Annual vegetable varieties are gossamer entities. Unlike a concerto that might be out of favor for a few years but is preserved because it is written on a sheet of paper, a carrot that has been grown for centuries can disappear in a year or two if no one grows it.

Growing an heirloom vegetable garden is an exciting variation on the usual array of current varieties such as 'Yolo Wonder' peppers, 'Silver Queen' corn, and 'Early Girl' tomatoes. It's stimulating to try the old-time yellow tomatoes, purple broccoli, and cylindrical potatoes, not to mention the feeling of kinship you'll have

with previous generations while you shell the same kind of beans your great-grandmother might have shelled.

Some of these old varieties have traits that make them valuable eating in their own right, while others may be good only for future breeding stock. The effect of acid rain, carbon monoxide, and salty irrigation water on plants, for example, could not have been predicted one hundred years ago. Some of the old varieties will grow well with less nitrogen or water; others are more salt tolerant. There will be many problems in the future that we can't foresee; therefore, it makes sense to keep as many plant-gene options as possible open for future generations.

How serious is the problem of annual vegetable variety erosion? Very! Thousands of varieties have already been lost. Kent Whealy, founder of Seed Savers Exchange, figures that only 20 percent of the pea varieties once in cultivation are still available. In the early 1900s a scientist compiled a list of 8,000 varieties of apples, and in 1981 the USDA could find only 1,000 varieties.

A great loss of varieties happened in the early part of this century when seed saving was discouraged and hybrid seeds were introduced. (In plant breeding, hybridizers cross specially selected strains and produce a second generation with desired characteristics.) Hybrid vegetables and grains have made American farms the most productive in the world, but, as with everything else in life, there have been trade-offs. Home gardeners have benefited from hybrids that are more disease resistant, more vigorous and higher yielding, but the cost has been high. Not collecting seeds means buying seeds and being dependent on seed companies, which means fewer options for home growing.

The erosion of home varieties is starting to snowball. The new wave of losses is a result of a growing national trend—the buying up and consolidation of many small seed companies by multinational corporations. The major seed companies, once owned by seedsmen, are now owned and run by business people. For example, ITT now owns Burpee; Monsanto owns Farmer's Hybrid; the Swiss corporation Sandoz owns Northrup-King; and Purex owns Ferry-Morse. Now the accountants as strongly as the seed people influence what is grown. And because farmers buy the great majority of seeds in this country, varieties of vegetables that are tailored for agriculture—extra-firm for shipping, simultaneous ripening of the whole crop—are now stressed. As a consequence, countless home varieties are being dropped.

You can help. You can save some of your own seeds. You can share them with others. You can join a seed-saving organization and grow some of the rarer varieties. Even some of the old woody carrot varieties and mealy potatoes have value, because some are particularly disease resistant. You can help also by spreading the word. Most of the media is flooded with the latest information on the newest hybrid. These hybrids are usually great, but we have relied too much on them, and an adjustment period is needed.

The panda and the snow leopard are endangered, and often we can do nothing more than send a check to a conservation organization or a letter to a senator. Saving heirloom seeds, however, has a direct impact on the problem. In addition, growing heirloom varieties is interesting; it's a great way to get a sense of history. Perhaps it will bring back a childhood memory and save you some money. You may very well discover that 'Howling Mob' corn and 'Purple' beans are the tastiest vegetables you have ever eaten.

Planning and Preparation

Because of the unpredictability of a first-time heirloom vegetable garden (that is, not knowing how well each variety will do in your garden and not knowing how well you will like each variety), you should not plan it as your only vegetable garden. Rather, it can be an exciting addition to some of your tried-and-true favorites.

To start your heirloom garden, you must obtain the seeds, thus, your introduction to seed saving. There are a number of ways to obtain seeds of heirloom species. The best way is to talk with some of your neighbors to find out if they have any varieties to share with you. If you don't come up with anything, contact Seed Savers Exchange or one of the other seed-saving organizations, or buy your seeds from one of the new seed companies that cater to heirloom growers. (See the lists of organizations and seed companies at the end of this chapter.)

Making your seed selections will take some research. There is much more variability with some of the old-time varieties than with hybrids in adaptability, viability, and yield. Some varieties taste better; some taste worse than what you're used to; some are just different. Some of the old string-bean varieties, for example, are particularly tasty, but each bean has a string down the side that is too tough to eat and must be pulled off; hence, the name *string* bean, right? You may like the taste but not the stringing.

Another characteristic of many of the old varieties is that they keep well. Before refrigeration it was critical that vegetables keep for long periods of time without rotting. Consequently, many of the old turnip, carrot, beet, and cabbage varieties can be stored very well in a root cellar. Another factor to consider when growing heirlooms is that while many of the varieties are disease resistant, others are particularly prone to certain diseases, and others have a very limited optimum-growth environmental range.

The limitations of some of the old varieties are what helped to make hybrids as popular today as they are. Hybrids offer adaptability, yield, and disease resistance. Remember, though, that one of the goals of growing heirloom plants is to make sure that we have the necessary starting points for future hybridization.

Begin by choosing six to eight varieties. The easiest families to start with are the legumes—beans and peas—and the solanaceae—tomatoes, peppers, and eggplants. Order a catalog from one of the recommended seed companies. Stick to open-pollinated varieties, no hybrids; the reasons will become clear as you read on.

You may want to order an heirloom vegetable kit from either Seeds Blum (the address is given at the end of this chapter), which carries a seed-saver's kit that includes nine varieties of vegetables, many of which are listed below, or from Roger A. Kline, Department of Vegetable Crops, Plant Science Building, Ithaca, NY 14853. Kline offers both large and small kits. The largest has twenty-two varieties, more than enough for a "demon" heirloom gardener. Some of the varieties in the

Carl Barnes of Oklahoma has been collecting and growing heirloom varieties of corn since 1946. His dedication to saving old corn varieties includes hand-pollinating the varieties he grows in order to prevent cross-pollination. He has been instrumental in organizing a group called CORNS.

large kit are 'Alaska' pea, 'Black Mexican' corn, 'Drumhead Savoy' cabbage, 'Jacob's Cattle' bean, 'Lady Finger' potato, 'Long Season' beet, 'Ponderosa' tomato, 'Purple-top Strap-leaf' turnip, 'Red Wethersfield' onion, and 'White Bush Scallop' squash. All kits include detailed seed-saving information.

Or you may want to choose from the lists that Jan Blum, owner of one of the new seed companies that is devoted to heirloom seeds, has put together. She has chosen heirloom vegetable varieties that she thinks are valuable and superior. The seeds are available from a number of the seed companies that carry heirloom seeds (an annotated list of those companies appears at the end of this chapter). If you are a beginning heirloom gardener and seed saver, Blum recommends that you start with the following varieties: 'Black Valentine' bean, 'Blue Coco' bean, 'Blue Pod' pea, 'Jacob's Cattle' bean, 'May King' lettuce, 'Oakleaf' lettuce, 'Persimmon' tomato, 'Ruby King' pepper, 'Super Italian' paste tomato, 'Tall Telephone' pea, and 'Wren's Egg' bean.

For experienced gardeners and seed savers, she recommends the following varieties because they offer more of a challenge: 'Dutch White Runner' bean, 'Early Scarlet Horn' carrot, 'French Breakfast' radish, Good King Henry (a type of green), purple broccoli, red celery, sea kale, 'Shoepeg' corn, and 'Windermoor Wonder' cucumber. Some of the varieties, such as the celery and the broccoli, are more challenging because they are hard to grow, but most of the items on the list are there simply because they need hand-pollinating or because the seed-saving process is more complex than for those on the beginner's list.

A Prototype Heirloom Vegetable Garden

A good way to start your seed-saving adventure is to use the accompanying garden as a guide. Choose a part of your yard that receives at least six hours of sun each day. The layout of this garden is north to south, because you don't want taller plants such as corn and pole beans to shade the shorter vegetables. I have chosen a summer heirloom garden to start because most of the vegetables are easy to grow. If you have questions, read the information in *Vegetables: How to Select, Grow, and Enjoy* by Derek Fell. The heirloom varieties are grown the same way that modern vegetables are. Take note of the layout; not only is it important to have taller vegetables at the back, but when you are seed saving, you must try to isolate the plants that may cross-pollinate. Therefore, the

different bean varieties have been separated by rows of other vegetables.

You can plant heirloom varieties of corn and cucumbers in your garden if you can isolate them; however, if you or your neighbors are growing other varieties of cucumbers or corn within 300 feet, you cannot save the seeds because the pollen from the other varieties may be carried to your heirloom plants, pollinating them and changing the next generation of the heirloom varieties.

Saving Seeds

People stopped regularly saving seeds early in this century when hybrid seeds—seeds produced by selectively bred plants—were introduced. Because hybrid seeds do not come true from seed—that is, succeeding generations are not like the parent plant—saving seeds was no longer worthwhile. Hybrid seeds virtually guaranteed the seed companies that their customers would return year after year. Over the last sixty or seventy years the American public has been so conditioned to buy seeds for the latest hybrids that a generation or two of gardeners has not learned how to save seeds from favorite plants.

As I said earlier, I never even thought about saving my own seeds when I started vegetable gardening. Seeds, in my experience, came in beautiful packages, not from my plants. I have just recently begun to learn about seed saving and have been amazed at how simple and satisfying it is. I keep a few 'Dutch White Runner' beans each year for the next year's crop. When they are completely dry, I freeze them for a day to kill any weevil eggs that may be in them, and label them—that's all there is to it. Once I went through the process, I felt like a chump for having faithfully sent off to Maine every spring for a new package of 'Dutch White Runner' beans—an open-pollinated variety that I could have saved easily myself.

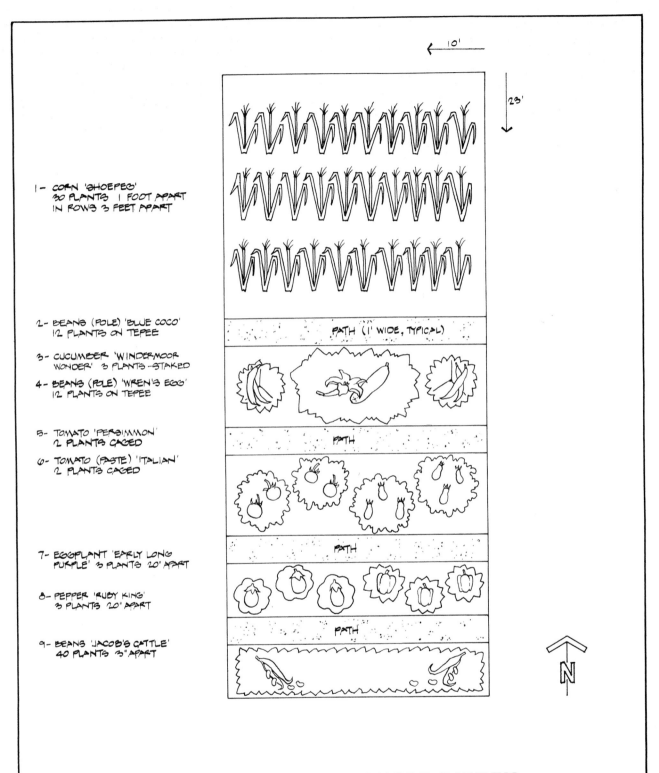

1 – CORN 'SHOEPEG'
    30 PLANTS 1 FOOT APART
    IN ROWS 3 FEET APART

2 – BEANS (POLE) 'BLUE COCO'
    12 PLANTS ON TEPEE

3 – CUCUMBER 'WINDERMOOR
    WONDER' 3 PLANTS –STAKED

4 – BEANS (POLE) 'WREN'S EGG'
    12 PLANTS ON TEPEE

5 – TOMATO 'PERSIMMON'
    2 PLANTS CAGED

6 – TOMATO (PASTE) 'ITALIAN'
    2 PLANTS CAGED

7 – EGGPLANT 'EARLY LONG
    PURPLE' 3 PLANTS 20" APART

8 – PEPPER 'RUBY KING'
    3 PLANTS 20" APART

9 – BEANS 'JACOB'S CATTLE'
    40 PLANTS 3" APART

THE HEIRLOOM VEGETABLE GARDEN

I want to begin this explanation on how to save seeds with a review of the birds-and-bees information we think we know all about, until we are called upon to explain it. The reproduction of seed plants involves the transference of pollen, which contains the sperm cells produced by the male flower part, the stamen, to the stigma, which contains the ovary, the female organ. This transfer process is called *pollination*. Once a plant has been pollinated, seeds form. If the pollen from a flower fertilizes the ovary of the same flower, the process is called *self-pollination*. To self-pollinate, a flower must have both stamen and stigma; such a flower is called a *perfect* flower. Beans and peas have perfect flowers and are usually self-pollinated. When there is a transference of pollen, either between flowers on the same plant or between flowers on different plants, the process is called *cross-pollination*. In that case, pollen is carried from flower to flower either by an insect or by the wind. Corn, squash, broccoli, and beets are cross-pollinated.

In seed saving your aim is to preserve existing varieties unaltered. To do so, it is necessary to avoid cross-pollination of the plant you intend to preserve. Say, for example, that you have a banana squash plant situated next to a zucchini plant. Along comes a bee that visits a male flower on the banana squash plant then flies to a female flower on the zucchini plant, transferring pollen from banana squash to zucchini—cross-pollinating the zucchini. If you planted the seeds from the pollinated zucchini the next year, the result would be a cross between the two plants. Sometimes the cross produces a good offspring, and that's one way we get new varieties. Usually, you'll just get a weird squash. I remember once letting some squash plants mature that had sprouted in the compost pile. I got a cross between a striped summer ball squash and an acorn squash: a striped, tough-skinned, stringy summer squash.

You can see that when you intend to save the seeds of your plants in order to preserve varie-

ties over the generations, you must always take steps to prevent cross-pollination. With plants such as beans, which have perfect flowers and usually pollinate themselves before they open, cross-pollination is seldom a problem. Others, such as plants in the squash and cucumber family, cross-pollinate readily and must be planted in isolation to ensure that the variety will remain pure.

There are a number of ways to isolate plants. First, you can plant only one variety of each type of vegetable, since cross-pollination does not occur between different genera. Second, you can plant potential cross-pollinators far from each other. Some varieties need only one hundred feet between them; others require half a mile. This is where your research—getting information from books on the subject or from nurseries that specialize in open-pollinated varieties—pays off. Finally, you can use a physical barrier: a number of rows of tall corn between the species, or plant the species on either side of an existing building.

I have mentioned that saving the seeds of hybrids is wasted energy, since hybrid seeds don't reproduce true. A hybrid is analogous to a mule. You get a mule by crossing a horse with a donkey; that is, you cross closely related species to create a new entity. That is also how a hybrid is created. The second generation, the mule, however, is sterile (not *all* hybrids are sterile). When you want to produce another mule, you must again cross a horse and a donkey; mules don't beget mules. In plant breeding, hybridists cross specially selected strains to produce a generation that possesses desired characteristics as well as what is called *hybrid vigor* (unusually strong or productive plants). Because you don't know which parents were crossed to create your hybrid plant (it's all a trade secret), you cannot produce the offspring. When you save seeds, then, you have to know which are pure, or open-pollinated, varieties and which are hybrids. Those that are open-pollinated are the only ones you can reproduce consistently. To prevent confusion, seed nurseries label the hybrids. That information is indicated in the catalog and on the seed packet. You may notice the designation "F1 hybrid"—that is simply a form of hybrid.

In addition to knowing about pollination and hybrids, you must know the life cycles of the plants you are dealing with. While the life cycles of most of our vegetables are annual (maturing in one season), many are biennial, which means that they take two seasons to reproduce. Some popular biennials are beets, carrots, parsley, and chard; and these will not produce seeds the first growing season.

If you are a novice seed saver, you will benefit from reading the pamphlet *Growing Garden Seeds* by Robert Johnston, Jr. It is available from Johnny's Selected Seeds, Albion, ME 04910, for $2.50. For a complete discussion of seed saving, with lists of seed exchanges and seed sources, as well as a rundown on the whole seed-saving movement, see Carolyn Jabs's book *The Heirloom Gardener*.

Following are some basic guidelines for seed savers.

1. Learn to recognize plant diseases since some of them, particularly the viral ones, are transmitted by seeds.

2. Always label the seed rows and packaged seeds, because our memories sometimes play tricks on us.

3. Never plant all your seeds at once; the elements might wipe you out.

4. Learn to select the best seeds for the next generation. For seed saving, select seeds from the healthiest plants and from those producing the best vegetables.

5. To maintain a strong gene pool, select seeds from a number of plants, not from just one or two. (This advice does not apply to self-pollinating varieties; see the information on beans in this chapter.)

6. Get to know the vegetable families; members of the same family often cross-pollinate.

7. Only mature, ripe seeds will be viable.

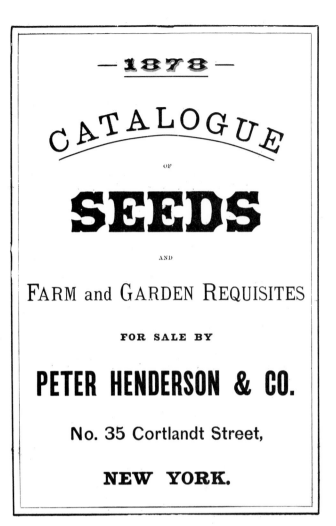

— 1878 —

CATALOGUE

OF

SEEDS

AND

FARM and GARDEN REQUISITES

FOR SALE BY

PETER HENDERSON & CO.

No. 35 Cortlandt Street,

NEW YORK.

Storing Seeds

Seeds must be stored carefully to ensure that they germinate in the next season. The greatest enemy of seed viability is moisture, so be sure to dry the seeds thoroughly before storing them. A good test of moisture content is to bite the seed; if you can't dent it, it's probably dry enough.

Another enemy is heat. Seeds must be stored in a cool, dry, dark place, or, if sufficiently dry and in a sealed container, seeds can be frozen too. They will stay viable for years in a freezer if properly packaged. Also, freezing helps protect the seeds from insects, not an uncommon problem of seed savers. (Don't freeze beans or peas, though; they need more air than freezing provides.)

Saving Beans

Beans are the easiest vegetable seeds to save. Most beans are self-pollinating, so you don't have to worry about cross-pollination when you plant them. In fact, you'll be able to grow 2 or 3 varieties with very few pollination problems. John Withee, one of this nation's most devoted seed savers, plants 250 varieties of beans every summer. He suggests planting varieties that are very different side by side; then, if any crossing does occur, the seeds that result will look quite different and you'll know that your selected variety has been altered. When harvesttime approaches, start choosing the plants that are the healthiest. With *snap* beans, let some of the healthy plants mature. They will be mature about six weeks after the eating stage. With *dry* bean varieties, allow them to mature as you would ordinarily. Beans usually ripen from the bottom to the top. Pick them as soon as the pods start to crack, so the beans won't fall to the ground and get damp. Don't pick the beans right after it has rained.

Do not save beans from diseased plants. Diseases borne by bean seeds are anthracnose and bacterial blight. The symptoms of anthracnose are small brown spots that enlarge to sunken black spots. Bacterial blight is characterized by dark green spots on the pods that slowly become dry and brick red. The most bothersome pest of bean seeds is the weevil.

After you thoroughly dry the bean seeds, package them in a breathable container, label them, and freeze them for for twenty-four hours to kill the weevils. Then put them in a cold, dark place. That's all there is to it.

John Withee has saved hundreds of heirloom varieties of beans. Here he poses with a box containing only a portion of his many varieties.

Sources of Information

Books

Bubel, Nancy. *The Seed Starter's Handbook.* Emmaus, Pa.: Rodale Press, 1978. Basic information on how to start most plants from seed as well as valuable botanical information on how to select and save your own seeds. A must for seed savers.

Fell, Derek. *Vegetables: How to Select, Grow, and Enjoy.* Tucson, Ariz.: H.P. Books, 1982. A marvelous compendium of basic vegetable growing.

Jabs, Carolyn. *The Heirloom Gardener.* San Francisco: Sierra Club Books, 1984. The definitive book on heirloom gardening. Covers the history of seed saving, gives sources of seeds as well as information on how to save seeds.

Jeavons, John, and Leler, Robin. *The Seed Finder.* Willits, Calif.: Jeavons-Leler Press, 1983. Detailed guide on where to find many of the old-time varieties.

Koopowitz, Harold, and Kaye, Hilary. *Plant Extinction—A Global Crisis.* Washington, D.C.: Stone Wall Press, 1983. The most thorough and complete book about our endangered ecosystem.

Mooney, Pat Roy. *Seeds of the Earth.* Ottawa, Canada: Inter Pares, 1979. A global look at the problem of the shrinking gene pool of edible plants.

Vilmorin-Andrieux, MM. *The Vegetable Garden.* Palo Alto, Calif.: Jeavons-Leler Press. Reprint 1976. A marvelous reprint of a classic that was first printed in 1885. It is a description of the old varieties, with information on how to grow hundreds of them. I counted fifty-five pages on peas alone.

Catalogs

Rural Advancement Fund
P.O. Box 1029
Pittsboro, NC 27312
Ask for "The Second Graham Center Seed and Nursery Directory"—a valuable catalog of seed companies that carry open-pollinated varieties of seeds. Catalog $2.

Demonstration Gardens

Many historic gardens grow heirloom vegetables and are interesting to visit. A list of these gardens is available from the Association of Living Historical Farms and Museums, c/o The Smithsonian, Washington, DC 20560.

Genesee Country Museum
P.O. Box 1819
Rochester, NY 14603
This demonstration garden is one of the most active and offers helpful information to those new to heirloom gardening.

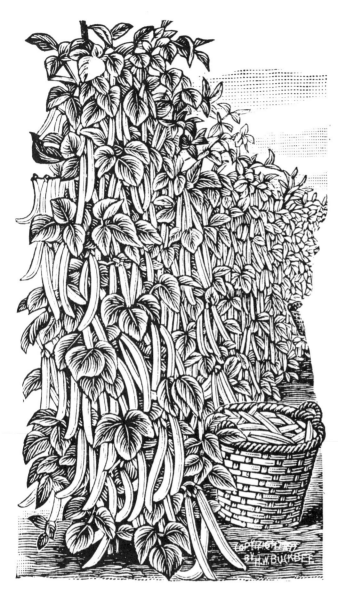

Monticello
P.O. Box 316
Charlottesville, VA 22902
Researchers are working hard to restore the vegetable garden at Monticello. It reflects as closely as possible the era and genius of one of our nation's most inspired gardeners: Thomas Jefferson. Visitors are welcome.

Nurseries

The seed companies listed below carry heirloom, open-pollinated varieties of vegetables. Most of these companies offer seed exchanges, as does the magazine *Gardens for All*, 180 Flynn Avenue, Burlington, VT 05401.

G. Seed Company
P.O. Box 702
Tonasket, WA 98855
G. Seeds offers a nice selection of heirloom beans, corn, tomatoes, and other vegetables. The company is willing to swap with you for varieties they don't have.

J.L. Hudson, Seedsman
P.O. Box 1058
Redwood City, CA 94064
This seed company sells only open-pollinated varieties and has a large selection.

Johnny's Selected Seeds
Albion, ME 04910
Johnny's sells seeds of many open-pollinated vegetables, particularly those that do well in northern climates.

Redwood City Seed Company
P.O. Box 361
Redwood City, CA 94064
Redwood carries a very large selection of open-pollinated, heirloom vegetables and the seed of many fruit trees. A brochure that covers heirlooms is available.

Seeds Blum
Idaho City Stage
Boise, ID 83707
Jan Blum raises her own seeds for many of the old varieties that are being dropped by larger seed companies. She also runs a seed exchange.

Seed Exchanges

A saved seed should be a shared seed. Help spread the wealth; join a seed exchange. Help spread the word; the more people who save and trade their seeds, the more seeds we all will have.

Native Seeds/SEARCH
3950 West New York Drive
Tucson, AZ 85745
This organization is devoted to seeking out and keeping in cultivation seeds from Southwest native crops as well as their wild relatives. A yearly membership is $10, which includes a newsletter. Seeds of these natives are available for a small fee.

Seed Savers Exchange
c/o Kent Whealy
203 Rural Avenue
Decorah, IA 52101
This is the place to start if you are interested in seed saving. Join Kent and hundreds of others in this membership organization. Membership is $6 for U.S. residents; $8 for Canadian residents. Membership entitles you to a directory of seed savers and what they want to trade, as well as information on seed saving. The directory is probably the most exciting seed catalog you will ever see; however, don't order seeds unless you are dedicated to growing and preserving these heirlooms.

Consumer Note

Seed saving is done primarily by enthusiastic gardeners and small seed companies, so there is a variation in the gardening skill of the growers and in the seeds. You might be exchanging seeds with an old-time gardener who could run circles around the average seedsman, or you could be exchanging seeds with a new gardener. The new gardener may not know how to recognize virus symptoms, say, or how to prevent cross-pollination. Be forewarned that although this has not been a large problem, there is a slight chance that you may get poor quality seeds, seed-borne diseases, or seeds that were not properly stored.

California quail

Chapter 6
The Wildlife Garden

If you have never experienced living near buffaloes and eagles, you certainly don't miss their presence. In fact, you probably are not even aware of their ever having been around. Nevertheless, those creatures, as well as many others, were once a part of our habitat. It could be, for example, that there was a buffalo migration path through your front yard. Or perhaps your yard was once the nesting site of eagles.

With a little research and imagination you can partially restore the natural state of your land by putting in plants native to your specific locale. The net effect will be not only a preserve for the plants you choose, but a protected retreat for many of the wildlife species that live in your ecological niche.

Your yard will be part of the ark, instead of a large expanse of Kentucky bluegrass with a mustache of shrubs across the front of the house, when you plant a number of different species that need preserving and that will serve as habitat for native animal species. If your design is well conceived, the result will be beautiful and maybe more unusual than any other yard in your neighborhood. In addition, it will give you pleasure and help preserve species.

There are a number of tacks you can take when planting with the express purpose of protecting your area's wildlife species. For example, if you are interested in providing a habitat for birds, butterflies, and small mammals, you can set up your yard as a haven for them. Another, less radical option is a conventional yard augmented with a bird house for purple martins, and, instead of forsythia, maybe a hedge of viburnum or elderberries for the cedar waxwings, and a colorful border with hollyhocks for the painted lady butterflies.

If you want to create a true wildlife preserve, you'll need to think not only about what kinds of wildlife you do want to attract but also which animals you don't want to attract. A few years ago a native brown bear meandered out of the wilderness south of the San Francisco area. He kept himself busy for days foraging up and down the creeks and in suburban backyards. Cocktail parties were arranged on the chance that he might appear. Obviously, there's "wild" life, then there's wildlife. Bears, mountain lions, and wolves are not the wildlife I expect you will want in your yard.

Still, even the less-alarming species, in terms of their size and wildness, require some careful consideration. For example, our backyard, even though in a suburban area, is near a creek. Occasionally our visitors include an opossum, a raccoon, an owl, and a bevy of quail. Unfortunately we also have too many squirrels and, occasionally, a skunk. A squirrel can go through a ripe apricot tree like a bejeweled matron picking over a box of mixed chocolates, tasting or knocking down ten apricots for every one it eats. Squirrels rip apart my macrame plant hangers to make their nests, and occasionally a raccoon gets into the garbage can. Sometimes we see a roof rat, and we know neighbors who had to spend the night in a motel waiting for a skunk to go back out through the "doggy" door at home. With wildlife you can't put up a turnstile and let in only those animals you want.

Fortunately, though, if you really want wildlife to be a part of your landscape, you can usually make the necessary arrangements to encourage the species you want and to discourage or guard against those you don't want. Raccoons can be kept out of garbage cans by using certain kinds of lids. Skunks can be prevented from getting under the house by screening all house vents. When squirrels overpopulate, you can control their numbers by trapping and relocating them. Encouraging (and discouraging) wildlife requires some preplanning on your part, but it is worth the effort. Despite my cursing at the squirrels, I remember the joy of watching baby hummingbirds learn to fly, of awaiting the arrival of the migrating woodpecker that visits us and hammers on the trees every year in May, and of seeing, one foggy morning, a stag staring in the kitchen window. I wouldn't trade any of those moments. However, realistic expecta-

Above While it is great to feed wildlife, you can't put up a turnstyle and let in only those animals you want. If skunks are prevalent in your area, pet food left outside is sure to attract them.

Opposite Purple martins are extremely beneficial in controlling insects in the garden. You don't have to provide them with a mansion as the owners of Middleton Gardens in South Carolina have done; a simple structure built well above the ground will suffice. At the end of this chapter is a list of books about how to attract birds and how to build a bird house for purple martins.

tions and good planning are definitely the keys to a successful wildlife garden.

I'd like to say a few words about expectations. Whereas we love birds, small fuzzy mammals, and Bambi, we generally say "yuck" to spiders, toads, and snakes. This brings me back to the main reason for changing our yards: As far as I am concerned, it is to reinstitute as closely as possible whole, natural habitats. A successful habitat is one that has as many niches filled as possible; some of the creatures that we are not fond of do belong. We all like butterflies, and many of them are becoming endangered because we don't like caterpillars or chewed foliage and flowers. Since the caterpillar has to eat foliage in order to become a butterfly, we have to tolerate chewed foliage or give up butterflies. Try hard to separate facts from prejudices. The black widow spider, the rattlesnake, and poison ivy are hazardous; but garter snakes, daddy longlegs,

and most toads are not. There are many books on how to encourage birds and small mammals, but there are no books devoted to how to encourage spiders, toads, and snakes. You will have to use your own senses and observation to teach you how.

All wildlife needs food, water, shelter, and areas for reproducing and rearing young. If you have a yard that is near a fairly wild area and has many mature trees and shrubs, you will need only to provide water in dry times and extra food in the winter. A more typical yard in this country, however, is the suburban yard— a large lawn, a few clipped exotic shrubs, and a small tree or two. If this is your situation, then you have many decisions to make. It will probably be necessary to remove some species and plant others, provide feeders and water sources, and reevaluate landscaping procedures because they are at cross-purposes with your goal.

How to Change Minds and the Landscape

Begin at the beginning. That is, recognize that by changing the emphasis in your mind and, consequently, in your yard, you are making a radical departure from the usual people-oriented garden—its goals, techniques, and procedures. So radical a change requires awareness, information, planning, sensitivity, and, sometimes, even tact.

You must realize that you will have to continually monitor and "translate" information you get from garden books and other sources because garden information in this country is primarily people oriented. The subjugation of nature, not the encouragement of natural systems, is often the goal. Because you are not living in the wilderness, a compromise usually must be made. For example, many woodpeckers need dead branches or trees to nest in, but garden books tell you to remove dead trees or to trim off dead branches for the good of the tree. You will have to determine your priorities. If the tree is your favorite or if it shades a south wall in summer or if the dead branch could fall and hurt someone, then it should probably be removed. Be aware also of your redefinition of the word "pests." An insect defined as a pest in a people-oriented landscape may be defined as food for spiders and birds in a wildlife-oriented one. Many such translations will have to be made.

Be realistic in choosing your goals. If all your neighbors spray their yards with pesticides and think that the only proper landscape scheme is a lawn and some clipped shrubs, then obviously you must scale down your expectations. If starlings are moving in or if neighborhood cats are having a field day, then changes will have to be made. As a rule, it usually pays to start slowly and continually monitor the situation, making changes when necessary.

For neighbors who are used to mown lawns and clipped hedges and who may be unnerved by your installing a thicket of shrubs and vines and putting in a meadow of unmown grasses and wildflowers, a little tact and discretion on your part will pay off. My inclination in the case where neighbors may be unsympathetic is to start slowly and to share your enthusiasm. Talk about your ideas for providing a home for a family of cardinals or robins. If you make your yard attractive and share your enthusiasm with your neighbors, you will probably recruit them to your cause, then everyone will benefit because the more neighbors that are involved, the more wildlife you all will have—and the more habitat the wildlife will have.

Join the National Audubon Society and the National Wildlife Federation. There are many good books about wildlife and a number of nurseries devoted to providing plants for wildlife (see the lists at the end of this chapter).

The National Wildlife Federation's Backyard Wildlife Habitat Program is composed of thousands of families who have decided to give wildlife a major place in their yards. If you meet a few requirements, for $2 you may register your yard and get information and encouragement for your garden. The program is for homeowners with three acres or less or for those with larger lots who want to register only a portion of three acres or less. The goals of the

program are to provide more refuges for indigenous animals and to share and document experiences so that others can profit from the experiences. To get information and an application for this program, write to Backyard Wildlife Habitat Program, National Wildlife Federation, 1412 16th Street NW, Washington, DC 20036. The application asks you to describe what steps you are taking to encourage wildlife. Once you are registered, you will receive useful information on how to get started and an occasional issue of *The Backyard Wildlifer,* a newsletter to keep you up to date on successful wildlife gardening techniques and on the latest books.

Before turning to the practical aspects of creating a wildlife preserve, I want to remind you that plant species are as crucial to the ark as animal species, perhaps more so. The reason for creating a wildlife preserve is not solely to protect endangered animals but to perpetuate the complex interdependence between plants and animals that is the hallmark of a natural system.

Above This yard in Colorado recently became the two-thousandth yard in the National Wildlife Association's Backyard Wildlife Program. It is filled with sheltering and fruit-bearing shrubs and is visited by many animals and birds.

Opposite Elderberries are a great favorite of birds—with what is left over you can make fabulous jam.

Planning and Preparation

Begin by assessing your yard. A large rural lot has many more options than a city lot, but both can make a valuable contribution and be augmented with a bird feeder and a bird bath and shrubs and trees that feed wild birds. Most people think about birds but forget about butterflies, bumblebees, and other insects. Select your flowers with insects in mind, and not just at their nectar stage. While it's fun to watch a butterfly flit around, the caterpillar must be fed. Dill, parsley, and fennel are food for the colorful larvae of many swallowtail butterflies. If you don't plant and share your dill, you probably won't have the swallowtails flitting around your zinnias.

Next, get some graph paper and plan in detail the changes that are to be made. Measure your yard and lay it out to scale on paper. Plan wildlife areas, clusters of shrubs, maybe a hedgerow, even a small pool. Select plants that will provide food all through the year. When doing your layout, it is helpful to have some of the basic texts that cover landscaping for wildlife. Also, get some nature guides for your part of the country. Collecting this resource material can be a family project. See the lists of books at the end of this chapter and at the ends of Chapters 1, 2, 3, 4, and 10.

Planting for Wildlife

Birds and animals need shelter. Your yard will be more hospitable if you provide many of the following: (1) many levels of vegetation, including low shrubs, ground covers, tall shrubs, and small and large trees; (2) vines; (3) plants with thorns to give protection from cats; (4) trees, stumps, and dead trees to provide nesting sites for woodpeckers, owls, and raccoons (If they did not die of a disease that will spread to other trees, keep as many tree stumps and dead trees as possible, but eliminate those that are near buildings and places where chil-

dren play and people walk.); and (5) bird houses, especially in young yards with few trees.

In addition, try to avoid the manicured yard because well-manicured yards eliminate many hiding places. Shrubbery should be allowed to branch to the ground; and leaf litter and old grass stalks are valuable for nesting materials and for burrowing mammals and insects.

Wildlife is attracted to a yard that provides food and water. Keep in mind that most animals and birds need food all year round. Use plants that seed or fruit at different times of the year. Food can be provided by food-producing plants and by bird and animal feeders. Again, avoid the manicured yard. Because I allow my cosmos and large marigolds to go to seed, my garden is visited all summer by flocks of yellow finches who scramble for the seeds. Leaf litter provides food for worms, who in turn provide food for robins. Leave a few aphids on some of your plants to provide food for lacewings and ladybugs.

Small fountains with moving water often attract more wildlife than still water, and they have the advantage of creating fewer mosquito problems. If you can put in a small pond with fish, which help control mosquitoes, you will have the best situation. If your source of water

Opposite Wildlife needs food, water, and shelter. Notice how bird houses and feeders are spotted around the yard. Notice, too, that almost every ornamental plant has a dual role: some provide food; others provide shelter for birds, insects, and small mammals. Also, nearly all are beautiful to look at or serve as windbreaks for the house. The vegetable garden is fenced for protection, and especially vulnerable plants, such as the strawberries, are placed close to the front door so the occupants will have some chance at the harvest.

1. Elderberry	12. Amelanchier
2. Bayberry	13. Winter creeper
3. Winterberry	14. Lilac
4. Butterfly bush	15. Native pines
5. Viburnum	16. Dogwood
6. Junipers, low	17. Mountain ash
7. Red maple	
8. Viburnum	
9. Blueberries	
10. Strawberries in containers	
11. Birches	

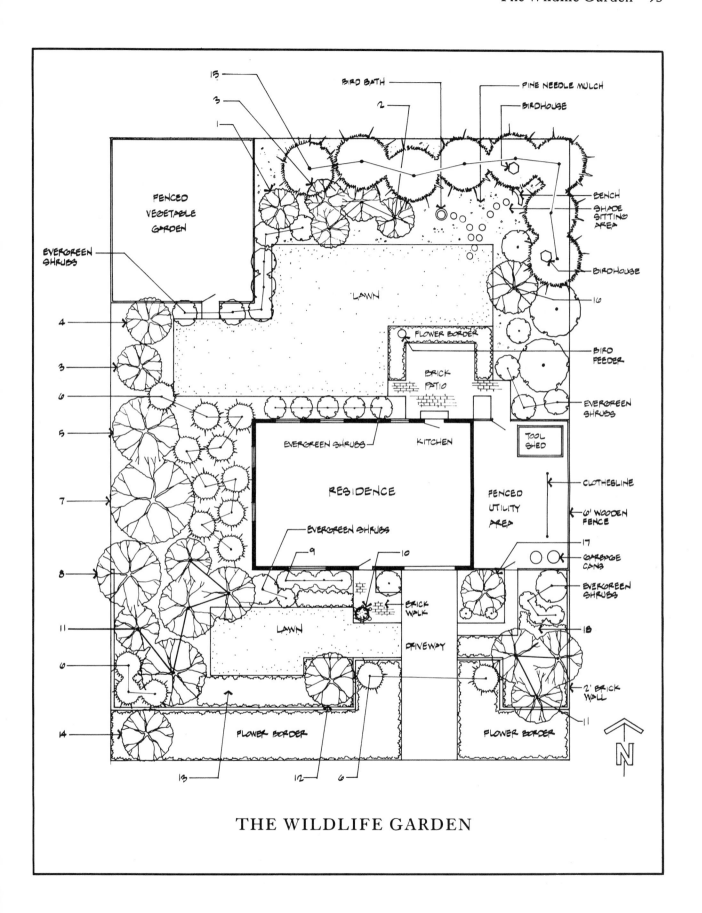

THE WILDLIFE GARDEN

is limited and still, such as a bird bath, change the water daily. Water should be out in the open, surrounded by lawn, for example, so that neighborhood cats cannot sneak up on the visiting wildlife. In the winter you may want to set up an immersion heater to keep the water from freezing.

When choosing the plants for your wildlife garden, concentrate on plants native to your area; they will attract the most wildlife. Be sure to provide a wide variety of trees, shrubs, and herbaceous plants; the more variety the more wildlife you will attract. Lawn areas surrounded by many layers of vegetation make successful wildlife gardens. There are a number of good books on the subject; one of the best is *Gardening with Wildlife,* published by the National Wildlife Federation.

Look over the model wildlife garden in this chapter to get some ideas for your garden. Notice that not just wildlife habitat is considered, but protection for the inhabitants of the house as well. The deciduous trees such as birch, red maple, and dogwood that provide food and shelter for birds have been situated where they shade the house in summer. Sheltering evergreens that provide safe nesting sites for birds are placed to form a windbreak from winter winds for the house. The vegetable garden has been fenced off from rabbits and small mammals, and if the residents want a bountiful harvest, the blueberry bushes, strawberries, and young seedlings in the vegetable garden will need the additional protection of bird netting.

The style of the yard is informal, and the shrubbery is meant to grow primarily unpruned because, as I mentioned earlier, unpruned shrubbery furnishes hiding and nesting places. The flower borders give much food to insects and birds as well as hours of pleasure to passersby. Large bowers of blooming and fruiting shrubs delight many songbirds and butterflies. Finally, bird feeders, bird houses, and a bird bath are included in the yard. These are particularly important to provide food, shelter, and water in new yards that are not yet well established and in older yards to give wildlife sustenance in the winter.

Be forewarned that most of the information for wildlife gardens is heavily weighted toward animals and is sometimes insensitive to the needs of native plants. For example, some of the plants recommended, although good sources of food for birds, can spread and crowd out acres of native plants. Native habitats are the most stable; it is equally important to preserve plants and animals.

Try to avoid planting particularly invasive weeds such as Japanese honeysuckle, Oriental bittersweet, multiflora roses, and purple loosestrife. Choose some of the plants on the following list, which includes plants that are usually well behaved. (But, again, check the list of "green invaders" on page 17 to make sure that the plants are not a problem in your particular area.) Ask local naturalists which plants on this list will be most attractive to your local birds, butterflies, and small mammals.

Opposite, clockwise from top The lowly opossum looks its best perched in a redbud tree.

A wood thrush is a welcome visitor to the garden. Plan for trees and shrubs that give nesting sites and protection.

A monarch butterfly sips from a tithonia blossom. Planting different species of flowers in your garden provides for many species of butterflies.

Page 98, clockwise from top left Many heirloom fruits, such as the 'Sonoma' melon and 'Pink Pearl' apple shown here, are extremely flavorful and should be preserved.

Jan Blum is the owner of one of the new seed companies that are interested in heirloom varieties. Here she is harvesting several of her eighty varieties of heirloom potatoes.

A close-up of some of Blum's heirloom varieties of potatoes, broccoli, cauliflower, and kale.

Page 99, clockwise from top left Brassia Edvah Loo.

Phalaenopsis Golden Sands 'Canary'.

The large white orchid is a cattleya hybrid Japhet type; the tall pink one is a *Doritaenopsis;* in the middle are three types of *Paphiopedilum,* or lady's-slipper orchids; and in the foreground are different types of *Phalaenopsis.*

Three different types of cattleya are growing in a moderate-to-warm windowsill garden. Top left, *C. Angelwalker x C. amethystoglossa;* lower left, *Lc. Cuiseag* 'Cuddles'; lower right, *Slc. Brillig.*

Opposite, clockwise from top left 'Old Blush' China climbing rose.

White Rugosa rose

'Cornelia' Hybrid Musk rose

Rosa damascena Trigintipetala

Plants for Birds

The following list of trees and plants will guide you in selecting plants that will attract birds to your garden.

Small Trees

Dogwood, *Cornus,* most species
Hawthorn, *Crataegus* species
Mountain ash, *Sorbus* species
Serviceberry, *Amelanchier* species

Large Trees

Birch, *Betula* species
Green ash, *Fraxinus pennsylvanica*
Hackberry, *Celtis occidentalis, C. reticulata*
Maple, *Acer rubrum*
Mimosa (silk tree), *Albizia Julibrissin*
Oak, *Quercus* species (native species in
    particular)
Persimmon, *Diospyros* species
Pine, *Pinus Strobus, P. edulis*
Tulip tree, *Liriodendron Tulipifera*

Vines

Bittersweet, *Celastrus scandens*
Five-leaf akebia, *Akebia quinata*
Virginia creeper, *Parthenocissus quinquefolia*
Winter creeper, *Euonymus Fortunei*

Shrubs

American cranberry bush, *Viburnum trilobum*
Cherry laurel, *Prunus Laurocerasus*
Elderberry, *Sambucus* species
Fire thorn, *Pyracantha* species
Juniper, *Juniperus* species
Myrtle, *Myrtus communis*
Rose, *Rosa* species (see Chapter 7)
Silverberry, *Elaeagnus commutata,*
    E. pungens
Winterberry, *Ilex laevigata*
Witch hazel, *Hamamelis vernalis,*
    H. virginiana

Perennials

Aster, *Aster* species
Black-eyed susan, *Rudbeckia* species
Chrysanthemum, *Chrysanthemum* species
Columbine, *Aquilegia* species
Statice, *Limonium latifolium*

Annuals

Amaranthus, *Amaranthus* species
Bachelor's-button, *Centaurea Cyanus*
Calendula, *Calendula officinalis*
Coreopsis, *Coreopsis* species
Cosmos, *Cosmos* species
Marigold, *Tagetes* species
Pink, *Dianthus* species
Sunflower, *Helianthus* species

Plants for Butterflies

Meadow and prairie gardens are wonderful habitats for butterflies, as are perennial flower borders. Consult *Theme Gardens* by Barbara Damrosch for more information. Different flowers and foliage plants attract different species of butterflies. The range of native butterflies and their food sources vary from region to region. Check with local wildlife experts to see which butterflies you are most likely to attract. Following is a list of plants that are attractive to butterflies.

Shrubs

Agave, *Agave deserti*
Blueberry, *Vaccinium* species
Butterfly bush, *Buddleia Davidii*
Ceanothus, *Ceanothus* species
Cherry, *Prunus* species
Dogwood, *Cornus* species
Lilac, *Syringa vulgaris*
Passionflower, *Passiflora* species
Spicebush, *Lindera Benzoin*
Willow, *Salix* species
Wisteria, *Wisteria* species

Perennials

Aster, *Aster* species
Chives, *Allium schoenoprasum*
Coreopsis, *Coreopsis grandiflora*
Daylily, *Hemerocallis* species
Goldenrod, *Solidago* species
Hollyhock, *Alcea rosea*
Lupine, *Lupinus* species
Phlox, *Phlox* species
Sage, *Salvia* species
Scabiosa, *Scabiosa caucasica*
Sedum, *Sedum spectabile*

Annuals

Dill, *Anethum graveolens*
Fennel, *Foeniculum vulgare*
Marigold, *Tagetes* species
Parsley, *Petroselinum* species
Stock, *Matthiola incana*
Sunflower, *Helianthus* species
Zinnia, *Zinnia* species

Protection—Just Good Sense

Foods that are appealing to humans are usually favorites of wildlife too. Therefore, if there are edible plants in your yard or your neighbors' yards, plan to protect them. If the gardens are not protected by fences, fence the areas, or don't encourage wildlife. Scarecrows are often useful (and fun to create). One way to save some of your fruit crop for yourself is to anticipate sharing it with the birds and plant extra. For example, plant two plum trees or two cherry trees and a mulberry tree instead of one plum tree or just cherries. I recommend using all three types of protection: netting, scarecrows, *and* sharing your harvest.

To make your house safe from unwanted visitors, batten down the hatches. Nail or board up crawl spaces; make sure screening is secure over vent holes in the attic and the basement. Retire doggy doors lest they become skunk doors. Garbage cans should be secured; clamped lids usually discourage raccoons, but not always. If raccoons continue to be a problem, keep the garbage cans locked in a garage, or attach a door spring to the handles of the can. Install a screen over the top of the chimney to keep swifts and bats from nesting there.

Check with the local board of health to find out if there are rats in your area. Many suburbs have them; they are not just an inner-city problem. If rats are a problem in your area, keep ivylike ground covers to a minimum and clean up debris. Don't leave trash piled around. Stack woodpiles neatly—off the ground. And, most important, don't leave food out for domestic animals.

There are many ways to protect your plants from wildlife. Here are a few. Wrap chicken wire around the trunks of young trees so the bark can't be eaten by rabbits and deer. Keep in mind that piled-up snow allows animals to reach farther up the trunk, sometimes as much as four to five feet higher. Take into account your local snowfall. Leave at least six inches of space between the wire and the trunk so that the critters can't reach in. If gophers are a problem in your area, set out young plants in chicken-wire baskets to protect the roots.

Control and protect your pets. To enjoy the benefits of wildlife in your yard, you must control your household pets. Cats are one of the biggest problems for birds and small mammals; keep them inside or put bells on their collars. Free-running dogs are a severe problem in rural and semirural areas; these pets run in packs and kill deer and other mammals, not to mention a neighbor's sheep and chickens. Pets should have their rabies shots regularly, in case they have an encounter with a rabid wild creature.

Providing for wildlife is a rewarding aspect of gardening. It is a project that will never be complete; the environment is always changing.

Rabbits are cute and sure to be a nuisance in a vegetable garden.

Sources of Information

Books

Damrosch, Barbara. *Theme Gardens*. New York: Workman Publishing, 1982. Good information on how to attract butterflies and hummingbirds to your garden.

National Wildlife Federation. *Gardening with Wildlife*. Washington, D.C.: National Wildlife Federation, 1974. A comprehensive book on the subject of gardening with wildlife. A must!

Ortho Books, Chevron Chemical Company editorial staff. *How to Attract Birds*. San Francisco: Ortho Books, 1983. Extensive information on birds and the plants that they prefer for food and shelter.

Rothschild, Miriam, and Farrell, Clive. *The Butterfly Gardener*. London: Michael Joseph, 1983. A must for butterfly lovers. It even covers raising butterflies in captivity.

Also see the books recommended at the end of the first four chapters and the Peterson field guides, which cover insects, birds, reptiles, and animals of this continent.

Nurseries

Dutch Mountain Nursery
7984 North 48th Street
Route 1
Augusta, MI 49012
This nursery has a large variety of shrubs, trees, and vines that are very valuable for wildlife. Catalog 25 cents.

Clyde Robin Seed Company, Inc.
P.O. Box 2855
Castro Valley, CA 94546
This nursery specializes in seeds of native wildflowers and shrubs. It has wildflower mixes for all parts of the country. Catalog $2. Also see the sources of information at the end of Chapter 1 for more information.

Wildlife Nurseries
P.O. Box 2724
Oshkosh, WI 54903
This company specializes in plants that provide food for wildlife, particularly for game birds and ducks. It has a good selection of seeds of plants for marshes and streamsides, and even sells tadpoles and baby ducks and turtles.

For additional information on nurseries, see the lists of nurseries at the ends of Chapters 1, 2, 3, and 4 and purchase the booklet *Nursery Source Manual*, a Brooklyn Botanic Garden publication. Send $3.05 to the Brooklyn Botanic Garden, 1000 Washington Avenue, Brooklyn, NY 11225, to obtain the booklet.

Organizations

National Audubon Society
950 Third Avenue
New York, NY 10022
This venerable old organization offers many publications with information on attracting birds to your yard.

National Wildlife Federation
1412 16th Street NW
Washington, DC 20036
An organization with a wealth of information for the homeowner who is interested in attracting wildlife.

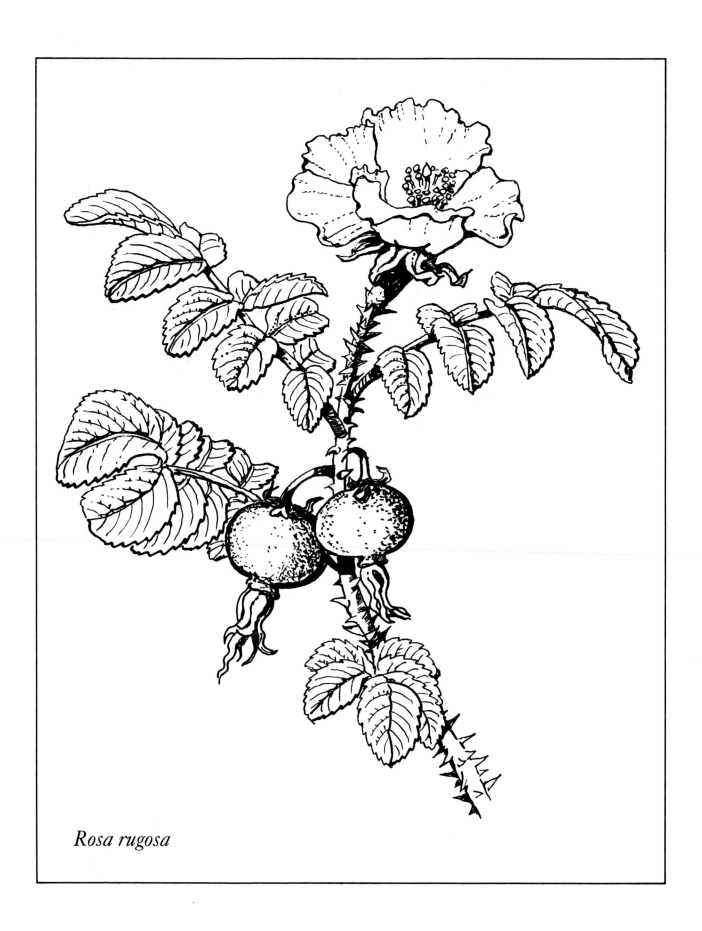

Rosa rugosa

Chapter 7
The Heritage Rose Garden

To many people, "roses" mean the old-fashioned roses of song, sonnet, and grandma's garden—roses that produce bowers of fragrant flowers, showers of shell pink petals on a warm day in June, or bouquets of rosebuds on a picket fence. These sentimental favorites bring to mind such names as Damask, Moss, Sweetbrier, and 'Maiden's Blush'. Instead of experiencing history only on paper, plant *Rosa damascena bifera* and enjoy, as did Ovid and Homer, its perfume and clear pink, double flowers. Or enjoy the ripe-apple smell of the Sweetbrier as Shakespeare may have. While these and other old roses have always been among people's favorite flowers, the recent quest for the new hybrid tea roses has meant that these old roses have been ignored for the last forty or fifty years. However, a new awakening in horticulture, fueled sometimes by nostalgia, sometimes by concern over the loss of old varieties, and often by despair at the amount of care many hybrid tea roses require, has caused a rapidly growing interest in heritage roses. The interest in and concern for heritage roses have developed none too soon. We could very well have lost a substantial amount of this antique gene pool.

Rose growing since the turn of the century has been devoted mainly to the latest hybrid tea roses. Each new introduction has been hailed as an improvement over those of previous years. Sometimes the improvements were truly improvements, and the roses were more cold tolerant or more disease resistant. Often, however, improvement simply meant different —a different color or a different bud shape. Fragrant roses, for example, are out of style, so some modern roses have no scent. Pesticides have become readily available, so some beautiful but quite disease-prone introductions were made. Water and fertilizer were plentiful, so some of the new hybrids are nourishment-greedy. The rose garden of the twentieth century is very high maintenance. And what has happened to the old-fashioned favorites? Well, some are extinct, others are still growing in grandma's garden and in old cemeteries, and a few are being propagated and sold by people like Pat Wiley, proprietor of America's best-known heritage rose nursery, Roses of Yesterday and Today.

In contrast to their hybrid cousins, many heritage roses are low-maintenance plants. In fact, according to Wiley, the most common mistake gardeners make with old roses is to treat them as they do modern hybrid tea roses. Hybrid tea roses need severe winter pruning, systematic summer removal of spent blooms, frequent fertilizing, supplemental watering, and, in most of the country, nearly weekly spraying for diseases and pests. To the contrary, once established, most old-fashioned roses are easy to care for.

According to another heritage rose authority, Beverly Dobson, *Rosa rugosa, R. rugosa alba,* and *R. rugosa Rubra* are absolutely disease-free. Further, the great majority of the old rose varieties require fewer petroleum products in the form of fertilizers and pesticides, can survive with less water, and are perfect examples of appropriate gardening.

Growing heritage roses makes sense in terms of conservation and ease of maintenance, but, more important, we should grow these roses so that generations to come, our descendants, can take a break from their computer consoles and refresh their senses with the scent of one of the heritage beauties. If we keep the Damask and Sweetbrier roses alive, our great-grandchildren will be able to have an experience in common with Shakespeare and Homer.

Pat Wiley is the owner of Roses of Yesterday and Today, one of the few nurseries devoted to heritage roses.

Heritage Roses

The rose family is vast. If you are a beginning gardener or don't want to spray your roses, choose from the following hardy types: Hybrid Musk, Autumn Damask, Damask, Gallica, Alba, Rugosa, Moss, Centifolia, Hybrid Moss, and species roses such as *Eglanteria, pendulina,* and *rubrifolia.* There are hundreds of varieties in these different classifications. If you are an experienced gardener or live in a part of the country where rose diseases are rarely a problem, you may want to choose from an even larger selection, such as the one given in Beverly Dobson's booklet on roses. Her booklet, described at the end of this chapter, gives information and availability of the majority of heritage roses.

In addition to choosing for disease resistance, you can make other choices as well when you select your heritage roses. Some types give a spectacular show of blooms once in the spring; other varieties bloom on and off throughout the growing season. A few of the old roses, such as some of the Hybrid Musks and Albas, can be grown in filtered sun, so if you have limited sun, choose one of those. If you live in a very cold area, choose from the most hardy varieties. Most of the old roses are cold tolerant, and some extremely hardy types can be grown as far north as the arctic.

Unusual and Easy-to-Grow Old Roses

Pat Wiley recommends the following old roses as being particularly disease- and pest-free.

'Delicata', Rugosa (1898). Flowers repeatedly; large double lavender pink blooms; produces large, colorful hips.

'Old Blush', China (1752). Flowers repeatedly; semidouble pink flowers.

'Perle d'Or', Polyantha (1884). Flowers repeatedly; pink to amber flowers; quite disease-free.

Rosa damascena Trigintipetala, Damask (prior to 1850). One annual flowering; cherry red flowers, red hips; disease-free plant.

'Safrano', Tea (1839). Flowers repeatedly; light apricot flowers; needs little fertilization or irrigation.

'Zephirine Drouhin', Bourbon (1868). Flowers repeatedly; bright pink flowers; no thorns; disease-free.

Modern Roses

Most modern hybrid tea roses need constant attention: spraying, fertilizing, and pruning. A few varieties are more disease resistant than the average, generally needing little spraying if planted in the right place—with full sun, good drainage, and away from a lawn where constant irrigation makes the environment too moist. Choose from the following list of fairly disease-resistant tea roses, but remember that most will require more care than their heritage cousins.

'Belinda', Hybrid Musk (1936). Flowers repeatedly; trusses of one-inch bright pink flowers; disease and pest resistant.

'Cornelia', Hybrid Musk (1925). Flowers repeatedly; coral to pink blooms; disease and pest resistant.

'Golden Fleece', Floribunda (1955). Flowers repeatedly; large yellow flowers.

'New Dawn', Climber (1930). Flowers repeatedly; pale pink flowers; disease-free foliage.

'Rosette Delizy', Tea (1922). Flowers repeatedly; yellow to red flowers; disease and pest resistant.

I asked Beverly Dobson, who gardens in New York, for her recommendations of disease-resistant, easy-to-grow, old roses, and she recommended the Rugosas, the Damasks, the Albas, the Centifolias, the Moss types, and the following varieties in particular.

'Celsiana', Damask (prior to 1750). One annual flowering; warm pink flowers.

'Leda', Painted Damask (before 1827). White or near white.

'Konigin von Danemark', Alba (1826). One annual flowering; pink.

R. gallica officinalis, Apothecary (before 1300). One annual flowering; light crimson.

'Rosa Mundi', Gallica (prior to 1581). One annual flowering; red stripes over pink ground.

Planning and Preparation

While roses can be spotted in the back of shrub borders and along walls and driveways, a rose garden has traditionally been the most graceful way to feature roses in a landscape. Roses come in many colors and shapes, and to show them off in all their glory, it helps to give them a jewellike setting. See the accompanying diagram, a good-size area organized to feature heirloom roses.

In planning your rose garden it helps if you define the area, as was done in the diagram, with a fence or boxwood hedge and paths of brick or gravel. Fencing and paths give the area form when the roses are dormant in winter, and they provide a strong design element that serves to unify the area. Rose plants, particularly the heritage varieties, have different forms and colors of flowers and need a strong design because they sometimes compete with each other for the viewer's eye. In the accompanying design, I placed Rugosa roses, with their crisp clean foliage and controlled form, in all the corners of the garden to further unify the design. You could probably use Rugosa roses in the same manner because they grow well in most parts of the country. Having laid the framework for a unified garden—paths, fencing, and the Rugosa roses—I then delighted in choosing one each of many other kinds of roses to fill in the planting beds. The resulting garden full of fragrances, representing a full spectrum of flower types and colors, shows off the great variety of the heritage rose.

Planting Roses

While most old roses are pretty tough, all perform best in good, well-drained soil and plenty of sun. Most of these rose bushes are large and need room to spread so they can be seen in all their beauty. Old roses can be situated in a rose garden or used in a landscape design. They can cover arbors, fences, and walls, or cascade over banks. Some varieties, such as some of the Rugosas, can be used as a hedge; others can stand alone as large fountain-shaped shrubs. Everywhere you use the heritage roses they produce a spectacular show of blooms and become a noteworthy focal point in the garden.

Purchase bare-root roses in late winter from local nurseries or, in the case of many of the old roses, from mail-order firms. Plant them as soon as possible after purchase. Unwrap them the night before planting and revitalize the roots with a solution of vitamin B_1.

Opposite Surround yourself with the many scents and colors of an old rose garden. The diagram shows a heritage rose garden laid out in a geometric shape, surrounded with a low hedge of lavender or boxwood to give it form throughout the seasons and to unify the area. I chose to repeat one of the sturdiest Rugosa roses, 'Delicata', in a number of places to further unify the garden. There is a wide choice of flower colors and shapes represented as well as a number of varieties that bloom throughout the whole summer.

1. 'Delicata' (lavender)
2. 'Safrano' (apricot)
3. 'Konigin von Danemark' (pink)
4. *Rosa gallica officinalis* (light crimson)
5. 'Leda' (white)
6. 'Penelope' (salmon pink climber)
7. 'Perle d'Or' (amber)
8. 'Celsiana' (pink)
9. *Rosa damascena Trigintipetala* (red)
10. 'Old Blush' (pink)

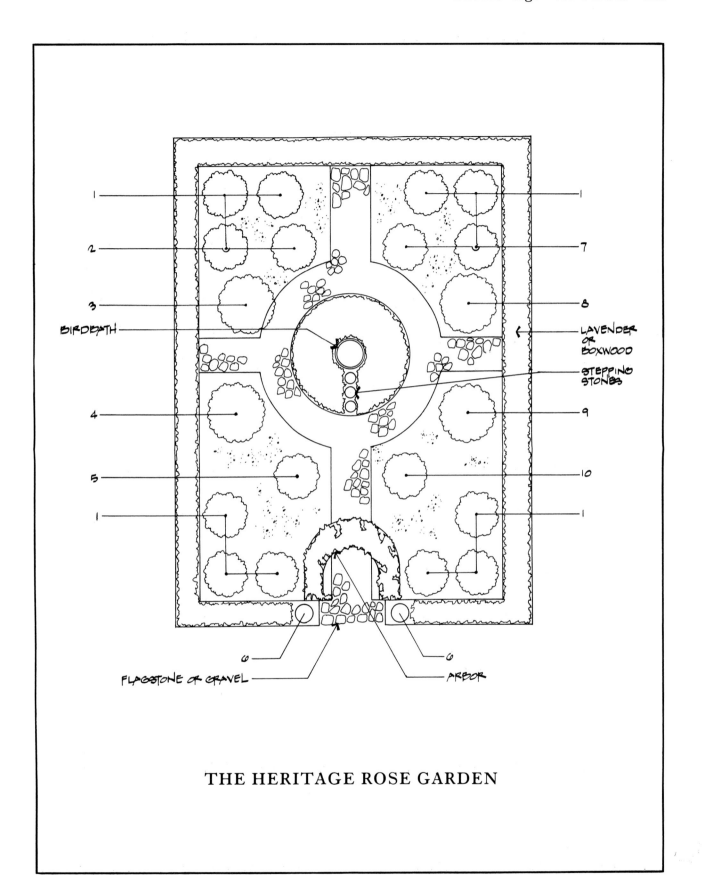

THE HERITAGE ROSE GARDEN

Dig a hole about two feet deep and at least eighteen inches across. Put two tablespoons of bone meal in the bottom of the hole, then partially fill it in with light, amended soil. Form the soil into a slight mound and gently mold the roots of the rose over the mound of soil. Fill in the rest of the hole and firm the soil around the roots, making sure the bud union (a swelling a few inches above where the roots begin) is about two inches above the soil line. Water very slowly and very thoroughly. It is critical to completely moisten the soil and to remove any air pockets. Keep your new rose moist for the first six weeks or so. After that, the watering schedule will depend on your climate. You can get general guidelines from local rose growers, but remember that in most cases old rose varieties can get along on much less water than their hybrid tea cousins. Once established, many old roses are quite drought tolerant, but to get the most blooms and lush growth in arid climates, give them an occasional deep watering.

Maintenance

Unlike hybrid tea roses, old roses should not be pruned severely. In fact, if you do prune them severely, you will probably cut off most of the buds; and, in the case of some of the large ramblers, you will get only a puny show instead of a large billowing mass of blooms. Prune heritage roses primarily to shape them, not to induce flowering. Varieties of old roses that bloom only once a year should be pruned *after* they bloom, not before. The varieties that bloom repeatedly throughout the year should be lightly pruned in late winter or early spring. Pat Wiley says, "Study your roses so that you begin to know their personalities. Some of the older varieties that bloom repeatedly should not be pruned except to remove weak or dead growth . . . their beauty is in a large plant with hundreds of small flowers, and if you prune them like you would a hybrid tea or floribunda,

you will not get a mass of blooms." After about two or three years, it is a good idea to remove a few old canes from all your roses because the new ones grow from the base of the plant.

Your old roses will benefit from yearly applications of manure or compost. If the foliage becomes pale, use supplemental applications of nitrogen. Most of the old roses are very pest and disease tolerant; that is, if they become diseased or pest ridden, they won't look their best, but they can *live through* the attacks. Some of the varieties on the list, particularly the Rugosas, almost never get diseases. Find out which rose diseases are a problem in your area and choose the varieties that are immune or resistant to them. Spider mites and aphids can occasionally be a problem on roses. Again, they won't kill the old-timers, but if looks are critical, you may want to spray occasionally with Safer's agricultural soap.

Moss rose

If you would be happy for a week, take a wife:
if you would be happy for a month, kill your pig:
but if you would be happy all your life, plant a
garden.

An Old Chinese Saying

Sources of Information

Books

Brooklyn Botanic Garden Handbooks. *Roses.* Vol. 6, no. 1. Brooklyn, N.Y.: Brooklyn Botanic Garden, 1980. A good, inexpensive, basic book on rose growing.

Damrosch, Barbara. *Theme Gardens.* New York: Workman Publishing, 1982. This book includes the plans for a marvelous old rose garden as one of its many gardens and information on a number of the old roses.

Griffiths, Trevor. *My World of Old Roses.* London: Whitcoulls, 1983. A delightful book that covers the whole range of old roses.

A large selection of books on old roses is available from Bell's Book Store, Attention: Barbara Worl, 536 Emerson Street, Palo Alto, CA 94301.

For more information on old roses and where to obtain them, send for the booklet *Combined Rose List 1982* by Beverly Dobson. It covers roses in commerce and cultivation, the rose registration since *Modern Roses 8,* as well as where to locate hard-to-find roses. Write to Beverly Dobson, 215 Harriman Road, Irvington, NY 10533. The cost of the pamphlet is $5.

Demonstration Gardens

Following is a list of public heritage rose gardens. The best time of the year to visit these gardens is in May and June.

Alfred L. Boerner Botanical Gardens
Hales Corners, WI 53130

Empire Mine State Park
Grass Valley, CA 95945

Mormon Museum
Salt Lake City, UT 84150

Mount Vernon
Mount Vernon, VA 22121

Reinisch Rose Garden
Gages Park
4320 West 10th Street
Topeka, KS 66604

Nurseries

Dynarose Limited (formerly Ellesmere)
Brooklin, Ontario L0B 1C0
Canada

Pickering Nurseries
670 Kingston Road
Pickering, Ontario L1V 1A6
Canada

Roses of Yesterday and Today (formerly
  Tillotson's)
802 Brown's Valley Road
Watsonville, CA 95076
Catalog $2. Send an additional 88 cents if you
want it mailed first class.

Organizations

If you are interested in joining Heritage Roses,
the heritage rose society, contact the member
nearest you.

Northeast:
Lily Shohan
R.D. 1
Clinton Corners, NY 12514

Northcentral:
Henry Najat
Route 3
Monroe, WI 53566

Northwest:
Jerry Fellman
947 Broughton Way
Woodburn, OR 97071

Southwest:
Miriam Wilkins
925 Galvin Drive
El Cerrito, CA 94530

Southcentral:
Vickie Jackson
122 Bragg Street
New Orleans, LA 70124

Southeast:
Charles G. Heremias
2103 Johnstone Street
Newberry, SC 29108

Consumer Note

Avoid planting the old multiflora roses.
Their growth is rampant, and they have become a serious invader in large parts of the
East and Northwest. Their thickets are impenetrable, and birds spread the seeds.

A wonderful way to acquire some of the old
roses is to visit old cemeteries and to ask
permission to take cuttings from some of the
heritage roses that have been planted there
through the years. Do not plant cuttings of
Moss, Alba, Damask, Gallica, or species roses
directly in the ground; graft them to a rootstock
such as 'Dr. Huey'. Many of the old roses are
so vigorous that they become rampant if they
are not grafted onto a more contained rootstock.

Birds occasionally spread rose seeds from
many of the old varieties. According to Pat
Wiley, though, it is not generally a problem because birds usually eat the seeds before they are
completely ripe. However, if your yard is adjacent to a wild area, keep an eye out for rose
seedlings in the vicinity of your roses. If you see
many seedlings, remove them and the parent
bush as well.

Cypripedium reginae

Chapter 8
The Orchid Garden

Orchids have a reputation for being exotic and difficult to grow. But, in fact, the orchid family, the largest family of flowering plants, with more than 35,000 species, contains some species that are so easy to grow that in many parts of the world people keep a few orchid plants just for their delight. Most are no more expensive than the average house plant. Their fanciful shapes, incredible colors, and unusual growth habits—some hang from trees—have long fascinated humans. Several hundred years ago tropical types were first introduced into Europe. Because they were rare, they developed a prestigious reputation. And because people believed orchids had to be kept in greenhouses, growing them became a hobby of the rich. The wealthy collectors became obsessed with imported varieties and put many orchid species on the road to extinction.

In the 1800s, orchids were so popular that auctions in Liverpool and London attracted a great deal of publicity. Orchid prices soared, with buyers often paying $500 for a single plant. Because people did not know how to grow them, orchids died by the thousands. English gardeners thought that plants coming from the tropics needed a hot, humid environment, so they placed orchids in stoves. The stoves combined heavily painted glass, coal fires, and hot-brick flues to simulate tropical conditions. There was no ventilation, and the bricks were doused continually with water to produce a steamy atmosphere. So many thousands of orchids died that one nobleman remarked that England had become the "grave of tropical orchids." Even though orchids died by the thousands, the novelty and beauty of those that survived inspired people to import still more.

Today not only the orchids, but the habitats that support them, are endangered. Thus one good reason to grow orchids is to provide a habitat for these lovely plants at a time when their own natural ecosystems are being destroyed by the inexorable press of land development.

Many varieties of orchids thrive in the house and, when given the right conditions, require no more care than other blooming house plants. In addition, with the proliferation of solar greenhouses, the subject of greenhouse-grown orchids becomes timely. Many of the cool-climate orchids thrive under cool greenhouse conditions; others tolerate or thrive in warm greenhouse conditions. The type of orchids you can grow depends on what kind of solar greenhouse you have and in what temperature range you keep it. Orchids rarely have pest problems that necessitate spraying.

I purposefully chose orchids over many other endangered species, such as cactuses and succulents, to illustrate that hybrids have a place in our garden plans. There is a growing fear that we are overrelying on hybrid plants. As a result, people categorically reject hybrids. The issue of hybrids in horticulture is a complex one. On the one hand, it is true that we have overrelied on hybrids in the vegetable garden (see the discussion of this subject in Chapter 5). On the other hand, the emergence of hybrid-orchid growing in this country has taken some of the pressure off the plants in the wild by cloning and propagating many of the wild species and hybridizing new plants, thereby producing a huge selection of fanciful, fairly easy-to-grow plants.

The number of choices available to the orchid grower far surpasses that of most other types of plants. With roses one gets a wide selection of colors and a few shapes; with fuschias and begonias, the same; but with orchids nature outdoes herself. Orchid flowers come in shapes so outrageous they are completely beyond human imagination. Orchids are festooned with plumes and pouches, protuberances and ruffles; the colors range from jade green to sunshine yellow, lavender, pink, orange, red, magenta, even brown. Some have blotches; some have stripes; others are crystal clear. Nowhere in the plant kingdom is there such variety.

Planning and Preparation

Orchids are herbaceous (nonwoody) perennials that occur as vines or clumping grasslike plants. Some bear a single, and usually spectacular, flower; others have many flowers. They grow in habitats from tropical rain forests to alpine meadows, from bogs to semidesert, and from sea level to 14,000 feet elevation. Most orchids are easy to grow once their basic requirements are known and met; others, however, are extremely difficult to grow.

Some orchids grow in soil and are referred to as "terrestrial"; their root systems have adapted to porous soils and humus. Other orchids grow on trees and are known as "epiphytes." Their roots have adapted to their aerial habitat. Good drainage is usually the key to healthy orchids; therefore, orchid nurseries sell a fast-draining potting mix blended especially for orchids. For some of the epiphytes there is no soil at all, just shredded bark or coconut fiber.

While some orchid varieties can be grown outdoors in some parts of this country, most should be treated as house plants or grown in a greenhouse. Many are well suited to the solar greenhouse. Orchid-growing temperatures are described by three designations: warm—daytime temperatures 75 to 85 degrees F., night 65 to 70; intermediate—daytime temperatures 70 to 80 degrees F., night 55 to 65; and cool—daytime temperatures 65 to 75 degrees F., night 50 to 55.

To bloom well, orchids need quite a bit of light. They will not grow well in a dark corner of a room; instead, they should be placed fairly near a bright window that faces east, south, or west. Plants should not receive hot, midday, summer sun. If orchids get too much sun, they turn yellow; if they get too little, they turn deep green and develop a soft, floppy growth habit. Nursery catalogs usually describe an orchid's light requirements as: bright—4,000 to 5,000 foot-candles (a southern or western window); moderate—1,500 to 4,000 foot-candles (a southern, western, or eastern window); or semi-shady—500 to 1,500 foot-candles (vary the distance between the plant and any window). About 3,000 foot-candles of light seem to be suitable for most orchids.

Most orchids like fairly humid conditions (60 to 65 percent humidity) and no strong drafts. These requirements can be met easily by placing the orchid containers on trays filled with pebbles and a half inch of water. Do not situate the plants near doors.

Purchase one of the beginning orchid-growing books recommended at the end of this chapter; most are not expensive. Assess the conditions in your home or greenhouse and choose the orchids that best fit those conditions. In addition, include at least one cattleya in your selection because it is the standard in orchid growing. Often directions for growing orchids will tell you what to do in relation to cattleya cultivation.

Even before you consider their fanciful shapes and wondrous color variations, you have to make many decisions in the process of selecting the orchids you want to grow. I asked Steve Hawkins at Rod McLellan's Acres of Orchids to choose ten readily available orchids that are suitable for beginning orchid growers. The following two indoor orchid gardens are his recommendations.

Two Windowsill Gardens

One garden is for houses that are kept on the cool side in the winter; the second is for houses that are kept warmer in winter or for those that are in warm parts of the country, such as in Florida or Hawaii.

First, there are some general guidelines that pertain to both gardens. For example, Hawkins has chosen both an east-facing and a south-facing exposure to show you how each is handled. The east-facing is optimum, but a south-

or west-facing window would be all right if you cover it with a sheer curtain to cut down on some of the bright sunlight. Make sure that the plant's leaves do not touch the window; the glass will be too cold for the plant. In addition, you should use a circulating fan to keep the air near the windows from becoming too cold. The fan will benefit the residents too because it will circulate the air, preventing the hot air from rising to the ceiling and the cold air from lying on the floor. Hawkins suggests a windowsill approximately eighteen inches wide for displaying the orchids. (A table or counter at the window would work well also.) To insure that the humidity around the plants is sufficient, he suggests placing the pots on trays that have pebbles in them, then filling the trays with water. The pebbles and water are not necessary if your house is equipped with a humidifier. Because orchids do not have lush foliage, they tend to look bare when grown by themselves. You will notice that the arrangements suggested by Hawkins leave room for other house plants that will grow under the same conditions.

The "Warm" Orchid Garden

For warm to intermediate greenhouses and homes, where daytime temperatures are between 70 and 80 degrees F., and nighttime temperatures are 60 degrees F. or warmer, choose a site where the temperatures are consistently warm and where there are no cold drafts or days when the temperature may drop to near freezing. An occasional 55-degree night is tolerable but not ideal. The orchids in the garden are described in the list below. The tallest plants and the varieties requiring the most light are located nearest the window. These orchid varieties bloom at different times of the year and will combine well with coleus, caladium, and philodendron.

Cattleya Greenwich, 'Cover Girl'. Pure green with a splash of purple at the edge of the labellum. Strong stems; blooms in the summer and fall. Intermediate temperature; moderate light.

Cattleya Gloriette, 'Superba'. Large blooms of light lavender. Dark purple labellum with a golden throat. Blooms in the late summer. Intermediate temperature; moderate light.

Phalaenopsis Toni Featherstone, 'Falcon Castle'. Dark pink striping on a pink background. Bold magenta-spotted labellums. Intermediate to warm temperature; semishady light.

Paphiopedilum Makuli. Blooms prolifically. White dorsal with green striping. Broad petals with delicate, chestnut spotting. Bronze pouch. Variegated foliage. Blooms in the summer and fall. Intermediate to warm temperature; semishady light.

Oncidium Carnival Costume, 'Summer Sprite'. Compact plants with a profusion of one-foot spikes at maturity. Rich gold with chestnut markings. Blooms in the summer. Intermediate temperature; moderate light.

The "Cool" Orchid Garden

This orchid garden is for a cool house, one where the winter temperatures range from 50 to 75 degrees F., or for an outdoor garden in a mild climate. The tallest plants and the ones that need the most light are nearest the window. The following selection of orchids will bloom at different times of the year and will combine well with different kinds of ivy and kalanchoe and grape ivy (*Cissus*).

Laelia Canariensis, 'Austin'. Produces silky soft yellow stars atop a foot-long stem. Blooms in the winter. Intermediate to cool temperature; moderate to bright light or outside in partial shade in mild climates.

Cymbidium Siempre, 'Summer Green'. Unusual summer bloomer. Icy green with delicate red lip markings and straight, upright spikes. Fragrant. Cool greenhouse; bright light or outdoors in partial shade in mild climates.

Above There are orchids with wondrous shapes; among them is this yellow fringed native, *Platanthera ciliaris*.

Opposite Orchids can be grown indoors on a shelf or table located near either a south- or east-facing window. Put up a sheer curtain if you have a south-facing window so the sunlight will not burn the orchid foliage. To give substance and variety to the window garden, include other kinds of house plants. Here the warm window garden includes coleus and caladium; the cool window garden has ivy and kalanchoe.

Warm Orchid Garden
1. *Phalaenopsis* Toni Featherstone, 'Falcon Castle'
2. *Cattleya* Gloriette, 'Superba'
3. *Oncidium* Carnival Costume, 'Summer Sprite'
4. *Paphiopedilum* Makuli
5. *Cattleya* Greenwich, 'Cover Girl'

Cool Orchid Garden
6. *Odontocidium* Big Mac, 'Saragossa'
7. *MacLellanara* Pagan Love Song, 'Golden Realm'
8. *Cymbidium* Siempre, 'Summer Green'
9. *Laelia Canariensis*, 'Austin'

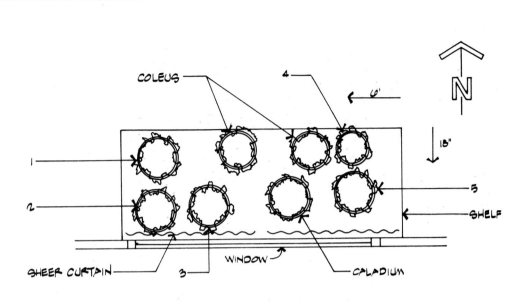

The "Warm" Orchid Garden

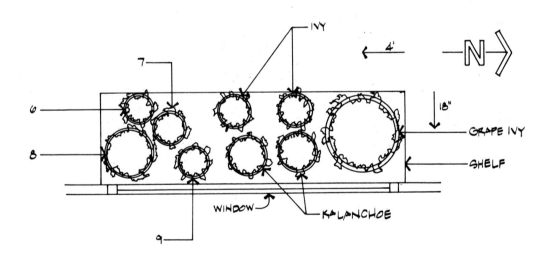

The "Cool" Orchid Garden

THE ORCHID GARDEN

Cymbidium Hunter's Point, 'Sunset'. Large blooms of gold to orange with red veining and barred lip. Blooms early to midseason. Two spikes per new bulb are not unusual. Cool greenhouse with bright light or outdoors with partial shade in mild climates. (This plant is not recommended for indoor growing.)

Odontocidium Big Mac, 'Saragossa'. Sprays of long-lasting chartreuse yellow with chestnut spotting. Flowers two or three times per year. Extremely strong grower. Cool to intermediate temperature; semishady light indoors or outside in heavy shade in mild climates.

MacLellanara Pagan Love Song, 'Golden Realm'. Three-to-four-foot spikes of iridescent chartreuse yellow stars with dark chocolate markings. Flowers four inches across. Blooms in the winter and spring. Intermediate to cool temperature; moderate light or outside in heavy shade in mild climates.

Maintenance

If conditions are right—proper lighting and humidity, good potting soil—orchids are quite simple to take care of. McLellan's Acres of Orchids recommends a compromise schedule of watering and fertilizing that works for all the orchids, so you won't have to keep separate schedules for each one. If you pot the plants in containers of similar size, try a schedule of watering once a week and fertilizing once a month. Use a high-nitrogen fertilizer (except for cymbidiums, which are fed with a low-nitrogen fertilizer from July to December). Closely watch your plants when you start this schedule. If necessary, change the potting medium to suit the watering schedule.

Orchids seldom have problems with pests and diseases. When they do, the pests are thrips, aphids, mealybugs, and scale. Orchid diseases are usually a form of root rot caused by too much water. Virus diseases are not usually a problem, unless you bring in new, diseased

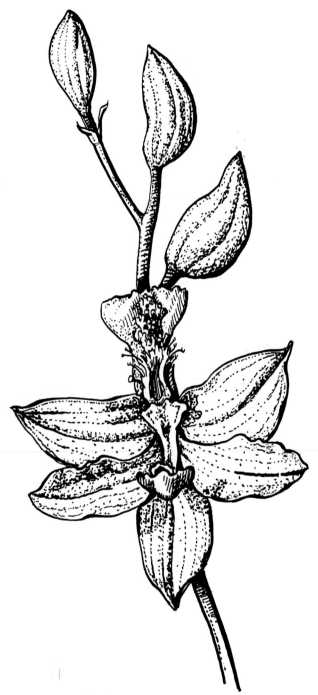

Calopogon tuberosus

plants and spread the virus to your old plants. Check the orchid books for remedies. As with most good pest control, though, prevention is the key.

Sources of Information

Books

American Orchid Society. *Handbook on Orchid Culture*. Cambridge, Mass.: American Orchid Society, 1982. A booklet covering many of the basics.

Dillon, Gordon W. *American Orchid Society, Beginner's Handbook*. Cambridge, Mass.: American Orchid Society, 1981. A fairly detailed book on most aspects of orchid growing.

Northern, Rebecca Tyson. *Home Orchid Growing*. 3rd ed. New York: Van Nostrand Reinhold Company, 1970. This book is a classic in its field, and if you have only one orchid-growing book, this should be it.

Oregon Orchid Society. *Your First Orchids and How to Grow Them*. Portland: Oregon Orchid Society, 1977. An inexpensive and pleasant way to get your feet wet.

Williams, Brian. *Orchids for Everyone*. New York: Crown Publishers, 1980. A beautiful book showing 200 orchids in color with extensive practical advice.

Williams, John G., and Williams, Andrew E. *Field Guide to Orchids of North America*. New York: Universe Books, 1983. A useful guide for looking at or photographing orchids in the wild.

Demonstration Gardens

Lahaina Orchid Exhibit
Highway 30
Lahaina, HI 96761
Over 300 varieties of orchids. Open daily.

Marie Selby Gardens
800 South Palm Drive
Sarasota, FL 33577
The center of orchid study in the United States; these people are interested in endangered species of orchids.

Nurseries

Alberts & Merkel Bros.
2210 South Federal Highway
Boynton Beach, FL 44335
Nursery open to the public.

Fennell's Orchid Jungle
26715 Southwest 157th Avenue
Homestead, FL 33031
Gardens open to the public.

Jones & Scully
2200 Northwest 33rd Avenue
Miami, FL 33142
Exhibits of orchids on the premises.

Rod McLellan Company
Acres of Orchids
1450 El Camino Real
South San Francisco, CA 94080
Large exhibit of orchids. Catalog 50 cents.

Orchids by Hausermann
P.O. Box 363
Department A
Elmhurst, IL 60126
Carries a large selection of orchids.

Fred A. Stewart Orchids
1212 East Las Tunas Drive
P.O. Box 307
San Gabriel, CA 91778
Nursery open to the public.

Organizations

For further information on orchids, join the American Orchid Society, 600 South Olive Avenue, West Palm Beach, FL 33402.

Consumer Note

A number of years ago my husband and I changed our fresh-water aquarium to a salt-water aquarium. How exciting it was to get new fish: the spectacular lion fish, the curious Humu Humu Nuku Nuku Apu Ah Ah, the graceful damsels, and the Moorish idols. They were much more interesting than the ordinary guppies and angel fish we were used to. Eventually, though, our delight changed to disappointment as one by one they starved themselves to death or contracted some exotic disease. Soon we realized that we were trying to care for *wild* creatures and that very little was known about their eating habits, diseases, and environment. They cannot even breed in captivity. To complete our disillusionment we found out that in Hawaii, where our fish had come from, natives spread household bleach in the water to stun the fish, thereby catching them easily and quickly. For every fish that ended up in someone's aquarium, hundreds of others died. Once we realized what the consequences of our fish collection were, the joy went out of the experience. We soon gave up our salt-water aquarium.

Orchids, cactuses, succulents, and other plants are often taken from the wild, usually to die in captivity. The plants, unable to reproduce, provide only a fleeting moment of pleasure for someone. And these plants represent only the tip of the iceberg; many others of their species end up withering in the sun behind some native hut, waiting to be taken to market. Taking fish, animals, and plants out of their native settings is a practice carried over from a time when there were fewer people on our planet. What may have been reasonable for hundreds is certainly not appropriate for millions. Like the leopard coat of our parents' generation that we no longer feel right owning, it no longer seems appropriate to take plants from the wild. We really don't have to anyway; we have a rich variety to choose from if we preserve our thousands of heirlooms, continue to propagate the thousands of plants already taken from the wild, and enjoy our new hybrid plants. We are gardeners blessed with choices and have no need to feel cheated.

Never collect plants from the wild unless you are rescuing a plant from the blade of a bulldozer. Be forewarned that some of our native terrestrial orchids are so difficult to grow that members of the orchid society stand up and cheer when someone gets one of them to bloom. Most orchids will not tolerate being transplanted and will not grow from seed; therefore, if you want to rescue one, get a knowledgeable person to help you. Perhaps it would be better to fight to have the plants left undisturbed. You can use the orchid guides to help you get to know native orchids. Collect pictures, not plants.

Nurseries of questionable ethics occasionally offer native, ground-dwelling orchids, such as various lady's-slippers and fringed habenarias, for sale. Avoid buying these and any other orchid that may have been collected from the wild. If you are an expert orchid grower, become involved with the American Orchid Society's program to save endangered orchids.

Never sneak orchids into the country. Besides the fact that you could end up going to jail or having to pay a whopping fine, you could introduce a new orchid pest or disease into this country.

When you start growing orchids, stay with the less expensive varieties for a while, so if you lose a few while you are learning, your cost will be minimal. Most orchids can be propagated by division, so you can save money by trading offshoots with other growers. If you do get orchids from a friend, be sure you are getting disease-free plants. If you cannot recognize most of the diseases, don't trade.

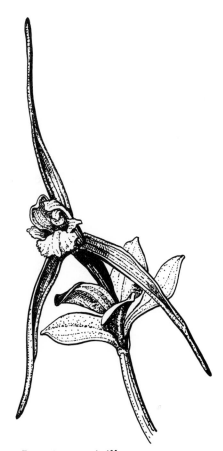

Isotria verticillata

PART THREE

PLEASURE GARDENS

Being a horticultural consultant at a party is a little like being a doctor, I imagine. Friends and acquaintances often ask what they should be doing to their gardens. Usually the questions go like this: Do I have to fertilize my lawn now? Is this the time to prune the wisteria? My plum tree is oozing sap—what should I do? In our culture, garden information gleaned from books, newspaper columns, and commercial nurseries is inevitably oriented toward what you *must do* to take care of plants. This book, while conveying many specifics about plant care, is intended as a celebration of what plants and gardening can do for you.

Instead of thinking, I have to mow the lawn now, or I have to clip the hedge before we go on a picnic today, imagine a trip to the garden as an inspiration for thinking, I wonder if there's a ripe strawberry, or I wonder if the cardinal found the nesting material I left yesterday. If the number of mandatory chores is reduced and the garden is planned to enhance your own personal pleasure, a garden can be a source of renewal, a refuge from the world.

An Integral View of Gardening

More and more often, people are trying to integrate the different parts of their lives. They are making choices based on what is best for the whole person. This approach is needed also in the garden. Gardening is not just a lawn and a few shrubs around the house, but a whole system, a part of life. Our "concrete, microchip life" takes its toll, and viewing the yard as just one more chore that needs to be done before the weekend is over deprives you of a healthful, calming experience. Most people find renewal in nature: that trip to the mountains or to the park lifts their spirits. Yet few homeowners walk around their yards feeling more than, I had better prune that tree, or I need to water.

Gardening can be therapeutic. While gardeners have always known that, governmental studies and professional observations have now made it official: Gardening has *proven* to be of great benefit to mentally disturbed and handicapped people, seniors, prisoners, and institutionalized people. Further, schools are finding that gardening is a way to teach children about such intangibles as the seasons, the flow of time, changes in nature, and life and death.

People who have long been involved with their own gardens can speak eloquently about the feelings of well-being they get from puttering in the yard, smelling the roses, picking the tomatoes, and watching the passing seasons. Surrounded by nature, their cares melt away.

What does the typical American yard, with its large lawn, mustache of evergreen shrubs, and few trees, do for us? Well, a yard gives you distance from the neighbor's stereo; it shows you can afford some land; and it gives the children a place to play. That large lawn can also function as a barrier to rodents, fire, and insects, and it keeps dust and mud out of the house. If the trees are large, deciduous, and well placed, they can keep the house cooler in the summer.

I have no argument about the fact that these are worthwhile considerations. But let's take another look at the garden and imagine what you *could* do there: visit the vegetable garden with your child to see if the peas sown a few days ago have germinated, get out your binoculars to spy on a nest of finches, pick sun-warmed raspberries, pick a nosegay of johnny-jump-ups, or curl up to read a book under a bower of heady jasmine—maybe that's what people mean when they tell you to "smell the roses as you pass through life." If you can add these dimensions to your yard, why be content with a lawn and a few shrubs? All of us, in our own varied ways, are seeking peace of mind, fulfillment, and a feeling of integration with the natural environment. A rich source of these rewards lies just outside the window.

There is the healthful exercise to be had from gardening, and, concurrently, that wonderful feeling of actively participating in the natural scheme of life. Sharing that experience with your children can result in many rich, sun-filled hours that later on will seem to have been idyllic.

We all, regardless of our ages and levels of experience, can learn from our contact with nature. Children come to understand birth, death, and renewal in the garden, and adults as well need hands-on exposure to these cycles to remind them of what is really important. Somehow a job deadline, a bank statement, or even a serious illness in the family slips into a different perspective during an afternoon or a weekend of gardening. The new perspective encompasses both the changefulness and the stability of the natural order. You can stand in the garden and think through natural connections until you've seen the links between yourself, your own plot of land, and the Milky Way itself. There's pleasure and balance in that kind of thinking.

On a less cosmic level, consider the great fun you can have in feeding, quite literally, your other pleasures. If you're a cook, why not extend your creative touch to growing the produce you prepare in the kitchen? Do you like Italian cooking? Grow pear tomatoes, basil, and arugula. French cooking? Grow fraises des bois, flageolets, and mache. Chinese cooking? Grow bok choy, fuzzy gourds, and yard-long beans. You'll lessen your dependence on the market and give new meaning to the word *fresh*.

Is making your home comfortable and pretty your particular source of enjoyment? Why let your pleasure end at the door? Think about designing your *total* environment, cooling and heating the inside by making good landscaping decisions outside. Plant shade trees against the south wall; put in evergreen windbreaks to soften the effects of winter winds. Reserve part of your garden as a year-round source of cut flowers for the house. Create natural beauty everywhere; the only limits to your choices are the regional ones that determine the particular varieties of plants you can grow.

If you love animals or butterflies or certain kinds of plants, such as cactuses or succulents, or if you would like to teach your children about these things, design your yard to support those species and watch them flourish. Plants give us a sense of our own place in the natural world. The gardens in Part Three are examples of ways your yard can be a source of joy.

If you give up the typical American habit of trying to dominate nature and begin to think about living with nature—as an active part of it— you'll come up with ways of designing your yard to reflect and enhance what you love. Your garden will be a source of joy and understanding and, ultimately, a place to feel at home and tranquil. Feel like going to bed? Taking a pill? Calling a therapist? Try rolling up your sleeves and doing some gardening instead.

Ficus carica

Chapter 9

The Gourmet Garden

Every week twenty years ago I tuned in to Julia Child's television program, "The French Chef." With great enthusiasm I followed her lead and made quiche, ratatouille, salade nicoise, crepes, and numerous other goodies. I, like many Americans, was being awakened to a whole new way of cooking and eating. Our gastronomy changed dramatically as a consequence of several factors: Julia's program and cookbooks, an upswing in our economy and the resulting societal changes, and increased education and travel. In the last two decades the improvements in cooking skills and the wide availability of exotic ingredients have changed the American palate. Twenty years ago only the very sophisticated or well-traveled person had heard of kiwis, tacos, pesto, shallots, and chutney. Now most people have.

If we take stock of gastronomy in the mid-1980s, we are led to the conclusion that eating more home-grown fruits and vegetables is the order. For instance, we are becoming more health conscious and have begun to cut back on salt, butter, and calories. We suspect there are unsafe additives and pesticides in our produce. If we grow our own food, we will ingest fewer chemicals. If we eat more fruits and vegetables, we have more roughage in our diets—the nutritionists tell us that is healthful.

Since the oil crisis, food prices have skyrocketed, and the high price of food has become an issue. It is expensive to eat well. Of particular interest to the gourmet cook is the fact that even though there is a huge selection of fruits and vegetables at the market, the quality is slipping. The hybridization of fruits and vegetables to make them as firm as cardboard for machine picking and packing and the early harvesting of unripe produce to ensure it withstands long-distance shipping have resulted in an ever-increasing choice of beautiful but tasteless produce: the nickel apple that costs a quarter and tastes like nothing.

Most home-grown produce is far superior to what you can buy. It's fresher and usually more succulent, and that is because it can be picked at its peak. However, several caveats are in order here. Some of the worst produce I have eaten has come from my garden. Cucumbers must be picked when they are young; they develop tough seeds as they mature. Pears that are allowed to ripen on the tree get grainy. Overripe melons are soft and mushy. The point I am making is that growing your own produce is only half of the answer to eating well; in addition, you must learn when each vegetable and fruit is at its peak. To do that, you must be diligent. Experiment: try picking at different times and see at which stage individual vegetables and fruits are most appealing to you.

You must have reasonable expectations for your home-grown produce. Some edibles that you buy from the grocery store can't be duplicated at home. For instance, commercially produced 'Thompson Seedless' grapes are larger and sweeter than those grown at home. Farmers spray a plant hormone, gibberellic acid, on the grapes to make them large, and they girdle the stems of the vines to prevent the sugars from migrating to the roots. Most homeowners do neither. Also, different soils and climates produce different tastes. My tomatoes in California have never had as much tomato flavor as those from my New England garden; and my California-grown onions are very hot, even when I plant the sweetest, mildest varieties. Through experimentation and adventurous selection of varieties you will develop a list of superior edibles for your own garden and table.

In order to learn which varieties of fruits and vegetables do well in your area, frequent farmers' and gourmet produce markets. If the produce is not labeled with the name of its variety, ask the produce manager or the farmer who grew it what it is. Keep a record of the varieties you prefer so that when winter bareroot planting season comes or when it is time to order seeds in the spring, you will know which varieties are your favorites. Learning about the different varieties will help you avoid the problem I so often see at the nursery: people standing in front of an array of bare-root fruit trees or at the seed racks scratching their heads, with no idea which varieties to choose.

Let's face it, many of us who enjoy gourmet cooking have a bit of the showoff in us, and I've noticed that it is getting harder to stay one up on everyone. Ten years ago I could go to a meeting of rare-fruit growers and come home to wow everyone with an exotic fruit—a kiwi, for example. Today everyone yawns. If you want to be out in front now, you must join the next gourmet frontier: home-grown produce. Home-grown corn, new potatoes, petits pois, as well as more unusual varieties such as adzuki beans, water chestnuts, quince, and loganberries, can be grown at home to produce rave reviews at the table.

A home vegetable garden can dramatically enrich your cuisine, and in most cases the unusual edibles are no harder to grow than common fruits and vegetables. As a rule, you must purchase the unusual edibles by mail or from specialty nurseries.

Gourmet Plants for the Outdoor Garden

I recommend the following plants and seeds for a beginning gourmet gardener; only a few of them are available in grocery stores, and all will enrich your table fare.

Avocados. 'Mexicola' avocados are my favorite; they taste like melted cashews. They are little and soft skinned, which is probably why they aren't found in grocery stores. In addition, if you have a greenhouse or live in a warm climate, you can try the exciting, new dwarf avocado, 'Whitsell'. It is a good, green-skinned avocado that growers have spent years producing. Pacific Tree Farms, 4301 Lynwood Drive, Chula Vista, CA 92010, is one of the first nurseries to carry this 'Hass'-type avocado.

Bamboo. Fresh bamboo shoots are sweet and succulent. Varieties that are easily grown in many parts of this country produce shoots in the spring or fall.

Beets. Yellow beets have made cooking with beets more versatile because, unlike red beets, they do not "bleed" into soups, stir-fried dishes, salads, and stews.

Corn. Hopi blue corn is easy to grow, makes incredible cornbread and tamales, and is almost never available at the grocery store.

Cucumbers. Armenian cucumbers have a wonderful cucumber taste and don't cause the burps that standard cucumbers give some people. My Indian friend says that they also make the best raita.

Elderberries. Elderberries make superb pies, jam, and wine but are rarely used for such.

Garlic. Elephant garlic is much easier to peel, and, while not as pungent as ordinary garlic, the large cloves are mild and tasty.

Ginger. Ginger that is grown outside in the summer and brought inside when it gets cold not only produces flavorful rhizomes but also tasty green shoots for use in salads and stir-fried dishes.

Heirloom fruits. Fruits that will elicit comments from your guests are 'Cox's Pippin', an antique apple from England; currants in the form of jelly; and quinces, which make the best baked "apples" you've ever tasted.

Herbs. Fresh herbs such as thyme, red basil, sage, pineapple mint, chervil, savory, and anise lend much more aroma and flavor to cooking than their dried equivalents and are at their best when picked only minutes before you use them.

Hops. Hops are easily grown, and they produce edible shoots every spring that are similar to asparagus. They can be cooked and served the same way as asparagus.

Nuts. There are new varieties of nuts available, especially the self-pollinating, pink-flowered, dwarf 'Garden Prince' almond. The North American Nut Growers Association is currently trying to develop a hardy pecan variety and a disease-resistant chestnut.

Oranges. 'Tarocco' oranges, sometimes called raspberry, or blood, oranges, have red, tangy juice that will make you yawn at ordinary orange juice.

Peaches. 'Indian Blood' peaches are deep red inside. Can them or make a beautiful red jam with them.

Salad greens. Flavorful greens such as sorrel, mache (corn salad), salad burnet, orach, and rocket (arugula) are flavorful additions to humdrum salads.

Fresh salad greens make a dramatic addition to your table fare. They grow well in containers and are beautiful in any garden.

Strawberries. Alpine strawberries are so delicate that they barely survive the trip from garden to table, much less by truck to store to home. Their fragrance alone is worth the experience of growing them.

Zucchini. Golden zucchini is a tasty and colorful addition to omelets, salads, and soups.

Gourmet Plants for the Greenhouse

Following is a list of delightful edibles that can be grown in a greenhouse.

Banana. Home-grown bananas are small but have much more flavor than those purchased at the store, and the leaves are wonderful to steam vegetables in: they impart a fragrance to the food. 'Enano Gigante' dwarf bananas are particularly well suited to greenhouse growing.

Cherimoyas. Succulent, creamy fruits that currently sell at $8 to $10 per pound and are considered one of the finest fruits in the world. They grow on large shrubs that are suitable for greenhouse growing, though the flowers will need to be hand-pollinated. 'Mariella' is a good variety to try.

Vanilla. Pods grow on an orchid vine that can be grown in the greenhouse. They are difficult orchids to grow but are a challenge for the experienced gardener and worth the effort.

Ethnic Cooking

Many ingredients for the different ethnic cuisines are easy-to-grow herbs and annual vegetables that can be grown in most parts of the country. Related varieties, such as string beans and the French haricots verts, are grown the same way their American cousins are; and vegetables such as sorrel, garland chrysanthemum, and mache are generally very easy to grow. To give you an idea of what is feasible in your garden, look over the following list.

Oriental Ingredients You Can Grow

Amaranth (pot herb). A hot to bland, depending on the variety, spinach-type vegetable. Use it in soups and stir-fried dishes, or steam it by itself.

Bitter melon (vegetable). A slightly bitter summer-squash-like vegetable. It can be stuffed with pork and herbs or used in stir-fried dishes or steamed like spinach.

Burdock, gobo (root vegetable). The leaves are eaten the way spinach is. The root, which is somewhat pungent, can be used as a root vegetable: steamed, stir fried, and in soups.

Chinese cabbage. A mild-tasting, sweet, succulent cabbage used in Chinese soups, stir-fried dishes, salads, and pickling.

Chinese okra. A sweet zucchinilike vegetable that can be eaten raw in salads. It can be stir fried, deep fried, simmered, or stuffed.

Chinese parsley (cilantro). A zesty herb that is used in many vegetable and meat dishes.

Daikon (radish). Grate and serve raw in Japanese cuisine, stir fry with shellfish, and pickle for Chinese cuisine.

Daylilies (golden needles). The buds of the daylily are sweet, tasty additions to Chinese soups and meat and vegetable dishes.

Fuzzy gourd (vegetable). A sweet summer-squash-like vegetable that can be steamed or used in stir-fried dishes and soups.

Garland chrysanthemum, shungiku (pot herb). A fragrant green that is used in soups and stir-fried dishes or steamed like spinach.

Sesame. A versatile plant that provides leaves, which can be cooked as a vegetable, and seeds, which add a characteristic nutty flavor to salads, stir-fried dishes, and vegetable dishes.

Yard-long beans. Tasty, very long string beans that are used in stir-fried dishes. They are fabulous as a dry-braised dish and can be used wherever string beans are.

Good sources of Oriental seeds are Redwood City Seed Company and Shepherd's Garden Seeds. The addresses of these companies are given at the end of this chapter.

French Ingredients You Can Grow

Alpine strawberries. The most delicate and aromatic of all strawberries. These small, wild-like strawberries will make any fruit salad or tart a special occasion.

Celeriac (root vegetable). A root vegetable with a sweet celery taste. Superb served julienne sliced in a remoulade and in salads and cooked dishes.

Chervil (herb). A mild herb that adds a subtle richness to egg dishes, seafood, and salads.

Courgettes (squash). This tender summer squash is versatile; it is enhanced by many different sauces and cooking techniques.

Haricots verts (beans). Tender, pencil thin, string beans that are great just by themselves or in soups, salads, and vegetable dishes.

Mache, corn salad

Mache (corn salad). A tender, subtle-tasting salad green.

Petits pois (peas). These are the small, incredibly sweet peas that make the regular varieties unacceptable by comparison.

Roquette (salad green). A rich salad green that adds a zesty flavor to bland greens.

Shallot. A relative of onion and garlic, the shallot has inherited the best of both. Useful where onion and garlic are featured.

Sorrel (pot herb). A slightly sour, succulent green that is fabulous in salads and soups.

Good sources of French seeds are Epicure Seeds Ltd., Le Marche Seeds International, and Shepherd's Garden Seeds. The addresses of these companies are given at the end of this chapter.

Mexican Ingredients You Can Grow

Chayote (vegetable). A versatile squashlike vegetable that adds a sweet, nutty flavor to soups and stews and is beautiful just steamed by itself.

Chilies. These peppers add authority to Mexican cuisine, and the fresh varieties add a perfume that dried chilies only hint at.

Cilantro (herb). A commonly used herb that tastes similar to parsley.

Jicama (vegetable). A very sweet, watery, crisp vegetable. It can be sliced into salads to add extra crispness and into soups and stews.

Nopales (cactus pads). Sliced cactus pads are an unusual vegetable; they are sweet and similar to string beans in taste. They can be steamed and fried and are sometimes smothered in sauces.

Tomatillo (vegetable). A close relative of the tomato, this tasty, small, green globe gives a richness to green salsa and is a treat fried, stewed, and in soups.

Good sources of Mexican seeds are Redwood City Seed Company and Shepherd's Garden Seeds. The addresses of these companies are given at the end of this chapter.

Indian Ingredients You Can Grow

Bitter melon (vegetable). A slightly bitter, tasty, squashlike vegetable you can use in dishes that feature its unusual taste.

Chilies. Fresh chili peppers give bite and the characteristic hotness to Indian food. Fresh chilies can be grated or chopped finely and used in chutneys, curries, soups, and pickles.

'Gypsy' peppers are outstanding—sweet, crisp, and thin-walled.

Cilantro (herb). A parsleylike herb that is dried and used in chutneys, curries, rice, and vegetable dishes. Use it fresh as a flavoring and garnish. You cannot do very much authentic Indian cooking without it.

Ginger. A succulent rhizome that adds a heady aroma and hotness to many Indian dishes, including curries, rice and lentil dishes, sweets, and pickles.

Fenugreek (herb). This herb is used fresh whenever possible. It is added to chutneys and spice tea and is used as a garnish.

Saffron (spice). A pungent, orange-colored spice obtained from the saffron crocus. It is used in Indian cooking to add an exciting taste to rice, curries, and sweets.

A good source of Indian seeds is Redwood City Seed Company, whose address is given at the end of this chapter.

An Italian Gourmet Vegetable Garden

When people think of Italian cuisine, they usually think of pizza, spaghetti, and other pasta dishes. While they are certainly Italian, those dishes make up only a small part of Italian cuisine. To my mind, Italian cuisine is marinated vegetables (bright red peppers, sweet onions, and mushrooms bathed in olive oil, vinegar, and herbs), eggplant parmigiana, deep-fried cardoon (a close relative of the artichoke), peas with prosciutto, and bagna cauda (raw vegetables dipped in hot butter and olive oil flavored with garlic and anchovies). It is antipasto, minestrone, pesto (a sauce of pureed fresh basil, olive oil, and garlic), and colorful salads with magenta chicories called radicchio and bright green endive and arugula. It was my good fortune to enjoy these dishes in Italy, and because most of these dishes are filled with fresh herbs and unusually succulent and colorful vegetables, I found that the only way to duplicate many of the taste sensations I had experienced was to grow some of the vegetables and herbs myself.

To really do justice to most ethnic cuisines, you need produce that is usually either not available in American grocery stores or, if it is available, is exorbitantly expensive; and Italian cuisine, I found, is no exception. It requires fresh basil, cilantro, and dill, for instance, and fresh fava beans, white Italian eggplant, 'Romanesco' broccoli with its sculptured conical heads and lively taste, scorzonera and ravanello (large brown and white radishes), squash blossoms, radicchio (red and striped chicories), and finnochio (sweet fennel). These are all outstanding vegetables that are seldom seen in this country, except in home vegetable gardens or in the fanciest restaurants.

If you want to experience some of Italy's best cuisine, put in a vegetable garden similar to the one illustrated here; it is based on the garden of Vicki Sebastiani, who is married to Sam Sebastiani, the president of Sebastiani Vineyards. Vicki has been a vegetable gardener since she was four years old and is often called upon to entertain hundreds of people and to contribute recipes to the winery's newsletter. Vicki's interest in vegetable gardening has grown to prodigious proportions. Last summer her garden included one hundred varieties of vegetables and herbs, most of them Italian. There were red, yellow, and white varieties of Italian tomatoes, white eggplant, Italian yellow and light green zucchini, giant cauliflower, variegated chicory, long beans, spaghetti squash, horseradish, and scarlet runner beans. Red and white flowers were interspersed among the vegetables and herbs.

Planning and Preparation

Vicki offers the following information for the aspiring Italian gourmet vegetable gardener. Most of the superior, authentic varieties of vegetable seeds are not available at nurseries. You must order them by mail early in the spring, or, if you are as fortunate as Vicki, get them in Italy when you visit there. She ordered most of her seeds from Gurney Seed and Nursery Company and W. Atlee Burpee Company. Some of the varieties that she bought in Italy can be purchased from DeGiorgi Company, Epicure Seeds, and Shepherd's Garden Seeds (the addresses of these companies are given at the end of this chapter). Each company carries a number of Italian vegetable and herb

Right Vicki Sebastiani grows 'Romanesco' broccoli in her Italian vegetable garden.

seeds. You will not, however, be able to buy seeds for some of the vegetables you see on the list. They are a challenge. Perhaps if you have Italian friends or neighbors, they will share some of their open-pollinated varieties with you. Perhaps you can visit Italy or find a seed source there.

Once you have gotten the seeds, choose a sunny, well-drained garden area and add large amounts of organic matter. Start the tomatoes, peppers, eggplants, squashes, and cantaloupes indoors early in the spring so that you can transplant them into the garden after all chance of frost has passed. When your soil starts to warm up in the spring, you can plant the seeds of some of the early vegetables, such as lettuce, peas, carrots, spinach, radishes, turnips, kohlrabies, cauliflower, broccoli, chicory, endive, fennel, and nasturtiums. Once the weather has completely warmed up, with no possibility of frost, you can plant the seeds of beans, dill, corn, and okra and transplant the tender plants that you started weeks before. Consult local authorities for exact dates for planting your garden. The varieties suggested in this garden have the same cultural requirements—water, fertilizer, and pest control, if any—as your usual varieties.

Following is a list of vegetables and herbs that is keyed to the layout of a variation of the Sebastiani gourmet garden. Notice that not all the vegetables and herbs are Italian; many are American. Vicki's garden is a very ambitious project and too large for the average family. so scale yours down to a more manageable size. Not all the plants were grown in the same season. Some are spring crops; others are summer and fall crops. The numbers preceding the plants are keyed to the diagram on page 141. Following the plant name there is often, in brackets, the name of a seed company. Those companies are either where Vicki obtained her seeds or where I have located the seeds or seeds of a very similar variety. Where there is no company name, Vicki obtained the seeds either in Italy or from local nurseries. Addresses of the seed companies are given at the end of this chapter.

1. Basil [Burpee]
2. Cavolfiore Precocissimo di Jesi (Italian white cauliflower)
3. Cavolfiore, 'Grodan' (Italian snow white cauliflower)
4. Cavolbroccolo d'Albenga, 'Bronzino' (spear-shaped Italian broccoli)
5. Cavolfiore di Sicilia, Catanese (Italian red cauliflower)
6. Cavolbroccolo, 'Romanesco' (Italian light green, small-speared broccoli) [Epicure, Seeds Blum]
7. Kohlrabi, 'Grand Duke' [Gurney's, Burpee]
8. Kohlrabi, 'Early Purple' Vienna [Gurney's, Burpee]
9. Pepper, 'Sweet Bell'
10. Pepper, 'Big Jim New Mex' [Gurney's]
11. Pepper, 'Spartan Garnet' [Gurney's]
12. Pepper, 'Fresno Chili Grande' [Gurney's]
13. Pepper, pepperoncini [Gurney's]
14. Pepper, jalapeno [Gurney's, Burpee]
15. Pepper, 'Santa Fe Grande' [Gurney's]
16. Alchechenge (small, Italian yellow pear tomato)
17. Tomato, 'Golden Boy' [Gurney's]
18. Tomato, 'Golden Delight' [Gurney's Early Yellow]
19. Tomato, 'Yellow Pear' [Gurney's, DeGiorgi]
20. Tomato, 'White Beauty' [Gurney's]
21. Tomato, 'Pink Delight' [Gurney's]
22. Tomato, 'Beefmaster' [Gurney's]
23. Okra, 'Clemson Spineless' [Gurney's]
24. Okra, red [Gurney's, DeGiorgi]
25. Squash, 'Golden Zucchini' [Burpee]
26. Squash, 'White Patty Pan' [Burpee, DeGiorgi]
27. Squash, 'Green Patty Pan' [Gurney's]
28. Squash, 'Gold Zucchini' [Gurney's]
29. Squash, Zucchetta Goldzinni (Italian yellow zucchini)

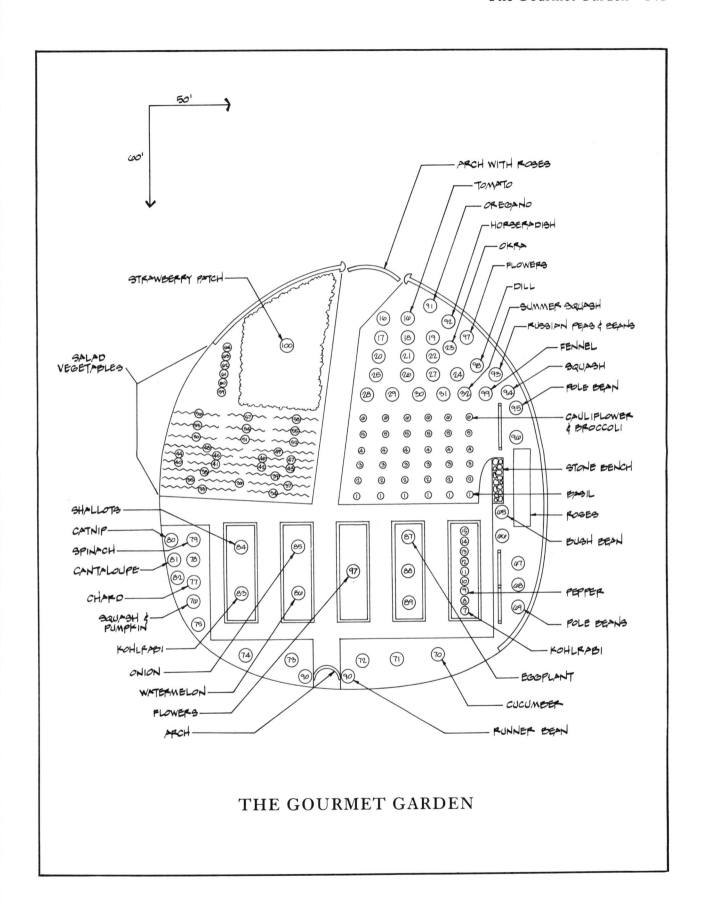

THE GOURMET GARDEN

30. Squash, Zucchetta Bianca Della Virginia (Italian light green zucchini)
31. Squash, 'Rich Green Zucchini' [Burpee]
32. Squash, 'Petite Crookneck' [Gurney's]
33. Nasturtium [Burpee]
34. Radish, 'Champion O' Giants'
35. Ravanello (Italian 24-inch white radish)
36. Radish, daikon [Gurney's, Burpee]
37. Scorzonera (24-inch brown radish, salsify) [DeGiorgi]
38. Sugar pea, 'Dwarf White' [Gurney's]
39. Turnip, 'Sweet White' [Gurney's]
40. Spinach, 'Iron Duke' [Gurney's]
41. Cicoria Invernale
42. Cicoria Palla di Fuoco Rossa
43. Cicoria, red variegated
44. Lettuce, green curled [Burpee]
45. Lettuce, 'Dark Green Boston' [Burpee]
46. Lettuce, 'Sweetie Leaf' [Gurney's]
47. Lettuce, 'Buttercrunch' [Gurney's]
48. Endive, 'Green Curled' [Burpee]
49. Carrot, 'Nantes Half Long' [Burpee]
50. Cicoria (Italian butter lettuce)
51. Cicoria Endivia (Italian curly endive)
52. Arugula (roquette, or rocket) [Shepherd's, Epicure]
53. Valeriana (Italian leaf lettuce)
54. Lattughino (Italian small-leaf lettuce)
55. Cicoria Rossadi Treviso (Italian red tight endive) [Shepherd's, Epicure]
56. Misticanza (mixed Italian lettuces)
57. Bieta Green (Italian leaf lettuce)
58. Lettuga (Italian red lettuce)
59. Prezzemolo (Italian parsley) [Epicure]
60. Parsley, single [Burpee]
61. Parsley, 'Extra-Curled Dwarf' [Burpee]
62. Parsley, 'Moss Curled'
63. Dandelion, thick-leaved
64. Dandelion, French
65. Bean, 'Bush Blue Lake' [Burpee]
66. Bean, 'Bush Yellow' [Burpee]
67. Experimental pole bean (entirely edible)
68. Bean, Fagiolo Rampicante (Italian green pole bean that can grow to 3 feet in length)
69. Bean, Fagiolo Rampicante Borlotto (Italian purple pole bean)
70. Cucumber, Citriolo Bianco Lunghissimo (Italian white cucumber)
71. Cucumber, 'West India Gherkin' [Burpee]
72. Cucumber, 'White Wonder'
73. Squash, cucuzzi (Italian edible gourd) [DeGiorgi]
74. Squash, 'Jumbo Pink Banana'
75. Squash, spaghetti [DeGiorgi, Burpee]
76. Pumpkin, 'Jack-O'-Lantern'
77. Bieta (Italian white chard)
78. Bieta Rosse (Italian red chard)
79. Spinach, New Zealand [DeGiorgi]
80. Catnip (for "Mouser," the cat) [Burpee]
81. Cantaloupe, 'Ambrosia' [Burpee]
82. Cantaloupe, 'Gospe's French'
83. Kohlrabi, 'Early White Vienna' [Gurney's, Burpee]
84. Shallots
85. Cippola (Italian white giant onion) [Epicure]
86. Watermelon, 'Petite Sweet' [Gurney's]
87. Melanzana bianca ovale (white Italian eggplant) [Seeds Blum]
88. Eggplant, 'Black Beauty'
89. Eggplant, Japanese
90. Scarlet runner beans [Seeds Blum]
91. Oregano
92. Horseradish
93. Russian peas and beans
94. Squash, 'Butter Bush' [Burpee]
95. Beans, 'Roma II' [Shepherd's]
96. Beans, 'Romano'
97. Flowers
98. Dill
99. Fennel
100. Strawberry patch

Clockwise from left Elwin Meader has been instrumental in introducing a number of superior vegetables and fruits to this country. Here he stands at his New Hampshire home with his hardy kiwi vine, which is able to stand temperatures as low as 25 degrees below zero F. The hardy kiwi, *Actinidia arguta,* is available from Michael McConkey, Edible Landscaping Nursery, Route 2, Box 343A, Afton, VA 22920.

The fruit of the hardy kiwi, shown in this close-up photograph, tastes just like its larger cousin that is available in the grocery store, but its skin is green and smooth; instead of peeling the fruit, you pop it into your mouth as you would a cherry.

Peter Chan of Portland, Oregon, is famous for his vegetable garden—it contains many Chinese varieties. Here he is examining a fuzzy gourd vine that grows much like cucumber vines do.

Sources of Information

Books

Harrington, Geri. *Grow Your Own Chinese Vegetables.* New York: Collier Books, 1978. Definitely the complete word on how to grow Oriental vegetables and herbs in this country.

James, Theodore, Jr. *The Gourmet Garden.* New York: E.P. Dutton, 1983. Extensive information on many superior types and varieties of vegetables and fruits.

Jeavons, John, and Leler, Robin. *The Seed Finder.* Willits, Calif.: Jeavons-Leler, 1983. The key to growing superior vegetables is knowing where to get the seeds. The authors have done a service to gardeners by providing information on where to get many of the best vegetable seed varieties.

Morash, Marian. *The Victory Garden Cookbook.* New York: Alfred A. Knopf, 1982. My favorite vegetable cookbook.

Organic Gardening and Farming editorial staff. *Gourmet Gardening.* Edited by Anne Moyer Halpin. Emmaus, Pa.: Rodale Press, 1978. Specific information on how to grow many unusual and superior vegetables.

Sunset Books editorial staff. *Sunset Italian Cookbook.* Menlo Park, Calif.: Lane Publishing Co., 1974. A good basic Italian cookbook.

Waters, Alice. *Chez Panisse Menu Cookbook.* New York: Random House, 1982. An inspiring cookbook by an author who feels that fresh, superior, home-grown produce is the starting point for outstanding cuisine.

Demonstration Gardens

The Boonville Hotel
Boonville, CA 95415
This is really a restaurant (although it may be a hotel in the future) that serves vegetables from the garden. You can see many outstanding varieties growing there and taste some in the restaurant.

Chicago Botanical Garden
Lake Cook Road
Glencoe, IL 60022
The botanical garden is opening a demonstration food garden and will start giving demonstrations and cooking classes.

Nurseries

W. Atlee Burpee Company
Warminster, PA 18974
Burpee has a wide selection of vegetable seeds
for the home gardener.

DeGiorgi Company
Council Bluffs, IA 51502
This nursery imports seeds of many of the
Italian vegetables as well as many of the stand-
ard varieties.

Epicure Seeds Ltd.
P.O. Box 450
Brewster, NY 10509
This seed company specializes in European
seeds.

Gurney's Seed & Nursery Company
Yankton, SD 57079
Gurney's has a large collection of unusual
vegetable varieties.

Le Marche Seeds International
P.O. Box 566
Dixon, CA 95620
This company specializes in French and heir-
loom vegetable seeds.

Redwood City Seed Company
P.O. Box 361
Redwood City, CA 94064
This company carries many varieties of Orien-
tal, Mexican, Indian, and open-pollinated
vegetable seeds.

Seeds Blum
Idaho City Stage
Boise, ID 83707
This company specializes in open-pollinated
seeds that often are old-time varieties. Many
are similar to some of the Italian varieties, and
some are the actual Italian varieties themselves.

Shepherd's Garden Seeds
7389 West Zayante Road
Felton, CA 95018
A gourmet seed company specializing in European varieties.

Chapter 10
The Child's Garden

My introduction to gardening was a delightful one. When I was four or five years old, my father gave me my own patch of soil under an ancient apple tree. It was near his vegetable garden, close enough so that we could chat and wonder together. In my plot I planted his extra seeds; I watered everything in sight, moved his extra strawberry runners, and watched marigolds and tomato plants sprout. While I sometimes helped him pick beans, plant corn, and mine for potatoes, I seemed to enjoy most moving plants around in my own garden. I treated my garden much like I treated my doll house: as something that needed constant rearranging. I seldom produced anything, and most of my plants died because they were weary from being moved. Nevertheless, I have wonderful memories of "gardening" with my father. Looking back on that experience, I can see what an ideal environment it was for learning. There were never any gardening dicta. I wasn't told, "You must not move your carrots." Instead, I moved my carrots and discovered that, instead of straight, succulent carrots, I got "many-gnarled things," multipointed corkscrews! I proved, to my satisfaction, at least, that plants don't like to be moved. In addition to learning a few specifics, I also learned about the birth of spring, the fullness of life in the summer, and the dying in the fall. Abstract principles became real.

My garden experience was not only experimental; if I asked specific questions, I usually got answers. And, most often, not answers phrased as facts, but more as sharing wonders. For example, I remember asking my father why he was spreading ashes from the fireplace in the garden. Instead of being told that ashes contain potash that can be used by the plants, I remember a discussion of how nature recycles everything. We speculated on where the smoke went and what happened to the heat and what was left that the corn could use. Instead of a teacher-pupil relationship, we shared in the experience of questioning. We wondered why mint had square stems and where our robins went in the winter. We commiserated with one another when the blue jays dug up our newly planted corn or when the cutworms ate to the ground the baby squash plants. We ate sun-warmed tomatoes together and enjoyed being among living things. I did not learn when or how deep to plant corn seeds or many other practical things; those I had to look up later in a book. What I learned was much more valuable —love for the garden and a respectful awe of nature.

I've shared my own childhood gardening experience because it seems the best way to illustrate that a child's garden will be the most enriching experience if it is filled with sharing and wonder, rather than with lists of "thou shalts" and "thou shalt nots." If my father had chided me about moving my plants around or made me spend hours weeding and raking, my feelings about gardening would probably be quite different from what they are. If my father had felt obliged to "teach" me gardening, he probably wouldn't have enjoyed having me in the garden as much as he did. Instead, our gardening was a pleasure for both of us.

Shared moments in the garden with children are rewarding, but in stressing only time in the garden itself, you might overlook other ways to experience nature. The growing experience can be felt in many ways. You can put out bird food in the winter during a storm or bring in the pussy willow as a celebration of spring or let a sweet potato or carrot that has started to sprout grow on the windowsill. Grow your own bean sprouts and let the children help. Instead of their just playing house under the card table, maybe they could create a greenhouse with a few house plants. Gardens are not isolated expressions of nature; they are an integral part.

I think children should have a garden experience so that they can grow up appreciating that they are part of the web of nature, not beings outside of it. And what a joy if they can experience it with a wonder that will stay with them all of their lives. Further, it seems important for children to grow up knowing that food does not originate at the corner market, but is a gift from the earth that they can participate in.

Getting Children Started in the Garden

Here are a few ideas to help you and your children find pleasure in the garden. If at all possible, get the book *Growing Up Green* (listed at the end of this chapter). It captures the essence of the whole experience, and I can't recommend it highly enough. If you have the space, give your child a growing area. It does not have to be a garden; it can be as simple as a planter box or a potato in a bucket of compost.

Help them send for their own seed catalogs and seeds. Children love to get mail, and receiving their seeds by mail is often half the fun. In addition, you may want to become involved with the local 4-H, a particularly good organization for older children that will also be a source of information for you if you are a beginning gardener. Another way to bring the love of gardening to your children is to try to get the school interested in a gardening program. You may want to volunteer your help.

If you are able to give your children garden space, start with plants that grow quickly and easily. Include at least a few edible plants in the project because they seem to provide more interest for children than flowers do. It certainly isn't necessary for the child to produce bushels of tomatoes or potatoes in order to enjoy gardening—remember my "moving" garden—however, it seems to help to guide them in a successful and fruitful direction because children usually get excited by producing something. My eight-year-old niece started gardening in Florida with strawberry plants that already had little, immature straw-

1 - SUNFLOWERS PLANTED
  1 FOOT APART

2 - CORN - 'KANDY KORN'
  4 ROWS WITH PLANTS
  THINNED TO 1 FOOT APART

3 - ZUCCHINI - 'GOLD RUSH'
  2 PLANTS PLANTED
  TOGETHER IN A HILL

4 - TOMATO - 'SWEET 100'
  IN A WIRE CAGE

5 - RADISHES - 'EASTER EGG'
  THINNED TO 2" APART

6 - BEANS - 'ROYAL BURGUNDY'
  PLANTED 6" APART

7 - STRAWBERRIES
  PLANTED 1 FOOT APART

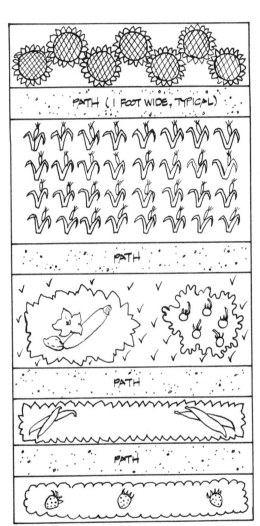

8'

16'

PATH (1 FOOT WIDE, TYPICAL)

PATH

PATH

PATH

N

THE CHILD'S GARDEN

berries on them. Because it was her first taste of gardening, the almost-instant return of ripe strawberries got her involved at the outset. We also planted two vegetables that usually do very well in Florida: tomatoes and sweet potatoes. Weeks later, when the tomatoes began to produce, she had already been "hooked." The sweet potatoes didn't produce worth a darn, but, then, that's gardening. It's not always a success, and that's part of the process too.

As you and your children are gardening together, not only can you share the wonder of nature, in addition, you have an opportunity to help stop the spread of insect phobias. Children learn by example, and before they grow up, they will see hundreds of commercials on television for insecticides, in which hysterical people run from bugs. To counteract that knee-jerk reaction, which accounts for a great deal of unnecessary pesticide usage and exposure, you can marvel at the spider in your closet and put it outside, instead of routinely clobbering it with the newspaper. I know that is difficult for many folks. Maybe all you can do is to say to your child, "I wish I didn't feel like killing the spider." That would, at least, acknowledge that your reaction to kill the spider is irrational.

It doesn't take a lot to change attitudes. One day I was visiting a neighbor whose children, aged seven, nine, and ten, were swimming in the pool. A very large stag beetle, flying near the surface of the water, was hit by a wave and fell in. The children immediately scrambled out of the pool in a panic, and their mother, who is afraid of insects, was trying to figure out how to get it out of the pool. With a dramatic flair, I reached down gently and allowed the beetle to climb on my hand, lifted it out of the pool, and put it on the deck. You should have seen everyone's face; it was as though I had bearded the lion in its den. As the beetle started to amble off, fear turned to fascination. I then went home and brought back my field guide to insects and showed the children how to look it up. As a result, these three children

became so interested in insects that they now occasionally show up at my house bearing "bugs" in a jar, wanting me to help identify them.

It seems to me that the best way you can give your children the gift of gardening is to enjoy it with them. Give them a supportive environment for their gardening experience rather than a list of how-to's. As Alice Skelsey and Gloria Huckaby say in their book, *Growing Up Green,* "Gardening is caught, not taught."

Planning and Preparation

Through the years, as a child and as an adult, certain aspects of gardening have tickled my soul. I have listed some of them here as a starting place for novice gardeners of any age.

Growing vegetables can be as simple as planting a dozen crocus bulbs in a container or as involving as planting a large vegetable garden. If your space and time are very limited, start small. A simple garden can be a large plastic bag of potting soil placed in full sun on a patio. Slit the bag, poke a few holes in the bottom, and put the bag where it won't stain the patio. Plant a few potatoes, two petunia plants, a cherry tomato, or a zucchini plant. Have your child water it occasionally and fertilize it once a month; then enjoy the harvest. Or you can order a packet of wildflower seeds from a catalog and sprinkle them over a small patch of prepared soil, making sure they stay moist for a few weeks. Let them grow while you and your children wonder which flowers will appear. Another simple but rewarding project is to buy a few dozen tulip bulbs in the fall and help your young child plant them. Little effort, much reward.

If you can, however, set aside a small piece of ground for your child's vegetable garden; then simply plant some or all of the annual vegetables and herbs listed below. These plants are, I think, a good place to start with children. There is nothing exclusively childish about the following list; it is a great place to start for any gardener, no matter the age and skill. The list contains particular vegetables and specific varieties that I personally find rewarding and interesting to grow. I am confident that it holds things of fascination for children, and for the child in all of us. You will notice that I recommend a number of vegetables and fruits that are unusual colors. Growing unusual vegetables often adds another element of wonder and excitement to gardening.

An alternative that you may find appealing is to get an entire children's garden that has already been preselected for you and your children, the Child's Garden in a Can, put together by Clyde Robin Seed Company. The can comes complete with seed packets designed by children, a well-written instruction booklet that older children can read and follow, and string and stakes. Information on Clyde Robin Seed Company can be found at the end of Chapter 1.

Magic Beans

Try 'Royalty' or 'Royal Burgundy' bush or pole beans. These are tasty, deep purple string beans that are fun to grow. My children used to call them "magic beans" because after they have been in boiling water for two or three minutes, they turn green (much to the relief of people who can't imagine eating bright purple string beans). Where does the purple go?

Beans must be blanched before freezing, or the beans will be very soft when thawed. Blanching (boiling for a few minutes) destroys the enzyme that makes beans turn mushy. Purple beans are their own barometer to tell you how long to blanch them; when they turn green they are properly blanched.

Pole bean plants are great for making a bean tepee. (See the accompanying drawing for directions on how to make a bean tepee.) Particularly appropriate for bean tepees are scarlet and 'Dutch White' runner beans; they grow fast and very tall, and in some parts of the country they attract hummingbirds. (See Chapter 5 for instructions on how to save some of your bean seeds for next year.)

Colorful Corn

Corn is a good crop for children. The seeds are large enough for little fingers to handle and they sprout quickly. Corn generally has few pests, and it grows very fast. Picking and shucking the corn are enjoyable endeavors. Corn takes a lot of room and has some basic cultural requirements that limit where it can be planted. Before you can decide where to plant it, you must know that corn is wind-pollinated; therefore, it must be planted in blocks, not in a long, single row or in double rows. Corn planted in single or double rows usually produces few kernels. In addition, because of cross-pollination, sweet corn must be separated from popcorn and cornmeal varieties. Consequently, if you want more than one type, one type must be separated from another by a building, or different types must be planted one hundred feet or so apart. Different varieties of sweet corn do not need to be separated because it doesn't matter if they cross-pollinate. If you have only a small area for gardening, try one of the dwarf corn varieties. Even though the plants are small, most varieties have fairly good-size ears. Of course, you may want to see what happens if you plant corn in single rows; often we learn better by experiencing the reasons for rules. And there aren't many other areas of experience where children can deviate from given rules and not have serious consequences.

If you want a lesson in cross-pollination, plant a block of sweet yellow or white corn within ten or fifteen feet of a block of Hopi blue corn. What will happen? You will probably get ears of yellow (or white) corn with a few purple polka dots and purple corn with yellow (or white) dots. The purple kernels in the yellow ear will be a little tough, and the yellow kernels in the purple ear will not grind as easily. That's why gardeners are advised not to plant those corn varieties close together. Most people are not bothered by the cross-pollination.

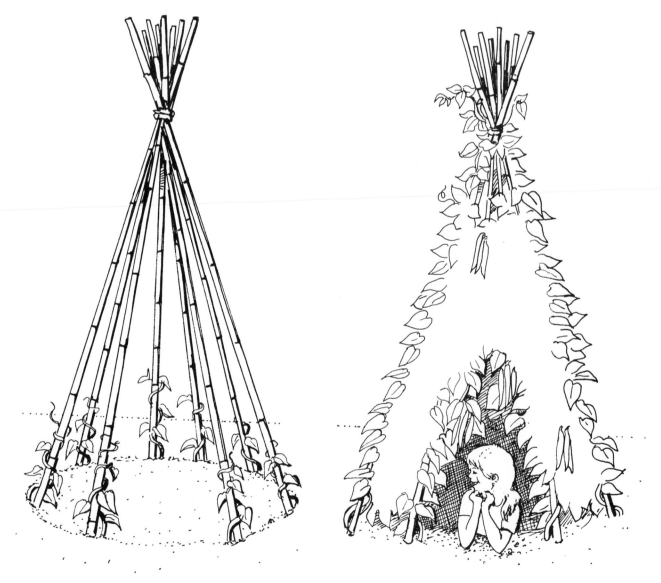

Regardless of what happens, the Hopi blue corn will make great cornmeal—blue corn is not usually eaten fresh on the cob. When the kernels are very dry, they will grind beautifully in the blender. Use the cornmeal to make some of the best cornbread and tamales you have ever tasted.

Grow popcorn, then pop it. There are all types of popcorn. Some varieties produce little yellow or white ears. 'Strawberry' popcorn produces miniature, rounded, reddish ears that look like large strawberries. For Christmas you can put strong wires in the ends and hang them on the tree or give them away as presents.

Dill, Fennel, and Butterfly Wings

Dill and fennel are closely related, fast-growing herbs. They should be planted in the spring and can be harvested throughout most of the summer. They grow easily, sometimes too easily, and often support the yellow-and-black-striped caterpillars of the swallowtail butterfly. In addition, because the nectar in the flowers is food for many other insects as well, the flowers become miniature entomology labs, often crawling with ladybugs, syrphid flies, and lacewings, all of which are predators of bothersome pests. The flowers are fragrant and useful in the kitchen, and they grow so readily that children can learn to share some of their garden with insects. Furthermore, dill and fennel are members of the same family, and the flowers, umbels, look the same. Knowing plant families is valuable for all gardeners. Related plants are carrots, caraway, anise, coriander, and celery.

Opposite Bean tepees are one of a child's favorite garden pleasures. Use wooden or bamboo poles to form a circle about four feet in diameter. Mulch the ground heavily with compost or other organic matter so that the soil will not get packed down. Outside the circle of poles plant vigorous varieties of pole beans, 'Sugar Snap' peas, or climbing peas such as scarlet runner beans.

Playhouse Bouquets

Children, like the rest of us, love flowers. Annuals such as marigolds, zinnias, cosmos, and pansies are easy to grow. Even easier for little ones to grow are bulbs such as crocus, hyacinths, and tulips. Make sure they don't put the bulbs in their mouths because some of them, such as daffodils and narcissus, are poisonous.

Gardening with flowers has infinite possibilities. Just being able to pick their own bouquets gives most children joy, not to mention taking daffodils to the teacher, arranging zinnias in a vase, drying statice and strawflowers for winter bouquets, making flower headbands, pressing wildflowers or johnny-jump-ups and mounting them to make greeting cards, making potpourri with fragrant roses, and decorating a May-pole with spring flowers. The pleasures of flowers seem endless.

Goobers—The Curious Nuts

There's something wondrous about peanuts. They flower, produce pegs from the flowers, and then the pegs burrow into the ground. A few months later when you pull up the plant, you will see clusters of peanuts hanging from the underground stems. Peanuts require a long, warm summer. If you live in a cooler area, choose Spanish peanuts because they can be grown farther north.

Potatoes—Nature's Treasure Hunt

If you plant potatoes in plenty of loose compost, you will have a large harvest and easy digging in the fall, even for little children. Harvesting potatoes is like going on a treasure hunt; it's one of my favorite gardening projects. Potatoes are started by cutting whole potatoes into pieces (each piece must have an eye) and planting each piece. If you try to grow potatoes purchased at the market, they usually rot in the ground before they sprout. Why? Because Americans don't like to see octopuslike white sprouts coming out of their potatoes; therefore, most potatoes have been sprayed with a growth-regulating hormone that inhibits sprouting.

One of the seed companies, Gurney's, carries blue potatoes, which are blue all the way through; all-yellow potatoes; and small, oblong, fingerling types. All are delicious and fun to grow.

Strawberries—Everybody's Favorite

Strawberries are rewarding for beginning gardeners because they are not too difficult to grow in most parts of the country. Combine some plants of a spring-bearing variety and plants of the ever-bearing type that will bear through part of the summer. If you have lim-

Peanuts are fun to grow. After they blossom, they send pegs down into the ground; the pegs develop into peanuts.

ited space, give your child his or her own strawberry jar. Strawberry plants can be put in all of the little pockets, or a combination of strawberries, violas, and alyssum can be planted.

Double Your Pleasure— Peppermint and Spearmint

Mint is easy to grow and pleasant to taste. Actually it is almost too easy to grow and can become a pest. Plant mint in a confined area. Dry some of the leaves by placing them in the oven, turned on to the lowest setting, and drink peppermint tea on a cold winter night. Have you ever noticed that mint has square stems?

Giant Jack-O'-Lanterns

Children love large pumpkins, so choose a large variety such as 'Big Max'. Plant the seeds as soon as frost is no longer a problem so there will be enough time to grow super-size pumpkins. In addition, your children can carve their initials on the fruits when they are just starting to form; then when the pumpkin is ripe, the initials will have grown and the jack-o'-lanterns will be personalized. Most jack-o'-lantern pumpkins don't make good pies, but the seeds are good when roasted.

Radishes—Red, White, and Black

Not all children like radishes, but if yours do, grow them because they are the fastest-growing edible. The seeds germinate quickly, and many varieties are ready to harvest in three to four weeks. There are many, many types of radishes: large, small, round, oblong, red, white; and some Oriental types are even black. Try the new radish called 'Easter Egg'; the radishes of this variety are different shades of red and pink.

Radishes grow best in the cool part of the year: spring and late summer. Use fertilizer and plenty of water so the plants will grow fast.

Squash and More Squash

If your child likes squash, zucchini is a good vegetable to grow. 'Burpee Hybrid' will produce nearly a zucchini a day, whether you want it or not. A golden variety, although not usually as prolific as the green, is sometimes better accepted by children. Chop up some of the flowers and float them in a bowl of soup. Spaghetti squash is interesting and delicious. When it's ripe, you can bake it, scrape out the strands of spaghettilike squash, and smother it in marinara or pesto sauce. Just writing this makes my mouth water.

Sunflower—King of the Garden

Sunflowers grow very big and tall, and young children get a charge out of being responsible for growing something so awesome. Sunflowers are a bonus for the birds. You and your children can present a sunflower head to the birds on Christmas morning.

Tomatoes and Their Horned Foes

Of all the types of tomatoes, cherry tomatoes grow the most easily and are just the right size for a child's mouth. 'Sweet 100' is a particularly tasty and prolific variety. Other varieties to try are one of the old-fashioned, large, fluted varieties; the small, yellow pear; or the striped 'Tigerella'. All of these will produce exclamations during "show and tell" at school. The seed companies mentioned at the end of Chapter 5 and at the end of this chapter are good sources for the seeds.

An interesting garden project involves the tomato hornworm, which is an extremely large caterpillar that thrives in most parts of the country and feeds on tomatoes. If you find a tomato hornworm on your plants, cut off the branch it's on (it will hold on for dear life), collect some foliage, and put the hornworm and the foliage in a large jar. (Hints on how to find a hornworm: Look for areas of the plant where whole leaves are missing. Then look for little piles of green geometric droppings; the caterpillar should be in the foliage above the droppings.)

Leave the hornworm in the jar while it eats its fill and pupates, probably a few days. Then remove the pupa from the jar and place it on top of the soil in a large flowerpot filled with potting soil. Watch it burrow down into the soil. Cover the pot with a plate and put the pot in a cool place for the winter. In late March or April bring in the pot, take off the plate, and

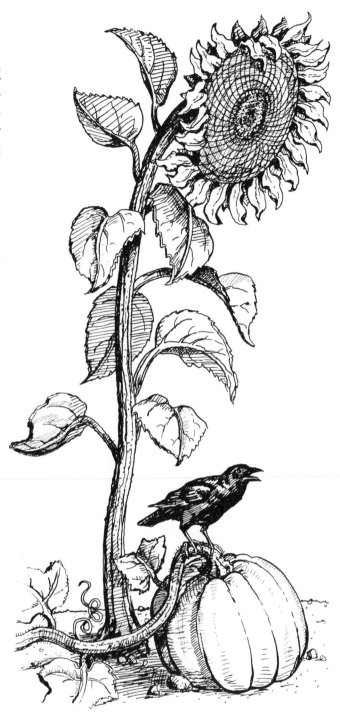

cover the pot with something that allows you to see what's going on, but that won't let the soon-to-emerge, large, spotted sphinx moth escape. Usually it will be a week or two before the moth emerges, and if you are exceedingly lucky, you may even see it come out and "pump up" its wings.

Sources of Information

Books

Brown, Marc. *Your First Garden Book*. Boston: Little, Brown and Company, 1981. A book of garden projects and delights for children.

Burnett, Frances Hodgson. *The Secret Garden*. New York: Lippincott, 1938. A classic story that I must have heard or read numbers of times. A wonderful, imaginative trip set in a garden.

Skelsey, Alice, and Huckaby, Gloria. *Growing Up Green*. New York: Workman Publishing, 1973.

Nurseries

Use the nurseries listed at the end of Chapter 5, particularly Johnny's Selected Seeds, Redwood City Seed Company, and Seeds Blum, to obtain varieties I have mentioned. Other companies that carry some of these varieties are listed below.

Gurney's Seed & Nursery Company
Yankton, SD 57079
Gurney's carries many vegetable seeds, including the purple beans and all kinds of seed potatoes.

Geo. W. Park Seed Company
P.O. Box 31
Greenwood, SC 29647
This company carries a wide range of vegetable and flower seeds.

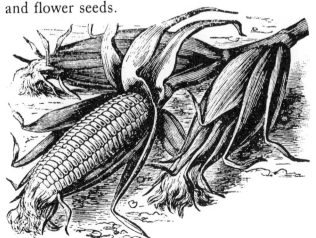

Chapter 11
The Moneysaving Garden

Who says money doesn't grow on trees? Homeowners expect their yards to cost them money. Few ever consider the possibility that instead of costing money, a yard actually can help save money. The average yard in this country consumes money in three major ways. First, hundreds of dollars are wasted because few yards are planned to take advantage of solar heating or basic cooling techniques for the house. Second, yards that have large lawns, particularly in the arid West, where constant watering is necessary, often have high maintenance costs. And, finally, few yards are designed to cut food and gift-giving expenses.

Heating and cooling experts estimate that up to 20 percent of air-conditioning bills and 20 to 30 percent of heating bills for residences can be cut by proper placement of the landscaping elements. The larger your yard, the more savings you can realize by strategically placing trees and shrubs. Well-placed evergreen shrubs and trees help cut down the effects of winter winds against the house; by removing evergreen shrubs and trees near the south-facing wall, the homeowner allows the winter sun to warm the wall. Conversely, in the summer, deciduous trees, shrubs, and vines can shade the south and west walls, preventing the heat from building up in the house. For more information on saving money through landscaping, see Ruth Foster's book, *Landscaping That Saves Energy Dollars*.

Lawn, the Great Money Sink

I've seen it happen time and time again. People who are on a tight budget think they cannot afford to spend a lot of money on the landscaping; so they go to the nursery, buy a package of grass seed, and turn most of their yard into a large lawn. There are few things you can do, particularly in the West, that will cost more over the long run. A lawn will nickel and dime you to death. Lawn mower, gas for the mower, lawn-mower maintenance, edger, water, sprinkler repairs, fertilizer, herbicides, fungicides, vacation maintenance: all for just a humdrum lawn. And a show-place lawn can cost you many hundreds of dollars a year. A well-maintained lawn needs to be aerated, thatched, reseeded, and top dressed every year. All of those expenses are just the tip of the iceberg. They don't even take into account that the lawn area could be covered with money-saving plants that would provide food for the table.

Lawn maintenance is big money in this country, and our whole system is set up to perpetuate it. If you have a lawn, use appropriate lawn maintenance techniques to save money and use fewer resources. Here are a few pointers.

1. Plan your lawn area to be as level as possible so that water and nutrients won't run off. Keep the lawn as small as possible. Don't plant lawn simply because you don't know what else to do.

2. Plan the area for ease of maintenance. Avoid spotting trees and shrubs in the lawn, and install mow strips (strips of concrete, brick, or wood that border a lawn and keep the wheels of the mower level at the edge, so when you mow, you also trim the edge), thereby cutting down on the amount of machine trimming. Furthermore, without trees the grass will grow thicker so that less weeding and fewer herbicides will be necessary.

3. No lawn grass species has low water or fertilizer needs, but some are a little better than others. Choose bluegrass and rye over bentgrass, which is a heavy feeder and needs lots of water. Breeders of grass seed are now aware of the problem and are hybridizing for grass varieties that use less water and fertilizer. Keep an eye out for new introductions.

4. Do not remove lawn clippings unless they are longer than an inch. Research has shown that turf is healthier and requires less fertilizer when the clippings are left in place. Grass clippings are equivalent to a 4-1-3 fertilizer, which means that two pounds of nitrogen per 1,000 square feet are saved on the average lawn. Contrary to popular opinion, thatch buildup is not a problem

5. Avoid so-called cheap fertilizer. It ain't! Nitrate fertilizers, in particular, are leached from the soil and volatilize into the air; plants get a quick fix of nitrogen, then soon need another shot. Except when the weather is cold, use organic manures or slow-release nitrogen fertilizers.

6. Mow the grass so it is 1-1/2 to 2 inches long. Most people cut the grass too short, causing it to thin out. Grass that is cut too short requires more water.

The Garden as Provider

Most homeowners realize that they can save money by growing some of their food, but few realize how much can be saved or how to make the greatest savings. A Gallup Poll conducted for *Gardens for All* (180 Flynn Avenue, Burlington, VT 05401) showed that in 1981 the average home gardener invested $25 in garden supplies and reaped $414 worth of produce. Those statistics related to an ordinary garden; an intensively grown vegetable garden can produce much more. Fruit trees and fruiting shrubs will provide additional food. An article in *The Family Food Garden* (November 1983) described a gardening family that grew $1,100 worth of crops for a family of seven on an acre in Minnesota. Dedicated gardeners obviously save a lot more money than those who want to be only somewhat involved.

Opposite Container gardening is possible even in an apartment or on a small patio. Three very productive varieties of vegetables that grow well in large containers are 'Gypsy' pepper, 'Gold Rush' zucchini, and 'Sweet 100' tomato.

Home-grown Gifts

A delightful way to save money is to plan your garden with gift giving in mind. At Christmas or for birthdays, homemade strawberry or kiwi jam, pickles, canned peaches, tomato juice, applesauce, dried fruit for a trail mix, and dried herbs are always a hit. So are dried-flower bouquets, so in the summer grow statice, strawflowers, yarrow, baby's breath, and many of the grasses with beautiful seed heads. Gifts from the yard are unusual and original.

If you occasionally buy flowers for the house, for a friend in the hospital, or if you enjoy taking a house gift when you go to a friend's house for a visit, consider growing your own cut flowers. If you are short on garden time, plant perennials and shrubs that are easy to grow and that produce flowers you can cut. Another idea for people who are short on time (aren't we all?) is to convert some of your lawn to a meadow and seed it heavily with wildflowers that are good for cutting. For winter giving consider growing and collecting some of the flowers and seed pods that dry well. Wreaths made of grapevines or wisteria can be dramatic when festooned with garlic heads and chilies for the kitchen, or with bittersweet and thistles for the front door.

Following is a list of flowers for cutting and for dried arrangements. Find out which ones will do well in your area.

The Home Florist

Have you priced flowers lately? Many exotic flowers are sold by the stem, which range in price from $2.50 to $5.00. You can add beauty to your home year after year by planting your flower garden today. The home florist always has a bouquet to give friends on birthdays and at other special times.

Perennials

Bird-of-paradise, black-eyed susan, chrysanthemum, coreopsis, forsythia, iris, lavender, lilac, lily, marguerite, old roses, Shasta daisy, and yarrow.

Annuals

Baby's-breath, bachelor's button, bells of Ireland, calendula, cosmos, marigold, nasturtium, nicotiana, pincushion flower, snapdragon, stock, sweet pea, and zinnia.

Bulbs

Anemone, daffodil, Dutch iris, freesia, narcissus, ranunculus, and tulips.

Flowers for Drying

Baby's-breath, bells of Ireland, Chinese lantern, globe amaranth, globe thistle, hydrangea, love-in-a-mist, money plant, safflower, statice, strawflower, yarrow, and many ornamental grasses.

Wildflowers

Black-eyed susan, California poppy (if seared), cattail, coreopsis, daisy, goldenrod, mullein, mustard, penstemon, prairie grasses, Queen Anne's lace, tiger lily, wild roses, and yarrow.

Kitchen Gifts

Dried herbs add zest to your cooking. You can change an ordinary salad, for example, into an interesting, tasty salad simply by adding some freshly dried herbs. A soothing cup of tea can be brewed from a mixture of several varieties of dried mint. Also, herbs, harvested from your garden and carefully dried, are an especially welcome gift.

Drying Herbs

Drying herbs is a simple, rewarding task. Dried herbs lose their potency with age, so you should renew your supply of them annually.

It is important when harvesting herbs—basil, borage, cilantro, marjoram, mint, parsley, oregano, rosemary, sage, and thyme—for drying that you pick those that have not yet flowered. Pick during the driest part of the day. If necessary, wash the plants quickly and pat them dry. On a piece of screening, carefully place the leaves in a single layer, with no overlapping. Leave the screens out in a warm room away from sunlight for five to seven days, stirring the leaves occasionally. If the air is very humid or if you must dry the herbs quickly, put them in a very low oven (140 degrees Fahrenheit) for a few hours, until they crumble fairly easily in your hand.

When the herbs are thoroughly dry, store them in airtight containers and put them in a cool, dark place. For gift-giving, put them in small jars and label them in a decorative manner.

Drying Flowers

Take a bouquet of home-grown, dried flowers to your hosts when you dine out or to a sick friend. Flowers are a personal, beautiful, inexpensive—when you grow your own—gift that is always appreciated. If you have no room in your garden for an individual cutting garden, interplant a few of the easy-to-grow, compact varieties in your perennial border or vegetable garden. Choose from globe amaranth, love-in-a-mist, safflower, statice, and strawflower: they are the easiest to grow and dry.

Harvest your flowers on a dry day just before they come into full bloom and bring them inside. Make small bunches of individual varieties and hang them in a warm, dry, fairly dark place—a dark corner of the kitchen or in the garage, perhaps. Once they are thoroughly dry, you can carefully arrange the flowers in baskets or vases and have them ready to give as gifts. Of course, you can enjoy them in your own home as well.

After you have become successful at drying the flowers mentioned above, try some of the following varieties: baby's-breath, bells of Ireland, celosia, Chinese lantern, goldenrod, grasses of all different types, heather, hollyhock, hydrangea, lavender, Queen Anne's lace, tansy, and yarrow.

Wreaths

Wreaths are cherished symbols and have been used by humans for eons. While they are usually associated with Christmas, wreaths of herbs, dried flowers, pine cones, and vines are enjoyed the year round. Useful as inexpensive house decorations and as gifts, wreaths from the garden are easily constructed.

A very simple wreath can be made of grapevines and other materials from the garden. Start with freshly pruned vines that are supple; dried-out vines will be hard to bend and weave. Determine the size of wreath you want to make: the thicker the vines, the larger the wreath should be because large vines are not as flexible as thin ones. If you want your wreath to be particularly symmetrical, start weaving it around a large bowl or round wastebasket. Because of the suppleness of the material and the ridges caused by the leaf stems, the woven vines tend to stay securely in place. When the wreath is the thickness you want, decorate it with clusters of dried flowers, herbs, grasses, and anything else that strikes your fancy.

While the price of seeds *has* gone up since the issue of this ad in a 1909 seed catalog, $15 worth of seeds can still produce hundreds of dollars worth of vegetables.

Opposite, top Shown here, early in the season, is a portion of Vicki Sebastiani's Italian vegetable garden. In the foreground are tomato plants on wire cages; farther back are melons; and in the raised beds are eggplants, onions, and young summer vegetables.

Bottom Succulent young vegetables from the gourmet grocery store are a treat few people can afford. From the author's garden, left to right, are 'Tiny Tim' cherry tomatoes; 'Gold Rush' zucchini; baby romaine lettuces; red, white, and yellow young beets; young wax beans; half-developed lemon cucumbers; and very young carrots.

Page 166, top The Fancys' backyard has been transformed from a basketball court to an edible landscape with raised beds. Ninety percent of the plants in the photograph are edible. Included are a number of dwarf citrus and fruit trees and numerous annual edibles, such as tomatoes, eggplants, summer squash, peppers, herbs, and strawberries. Flowers are added for color and for cutting. A true pleasure garden, it produces bounty as well as beauty. (Landscape design: Rosalind Creasy)

Bottom Fresh produce from the Fancys' garden enriches the quality and variety of food on the table.

Page 167, clockwise from left Nowhere is it written: Thou shalt not grow flowers with your vegetables.

A grapevine trained on a south-facing wall can perform the herculean task of saving money for you, and its lush green foliage is beautiful. In summer the leaves shade the house, thereby reducing air-conditioning expenses. In fall it produces grapes, to be eaten fresh or dried as raisins. In winter it loses its leaves, letting in the sun to warm the house, and in spring the prunings can be saved to make grapevine wreaths for gift-giving all through the year.

Grow your own ginger as a gourmet treat. Young green ginger shoots can be added to stir-fried dishes; and as a bonus, it is a lush green container plant.

Page 168, clockwise from top left Kate Gessert is harvesting salad makings from her cottage pleasure garden. Among the wonderful additions to her salad are homemade herb vinegars and edible nasturtium and chive flowers.

Children particularly enjoy picking flowers and strawberries from the garden.

Kate Gessert's frontyard flower/vegetable border delights passersby. The decorative kales and chrysanthemums are the real stars in early fall.

Even the smallest corner can produce a pleasure garden. Here bronze fennel provides leaves and flowers for a salad and also attracts butterflies. In the barrel are geraniums and violas; both have edible flowers.

Edible Gardens—Moneysavers

Time is one of the factors that determine how much money you can save by gardening. How much time do you have to garden and how much time do you have for harvesting and preserving food? For a vegetable garden, planting time is needed in the spring and quite a bit of time is needed for harvesting in late summer. For the garden I recommend, plan to devote a few days in the spring to prepare the soil and to start annual vegetables. If your space is limited and you are going to put in French intensive beds, you will need twenty or thirty additional hours the first year to install the beds. After your soil is prepared and the seedlings are in, you will need three or four hours a week throughout the summer to weed, to tie up vines, to put in transplants, to harvest, and perhaps to water.

Not only is time necessary, but so is timing: putting in the time when it is needed. If you are a teacher, say, you may have plenty of time in the summer but little when school starts. For you, picking beans through the summer or making delicacies from edibles that produce in spring or summer, such as pickled beets and strawberry jam, may be no problem. However, your dreams of canning spaghetti sauce and making salsa from your dozen tomato plants that ripen in September, when new students need attention, would be disappointing and frustrating.

Another factor to consider is garden space. Some people create a problem here where none exists; or, at least, if there is a problem, it is usually easily solved. Many folks tell me that they would like to have a vegetable garden, but they don't have the space. People seem to confuse having space with owning the garden. My partner and I gardened for years in a neighbor's unused dog run. Garden space abounds in this country. Many cities and towns have community gardens; if yours doesn't, you probably know a neighborly senior citizen or a friend who would be delighted to share space in return for some of your harvest. It doesn't take much room to produce a lot of food.

A final important factor is your selection of edibles. Dwarf fruit trees give more yield for the space than full-size trees. Pole beans yield more beans than bush types. Vining cucumbers and melons yield more produce than bush types. Choose from the following list of high-yielding vegetables and fruits those that grow well in your area.

Vegetables

Artichokes, asparagus, basil, beans, beets, chard, cucumbers, eggplants, garlic, leeks, lettuce, parsley, peppers, scallions, shallots, snow peas, sorrel, sprouts, tomatoes, and zucchini.

Fruits

Alpine strawberries, apples, apricots, avocados, blackberries, blueberries, cherries, chestnuts, grapefruits, kiwis, lemons, mangoes, oranges, papayas, peaches, pears, pecans, pineapples, plums, raspberries, rhubarb, and strawberries.

Here are some other suggestions for planning your moneysaving food garden.

1. Interplant quick-growing annuals such as radishes and lettuce among your slow-growing vegetables.

2. Plant seeds when possible. Vegetable plants from the nursery are expensive. Save your own seeds from year to year when possible. (See Chapter 5 for information on saving seeds.)

3. If your space is limited, plant in intensively prepared beds. (Read *How to Grow More Vegetables* by John Jeavons for instructions on bed preparation.)

4. Compost anything you can get your hands on. Some city park departments distribute

leaves and clippings to homeowners who want them for mulch and compost.

5. Use dwarf fruit trees whenever possible to produce more fruit from a limited area. The trees are dwarf, but the fruit is full size.

6. Replace barren ornamental plants with edibles. Many of the standard fruit trees and shrubs have long been overlooked as landscape material. Beautiful edibles such as blueberries, apples, almonds, plums, persimmons, and cherries, just to mention a few, have been overlooked in favor of flowering crabs, dogwoods, and forsythia.

7. If space is at a premium, avoid space-wasting plants such as winter squash, pumpkins, and corn.

8. Plant gourmet vegetables to help cut down on your entertaining costs.

Another way to save money is to preserve some of your harvest for winter eating, when produce prices are up. The most economical way to preserve some vegetables and fruits, such as carrots, potatoes, beets, cabbage, turnips, apples, and pears, is to put them in a root cellar; although drying is economical for apricots, peaches, plums, grapes, tomatoes, and herbs.

A Moneysaving Backyard

The accompanying diagram shows a very small backyard full of bountiful, yet beautiful, plants: they do double duty. There are genetic dwarf fruit trees: two apples, a peach, and a pear. These flowering and fruiting large shrubs make quite a delightful background for the patio area. On either side are black and red raspberry bushes trained on decorative trellises and clusters of blueberry bushes. On both sides of the patio and in the middle of the back planting bed is a combination vegetable and flower border, which is planted with extra-productive species such as tomatoes, snow peas, chard, peppers, and eggplants and flowers that are good for cutting, such as calendulas, statice, coreopsis, and baby's-breath.

The patio has containers for vegetables and herbs and is covered with an arbor that has two kiwi vines on it. Grapevines are espaliered on the south wall on either side of the house; with the kiwi vines on the arbor they provide shade on hot days and help cut air-conditioning bills. In addition, the grape prunings can be used to make wreaths in the winter.

Raspberries can be one of the biggest moneysavers in your garden.

Opposite A moneysaving garden can be as small as this patio garden, which includes many features: it shades the house in summer, it provides flowers for gift-giving, and it produces vegetables and fruits for the table.

1. Genetic dwarf peach, 'Honey Babe'
2. Genetic dwarf apple, 'Garden Delicious'
3. Black raspberries
4. Herb jar
5. Strawberries
6. Blueberries, three different varieties
7. Kiwi vine, female
8. Rhubarb
9. Grapevine trained on wall
10. Genetic dwarf pear, 'Golden Prolific'
11. Red raspberries
12. Peppers in container
13. Zucchini in container
14. Cherry tomato in container
15. Kiwi vine, male

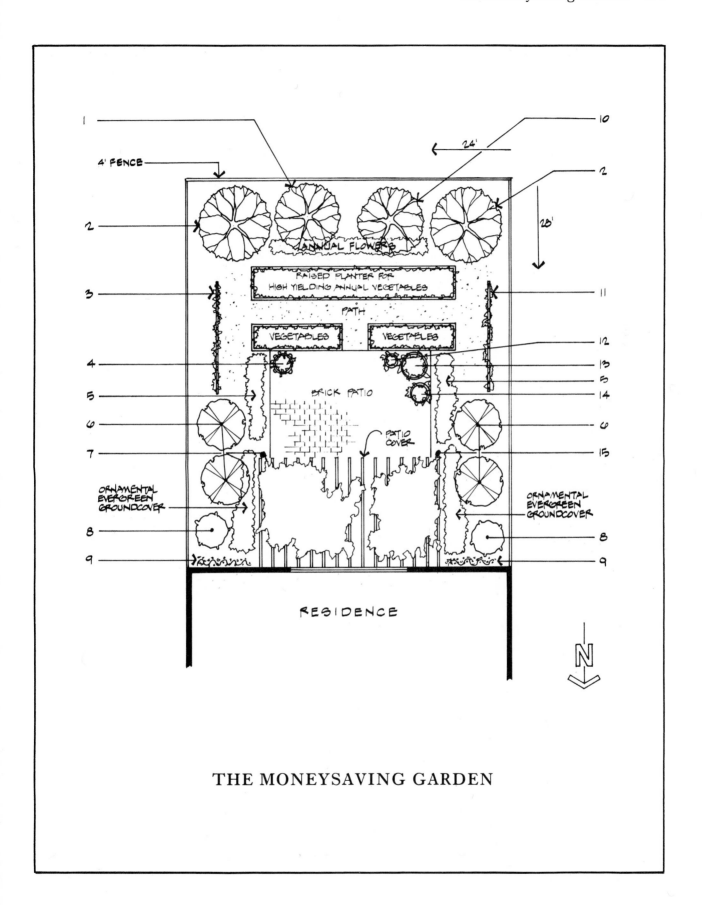

THE MONEYSAVING GARDEN

Recycled Materials

The materials are usually the most expensive items in any garden construction project. Projects using brick, stone, and concrete can make the budget groan. One way around the high cost of some of these items is to use recycled materials.

With the detailed plans in front of you, figure the dimensions of the items you want to construct. Then look at the list that follows and consider which recycled materials you may be able to use. If you must make adjustments, it will be simpler to make them on paper than after you have begun construction. For instance, railroad ties generally come in eight-foot lengths. They are hard to cut; therefore, if you are using them for a planter, it would make sense to design the planter with eight-foot increments in mind.

Recycled materials are available from a number of different sources, and one source may even be your own yard. I recycled the grapestakes from my own fence after the posts and stringers had rotted away. I reused bricks from my old patio that was buckled by some very invasive tree roots. I didn't have enough bricks to make the new patio as large as I wanted, so I purchased 400 new ones, then made a pattern that combined the old and the new bricks. (You can see my recycled backyard, with its brick patio, grapestake fence, and railroad-tie planter on page iv.) Other sources of recycled materials are contractors, demolition yards, nursery supply houses, and friends and neighbors.

1. Concrete. Recycled concrete, broken into 12-inch to 24-inch pieces, can be used as paving material for patios, paths, utility areas, retaining walls, and steps. You can recycle concrete from your own yard or from a nearby demolition project. If you decide to have the contractor dump a load of broken concrete in your front yard, you will have a disposal problem; that is, what to do with the pieces that are stained or too large or too small to use in your project. To avoid that problem it may be better to pick up the pieces at the demolition site. Concrete is very heavy, and only a limited number of pounds can be carried at one time in the average car. Therefore, it behooves you to locate the concrete as close as possible to your yard. You will find concrete of different shades of gray and beige and made with different types of aggregates. Try to choose batches of compatible colors when combining concrete from more than one source. For paths, pieces of broken concrete can be set in sand and mortared in place or left unmortared and planted between the cracks with herbs or low groundcovers. For walls less than two feet high, the pieces can be mortared, or the areas between the slabs can be filled with soil and planted with cascading types of flowers and herbs. Walls over two feet high, of any type of material, including recycled concrete, should be built by a licensed contractor and overseen by a structural engineer.

2. Old lumber can be gathered from demolition sites, old barns, and sometimes from the beach. Used telephone poles and railroad ties are usually available from nursery supply houses. Pieces of new wood, usable but often in short lengths, are sometimes available from construction sites. Usually it is wood suitable for inside construction, which must be painted or treated with wood preservative if you are going to use it outside.

Old railroad ties are probably the most versatile recycled construction material of all. They can be placed horizontally for steps, planters, short walls, and decking; they can be placed vertically for retaining walls. Their major drawback is their price. Railroad ties have been treated with creosote, which, while protecting the wood from the elements, can sometimes ooze out and get on clothing or stain carpeting when it is tracked inside on shoes.

Sources of Information

Books

Contact your local university extension office for brochures and booklets on how to grow fruits and vegetables in your area and how to preserve them.

Foster, Ruth. *Landscaping That Saves Energy Dollars.* New York: David McKay Co., 1978. A detailed text covering the many ways that landscaping can help cut energy bills.

Jeavons, John. *How to Grow More Vegetables.* Palo Alto, Calif.: Ecology Action of the Midpeninsula, 1974. A primer on French intensive gardening.

Schuler, Stanley, and Schuler, Elizabeth Meriwether. *Preserving the Fruits of the Earth.* New York: Dial Press, 1973. A book that is hard to find but worth looking for. It covers in detail how to preserve nearly everything.

Nurseries

Pine Tree Seed Company
P.O. Box 1399
Portland, ME 04104
Pine Tree is an unusual vegetable seed company because it sells inexpensive packages of vegetable seeds that contain only a few seeds of each variety—after all, how many of us use fifty tomato seeds?

Consumer Note

Sometimes homeowners get carried away and buy unnecessary equipment. Avoid, as much as possible, buying rarely used yard tools and gadgets. Consider renting a large tiller rather than buying one—it's probably cheaper in the long run. In addition, when you do buy tools, buy good ones. A fine fork and shovel made of forged steel with hardwood handles can last a lifetime; cheaply made tools often last only one season.

Smith & Hawken Tool Company
25 Corte Madera Avenue
Mill Valley, CA 94941
This company is known for its vast collection of superior garden tools.

Chapter 12
The Cottage Garden

The early Puritans left their mark on us in a number of subtle ways, some of which make life a series of joyless tasks. Sometimes I think their devotees must write garden books. The tone of many of the how-to books reeks of rules, admonitions, and dicta. How about a garden that is programmed to give you joy, to take care of you. Previous chapters of this book have given you ways to cut down on many of the usual garden chores, thus leaving you more time to spend in a meaningful way. This chapter is designed to give you the means to glory in the new-found time. The cottage garden is an outright celebration of what a garden can do for every part of you: colors to see, textures to touch, fragrances to smell, bird calls to hear, and myriad tastes for the palate. And, of course, we can't forget the most important part, your soul. You will experience the renewal of life, that primordial urge to believe in the future. You will put your fingers on the emerging carrot seedlings, anticipate the taste of the first tomato, and feel delight when the hummingbird visits the sage and the monarch butterfly sips from the dew collected by the nasturtium leaf.

I am suggesting that you plant a rather hedonistic variation of the traditional mixed border. Put it where you usually see a conventional shrub or flower border—along a fence line, for instance, or along a walk or driveway, next to the patio, or along shallow hillsides. Fill it with joy, with colors, tastes, fragrances, and even tactile pleasures—a swath of flowers and foliage.

The mixed border, sometimes called the perennial border since it usually includes a large number of perennially blooming plants, has been in fashion since the late nineteenth century. It has its roots in the English cottage garden, and, at its best, the border is a subtle work of form, texture, and color—all used together to delight the soul. Properly planned, the border changes with the seasons.

Traditionally the staples in the mixed border were nonedible flowers, mostly perennials, with a sprinkling of annuals for quick color. Popular perennial flower choices for this type of ornamental border were iris, peony, phlox, dahlia, daisy, chrysanthemum, poppy, and the like. A new variation in today's perennial border is the addition of beautiful edibles such as ruby chard and flowering kale; plus a number of savory and attractive herbs such as variegated sage and dill; edible flowers such as nasturtium and carnation for your salads and desserts; and, to add still another dimension, fragrance, choose sweet-smelling lavender and stock. For many more choices, see the lists of flowers and beautiful edibles later in this chapter.

Think of the pleasure these gardens can give. Imagine having your barbecue on the back patio surrounded by bright borders of nasturtiums, violas, geraniums, and many herbs and edibles. You could reach over and pick a few leaves of spicy basil to put on your guest's still-warm tomato slices. Then you could harvest some of the nasturtium and viola flowers to add zip to your salad. Throughout the meal the fragrance of alpine strawberries would hint of the dessert to come, and the light fragrance of peppermint geraniums and lavender would perfume the air.

Your cottage garden could be near the front walk to welcome guests with fragrance and color. Or if your space is limited, you could even plant your pleasure border in the strip between the street and the sidewalk the way the Gessert family did in Oregon. (See page 178 for a detailed description of their garden.)

In planning your pleasure border, keep in mind these simple guidelines.

1. Make the border less than three feet wide, or provide a path or access on both sides of the beds so you'll be able to pick flowers and edibles and perform maintenance tasks.

2. Choose plants that require the same soil, water, and exposure.

3. If you are covering a large area, your design could depend on large quantities of one or two types of plants to unify the border, to create a theme to pull the border together for the eye.

4. There are two ways to work with color in these flower borders: (1) you can limit yourself to three or four basic colors, with one of them serving as an accent (for example, use red, orange, and yellow with an accent, a dash of blue); or (2) work with variations on one color theme (combining blues, lavenders, and pinks, for instance). Or throw caution to the wind, put in your favorite plants, and see what happens. Some people think that all flowers go well together, others don't; it seems to be a matter of personal taste. While it addresses itself to only a few edibles and herbs, a good resource on color design with plants is *Gardening with Color—Ideas for Planning and Planting with Annuals, Perennials, and Bulbs* by Margaret Brandstrom Pavel.

5. Think about the height your plants will be when they are full-grown. Consider height as a distinct design element; thus, tall plants will be at the back of the border while shorter ones will be toward the front.

6. Try to choose as many "double-duty" plants as you can; that is, choose those that have both colorful flowers as well as edible or fragrant flowers.

7. Choose attractive varieties of edibles for your border. Some vegetables and some varieties of vegetables are not particularly suited to a mixed border. For example, large vining squashes and pumpkins usually climb all over their neighbors; brussels sprouts usually get top-heavy and rangy with age; potatoes need to die back and turn yellow before they can be harvested. (See the list of suitable edibles later in this chapter.)

Caution: Because, for the most part, you are using edible plants and flowers to fill these borders, exclude ornamental plants that are poisonous. Poisonous flowers you might be tempted to use but should avoid are sweet peas, autumn crocus, bleeding-heart, foxglove, lantana, and larkspur. Also, don't interplant the edibles with ornamentals that need to be sprayed with pesticides.

Planning and Preparation

"Choose a sunny area where you would like to see your pleasure garden. Then envision the area as a three-dimensional painting or a colored sculpture—with lots of textures, colors, and shapes. Only what *you* are creating grows! The fact that you are creating a work of living art adds a whole dimension of chance and excitement to the creation." So says Kate Gessert, an experienced pleasure gardener and author of the book *The Beautiful Food Garden.* Unlike many food gardeners, she has been interested not only in how vegetables and fruits grow and taste, but also in how those edibles look in the garden. In fact, she was so interested that she managed a test plot of over one thousand varieties of annual vegetables at Oregon State University. As overseer, she evaluated the ornamental aspects and tastiness of the plants and included much of the information in her book. In an effort to share her experience and her vision of a pleasure garden, she has put together the following comments and recommendations.

"When you put in your pleasure garden, first, make sure that you have chosen a sunny, well-drained site. Next, incorporate plenty of organic matter; healthy plants are beautiful and productive plants.

"I love the way gardens are when various kinds of plants are all mixed up together. I enjoy working in these gardens, being in the middle of them, looking out into a forest of deeply cut zucchini leaves, big round seed heads of leek, graceful, sweetly scented lily flowers, and rampant caged tomatoes.

"I also enjoy the planning process, dreaming in winter and spring about what we'll grow the

The Gesserts enjoy the continual changes in their sidewalk flower/vegetable border. (If your sidewalk garden has heavy automobile traffic nearby, rinse your vegetables in a 5-percent vinegar solution to remove the lead that may be deposited on them.)

next season. In particular, I enjoy planning the flower-vegetable-herb bed that we plant in front of our house in the planting strip between the sidewalk and the street.

"In spring, after working in plenty of organic matter, I sowed kale, leeks, and parsnips. Later, I added rhubarb chard, celery, and chrysanthemums, with short-term fillers—coriander, lettuce, and California poppies. These were replaced in late summer by carrots and ornamental kale, which really came into full color after the first frost. That fall the rhubarb-chard leaves turned a deep mahogany, and nearby were the yellow and red chrysanthemums and the bright green foliage of parsnips and carrots. In another part of the bed I used cooler colors: grayish foliages and pink and purple flowers. With the purple-leaved 'Coral Queen' flowering kale, I planted 'Fragrance' carnation, burnet (a cucumber-flavored herb with a rosette of delicate blue green foliage), fall 'Violet Carpet' aster, 'Dwarf Blue Scotch' curly kale, leeks, artichokes, and wine red and lavender chrysanthemums. The combination was spectacular!

"Now it's late fall, and we're mulching the borders and planting spring bulbs. Already we are planning next year's pleasure; we will enjoy snowdrops near the burnet, ornamental alliums near the leeks, and iris reticulata near the ruby chard."

Look at the accompanying plans and pictures of the bed Kate designed. In particular, notice the arrangement of the different plants. The vegetables such as leeks and carrots, which you usually associate with long, straight rows, are clumped together instead. Nowhere is it written that vegetables have to grow in straight rows. In fact, that is not usually the most productive configuration. Straight rows have met the cultural needs of agriculture and its equipment, but the home gardener can produce more food per square foot by using wide rows or clumps. As Kate says, "Ornamental plants seldom look their best in long, straight rows—picture tulips or daffodils planted that way. Vegetables look best in clusters and arranged in pleasing shapes."

Choose your pleasure plants from the list that follows. On the list there are plants that give fragrance, taste, and a bounty of color and texture. Some of the flowers are edible and are delightful in salads or floating on a clear soup; many of the flowers are suitable for cutting and drying. Think how nice it will be to save money on flower buying, as well as to give bouquets

that don't have a "canned" appearance, as so many purchased ones do. And they're always the same varieties of flowers. Your bouquets will have an individual touch that reflects you, not the florist. Check to make sure that the flowers and vegetables you choose grow well in your area.

Opposite To get the most out of your cottage border, plan for as long a season as possible. As you can see here, the Gesserts make substitutions for spent plants and think ahead to the next season, taking advantage of every square inch of garden area.

1. Alyssum
2. Asparagus, interplanted with kochia in the summer
3. Coreopsis, 'Brown Eyes'
4. Dahlia, 'Terpo'
5. Artichoke, 'Green Globe'
6. Chrysanthemum, lavender and burgundy red, interplanted with 'Barrett Browning' narcissus in the fall
7. Anemone, 'Max Vogel'
8. Dahlia, pink
9. Clarkia in the spring; *Zinnia linearis* in the summer
10. Helenium, 'Butterpat'; interplanted with 'Carbineer' narcissus in the fall
11. Swiss chard, 'Rhubarb'
12. Chrysanthemum, 'Freedom'
13. Parsnip, 'Hollow Crown Improved'
14. Bunching onion, 'Japanese'
15. Kale, 'Dwarf Blue Curled Vates'
16. Leek, 'Unique'
17. Celery, 'French Dinant'
18. Chrysanthemum, 'Fireside'
19. Lettuce, 'Red Salad Bowl' in the spring; 'Portola Giant' gaillardia in the summer
20. Sage, 'Joseph'
21. Sage, 'Broadleaf'
22. Viscaria, 'Maggie May', in the spring; 'Coral Queen' flowering kale in the late summer
23. Aster, 'Violet Carpet'; interplanted with snowdrops in the fall
24. Petunia throughout the summer; interplanted with 'Minnow' narcissus in the fall
25. Coriander in the spring and summer; 'Early Red Ball' beets in the late summer
26. California poppy, 'Sundew'; 'Royal Chantenay' carrots in the late summer
27. Thyme, 'Dwarf Compact'
28. Carnation, 'Fragrance', interplanted with *Iris reticulata* in the fall
29. Burnet
30. Thyme, creeping

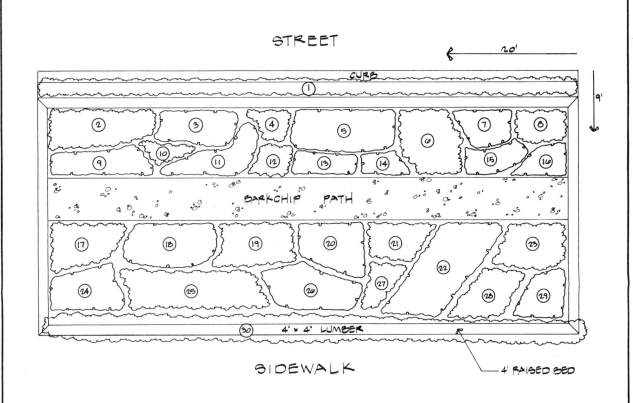

THE COTTAGE GARDEN

Edible Flowers

Borage, *Borago officinalis*
Calendula, *Calendula officinalis*
Carnation, *Dianthus Caryophyllis* species
Chamomile, *Matricaria recutita*
Chrysanthemum, *Chrysanthemum morifolium*
Cottage pink, *Dianthus plumarius*
Daylily, *Hemerocallis* species
Dill, *Anethum graveolens*
Fennel, *Foeniculum vulgare*
Garlic chives, *Allium tuberosum*
Geranium (scented), *Pelargonium* species
Gladiolus, *Gladiolus* species
Hollyhock, *Alcea rosea*
Johnny-jump-up, *Viola tricolor*
Lavender, *Lavandula officinalis*
Nasturtium, *Tropaeolum majus*
Peony, *Paeonia* species
Petunia, *Petunia hybrida*
Poppy, *Papaver* species (not opium)
Primrose, *Primula vulgaris*
Rose, *Rosa* species
Safflower, *Carthamus tinctorius*
Squash blossoms, *Cucurbita* species
Tulip, *Tulipa* species
Viola, *Viola cornuta*

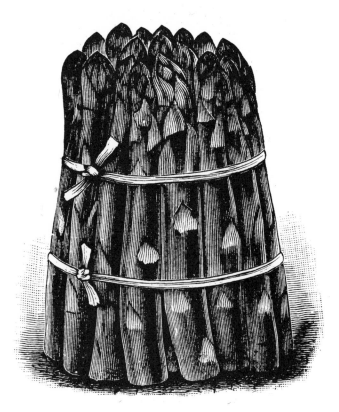

Recommended Varieties of Edibles

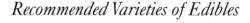

Artichoke, 'Globe'
Asparagus, 'Mary Washington'
Basil, 'Dark Opal', Sweet
Beans (bush), 'Royal Burgundy', 'Tender Crop', 'Rhemus'
Cabbage, 'Red Danish', 'Red Savoy', 'Stonehead', 'Ice Queen'
Celery, 'Summer Pascal', 'Burpee's Fordhook'
Chard (Swiss), 'Rhubarb'
Chrysanthemum greens, Shungiku types
Eggplant, 'Midnight', 'Japanese Purple Pickling', 'Black Beauty'
Endive, 'Green-Curled Ruffec'
Kale, 'Green-Curled Scotch', ornamental types

Lettuce, 'Dark Green Cos', 'Oakleaf', 'Red Salad Bowl', 'Salad Bowl'

Mustard, 'Fordhook Fancy', 'Prizewinner Curled Long'

Okra, red

Parsley, 'Champion Moss Curled', 'Dark Green Italian', 'Deep Green'

Peanuts, most varieties

Peas, 'Novella'

Peas (edible pods), 'Sugar Ann', 'Dwarf Gray Sugar'

Peppers, 'Red Chili', 'Hot Hungarian Yellow Wax', 'Golden Bell', 'Gypsy'

Strawberries, most varieties, particularly Alpine

Tomatoes, 'Floramerica', 'Roma', 'Red Cherry', 'Salad Master'

Zucchini, 'Gold Rush', 'Delicata', 'Bush Table Queen'

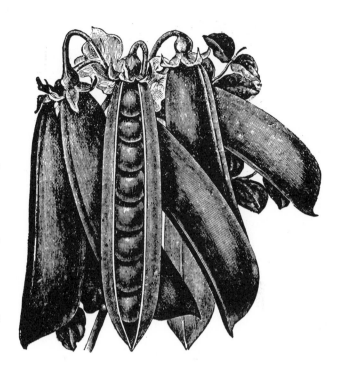

Herbs for a Decorative Border

Borage, burnet, chamomile, chives, dill, fennel, perilla, saffron crocus, and sage.

Flowers for a Decorative Border

The following list contains flowers that combine well with the edibles listed above; the starred flowers include varieties that are particularly good for cutting.

anemone*

baby's-breath*

bachelor's-button*

coreopsis*

cosmos*

forget-me-not

lobelia

marigold*

nicotiana

penstemon*

pincushion flower*

rudbeckia*

salvia*

santolina

snapdragon*

statice*

strawflower*

stock*

sweet William*

tansy

tithonia*

yarrow*

zinnia*

Sources of Information

Books

Creasy, Rosalind R. *The Complete Book of Edible Landscaping*. San Francisco: Sierra Club Books, 1982. How to use edible plants for beauty in the garden. It covers fruits and vegetables for the whole country.

Diamond, Denise. *Living with the Flowers*. New York: Quill, 1982. This book literally brings flowers into your life. It covers the subjects of edible flowers, how to dry flowers, gardening with flowers, even flower fairies.

Gessert, Kate Rogers. *The Beautiful Food Garden*. New York: Van Nostrand Reinhold Co., 1983. Gessert's book covers in great detail how to landscape with edibles and combine flowers and vegetables, as well as selections of the most beautiful vegetables and herbs.

Midda, Sara. *In and Out of the Garden*. New York: Workman Publishing, 1981. A poetic, visual delight for those who love living things.

Pavel, Margaret Brandstrom. *Gardening with Color—Ideas for Planning and Planting with Annuals, Perennials, and Bulbs*. San Francisco: Ortho Books, 1977. This book describes how to use flowering plants in the garden.

White, Katherine S. *Onward and Upward in the Garden*. New York: Farrar, Straus & Giroux, 1979. One woman's delightful view of gardening.

Nurseries

The following nurseries have excellent selections of ornamental annual vegetables and edible flowers.

Nichols Herb and Rare Seeds
1190 North Pacific Highway
Albany, OR 97321

Geo. W. Park Seed Company
P.O. Box 31
Greenwood, SC 29646

Redwood City Seed Company
P.O. Box 361
Redwood City, CA 94064
Catalog 50 cents.

Seeds Blum
Idaho City Stage
Boise, ID 83707
Catalog $1.

Acknowledgments

No one person has the range of garden experience and technical expertise represented in this book. I needed help from many different people. Numerous authorities in many specialized horticultural fields shared their knowledge. A host of plant people—passionate gardeners—generously shared their gardens and vast experience. And, of course, there was the guidance of numerous book people—people whose passion it is to produce a beautiful and meaningful book.

Let me start with my friends and cohorts whose involvement with this book was global. Marcie Hawthorne, whose love of life is brought to the world through her pen, not only illustrated this book but also was directly involved with many other aspects. When I needed photos of Italian vegetables, she grew the vegetables. When I needed information on chaparral gardening or when I needed to locate other gardeners, she helped. In addition, and of most importance, Marcie was my soulmate, lending her support and inspiration whenever it was needed. Another valuable source of support and information came from Kit Anderson of Gardens For All in Vermont. Her hospitality made my northeastern research a joy, and often I have called her for information and resources. Kate Gessert of Oregon generously shared her gardening expertise and contacts, located photos and gardens, and gave me a base of operations while I learned about northwestern gardens. Suzanne Lipsett is editor par excellence; her organizational and editing help was invaluable. Robert Creasy generously tutored me in the ways of the computer and helped me hone my photographic skills; and his high standards are evident throughout the book. Jane McKendall, my business partner and dear friend, kept things running smoothly and provided an always-available ear to help me think things through. Daniel Hawthorne gave enthusiastic support, and his meticulous construction of my garden gave me the perfect environment for my research. Karla Patterson, director of education at the Morton Arboretum, made my study of the prairie as rewarding and inspirational as possible, and Peg Creasy was my guide and noble assistant on tours of the East Coast. I thank them.

Throughout my years of research many experts in horticultural and environmental fields were generous with their help. They were: Pat Armstrong, Morton Arboretum, an expert on prairie restoration; Russell Beatty, landscape architect, University of California at Berkeley; Faith Thompson Campbell, Natural Resources Defense Council; Craig Tufts, National Wildlife Fund; Ruth Troetschler, biologist and bird enthusiast; Roger Del Moral, professor of environmental botany, University of Washington. Native plant authorities who assisted me were Barry Coate, horticultural consultant; Art Kruckeberg, professor of botany, University of Washington; and Cliff Schmidt, professor of botany, San Jose State University. Wildflower experts who assisted me were Steve Atwood, Clyde Robin Seed Company; the staff of Vermont Wildflower Farm; and Judith Lawry, Larner Seeds. Heirloom vegetable experts were Jan Blum and Karla Prabucki, Seeds Blum; Carolyn Jabs, writer and expert on heirloom seeds; and John Withee, heirloom bean expert. Rose authorities were Beverly R. Dobson and Pat Wiley, owner of Roses of Yesterday and Today. Authorities on orchids include Steve Hawkins and Marvel Sherril of McLellan's Acres of Orchids, Rebecca Tyson Northern, Randy Peterson, and Sue Johnson.

In addition I received help in locating information and gardeners from John Dotter, administrator of Prusch Park, San Jose, California; Robert Kourik, edible landscaper, Sonoma, California; Steve Frowine, Burpee Seeds, Warminster, Pennsylvania; the staff of Gardens For All, Burlington, Vermont; Grigsby's Cactus Gardens, Vista, California; Geo. W. Park Seeds, Greenwood, South Carolina; *Organic Gardening and Farming* magazine staff, Emmaus, Pennsylvania; and Jamie Jobb of The Howe Homestead of Walnut Creek, California. The staff of a number of arboretums were extremely helpful, including Longwood Gardens, Kennet Square, Pennsylvania; Missouri Botanical Garden, St. Louis, Missouri; and the Morton Arboretum, Lisle, Illinois.

Besides the gardens described in this book, the following people shared their gardens with me: Patricia and Milton Clauser of New Mexico, heirloom roses; Ann Cooper of Colorado, wildlife garden; Adele Dawson of Vermont, herb and vegetable garden; Gail, John, and Kathy Gallagher of Florida, child's garden; Carolyn Jabs of New Hampshire, bird sanctuary and woodland garden; Arvind and Bhadra Fancy of California, edible landscape and East Indian vegetable garden; Elwin Meader of New Hampshire, edible research garden; Patricia Turner of New Mexico, heirloom rose garden; and Sandra and Robert Wheeler of Oregon, meadow planting and edible garden.

The actual crafting of this book has received care and attention from a number of people. Maggie Gage, editor and garden writer, provided invaluable tutelage and groundbreaking work on my first book, much of which is reflected here. Larry Breed, proofreader and English language maven, spent hours making sure the text was correct. Ray Ten rendered the diagrams of the many gardens with a sure hand and gave them his special style. Thanks also go to Laura Creasy, Dayna Breeden, Hetty Williams, and Stephanie Disman for clerical support. Special thanks go to Diana Landau of Sierra Club Books, to Carolyn Robertson, and to Jim Robertson and the staff of The Yolla Bolly Press, Barbara Youngblood, Juliana Yoder, and Aaron Johnson, who gathered all the elements and gave the book form.

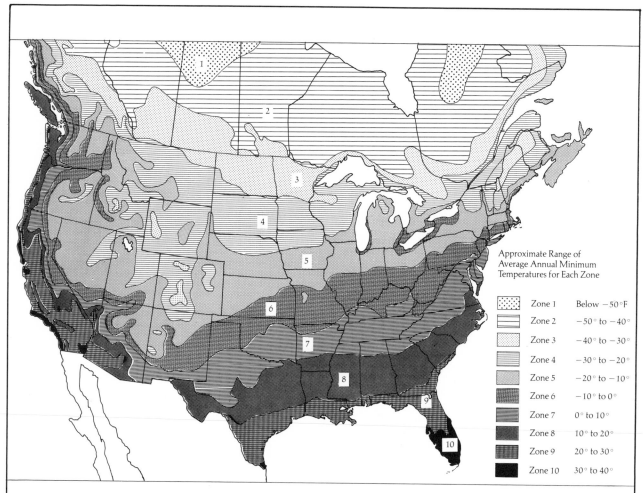

Approximate Range of
Average Annual Minimum
Temperatures for Each Zone

	Zone 1	Below −50°F
	Zone 2	−50° to −40°
	Zone 3	−40° to −30°
	Zone 4	−30° to −20°
	Zone 5	−20° to −10°
	Zone 6	−10° to 0°
	Zone 7	0° to 10°
	Zone 8	10° to 20°
	Zone 9	20° to 30°
	Zone 10	30° to 40°

It is critical to choose the right plant for the climate. This map of hardiness zones in the United States (adapted from a map prepared by the U.S. Department of Agriculture) is helpful when you start selecting your plants. Most garden texts refer to this map. To determine which plants are native to your area, however, you'll need to know more than simply how hardy a plant may be. Look at the map on page 9 for more information on which plants may be well adapted to your garden.

ZONE MAP

Bibliography

American Orchid Society. *Handbook on Orchid Culture.* Cambridge, Mass.: American Orchid Society, 1982. A booklet covering many of the basics.

Bienz, Darrel R. *The Why and How of Home Horticulture.* San Francisco: W.H. Freeman, 1980. A comprehensive collection of information on basic plant care. The book answers most of the horticultural questions that the average gardener might ask.

Brookes, John. *Room Outside: A New Approach to Garden Design.* New York: Penguin Books, 1979. This book places the garden where it belongs—as part of the family's living space. Examples of livable gardens are given.

Brooklyn Botanic Garden Handbooks. *Gardening with Wild Flowers.* No. 38. Brooklyn, N.Y.: Brooklyn Botanic Garden. How to incorporate wildflowers in your garden. This handbook is available for a small charge from Brooklyn Botanic Garden, 1000 Washington Avenue, Brooklyn, NY 11225.

———. *Roses.* Vol. 6, no. 1. Brooklyn, N.Y.: Brooklyn Botanic Garden, 1980. A good, inexpensive basic book on rose growing.

Brown, Marc. *Your First Garden Book.* Boston: Little, Brown and Company, 1981. A book of garden projects and delights for children.

Bruce, Hal. *How to Grow Wildflowers and Wild Shrubs and Trees in Your Own Garden.* New York: Alfred A. Knopf, 1976. Valuable cultural and source information. East Coast oriented from an environmentalist's viewpoint. This text includes an encyclopedia of wildflowers and their sources.

Bryan, John E., and Castle, Coralie. *The Edible Ornamental Garden.* San Francisco: 101 Productions, 1974. The authors give numerous suggestions of plants to use and ways to enjoy your garden.

Bubel, Nancy. *The Seed Starter's Handbook.* Emmaus, Pa.: Rodale Press, 1978. Basic information on how to start most plants from seed as well as valuable botanical information on how to select and save your own seeds. A must for seed savers.

Burnett, Frances Hodgson. *The Secret Garden.* New York: Lippincott, 1938. A classic story that I must have heard or read numbers of times. A wonderful, imaginative trip set in a garden.

Carr, Anna. *Rodale's Color Handbook of Garden Insects.* Emmaus, Pa.: Rodale Press, 1979. A valuable source that will help you identify the insects in your garden—both the friends and the foes.

Cocannouer, Joseph A. *Weeds—Guardians of the Soil.* Old Greenwich, Conn.: The Devin-Adair Company, 1980. The author presents an unusual view of weeds: he praises them. He demonstrates how controlled weeds can give you insight into the composition of your soil, enrich your diet, control erosion, and improve soil fertility.

Creasy, Rosalind R. *The Complete Book of Edible Landscaping.* San Francisco: Sierra Club Books, 1982. How to use edible plants for beauty in the garden. It covers fruits and vegetables for the whole country.

Crockett, James Underwood, and Allen, Oliver E. *Wildflower Gardening.* Alexandria, Va.: Time-Life Books, 1977. A general view of the subject, with specific information on a number of wildflower species.

Damrosch, Barbara. *Theme Gardens.* New York: Workman Publishing, 1982. This book includes the plans for a marvelous old rose garden, a butterfly garden, and a hummingbird garden.

Davison, Verne E. *Attracting Birds from the Prairies to the Atlantic.* Thomas Crowell Co., 1967. This book provides good information on more than 400 species of birds.

Diamond, Denise. *Living with the Flowers.* New York: Quill, 1982. This book literally brings flowers into your life. It covers the subjects of edible flowers, how to dry flowers, gardening with flowers, even flower fairies.

Diekelmann, John, and Schuster, Robert. *Natural Landscaping, Designing with Native Plant Communities.* New York: McGraw-Hill Book Co., 1982. Basic information on landscaping with natural ecosystems, including prairies.

Dillon, Gordon W. *American Orchid Society, Beginner's Handbook.* Cambridge, Mass.: American Orchid Society, 1981. A fairly detailed book on most aspects of orchid growing.

Duncan, Wilbur H., and Foote, Leonard E. *Wildflowers of the Southeastern United States.* Athens, Ga.: University of Georgia Press, 1975. A useful guide for identifying wildflowers.

Du Pont, Elizabeth N. *Landscaping with Native Plants in the Middle-Atlantic Region.* Chadds Ford, Pa.: Brandywine Conservancy, 1978. A valuable resource for gardeners wanting a woodland garden on the Atlantic coast.

Fell, Derek. *Vegetables: How to Select, Grow, and Enjoy.* Tucson, Ariz.: H.P. Books, 1982. A marvelous compendium of basic vegetable growing.

Foster, Ruth. *Landscaping That Saves Energy Dollars.* New York: David McKay Co., 1978. A detailed text covering the many ways that landscaping can help cut energy bills.

Gessert, Kate Rogers. *The Beautiful Food Garden.* New York: Van Nostrand Reinhold Co., 1983. Gessert's book covers in great detail how to landscape with edibles and combine flowers and vegetables, as well as selections of the most beautiful vegetables and herbs.

Griffiths, Trevor. *My World of Old Roses.* London: Whitcoulls, 1983. A delightful book that covers the whole range of old roses.

Harrington, Geri. *Grow Your Own Chinese Vegetables.* New York: Collier Books, 1978. Definitely the complete word on how to grow Oriental vegetables and herbs in this country.

Hartmann, Hudson T., and Kester, Dale E. *Plant Propagation—Principles and Practices.* 3rd. ed. Englewood Cliffs, N.J.: Prentice-Hall, 1975. This book provides detailed information on the propagation of plants by seed, layering, grafting, and cutting.

Holm, LeRoy G. et al. *The World's Worst Weeds.* Honolulu: The University Press of Hawaii, 1977. A technical description of agricultural weed problems.

Jabs, Carolyn. *The Heirloom Gardener.* San Francisco: Sierra Club Books, 1984. The best and most complete book on the subject of the extinction of domestic edible plants. A must for gardeners who want to become involved with heirloom plants and seed saving.

James, Theodore, Jr. *The Gourmet Garden.* New York: E.P. Dutton, 1983. Extensive information on many superior types and varieties of vegetables and fruits.

Jeavons, John. *How to Grow More Vegetables.* Palo Alto, Calif.: Ecology Action of the Midpeninsula, 1974. A primer on French intensive gardening.

Jeavons, John, and Leler, Robin. *The Seed Finder*. Willits, Calif.: Jeavons-Leler, 1983. The key to growing superior vegetables is knowing where to get the seeds. The authors have done a service to gardeners by providing information on where to get many of the best vegetable seed varieties.

Jekyll, Gertrude. *Color Schemes for the Flower Garden*. Rev. ed. Salem, N.H.: The Ayer Co., 1983. Jekyll has profoundly influenced the modern garden. This revised classic can give you hours of pleasure, helping you to create a living painting.

Koopowitz, Harold, and Kay, Hilary. *Plant Extinction—A Global Crisis*. Washington, D.C.: Stone Wall Press, 1983. The best book for concerned homeowners. It gives extensive information about our endangered ecosystem and speaks extensively about invasive weed species.

Kruckeberg, Arthur R. *Gardening with Native Plants of the Pacific Northwest*. Seattle: University of Washington Press, 1982. A great resource for northwesterners, this book includes growing information for the Northwest as well as detailed information on species for the garden.

Larcom, Joy. *The Salad Garden*. New York: The Viking Press, 1984. A fantastic book that gives all the information you could ever want about salad vegetables. You will never again be without a salad garden of some sort.

Lenz, Lee W., and Dourley, John. *California Native Trees and Shrubs for Garden and Environmental Use in Southern California and Adjacent Areas*. Claremont, Calif.: Rancho Santa Ana Botanic Garden, 1981. This book is excellent for the gardener who is just beginning to use native plants.

Logsdon, Gene, and the editors of *Organic Gardening and Farming*. *The Gardener's Guide to Better Soil*. Emmaus, Pa.: Rodale Press, 1975. This book covers the subject in an uncomplicated and enjoyable way, emphasizing that a rewarding garden experience and healthy carefree plants begin with good garden soil.

Midda, Sara. *In and Out of the Garden*. New York: Workman Publishing, 1981. A poetic and visual delight for all people who love living things.

Miller, G. Tyler, Jr. *Living in the Environment*. Belmont, Calif.: Wadsworth Publishing, 1982. A comprehensive text on environmental theory and practice. A must for those who were educated before environmental studies were required in the school curriculum.

Mohlenbrock, Robert H. *Where Have All the Wildflowers Gone?* New York: Macmillan Co., 1983. An excellent discussion of the wildflower problem.

Mooney, Pat Roy. *Seeds of the Earth*. Ottawa, Canada: Inter Pares, 1979. A global look at the problem of the shrinking gene pool of edible plants.

Morash, Marian. *The Victory Garden Cookbook*. New York: Alfred A. Knopf, 1982. My favorite vegetable cookbook.

National Wildlife Federation. *Gardening with Wildlife*. Washington, D.C.: National Wildlife Federation, 1974. A comprehensive book on the subject of gardening with wildlife. A must!

Nichols, Stan, and Entine, Lynn. *Prairie Primer*. Madison: University of Wisconsin—Extension, 1978. A marvelous little book for beginners that has all the basics.

Niehaus, Theodore F., and Ripper, Charles L. *A Field Guide to Pacific States Wildflowers*. Boston: Houghton Mifflin, 1976. This book is helpful in identifying wildflowers

Northern, Rebecca Tyson. *Home Orchid Growing*. 3rd ed. New York: Van Nostrand

Reinhold Company, 1970. This book is a classic in its field, and if you have only one orchid-growing book, this should be it.

Organic Gardening and Farming editorial staff. *Gourmet Gardening.* Edited by Anne Moyer Halpin. Emmaus, Pa.: Rodale Press, 1978. Specific information on how to grow many unusual and superior vegetables.

Ortho Books, Chevron Chemical Company editorial staff. *All About Perennials.* San Francisco: Ortho Books, 1981. This book is primarily about water-loving nonnative plants; however, it has valuable information about how to work with perennial flower borders and flower color.

_____. *How to Attract Birds.* San Francisco: Ortho Books, 1983. Extensive information on birds and the plants they prefer for food and shelter.

_____. *The World of Cactuses and Succulents.* San Francisco: Ortho Books, 1977. How to grow, select, and maintain cactuses and succulents.

Oregon Orchid Society. *Your First Orchids and How to Grow Them.* Portland: Oregon Orchid Society, 1977. An inexpensive and pleasant way to get your feet wet.

Pavel, Margaret Brandstrom. *Gardening with Color—Ideas for Planning and Planting with Annuals, Perennials, and Bulbs.* San Francisco: Ortho Books, 1977. This book describes how to use flowering plants in the garden.

Perry, Bob. *Trees and Shrubs for Dry California Landscapes.* San Dimas, Calif.: Land Design Publishing, 1981. Valuable information about drought-tolerant plants; color prints.

Peterson, Roger Tory, and McKenny, Margaret. *A Field Guide to Wildflowers of Northeastern and North Central North America.* Boston: Houghton Mifflin, 1968. An excellent field guide.

Rickett, Harold William. *Wild Flowers of the United States.* 6 vols. New York: McGraw-Hill Book Co., 1966-70. This is the perfect book for wildflower mavens.

Robinson, William. *The Wild Garden.* Rev. ed. London: Century Publishing, 1983. A revised classic that is particularly appropriate today. Robinson's outrage at the traditional formal borders and controlled gardens of his day inspired him to expound his theory of gardening, one that respects and uses native and wild plants. While most of the plants discussed in this book are for English gardens, the ideas and designs are appropriate everywhere.

Rock, Harold W. *Prairie Propagation Handbook.* Hales Corners, Wis.: Milwaukee County Department of Parks, 1981. This basic text is necessary for those who are interested in maintaining a prairie garden.

Rothschild, Miriam, and Farrell, Clive. *The Butterfly Gardener.* London: Michael Joseph, 1983. A must for butterfly lovers. It even covers raising butterflies in captivity.

Santa Barbara Botanic Garden. *Native Plants for Southern California Gardens.* No. 12. Santa Barbara: Santa Barbara Botanic Garden, 1969. Detailed information on California native plants and the growing conditions they prefer.

Saratoga Horticultural Foundation. *Selected California Native Plants with Commercial Sources.* 3rd ed. Saratoga, Calif.: Saratoga Horticultural Foundation, 1983. This book is particularly helpful in finding sources for the native plants you want.

Schuler, Stanley, and Schuler, Elizabeth Meriwether. *Preserving the Fruits of the Earth.* New York: Dial Press, 1973. A book that is hard to find but worth looking for. It covers in detail how to preserve nearly everything.

Skelsey, Alice, and Huckaby, Gloria. *Growing Up Green.* New York: Workman Publishing, 1973. A guide for parents and children and how they can share the wonder of living things. A gem!

Smith, J. Robert, and Smith, Beatrice S. *The Prairie Garden*. Madison: University of Wisconsin Press, 1980. A useful book that describes in detail seventy native prairie plants and how to use them in your yard. In addition, it details how to collect seeds, raise your own plants, and maintain a prairie.

Smith, Ken. *Western Home Landscaping*. Tucson, Ariz.: H.P. Books, 1978. A helpful book for home landscapers. It has quite a bit of information on drought-tolerant plants and how to put in a drip irrigation system.

Southern Living editorial Staff. *Southern Living—Growing Vegetables and Herbs*. Birmingham, Ala.: Oxmoor House, 1984. This marvelous book discusses vegetable culture and cooking techniques for southern gardeners.

Sunset Books editorial staff. *New Western Garden Book*. Menlo Park, Calif.: Lane Publishing Co., 1979. This book is a must for all western gardeners; it's considered the bible of West Coast gardening.

_____. *Sunset Italian Cookbook*. Menlo Park, Calif.: Lane Publishing Co., 1974. A good basic Italian cookbook.

Vilmorin-Andrieux, MM. *The Vegetable Garden*. Palo Alto, Calif.: Jeavons-Leler Press. Reprint 1976. A marvelous reprint of a classic that was first printed in 1885. It is a description of the old varieties, with information on how to grow hundreds of them. I counted fifty-five pages on peas alone.

Waters, Alive. *Chez Panisse Menu Cookbook*. New York: Random House, 1982. An inspiring cookbook by an author who feels that fresh, superior, home-grown produce is the starting point for outstanding cuisine.

White, Katherine S. *Onward and Upward in the Garden*. New York: Farrar, Straus & Giroux, 1979. One woman's delightful view of gardening.

Williams, Brian. *Orchids for Everyone*. New York: Crown Publishers, 1980. A beautiful book showing 200 orchids in color with extensive practical advice.

Williams, John G., and Williams, Andrew E. *Field Guide to Orchids of North America*. New York: Universe Books, 1983. A useful guide for looking at or photographing orchids in the wild.

Wilson, William H. W. *Landscaping with Wildflowers and Native Plants*. San Francisco: Ortho Books, Chevron Chemical Company, 1984. A most valuable and up-to-date book covering in detail most of the many ecosystems in this country. The book contains numerous lists of native plants to choose for your landscape as well as information on how to plant and maintain them.

Index

Italicized page references indicate illustrations.

A

Acacia melanoxylon, 18
Acer species, 38, 101
Acres of Orchids, 119, 124
Actinindia arguta, 143
African daisy, *31*
Agave deserti, 102
Ailanthus altissima, 18
Akebia quinata, 101
Albizia Fulibrissin, 101
Alcea rosea, 102, 180
Allium schoenoprasum, 102
Allium tuberosum, 180
Aloe polyphylla, 74
Aloe species, 62
Alpine strawberry, 136, 137
Amalia orchid, 74
Amaranth, 136
Amaranthus species, 101
Amelanchier species, 38, 101
American cranberry bush, 101
Amorpha canescens, 49
Andropogon Gerardii, 48
Andropogon scoparius, 49
Anemone lancifolia, 32
Anemone patens, var. *Wolfgangiana,* 49
Anemone: tree, 61; woodland, *32*
Anethum graveolens, 102, 180
Annuals: for birds, 101; for butterflies, 102; for cutting, 162; in meadow garden, 28
Aquilegia canadensis, 22
Aquilegia species, 101
Arctostaphylos, 61
Artotheca calendula, 62
Arctotis species, 62
Ariocarpus agavoides, 74
Asclepias tuberosa, 30, 49
Aster novae-angliae, 49
Aster species, 49, 101, 102
'Austin' orchid, 102
Avocado, 134
Aztekium Ritteri, 74

B

Bachelor's button, 101
Backyard Wildlifer, The, 93
Bacterial blight, 84
Bamboo, 18, 134-135
Banana, 136
Baptisia leucantha, 50
Baptisia leucophaea, 49
Barnes, Carl, 79
Bean: 'Dutch White' runner, 151; haricots verts, 137; 'Royal Burgundy', 151; 'Royalty', 151; yard-long, 136
Beans: diseases of, 84; freezing seeds of, 84; saving, 84
Bean tepee, *152*
Beet, 135
Bellis perennis, 18
Berberis Thunbergii, 18
Bermuda grass, 18
Betula species, 38, 101
Biennial vegetables, 83
Big bluestem, 48
Bird-food violet, *50*
Bird houses, *91,* 94
Bitter melon, 136, 138
Bittersweet, 101; Oriental, 15, 17, 18
Blackberry, 17; Himalayan, 18
Black-eyed susan, *29,* 101
Blazing-star, 49
Blueberry, 102
Blue-eyed grass, *50*
Blue vanda orchid, 74
Borago officinalis, 180
Border: chaparral flower, *57-58*; mixed, *175*; perennial, *175*; prairie, 47
Bottle gentian, *71*
Bougainvillea species, 62
Bracken fern, 18
Brassia Edvah Loo, *99*
Brazilian pepper, 15, 17, 18
Broadleaf cycad, 74
Broccoli, 'Romanesco', *139*

Buckwheat, 61
Buddleia Davidii, 102
Buffalo grass, 46
Bulbs, 153, 162
Burdock, 136
Burning restrictions, 46
Bush poppy, 61
Butterfly bush, 102
Butterfly, monarch, *97;* swallowtail, *153*
Butterfly weed, *30, 49*

C

Cabbage, Chinese, 136
Cactus, endangered species of, 74
Cactus pads, 137
Cajeput tree, *16,* 18
Calendula officinalis, 31, 101, 180
Caliche, *56*
California buckeye, *56*
California fuchsia, 61
California lilac, *57,* 61
California poppy, *55,* 61
California quail, *88*
Calopogon tuberosus, 122
Camassia Leichtlinii, vi
Cape honeysuckle, 62
Capeweed, 62
Carnation, 180
Carpenteria californica, 61
Carissa species, 62
Carthamus tinctorius, 180
Carya ovata, 39
Casuarina, 15
Casuarina equisetifolia, 18
Catalpa speciosa, 38
Caterpillar, dill, *153*
Cattail, 17, 18
Cattleya Angelwalker x *C. amethystoglossa, 99*
Cattleya Gloriette, 120
Cattleya Greenwich, 119
Ceanothus species, *31, 57,* 61, 102
Celastrus orbiculatus, 18
Celastrus scandeus, 101
Celeriac, 137
Celtis occidentalis, 101
Celtis reticulata, 101
Centaurea Cyanus, 101
Cercis occidentalis, 61
Chamomile, 180
Chaparral garden, *31, 55-65;* design hints for,

58-59; diagram of, *63;* flammable plants in, 57; flower borders in, *57-58;* maintenance of, 60; native plants for, 61; nonnative flowering plants for, 62; planning of, *56-59*
Chayote, 137
Cherimoya, 136
Cherry, 102
Cherry laurel, 101
Cherry tomato, 'Sweet 100', 156, *161;* 'Tiny Tim', *165*
Chervil, 137
Chicory, 18
Child's garden, 147-157; diagram of, *149;* planning of, 150-151
Child's Garden in a Can, 151
Chili pepper, 137, 138
Chinese cabbage, 136
Chinese okra, 136
Chinese parsley, 136
Chipmunk, *105*
Chive, 102; garlic, 180
Chrysanthemum, 101, *168,* 180; garland, 136
Chrysanthemum Leucanthemum, 18
Chrysanthemum morifolium, 180
Chrysanthemum species, 101, 180
Cichorium Intybus, 18
Cilantro, 136, 137, 138
Cistus species, 62
Clarkia amoena, 88
Columbine, 101
Compass plant, *44,* 48
Coneflower, *30,* 49, *50*
Conservation of plant species, 19, 69-75
Coreopsis grandiflora, 102
Coreopsis palmata, 49
Coreopsis species, 49, 101, 102
Cortaderia jubata, 18
Corn, 135, 151-153
'Cornelia' musk rose, *100*
Corn salad, *137*
Cornus Nuttallii, 39
Cornus species, *34,* 38, *39,* 101, 102
Cosmos species, 101
Cottage garden, 175-184; diagram of *179;* guidelines for, 176; planning of, 177-178; recommended edibles for, 180
Courgettes, 137
'Cover Girl' orchid, 119
Crataegus species, 101
Cream wild indigo, 49
Cross-pollination, 80, 82
Cucumber, 135; lemon, *165*

Cucurbita species, 180
Cymbidium Hunter's Point, 122
Cymbidium Siempre, 120
Cynodon Dactylon, 18
Cypripedium reginae, 116
Cytisus scoparius, 18

D

Daffodil, *32*
Daikon, 136
Daisy: African yellow and white, *31, 62;*
    English, 18; oxeye, 18
Daylily, 102, 136, 180
Deer-resistant plants, 60
Dendromecon, *31*
Dendromecon rigida, 61
Dianthus Caryophyllis species, 180
Dianthus plumarius, 180
Dianthus species, 101
Dietes vegata, 62
Digitalis, 70
Digitalis purpurea, 18
Dill, 102, 153, 180
Dill caterpillar, *153*
Diospyros virginiana, 38, 101
Dodecatheon Meadia, 50
Dogwood, *34, 38, 39,* 101, 102
Douglas iris, 61
Drought-tolerant garden, *59-60,* 61-62
Drying: flowers, 163; herbs, 163
'Dutch White' runner bean, 151

E

Echinacea pallida, 49
Echium fastuosum, 31
Echium species, 62
Ecology lawn, 47
Ecoscaping, 8, 14
Ecosystems map, *9*
Eglanteria species, 108
Elaeagnus commutata, 101
Elaeagnus pungens, 101
Elderberry, *92,* 101, 135
Encephalartos latifrons, 74
Endangered plant species, 8-10, 74; saving, 2
English daisy, 18
English ivy, 15, 18
Equisetum hyemale, 18

Eriogonum species, 61
Eschscholzia californica, 54, 61
Ethnic ingredients, 136-142
Eucalyptus species, 18
Euonymus alata, 40
Euonymus Fortunei, 101
Evening primrose, 61

F

'Falcon Castle' orchid, 120
Family Food Garden, The, 160
Feijoa Sellowiana, 62
Fennel, 102, 153, *168,* 180
Fenugreek, 138
Ferns in a woodland garden, 40
Ficus carica, 132
Fire orchid, 74
Fire thorn, 101
Five-leaf akebia, 101
Florida holly, 15
Flower borders, 176, 181; chaparral, *57-58*
Flower, perfect, 82
Flowers: for birds, 101; for butterflies, 102;
    for child's garden, 153; for cutting, 161-162;
    drought-tolerant, 62; drying, 162, 163;
    edible, 180; native, in a meadow, 26;
    poisonous, 176
Foeniculum vulgare, 102, 180
Forbs, 45
Fortnight lily, 62
Fountain grass, 18
Foxglove, *18*
Fraxinus pennsylvanica, 101
Fraxinus species, 38
Freezing seeds, 83, 84
Fremontodendron californicum, 31, 61
French ingredients, 137
Fruits: heirloom, 135; high-yield, 169
Fuzzy gourd, 136, *143*

G

Galium verum, 18
Galvezia speciosa, 61
Garden construction, materials for, 172
Garden, drought-tolerant, *59-60,* 61-62
Gardening: benefits of, 130-131; equip-
    ment, 173
Gardens. *See specific types*

Garlic, 135
Garlic chive, 180
Gene pool, 72
Genetic engineering in plants, 70
Geranium, 62, 180
Gessert, Kate, 177-178
Geum triflorum, 50
Giant pitcher plant, 74
Gibberellic acid, 134
Gifts from the garden, 163
Ginger, 135, 138, *167*
Gladiolus species, 180
Glechoma hederacea, 18
'Golden Realm' orchid, 122
Goldenrod, 18, 102; stiff, *50*
'Gold Rush' zucchini, *161*
Gopher, *59,* 60, 103
Gourd, fuzzy, 136, *143*
Gourmet garden, 133-145; plants for, 135-142
Grapevine, *167*
Grass. *See specific varieties*
Grass seeds, native, 53
Green ash, 101
Green invaders. *See* Invasive species
Green pitcher plant, 74
Greens: French salad, 137; salad, 135
Grevillea species, 62
Ground ivy, 18
Grouse, *50*
Growing Garden Seeds, 83
Growing Up Green, 148, 150, 157
'Gypsy Pepper', *138, 161*

H

Habitat: for butterflies, 102; for birds, 102;
    natural, as part of garden, 1-2, 8, 35;
    successful for wildlife, 91
Hamamelis vernalis, 101
Hamamelis virginiana, 101
Haricots verts bean, 137
Hawthorn, 101
Hedera Helix, 18
Hedera species, 18
Heirloom fruits, 135
Heirloom vegetable garden, 77-87; diagram of,
    81; planning of, 78-80; sources of seeds for,
    86; suggested varieties for, 79-80
Helianthus species, 101, 102
Hemerocallis species, 102, 180
Herbal medicine, 70-71

Herbs, 135, 176; for a decorative border, 181;
    drying, 163; pot, 136, 137
Heritage rose garden, 107-115; diagram of,
    111; maintenance of, 112; planning of, 110;
    planting of, 110
Heritage rose society, 115
Heritage societies, 2
Heteromeles arbutifolia, 61
Hickory tree, *39*
Holly, 38; Florida, 15
Hollyhock, 102, 180
Home-grown gifts, 161
Honeysuckle, Cape, 62
Hops, 135
Hornworm, tomato, 156
Horsetail, 18
Hybrid vigor, 82
Hypericum calycinum, 18

I

Ilex species, 38, 101
"Immigrant" plants, 7
Indian grass, 49
Indian ingredients, 138
Indigenous species. *See* Native plants
Invasive species, 14-18, 96, 115
Ipecac, 70
Ipomoea species, 18
Iris, bearded, *31,* 62
Iris Douglasiana, 61
Iris reticulata, 178
Iris Shrevei, 53
Iris species, 62
Ironwood, 18
Irrigation: drip system of, *59;* of meadow
    garden, 28; in U.S. Southwest, 56
Island bush snapdragon, 61
Isolation of plants to prevent cross-
    pollination, 82
Isotria verticillata, 125
Italian garden, 138-142, *165;* diagram of, *141*
Ivy, 18

J

Japanese barberry, 18
Japanese honeysuckle, 14, 15, 18
Japanese knotweed, 18
Jicama, 137

Johnny-jump-up, 180
Juniperus species, 39, 101

K

Kitchen gifts, 163
Kiwi, *143*
Kniphofia Uvaria, 62
Kudzu, *13, 14,* 18

L

Laelia Canariensis, 102
Laelia jongheana, 74
Landscaping with native plants, 11-14
Lantana species, 15, 18, 62
Lavandula officinalis, 180
Lavandula species, 62, 180
Lavender, 62, 180
Lawn maintenance techniques, 160
Lawns, cost of, 159-160
Lc. Cuiseag 'Cuddles', *99*
Lead plant, 49
Lead, removal of from vegetables, 177
Lemon cucumber, *165*
Leptospermum species, 62
Liatris aspera, 49
Liatris punctata, 49
Liatris pycnostachya, 49
Liatris spicata, 49
Lilac, 102; California, *57*
Lily: fortnight, 62; moist meadow, *21*
Limonium latifolium, 101
Limonium Perezii, 62
Lindera Benzoin, 102
Liquidambar Styraciflua, 39
Lifiodendron Tulipifera, 39, 101
Littauer, Deveda and Ernest, 59, 60-61
Little bluestem, *49*
Living rock cactus, 74
Lonicera japonica, 18
Lupinus arboreus, 61
Lupinus nanus, 25
Lupinus species, 25, 61, 102
Lythrum Salicaria, 18

M

Mache, *137*
MacLellanara Pagan Love Song, 122

Malus 'Dorothea', 40
Maple tree, 38, 101
Matricaria recutita, 180
Manzanita, 61
Marigold, 101, 102
Mattiola incana, 102
McLellan's Acres of Orchids, 119, 124
Meadow in a Can, *25*
Meadow: definition of, 23; managed, 24
Meadow garden, 23-33; advantages of, 24;
    diagram of, *27;* limitations of, 24;
    maintenance of, 28; planning of, 24-26;
    reseeding of, 28; seeding of, 25-26
Melaleuca, 15, *16*
Melaleuca quinquenervia, 16, 18
Melon, 'Sonoma', *98*
Mexican ingredients, 137-138
Milkweed, 17
Mimosa, 101
Mimulus, 21, 61
Mint, 154
Moist meadow lily, *21*
Monarch butterfly, *97*
Moneysaving garden, 159-173; diagram of,
    171; planning of, 169-170
Monkey flower, 61
Morning-glory, 18
Moss rose, *112*
Mountain ash, 101
Mountain sweet pitcher plant, 74
Mowing: of meadow garden, 28; of prairie
    garden, 48
Mulching, 59
Multiflora rose, 17, 18, 115
Myrtle, 101
Myrtus communis, 101

N

Nasturtium officinale, 18
Natal plum, 62
National Wildlife Association's Backyard
    Wildlife Habitat Program, *93*
Native grass seeds, 53
Native plants, 8-12; that aid erosion control,
    57; characteristics of southwestern, *56;*
    communities of, *9;* definition of, 20-21; for
    drought-tolerant garden, 61; flammable, *57;*
    guidelines for working with, 11-12; help in
    growing, 10-11; hybrids of, 21; illegal
    removal of, 74; maintenance of, 13; in a

meadow, 26; planning for use of in land-scaping, 13-14; renewed interest in, 10; rescuing, 19; setting goals for use of in land-scaping, 12; special germination requirements of southwestern, 56; trees, 40
Natural gardening, 8
Nepenthes rajah, 74
Nerium Oleander, 62
New England aster, 49
New Zealand tea, 62
Nopales, 137
Northern dropseed, 49
Nuts, 135

O

Oak, scrub, 62
Obregonia Denegrii, 74
Odontocidium Big Mac, 122
Oenothera Hookeri, 61
Okra, Chinese, 136
'Old Blush' rose, *100*
Oncidium Carnival Costume, 120
Open-pollinated vegetables, 72, 73; sources of seeds for, 86
Opossum, *97*
Orange, 135
Orchid: endangered species of, 74; history of culture of, 117-118; needs of, 118-119; yellow fringed native, 120
Orchid garden, 117-125; cool, 120-122; diagram of, *121;* maintenance of, 122; planning of, 118-119; warm, 119-120; in windowsill, 119-122
Oriental bittersweet, 15, 17, 18
Oriental ingredients, 136-137
Osteospermum, 31
Oxeye daisy, 18

P

Pachypodium namaquanum, 74
Paeonia species, 180
Pampas grass, 15, 17, 18
Panicum virgatum, 49
Papaver species, 180
Paphiopedilum, 99
Paphiopedilum Makuli, 120
Parsley, 102; Chinese, 136
Parthenocissus quinquefolia, 101

Pasque flower, 49
Passiflora species, 102
Passionflower, 102
Peach, 135
Peanut, *154*
Pelargonium species, 62, 180
Pendulina species, 108
Pennisetum grass, 17
Pennisetum setaceum, 18
Penstemon, *61*
Penstemon cordifolius, 61
Peony, 180
Pepper, 'Gypsy', *138, 161*
Perennials, 176; for birds, 101; for butterflies, 102; for cutting, 162; in meadow garden, 28
Perfect flower, 82
Periwinkle, 18
Persimmon, 38, 101
Pests. *See individual name*
Petalostemon purpureum, 49, 50
Petits pois, 137
Petroselinum species, 102
Petunia hybrida, 180
Phalaenopsis Golden Sands 'Canary', *99*
Phalaenopsis Toni Featherstone, 120
Phlox species, 102
Pineapple guava, 62
Pink, 101; cottage, 180
'Pink Pearl' apple, *98*
Pinus species, 39, 101
Plant isolation, 82
Plant rustling, 74
Plants: for birds, 101; for butterflies, 102; as contraceptives, 70; for cottage border, 178, 181; deer-resistant, 60; endangered, 8-10, 74; for greenhouse gourmet garden, 136; life cycles of, 83; for outdoor gourmet garden, 134-136; prairie, 48-50; reasons for diversity of in U.S., 10; for wildlife, 96, 101-102. *See also* Native plants
Plant species, saving, 19, 69-75
Platanthera ciliaris, 120
Plumbago auriculata, 62
Plum, natal, 62
Poisonous flowers, 153, 176
Pollen, 24
Polygonum cuspidatum, 18
Pollination, 82. *See also* Cross-pollination
Pomegranate, 62
Popcorn, 153
Poppy, 180

Populus tremuloides, 39
Portulaca olerace, 18
Potato, 154
Pot herbs, 136, 137
Prairie border, 47
Prairie coreopsis, 49
Prairie, definition of, 45
Prairie garden, 45-53; diagram of, *51;* and fire, 47; local ordinances affecting, 46; mainte-nance of, 48; mowing of, 48; planning of, 47-51; problems with establishment of, 46-47; recommendations regarding, 47-48; seeding of, 47; soil for, 47
Prairie grass seeds, sources of, 53
Prairie patch, 47
Prairie plants, 48-50
Prairie smoke, 50
Preserving produce, 170
Pride of Madeira, *31*
Primrose, 180; evening, 61
Primula vulgaris, 180
Pruning, 60; of roses, 112
Prunus Laurocerasus, 101
Prunus species, 102
Pseudotsuga Menziesii, 40
Pteridium aquilinum, 18
Pueraria lobata, 13, 18
Pumpkin, *155, 156*
Punica Granatum, 62
Punk tree, 18
Purple loosestrife, *15,* 18
Purple martin house, *91*
Purple prairie clover, *49, 50*
Purslane, 18
Pyracantha species, 101

Q

Quail, California, *88*
Quercus agrifolia, 62
Quercus species, 39, 101
Quinine, 70

R

Rabbit, *103*
Radish, 115; daikon, 136
Rare and Endangered Native Plant Exchange, 71
Raspberry, *170*

Ratibida pinnata, 49
Recycling construction materials, 172
Redbud, 61, *97*
Red-hot-poker, 62
Renanthera Imschootiana, 74
Reproduction of seed plants, 82
Rhus ovata, 61
Rock rose, 62
'Romanesco' broccoli, *139*
Root rot, prevention of, 59
Roquette, 137
Rosa damascena bifera, 107
Rosa damascena Trigintipetala, 100, 109, 110
Rosa gallica officinalis, 110
Rosa multiflora, 18
Rosa rugosa, 106, 108
Rosa rugosa alba, 108
Rosa rugosa Rubra, 108
Rosa species, 101, 180
Rose, 101, 180; controlling spread of, 115; 'Cornelia' musk, *100;* disease-free, 108, 109; grafting of, 115; hardy heritage, 108-109; modern, 109; Moss, *112;* multiflora, 17, 18, 115; needs of, 110, 112; unusual, 109; 'Old Blush', *100;* white Rugosa, *100*
Rose garden, heritage, 107-115
Rosemary, 62
Roses of Yesterday and Today, 108, 115
Rosmarinus species, 62
'Royal Burgundy' bean, 151
'Royalty' bean, 151
Rubrifolia species, 108
Rubus procerus, 18
Rudbeckia species, 101
Rugosa rose, white, *100*

S

Safer's agricultural soap, 112
Safflower, 180
Saffron, 138
Sage, 61, 102
Salad greens, 135; French, 137
Salix species, 102
Salvia species, 61, 102
Sambucus species, 101
'Sargossa' orchid, 122
Sarracenia Fonesii, 74
Sarracenia oreophila, 74
Scabiosa caucasica, 102
Schinus terebinthifolius, 18

Scotch broom, 14, 15, 17 18
Scrub oak, *62*
Sea lavender, 62
Sebastiani, Vicki, 139
Sedum species, 62, 102
Seed banks, 2
Seed exchanges, 86
Seed Savers Exchange, 77, 78
Seed saving, 73, 80-83; basic guidelines for, 83
Seeds: germination of, 47, *56*, 60; obtaining, 47, 65, 78-79; stratified, 47; storing, 83. *See also* Prairie grass seeds; Native grass seeds; Wildflower seed mixes
Senecio Greyi, 62
Sequoia sempervirens, 40
Serviceberry, 101
Shallot, 137
She-oak, 18
Shooting-star, *50*
Shrubs: for birds, 101; for butterflies, 102; in a woodland garden, 36, 37
Shungiku, 136
Sideoats grama, 46, *50*
Silverberry, 101
Sisyrinchium albidum, 50
Sisyrinchium angustifolium, 50
Sisyrinchium californica, 88
Sisyrinchium campestre, 50
Skunk, *90*
Slc. Brillig, 99
Solidago canadensis, 18
Solidago rigida, 50
Solidago species, 102
'Sonoma' melon, *98*
Sorghastrum nutans, 49
Sorrel, 137
Spaghetti squash, 155
Sphinx moth, 156
Spicebush, 102
Spiral aloe, 74
Sporobolus heterolepis, 49
Squash, *155*
Squash blossoms, 180
Statice, 62, 101
Stock, 102
Strawberry, 154; alpine, 136, 137
Succession, 13; role of in meadows, 24
Sugarbush, 61
'Summer Green' orchid, 120
'Summer Sprite' orchid, 120
Sunflower, 101, 102, *156*
'Sunset' orchid, 122

'Superba' orchid, 120
Switch grass, 49
Syringa vulgaris, 102

T

Tagetes species, 101, 102
Tecomaria capensis, 62
Tithonia, *97*
Tomatillo, 137-138
Tomato, 156; cherry, *161, 165*
Tomato hornworm, 156
Toyon, 61
Tree anemone, 61
Trees: ailanthus, 14, 18; ash, 38; birch, 38, 101; for birds, 101; catalpa, *38;* dogwood, *34, 38, 39,* 101; Douglas fir, 40; eucalyptus, 18; green ash, 101; hackberry, 101; hawthorn, 101; hemlock, 40; hickory, *39;* maple, *38,* 101; mimosa, 101; mountain ash, 101; oak, *39,* 101; persimmon, 38, 101; pine, *39,* 101; punk, 18; quaking aspen, *39;* redwood, 40; serviceberry, 101; silk, 101; sweet gum, *39;* tulip, *39, 101;* in a woodland garden, 35-36, 38-41
Trillium, *19*
Tropaeolum majus, 180
Tsuga heterophylla, 40
Tulipa species, 180
Tulip tree, 39, 101
Typha latifolia, 18

V

Vaccinium species, 102
Vanda coerulea, 74
Vanilla, 136
Vegetable garden: benefits of, 133; gourmet, 133-145; heirloom, 77-87
Vegetables: in a cottage border, 177-178; high-yield, 169; open-pollinated, 72, 73; planting in clumps, 178; in a woodland garden, 36
Viburnum carcephalum, 40
Viburnum tomentosum, 40
Viburnum trilobum, 101
Vinca major, 18
Vines for birds, 101
Viola, 180
Viola cornuta, 180
Viola pedata, 50

Viola tricolor, 180
Virginia creeper, 101

W

Watercress, 18
Watering of chaparral garden, *59*
Water for wildlife, 94-96
Weeds, 13, 14-18; controlling, 17; definition of, 14; as foes in natural areas, 14; guidelines for identifying, 17; in a meadow garden, 28
White Rugosa rose, *100*
White wild indigo, 50
Wildflower seed mixes, 15, 17; sources of, 33, 53
Wildflowers: for cutting, 161, 162; in a woodland garden, 40
Wildlife: needs of, 91, 94-96; protection from, 103
Wildlife garden, 89-105; diagram of, *95;* planning of, 94-96; plants for, 96, 101-102
Willow, 102
Winterberry, 101
Winter creeper, 101

Wisteria species, 102
Witch hazel, 101
Woodland anemone, *32*
Woodland garden, 35-43; diagram of, *41;* guidelines for converting existing garden to, 37; guidelines for starting new, 37; planning of, 36-37; size of, 35; soil for, 37
Woodthrush, *97*
Wreaths, 163

Y

Yard-long bean, 136
Yards, 159
Yellow bedstraw, 18
Yucca species, *65*

Z

Zauschneria californica, 61
Zinnia linearis, 178
Zinnia species, 102
Zone map, 186
Zucchini, 136; 'Gold Rush', *161, 165*

Enterprise Web 2.0 Fundamentals

Krishna Sankar

Susan A. Bouchard

Cisco Press

800 East 96th Street

Indianapolis, IN 46240

Enterprise Web 2.0 Fundamentals

Krishna Sankar
Susan A. Bouchard

Published by:
Cisco Press
800 East 96th Street
Indianapolis, IN 46240 USA

Printed in the United States of America

First Printing April 2009

Library of Congress Cataloging-in-Publication Data is on file.

ISBN-13: 978-1-58705-763-2

ISBN-10: 1-58705-763-8

Warning and Disclaimer

This book is designed to provide information about Web 2.0 technologies. Every effort has been made to make this book as complete and as accurate as possible, but no warranty or fitness is implied.

The information is provided on an "as is" basis. The authors, Cisco Press, and Cisco Systems, Inc., shall have neither liability nor responsibility to any person or entity with respect to any loss or damages arising from the information contained in this book or from the use of the discs or programs that may accompany it.

The opinions expressed in this book belong to the authors and are not necessarily those of Cisco Systems, Inc.

Trademark Acknowledgments

All terms mentioned in this book that are known to be trademarks or service marks have been appropriately capitalized. Cisco Press or Cisco Systems, Inc., cannot attest to the accuracy of this information. Use of a term in this book should not be regarded as affecting the validity of any trademark or service mark.

Corporate and Government Sales

The publisher offers excellent discounts on this book when ordered in quantity for bulk purchases or special sales, which may include electronic versions and/or custom covers and content particular to your business, training goals, marketing focus, and branding interests. For more information, please contact: **U.S. Corporate and Government Sales** 1-800-382-3419 corpsales@pearsontechgroup.com

For sales outside the United States please contact: **International Sales** international@pearsoned.com

Feedback Information

At Cisco Press, our goal is to create in-depth technical books of the highest quality and value. Each book is crafted with care and precision, undergoing rigorous development that involves the unique expertise of members from the professional technical community.

Readers' feedback is a natural continuation of this process. If you have any comments regarding how we could improve the quality of this book, or otherwise alter it to better suit your needs, you can contact us through email at feedback@ciscopress.com. Please make sure to include the book title and ISBN in your message.

We greatly appreciate your assistance.

Publisher: Paul Boger

Associate Publisher: Dave Dusthimer

Cisco Representative: Erik Ullanderson

Executive Editor: Brett Bartow

Cisco Press Program Manager: Anand Sundaram

Development Editor: Andrew Cupp

Managing Editor: Patrick Kanouse

Copy Editor: Margo Catts

Project Editor: Mandie Frank

Editorial Assistant: Vanessa Evans

Technical Editor(s): Praveen Shah and Tom Wesselman

Composition: Mark Shirar

Cover and Interior Designer: Louisa Adair

Proofreader: Elizabeth Scott

Indexer: Tim Wright

Americas Headquarters	**Asia Pacific Headquarters**	**Europe Headquarters**
Cisco Systems, Inc.	Cisco Systems (USA) Pte. Ltd.	Cisco Systems International BV
San Jose, CA	Singapore	Amsterdam, The Netherlands

Cisco has more than 200 offices worldwide. Addresses, phone numbers, and fax numbers are listed on the Cisco Website at www.cisco.com/go/offices.

CCDE, CCENT, Cisco Eos, Cisco HealthPresence, the Cisco logo, Cisco Lumin, Cisco Nexus, Cisco StadiumVision, Cisco TelePresence, Cisco WebEx, DCE, and Welcome to the Human Network are trademarks; Changing the Way We Work, Live, Play, and Learn and Cisco Store are service marks; and Access Registrar, Aironet, AsyncOS, Bringing the Meeting To You, Catalyst, CCDA, CCDP, CCIE, CCIP, CCNA, CCNP, CCSP, CCVP, Cisco, the Cisco Certified Internetwork Expert logo, Cisco IOS, Cisco Press, Cisco Systems, Cisco Systems Capital, the Cisco Systems logo, Cisco Unity, Collaboration Without Limitation, EtherFast, EtherSwitch, Event Center, Fast Step, Follow Me Browsing, FormShare, GigaDrive, HomeLink, Internet Quotient, IOS, iPhone, iQuick Study, IronPort, the IronPort logo, LightStream, Linksys, MediaTone, MeetingPlace, MeetingPlace Chime Sound, MGX, Networkers, Networking Academy, Network Registrar, PCNow, PIX, PowerPanels, ProConnect, ScriptShare, SenderBase, SMARTnet, Spectrum Expert, StackWise, The Fastest Way to Increase Your Internet Quotient, TransPath, WebEx, and the WebEx logo are registered trademarks of Cisco Systems, Inc. and/or its affiliates in the United States and certain other countries.

All other trademarks mentioned in this document or website are the property of their respective owners. The use of the word partner does not imply a partnership relationship between Cisco and any other company. (0812R)

About the Authors

Krishna Sankar is a Distinguished Engineer with the Software Group at Cisco. He is currently focusing on different forms of the emerging collaborative social networks (as opposed to current functional coordination networks) and other strategic Web 2.0 mechanics inside and outside Cisco. His external work includes the OpenAJAX Alliance, OpenSocial, next generation infrastructure projects such as Ruby on Rails, OAuth, ZooKeeper and Vertebra, as well as the Advisory Board of San Jose Education Foundation. His interests lie in Cloud Computing, highly scalable web architectures, social and knowledge graphs, intelligent inference mechanisms, iPhone programming, and Lego Robotics. Occasionally he writes about them at doubleclix.wordpress.com.

Susan A. Bouchard is a senior manager, Business Development with US-Canada Sales Planning and Operations at Cisco. She focuses on Web 2.0 technology as part of the US-Canada Collaboration initiative. Susan's presentations include

- Cisco Systems Case Study: Collaboration, Innovation and Mobility—The Productivity Triple Play on behalf of Dow Jones at the Gartner Customer Relationship Management Summit, September 2008

- Cisco Systems Case Study: EA Foundation Delivers Mobile Service Value at Shared Insights' Enterprise Architectures Conference, March 2007

- Cisco Systems Case Study: Architecture Review Process—Improving the IT Portfolio at DCI's Enterprise Architectures Conference, October 2005

Susan joined Cisco in 2000, and as a Member of Technical Staff helped to establish the Sales IT Partner Architecture Team and led the Cisco Enterprise Architecture Standards & Governance program for five years. Prior to joining Cisco, she was a Computer Scientist with the Department of the Navy, managing the Navy's e-commerce website for IT products and services. Susan led other software development and support programs for the Navy and Marine Corps in the areas of database administration, artificial intelligence and robotics.

About the Technical Reviewers

Praveen Shah is a tech-savvy management consultant and entrepreneur with an 18-year track record of helping 75+ Fortune Global 500s, SMBs, and early-stage startups successfully launch, grow, and optimize their businesses. He counsels CXOs and SVPs of high-tech, software, services, Internet, telecom, manufacturing, and semiconductor clients on business model, innovation, globalization (offshoring, outsourcing), Web 2.0/3.0, operations improvement, supply chain, and demand-driven planning.

In 2002, he founded Mobity LLC (www.mobity.com), a business consulting and angel investment firm. Before, he held senior management positions with Quovera, KPMG Consulting (BearingPoint), Iacocca Institute (Lehigh University), and Philips Consumer Electronics. He holds an M.S. in manufacturing systems engineering from Lehigh University (U.S.A.) and a B.S. in mechanical engineering from the University of Pune (India).

Outside work, Praveen always finds time to avidly read, meet friends and family, travel worldwide, take photographs, watch movies, and follow cricket. Beyond professional subjects, other topics of his interest include quantum physics, cognitive sciences, positive psychology, and secular spirituality.

Praveen lives in Mountain View, CA with his wife Pallavi and son Mohnish. He can be reached at http://www.linkedin.com/in/praveenshah or at Praveen.Shah@mobity.com.

Tom Wesselman is a senior manager in the office of the CTO responsible for the long-term strategy for Cisco Communication and Collaboration products, building on the foundation of unified, IP-based communication to add social networking, collaboration, and Web 2.0 interfaces and applications. Before that he ran engineering for Cisco Unified Personal Communicator, partnerships for the initial release of Cisco Network Admission Control, and engineering for Cisco Unity Unified Messaging.

Dedications

I dedicate this book to two folks—from very different ends of life's spectrum—who, in my perspective, make all the difference in the world: to my mother Rajam Krishnan, who always makes me feel special, and to President Barack Obama for making this country special. With a mother's love and a leader's inspiration, the two most important influences in life, one will achieve wonders.

—Krishna

I would like to dedicate this book to my family, especially my mother, Beryl Bouchard, for always encouraging me to pursue my education, and my two younger sisters, Kim and Trista, for leading the way.

The confidence gained from excelling in school has helped me believe in myself and know that, even in the most adverse times, I could choose my course, see it through, and succeed.

—Susan

Acknowledgments

From Krishna: We are literally standing on the shoulders of giants—this book wouldn't have been possible without numerous blogs, newspaper and magazine clippings, and columns and articles. Our first acknowledgements go to all the references for their observation and careful reporting of the past, present, and future of the Web 2.0 phenomenon. You can find a list of these references in the Appendix, "References." Although we have diligently added reference pointers, it is possible we might have unintentionally missed a few—our apologies for any mistakes. Many times I just quoted the sources because they have articulated it so well and I could do no better.

Next, we thank our reviewers Praveen and Tom. Guys, thanks for your diligence and suggestions. It is a pleasure working with you. Of course the crew at Cisco Press—Brett, Andrew, Mandie, Margo, Vanessa, Louisa, Tim and others whom we haven't "met"—are the best. They turned a set of random musings into a coherent book! Their support, encouragement, and occasional push-backs resulted in the book you are holding in your hand (or on your screen!).

My co-author Susan has been with me through the thick and thin, offering support when I thought it was impossible, and delivering chapters ahead of me(!). She was always ready to take on another chapter even with her busy schedule.

Inside Cisco I wish to thank David Bernstein, who was supportive of this effort from the very beginning. His encouragement, not only for this book but also on a multitude of other areas, has made a great impact on me. Our "grand-boss" Don Proctor always was there for me, an email away, always ready with his thoughts and insights. And he had no hesitation to write a forward, in spite of his very busy schedule. Debbie Law always had a smile and an encouraging word whenever I needed them. Thanks Debbie. Steve "IEEE" Diamond has a special place, a big place ;o). And I appreciate the help and encouragement from Ann McArtor in getting the forward done, as well as for her encouraging words.

On the home front, I'm beholden to Subbalakshmi "Usha," the "rock of our family and the love of my life", and little "Yellow Beard Pirate" Kaushik, who most probably marks the passage of the last year as the "Nintendo years" from Gameboy to DS to Wii! One couldn't ask for better family and support. I wish and hope that I can spend more time with them. Actually he is calling me to play Wii Golf—we have a play date with Tiger and later need to help Professor Layton as he solves puzzles at the curious village of St. Mystere; now that I have completed the book, I have no excuses. See you all soon, in a bookstore nearby (or a website far, far away), and happy surfing!

From Susan: Heartfelt thanks to Donna Rhode and Jim Grubb for their executive sponsorship and leadership in the Web 2.0 space and to Krishna Sankar for the opportunity to co-author this book. And special thanks to Bill Ward, for helping me better prepare for the fierce conversations along the way.

Contents at a Glance

Introduction   xviii

Chapter 1   An Introduction to Web 2.0   3

Chapter 2   User-Generated Content: Wikis, Blogs, Communities, Collaboration, and Collaborative Technologies   33

Chapter 3   Rich Internet Applications: Practices, Technologies, and Frameworks   77

Chapter 4   Social Networking   91

Chapter 5   Content Aggregation, Syndication, and Federation via RSS and Atom   125

Chapter 6   Web 2.0 Architecture Case Studies   143

Chapter 7   Tending to Web 3.0: The Semantic Web   161

Chapter 8   Cloud Computing   181

Chapter 9   Web 2.0 and Mobility   203

Chapter 10   Web 2.0 @ Cisco: The Evolution   231

Chapter 11   Cisco's Approach to Sales 2.0   267

Appendix   References   307

             Index   348

Contents

Introduction   xviii

Chapter 1   **An Introduction to Web 2.0   3**

What Exactly Is This Web 2.0 and Why Should We Care About It?   3

Social Aspects of Web 2.0   5

Business Aspects of Web 2.0   6

Web 2.0 Versions and Generations   11

Web 2.0 CE Versus EE   14

Challenges to Web 2.0 EE Adoption   16

Characteristics and Memes of Web 2.0   16

User-Generated Content   18

Rich Internet Applications (RIA)   18

Social Networks   19

Cloud Computing   19

Web-Centric Development and Architectural Models   19

Data   21

Mashups   22

Scale Free and Long Tail   23

Mobility   24

Web 2.0 at Cisco   24

Web 2.0–Centric Products from Cisco   25

How Cisco Is Leveraging Web 2.0 Internally   27

Chapter 2   **User-Generated Content: Wikis, Blogs, Communities, Collaboration, and Collaborative Technologies   33**

Evolution of User-Generated Content (UGC)   35

Personal Webpages   35

Blogs   37

Wikis   46

Bookmarking and Folksonomies   54

Photos and Videos   60

Communities   63

Collaboration   65

Collaborative Technologies   65

Cisco TelePresence   65

WebEx   67

Unified Communications   69

Chapter 3   Rich Internet Applications: Practices, Technologies, and Frameworks   77

What Exactly Is an RIA and Why Do We Care About It?   77

A Techno-Business Tour Through the RIA Land   79

Web 2.0 RIA Technologies, Standards, and Frameworks   84

  Ajax   85

  HTTP Architectural Constraints   87

  OpenAjax   88

  Ruby on Rails Framework and Infrastructure   89

Chapter 4   Social Networking   91

State of the Union and Business Value of Social Networks   92

  Characteristics of a Social App   94

Social Network Ecosystems and Players   96

  Facebook: A Complete Ecosystem   96

  Facebook Platform   96

  Facebook Applications   98

  Facebook Platform and Architecture   99

  Weaving a Facebook Application   103

  LinkedIn: The Corporate Hangout for Jobs and Connections   104

  MySpace: The Teen Social Network Site   105

  Friendster: Where It All Began   106

  Ning: A Generic Social Site Hosting Platform   106

  Jive: An Enterprise Platform   107

  Socialtext: A Hosted Enterprise Collaboration Tool   107

  Awareness: An Enterprise Social Media and Web 2.0 Communities Platform   108

  Google: Social Network Interoperability Interfaces   108

  Microsoft: Enterprise Content Management with Social Network Features   108

  IBM: Making Collaboration a Corporate Priority   109

  Twitter: In a New Category by Itself—Microblogging   111

Social Networking Standards and Interfaces   113

  OpenSocial   114

  OpenID   115

  OAuth   117

  Other Social Networking Standards   117

Challenges in the Social Networking Industry   118

  Relevance and Nature   118

  Openness and Data Portability   118

Security and Privacy   119

Data Ownership   120

Worldwide Acceptance and Localization   121

Chapter 5   Content Aggregation, Syndication, and Federation via RSS and Atom   125

Business View of Information Distribution   127

RSS   129

RSS 2.0 Information Architecture   131

RSS 2.0 Modules   133

How RSS Works   134

RSS at CISCO   135

Cisco RSS Publishing   136

Cisco RSS Consumption   137

Enterprise RSS Best Practices   137

Atom   139

Atom Information Architecture   140

Chapter 6   Web 2.0 Architecture Case Studies   143

Web 2.0 Infrastructure Architecture: Scale, Concurrency, and Distributability   144

Web 2.0 Infrastructure Architecture Case Studies   145

eBay   146

YouTube   147

Amazon   148

Google   149

Twitter   151

Flickr   152

Technologies for Scalable Architectures   152

Case for MapReduce and Its Cousin Hadoop   154

Scalable Interfaces   155

Web 2.0 Development and Deployment   156

Chapter 7   Tending to Web 3.0: The Semantic Web   161

A Business Definition of the Semantic Web   161

A Business View of the Semantic Web   163

Semantic Web Origins—From Aristotle to W3C   167

Inner Workings of Semantic Web Technologies   168

Resource Description Framework   169

Web Ontology Language   172

SPARQL   175

Enterprise Applications of the Semantic Web   176

   Social Media, Education, and the Semantic Web   176

   Semantic Web SaaS Platform   177

   Semantic Web Support in Databases   178

   Other Enterprise Applications   178

Chapter 8   Cloud Computing   181

Cloud Computing and Its Relevance   181

   Cloud Computing Eco System   184

Cloud Computing Business Value   188

Cloud Computing Offerings from Major Vendors   190

   Amazon   192

   Google   195

   Microsoft   195

   Live Mesh   195

   Azure   195

   IBM   197

   Sun   197

   Other Companies   198

Enterprise Adoption of Cloud Computing   198

Chapter 9   Web 2.0 and Mobility   203

Evolution of Mobile Web Technology   204

   Generations of Mobile Phone Technology   204

   Mobile Devices   206

   Voice Recognition and Position Location Technology   211

   Developing Applications for Mobile Devices   211

Mobile Web Applications and Websites   213

   Mobile Webapps   213

   Web Portals and Wireless Application Service Providers   216

   Mobile Social Networking   219

Mobile Web at Cisco   222

   Cisco.com Mobile   222

   Cisco Text Messaging Services   223

   Cisco Mobile Intranet Services   224

   Cisco Mobile Sales Information Services   226

   Cisco's Mobile Web Strategy   227

Chapter 10   Web 2.0 @ Cisco: The Evolution   231

Intranet Strategy Group   235

Blogs   236

Discussion Forums   241

Wikis   245

Connecting People, Information, and Communities   250

Video   255

Communications Center of Excellence (CCoE)   256

Communication and Collaboration Board   261

Cisco 3.0   262

Chapter 11   Cisco's Approach to Sales 2.0   267

Web 2.0 Changes Sales Processes   267

Sales 2.0   268

Cisco Sales Explores Web 2.0   269

Connected Communities   270

Finding Expertise   270

Mobile Sales 2.0   271

Web 2.0 Explorers   272

Mashups   273

Salespedia   274

WebEx Connect Initiative for Sales   275

Sales Innovation via iFeedback   276

U.S.-Canada Sales Theater Initiatives   278

Sales Planning & Operations   279

Scale the Power   281

Administrator Training   282

Collaboration Portal   282

Collaboration Guide   282

Collaboration Hot Topics   286

Collaboration Library   288

Collaboration Cockpit   289

Web 2.0 Committee   290

Worldwide Sales Collaboration Board   290

Advanced Technology   291

Specialist, Optimization, Access, and Results   292

Five to Thrive   295

Worldwide Channels   297

Cisco to Partner   299

Partner to Partner   300

Marketing   303

Collaboration Consortium   303

Appendix   References   307

Index   348

Forward by Don Proctor

Recently, a friend who is an executive at a California-based consulting firm asked me, "What *is* Web 2.0, anyway?" Jamie is pretty tech-savvy, lives on his Blackberry whenever his laptop can't be conveniently connected, and has three 20-something children immersed in social networking. Yet he wasn't quite sure what Web 2.0 was, or just when Web 1.0 ended and Web 2.0 began.

If you have been wondering the same thing—maybe you have the feeling that something interesting is going on, but you're not quite sure what it is and how much you should care—this book was written for you. It will give you a thorough introduction to Web 2.0, explaining it in technological, sociological, and business terms. Perhaps more important, it will show you how to integrate Web 2.0 into your own organization.

Going back to Jamie's question, the simplest answer is that Web 1.0 was an information source and Web 2.0 is an experience.

Web content in the first generation was completely controlled by its immediate owners. They decided what appeared on their sites and they or their employees were the only ones who could modify it. The success of their sites depended on how well they read their target audiences and how accurately they could anticipate what kind of information people would look for. It was one-way communication and there was really only one way to get to it: through a computer.

Today, in the Web 2.0 world, users are accessing the Web through laptops, PDAs, smart phones, and their televisions, not just to find things but to do things. A rich, user-friendly interface is a major characteristic of Web 2.0, intended to engage users in participating in some way, and participate they most enthusiastically do. Now they are often the co-creators of web content.

To take just one example, Wikipedia is an online encyclopedia in 10 languages with millions of entries that are written, edited, and continually updated by its users. Even for sites where users play a much smaller role in generating the content, companies are creating new Web 2.0 channels, such as blogs and wikis, which make possible interactive—and public—discussions outside of corporate control. We're also seeing entirely new communications channels emerge, such as the rapid-fire messaging services Twitter and Yammer, as the main vehicle for communicating. A new kind of conversation is replacing one-way communication, and it is changing the way companies engage with their audiences.

One reason Web 2.0 is so relevant to business today is because it's at the heart of a number of fundamental market transitions that are having an impact on many different kinds of industries, from consumer-packaged goods to energy to high tech. Some of the transitions are technology-based, some are sociological, and others are business model transitions.

One of these is *inter-company collaboration*. No word better represents what Web 2.0 is about than collaboration, and Web 2.0–enabled technologies are creating a new wave of collaboration in business. Collaboration in the work group has been with us for as long as we've had IT and even before, if you go back to more traditional methods, such as talking. But a few years ago, we started to see a transition from work group–based collaboration to more cross-functional collaboration, where a project might involve not only a marketing department, but development, manufacturing, and services departments as well.

Where it gets exciting is the third wave of collaboration on which we are embarking now: inter-company collaboration, or collaboration that happens between completely separate organizations. It means that you can collaborate seamlessly across firewalls with your critical ecosystems of partners, your supply chain, your customers, and even your customers' customers. It's not simply about bilateral partnerships, but about whole ecosystems in a particular industry that can act together in a new way. That's a pretty fundamental shift, even beginning to reshape what industries look like. As eBusiness was to the 1990's, collaboration will be to the next decade, a critical growth-driver, and much of it will be delivered through Web 2.0–enabled technologies.

Another important market transition propelled by Web 2.0 is *crowd sourcing*, or distributed co-creation of content. Wikipedia, Amazon, YouTube, and other well known companies today use crowd sourcing; that is, they turn over content creation to a potentially huge audience of users. It's paying off. The social networking site, Facebook—as I write, the fifth most trafficked site on the Internet in the United States—is entirely based on information provided by 6,000,000 users self-aggregated into 55,000 networks.[1] Over on YouTube, an estimated 80% of the tens of millions of videos that have been uploaded have come from amateurs, in hopes of getting their content viewed, discussed, and rated.[2] When users create the content on a site, they are invested in it; they identify with it, pay attention to it, and tell others about it. It's less about the tools they use than in the collaborative experience they create, and how that is leveraged to create highly functioning communities.

Communities can be very powerful if you understand how they operate, and many companies are learning to use Web 2.0 tools to engage their employees and to create communities where they didn't previously exist. At Cisco, our directory of more than 65,000 employees is being enhanced so that it can be searched not by just by name but by area of expertise or personal interest. Employees can create profiles stating their skill sets, their hobbies, and just about anything they care about. One employee's profile ranged from "email authentication" to "Duke basketball." Using those profile tags, other employees looking for technical assistance or fellow fans can find them. Our CEO was one of the first to create a profile.

These examples are just a taste of what is in store in Krishna Sankar's lively journey through the Web 2.0 world. The goal of this book is to shine some light on Web 2.0 and the changes it is ushering in, as well as to offer some ideas and strategies to help you and your business make the most of it. At Cisco, we have leveraged Web 2.0–enabled technologies and Web 2.0–related practices to increase productivity, accelerate innovation, and retool basic business processes for greater efficiency and faster decision-making. Susan has some good highlights on our internal activities. But you don't have to work for a large enterprise to want to understand Web 2.0. The lines between consumers and business are blurring as the digital generation comes of age, and Web 2.0 is going to touch you almost regardless of who you are or what you do.

Don A. Proctor
Senior Vice-President, Software Group
Cisco Systems, Inc.
References:

[1]Facebook stat source: http://www.facebook.com/press/info.php?statistics

[2]YouTube stat source: http://mediatedcultures.net/ksudigg/?p=163

Forward from David Bernstein

To appreciate the significance and breadth of the term "Web 2.0," one has to ponder at first, just what was "Web 1.0," and more significantly, "Internet 1.0" before that? Many people rightfully trace the roots of the Internet back to 1961, when Leonard Kleinrock from MIT wrote the first paper on packet-switching theory. Others point to 1966 and 1967 when the first ARPANET plans were made and design meetings were held. From there, the progress of actually building a network was pretty rapid, from the original four hosts (UCLA, SRI, UCSB, and the University of Utah) on the ARPANET in 1969 to the development of TCP in 1974 by Vint Cerf and Bob Kahn, and to technologies such as DNS in 1984—the year that the number of hosts exceeded 1,000—to 1991, which in my opinion, is really the birth date for Web 1.0.

In 1991, collaboration became a key part of the Internet, with, on the one hand, the formation of the Commercial Internet eXchange (CIX), and on the other hand, the release of the client and server technologies of the World Wide Web (WWW), released by CERN and as authored by Tim Berners-Lee.

The CIX allowed various carriers of TCP traffic to exchange traffic carried by one network but destined for another. Because the CIX was designed around Layer 3 and 4 interoperability, any application using TCP and IP traffic could now view the "Internet" as one large, interconnected, *collaboration-ready* platform.

The introduction of the browser, which could talk to many web servers on the same page, and the web server, which could serve up content and formatting instructions to several browsers at once, was just what the new substructure needed.

What is interesting about the coincidence of these two key technologies is that they are so different and yet so interdependent. CIX was, essentially, one router; the WWW browser and server, otoh, was software, which ran on client workstations and UNIX servers, respectively. Without coordination from the routing layer to the server layer to the client layer, the collaboration system we call "Web 1.0" could never have technically existed. There is an interconnected and interdependent relationship between the networking infrastructure and the enabling upper-layer software far more fundamental than the sockets interface definition, which many engineers would point out.

It is not a coincidence that the WWW technologies were introduced to the world at the same time that the global commercial Internet became interconnected. Collaboration is a top-to-bottom driving phenomena which, in 1991, through the curious combination of the router, the web server, and the browser, gave us "Web 1.0."

As the tremendous pace of innovation around the Internet continues, and the phenomena known as "Web 2.0" has come upon us, the fundamental parallelism and interdependence of technologies across all layers—from the network router all the way up to server-and-user-experience-software—has not changed. This explains both why Cisco is in the Web 2.0 business in the first place, and why Krishna has taken the time to write about the breadth and depth of this phenomenon and connect all these dots for us.

From his vantage point as a Distinguished Engineer in the Software Group, Krishna has been connecting these dots for the company for some time. Here in the Software Group, which consists of approximately 7,500 full time employees, we produce everything from the embedded operating system that powers our routers and switches, to the management systems that configure and control those networks, to the systems that implement voice and telephony over the networks, to the web-based meetings and "groupware" software you know as WebEx. From this background, Krishna sorts through all the misinformation and misunderstandings about Web 2.0 to deliver a comprehensive eagle-eye view of how the network has enabled breathtaking new ways for people to live, work, play, and learn.

Follow Krishna and Susan as your guides to this interesting journey as they take you from blogs, wikis, meetings, clouds, and all sorts of Web 2.0 technologies that are living, breathing examples of thinking about collaboration from the full stack of networking to the user experience. I know as an executive here in Cisco that Krishna has been invaluable to me and my peers as a guiding light in this exciting journey. I am hopeful that you will take away both a deep understanding of the Web 2.0 phenomena as well as an understanding of why Web 2.0 is our "bet the company" strategy!

David Bernstein
VP and General Manager, Software Group
Cisco Systems, Inc.

Introduction

In studying and/or promoting web-technology, the phrase Web 2.0 can refer to a perceived second generation of web-based communities and hosted services—such as social-networking sites, wikis, and folksonomies—which aim to facilitate creativity, collaboration, and sharing between users. The term gained currency following the first O'Reilly Media Web 2.0 conference in 2004. Although the term suggests a new version of the World Wide Web, it does not refer to an update to any technical specifications, but to changes in the ways software developers and end-users use the web.

—Wikipedia

The emergence of Web 2.0 isn't tied to a specific technology or tool. It's a collection of advanced capabilities growing out of technologies such as Java, Ajax, and specialized markup languages that simplify sharing and repurposing of web content. These rich and interactive features change the web experience in notable ways:

- They allow users to participate without regard to geography

- They democratize information

- They allow new ideas, products, and features to emerge

The change in the nature of how content is created and these next-generation features are ushering in new opportunities for marketing, customer service, business intelligence, and internal communication. Web 2.0 is perhaps most evident in the consumer marketplace with social networking sites, mash ups, and video sharing services. This is the "play" part of Web 2.0. But this collaborative technology will make huge advances in the business effectiveness with online collaborative tools.

Just as users play a key role in a consumer-based Web 2.0 world of blogs, wikis, communities, and collaboration, they, and the content they create, are critical to the success of Web 2.0 in business as well. Blogs, for example, are changing the marketing landscape and provide an exciting new way to gain valuable customer feedback. Wikis create valuable enterprise knowledge management assets, enabling improved customer service. Bookmarking and folksonomies enable an organization to share information and to define and tag content in ways that facilitate and accelerate search and retrieval. Photos and videos make content more visual, more personal, and more human. They can also become a valuable business asset: a customer video testimonial from a known expert helps sell product.

Web 2.0 technologies enable more effective collaboration and knowledge-sharing, improve decision-making, and accelerate productivity and problem-solving among employees, partners, and customers. Collaborative technologies are key enablers, increasing productivity and reducing travel time and expense. More importantly, collaborative technologies enable business managers to re-engineer and transform their business function, department, or process to reap the business value Web 2.0 and the Mobile Web can enable.

Goals, Objectives, and Approach

A little into the writing of the book, we realized that Web 2.0 is very vast and could fill a thousand-page book! So our challenge was to see what areas we should leave out to cut through the hyperbole, the hype, the billion dollar valuations, and the security threats and still provide the readers with an introduction to the social and business characteristics of Web 2.0 as well as a glimpse of the technologies behind it.

Another challenge we had was to get the right level of detail on the topics we selected. We wanted this book to be not a guided tour but a hitchhiking experience, where sometimes the stops are quick (as in a quick look at UI or wikis), sometimes the detours linger longer (such as in social networking and cloud computing), and sometimes you need to dig deeper via the hundreds of links and references to experience the inner details.

Many of you already have some exposure to various pieces of Web 2.0, but few have a full appreciation for all the vectors of Web 2.0. In this book, we aim to provide a cohesive, coherent view of both the underlying technologies and the potential applications to bring readers up to speed and spark creative ideas about how to apply Web 2.0.

This book does not have ROI calculations or project plans. It also does not rely on extensive code fragments or programming aspects. The major challenge we faced was of omission rather than inclusion. We had to find those key pieces of Web 2.0 that would make an enterprise tick.

An complete understanding of Web 2.0 does not come just from reading a book. One has to also experience the various collaborative formats that make up Web 2.0 by creating an account in facebook.com, developing a wiki, or reading a blog about some topics of interest, or better yet by writing a blog or participating in a collaboration-based wiki.

Who Should Read This Book?

The primary target audience is anyone who has a need to understand Web 2.0 technologies. This includes program managers, marketing managers, business analysts, IT analysts, and so on, who either have to market Web 2.0 or understand enough to engage in Web 2.0 systems development. The audience also includes executives, in any field, who need to understand the Web 2.0 phenomenon.

A secondary audience is the engineers who are working on traditional legacy systems and who want to understand the opportunities Web 2.0 brings. They need an in-depth conceptual view to see how everything fits and also an evaluation of the hottest technologies.

This book does not assume any special knowledge other than general computer literacy and an awareness of the Internet and the web.

Strategies for Experiencing Web 2.0

Using Web 2.0 is like swimming: You cannot really learn it or in this case understand it by standing on the land; you need to immerse yourself in it. We have included many reference URLs to visit that will give you more in-depth information on various aspects of Web 2.0. We urge you to visit these URLs. They are listed in the appendix. You can find an electronic version of the appendix, with all the URLs conveniently hot linked, at the book's website. Keep in mind that because of the dynamic nature of the web, some links might no longer function depending on when you are reading this book.

Enterprise Web 2.0 Fundamentals Companion Website

You can find the book's companion website at http://www.ciscopress.com/title/1587057638.

How This Book Is Organized

Although you can read any chapter alone and get a full understanding of that particular aspect of Web 2.0, we recommend you read Chapter 1, "An Introduction to Web 2.0," which outlines Web 2.0 and gives you an overview of Web 2.0 that should enable you to see how the pieces fit together. After you have a good feel of the various elements that make up the world of Web 2.0, you are free to roam around! But please make sure, at the end, you do visit all the chapters to get an idea of all that Web 2.0 entails. And poke through the URLs listed in the appendix to get a full Web 2.0 experience.

The following is a summary of each chapter:

- Chapter 1, "An Introduction to Web 2.0," is the starting point. It details the various aspects—business and technology—of Web 2.0 and sets the stage for the rest of the book.

- Chapter 2, "User-Generated Content: Wikis, Blogs, Communities, Collaboration, and Collaborative Technologies," describes the importance of the user and user-generated content in a Web 2.0 world. It identifies how blogs, wikis, communities, collaboration, and collaborative technologies are creating business value.

- Chapter 3, "Rich Internet Applications: Practices, Technologies, and Frameworks," describes the essential technologies and business implications behind rich user interfaces and interactions.

- Chapter 4, "Social Networking," details the multi-dimensional aspects of social networking—business value, opportunities, and technologies—from Facebook to Twitter and from standards to offerings from the big enterprise players.

- Chapter 5, "Content Aggregation, Syndication, and Federation via RSS and Atom," is about the two-way interactions of Web 2.0, including the capability to collect and publish individual contributions via RSS feeds and Atom.

- Chapter 6, "Web 2.0 Architecture Case Studies," looks at the most successful web applications like Twitter, eBay, Amazon, and Google and talks about the infrastructure and architecture aspects of Web 2.0 from a development perspective. Web 2.0 definitely has a new feel for application interfaces, protocols, distributability, and scalability.

- Chapter 7, "Tending to Web 3.0: The Semantic Web," describes one of the most important next-generation web technologies: the Semantic Web. An introduction to this concept is followed by details of the various aspects of the Semantic Web.

- Chapter 8, "Cloud Computing," details a very important development that has lasting impact: cloud computing. This chapter looks into the business practices and the technology stacks that make up the domain of cloud computing.

- Chapter 9, "Web 2.0 and Mobility," focuses on the evolution of Mobile Web technology and examines generations of mobile phone services. The chapter touches on a number of mobile devices and key mobility features, such as voice recognition and position location. It provides examples of the types of Mobile Web services available today and identifies Cisco's efforts to create Mobile Web applications, particularly in sales.

Chapters 10 and 11 provide a set of Cisco case studies of Web 2.0 technology adoption:

- Chapter 10, "Web 2.0 @ Cisco: The Evolution," describes the evolution of Web 2.0 technologies at Cisco Systems, Inc. It provides basic steps and best practices for leveraging blogs, discussion forums, and wikis based on Cisco experience.

- Chapter 11, "Cisco's Approach to Sales 2.0," focuses on how Web 2.0 is changing the selling process and how Cisco Sales is leveraging Web 2.0 technology to transform how it does business through more effective communities, collaboration, and collaborative technologies.

\<monologue\>

When we proposed this book, Web 2.0 (and the Web 2.0 society) was very young—cloud computing was not even in the public consciousness, investment banking was still a profession, and social networking was still mainly a teenager's place. Times have changed since 2007. And though things are changing rapidly because of the nature of ideas and technologies and their implementation, this book does provide solid information on the fundamentals and themes of Web 2.0 from which you can dive in. With that in mind let us begin the journey I call "A Hitchhiker's Guide to Web 2.0 Enterprise Edition." But don't panic! Of course the official title is "Enterprise Web 2.0 Fundamentals."

\</monologue\>

CHAPTER 1

An Introduction to Web 2.0

This chapter starts out by introducing Web 2.0 across a set of multi-dimensional aspects: social, business, and technological. It goes through the Web X.0 generations, including their salient characteristics and transition points, and describes the challenges of Web 2.0 EE (Enterprise Edition) versus Web 2.0 CE (Consumer Edition). The chapter then proceeds to summarize the nine characteristics that define the locus and trajectory of Web 2.0. The chapter ends by sharing some of the agonies and ecstasies of the Web 2.0 journey at Cisco. All of these introductions provide the basis for more detailed discussions of these and other topics in the chapter to come.

What Exactly Is This Web 2.0 and Why Should We Care About It?

Most people, at one time or another, have questioned the wisdom and the hype behind Web 2.0, because there is really no precise definition of Web 2.0. It is almost impossible to define Web 2.0 without hand waving and a lot of animation. So how can you tell whether it is hype or real, and more important, what parts of it are important to your enterprise and what parts of it would be employed by your competitors?

The following is a brief introductory list of what Web 2.0 is. This chapter and the rest of the book go on to develop these themes further with examples and narratives as they progress:

- Web 2.0 is a convergence of social and business practices rather than a technology transition. In fact, many of the technologies that make up the Web 2.0 substrate were developed during the early 90s.

- Although Web 1.0 was mainly brochure-ware with data being published by companies, the data flow in Web 2.0 is both ways. In fact, the user-generated content such as blogs, wikis, and video have surpassed the amount of data created by enterprises and media companies.
  Another aspect of user-generated content is analytics—what people look at, what they select, what they bring together—and the capability to derive inferences from these analytics. The inferences then add to the user experience in areas such as movie recommendations, book recommendations, up-selling, and cross-selling of products.

- Web 2.0 has an element of rich user experience enabled by web applications developed using technologies termed as RIA (Rich Internet Applications).

- An important and sustaining element of Web 2.0 is social networking as well as the development of communities.

Although a short definition is difficult, the impact of Web 2.0 on the society is not. From the 2008 presidential election to the way enterprises make money to the judicial system, Web 2.0 has made its mark and is continuing to do so as the following examples illustrate:

- The U.S. presidential campaign of 2008 will be remembered as marking the evolution of social networks into the popular culture as a change agent. "The Facebooker Who Friended Obama" cries *The New York Times* and says "The campaign's new-media strategy, inspired by popular social networks such as MySpace and Facebook, has revolutionized the use of the web as a political tool,"[1] As Marc Andreessen observed,[2] the Obama campaign successfully employed the social networking approach and philosophy as the engine for fundraising as well as volunteer coordination.

- Social networking, which is an important part of Web 2.0, also is playing a crucial part in the judicial system. In "Web Networking Photos Come Back to Bite Defendants" ABC News[3] reports how a defendant got harsher sentencing after the judge viewed photos from a party in Facebook. "The pictures, when shown at sentencing, not only embarrass defendants but also can make it harder for them to convince a judge that they're remorseful or that their drunken behavior was an aberration."

- User-generated content, such as blogs, are an integral part of Web 2.0, and bloggers have started to be treated like news reporters. *The New York Times* says "The year of the political blogger has arrived."[4] It seems the Democratic and Republican conventions issued credentials to bloggers, invited them to attend the conventions, and one even had an 8,000 square foot two-story tent with wireless coverage! Moreover, the credentials included access and coverage like that of traditional media—even work with state delegations with unlimited floor coverage! "D.N.C. organizers said the recipients of these credentials were chosen by looking at the posts and mission statements of the competing blogs, and at the traffic these sites generated." In short, like newspaper circulation, blog traffic is a measure of the power of the press—er...the digital press!

As the examples illustrate, Web 2.0 is a phenomenon, and it is not solely a technological one, but has social and business aspects as well, as it turns out (more, later in this chapter). That fact needs to be understood and leveraged, in our work, life, play, and in between!

A Word About References and Links in this Book
Although the chapters provide thorough explanations and examples to illustrate Web 2.0, to get a true feel for Web 2.0 you should also *experience* it. Also, unlike other domains, there are tons of reference materials at various sites that we referred to write the chapters. We struggled with how to handle the numerous links, without which the book would not be complete. We could have omitted them, but then you would not be able to get more details as quickly on interesting topics at hand or have a sort of guided tour of the Web 2.0 world. So we included all the links. In fact, the "Resources" appendix has a compilation of all of the links, references, and resources by chapter. We urge you to explore these links to bring the concepts presented in this book to life.

Each reference in a bracketed number points to the corresponding information in the appendix. If you are reading the PDF version of this chapter, the bracketed numbers are hyperlinked to the resource for your convenience.

The term *Web 2.0* was coined by Dale Dougherty[5] and it stuck as a moniker. In fact, "Web 2.0" was the most cited term in Wikipedia in 2006.[6,7] Some of the best reading on Web 2.0 is Tim O'Reilly's pioneering article "What is Web 2.0?"[5] Among many insightful concepts in that article, what struck me as the most relevant to the application of Web 2.0 in enterprises are the transitory trends from Web 1.0 to 2.0, such as from "personal web sites to blogging" and from "publishing to participation".

If we want to understand the relevance and context of Web 2.0, we have to understand it through its roots—the blogsphere. Let us hitchhike through the blogsphere, seek out insightful definitions, analyze them, and also explore whether they give us an insight into the future:

- Rich McManus[8] writes quoting Nova Spivack, that "Web 2.0 is a decade not a technology...more about defining the character of each era, rather than trying to define a web era as a set of technologies..." [9] and offers the categorizations Web 2.0 = social, 3.0 = Intelligent Web and 4.0 as AI.

- The O'Reilly Report[10] offers the definition, "Web 2.0 is a set of economic, social, and technology trends that collectively form the basis for the next generation of the Internet—a more mature, distinctive medium characterized by user participation, openness, and network effects."

- A Gartner report says[11] Web 2.0 "...refers to a set of technology, community, and business models that characterize today's leading websites."

In short, Web 2.0 is defined by its *enablement*, not by its technologies. Web 2.0 gives a new frame of reference to the Internet, a new tone if you will, beyond just technologies—one of new business models, economic models, and social models defined by usage and participation and supported by appropriate technologies.

The following sections leave the technology aside and take a quick look at the societal and business impacts and Web 2.0's role in those aspects of life. Naturally the rest of the book will take a deeper look at the practices and technologies behind these realms of Web 2.0, with a focus on the enterprise.

Social Aspects of Web 2.0

Two classic examples that show how Web 2.0 has influenced the social and political arena can be found in the United States and in the United Kingdom.

The U.S. presidential election of 2008 proved to be a show of the influence of Web 2.0 artifacts in many ways, from social networking to unprecedented donations via the web to YouTube videos affecting the way information (and misinformation) is produced and consumed. "Online media changes political landscapes" says MSNBC[12] and claims "Obama's campaign is, in many ways, the quintessential "YouTube" operation." Barack

Obama continues to be adept in leveraging the web. In fact, he announced his vice presidential pick via text message at 3:00 a.m. And you could have registered to get his text message as shown in Figure 1-1.

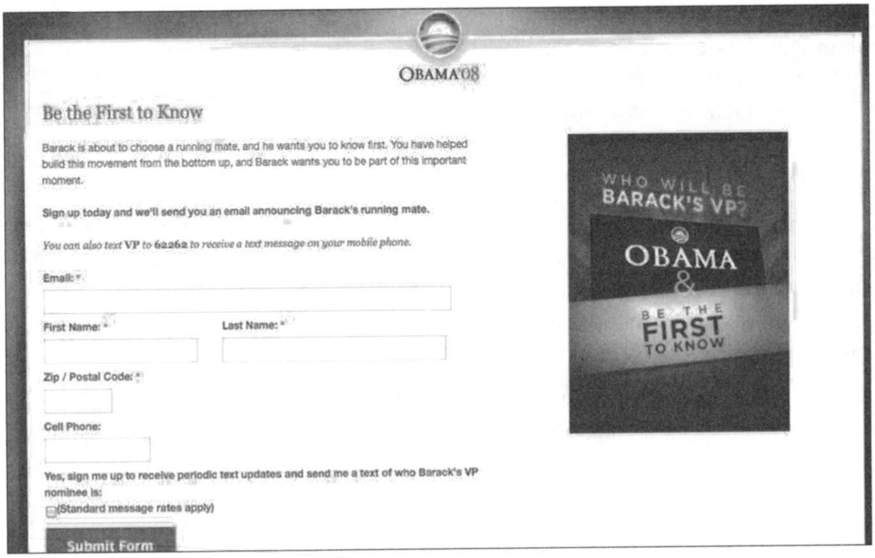

Figure 1-1   *Register to get Obama's VP pick by text.*

In the United Kingdom Lords of the Blog is a good example of Web 2.0's positive influence on governing. Slashdot reports[13] that the House of Lords have launched YouTube videos to communicate with the young generation. They also have a blog in Wordpress,[14] as shown in Figure 1-2. The Lords of the Blog is interesting because it is not a promotion by a political party, but is being chaperoned by the Hansard Society[15] (an independent, non-partisan society to promote democracy) and declares "Each Member will make a regular and short written entry providing an insight into the business of the House of Lords, and their own particular activity in and around the Lords Chamber." It is working; there are lots of interesting blogs from the members of the house.

A perfect, if not unfortunate, business example of Web 2.0's influence on the society is what happened to UAL stock on September 9, 2008.[16] The Google news bot picked up an old story (2002) about UAL being at the verge of bankruptcy. The story that prompted a selloff of UAL stock and then it was blogged many times in investor and other blogs, bringing down the stock to $3 from $12, a loss of $1.14 billion. Eventually the stock recovered to $10, still permanently wiping out $300 million—for no justifiable reason!

Business Aspects of Web 2.0

Social networking, even though it is a heavily consumer-oriented artifact, can be leveraged by businesses in a spectrum of ways, including interactions during research and development to communities, blogs for service and support, marketing activities to the web crowd, and for internal productivity. As pointed out by Nitin Karandikar in an excellent blog,[17]

Figure 1-2   *Lords of the Blog.*

other forces and trends are in the play as well. Generational shifts as well as the expectation from informed customers (and employees) create an imperative to embrace and extend the Web 2.0 paradigms inside modern corporations. Of course, there are challenges in adapting primarily consumer technologies—security, relevance, and compliance being the primary ones. So there is a balance somewhere. A *PC World* interview talks about how companies should avoid the "Kumbaya Zone—the place where social media is ultimately a time-waster and has little business value"[57] and focus on beneficial interactions like the use of Twitter by Comcast to improve customer service. Many believe that the floodgates are already open,[18] resistance (from corporate IT folks) is futile, and it is better to join the crowd and find ways of enabling and profiting from the Web 2.0 phenomenon.

A good example of how a company is successfully employing Web 2.0 consumer participation concepts is the Salesforce IdeaExchange. Salesforce IdeaExchange is a community engagement[19] vehicle to solicit and prioritize the various feature sets that SalesForce.com should be adding to its services. (By the way, SalesForce.com is a cloud/SaaS—software as a service—offering. You'll learn more about those Web 2.0 concepts later in this chapter and throughout the book.) The Salesforce IdeaExchange (see Figure 1-3) site has capabilities to post an idea, discuss posted ideas as a community, and vote for ideas that one is passionate about. The interesting observation about the IdeaExchange is that it enables the company to engage its users at the research and development stage of its product Salesforce.com as the users are voting for features that could be incorporated in future versions of the product.

Figure 1-3   *Salesforce.com IdeaExchange.*

The benefit is that now the user community is engaged even before development of features. This is a classic Web 2.0 concept of participation and user-generated content that has multiple advantages, including a better product management strategy and greater ability to acquire and keep enthusiastic users. Moreover, because the ideas are hosted in a public forum[20] and voted on by users, popular ideas will move up the stack, making it easy and effective for product management to prioritize feature sets. This is Web 2.0 EE at its best—businesses leveraging community, user-generated content, collaboration, and the human network. They even have T-shirts (see Figure 1-4) for folks whose ideas were incorporated into Salesforce.com!

In ideas under construction, Salesforce actually gives users a "first-hand insight into what ideas we are considering on our roadmap over the next twelve months," a "most accurate and timely snapshot of where we are focusing our energy this year."[19] How poetic—a company whose products focus on sales, executing perfectly on the sales management of their own products!

Their Web 2.0 offers don't stop there. Salesforce is offering the IdeaExchange infrastructure as a service (see Figure 1-5), which companies like Starbucks are using to launch their own IdeaExchange[21] called myStarbucks Idea, as shown in Figure 1-6.

MyStarbucks Idea is an excellent example of how Web 2.0 is succeeding in building a multi-dimensional community by an enterprise around its products. The myStarbucks idea not only enables employees and users to suggest new product ideas, but also the

Figure 1-4   *The Salesforce.com IdeaExchange T-shirt for user participation.*

Figure 1-5   *Salesforce.com IdeaExchange as an SaaS Offering.*

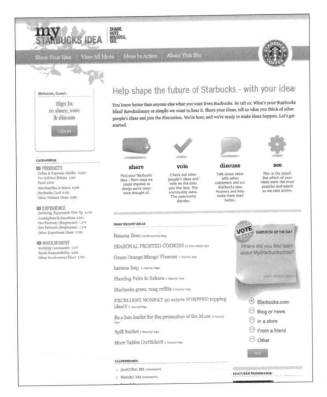

Figure 1-6 *Starbucks hosts myStarbucks Idea.*

community covers a wide range of ideas such as experiences (like ordering and payment, atmosphere, location, and employees) as well as community involvement issues such as social responsibility. They also have polling and previews of new products.

Web 2.0 is not kind to all industries and many industries will have a hard time responding to the Web 2.0 way. The blog "Responding to Disruptive Innovation: Threat or Opportunity?"[22,23] has a good view of the Web 2.0 technologies and the response from established industries.

One industry that is reeling from the Web 2.0 technologies is the newspaper industry. The article "How Newspapers Tried to Invent the Web and Failed"[24] is a good read on the challenges the newspaper industry faces and their responses. One would then assume that all newspaper companies would suffer. Not so, says the blog. For example, *The New York Times* is leveraging the Web 2.0 paradigm successfully whereas *The Washington Post* doesn't get it. For example, as of July 2008 *The Washington Post's* website mirrored its printed page while *The New York Times* had more Web 2.0 native capabilities such as thread, presence, Twitter, and blogs. This brings out an important aspect of Web 2.0 EE: Just putting on a façade of Web 2.0 is not enough to expect return; companies must restructure and reengineer the back-end business processes and innovate on business models. During the 2008 presidential campaign I frequented *The Caucus New York Times* live blog. I visited the live blog[25] to "view" the first 2008 presidential debate, where *The New York Times* provided not only live blogging but live streaming as well. And the debate video, in its entirety or as highlights, was available at *The New York Times* site to be viewed anytime. This is Web 2.0 participatory publishing(via blogs and videos) working its magic.

As the newspaper industry continues to be threatened by the web technologies, the radio industry is in the same predicament. NPR has an antidote: social networking. SMN reports[26] that "National Public Radio is boosting its digital ambitions in search of larger and younger audiences, beginning with—(the) introduction of social-networking features akin to Facebook." The insights from NPR folks are illustrative of the challenges and power of Web 2.0: "...these digital initiatives are aimed at capturing and retaining audiences—particularly younger people who aren't habitual radio listeners but who represent the future for fundraising at NPR's member stations" and "...to be realistic, the Internet is a fast-moving place. That makes everybody nervous on one level, and everyone sees new opportunities on another." NPR is also providing APIs[27] (Application Program Interfaces) to their content—music, artists, programs, bios, columns and series—as far back as 1995, so that developers can create mashups and facilitate interfacing with iPods and widgets. Who would have thought of Web 2.0 APIs from NPR? Well, when it starts affecting your donor base, things happen fast.

Another enterprise example is the A-space and Intellipedia hosted by the intelligence community. In an article (shown in Figure 1-7) titled "SpySpace or Faceless Book," the San Jose Mercury News talks about how the intelligence community is developing a classified A-Space, which will have blogs and a Wikipedia-like site called Intellipedia, as well as searchable databases.

Although it is comforting to note that even the CIA has problems in common with those mere mortals involved with corporations, it is also a little unsettling to see CIA embracing social networking—even if it is a faceless book. Of course, on second thought, this is not that far off; leveraging consumer technologies makes a lot of sense considering the scale of information management and collaboration the agencies have to perform. But be careful if you are poking somebody in the faceless book.

Web 2.0 Versions and Generations

Although you could simply dismiss the web versioning system, there is a method to its madness. In fact, each version has very specific and salient characteristics and the transition points become very clear. It helps to look at the generations of the web from an evolutionary perspective and not see Web 2.0 as one single web, but many smaller, evolutionary webs. Although there is certainly always room for debate, this section gives you a 30,000 foot view and examination of the versions.

The web technologies have matured from α-stage to β-stage, in the early stages, and then thru versions 1.0, 1.5, and finally 2.0. Many suggest that Web 3.0 is also a legitimate version. The general consensus is that the semantic web is Web 3.0, and this is covered later in the book.

One can cut it in many ways, but thus far there are three distinct stages of the web: 1.0, 1.5, 2.0. We could even call it Web, Web Reloaded, and Web Revolutions as the Matrix

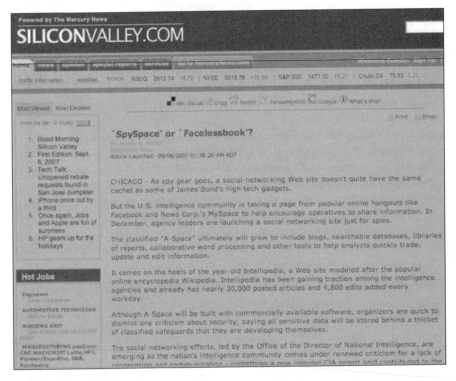

Figure 1-7 *Web 2.0 in the intelligence community—A-space or faceless book.*

movies did. A good depiction of the growth of the Internet is shown in the website "The 50 Most Significant Moments of Internet History."[28]

Each version of the web has its own expectations and beliefs, as shown in Table 1-1.

Table 1-1 *Definitions, Beliefs, and Expectations of Web Versions*

Generation	Examples
Web 1.0	Dancing bears
	Static brochureware
Web 1.5	eBay
	Amazon (first generation)
Web 2.0	Waltzing bears
	Google, YouTube
	Facebook, MySpace
	Amazon (second generation), Netflix
Web 3.0	Bears that know your favorite dance

Table 1-1   *Definitions, Beliefs, and Expectations of Web Versions*

Generation	Examples
	Semantic web

The first incarnation of the web was akin to dancing bears: it is not how well they dance, but the fact that they can dance itself is novel enough. This version of the web, dubbed Web 1.0 after the fact, involved mostly static brochure-ware types of applications, which were very useful by themselves. There were few dynamic capabilities, very little context, and almost no interactivity. Moreover, the websites did not leverage the intelligence inferences from the user interactions.

Then came the Web 1.5 era of electronic commerce, with sites such as eBay and first generation of Amazon. One could not only buy books, toys, and a whole host of other things online, but also auction any surplus. The reason for the 1.5 version moniker is that other than the commerce layer, the rest of the web was still relatively static. Of course, during the end of the 1.5 era, companies such as eToys and WebVan came into existence—you could get groceries on the web, how interesting—and then disappeared, creating the Internet bubble and the inevitable burst. As the site "The 50 Most Significant Moments of Internet History"[28] points out, the defining moments of Web 1.0/1.5 were the beginnings of Yahoo! (1994), Amazon, and eBay (1995), and the merger of AOL and Time Warner (2000).

In both the stages, Web 1.0 and Web 1.5, the technologies were pretty straightforward: HTML rendering with backend servers doing transaction-level processing. By this time, the Internet bubble came and went, and the web started becoming a bona fide application platform. Even more important, it started attracting lots of repeat dedicated users. Improvements in User Interface (UI) technologies like AJAX, the increase in speed of computers, and the strides in bandwidth and connectivity ushered in the era of Web 2.0. Now the bears can waltz, or the other way round: If the bears are not waltzing, the users are not interested anymore. We need search, we need intelligent inferences, we need interactivity, we need speed, we need rich multimedia; all characteristics of Web 2.0. Now we not only want to buy stuff, but also want to read all the 1-star reviews as well as see what others who bought similar items also bought. We want to keep a wish list, we want to set up and manage invite lists electronically, we want to meet folks who will be at the city we visit, we want to share our photos, our thoughts, our ideas, we want to debate about politics, we want to keep a list of movies to watch, we want to communicate with companies about what they should make—and all online, of course. This where the web is now; this is Web 2.0. And notice that although none of this is defined by any particular technology, a host of technologies are behind it. As the site "The 50 Most Significant Moments of Internet History"[28] points out, the defining moments of Web 2.0 are the launching of JavaScript, weblog, Blogger, Wikipedia, and Digg—most of which are related to user-generated content.

Of course, the technology is not static; neither is the social and business progress. Web 3.0 is the next frontier that holds the age of intelligent information and the semantic web (covered in more detail in Chapter 7, "Tending to Web 3.0: The Semantic Web"). In Web 2.0, context and meaning are still externalized in the programs, servers, and protocols; the data still is pretty much anemic in terms of meaning. In the case of Web 3.0, when powered by semantic web technologies, the data will be annotated with meaning, context, and most important, the relationship with other data.

The transition is slowly happening. For example, you can code geocode your pictures and keep the information, as annotation, with the photos in Flickr. This enables others to see the photo from a geographical context, for example in a map. One can click the Fisherman's Wharf in Google Maps and get to pictures others have downloaded in Flickr! In another example, the popularity of the web also has created challenges that the semantic web might help us face. One just has to search for something to see the thousands of links returned. It takes a lot of time just to get to the right information and many times the right information is buried so deep that one misses it. This is where Web 3.0 artifacts such as semantic search and different methods of navigation come into the picture. Web 3.0 promises to improve on the data layer with better search, bigger distributed databases, intelligent search across multimedia, improved conversation between applications, and more mobility capability.[29,30,31]

A good insight into the evolution of the web is to track popular sites across a span of years, as Forbes did[32] from 2005 to 2008. This list has lots of information (about user-clicks and time spent in sites as well as the appearances, moves, and drops of the top 20 sites), which provokes a multitude of insights and inferences. A few quick observations and trends relevant to us from the context of web versions are

- The rise of user-generated content as evident from Wikipedia (ranked 57th in 2005 to 9th in 2008), YouTube (ranked 6th in 2008), and blogger (ranked 12th in 2008).

- The "maturing" of social networking from a teen phenomenon to mainstream as Facebook climbed from 236th in 2005 to 16th in 2008 while the teen social network MySpace went down from 18th in 2005 to near 25th in 2008.

- Increasing use of the Internet as a part of normal living activities, as evident by Craigslist coming in at 20th in 2008, and Ask, About, Weather, and eBay all still in the top 20 ranks in 2008. Moreover, there is tremendous increase in the number of people visiting all the top 20 sites and users spend more time there.

Web 2.0 CE Versus EE

From the beginning, Web 2.0 found its roots in the consumer space, be they social networking in the schools and universities (and found acceptance among the teenage population) or sharing videos and photographs or even multimedia sites for movies and music videos. This is the Web 2.0 Consumer Edition (CE).

At the same time, enterprises are realizing that many applications require the use of Web 2.0 practices, such as forming a community of users for sharing ideas, supporting existing products, marketing to the new web savvy crowd, or even increasing internal productivity. Although there are "cool" applications in the Web 2.0 CE space, they are also less secure and lack enterprise-grade controls for compliance and regulatory requirements. Also the architecture and the development practices of the Web 2.0 CE applications are different from established enterprise development practices. Moreover, the enablement of new business models, and the desire and need to innovate, cut costs, connect with customers, improve efficiency and productivity—in other words, business drivers, rather than "cool" interfaces—will and must pull Web 2.0 into the enterprise. In short, Web 2.0 Enterprise Edition is the application and an adaption of the Web 2.0 Consumer Edition.

Web Generations and People Generations

An interesting observation is the relation between generations of people and the web generations. In fact, there is a correlation between the perception and acceptance of technology and generations.

The technologies we grow up with until around 20 years of age are natural to us. They are common and we know how to use them simply because of ubiquity. We do not even "see" them. More importantly we expect them to be available in all parts of our life—during work, play, learning, and all times in between. Generally from 20–40 we have a fascination when we encounter new technologies. If they serve a need we will and usually can learn them fairly easily. After 40, new technologies can become unnatural to the point that often we would rather not deal with them if older options are still available. Of course, there are always exceptions.

One important consequence of this insight is that as the work place is increasingly represented by a new technology generation, the tools and interactions need to dramatically change too. In fact, there are observations about Generation Y[33] that say that the digital native—who is social-networking savvy, socially conscious about issues on politics, the environment, and the like—will need tools in the workplace that mirror the apps they are already used to when they join the work force. And because they are natural with tools like social networking, media, and the rest, they can get business done in the same way. The business drivers create a need for Web 2.0 EE, and the fact that younger employees and customers will embrace this will make the change management easier, but they will not be the sole reason to cause the adoption of Web 2.0 EE.

One challenge of Web 2.0 CE that enterprises need to solve is that there is too much of it. There are many choices[34] and competing services. For example, there are at least five top social networks (Facebook, MySpace, bebo, LinkedIn, and hi5), multiple news rating sites (like Digg and reddit), and many RSS feed sites. Even Twitter has many clones.[35,36] But in an enterprise world, although the capabilities like social networking, news readers, and rating services are essential, only one or two in each category would be enough. Or better yet, an aggregator that monitors the sites with the capability to summarize and interact with the respective sites as needed would be effective. For example, if a marketing person wants to get an idea of the appropriate people in various organizations, a syndicator program could show a combined result—which is much more efficient than a bunch of marketing folks churning through the public sites.

One good way to get a view of the best applications in the consumer space is to look at the Webware 100 winners, as voted on by Internet users.[21] The categories include audio, commerce, browsing, e-commerce, communication, and productivity. The winners in 2008 include Google Maps, Twitter, Facebook, Blogger, Drupal, and Wikipedia.

Enterprises have successfully incorporated structures and primitives from the Web 2.0 Consumer Edition into the Web 2.0 Enterprise Edition. From the intelligence community embracing social networking[37] to the Salesforce IdeaExchange, there are lots of successful stories. When looking at the relevance of Web 2.0 technologies, one also needs to consider their stage in the emerging technology evolution. One tool you can use to evaluate the stage of an emerging technology is known as the Gartner Hype Cycle.[38]

In the Gartner 2008 Emerging Technology Hype Cycle, although Web 2.0 itself is going through a disillusionment stage (showing they fail to meet the high expectations they have created), technologies such as wikis and social network analysis are becoming stable; technologies such as cloud computing and social networking platforms are developing.

Challenges to Web 2.0 EE Adoption

Web 2.0 technologies are not without major challenges—security, privacy, and compliance to name a few important ones. For example, Forbes[39] talks about how because of scale, a single vulnerability can create havoc across different sites such as DHS (Department of Homeland Security), the United Nations, and the British government. As a book about fundamentals this book does not go into the security topics of Web 2.0, but after you've used this book to learn the basics you need to move on to robust security resources when implementing Web 2.0 applications. Always be aware of security and privacy issues, as well as the regulatory environment and the contexts in which your company operates. These issues should not be cause to avoid the Web 2.0 paradigm, but one has to build in the appropriate isolation, controls, and policy to be compliant of applicable regulations as well as common best practices and business considerations.

Characteristics and Memes of Web 2.0

If you ask 10 people what the basic characteristics of Web 2.0 are, most probably you will get more than 10 different answers. Eric Schmidt, CEO of Google, has a very interesting answer to the "What is Web 2.0" question, which is of course captured at YouTube.[40] Although the answer is a little imprecise, his points are very valid. According to Schmidt, "Web 2.0 is a different way of building applications" and "future web applications will be relatively small, very fast, with data in the cloud, can run on any device and (are) distributed virally." This is a very different application model with low barriers to entry and developed with new tools based on newer concepts, architectures, and development models. As Tom, our reviewer points out, this definition is all technology and deployment, which is one view.

A good calibration point, to understand the memes, is the state of the Web 2.0 conferences at any given point in time. Even though one shouldn't take the conferences too seriously, the recurring themes and the buzz, at these gatherings of the industry and users, are an indication of the ideas that have captured the mindshare of pragmatic industry applications. Recently we attended the Web 2.0 Expo 2008 in San Francisco. Along with the registration packet was a set of word stickers (see Figure 1-8) you could use to customize your pass and presumably start conversations. Most of the words try to summarize what was considered Web 2.0 at the time. Of course, new domains such as cloud computing have emerged since and are missing from the stickers. It would be instructive to compare this set to next year's words.

Tag your badge holder above your badge with these stickers and get conversations started.

We're hiring Launching soon! Fund us! Hire me!
I'm looking for a I♥ email Ask me about
I'm curious about angel venture capital s your
business model APIs virtual lifestreaming
cloud my computing iPhone reality funding
data portability open source social media
local search widget application frameworks
and tools browser enhancements research
usability the social graph collective intelligence
personal informatics web global design tagging
mashups analytics Asia metrics community
social capital semantic web SEO SMO enterprise
web ops hacker analyst n00b cynic veteran
corporate suit microblogging RSS entrepreneur
social networking mobile web user generated
startup web metrics buzz comics gaming
web viral performance blogs UGC accessibility
lang=(_____) gamer work-life balance
convergence art crowdsourcing Europe music

Figure 1-8 *Badge tags for the Web 2.0 Expo 2008 conference.*

The Web 2.0 meme map, as shown in Figure 1-9, is a good reference[5] on the characteristics of Web 2.0. Ed Yourdon has a set of comprehensive Web 2.0 presentations[41] that cover all aspects of Web 2.0.

Figure 1-9 *Web 2.0 memes.*

Microsoft has a good article[42] that explains Tim O'Reilly's Web 2.0 article. One reason Microsoft's article is interesting is because it appears in the category "Enterprise Architectures, Patterns, and Practices." Whereas Tim[5] talks about the Web 2.0 CE and the Web 2.0 memes point out participation, design, recommendation, and so on, this book's focus is on Web 2.0 EE and you need to understand in a pragmatic way what exactly these higher-level abstractions mean for day-to-day business and systems development. From that perspective, it's time to quickly look at the main characteristics and memes of Web 2.0 EE. The remainder of this section goes into the nine characteristics of Web 2.0:

- User-generated content

- Rich Internet applications (RIA)

- Social networking

- Cloud computing

- Web-centric development and architectural models

- Data

- Mashups

- Scale free and long tail

- Mobility

User-Generated Content

This is the first meme, in that participation and asymmetric two-way contribution are the cornerstones of Web 2.0 architectures and are very relevant to corporations. This includes YouTube videos, blogs, wikis, *pedias, social bookmarking, folksonomies, and social tagging. It also includes the click streams, the interactions with various websites—the ratings one might add, what you buy, what you buy along with what you buy, what you look at before you buy, and even what you watch on your VCR! The click streams become recommendations and inferences when processed through classifiers, clustering systems, Bayesian machines, and other mathematical processing. Chapter 2, "User-Generated Content: Wikis, Blogs, Communities, Collaboration, and Collaborative Technologies," covers these topics in more detail.

Rich Internet Applications (RIA)

Another important characteristic ushered by AJAX and now with tools like Flex from Adobe and Silverlight from Microsoft is the general makeup of the user interface as well as new interactive models. The web user interface (UI) has become more dynamic and multimedia rich as well as responsive. Again, UIs, frameworks, platforms, and even the patterns that are common in the consumer world are very relevant to Web 2.0 Enterprise Edition.

Chapter 3, "Rich Internet Applications: Practices, Technologies, and Frameworks," covers these topics in more detail.

Social Networks

Social networking and social media in general has become the most popular meme of Web 2.0. Web applications such as MySpace and Facebook have become poster children of the Web 2.0 phenomenon. As of February 2009, Facebook has 175 million users and 50% of them visit the site at least once a day. Even more interesting is the fact that many of the users visit the site more than 50 times a day. And as Marc Andreessen[2] points out, with its millions of users, Facebook is equivalent to the sixth most populous country in the world.

Cloud Computing

Cloud computing is a very recent phenomenon and has lasting impacts on how infrastructures are architected, bought, and deployed. In the cloud computing model, compute and storage infrastructures are available to use as a utility rather than only within one's own infrastructure. The utility model extends from just the computer hardware to platform service to complete applications (like CRM) as an external service. One of the more interesting Web 2.0 patterns is the concept of software above devices, which means software that is accessible by all devices all the time; and now with cloud computing, this pattern, extended as "software above an IT shop," is becoming a reality. Cloud computing is a tactical optimization as well as a strategic architectural artifact. It is tactical optimization, because if you have ad-hoc applications that need to run for a certain period of time (like a survey or some analysis), you can run them in a cloud infrastructure like the Amazon EC2. But it is also strategic because now enterprise business stakeholders (and the IT counterparts) can work beyond the constraints of finite compute bandwidth and asset optimization to an era of just-in-time infinite processing power, which is flexible. Chapter 8, "Cloud Computing," has a thorough discussion of cloud computing.

Web-Centric Development and Architectural Models

Web 2.0 ushers in a different class of applications, architectures, and models. This is why I liked Eric Schmidt's comment mentioned earlier in this chapter that "Web 2.0 is a different way of building applications." First the applications are hosted with a fast feature velocity (that is, their features need to be added or updated at a much faster pace than those of normal desktop or business applications), which blends well with development methodologies such as agile and scrum. Whereas traditional version deliveries occurred in around 12 months, now in many cases there can be more than one software delivery per day. And applications such as Google are on a perpetual beta. Naturally all apps cannot sustain a daily drop (ie daily software update delivery) and a perpetual beta status—mission-critical apps need a little more systemic development and a deliberate delivery schedule. Another impact of Web 2.0 is the requirement for massive scalability because of the unstructured nature of the data as well as the requirement for petabyte-scale computations. This has given rise to frameworks such as MapReduce, Hadoop, and BigTable, which make massive levels of parallel processing like searching through billions of web pages or processing user analytics from very busy websites easier and faster. Finally, new interface models such as JSON (JavaScript Object Notation) and REST (Representational State Transfer) are becoming popular, as opposed to SOA (Service-Oriented Architecture) and web services. Although this might be a little controversial in certain circles, we cannot deny the unmistakable shift in the architectural styles and programming models in the development of Web 2.0 applications. Chapter 6, "Web 2.0 Architecture Case Studies," covers these topics in more detail.

Lessonopoly: Anatomy of a Web 2.0 App

I am volunteering as a technical advisor for the Silicon Valley Education Foundation,[43] chartered with improving the education ecosystem for teachers, parents, students, and administrators. One of our multi-stage initiatives is Lessonopoly,[44] a site to help teachers manage the classroom and lessons (see Figure 1-10).

We are working on a few Web 2.0 features to make this effective. We want to enable sharing of lesson plans not only in the respective school districts but also across the country. And we want to make collaboration seamless between schools and groups. For example, it would be cool if two groups of children from schools far way from each other could work from the same lesson plan and collaborate on a combined field trip. The Web 2.0 features we are trying to incorporate include:

- Collaborative creation of lessons
- A derivative-based, repurposable, remixable, on-demand interchange multi-media content capability
- Ability to meaningfully stitch a fabric (of lessons, in this case) from a vast sea of materials that differ in content grade, content relevance, granularity, and format diversity
- Ability to perform semantic searches on the federated content with contextual attributes meaningful to teachers
- Social networking and other second-order artifacts (such as the already mentioned simultaneous field trip based on a shared lesson plan)

The point here is that to develop such a substrate, we need very different tools (content management, tagging, and searching), development models (agile, scrum), and architecture paradigms (semantic web and data annotation).

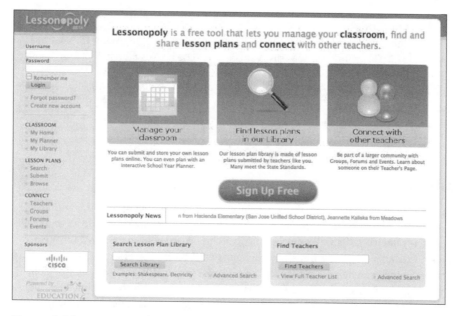

Figure 1-10 *Lessonopoly.*

Data

Data is a consequence of the participatory nature of Web 2.0. We all know that the blogs, wikis, YouTube videos, and the like are creating a lot of data and it is becoming more difficult to zero in on the exact information you are looking for on the web. Google recently reached the milestone of 1 trillion unique URLs.[45] (Maybe that is not surprising because it looks as if Google fetches all those trillion URLs every time you do a single search.) Data has always been a huge part of the web. In Web 1.0, data was static and it was one way. In the Web 2.0 era, the relevance of data is that users create data (via wikis, blogs, photos in Flickr, and video in YouTube) resulting in an asymmetry as well as a challenge to publish the right data to the right people; even just finding all the user-generated content on areas in which one is interested is a challenge. Chapter 5, "Content Aggregation, Syndication, and Federation via RSS and Atom," addresses some of the ways of taming the user-generated data. Another major impediment is to capture the relationship between the vast numbers of data elements on the web so that programs can intelligently search and retrieve appropriate data. The Semantic Web is addressing this domain, and you can read all about it in Chapter 7, And finally, the analytics from web applications offer ample opportunities to make intelligent inferences, as Amazon and Netflix do. Amazon shows us what others have bought after buying similar things in our cart using intelligent data mining; Netflix does the same in making movie recommendations.

Multimedia Tiger Effect
An interesting thing happened on June 7, 2008, at around 1:30 p.m.[45] Many ISPs started noticing high load. Their first reaction was that this could be a virus attack, but they found none. As it turned out, the root cause was viral—of the Tiger kind. Tiger Woods was playing at the U.S. Open golf tournament and the action was dramatic. Lots of folks were watching the descent and the eventual comeback of Tiger Woods in the final holes of the tournament via streaming video.

Mashups

Web apps are increasingly becoming mashups where content is combined, annotated, and aggregated from different sources. At a technology level, mashups are a combination of UI frameworks as well as web-centric architectural constructs. As a business strategy, mashups are very interesting. Mashups can create very effective websites and interfaces, which can help many aspects of business, especially the participatory one. For example, mashups have found popularity in real estate selling/valuation sites such as Zillow. But there are also challenges for effective cross-domain mashups, including the fact that the browser security model allows browsers to provide contents from only the original URL and also restricts the browser to two connections. Consortiums such as the OpenAJAX Alliance[46] are working on this challenge along with the browser vendors. It is almost certain that a cross-domain, multi-site mashup with an effective Web 2.0 trust fabric will be a feature in the next versions of the browsers. Mashups are covered in Chapter 3.

Mashups: When Starbucks Closed a Few Shops
A good consumer example of a mashup is what happened when Starbucks announced that they would close a few coffee shops. Now as every coffee lover knows, the first question many had was, "Is my Starbucks on the list?" Within a few hours the Seattle Times published a mashup[47] (shown in Figure 1-11) showing the locations of all the Starbucks closings. The site is not generated by hand or any single program, but is a mashup—two sources combined into one site, that is, an overlay of the list from Starbucks, which was passed on to Google Maps via APIs (Application Program Interfaces). In fact, the mashup first showed all blue rumored closings and then was updated with green confirmed closings. So the map overlay is not only a spatial rendering but also a dynamic temporal display. This is consumer Web 2.0 in action.

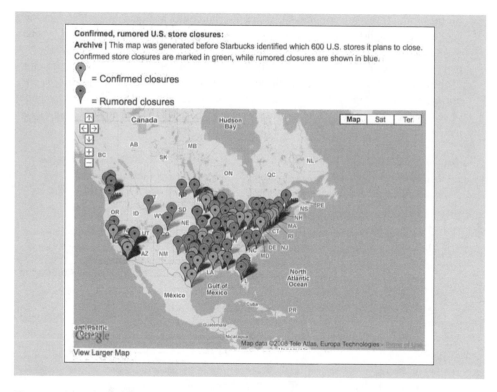

Figure 1-11 *Starbucks closing mashup.*

Scale Free and Long Tail

Another important aspect of Web 2.0 is the scale-free nature of the applications and, on the flip side, the ability to leverage the long tail.

In a scale-free web world, there is no upper or lower limit to the number of users that visit a site. Some applications become enormously popular, and the corresponding websites draw enormous hits. This could be momentary or might last a long time. A tense moment in a popular golf tournament or a mention in Slashdot can propel the popularity of a set of websites and the infrastructure can crash because of the heavy load. As there is no upper bound, you really cannot build your web infrastructure for these kinds of peak loads. But you need to make sure the website does not crash under very occasional heavy load and need to provide ways to recognize and then recover gracefully.

Long tail[48] is the flip side of the scale-free property. Long tail is the concept that, although there are a some products (for example, new books, movies, songs) that are very popular and sell a large number of single products, there are also smaller markets that prefer many related products that are rare or less well known (for example, old TV sitcoms, old movies, and rare books). Chris Anderson first proposed the concept and writes voraciously about it.[49] Whereas in the pre web 2.0 eras it was not easy to develop a market for the products that are not popular, Web 2.0 technologies and business models make it very easy to establish a market for a large number of products that are demanded by a few users. A good example of this phenomenon is the music industry. There are a few who make the million mark who sell well via traditional and online delivery channels, but a lot of the less famous music CDs are in the long tail, and also have a good market[50] via on-line music portals. Figure 1-12 illustrates this. You can see the long tail in the large number of selections sold online by Rhopsody, whereas Walmart sells a large number of fewer selections that are popular.

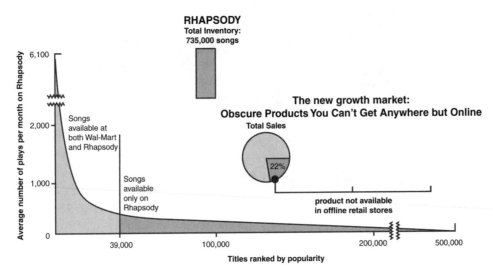

Figure 1-12   *Long tail in music.*

Mobility

As cell phones and the cell phone networks have become pervasive and powerful, Mobile Web has become a moniker for Web 2.0. From multi-media to social networks to Amazon, all the Web 2.0 sites have a mobile footprint. In fact, you can stream live video from mobile phones to the Internet directly (http://qik.com/). One of the profound influences in the mobile world is the introduction of the iPhone. It not only has a powerful operating system but also has an infrastructure for developers to distribute applications. Mobile applications not only span the multi-media world but also other services such as location-based services. In fact, the Obama '08 Campaign was astute enough to develop a mobile application, as shown in Figure 1-13. Chapter 9, "Web 2.0 and Mobility," covers this domain.

Web 2.0 at Cisco

Cisco has been in the forefront of Web 2.0—from the use of the technologies internally as well as incorporating the Web 2.0 patterns in products.[51] In fact, Cisco's mantra is "connect, communicate, and collaborate." This section takes a quick look at both sides—internal

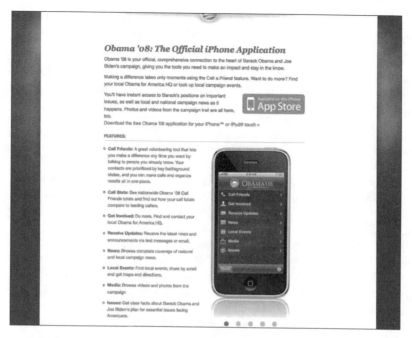

Figure 1-13 *Obama '08 iPhone application.*

use as well as features in Cisco's products. Chapter 10, "Web 2.0 @ Cisco: The Evolution," and Chapter 11, "Cisco's Approach to Sales 2.0," cover these Cisco Web 2.0 topics in more detail. The FastCompany article "How Cisco's CEO John Chambers Is Turning the Tech Giant Socialist"[52] offers insights into the whys behind Cisco's use of Web 2.0. A summary is shown in the list below:

- Better decisions through collaborative decision making—"a distributed idea engine where leadership emerges organically," as John Chambers puts it

- A culture of sharing to "democratize strategy and distribute leadership in order to stimulate innovation"

- Increased productivity and efficient information access, be they video demos of Cisco's products or a discussion chain on a new idea or engineering updates

- Use of community to help solve problems—engineering, product support, sales, HR, or marketing. A good example is the blogs showing the marketing folks how to position Cisco's products against competitors

- And, most important, more customer-centric approach, leveraging Web 2.0 memes for better, faster, and more innovative interactions and partnering with customers

Web 2.0–Centric Products from Cisco

Cisco believes that collaboration and Web 2.0 will transform business and is on a path to provide enterprises, service providers, small businesses, and homes with a wide array of products and services.[53] As part of this commitment, Cisco unveiled its collaboration portfolio, featuring Unified Communications, video (telepresence), and a Web 2.0 applications platform called WebEx Connect on September 24, 2008.

Webex Connect[54] is interesting from a Web 2.0 perspective. It has an array of communication and collaboration framework capabilities, ranging from the capability to create mashups, to composite applications, to IMs and email.

iPhone Game and Routers

An example of how Cisco is using the different aspects of Web 2.0 effectively can be seen from the iPhone game "Cisco Edge Quest 2 Mobile."[55] Figure 1-14 shows sample screens from the game. The game takes a player through five lanes of network traffic facing ever-lurking obstacles. The player, using the touch controls, maneuvers the craft through levels with increasing demands on the IP networks. The player earns game points in terms of packets repaired with bonuses for speed upgrade and network uptime. The game has three levels, and after each level is completed, informational marketing messages like "Cisco ASR 9000 can significantly reduce the mobile backhaul for 3G/4G video" are displayed. The aim of the game is to understand how the Cisco ASR 9000 router is transforming the mobile Internet. It is an interesting combination of gamesplay, mobile network, iPhone, and clever user interfaces—all characteristics of a well written Web 2.0 application, and that too with a business goal. What more could you ask for as an example of Web 2.0 EE? This example not only shows how an enterprise can innovate based on Web 2.0, but also the breadth of scope and application of iPhone as a development platform.

Figure 1-14   *Cisco Edge Quest 2 Mobile.*

How Cisco Is Leveraging Web 2.0 Internally

Cisco's internal mechanics and mechanisms are very similar to what it enables through its products and is aimed at providing the next-generation workforce a collaborative and participatory working atmosphere through the connect, communicate, collaborate, and learn themes, as Figure 1-15 shows.

Figure 1-15   *Goals of Cisco's internal Web 2.0 efforts.*

An important part of any initiative is the proper sponsorship and support from senior management, as well as resource allocation. For the Web 2.0 collaboration and collaboration platform, Rebecca Jacoby (CIO) and Blair Christie (SVP Corporate Communications) are executive sponsors. A Communications & Collaboration Delivery Team (CCDT) has been formed out of Communications & Collaboration IT (CCIT) and Corporate Communications Architecture (CCA) to lead this work.

Internally, all Cisco employees use the web for applications such as expense reports, HR applications, and so forth. All the internal information is available from a very well organized website, CCoE (Communications Center of Excellence), with more details available to you by navigating to different sub-sections. Cisco has new initiatives around the business and social aspects of Web 2.0 in a variety of application domains, spanning from audio/video conferencing to content management and social networking. Figure 1-16 shows an example of the details available for the social networking technology. An employee can get more details by clicking on the links.

From a business perspective, Cisco has a few initiatives such as Cisco 3.0 (which has two aspects—transforming the company internally and transforming relationships with customers); transforming command and control to collaboration/teamwork; and achieving a future organizational structure based on councils, boards, and workgroups. All these business goals are enabled by IT and Web 2.0 technologies.

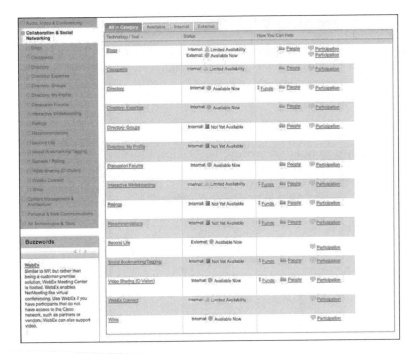

Figure 1-16 *CCoE web page for social networking technology.*

From a technology perspective, Cisco has categorized the initiatives into big buckets with associated technologies and tools, as shown in Table 1-2. As the table shows, most of the tools—such as blogs, Ciscopedia, social bookmarking, tagging, and so forth—are all Web 2.0 artifacts.

Table 1-2 *Cisco's Technologies and Tools Table*

Technologies	Tools
Audio, video, and conferencing	B2B IP video, Cisco TV live broadcasting, podcasts & vodcasts, telepresence, and web conferencing
Collaboration & social networking	Blogs, Ciscopedia, directory with expertise, search profiles and groups, discussion forums, wikis, social bookmarking, and tagging
Content management and architecture	Portal framework, enterprise search, web analytics, web content management, and UI templates
Personal and web communications	Dashboard, email, enterprise news, instant messaging, IP phone, wireless, RSS, and voicemail

Each technology is then decomposed into initiatives with more granularity, with deliverable capabilities, and with a timeline, as shown in Figure 1-17.

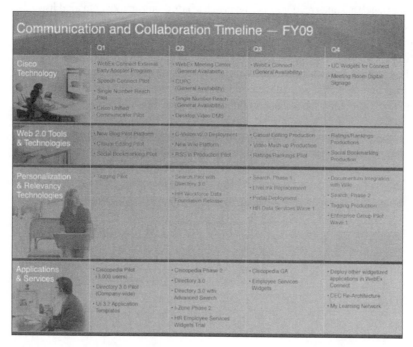

Figure 1-17   *CCDT roadmap.*

All these initiatives then turn into individual projects and go through a vision-poc-development-beta-release cycle.

In Short

For better or worse, David Brooks' New York Times opinion article,[56] "The Outsourced Brain," might best sum up Web 2.0 and the future of the web:

> "I had thought that the magic of the information age was that it allowed us to know more, but then I realized the magic of the information age is that it allows us to know less.
>
> Musical taste? I have externalized it. Now I just log on to iTunes and it tells me what I like.
>
> Personal information? I've externalized it. I'm no longer clear on where I end and my BlackBerry begins.
>
> Wherever there is a network, I'll be there.

Wherever there's a TiVo machine making a sitcom recommendation based on past preferences, I'll be there.

Wherever there's a Times reader selecting articles based on the most emailed list, I'll be there. I'll be in the way Amazon links purchasing Dostoyevsky to purchasing garden furniture."

So now it's time to explore this phenomenon in more detail and from the perspective of the enterprise. This book organizes the various Web 2.0 concepts touched on here into various chapters of their own. It is best to read them sequentially to grow your understanding of the topics, terms, and technologies, but you can skip to particular topics of interest if you like.

<monologue>

This chapter contains the keys to what makes Web 2.0 different. First, we can now generate content as a natural extension of "The Way We Work, Live, Play and Learn [SM]." In Web 1.0, for example, you'd take a few photos and email them, or perhaps publish them on your personal web page, to share those moments with family and friends. Along comes Web 2.0, and now Flickr and Facebook maintain your photos on their sites. Web 2.0 makes it easier to generate and share information—often richer, location-based, time-stamped information—with context. Mobile devices enable you to upload and tag your moments, as a natural part of each moment, where and while they happen.

Second, although you can notify family and friends of new photos you've posted on Facebook, for example, others who are interested can view them as well. Now whenever and wherever you like, you can search through the moments of your life and the millions of moments from other people's lives posted on these sites. That's the connectedness, the human network part of Web 2.0.

</monologue>

User-Generated Content: Wikis, Blogs, Communities, Collaboration, and Collaborative Technologies

Since its inception, the web has comprised millions of pages of content. Most Web 1.0 content came from traditional media and content publishers. In Web 2.0, the traditional content consumers—citizens and users themselves—create most of the content. This chapter discusses how users are critical to the success of wikis, blogs, collaboration, and communities. In particular, it

- Describes the emergence of user-generated content, a key feature of Web 2.0

- Discusses blogs and shows how they are changing the marketing landscape and providing customer feedback

- Examines wikis and identifies how examples, such as Wikipedia, create valuable knowledge management assets

- Explains the value of social and enterprise bookmarking, as well as folksonomies

- Identifies the value of photo and video sharing, highlighting Flickr as an example

- Showcases communities and explains why they're so important

- Defines collaboration and its impact to the business

- Explores collaborative technologies, such as TelePresence, WebEx, and Unified Communications

This chapter explains how Web 2.0 technologies enable users to create and share content, form communities, connect, communicate, collaborate, and learn. It also explains how enterprises can leverage Web 2.0 technologies and business models to create value.

The business value of Web 2.0 is that it enables sharing information and collaborating with colleagues in new ways to solve new and long-standing problems. It's the technical expert, for example, giving a demo or answering customer questions, capturing the questions and answers on video and tagging key points. The expert then uploads the video to a shared technical FAQ database, adding it to his/her portfolio of technical knowledge available for the less experienced to access as required. This enables the expert to share his knowledge with others, spend less time answering redundant questions, and focus on solving key problems or improving his skills. As organizations find themselves in the midst of a shortage of experienced technical experts, this is one way to help their scarce experts scale, or meet the multitude of demands for their time and expertise.

Web 2.0 technologies make it easier for individuals to share information and to provide context, such as date, time, etc., along with that information. The human network, connected via Web 2.0 technology, can take those discrete pieces of information provided with context, and assemble them to create the "big pictures," something single individuals or a few individuals working together might never accomplish. This works much the same way as some amazing new software which takes individual snapshots, from different cameras and diverse user perspectives, and combines them almost seamlessly to create amazing, new, 360° panoramic views.

Thanks to Web 2.0 social networks, much more diverse communities of interest can form and share knowledge and information. A city travel guide hosted on the web can now offer a more complete, panoramic, and up-to-date picture of a location, providing views of city landmarks, current weather conditions, photos and menus of nearby restaurants, and other points of interest. Residents, local businesses, chambers of commerce, and so on, using Web 2.0 can contribute to the guide in real-time. These communities enable knowledge to be aggregated, analyzed, and discussed in ways never before possible.

As we focus on tough business, economic, and technical issues, the disparate puzzle pieces are coming together from the global population to form detailed, big pictures of problems and situations. Consider a website focused on a specific illness or medical condition. Now information from patients, doctors, scientists, and researchers from around the world can be assembled, analyzed, and discussed by the communities concerned. These communities might devise a cure that individual members might never have discovered on their own, or perhaps yield a better, more effective solution or cure. Web 2.0 enables the world to connect, communicate, collaborate, and learn—that's the power of the human network!

As the web continues to grow, business needs to understand how to harness and leverage the power of this growing web usage. In its Benchmark 2008 series, Forrester Research, a leading independent technology and marketing research firm, identified several trends affecting Web 2.0. In North America, for example, three-quarters of adults are actively online for an average of 15 hours per week, including a majority of boomers and seniors. Forrester defines active web usage as being online at least monthly. Generally, the most frequent web users are younger adults.[1] In households in the United States, more than 50% have broadband, 81% have a personal computer (PC), and 50% of those have more than one.

Mobility is also a growing trend, as three-quarters of adults in the United States have a mobile phone.[2] 80% of North American homes have a mobile phone. That number increases to 91% where the head of household was born between 1979 and 1994, in a cohort known a Generation Y. Mobile devices are seemingly ubiquitous and mobile service has extended from voice to a wide variety of data applications. A growing number of users access, create, and upload web content via their mobile phones. The heaviest mobile web users favor three phone brands: RIM BlackBerry, Palm Treo, and Apple's iPhone.[3]

Forrester also offers insight into spending on enterprise Web 2.0 technologies globally over the next five years, predicting strong growth to $4.6 billion by 2013, with the greatest share going to social networking, Really Simple Syndication (RSS), and mashups. Forrester also predicts that over the next five years enterprise collaboration software will subsume enterprise Web 2.0 tools, becoming part of the enterprise fabric. Web 2.0 will, however, have a major impact on product marketing and workforce optimization over the next five years.[4]

Many enterprises are just beginning to grasp the important role the user plays and the need to support, enable, and encourage user participation in enterprise Web 2.0 initiatives and technology roll-outs. But, more importantly, business managers need to understand how to harness and leverage user-generated content: blogs, wikis, folksonomies, videos, and communities. They also need to recognize that collaboration and collaborative technologies described herein can help them to reengineer and transform their own business functions, departments, or processes and reap the benefits of Web 2.0. These themes will recur throughout the book, particularly in later chapters that explore mobility and Web 2.0 at Cisco and in Cisco Sales, when more specific implementations of Web 2.0 are discussed.

Evolution of User-Generated Content (UGC)

This section begins with a brief overview of the evolution of user-generated content (UGC) and explains the importance of the user in Web 2.0. Then it's time to explore a number of technologies enabling users to create and share content, photos, video, and so on in new and unique ways. Blogs, for example, enable users to comment on everything, your company included. This impacts marketing and provides an unprecedented opportunity to get feedback from customers. Wikis enable users to share information and develop knowledge repositories.

These valuable business assets can increase productivity and improve customer support and customer satisfaction, so much that customers will pay a premium for content your users and customers help create. Bookmarking and folksonomies enable the organization to share information and to define and tag information to facilitate and accelerate search and retrieval. Photos and videos make content more visual, more personal, and more human. They can also provide strategic value because a customer video testimonial from a known expert can help to sell products. So, how did user-generated content get its start?

Personal Webpages

The millions of pages of web content in existence include personal web pages created by end-users to share information about themselves or their families, a topic they are interested in, even a home-based business. When a user owns all the content of a domain name or website address, the pages are referred to as a personal website.[5] Internet Service Providers (ISPs) such as AOL (http://www.aol.com), formerly America Online, founded in 1983, enabled users to create personal web pages on AOL Hometown until 2008, when the service was eliminated.[6] Web hosting sites, such as the original GeoCities (http://www.geocities.com), founded in 1994, enabled users to place personal web pages in one of six thematic neighborhoods, such as SiliconValley for technology-related pages.

GeoCities was the fifth most popular website and had signed a million users by 1997. It went on to be acquired by Yahoo! in 1999, when the neighborhoods were replaced by URLs in the form http://www.geocities.com/membername. Although GeoCities' free hosting services were popular in the 1990s, they have become less so as the costs of hosting a personal website have decreased and other options gained popularity. However, by 2008 the GeoCities domain attracted nearly 180 million visitors annually, clearly indicating a following for the content it provides.[7]

In 2008 Optenet, a global IT security company, reported that at the end of 2007 the number of websites worldwide exceeded 155 million, largely because of the growth of personal web pages and blogs. The study also indicated an increase in the number of personal web pages since 2006 of more than 455%.[8] UGC is a term, used in web publishing and content production since 2005, which refers to publicly available content created by end-users. It includes all forms of digital media, frequently asked question (FAQ) databases, blogs, wikis, photos, and video. Amazon.com, for example, leverages UGC in the form of user product reviews.

There are some costs associated with leveraging UGC. For example, UGC is often monitored by site administrators to ensure it is relevant, inoffensive, and doesn't infringe on copyrights.[9] Organizations leveraging UGC must also consider whether or not such content increases site and content findability through search, traffic, engagement, and, most importantly, return visits.[10] The capability of popular sites to build traffic, a quality known as stickiness, is all about making content so compelling that users want to spend time on a site, enjoying it so much they don't want to leave. UGC can make a site more accurate and useful, but also give it more meaning and purpose.[11] Often, stickiness leads to the formation of another Web 2.0 phenomenon discussed later in the chapter, communities.

User-produced content is also referred to as consumer-generated media (CGM), in that the web provides a forum where consumers can publicly post comments, opinions, and experiences they want to share with others. It also provides an avenue for the consumers' combined voices on a variety of topics, concerns, companies, and products to be published and to be heard. This online consumer buzz, if you will, stems from blogs, message boards and forums, newsgroups, and online review and feedback/complaint sites. Its importance should not be downplayed because research shown in Figure 2-1 indicates that consumers trust their fellow consumers far more than advertisers. So, user- and, more specifically, consumer-generated content can be critical to marketing success.[12]

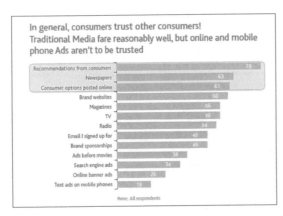

Figure 2-1 *Consumer trust in various forms of advertising.[12]*

By its very nature, CGM is becoming easier and less expensive to create and distribute while simultaneously becoming more prolific and impactful. This fact is also dramatically changing the marketing process: Marketers can no longer control medium or message. Since CGM data shows up in search results, media, analysts, and competitors all have access to this content. Marketers and business intelligence professionals are beginning to leverage blogs and wikis to influence, measure, and analyze consumer sentiment in real-time, with actionable and impactful results.

Sites such as Amazon (http://www.amazon.com) have figured out the strategic value of user reviews and ratings. Amazon uses consumer-generated comments, product ratings, and buying habits as a basis for identifying similar products a customer is likely to buy. If a customer, for example, shows interest in a particular book, they are offered selections of other books they might be interested, based on books other buyers, with similar buying habits or interests, have bought.[13]

Blogs

Blogs are considered part of social media. They are web-based tools that enable people to share and discuss information.[14] A blog, short for "web log," is a website that enables an individual user, the blog owner (blogger), to publish opinions or commentary on news or events—in essence to broadcast, without using a big media channel. A blog may also contain graphics, personal photos or videos, links to related content or sites, and even links to other blogs. The owner blogs, or regularly maintains or adds comments or entries to the blog, to attract and retain an audience or following.

Blog entries are usually displayed in reverse order chronologically to keep fresh content at the top. Blogs with very short posts are referred to as micro-blogs. One of the challenges with blogs is that searching them requires a specialized blog search engine, such as Technorati, described later. Some blogs serve as online diaries, whereas others focus on a particular topic or leverage a particular media, for example, audio (podcasts) or video (videoblogs). The word *blog* has come to loosely mean any media used to express an opinion.[15]

A number of key differences between a blog and a personal web page are worth emphasizing. A blog broadcasts information, but enables readers to comment, whereas a personal web page broadcasts information only one way. A blog, therefore, enables a conversation as readers leave comments, links, and trackbacks, which notify the author when someone links to his or her content. The blog comment feature enables a community to form and to discuss the bloggers opinion or information presented on the blog.

Blogs are as easy to write as email because web design and Hypertext Markup Language (HTML) skills are not required. A user can generally subscribe to a blog and receive new content automatically via email or, if a news or blog reader is used, via RSS. Most websites must be visited to see changes, although many now enable users to subscribe to RSS feeds for select portions of their site. The ease and simplicity of blogging has enabled millions of people who would have never created a website to create blogs, including video blogs.[16][17]

Early digital communities, such as Usenet, CompuServe, and Bulletin Board Services (BBS), enabled users to keep running accounts of their lives in the form of online diaries, written in a web protocol, such as Gopher. In the 1990s web forum software, such as WebEx, enabled topically connected, running conversations between messages on message boards. These evolved into early blogs, as websites containing commentary were manually updated to link to articles and other content. As tools evolved, it became easier for a larger, less technical population of users to produce, post, and maintain web articles in reverse chronological order.

Video blogs, sometimes abbreviated as vlogs, gained popularity in 2005, around the launch of the most popular video sharing site, YouTube, discussed later. They often leverage RSS to enable distribution on the web and automatic playback on PCs on mobile devices. In addition, the convergence of mobile phones and digital cameras now enables video of an event to be uploaded to the web, where and while it happens.[18] A joint project from Reuters and Nokia, for example, enables a journalist, using a mobile phone in the field, to file multimedia content to an editor-controlled blogging platform. Wavelog has launched a similar blogging application, enabling users with mobile phones running the Symbian operating system, discussed in Chapter 9, "Web 2.0 and Mobility," to post to Wordpress blogs, hosted on Wordpress.com or self-hosted.[19]

Users can create blogs on specialized blog hosting services or use blog software, a specialized form of content management software, and host them on their own computer or regular web hosting service.[20] Popular blog platforms include

- Blogger (http://www.blogger.com), available through the website shown in Figure 2-2, was launched in August 1999 by Pyra Labs, and as one of the earliest dedicated blog-publishing tools it helped popularize the blogging format. Blogger was acquired by Google in February 2003 and in 2007 was ranked 16 on the list of top 50 domains in terms of unique visitors.[21]

- ExpressionEngine (http://expressionengine.com), available through the website shown in Figure 2-3, is a popular blogging software platform which stemmed from a product called pMachine Pro, released in 2001 by pMachine (now EllisLabs).[23]

- Movable Type (http://movabletype.com), available through the website shown in Figure 2-4, was released in 2001 by Six Apart and re-licensed in 2007 under the GNU General Public License as free software. It was one of the first blogging platforms to support multiple authors.[25]

- TypePad (http://www.typepad.com), available through the website shown in Figure 2-5, was launched in 2003 and was one of the first blogging platforms to enable users to easily create static web content pages as well.[27]

- WordPress (http://www.wordpress.com), available through the site shown in Figure 2-6, appeared in 2003 and provides software users can download to create and host a blog on their own system. WordPress added hosting services in 2005 and launched its iPhone application in July 2008.[29]

Key features of these popular blog platforms are listed in Table 2-1.

Figure 2-2   *Blogger.[22]*

Figure 2-3   *ExpressionEngine.[24]*

Figure 2-4   *Moveable Type.[26]*

Figure 2-5   *TypePad.[28]*

Figure 2-6   *WordPress.[30]*

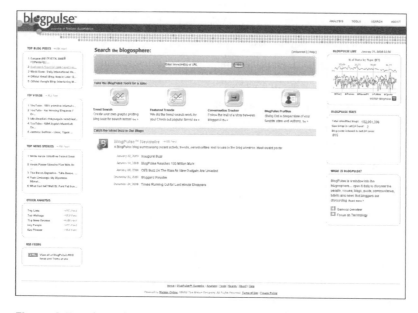

Figure 2-7   *BlogPulse.[38]*

Table 2-1   *Key Features of Popular Blog Platforms[31]*

Service	Key Features
Blogger	Offers free blog hosting services
	Provides customizable blog design templates
	Enables photo sharing
	Blogging files can be downloaded to other servers for hosting[21]
Expression-Engine	Software supports multiple authors
	Powerful template engine
	Modules and community plug-ins for mailing lists, photo galleries, forums
	Personal and commercial licensing[23]
Movable Type	Software that supports multiple authors
	Provides customizable blog design templates
	Tags and categories aid post organization
	What you see is what you get (WYSIWYG) posting and editing
	Provides spellchecking
	Enables photo and video sharing
	Licensing for personal, commercial, educational use
	Enables users to create static web pages[25]
TypePad	Fee for service hosting
	Enables users to create static web pages
	What you see is what you get (WYSIWYG) posting and editing
	Quick posting of photos and videos[27]
WordPress	Open source blog publishing application
	Offers free blog hosting services
	Provides multiple blog design templates
	Tags and categories aid post organization
	Provides spell checking and rich-text editing
	Supports site traffic measurement and statistics
	Integrates spam-fighting tool, Akismet[29]

Social networks, such as Facebook and MySpace, support blogging, as well, but are not meant to be used by professional bloggers, who blog about their industry or profession in an unofficial capacity. Social networking site blogs are also not intended as a means for starting a business, although some businesses have found they offer a way of reaching the young, hip audience that frequents the sites.[31]

Although there's some debate over who wrote the first blog, the popular news service CNET announced that blogs turned 10 in 2007.[32] Some bloggers have gained a large enough following to be considered professional bloggers, identified by topic, or even by country. The pressure to maintain this following can sometimes become intense. At the end of 2007, popular ZDNet blogger Marc Orchant suffered a massive heart attack.[33] The following month, Om Malik reported that the pressure of becoming a name brand and feeling tied to his machine had led him to have a heart attack.[34]

Daniel Lyons, a senior editor at *Forbes* magazine at the time, authored a popular blog titled "The Secret Diary of Steve Jobs." Lyons parody on Steve Jobs, co-founder, Chairman and Chief Executive Officer of Apple, Inc., led to Lyons become known as the "Fake Steve Jobs." When Lyons and Alex Schulman, the author of Sweden's most popular professional blog, quit blogging, their quitting made the news.[35][36] But because perhaps thousands of others stand ready to fill their shoes, what impact do popular blogs such as these have on business?

For starters, blogs offer unprecedented opportunities for business, particularly in the area of marketing, because they enable customers to comment on everything, including your company as well as your products. Blog sentiment, which captures the combined consumer voices, impacts marketing and provides business an unprecedented opportunity to track, analyze, and benefit from consumer sentiment and customer feedback, through such services as

- BlogPulse (http://www.blogpulse.com/), a service of Nielsen BuzzMetrics, is available through the site shown in Figure 2-7. It enables marketing teams to search blogs, track blog statistics, and discover trends in customer sentiment.[37]

- Google Trends (http://www.google.com/trends), whose site is shown in Figure 2-8, provides graphs showing how frequently a search term is entered versus the total number of searches in a variety of languages and global regions.[39]

- Technorati (http://www.blogpulse.com/), whose site is shown in Figure 2-9, provides marketers with access to blog content on a variety topics, including business, politics, sports, entertainment, and technology, organized by channels. It also looks for trend and patterns in near real-time and offers the ability to search the blogosphere, the collective community of all blogs.[41]

According to Technorati's "State of the Blogosphere 2008," blogs are here to stay. Highlights of worldwide statistics of this global phenomenon include

- 184 million users have started a blog.

- 346 million, 77% of active web users, read blogs.

- 1 million blog posts occur per day.

- 75% of bloggers measure the success of their blog in terms of personal satisfaction.

- Mean annual revenue from blogs that contain advertising is $6,000.

- Revenue from blogs with advertising and 100,000 or more unique visitors per month exceeds $75,000.

Figure 2-8   *Google Trends.[40]*

Figure 2-9   *Technorati.[42]*

The United States is home to 48% of the global blogging population, where

- 26.4 million have started a blog.

- 60.3 million active web users read blogs.

- 57% of bloggers are male.

- 74% bloggers have college degrees.

- 42% bloggers have some graduate work.

- 34% bloggers are between 25–34 years of age.

- The highest concentration of bloggers is in the San Francisco Bay area, followed by New York City, Chicago, and Los Angeles.

- Almost 95% of top newspapers have reporter blogs.

According to Technorati's six-part report, it is sometimes difficult to distinguish blogs from traditional media and content publishing and the lines between types of blogs blur as well.

Of active bloggers surveyed, 79% identified themselves as personal bloggers, 46% as professional, and 12% as corporate bloggers, who blog in an official capacity for their company. Many bloggers also identified themselves in a secondary category as well, indicating they either maintain a second blog or blur the lines of content in their blog, adding personal content into their corporate blog, for example. The report makes interesting reading for bloggers or those who frequent blogs.[43][44]

Companies find strategic business value in mining the rich source of customer sentiment and feedback popular buzz-tracking services provide, and each service has its pros and cons, shown in Table 2-2.

These services exist because companies find strategic business value in mining this rich source of customer sentiment and feedback.

At Cisco and other companies, enterprise business intelligence teams analyze and interpret the numbers to see whether consumers are responding to the company's green initiative. Some companies are even beginning to identify ways to influence through this new medium, tracking an emerging group of professional bloggers with a following on a particular topic or technology. The result has been a major change in the way companies go to market and leverage the blogging medium as part of their marketing strategies. A good example is found in Cisco's Data Center 3.0 Blogging Initiative, described in Chapter 10, "Web 2.0 @ Cisco: The Evolution." The initiative leveraged the blogosphere, influencing popular professional bloggers in the data center space to successfully market Cisco's latest Data Center product at a very low cost compared to traditional product marketing launches.

Blogs provide business value as a means of obtaining customer feedback, getting the company's message out, forming communities, and gathering company content. Many large companies, such as Google and Yahoo!, maintain company blogs. Companies such as Cisco and Microsoft have enabled official blogs and employee blogs. General Motors, Jupitermedia, and Sun Microsystems executives write blogs as a way of getting their message out to the company. Some C-level executives, such as Cisco CEO John Chambers, create video blogs. Smaller companies use blogs to raise their company's profile.

Table 2-2   *Pros and Cons of Popular Buzz-Tracking Services[45]*

Service	Pros	Cons
BlogPulse Trend Search	Useful if looking for information like, "How many people have blogged about McCain versus Obama in the past two months?" Useful if you want to compare 2–3 sites and watch number of blogs linking to them over period of time	Tracks only blogs (or sites with feeds) Can compare only three terms per search Shows information for fixed time-frame: 1, 2, 3, or 6 months Graphs can be generated only from the BlogPulse website[37]
Google Trends	Queries Google's extensive database Can find which queries originate from which regions of the world (including cities) Can limit searches to individual months, years, or a date range	Doesn't provide real statistics or numbers Graphs are only relative, giving no information about the real search data[39]
Technorati Charts	Tracks millions of blogs Tracks how many blog posts mentioned a particular keyword or phrase in a given time Generated in real-time Can be embedded in websites Provides simple URL with search parameters	Cannot compare two search terms in a single chart[41]

Blogs also provide means of becoming a known expert on a topic or an industry, and some are even credited with giving large companies a human face. Robert Scoble, known for his popular tech blog, *Scobleizer*, who became popular while he worked at Microsoft, is one example of someone who went on to become a professional blogger. Blogs also provide a means of forming communities, and for a minimal investment can yield qualitative feedback: One can see how popular a post is by the number of views and comments.[46][47] Corporate and company employee blogs offer a wealth of company and product-related content, yielding exceptional search results retrieved on key company and industry terms and offering insight into leader and employee sentiment.[48]

Wikis

The first wiki was named for the fast "Wiki Wiki" shuttle that runs around Honolulu International Airport. "Wiki" means fast in Hawaiian.[49] That site, developed by Ward Cunningham in 1995 for the Portland Pattern Repository, focused on gathering patterns in software development. Described by Cunningham as "The simplest online database that could possibly work," a wiki enables users using any browser to create and edit web pages using a simple syntax. Because wiki supports hyperlinks, pages can be cross-linked together easily.[50]

As mentioned earlier, one of the main differences between web pages and blogs is that while web pages enable a single user to share information, blogs enable single or multiple users to share information, start conversations, and form communities of interest. Wikis enable users to share information and form communities of interest. The key difference is that wikis enable users to co-create, to collaboratively develop content that often develops into shared knowledge repositories.

Users can create wikis on specialized wiki hosting services, called wiki farms, or use wiki software and host them on their own computer or regular web hosting service.[51] WikiMatrix (http://www.wikimatrix.com) enables users to find and compare features of wiki platforms so that they can choose the one that fits their needs. A number of solutions integrate wikis with other Web 2.0 capabilities, providing hosted or on-premise services. Popular wiki platforms include

- Clearspace (http://www.jivesoftware.com), a collaboration and knowledge management tool from Jive Software, whose website is shown in Figure 2-10, integrates wikis and many other Web 2.0 capabilities into a single user interface.[52] Clearspace unifies wiki pages, blogs, discussions, and instant messenger into a single application that supports email integration, RSS, and much more. Documents, for example, can be organized into spaces by topic, making them much easier to find.[53] Users can create and update their profiles.

- Confluence (http://www.atlassian.com/software/confluence/) is a popular web-based corporate wiki developed by Altassian Software, whose site is shown in Figure 2-11.[55]

- DocuWiki (http://www.dokuwiki.org/dokuwiki) is very simple to use and is targeted toward workgroups, teams of developers, and small companies.[57]

- Google Sites (http://sites.google.com) provides structured wiki launched by Google as part of Google Apps, replacing Google's previous web page creation service. Google Sites began as JotSpot, a company founded in 2004, focused on enabling something they called an application wiki—a shareable, easy-to-edit wiki-like environment in documents, spreadsheets, calendars, and so on. Google purchased JotSpot in October 2006.[58][59]

- MediaWiki (http://www.mediawiki.org/wiki/MediaWiki) web-based wiki software initially released in 2002, which serves as the foundation for Wikipedia and all wikis hosted by Wikia, both of which are described later in this section.[60]

- PBwiki, short for PeanutButterwiki (http://www.pbwiki.com), is a commercial wiki farm founded in 2005 as a free/premium hosted wiki service, whose goal is to enable wiki creation to be as easy as making a peanut butter sandwich. Figure 2-12 provides a view of their website.[61]

- Socialtext (http://www.socialtext.com), whose site is shown in Figure 2-13, was founded in 2002. The company offers a wiki-centric, enterprise social software platform designed to enable employees to more effectively manage and share information and collaborate with colleagues.[63]

Figure 2-10   *Clearspace.[54]*

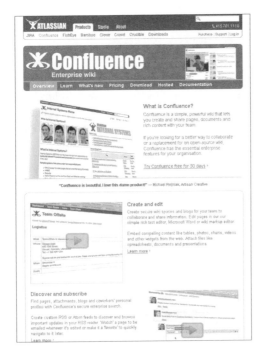

Figure 2-11   *Confluence.[56]*

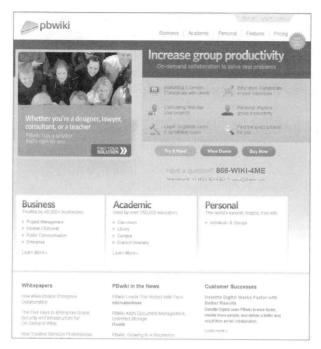

Figure 2-12   *PBwiki.[62]*

Figure 2-13   *Socialtext.[64]*

- TikiWiki CMS/Groupware (http://www.tikiwiki.org), more commonly known as TikiWiki, got its start in 2002. It can be used as a structured wiki, a blogging system, a collaboration platform, or a bug tracking system, for example.[65]

- Wetpaint (http://www.wetpaint.com), founded in October 2004, provides a simple, easy-to-use wiki hosting service, enabling non-technical users to collaborate online.[66]

- Wikia (http://www.wikia.com), originally called Wikicities, founded in 2004 by the founder of Wikipedia, hosts large community wikis that use the MediaWiki engine.[67]

Table 2-3 provides key features of these popular wiki platforms.

Wikipedia (http://www.wikipedia.org/), shown in Figure 2-14, is one of the best examples of how a community can work collaboratively to build a knowledge base or encyclopedia of content. Started in 2001, the global user community has helped grow the site into the massive, popular site it is today, containing more than 10 million articles in more than 250 languages, with more than 2.6 million articles in English alone. Users need to be aware that newer content sometimes contains misinformation, whereas older articles are generally more accurate. The value of this online encyclopedia versus a paper-based one is that the content is being constantly updated.[52] Wikipedia runs on a free, collaborative editing software package called MediaWiki.[69]

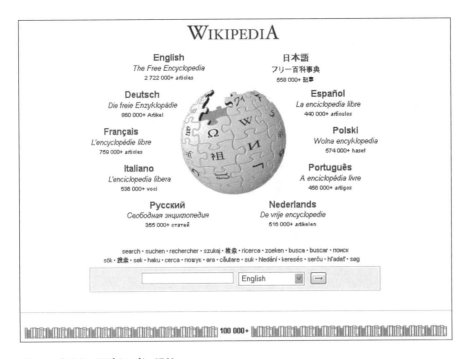

Figure 2-14   *Wikipedia.[70]*

Table 2-3 *Key Features of Popular Wikis[68]*

Platform	Key Features
Clearspace	Integrates wiki, blog, discussion forums, IM chat, and VoIP under a single user interface
	Supports RSS
	Email integration
	Personal user profiles
	Reputation and reward system for participation
	Hosted or on-premise solution[54]
Confluence	Web-based corporate wiki
	Complements Jira, the company's bug tracking solution
	Hosted or on-premise solution[55]
DocuWiki	Easy to use
	Standards-compliant wiki system
	Good choice to write documentation for a small or medium company
	Eases creation of structured content
	Has a powerful syntax
	Data files can be read outside the wiki
	Helps teams and workgroups collaborate while working on projects
	Data stored in plain text files
	No database required[57]
Google Sites	Structured wiki
	Part of Google Apps
	Began as JotSpot, company known for its application wiki[59]
MediaWiki	Free software package licensed under the GNU General Public License (GPL)
	Most popular wiki software on the web
	Runs Wikipedia, world's largest online encyclopedia
	Supports many languages, website user styles, multimedia, and extension features
	Provides index of content items, edit tracking, talk pages
	Suitable for personal, educational, and business use[60]
PBwiki	Simple, easy-to-use wiki
	Offers free/premium hosted wiki service[61]

continues

Table 2-3   *Key Features of Popular Wikis[68] (continued)*

Platform	Key Features
Socialtext	Socialtext Workspace, an enterprise wiki integrated with social networking capabilities
	Socialtext Dashboard, similar to iGoogle or NetVibes
	Internal and external widgets
	Collaborative weblog publishing
	Socialtext Miki mobile capability
	Email integration
	Searching[63]
TikiWiki	Powerful open-source groupware and content management system
	Written in PHP, a popular scripting language used to create dynamic web pages
	Can be used to create websites and intranets
	Offers great resources if used as a collaboration tool: forums, chat rooms, poll taking, blog, file and image gallery, FAQ, and calendar[65]
Wetpaint	Simple, easy-to-use three-step wiki creation wizard
	WYSIWYG editor
	Wide gallery of style templates
	Ability to comment on each wiki page
	Hosting service for non-technical users[66]
Wikia	Hosts large community wikis using the MediaWiki platform[67]

Now let's explore the business value of developing wiki sites integrated with other Web 2.0 capabilities, using a tool such as Socialtext, from an enterprise perspective.

With an enterprise wiki at its core, Socialtext enables users to do their work on group-editable wiki workspaces, organized by topic, in which they can collaborate and build upon one another's ideas. Instead of sending out a presentation, for example, Socialtext enables users to reduce email and

■   Create a page around the presentation

■   Organize notes on how and when to use the material

■   Embed a video of someone making the presentation

■   Provide a link to speaker notes

■   Attach a related customer story PDF file

■   Include a non-disclosure agreement (NDA) for signature

■   Provide links to related content

- Notify users when content changes by enabling the ability to "watch" a page for changes

The capability to watch content provides users with a set of unique individual and team content filters to match priorities, offering relief from information overload of both internal and external content.[71]

Socialtext also has a number of other interesting features: Socialtext Dashboard, Socialtext People, Collaborative Weblogs, and Socialtext Miki. Socialtext Dashboard, shown in Figure 2-15, provides the user with a personal dashboard, similar to iGoogle and NetVibes.

Administrators can also create group or function-specific dashboards. Users can select, customize, and add any number of both internal and external widgets to these dashboards. Socialtext supports open standards: External widgets developed on the OpenSocial gadgets standard work on Socialtext, and internally developed Socialtext widgets work in iGoogle. Socialtext People, is referred to as "Facebook for the Enterprise," by Mashable.com.

Socialtext provides a user directory containing profile information such as expertise and skills, like Jive Clearspace, which is also considered an enterprise facebook-like solution. Socialtext also makes it possible to subscribe to a user's profile and stay current on their activities. Unfortunately, wiki-based Socialtext appears to lack some of Clearspace's latest collaboration functionality, such as its project management features. Socialtext offers four business solution areas designed with specific users in mind:

- Collaborative Intelligence: For sales and marketing users

- Participatory Knowledgebase: For service and support departments

- Flexible Client Collaboration: For professional service divisions

- Business Social Networks: For partners and customers

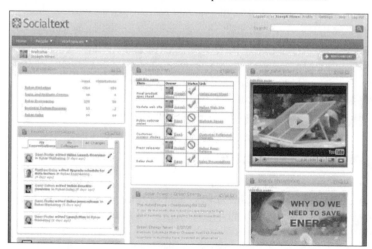

Figure 2-15 *Socialtext Dashboard.[72]*

These spaces capture the essence of social patterns and map them to a business context.[73] Socialtext enables blogging via Collaborative Weblogs designed to enable employees to collaborate by building on ideas of their colleagues. Users can add new posts or enter comments in-line and see a full history of all revisions to the conversation, a feature not found on other weblog offerings. Socialtext wants to facilitate and foster open and trusting relationships, enabling a company to make decisions and respond more quickly to change. Its product enables social networking so people can stay connected, form new networks, and discover fresh ideas from the farthest edges of the network.[74]

Socialtext even has a mobile site (http://www.socialtext.net/lite/login), enabling users to log in and access content via Socialtext Miki, an application designed to enable users to view or search content stored on Socialtext wikis, including a number of public wikis, via BlackBerry, Palm Treo, Windows Mobile devices, and others.[75] The real key is that Socialtext enables enterprises to leverage the benefits of Web 2.0 technologies tied up together instead of each one as a siloed, separate application, so that connections, communications, content, and collaboration are combined in one package. Socialtext developers are working on a collaborative spreadsheet capability called SocialCalc and have a great set of video demos (http://socialtext.blip.tv/) of these capabilities.

Wikis and the knowledge bases they enable, like Wikipedia and Socialtext's Wiki Workspaces, can provide significant strategic value to the enterprise, particularly in the areas of employee productivity and customer service. Wikis are becoming valuable business assets that can increase employee productivity and knowledge sharing. A good example is found in Cisco's Manager Portal, described in Chapter 10. This internal site served as an information source, providing a description of the project, a list of team members linked to Cisco Directory, weekly project updates, and links to release status documentation.

Wikis can also improve customer support and customer satisfaction, so much so that customers will pay a premium for content users and customers themselves help create, often at very little cost to your company. The Remote Operating System (ROS) wiki, also described in Chapter 10, enabled multiple users to contribute content documents describing various aspects of network management. It facilitated continuous improvement of the content, enabling users to refine each document over time, based on peer review.

The resulting knowledge base, consisting of hundreds pages of content, saves customers and employees countless hours of network diagnosis and problem-solving. ROS has been so well received that customers often subscribe to Cisco's ROS just to gain access to the knowledge base.[76] Now, let's turn our attention to other important examples of user-generated content: social and enterprise bookmarking, as well as folksonomies.

Bookmarking and Folksonomies

Social and enterprise bookmarking and folksonomies enable the organization to more effectively share information, and they facilitate and accelerate information search and retrieval. Social bookmarking enables users to manage bookmarks—web page locations known as URLs—for sites they wish to remember or share with others. The notion of shared online bookmarks originated in April 1996, with a free service called itList (http://www.itlist.com), shown in Figure 2-16, which enabled public and private bookmarks.[77]

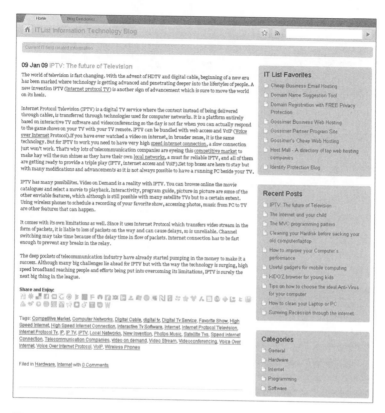

Figure 2-16   *itList.[78]*

In the three years that followed, other free online bookmark services emerged, such as HotLinks, Backflip, Clip 2, Blink, and ClickMarks, providing folders for organizing bookmarks, some even automatically. However, these companies lacked a business model for making money, so as the dot-com bubble burst, this first generation of social bookmarking companies closed.[79]

Delicious (http://delicious.com/), founded in 2003 and formerly known as Del.icio.us, pioneered the use of tags, and is said to have invented the term "social bookmarking."[80] Their site, shown in Figure 2-17, lists popular tags. These tags help identify and categorize the bookmarks more effectively, making it easier to store, organize, and search bookmarks. The social aspect refers to the capability to share bookmarks with others, offering them insight into your interests, while providing them with pointers to new information. The more these sites are used, the more valuable they become.

Many social bookmarking solutions also provide RSS feeds, notifying users when new sites are tagged, saved, and shared, enabling them to follow topics of interest. Table 2-4 provides key details on many popular social bookmarking services, with screenshots of some of their homepages shown in Figure 2-17 through 2-22.

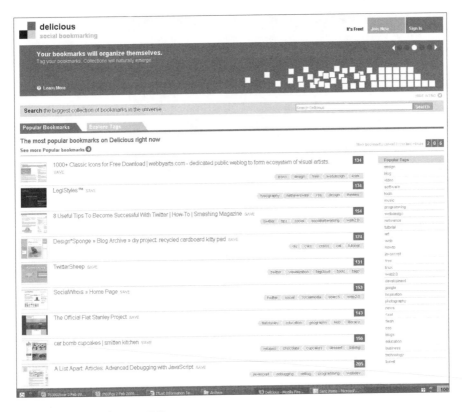

Figure 2-17   *Delicious.[81]*

From a business standpoint, social bookmarking services, particularly designed with the enterprise in mind, offer considerable untapped potential. Dogear, for example, enables users to bookmark pages within their companies' intranets and share them with others. Because Dogear also leverages enterprise directories to authenticate a user's identity, users are able to more easily find subject matter experts (SMEs) within the company. Someone looking for an expert on Web 2.0, could look at the Dogear'd Web 2.0 tag, see who has been using it, then look at that person's bookmarks, blog, contact information, and so on to narrow down the search. Sharing bookmarks in this way also sparks collaboration and sharing other resources across the organization.[88]

Table 2-4   *Key Details on Social Bookmarking Services[82]*

Service	Launch	Key Details
Delicious	12/03	http://delicious.com/
		Pioneered tagging
		Coined term "social bookmarking"
		Acquired by Yahoo! in 2005[80]

Table 2-4 *Key Details on Social Bookmarking Services[82] (continued)*

Service	Launch	Key Details
Furl	01/04	http://www.furl.net/
		For File Uniform Record Locator
		Purchased by LookSmart in 2004
		Developed for library community
		Members can store searchable copies of web pages, which remain accessible to members even if source page content is removed or changed
		Members receive 5GB storage space
Simpy	05/04	http://www.simpy.com/simpy/Splash.do
		Users create "topics" to track other users' bookmarks
		Developed to enable organizing links
		Supports RSS
CiteUlike	11/04	http://www.citeulike.org/
		Sponsored by Springer, developer of one of largest scientific databases
		Developed for academics/researchers
		Supports RSS
Connotea	12/04	http://www.connotea.org/
		Sponsored by Nature Publishing Group
		Developed for scientific community
Stumbleupon	2004	http://www.stumbleupon.com/
		Users discover, ratem and share web pages, photos, and videos
		Provides recommendations based on user/peer ratings and preferences
		Acquired by eBay in 05/07 for $75M[83]
Ma.gnolia	2006	http://ma.gnolia.com/
		Comparable to Delicious and Simpy
		Users can form groups to share common collection of bookmarks[84]

continues

Table 2-4   *Key Details on Social Bookmarking Services[82] (continued)*

Service	Launch	Key Details
Faves aka Blue Dot	2006	http://faves.com/home Comparable to Delicious Shows users "faves"—favorite sites, recently shared by their friends Known as Blue Dot until 2007[85]
Diigo	2006	http://www.diigo.com Users can tag (attach sticky notes to) web pages and share with others[86]
Connectbeam	2006	http://www.connectbeam.com/ Offers service aimed at enterprise, enables business to harness organization's collective intelligence[87]
Dogear	2007	http://www-01.ibm.com/software/lotus/products/connections/dogear.html Part of Lotus Connections suite Enables enterprise users to bookmark pages within their intranet Uses enterprise directories to authenticate users, then identify and leverage their expertise[88]

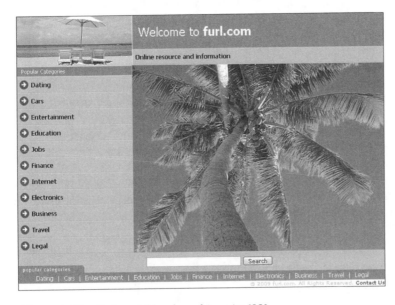

Figure 2-18   *Furl social bookmarking site.[89]*

Figure 2-19   *Stumbleupon social bookmarking site.[90]*

Figure 2-20   *Faves social bookmarking site.[91]*

Although social bookmarking has been successful on the web, most businesses have been slow to adopt it. This stems primarily from the lack, until recently, of tools such as Dogear that are designed specifically for enterprise use. Dogear enables business users to search and bookmark content inside and outside a company. In large organizations it provides a means of connecting users who might never have met ordinarily. Even if only 15% of the enterprise actively bookmarks content, the remaining 85% can benefit, particularly if their tags are leveraged by the enterprise search engine.

One key advantage of social bookmarking use in the enterprise is that the tags used to categorize bookmarks form taxonomies. These classification systems enable users to search for, and more easily find, content of interest. Taxonomies created through social bookmarking are called "folksonomies," combining "folks" and "taxonomies." As enterprise users acting as intelligent search engines tag content, certain patterns begin to emerge. Enterprises are just beginning to realize the power of pooling the collective wisdom of their employees through social bookmarking and folksonomies to enable faster, more effective information discovery and knowledge sharing.[92] Now let's examine another phenomenon that's taken hold: sharing photos and videos.

Photos and Videos

Most readers would agree that user-generated content, such as photos and videos, make web content more visual, more personal and more human. Flickr (http://www.flickr.com), Facebook (http://www.facebook.com), and YouTube (http://www.youtube.com/) are three of the most popular web-based sites enabling users to do so. Flickr, shown in Figure 2-21, was launched in February 2004, by Ludicorp, a company based in Vancouver, British Columbia. Flickr initially enabled users in multi-user chat rooms to exchange photos and evolved into a site enabling users to upload, file, and share photos and videos, becoming a popular photo storage site for bloggers. Yahoo! acquired Ludicorp and Flickr in March 2005, moving all content to servers located in the United States.[93]

Part of Flickr's popularity has been fueled by digital camera users, who print fewer photos but still want to share their photos and videos with family and friends.[94] One of the most popular sites on the web, Flickr boasts over 3 billion photos. Flickr's popularity has begun to wane as other sites, such as Facebook, combine the capability to share photos with other popular social networking features. As previously mentioned, sites such as Socialtext are beginning to combine previously siloed Web 2.0 technologies together, enabling enterprises to reap their combined value through dashboards providing access to contacts, communities, content, and collaborative tools and technologies.

Facebook, shown in Figure 2-22, hosts over 10 billion photos.[96] Like Flickr, Facebook was launched in February 2004 to put on the web the popular practice of providing new students and staff of Harvard University with photos of those already on campus.

The Facebook site, like the paper-based Facebook of Harvard university students and staff that preceded it, enabled new members to get to know each other and quickly become part of the community. Its use spread across Ivy League schools and Facebook now enables users to join networks organized by affiliation (school or workplace) or by location (city or region). Facebook enables users to share photos and videos, but users can

Figure 2-21   *Flickr.[95]*

Figure 2-22   *Facebook.[97]*

also update their personal profiles, add friends, notify friends about themselves, and send them messages.[98]

With more than 120 million active users, Facebook has become the fourth most heavily trafficked website and the most heavily trafficked social media site. As it pertains to the topic at hand, Facebook is the world's number one site for photo-sharing, with more than 30 million user-generated photos being uploaded each day.[99] This came home most profundly a few months ago when someone from high school found me on Facebook and reached out, connecting me to photos of his family, our former schoolmates, his friends, and he to mine, and so on. But now let's turn our attention to the most popular video-sharing site.

YouTube, shown in Figure 2-23 and founded in February 2005, made its official debut six months later. The popular site uses video technology in Adobe Flash format to display user-generated video content. Google acquired YouTube in 2006 and the site enables registered users to upload an unlimited number of videos, including TV and movie clips, music videos, videoblogs, and short, original videos, which both registered and unregistered users may view and comment on.

Figure 2-23   *YouTube.[103]*

YouTube also enables users to subscribe to video "channels" or content feeds. YouTube Mobile (m.youtube.com) launched in 2007, enables many popular videos to be viewed via web-enabled smartphones, discussed in Chapter 9. [100] Nearly 79 million users made over 3 billion YouTube video views in January 2008.[101] Special moments, once captured in photos, are now preserved and relived through video, which can be inserted into Facebook and other sites so anyone can share them.[102]

Like popular social bookmarking sites, Flickr, Facebook, and YouTube enable users to browse and tag user-generated content. Flickr, for example, supports free-form photo tagging, modeled after Delicious. Tags can be added to photos as they're being uploaded or later when they're displayed. The main difference in these Delicious and Flickr tags is that Delicious tags are usually created by users of content written by others.

Flickr tags are primarily added by individuals to help manage their own content, although a small number of users also upload and tag photos created by others.[104] YouTube content can also be tagged, so that when a user selects a video, related videos appear to the right onscreen. Related videos are identified by title and by user-created tags.[100] So what impact do photo and video social media have on business?

First, from a business perspective, photos and videos created by employees, customers, and partners can be considered key marketing assets. A customer photo taken with a popular product, or better yet, a video testimonial on behalf of a company or product from a customer or a known expert can help sell products, especially if it is posted on your company website for other customers to see.

Second, photos and videos can also become key parts of product reference material and training aids. A photo or video of a product assembly or linkage can augment documentation, and often express more detail in a shorter time span. New hires can quickly come up to speed if they make use of video training from experts. So it's important for business managers to consider how to enable users to create, share, and leverage this medium as a way of preserving and sharing business knowledge, developing communities, and perhaps even increasing collaboration effectiveness, as you will see in the next sections.

Communities

Communities play a significant role in a Web 2.0 world. Traditionally, the word "communities" has represented a group of people living and interacting in one physical location.[105] The advent of the web, and particularly Web 2.0, has forever changed that. Now, when a group of people interact online via email, instant messaging, and online social networks, they are said to form an online, virtual community or e-community. These communities enable both social and professional groups to interact, often to share knowledge and information via the web.

A community affiliation may be represented by something as simple as an email distribution list, for example, used mainly to disseminate information to its members. The members, in turn, may not know one another, but still share a sense of community from being part of the list and "sharing" information imparted by it. In fact, virtual communities depend on sharing and interaction between community members, which is part of an unwritten contract between them. When community members interact often enough virtually, they form stronger interconnections, called social networks. Web 2.0 is characterized by the virtual communities presented earlier in this chapter: Delicious, Flickr, and Facebook.[106] And how is this affecting business?

The importance of online, virtual communities has recently begun to be realized. Depending on the type of business, virtual communities may be organizational, as in a group of Sales account managers; regional, as in a group of manufacturers on the West Coast; or topical, such as in a Green team focused on a company's carbon footprint. A number of tools and technologies have begun to emerge, enabling business managers to create and nurture such communities. Some of those are identified later, in the "Collaborative Technologies" section of this chapter.

What's most important to remember is that Web 2.0 technologies now enable users to interact with individuals of a like mind, around the world, instantly, something Cisco describes as "The Human Network Effect."[107] This network, and capability to leverage its full potential, has significant ramifications for businesses managers needing to foster the ability to gain access to information, knowledge, and expertise distributed across a global workforce.

Communities and the networks they form are important to driving business results. Employee-to-employee (E2E) communities contribute to business success, but so can partner-to-partner (P2P) and customer-to-customer (C2C) communities. Members of these communities can help each other through knowledge- and information-sharing, accelerating the ability to find information and solve problems. Chapter 10 discusses how Cisco has formed and leveraged its E2E intranet community to drive Web 2.0 adoption. It also describes how Cisco worked to build an E2C and C2C communities among its customers, for example.

Chapter 11, "Cisco's Approach to Sales 2.0," describes how communities, such as the Systems Engineering community, through its Technology Solutions Network, help connect the dots, working together and supporting each other. It also describes how Cisco has expanded its reach into its Channel Partner community, establishing a P2P network through the annual Partner Summit, and leveraging that network to gain valuable partner feedback. This feedback enables the company to better understand partner needs and establish programs to address those needs.

But it is perhaps through communities enabling employee-to-partner-to-customer interactions that the most impactful business transformation can occur. Business is only just beginning to realize the value of these end-to-end communities in accelerating communication, decision-making, business processes, and delivery of results. Take, for example, a customer's ability to share feedback on a product with one of your supply chain partners, and then jump on a web conference with your product's design team to brainstorm a more effective product design for the next release. A product-feedback-redesign process that might have taken 5–6 discussions and design sessions, over several weeks, can be accelerated and fit into 1–2 sessions in a few days, perhaps even in a few hours. These are the types of interactions enabled within Web 2.0 communities, through a process called collaboration.

Collaboration

Collaboration, from the term "co-labor," means working together toward a common goal. Collaboration can occur between two or more individuals or organizations, and is a recursive process, meaning it is often applied repeatedly. Throughout this chapter you have seen examples of groups interacting, sharing knowledge, and learning from one another through blogs, wikis, bookmarking, and folksonomies, even photo- and video-sharing. But collaboration is often applied to problem-solving as well.[108]

Collective wisdom of a diverse community, often referred to as the "wisdom of the crowds," can yield results that are generally more creative, innovative, and often more complete. As groups work together, they aggregate information that would not have been available solely to any individual member. Collaboration can, therefore, build consensus and lead to better, more informed decisions than individual members would have come to on their own.[109] So how can this be applied?

Business managers and organizations can leverage collaboration to increase knowledge-sharing, improve decision-making, and accelerate productivity and problem-solving. Cisco employees, customers, and partners lead by example, using collaborative technologies to communicate and collaborate with each other. Collaboration enables new ways of interacting between functional business units and across employee, partner, and customer organizations. The next section describes how Cisco technologies, for example, have enabled the company, and many of its partners and customers, to reduce travel expenses, improve productivity, enhance speed of delivery and quality of customer service, and increase sales. So let's focus on these technologies and describe how they are being used to foster and increase collaboration in ways that yield business value.

Collaborative Technologies

Companies have begun to develop a number of technologies to enable and increase collaboration between employees, partners, and customers, establishing communities, increasing collaboration, and yielding significant business benefits. Cisco, for example, has a suite of technologies that enable collaboration within the organization and across its partners and customers: Cisco TelePresence, WebEx, and Unified Communications. This section describes the challenges these technologies are designed to solve, describes each technology in some detail, and explains how Cisco employees, partners, and customers are using the technologies to deliver business value. The first place to focus attention on is how Cisco is using one of its latest technologies, TelePresence, to host key meetings.

Cisco TelePresence

Many companies, like Cisco, host Quarterly Business Review (QBR) meetings with partners and customers. These events often, despite a good deal of logistical and schedule coordination, result in spotty attendance. Generally, these meetings also require considerable travel time and expense for highly paid executives to gather in one location. Collaborative technologies, such as TelePresence, change all that, enabling Cisco, customers, and partner executives to hold regular meetings, virtually face-to-face, and collaborate "live" on critical business planning and decision-making.

Bringing partners and customers together leveraging TelePresence has also proven to be a successful sales tool. Cisco invites partners and customers to visit Cisco offices to see for themselves how effective the technology is. Partners and customers quickly see the advantage of leveraging TelePresence internally and also with their own partners and customers. The savings on travel expenses alone helps customers offset their total cost to deploy TelePresence internally. One example, Nexus (http://www.nexusis.com/), a premier provider of Cisco's Unified Communications solutions, estimates their TelePresence deployment costs will be offset by travel expense savings within three years.[110]

Cisco TelePresence, shown in Figure 2-24, enables face-to-face meetings between individuals and groups in geographically dispersed locations in real time. It delivers a high-quality, "in person" experience, creating a "room within a room" around a single, virtual conference table. Using advanced audiovisual and interactive technologies, it renders spatial and discrete audio and life-size, high-definition images.[111] Attendees report a sense of truly being across the table from other meeting participants.

Cisco now hosts its Quarterly Business Reviews (QBRs) virtually with many of its Channel partners via TelePresence. This eliminates travel costs and executive downtime and has resulted in marked improvements in attendance and the same, if not, better attendee satisfaction, based on their feedback. The next technology to examine is WebEx, the newest technology in Cisco's portfolio, which is changing customer and partner technical support.

Figure 2-24 *Cisco TelePresence.[112]*

WebEx

As technologies become increasingly complex, many companies, like Cisco, are faced with the challenge of having enough skilled, deep technical experts to solve partner and customer problems. Historically, technical experts have done most of their work onsite, which meant traveling 60-80% of their time, wasting valuable time and energy that could be put to more productive use. Collaborative technologies, like WebEx, change all that, enabling a smaller pool of highly specialized technical experts available virtually to solve technical problems.

WebEx conferencing enables desktop, presentation, and technical document sharing, enabling problem-solving and collaboration on solutions. Bringing partners and customers together via WebEx has also proven to be a successful sales strategy. As soon as partners and customers see how WebEx works, they're eager to use it internally and leverage it with their own partners and customers. Like TelePresence, WebEx offers significant savings on travel time and expense.

WebEx, a Cisco company, provides a suite of tools designed to increase employee, partner, and customer productivity. WebEx applications support online meetings and web and video conferencing through the services it offers under the name WebEx Centers, shown in Figure 2-25.

The following list identifies key features of the Cisco WebEx Center products:

- WebEx Meeting Center: Hosted conferencing solution enables secure application, presentation, and document-sharing between multiple parties in real time, both internally and externally.

- WebEx Event Center: Hosted, Webcast conferencing solution, similar to Meeting Center, optimized for larger audiences, and supporting the complete event cycle, end-to-end. Manages live and recorded event planning, promoting, presenting, lead tracking, follow-up, and analysis.

Figure 2-25 *Cisco WebEx Centers.[113]*

- **WebEx Sales Center:** Customized online portals provide on-demand access to team selling features, including meeting schedules, sales team contact information, and selling collateral. Enables online sales training and demos, including an attention indicator and the ability to establish customer portals.

- **WebEx Training Center:** On-demand delivery of interactive, online instruction, using rich media. Supports rich online training features, including breakout rooms, as well as quizzing, polling, and remote testing of training participants and hands-on labs.

- **WebEx Support Center:** Application enabling support organizations, such as IT, to deliver real-time support remotely. Enables remote access to system information: desktop, application view, and control; file transfer, reboot, and reconnect; and WebACD (Automatic Call Distributor) and support escalation. Enables organizations to decrease call resolution time, minimize onsite visits, and reduce overall support costs.

WebEx also offers on-demand collaboration services through its WebEx Connect platform, shown in Figure 2-26.

WebEx Connect is a software-as-a-service (SaaS) platform and Web application combining real-time collaboration with personal and team spaces and data services via widgets. Core collaboration services include

- Access to contacts, with presence and instant messaging

- Personal My WebEx workspace with access to calendar and personal files

- Shared team workspaces with document sharing and discussion threads

- Voice over IP (VoIP) and video communication, including click-to-call

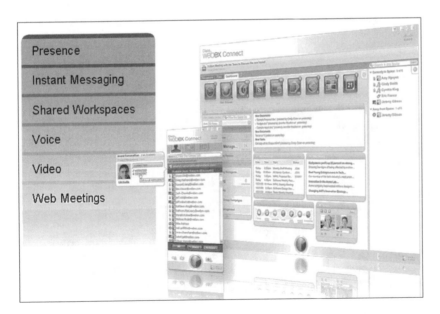

Figure 2-26   *Cisco WebEx Connect.[113]*

- Video- and web-conferencing, including one-click web meetings and one-to-one desktop sharing

- Integrated access to the suite WebEx meeting services

Connect also provides an open widget development platform. It supports the creation of simple mashups to fully customized applications that can be delivered through portals, websites, and proprietary clients. Connect offers infinite ways to improve collaboration between employees, partners, and customers.[114]

Connect offers the ability to not only accelerate but completely transform business processes, such as technical support. Cisco's highly skilled systems engineers, for example, now establish a WebEx session with a customer's or partner's less experienced on-site engineer to solve technical problems. The skilled expert may take control of the on-site engineer's computer to walk step by step through the problem and/or leverage the on-site engineer as his or her eyes and hands. The added benefit is that customer and partner engineers gain knowledge and experience from this hands-on training.

Cisco's systems engineers have begun using WebEx to host technical seminars, extending the training opportunities. These webinars enable Cisco to provide and record training on its products and services to a much larger audience of customers and partners, who can view or review the recorded material at their convenience. The use of WebEx eliminates much, if not all, travel time and helps to restore skilled expert job satisfaction and work-life balance, while improving the skill set and job satisfaction of the newly trained experts.

But the ways Cisco partners are using this technology internally and with their partners and customers are perhaps even more compelling. Nexus, for example, is leveraging WebEx and TelePresence to train new hires. Nexus now hosts two-hour training sessions for new hires, eliminating the time and expense for their travel to Nexus headquarters and accelerating their integration into the organization. Students can also replay the recorded training sessions as required as a refresher.[110] Now, let's move on for a brief discussion of ways Cisco's Unified Communications solutions are enabling collaboration, particularly for our customers.

Unified Communications

The ability to reach the right person in a timely fashion is a key measure of business agility. Historically, as most employees spent the majority of their time at their desks, with desktop phones at their sides, this was fairly easy. Today, reaching them is much more complex. Many workers are highly mobile and use both wired and wireless phones, as well as varied communication methods: email, fax, instant and text messaging, and audio- and video-conferencing.

Cisco Unified Communications (UC) addresses complex challenges, such as these, by integrating communication and collaboration with applications and processes that define and run the business. Cisco's UC solutions offer users a media-rich collaboration experience, using the network as a platform to unify voice, video, data, and mobile applications on fixed and mobile networks to its more than fifty thousand UC customers.[115] Unified Communications include capabilities shown in Figure 2-27.

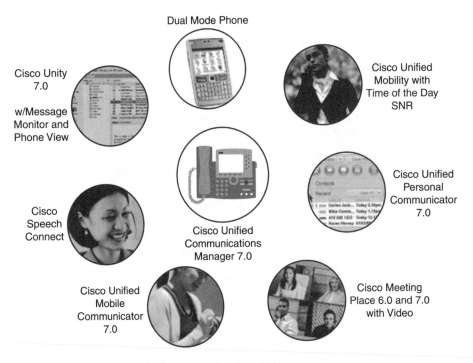

Figure 2-27   *Cisco Unified Communications.[116]*

Cisco UC capabilities include:

■   Cisco Unified Communications Manager (CUCM) manages calls from either a wired IP phone or mobile device, offers the capability to move between campus wireless and external cellular networks, supports dual-mode devices, offers single-number reach and single-business voicemail.

■   Cisco Unified MeetingPlace (CUMP) integrates voice and video and integrates with CUPC and Microsoft Office Communicator.

■   Cisco Unified Mobile Communicator (CUMC) extends UC to mobile phones and smartphones, integrates directories and presence, offers single business–number reach, office voice mail notification and playback, call logs, and CUMP conference notifications.

■   Cisco Unified Personal Communicator (CUPC) provides Instant Messaging, voice, video, and web conferencing.

■   Cisco Unified Video Advantage (CUVA) enables multipoint video calls.

■   Cisco Unity Voicemail enables secure messaging, message monitoring, interrupted session recovery, visual message locator, speech access, mobile voice messages, and integration with CUPC.[116]

Over the past few years many companies deployed Voice over IP (VoIP) networks to achieve cost savings. Today, UC offers the capability to increase productivity, enable mobility, and transform business processes. Unified messaging (UM) enables access to email, voice mail, and fax via a common interface on either phone or computer, so recorded messages can be easily reviewed, sorted, saved, filed, forwarded, or answered. Because UC enables real-time access to contact lists and their presence (availability) indicators, automatic dialing, and conferencing, its scope is much broader than UM.

The main focus of UM is increasing employee productivity. UC, however, enables mobility and makes it possible to improve, accelerate, and transform business processes. UC enables tight integration of communication and business process, helping to ensure the right person, or even multiple people at the same time, can be reached quickly via their preferred devices and communication methods.[117]

Let's take a moment to examine exactly how Cisco's Unified Communications solutions enable employees, partners, and customers a rich collaboration experience and support seamless mobile collaboration. Figure 2-28 below shows a scenario of how collaboration is enabled and enhanced by Cisco UC throughout a typical business day.

The following is a more detailed explanation of Figure 2-28:

- 9 a.m.—Lead weekly sales meeting, enhanced through videoconferencing.

- 11 a.m.—Use Speech Connect while driving to a customer meeting to reach your account manager and discuss the customer account.

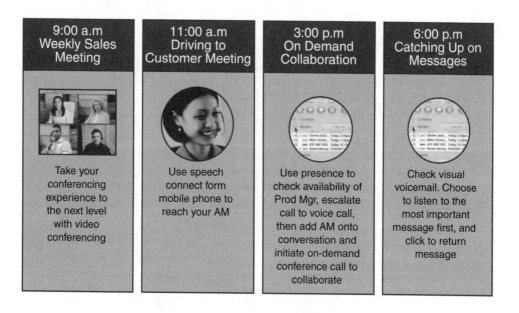

Figure 2-28 *Cisco Unified Communications' rich collaboration experience.*

- 3 p.m.—Use presence to check availability of a product manager, escalate call to voice call, then add your account manager on to the conversation and initiate an on-demand conference call to collaborate on customer feedback on your product.

- 6 p.m.—Catch up on voicemails by checking visual voicemail. Choose to listen to the most important message first, and use one-click to reply or return the call.

Figure 2-29 shows how the Cisco UC solutions enable seamless mobile collaboration between employees, partners, and customers throughout a typical business day.

Here is a more detailed explanation of Figure 2-29:

- 11 a.m.—While waiting for a rental car at the airport, with mobile presence set to available, engage in secure text messaging with your regional manager.

- 12 noon—You receive an important customer call, placed to your business phone, on your mobile phone, as you park in the Cisco parking lot.

- 12:10 p.m.—As you get to your cube, your active customer call is automatically handed off from your mobile phone to your IP desk phone.

- 1 p.m.—As you head off to the cafeteria for lunch, your on campus dual-mode phone automatically registers as a wireless extension of your IP desk phone and your next call is routed directly to your mobile over the Cisco Unified Wireless Network.

Obviously, these scenarios provide some insight into how UC technologies enable and enhance collaboration throughout a typical business day.[116] But perhaps the most compelling stories on the business value of collaborative technologies come from our customers.

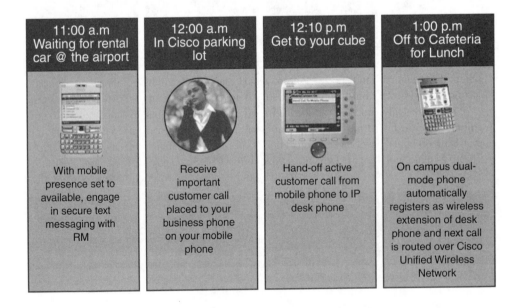

Figure 2-29 *Cisco Unified Communications seamless mobile collaboration.*

Nexus, for example, reports that they combine CUPC with WebEx to gain productivity and efficiencies, giving them increased "reachability." Single-number reach, leveraging presence indicators or CUPC, enables customers to connect more quickly to reach Nexus employees the first time, nearly every time, enabling faster communication and collaboration on important business concerns. And, when Nexus does miss a call, there is a significant decrease in the number of calls needed to respond to a customer. Much of the usual phone tag is eliminated by increased availability.

In general, Nexus and their customers are now talking within one or two calls. So what's the business impact? This decrease in the time to respond to a customer call improves Nexus' employee productivity and customer satisfaction. Nexus employees also report that they love being able to conference call, or to leave the office and push one button to transfer a call to their Smartphone versus losing time hanging up and having to call the customer back.

Finally, there's what we like to call the "domino effect" that partners' and customers' showcasing Cisco's collaborative technology enables. Nexus, like Cisco, uses everything they sell. They recently reported that one of their customers, SchoolsFirst Federal Credit Union (http://www.schoolsfirstfcu.org/), seeing the effectiveness WebEx and TelePresence in their interactions with Nexus, decided to trial videoconferencing technologies in several of their branches located in southern California.

Like the engineering virtual expert model described earlier, SchoolsFirst realized they could pool their loan and investment officers centrally. That enabled SchoolsFirst loan officers to be available to more customers located in their dispersed branch offices during more hours. Rather than have the officers travel from branch to branch, losing valuable face time with customers, the officers stayed in one location and the customers reached them via collaborative web technology.[118] We expect to see this sort of domino effect more and more as the business value of
WebEx, TelePresence, and Unified Communications collaborative technologies continue to be realized by Cisco partners and customers themselves, and their partners and customers.

In Short

After reading this chapter, you should be thinking "it's all about the user," and you'd be right. Users have been driving the web evolution since the creation of the very first web pages. What makes the user so important to Web 2.0 is the fact that users can create and share content, photos, video, and so on in more new and unique ways than ever before. Through blogs, users can comment on anything and everything, including your company, changing the way marketing works and providing a fantastic opportunity to gather customer feedback.

Users can leverage wikis to share information and develop knowledge repositories, which managed correctly, can create a valuable and revenue-generating business asset. Bookmarking and folksonomies play an important role, helping the organization to again share information, but to define and tag information in ways that accelerate search and retrieval. Photos and videos can not only help to make content more visual, more personal, and more human, but again, can serve as a business asset because nothing sells a product better than a satisfied customer video testimonial, particularly if that customer is a known and respected expert in the field.

One key takeaway is that collaboration is one way to increase knowledge-sharing, improve decision-making, and accelerate productivity and problem-solving amongst employees, partners, and customers. Applications like Socialtext combine the benefits of many Web 2.0 technologies, putting contacts, communities, content, and collaboration together in one dashboard. You've also seen how collaborative technologies are key enablers, increasing productivity and reducing travel time and expense.

Cisco TelePresence enables executives to hold "virtual" face-to-face meetings, increasing attendance while eliminating travel time and expense. WebEx enables highly specialized technical experts to solve technical problems remotely, training less skilled engineers and improving job satisfaction and work/life balance. Unified Communications offers the capability to increase employee productivity and reachability. UC also enables mobility and makes it possible to improve, accelerate, and transform business processes.

We hope this chapter has helped you to understand how to harness and leverage user-generated content: blogs, wikis, folksonomies, videos, and communities, as well as collaboration and collaborative technologies described here to reengineer and transform your business function, department, or process and reap the value Web 2.0 can enable. And do take advantage of the examples provided in the final chapters, which describe ways Cisco has already begun to do so.

<monologue>

When I think of Web 2.0, the first and foremost characteristic that comes to mind is the slick user interface, with eye-catching images as well as the multi-media rich videos. Of course, I also think of the banner ads. True to this thought, the tipping point to Web 2.0 indeed was the improvements in tools and frameworks to develop effective user interface (UI), especially client-side scripting, Ajax, and the concept of mashups. Who can forget Craig's List on Google maps? A simultaneous or parallel concept was the arrival of web applications that served as viable platforms for various activities, shopping being the foremost. Of course, now we have Rich Internet Applications (RIA) [1] development systems such as AIR and Silverlight, which rival the capabilities of desktop interfaces. In fact, for the first time, InfoWorld created a new category called "Best Rich Internet Application Platform" [2] for its technology awards. RIA has achieved the level of a platform alongside traditional development environments. Take a look at how the website capzles [3] captures multimedia stroylines and you will see what a slick user interface looks like. (Thanks to our beloved reviewer Praveen for this pointer.) And people are now more regularly talking in terms of the user interface feel, mental bandwidth to use an interface [4], and interaction audits!

</monologue>

Rich Internet Applications: Practices, Technologies, and Frameworks

This is a person-behind-the-curtain chapter. You will not see any slick UI technical procedures, but you will read about practices, frameworks, and concepts that can enable a slick web application. Enterprises face choices in this area. For example, "Should an app be a web application or traditional?" and "What frameworks should we use for a web application?" and "Could we use open source frameworks?"

Although one cannot definitely answer all these questions for every circumstance, this chapter does point out what is available and the position of those frameworks and platforms in an enterprise development ecosystem. As a result, this chapter is broad in scope as it deals with multiple technologies and business aspects, ranging from user interface to frameworks to concepts. The focus is more on technology than business simply because the big business idea is the rich user interaction and, as you will see, there are many ways to achieve the goal. If the topic list in this chapter looks like a daunting tech laundry list with names like Ajax, Comet, Ruby, and such, don't despair. They are explained with the book's audience in mind. The key to the selection of technologies, frameworks, and relevant application comes down to the business as well as development preferences. For example, Twitter chose Ruby on Rails, whereas WebEx is built with the Dojo framework. Each framework/technology has its own quirks and advantages, but they all evolve quickly because of the nature of the development methods as well as the public nature of the Internet. The best strategy is to have an understanding of the lay of the land, make a rational selection, and then focus on it—there are no right or wrong choices.

What Exactly Is an RIA and Why Do We Care About It?

This was the first question our editors asked me to clarify: Tell why this is relevant, what the choices are, and who makes them. Fair questions indeed! This first section strives to answer those questions.

RIA stands for Rich Internet Application, and is a category of very slick applications that leverage multi-media, high-definition graphics, and a highly interactive user experience. Usually RIAs are identified with consistent brand experience in a multimedia world. Movie and game introductions, new product launches, high-end consumer products, and general corporate websites are ideal candidates for RIAs. The operative term is "engaging experience," and the experience need not be just for movie websites. For example, MarketReplay [5] is a stock market playback and analysis tool from NASDAQ and it is offered on a subscription basis. Also as Web 2.0 evolves, RIA takes on new meanings. Let us quickly look at the world of RIA.

First of all, a rich internet application is not about just a slick user interface; it is also about the feel and how the various elements interact. For example, if the web page is refreshed for every click, the flow is broken; but if only parts of the page are refreshed, (say using AJAX technologies), the feel for the user is very different.

Second, RIAs are also about issues like feature velocity (that is, the speed at which new features can be incorporated into a website or web application) and availability of new functionalities; issues which are of interest not only from a development perspective but also in a business sense. The business should be able to conceptualize and then specify the additional features that make a web application more useful to its users; the developers should be able to incorporate them elegantly and in a timely manner, all of which calls for frameworks such as Rails and Dojo.

Third, a rich user interface is great, but the businesses and business models it enables are even greater. In the enterprise world, instead of an employee logging into ERP, email, IM, CRM, and multiple other systems, all these apps can now be brought into one personal portal that the employee can access through any device (PC, phone, and so on) from any place. Or, at the back end, the tasks can be segregated out, and one company can provide tax calculations, another can provide shipping charges and arrival date, another can provide an up-to-date spec sheet, and so on. Further, with tools such as widgets and gadgets a browser can provide rich apps, radically changing the enterprise app deployment paradigm.

Fourth, RIAs are not limited to phones and PCs. They are coming to your living room via a TV near you. In the Consumer Electronics Show in 2009, the Yahoo widget engine is embedded in Samsung TVs [6] and suddenly all the cool RIAs can be run on TVs.

Fifth, the browser as an application platform will change the face of enterprise applications. In fact, people are already claiming that the browser might be the next operating system [7]. There are many reasons for this transition, ranging from better security due to faster and automatic patching of vulnerabilities, to the capability to distribute application updates faster, to relatively simpler application development cycles. The popularity of browsers will naturally cement the RIA development platform as the primary application development vehicle. Of course, this development will not come immediately, but coupled with other trends such as the Virtual Desktop, this transition might be accelerated.

And finally, enterprise portal/portlet standards such as JSR168 and JSR286 are relevant here. Even if these do not fall in the rich Web 2.0 UI technologies, they are key to many enterprise software and functions. Although I do not plan to cover portals in this chapter, we recommend that they be considered along with other application architecture choices.

This brings us to the question of choices—who makes them and why. Earlier it was relatively easy: Choices were mostly technology related, such as whether to use Java back end and HTML front end or a PHP site or some other discrete combinations. But in the RIA world, the choices are not technical or clinical. First of all, the business goal has lots of influence on the choices: A database-based application might be built more easily by Rails, whereas a multimedia-intensive application for a movie website might be better off using Adobe AOR or Microsoft's Silverlight. The developer preference also needs to be factored: A PHP shop will use a PHP framework such as Zend, whereas a Python shop will be comfortable with Django, and of course JavaScript folks would prefer Prototype or the Dojo toolkit. In short, today's choices are more interdisciplinary and depend on the situation.

Mashups   It is no doubt that mashups have become a hit in the Web 2.0 world. Let us take a quick look at mashups and their relevance.

Mashups are the most useful Web 2.0 mechanics. Essentially mashups are combinations of two websites [8], for example real estate data (house for sale) and Google Maps. A good example of the multitude of mashups just on Google Maps is on the Google Maps Mania site, which lists 100 Google Maps mashups [9]. The list spans from a brewery map [10] to movie filming locations. There are useful mashups such as the ones that show telephone area code and zip code on a map. All this is done by mashups of data with Google Maps. Another interesting mashup mixes Flickr and Google Maps to show pictures from various parts of the world [11].

Mashups enable you to incorporate a different perspective or multiple perspectives by combining information at website level. There are lots of new ideas around mashups—mapping to messaging to music to shopping [12]—but all center around combining websites using interfaces provided by the websites. The combining can be done either at the web server or on the client browser.

ReadWriteWeb has a good article [13] on the business aspects of mashups. Although mashups can be very effective, they also have a few drawbacks, including the lack of a service-level agreement, lack of speed, and the limited functionality that comes from being restricted to the APIs exposed by the websites. But you can develop an effective mashup site with some aspects controlled by you and other parts coming from well known websites (for example, data you get from an internal source rather than Google Maps).

Lots of mashup websites provide value in the consumer space, such as Zillow or Movoto for real estate or Netvibes for personalized portals or even Zimbra or Zoho.com in the enterprise space. Zimbra and Zoho are better examples of RIA than they are pure mashups, but they do include elements of mashups.

A Techno-Business Tour Through the RIA Land

Now that you know what rich Internet applications do, it's time to take a look behind the scenes, at how and why they are built. There is no doubt that new web applications are becoming an essential part of life. Amazon and other shopping sites, Google Maps, and others testify to the power of the new breed of web applications. Moreover, web applications are replacing desktop applications.

Naturally, the new breed of RIAs are made possible by new developments in user interactions, as well as the capability to crank out web applications by using newer programming languages as well as frameworks. Instead of sending back and forth big HTML pages, one can now send small pieces of data between the browser and server. This makes web applications a lot more responsive and dynamic, for an excellent user experience. New interactive models are being developed. For example, instead of an Evite-like one-way party, you can use publish/subscribe among an ad-hoc group to find the best place and time (www.renkoo.com), using technologies such as Comet and OpenAjax Hub.

There are also challenges. With dynamic and interactive technologies, websites are not homogeneous anymore. The websites are accessed via a multitude of devices which include fully functional computers, handhelds, and even printers. All these different access modes require different presentation and sometimes different content as well. Moreover, a majority of access is by non-human methods (such as search and mashup) and these create a challenge because much of the content (such as rich video and Ajax) is invisible to search engines. These challenges are being addressed by various vendors. For example, Adobe is working on searchability of dynamic websites, whereas OpenAJAX is proposing ideas around device profiles.

The first thing to do is take a good look at all the facets of rich Internet applications and then dig deeper into them. As the applications' focus moved from client/server to the Internet, one of the major hurdles to leverage web architectures was the lack of good user experience and that led to the various technologies and development tools and frameworks for client-side and server-side processing. Before going into the details, it's best to get a view of the topology. Figure 3-1 shows a schematic view of a web page flow.

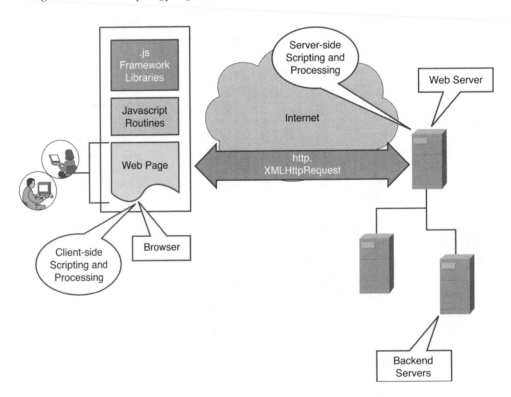

Figure 3-1   *Web page flow schematic.*

The focus in Figure 3.1 is the web page, which runs inside a web browser, and the capabilities you can build in that space. Web 2.0 has ushered in the era of web applications that live in web servers and other back-end servers and interact with a user via the web browser. All the work related to RIA is to make the web user experience better than the desktop counterpart's user experience. Although web applications have come a long way from static HTML pages, there are still challenges.

If you refer back to Figure 3.1, you can see that the browser interacts with the web server over the Internet via the HTTP protocol. The web page itself has many parts, including the part that is seen by the user, site-specific JavaScript programs, and framework routines and style sheets. The web server itself is not a single entity; it actually is the front end for a set of servers that manage different aspects—shopping carts, e-commerce, catalogue servers, search servers, ad servers, inference servers, and so on. In fact, a single web page is the result of a lot of work by many servers. For example, a web page from Amazon.com requires around 150 services. Each service has different sources for information and data, as well as different processing models. A modern web page has come a long way from static content that had no interactivity except for a few page counters and a few CGI attributes.

Another important point to remember is the division of labor between the server and the client. There is processing happening at the client side in the browser and there is also server-side processing done by various server-side frameworks. When you design a web page or a set of web pages, you can add markers in Python or Ruby or other scripting languages, and when a user requests a page, these markers would be processed by an appropriate server-side scripting engine.

For example, if you want to display a page with a list of books, you might design the page with all the graphics and text surrounding the page and add a Ruby marker for a table to display a list of books from a database, based on the query from the user. The user would request a list of books with some criteria (for example, title contains "Bond") which would be sent to the web application that runs the list page, which in turn would query the database and fill in the list with the names returned from the database in the table you had marked. In fact, web applications built mainly on databases have become common, and that prompted the advent of the Ruby on Rails server-side framework, covered later in this chapter.

The client-side processing is slightly different. For example, if this sample list of books had multiple pages, it would be wasteful to query the server for every page and redisplay the web page. Instead, you can query the server for the next page, get that data, and refresh the web page table rather than the whole page. Also, if there are lots of graphics the full-page-back-and-forth scheme takes a long time, but get-the-data-for-next-page-and-refresh-only-the-table scheme is much faster and thus results in a better user experience. In fact, that is the secret of XMLHttpRequest and Ajax.

To recap, web applications need a browser-based user interface that is dynamic, interactive, and responsive. That is exactly what Ajax and RIA frameworks provide. They also enable you to develop and maintain web applications easier and faster, and that is where server-side frameworks such as Ruby on Rails excel.

Now that you have graduated from Web Page 101, armed with this understanding look at the various elements that are part of the journey from static web pages to dynamic RIA frameworks and their business relevance. Table 3-1 lists the major technologies, their characteristics, and their relevance.

Table 3-1   *Key RIA Technologies*

Technology	Relevance
HyperText Markup Language (HTML)	Embed the various display characteristics of a web page's content in a browser, for example, tables, headings, placement of graphics, and so on.
	So far, HTML has been a presentation technology, but folks are working on the next generation version, HTML 5, which has many more capabilities [14]. Although a pervasive ubiquitous HTML 5 is a couple of years away, it is clear that HTML will have more Web 2.0 capabilities in the future.
HyperText Transfer Protocol (HTTP)	Used to exchange content and instructions between a web server and a browser. The protocol is understood by all the infrastructure devices such as firewalls, routers, and load balancers.
	HTTP is the most widely used protocol on the Internet.
Cascading Style Sheets (CSS)	This is an interesting development for separating content from presentation. Using CSS, one can change the look and feel of a web page without actually changing the content.
	CSS is very relevant to business because it gives the flexibility to display the same content with different branding, for example, one for enterprise customers and one for Small and Medium Businesses (SMB), or one type of web page for summer and another type for winter.
JavaScript	Scripting language used to write program snippets that are processed in the browser. In short, JavaScript is a language for client-side scripting. JavaScript has no relation to the popular language Java (outside of the name). It was called Mocha and LiveScript, but later became JavaScript[15].
	JavaScript is based on a Document Object Model (DOM) and event-driven program snippets, which is very different from traditional monolithic programs. Naturally the scope is also limited to interactions in a web page.
	JavaScript has become the essential component for interactive, dynamic web pages.
	The browser is in a stand-alone sandbox, which means normally it cannot execute anything outside itself. So all the JavaScript needs to run a web page is downloaded from the web server every time. If you are using frameworks such as Doo, they also need to be downloaded in addition to the site-specific code. Thus, over-use of JavaScript is not effective.
AIR	AIR is Adobe's [16] rich Internet application platform.
	The AIR platform has a design-time component that developers use to create web applications, as well as a runtime component that users need to download and install before they can run the AIR applications. The download can be automated and thus is easy for the user. AIR platform supports applications developed with JavaScript, CSS, and other technologies, as well as Adobe's Flex and Flash.

Table 3-1 *Key RIA Technologies (continued)*

Technology	Relevance
SilverLight	Silverlight is Microsoft's framework [17] for rich Internet applications. It also is a runtime component with associated development kit.
XMLHttpRequest (XHR)	XMLHttpRequest, as the name implies, is a method for a browser to exchange data with web server [18]. It is this mechanism that makes it easy to update parts of a web page without getting the whole page again from the web server.
Extensible Hypertext Markup Language (XHTML)	Usually web page contents are marked by HTML. But HTML are difficult to transform (for example to display in a mobile phone). Marking up a web page with XHTML makes it easier to transform.
Asynchronous JavaScript and XML (Ajax)	Nowadays, Ajax is a catchall phrase for a set of client-side processing capabilities that include XMLHttpRequest, XHTML, CSS, JavaScript, and the DOM model of processing. From a business perspective, a web application needs to have Ajax technologies because it results in better performance and an enhanced user experience. Of course, it is not a technical necessity. In addition, it is easier to talk about these client-side processing technologies in aggregate than separately.
OpenAjax	OpenAjax Alliance [19] is a consortium that focuses on enabling the use of Ajax technologies. The members work together to address challenges and problems either by developing lightweight frameworks or by working with browser vendors to add capabilities into the browsers.
JavaScript Object Notation (JSON)	This is a lightweight data format to exchange data between a browser and a web server. JSON is a IETF specification [20] RFC4627. From a business perspective, use of JSON as a data exchange format makes interoperability and extensibility easer and faster than proprietary formats.
Ruby on Rails (RoR)	Rails is a server-side framework for developing database-based websites. The Ruby programming language is used when developing within Rails. The RoR framework has features that make development and maintenance of websites easy. The features include built-in capabilities for testing, a REST (representational state transfer)–based URL scheme, model-view-controller pattern–based interactions, routing primitives, and extensibility (by using the Ruby language). The business reasons for using the RoR framework are the ability to develop web applications faster as well as the ease with which the web applications can be maintained.
Dojo	Dojo is an open source Ajax toolkit consisting of 26K of JavaScript functions for "DOM manipulation, Animations (like wipe and slide), Ajax, Event and keyboard normalization across different browsers, Internationalization (i18n) and Accessibility (a11y)" [21].

continues

Table 3-1 *Key RIA Technologies (continued)*

Technology	Relevance
	Dojo also has add-ons (DooX, or Doo Extensions) and widgets (Dijits, short for Doo Widgets). For example, progress bars, buttons, spinners and sliders, tooltips, an editor, modal dialogs, tab containers, and form widgets are part of the widgets, and bigger controls such as grids, analytics and charting are part of the extensions. For a rich UI, one either has to develop widgets from scratch or use a toolkit such as Dojo. And for consistency, reliability, breadth, and uniformity, use of Dojo is recommended.
Yahoo Widgets and Google Gadgets	The widgets/gadgets [22], [23] are mini-applications like weather displays, stock tickers, calendars and so forth. Usually the widgets/gadgets run on the desktop, not inside a browser, and they can be ported to run on other devices. In fact, at the CES 2009 show, Samsung showed TVs running Yahoo widgets! The Google gadgets come as part of the Google desktop search package, whereas the Yahoo Widgets can be downloaded on their own. From a business perspective, it is instructive to apply the models and develop nifty gadgets/widgets that make sense, such as widgets displaying order status or activities on a product community page or any other information customers and partners would find useful. When selecting a functionality for a gadget, ease of use, aesthetics (remember users are going to look at it constantly or at least multiple times), and relevance are the key. And as the widget engines become available in TVs and other consumer products, the business relevance and potential of this technology will increase tremendously.

Web 2.0 RIA Technologies, Standards, and Frameworks

It's time to look at the evolution of Web 2.0 RIA technologies in a little more detail. As you will see, evolution is the right characterization (rather than revolution). Many technologies such as Ruby and components of Ajax have been around for a long time; some such as Microsoft's SilverLight and Adobe's AIR are new. The key is that at this time, all of them have reached a critical mass and are taking off. This section digs deeper to understand the underpinnings of some of the specific technologies, frameworks, and standards, but don't worry: You won't dive into code (yet).

Ajax

The term *Ajax* was coined by J.J. Garrett [24] in 2005. His definition of Ajax still holds true. He defines the five elements of Ajax as

- Standards-based presentation, using XHTML and CSS

- Dynamic display and interaction, using the Document Object Model

- Data interchange and manipulation, using XML and XSLT (eXtensible Stylesheet Language Transformation)

- Asynchronous data retrieval, using XMLHttpRequest

- JavaScript, binding everything together

As JJ mentions, Ajax is not something that you download, but a way of developing web applications—especially the client-side processing techniques. This was in 2005 and since then, a few changes have happened. First is the popularity of server-side processing and development frameworks such as Ruby on Rails; another change is the use of JSON as the data interchange format. Although Ajax was once an acronym for Asynchronous JavaScript And XML, it is not an acronym anymore because of the technology changes.

Although the underlying technologies are evolving, the business advantages of Ajax, such as ability to transform content based on style sheets (CSS), the ability to achieve dynamic and high-performance user experience and most of all the ability to develop and add features faster, still hold true.

The history of the Ajax technologies [25] is interesting. The idea of asynchronous loading of data was started by Microsoft in 1996 and Microsoft had the XMLHttpRequest capability in the Internet Explorer browser in 1999. JavaScript itself was part of Netscape Navigator in 1995 and later became an ISO standard.

The War of the JavaScript Engines: SquirrelFish Extreme Versus V8 Versus TraceMonkey

How much mindshare do Ajax technologies have, one might ask. The answer is a lot! For example, one of the criteria the browsers brag about is the speed of their JavaScript engine. Apple's SquirrelFish Extreme, Google's V8, and Firefox's TraceMonkey are the three JavaScript engines in the respective browsers Safari, Chrome, and Firefox.

Firefox always has been the web standard in terms of AJAX technologies, with the original advent of JavaScript from Netscape.

Of late, Goggle entered the fray with its own browser and newer, faster processing models. It even has a cartoon series [26] to explain its browser Chrome. The emphasis on web applications (Figure 3-2) and the speed of JavaScript (Figure 3-3) is unmistakable.

Not to be outdone, Apple introduced the SquirrelFish Extreme JavaScript engine [27] which is claimed to be 35% faster than the V8 engine Google's Chrome has [28], [29].

Figure 3-2   *Google's Chrome introduction via a cartoon series (page 1 of 39).*

Figure 3-3   *Google's Chrome introduction via a cartoon series (page 2 of 39).*

Figure 3-4 shows the performance comparisons. The web community was excited [30] with positive press and comparisons galore.

Apple's engine boasts of exotic capabilities like "Polymorphic Inline Cache" and "Context Threaded JIT." Although these are totally cryptic to a business user, one thing is certain: If you base your web applications on Ajax, they will get faster on newer versions of the browser and the capabilities to achieve better user interaction will increase. As one blogger puts it [31], "Everybody is working hard to improve performance, standards compliance, and stability. The end result will definitely be a more open web, with richer content and more advanced applications than in the past." We couldn't say it any better.

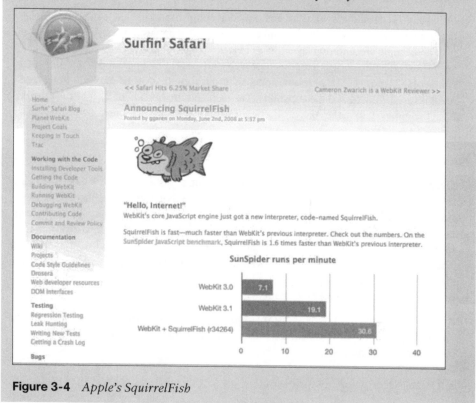

Figure 3-4   *Apple's SquirrelFish*

HTTP Architectural Constraints

One might ask, what exactly is preventing a complete merger of the desktop and a browser, and why might we go to all the trouble of various technologies for web applications? It all is attributable to the architectural and protocol considerations of HTTP and the constraints placed on the browser execution environment.

HTTP semantics dictate a request-response exchange between the browser and the web server, with the browser requesting a web page and the web server responding with an HTML page. The web server or any other server in the Internet cannot "reach out and touch" a browser. This is for security reasons; just think what would happen if all the spammers could directly access your browser.

Another semantic is that only the server to which the browser sent requests can respond back, and it can use only two connections. And the browser executes in a sandbox, which means it cannot get to the computer's file system or execute any arbitrary programs. The only place a browser can access is the cache and the cookies. This is why using a browser as an application execution platform is very challenging, and that is the reason HTML 5 and newer browsers with faster capabilities are all-important for the future of web applications based on rich user interactions.

Originally, HTTP and HTML were positioned as simpler markup, exchange, and display technologies, and browsers implemented that concept. They were intended to serve as a pure and simple presentation layer. But HTTP as a protocol and HTML as a markup gained such enormous popularity that now most web traffic is HTTP (including voice and video). Neither HTTP not HTML were envisioned as application platforms. Ajax and other technologies are trying to add the capability. The next section quickly dives into the efforts from the industry to make Ajax a richer platform for web applications.

OpenAjax

OpenAjax is an alliance of "vendors, open-source initiatives and web developers dedicated to the successful adoption of open and interoperable Ajax-based web technologies" [19]. An insight into the various activities of OpenAjax reveals the current state of the web applications domain and provides a peek into where the technologies need to evolve in the future. For example, the Runtime Advocacy Task Force has a long wish list (What does the Ajax community want from future browsers?) for the browser vendors to address, [32] and the Gadgets task force has proposals for interoperability among widgets as well as definitions driven by a lightweight metadata format.

A quick look at the browser wish list that OpenAjax members would like the browser vendors to implement in next-generation browsers is very illuminating of the current browser technologies. The most requested features include

- Better security for cross-site scripting
- Better and faster JSON parsing, UI layout, positioning and styling support
- Enhancements for XMLHttpRequest protocol and processing
- Offline support
- Various performance enhancements, as well as various JavaScript features

These requests come from the various companies that make a living developing web applications, and so are very relevant to businesses thinking of developing future web applications. Of course, all the features will not be available from all the browsers immediately. But an understanding of the requests by OpenAjax is a must if you want to understand the limitations and cautions (for example, mashup security) when designing web applications.

Ruby on Rails Framework and Infrastructure

Ruby on Rails (RoR as it is affectionately called) is an open source web development framework [33] that focuses on making the development and maintenance of database-based websites fast and easy. Having said that, there is nothing that prevents the use of RoR for any type of websites, whether they have a database behind them or not. RoR was developed by David Heinemeier Hansson and of course now there are lots of folks working on the open source project. It is interesting to note that RoR evolved from David's work at 37Signals, a web applications company. Originally 37Signals wanted to develop BaseCamp, a web-based project management tool, and they started using the Ruby language for that project. As the project progressed, David realized that many of the routines they were developing could be used for a variety of web projects, so he extracted the essential frameworks as Ruby on Rails and the rest is history. Now there are a large number of websites and applications that use the RoR framework, [34] including the popular Twitter.

The RoR framework and its programming model is so popular that competing frameworks such as Merb emerged. And thanks to the power of collaboration and open community, the two frameworks are merging in the next major version of Ruby. [35] When a platform is moving toward its third version and there are multiple frameworks based on its pattern, one can be relatively comfortable in developing business applications based on that platform.

Model-View-Controller: A Business Design Pattern?   One of the advantages of Ruby on Rails is that it is built on a Model-View-Controller (MVC) pattern. Whereas design patterns are more technological, the MVC pattern has business implications; we think the MVC pattern helps to frame a web application. Essentially the MVC splits logic into three buckets:

- **The View:** What the user sees and the various aspects of that display
- **The Controller:** The actions to be taken for the various view elements
- **The Model:** The database and other related logic

The MVC pattern is very much a business view of web apps, and that is why a framework based on MVC makes sense for developing web apps. The business is concerned mainly with the View (and to some extent with the Controller for the business flow). With this separation conveniently captured in the MVC pattern, business can specify systems in a clear and concise manner while developers can implement them congruently. Moreover, as the web application architecture and implementation reflect the layers clearly, the applications end up very flexible for easier enhancements and maintenance throughout the life of the web application.

In Short

Rich Internet applications and web applications are becoming a major force in the world of Web 2.0. The trend is accelerated by the rich interactive user experience provided by technologies and frameworks such as Ajax, SilverLight, Ruby on Rails, and so forth. These technologies not only provide effective, dynamic, interactive, and fast user interfaces but also enable developers and business to crank out web applications faster and maintain them efficiently. Moreover, the browser vendors are adding more capabilities as well as faster processing of Ajax technologies.

<monologue>

The U.S. presidential campaign of 2008 will be remembered as the evolution of social networks into the popular culture as a change agent. In "The Facebooker Who Friended Obama," *The New York Times* says "The campaign's new-media strategy, inspired by popular social networks like MySpace and Facebook, has revolutionized the use of the Web as a political tool." President Obama was quoted in Time,[1] saying, "What I didn't anticipate was how effectively we could use the Internet to harness that grassroots base...one of the biggest surprises of the campaign (was) just how powerfully our message merged with the social networking and the power of the Internet."

Just as social networking enabled a candidate to overcome the old school, social networking also is playing a crucial part in the judicial system. In "Web Networking Photos Come Back to Bite Defendants" ABC News reported how a defendant got harsher sentencing after the judge viewed photos from a party in Facebook: "The pictures, when shown at sentencing,...can make it harder for them to convince a judge that they're remorseful or that their drunken behavior was an aberration."

As an ultimate sign of the times, Stanford University is teaching parents Facebook skills[2] and how Facebook is influencing the lives of their kids.

The wealthy and rich are different, of course. Now they have special-invite-only social networking sites, as reported by Forbes.[3] What else do we need as the proof that social networking is a legitimate fire-breathing industry?

</monologue>

Social Networking

Social networking and the larger social media domain combine many Web 2.0 tenets.[4,5] These include user-generated content (information about the user, what users are doing, and photos and videos), interactive and dynamic web application platforms (such as Facebook, MySpace, and Twitter), communities (such as Ning), tagging and bookmarking, mobility, inferencability (for example, recommendations based on common interests of a group of people), and a wide consumer audience from teenagers to baby-boomers. Of all the Web 2.0 technologies, social networking, and social media in general, might be the one single area that has the maximum impact on organizations, and the impact is multi-dimensional. Just imagine: Facebook and MySpace, between them, have more than 150 million users and around 75 million unique hits every day. Social networks can influence the products you develop, the services you offer, and the way you are organized to accomplish the vision and mission of your business. Social networking affects your customer interactions, before and after they buy your services and products, as well as the interactions with your employees. In short, social networking will influence a spectrum of business systems—from internally facing apps (to increase employee productivity through collaboration and better information quality), to external marketing, to self-supporting customers, to driving product development. It is even influencing future datacenter architectures. Intel and Facebook are working on a next-generation data center.[6] Intel plans to deliver server configurations and energy-efficient processors to "meet processing needs of the company's increasingly rich media applications that span videos, music, photos, and more." Even search is not immune from the attack of the giant social networks. There are talks about Faceboogle, a combination of search and social networking that would kill search as we know it.[7]

The impact of social networking does not stop at sharing tastes in music or poking friends but also influences higher causes. *Network World*[8] declares "If there is any doubt to the power of social media, social networking, and social software, then nonbelievers may need to think New Orleans." The social networking artifacts such as blogs, wikis, photos, images, mashups, and social connections for various activities like Help Rebuild New Orleans provide citizens a voice against waste and inefficiencies and even helped uncover shoddy drainage pump work.

I found the summary from Graphing Social West conference[9] a good snapshot of the social networking space. "The social application space has gotten big fast and will get a lot bigger; social objects are at the center of healthy micro-communities and linking people who do not know each other; there's money to be made, and advertising is only part of it; and social networks are a powerful new force for fund raising!"

Note: Of course, social networking is not limited to humans; Dogster is a social networking site for dogs and Catster is probably not far behind. As bizarre as these social networks might sound, they are probably of extreme interest if you sell dog food or cat food.

Social networking is not limited to websites. Even MP3 players like Zune offer social networking[10] capabilities. Basically users can download music that their friends have recently played or have tagged as favorites. Mobile social networking such as Facebook on your Blackberry and social networking applications on the iPhone are other examples of the wide reach of social networking.

Social networking is not just a 21st-century phenomenon. In fact, as a study from Harvard and U.S. San Diego[11] shows, social networking has been ingrained in the human culture—from influencing behaviors to quitting smoking to obesity. The study concluded that one's behavior is dependent not only on the immediate social circle but also by people beyond one's social horizon. Maybe the social networks are nothing but a digital incarnation of basic human nature.

Enough philosophic waxing. Back to the main topic. This chapter looks at the domain of social networking, its platforms, its companies, its standards, and finally the challenges this emerging domain faces. Occasionally the chapter will dive deeper into a platform or a specific issue. The chapter concludes with a discussion on social networks and the enterprise.

State of the Union and Business Value of Social Networks

Like many other technologies, social networking originated in the consumer space—especially with teens and students—and now has found a permanent place in the business world. But it is okay to grab concepts and best practices from consumer space; in fact you will see that most of the examples are from the consumer space, but with an enterprise perspective!

From an external focus and marketing perspective, social networks are very important. Businesses need to address the hundreds of millions of social networkers—the demographics are hard to miss. Businesses need to understand the sites they visit, their social and connection activities, and the things they do and are interested in, as well as the viral nature of this medium. The viral nature is especially important to understand. It can work for you (a product can take off) and against you (customer unhappiness can spread very quickly). Social networking also enables community building, collaboration, and building relationships engaging with others at various levels including sharing interests, experiences and media like photos and videos. Communities and relationships usually build around causes (political, charity, volunteering) or common interests (music, reading). An interesting application of enterprise community is TimesPeople,[12] which is a social network for readers of *The New York Times* for sharing interesting things one finds in *The Times*. The interface is also very clever: TimesPeople appears as a toolbar in the NYTimes page, as shown in Figure 4-1. Although this is a consumer application, it has the enterprise relevance of a customer community.

Figure 4-1   *TimesPeople toolbar.*

From a customer interaction perspective, the major business benefit of social networking is in increasing responsiveness to the market place, making the company or business unit approachable to customers from all sides.[13] Communities, R & D forums, and support networks all fall in the social networking category. When combined with the viral nature of social media, rich customer interaction (at all stages of products and services) will become the major requirement for social networking systems in an organization.

Although corporations can hardly find business justification for developing and supporting consumer social networking applications that tell users what movie star they are like or play Hold 'Em poker, social networks do offer a powerful business-relevant platform for internal applications. From an internal perspective, social networking offers unprecedented opportunities for productivity and better working conditions in many ways: enabling employees to find the right information and the right person to talk to for more relevant details; leveraging the wisdom of crowds in tagging, bookmarking, and reading materials; and improving communication by giving employees more information about co-workers inside and outside the company. In fact there are a lot more advantages—you be the judge after reading through this chapter and going through all the hundreds of links!

Enabling employees to navigate through corporate hierarchies via a social graph and a knowledge graph over a Facebook-like platform is very real and can improve employee productivity. After all, most work is done via the informal social connections, which, many times, are independent of the formal hierarchy. Being able to harvest the knowledge graph would be especially powerful. Another social networking application in intercompany collaboration is the capability to search for expertise and then extend that connection to enable collaboration. For example, Best Buy is leveraging its home-grown social network[14] called Blue Shirt Nation (which, many claim, is the biggest corporate social network) for knowledge exchange between employees, project management, and executive communication. Another example application of social networking in the enterprise setting is IBM[15] where social media is employed not only for internal productivity but also as a vehicle to engage IBM alumni for professional networking. Another interesting application of the social graph is for social network analysis. MWH, an engineering firm, uses social network analysis to improve collaboration and identify communication bottlenecks.[16] Other companies such as Microsoft and Pfizer are also employing this technique to analyze work-force dynamics with the business goal of improved communication and increased productivity.

Social networking applications have their challenges as well—from security and privacy to compliance to corporations banning them to data portability issues to mushrooming frivolous applications to viruses to copyright violations! Gartner has a good discussion on corporations banning social networking applications,[17] and concludes that "Though not quite ready for use in enterprise applications, Facebook, Twitter, and the others can prove valuable in helping colleagues and customers connect, so long as businesses employ a trust model and appropriate usage policies."

Let us focus on the narrow social networking domain and explore different aspects—the good, the bad, and the ugly.

Characteristics of a Social App

Even though we discuss platforms and APIs in more detail, it's a good idea to take a quick look at what a social application is as a background for the rest of this chapter.

A social application is an interesting twist to normal applications. First of all, they focus on social interactions rather than the traditional user interface. Second, the recurring theme in almost all the popular social networking applications is that they are simple in a conceptual sense but have a very high connectivity quotient. Of course, a few of them also have very high valuation—AOL bought Bebo for $850 million![18] Third, using them is a social experience—which means meeting friends, finding people with common tastes, connecting with people who know things and are willing to share with others, and forming gatherings and communities. Finally, they are "good applications that facilitate fun and meaningful social expressions."[19] The OpenSocial site social design practices[19] gives us a glimpse of a good social application:

- **Engaging:** The recommendation is that you have 30 seconds to make a good first impression! The attributes that get the attention include:
  - Focus and clarity (that is, have a core function and make sure it is crisp and clear)

- Interesting content from the very beginning (have initial data and then make sure the site is populated with data from friends and things of interest that are related to the main theme)
- Ownership properties (that is, make it easy for users to add data as well as customize)

- **Look and Feel:** The application should be distinctive yet have the social touch. As you will see later, the Facebook platform does a good job—they even have added markups to HTML!

- **Self-expression:** Profiles, preferences, and tastes all make up the user's perspective. The application should form an extension of the user around those characteristics.

- **Dynamic:** Users' tastes change, friends change, and users evolve. An application should be able to accommodate these changes.

- **Expose friend activity and a browsable social graph:** This is very important to keep users engaged.

- **Communication and communities:** The ability to communicate easily (short messages, "walls" on which to write stuff, and pokes all are forms of social communication) and the capability to form communities are essential.

- **Perform real-world tasks:** Sharing interests, sharing pictures of events like a vacation, finding like-minded people, or developing a community are the kinds of interactions people want from a social network.

You will see more details about social applications in the sections dealing with platforms like Facebook and MySpace, as well as the OpenSocial APIs, later in this chapter. From a corporate perspective, there are three main areas of focus:

- Use the social networking platform as a marketing tool to leverage the viral aspect of social networks. The social networking domain is hard to ignore as there are lots of users of the various social networking sites and, corporations need to make sure that they conform to the norm and expectations of the social network domain.

- Use the social networking platform to develop useful applications.

- Use the social networking platform to integrate with internal social networking applications; now there is a way to interface with consumer social networks and have internal controls, policies, compliance, and security!

Facebook also has similar guiding principles for good social applications.[20] In their view, the characteristics of good social applications are that they are meaningful (social, useful, expressive and engaging), trustworthy (secure, respectful, and transparent) and well defined (clean and intuitive, fast and robust).

A good example of the innovative use of existing tools for building a social network is Universal McCann, who used Microsoft's Sharepoint and NewsGrator's RSS platform. In their view,[21] an effective social platform "only requires users to enter a little bit of basic information (such as name, title, and most high-level work interests), and Social Sites does the rest, feeding users relevant information and allowing them to tag pieces of content they find interesting or want to share with colleagues."

Social Network Ecosystems and Players

The best way to understand a domain is to look at the offerings from various companies—from established players to new startups. With that in mind, this section looks at some of the representative offerings. It not only covers the end-user feature sets, but also takes a good look at the developer platforms. Although the features offered by the websites themselves are interesting, it is the programmatic interfaces (and the platforms) that are more relevant to the enterprise.

Facebook: A Complete Ecosystem

Facebook actually is a book given to students in the Phillips Exeter Academy (where the founder Mark Zuckerberg studied) so that the students can become familiar with each other.[22] Mark Zuckerberg started the Facebook website in 2004, first as a site for Harvard students and then later for college students and in 2006 as a public website.[23]

Facebook Platform

The most interesting aspect of Facebook is the development platform and the developer support the company offers. The Facebook developer platform was announced at the annual f8 conference on May 24, 2007.[24] Mark Zuckerberg, in his keynote, introduced the platform as having deep integration with the Facebook website and pointed out the capability for any application written on the platform to leverage mass distribution through the social graph—in short, a platform based on a social graph, distributed via the social graph, and consumed in the context of a social graph! The three themes of the Facebook platform—deep integration, mass distribution, and new opportunity—have been consistent since its inception and are displayed prominently, as shown in Figure 4-2.

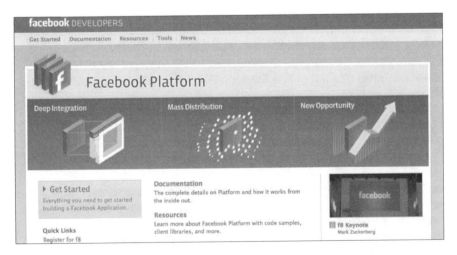

Figure 4-2   *Facebook platform themes.*

As of July 2008, Facebook had more than 400,000 developers who have written about 24,000 applications,[25] and as of March 2009 they had 660,000 developers and 52,000 applications.

Facebook Conferences and Developer Gatherings

The annual Facebook conference, f8, is as original as social networking. It was named to reflect the 8 hours of developer "Hackathon," following the keynote. During the Hackathon, attendees develop new interfaces, apps, and so on, and the Facebook engineers are at hand to help them! During the sessions, there are other activities like rock music, games, and lots of food and Red Bull to drink![26]

The f8 starts at 12:00 p.m. lasts for eight hours (and four hours of after-f8 party from 8:00 p.m.–12:00 a.m.!). This year (2008) it was sold out even after 100 more tickets were added! Mark, in his keynote, introduced Facebook Connect. It was rumored that he might introduce a micropayment infrastructure, but there was no mention of it in f8-2008.

Another interesting developer gathering is the Facebook developer garage[27] where folks who develop facebook applications gather and exchange ideas. The garage is organized across the globe by developers; the gathering can be small or big. Facebook even has guidelines for organizing developer garages.[28,29] One interesting feature of a developer garage is the logos, some shown in Figure 4-3. We can see that the developers have taken pains to develop a location-based brand for their gathering!

Figure 4-3   *Facebook garage logos from across the globe.*

Facebook Applications

Although Facebook applications are numerous, they show a highly scale-free distribution, with a short head and no long tail,[30] which means a few applications become immensely popular and the rest are used by only a few. The analytics are hard to come by, http://adonomics.com/ being the best. The top application, Superwall, has around 500,000 users, and had a peak of 4 million users. A competing application, Funwall, has approximately 1.6 million users (from a peak of approximately 5.5 million users). There are about 5 million users on applications such as Funwall and Superwall, Hug Me, Horoscopes, Likeness, Top Friends, and Superpoke. The Facebook application for iPhone went from 0 to a million users within a few weeks of the introduction of iPhone 2.0.[31]

The apps themselves are social in nature, enabling users to share videos, pictures and graffiti with friends (Superwall, Funwall), keep in touch with fiends (Top Friends), share movie reviews and compare movie taste with friends (Movies), play card and word games (Texas Hold'Em Poker, Scrabble), and share/track music users and their friends listen to (iLike).

One example of a Facebook application that transcends the online and offline/pen-and-paper world is Scrabulous. In fact, the game was so successful that Hasbro, the company that owns Scrabble, has sued the developers of Scrabulous. [32,33] Scrabulous got mindshare by initially drawing around 500,000 users a day (2.7 million active users, 70 million page views), whereas the "official" Scrabble Facebook game, launched recently, has only around 20,000 users. In fact, there is now a "Save Scrabulous" Facebook group.[34] Finally, on June 29, 2008, Facebook shut down Scrabulous for U.S. and Canada users[35]—a vivid demonstration of life in the fast lane of social networking application–land! Of course, the saga continues, with the creators of Scrabulous creating an app called Wordscraper with round tiles,[36] and with Facebook shutting down Scrabulous all over the world.[37] And even though the legal drama is interesting to watch,[38] the important conclusion to draw is that the Facebook platform is becoming a sought-after platform by developers and corporations.

Honesty Box[39] is another interesting app. One can leave anonymous messages to one's friends, either positive or negative. Circle of Friends is another app that expands one's circle via connections to other like-minded people—a typical social graph application.

The experience of applications like iLike exemplify the Facebook platform. At first iLike was a traditional website for a social music discovery service, and it later grew very quickly as a Facebook application. It is reported that as a Facebook application iLike grew in one week what it took its traditional site six months. iLike is now the tenth most popular Facebook application. Of course, the nature of the application (social sharing) made it highly suitable for the Facebook platform.

The Facebook ecosystem is getting crowded and is reaching its next stage, with bigger ecosystems, monetizing models for apps, and a payment infrastructure, as well as the capability for rating the applications.[34,40]. Windows Live Search is adding APIs; applications such as SocialCalendar are partnering with other giants like Amazon.com to add features such as Gift Giving (http://www.socialcalendar.com/). Even though the micro-payment infrastructure didn't make it in time for f8-2008, some form of monetizing system will certainly be in place soon.

Facebook Platform and Architecture

The Facebook architecture is interesting and instructive in terms of what a Web 2.0 architecture would look like. The Facebook platform acts as an intermediary for your application. For a user, the application lives in Facebook and has the look and feel of Facebook, as well as a set of distinctive social network elements and features. But in reality, the application back end lives in an application server and it interacts with the user via Facebook servers. Figure 4-4 shows a simplified view of the Facebook architecture.

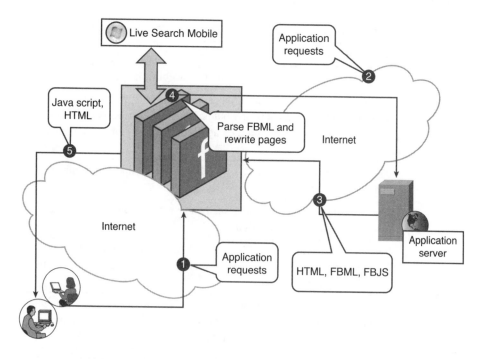

Figure 4-4   *Facebook platform architecture overview.*

The numbered steps in Figure 4-4 are as follows:

Step 1.   A user interacts with the application in Facebook's website and sends a request.

Step 2.   Facebook in turn sends the request to the third party's application server.

Step 3.   The application, depending on what it wants to do, creates web pages with normal HTML contents as well as markups for Facebook platform components such as FBML (Facebook Markup Language) and FBJS (Facebook JavaSCript). FBML is the markup language for incorporating data stored in the Facebook datastore, and FBJS is the capability to add program snippets specific to the Facebook platform.

Step 4.   The Facebook platform parses the page, acts on the markups, incorporates information datasets stored in the Facebook platform (like list of friends, related events, and other materials), and sends out normal HTML, JavaScript, and the like.

Step 5.   User sees a Facebook application and interacts with it.

The basic Facebook building block datasets shown in Table 4-1 are used to build applications.

Table 4-1   *Facebook application building blocks*

Building Block	Description
Profile	Profile is the on-line representation of a Facebook entity.
Friend	Friends, of course, are what social networks are all about. A user has a list of friends, who in turn have attributes. Usually a Facebook application operates on one's friends and their attributes, such as interests or movies they like.
Page	Page is a combination of HTML, FBML, JavaScript and other similar elements. Usually page is a frame.
Group	A group is made up of people. Usually a group has some overarching goal and activities associated with it.
Photos	Image data are uploaded to Facebook and are kept in albums. Photos can have tags. There is a workflow[41] associated with how a photo becomes part of an album.
News feeds & events	News feeds are notifications about some activity, for example when you comment about a photo or add a new video. Facebook applications can originate events and reflect then as feeds.
Requests & invitations	Requests are initiated from applications. For example, if someone wants you to be a friend that is a request; some applications might want you to join a group; that is an invitation.
	The difference between a News feed and a request is that a request needs the user to do something, such as allow an application or grant a person to become one's friend while a News feed is a notification.
Wall	A wall essentially is a frame on which friends can write things.

Of course, the dataset in Table 4-1 will change as the platform evolves.

Accessing Profile Information Dataset by Facebook Applications
The dataset is stored in Facebook and the applications access the information. Of course, Facebook has privacy and opt-in mechanisms. For example, if you add Funwall to your page, the pop-up shown in Figure 4-5 appears. Each application has its own terms of service in addition to Facebook's terms of service.
Even though I wanted to have the Funwall application, I did not click the Allow button. I was a little uncomfortable in allowing an app access to my profile.

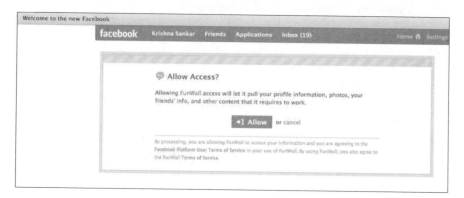

Figure 4-5   *Facebook security pop-up.*

The Facebook platform components provide interface and integration points to these datasets. The current Facebook platform components are

- **APIs:** REST-like interfaces to the Facebook data elements to add social context to the application. The advantage of the API interface is that programs written in any language can send an HTTP GET or POST request to the Facebook REST server.[42] Examples include
    - The events.get API call fetchs all the visible events.[43]
    - Friends.arefriends returns Yes if two users are friends.[44]
    - Friends.get returns all the IDs of the friends of the current user.[45]

Of late, the APIs are being expanded to create an ecosystem. For example, as I am writing this chapter, Microsoft announced that they are adding a Facebook API interface to Windows Live Search.[46]

- **FQL:** Facebook Query Language enables an application developer to embed SQL-like statements to access the Facebook data elements. Basically FQL is an alternate data access mechanism to the EST APIs. Examples include
    - To get all events one would send the query `SELECT eid, name, tagline, nid, pic, pic_big, pic_small, host, description, event_type, event_subtype, start_time, end_time, creator, update_time, location, venue FROM event WHERE eid IN (SELECT eid FROM event_member WHERE uid=uid AND rsvp_status=rsvp_status) AND eid IN (eids) AND end_time >= start_time AND start_time < end_time`.[43]

- To see whether two users are friends, the FQL would be `SELECT uid1, uid2 FROM friend WHERE uid1=uid1 AND uid2=uid2`.[44]
- To get all the friends of a user, the FQL would be `SELECT uid2 FROM friend WHERE uid1=loggedInUid`.[45]

- **FBML:** Facebook Markup Language is very interesting. It gives the applications the SI (social interface) experience (also known as the UI of a social networking) as well as deep integration to the Facebook platform. When you use FQL or APIs, it is essentially your application with Facebook data. But when you also embed FBML in your app, it becomes an integrated Facebook application.

FBML essentially is extensions/tags to HTML. The tags fall into four categories: [47]

- **Social data tags:** The most interesting set of tags about users, groups, and profiles. For example, the `Fb:name` tag displays the name of a user. The Facebook platform renderer knows about the context—such as the user's choices and preferences, including privacy settings—and so it renders appropriately.

- **Sanitation Tags:** These enforce the Facebook website standards, such as displaying a flashing image until a user interacts with it (using the `Fb:swf` tag).

- **Design Tags:** These define page design elements such as tabs (`Fb:tabs` and `Fb:tab-item`). In the case of tabs, the developer defines `Fb:tab-items` in `Fb:tab` tags and the Facebook renderer displays tabs at the appropriate location with the proper colors and uniform behavior (on mouse click or other defined user action). So the developer decides what to show and the Facebook platform decides how to show it. That way, if the Facebook look and feel changes in the future, the app still looks like other Facebook apps. Figure 4-6 shows the rendering.

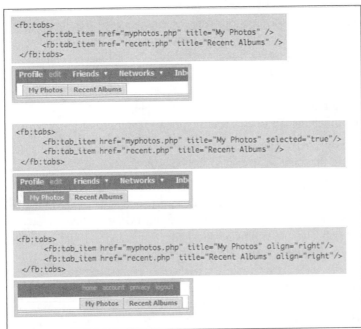

Figure 4-6 *FBML rendering example.*

- **Component Tags:** These provide more aggregate widget-like capabilities. The `Fb:comments` tag is a good example: It provides a full-fledged comment board where users can add and view comments on photos and so on.

- **Control Tags:** These are advanced tags for controlling the views, like `fb:visible-to-owner`. The reason for these control tags is that the developer does not know *a proiri* the context of an application (for example, the name and id of a user or the friends of user) so the developer inserts appropriate control tags—kind of declarative instructions to the renderer.

- **FBJS:** Facebook JavaScript adds JavaScript support. Again, like FBML, Facebook has a JavaScript parser, and social networking–related capabilities are embedded in JavaScript.

Weaving a Facebook Application

Now you can see how to weave an app on the Facebook platform. Figure 4-7 shows the essential elements of a Facebook application.[48]

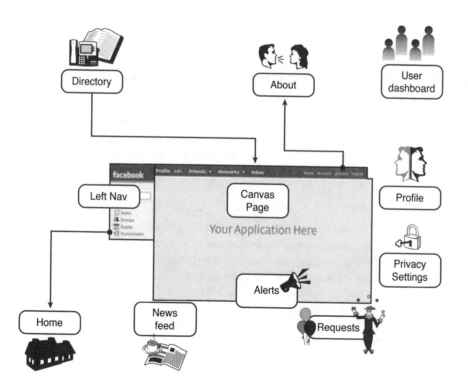

Figure 4-7   *Elements of a Facebook application.*

A social network application is not a single user–centric app, but a user and friends–centric app, which means an application developer should look at how a user and his or her friends use the app. It is not user interaction or user interface (UI) but social interaction (SI) that defines an application; the focus is on social behavior. The elements of the Facebook application platform reflect this paradigm.

The "real estate" of an application is the canvas page that renders as HTML in the browser, a web page written in FBML and interpreted by the Facebook servers or an external web page in a frame. The canvas page has multiple tabs as well as an application menu and a bookmark menu.

The application directory is an important element because that is where users usually get their first glance at an application.

Of course, alerts, feeds, and requests, along with the various profile artifacts, will work in conjunction to make the Facebook application and provide the social networking experience.

There are developer tools like the Facebook Test Console[49] to test the apps, as well as the Platform Status Feed.[50]

We have looked into Facebook in as much detail as a general Web 2.0 book allows. Naturally there are web pages to visit, voluminous book to read, and more important, sample applications to be developed before one can become an expert Facebook app developer.

LinkedIn: The Corporate Hangout for Jobs and Connections

LinkedIn is a social site where corporate folks feel at home. With a tagline "LinkedIn: Relationships Matter"[51] and characterized as "A networking tool to find connections to recommended job candidates, industry experts, and business partners" it certainly couldn't miss the corporate world. In fact, it has around 25 million users from more than 100 industries.

I found the description in TechCrunch[52] as "the boring social network that won't find you a date but may land you a job" very interesting but accurate in many ways. In fact, LinkedIn specializes on professional relationships and its site reflects that—the personal profiles have current position as the first item with past positions, education, recommendations, and other details. The search facilitates finding people associated with companies, and searches like "Who do I know from this company" are common. LinkedIn facilitates introductions by exposing the essentials of a social network—that is, how far away is a person socially in the friend-of-a-friend realm. One can follow the social chain, for example, to send an email to a person four contacts away and LinkedIn forwards the email through the chain; it does not expose the links, so the originator knows only the first-level contact, who is in the originator's friends list.

Some of the innovations starting to appear in LinkedIn include company directory,[53] native iPhone application, the LinkedIn intelligent applications platform, and the OpenSocial interfaces.

MySpace: The Teen Social Network Site

Until around the middle of 2008, MySpace was the most popular social networking website with more than 150 million users[54]. In terms of the total numbers of users, it is believed that MySpace still is bigger than Facebook.

It all started as eUniverse, a music promoting community selling CDs, and with the right vision grew to a juggernaut "Social networking at warp speed," as Brad Greenspan (the original chairman) puts it. Although MySpace is known for its audience of 13–16 year olds, it also has a good grip in the 18+ market. Brad Greenspan's blog[55,56] has a good snippet of MySpace's history. Naturally Wikipedia[57] has the complete set of information. MySpace is owned by News Corporation's Fox Interactive media. They paid around $600 million for it in 2005.[58]

Note: MySpace was not the first mover in this space; it was Friendster. In fact, many of the initial employees and developers of MySpace were in Friendster and they thought a better social networking site was in order. Eventually MySpace became the premier social networking site. It is interesting to see why MySpace succeed while Friendster languished. The main reasons, according to Brad, are

- A good technology and team from eUniverse

- A good initial user community—around 20 million users from eUniverse

- Financial and other infrastructures from eUniverse

Although MySpace was the biggest social networking site in 2007 in terms of page visits, Facebook has taken over that honor as of July 2008.[59]

In fact, the rivalry is very real and the battlefield is not only restricted to acquiring users across the world but is also extended to architecture, platform, and site design. In fact the development platform is the differentiator. At least, for now, Facebook has the technology lead on social networking platform, though maybe not for too long. In June 2008, MySpace went through a UI redesign that extended from navigation to search to home page to editing.[60] This was a direct response to the growing sophistication of Facebook. In fact, ARS Technical characterized it as the era of social network wars.[61] Usability, ease of community building, and global audience were all major themes for the redesign. MySpace has real homepage capabilities, where you can add a background and change the layout. Facebook has strict look and feel conformance and does not allow as much freedom for customization.

Of interest to enterprise folks is the MySpace Developer Platform (MDP).[62] The following are the key characteristics of MDP:

- MySpace is a big proponent of OpenSocial (Facebook is not).[63]

- MySpace also has an application development model consisting of application profile, a canvas, modules, and home page.[64]

- It has REST resources for normal social artifacts such as friends, videos, profile, albums, and so on.[65] It even has a REST URL for mood! The GET to the URI `/v1/users/{userid}/mood` gets mood of the person (identified by `userid`) and a PUT updates that person's mood. (Of course, this works only if you have access to the user.)

- MySpace has a cohesive data availability policy that respects privacy as well as secure access based on open standards such as OAuth.[66] Mechanisms such as access delegation based on access tokens makes it easy for users to provide restricted, temporal access to pieces of information while keeping all data secure and private.

- MySpace has very clear guidelines for applications.[67] It is interesting to read the guidelines, which include "MySpace Applications and MySpace Application Content (including any Advertising) must not contain, reference, promote or link to
  - Alcohol content targeted to users under ages 21;
  - Dating content targeted to users under age 18."
  - Age appropriateness is a challenge for MySpace and it does a good job of maintaining the required standards.

- The data availability adds another dimension to the MySpace platform controls and again, there are strict guidelines.[68]

- MySpace has a stated process for twiddling out bad apps, and the process is well stated.[69]

Note: All in all, from my research, the impression I got was that MySpace is an exciting place, possibly reflecting its heritage of playfulness, rather than a full-fledged developer destination. In my opinion, for a corporate platform, Facebook is better than MySpace.

Friendster: Where It All Began

A discussion about social networking will not be complete, or for that matter even start, without a discussion on Friendster. Most probably Friendster is the pioneer in social networking, and like many domains Friendster did not achieve financial success and fame as the other ones who came later, such as Facebook and MySpace. *The New York Times* chronicles the rise and fall of Friendster.[70] The main reasons were business (too much focus on other companies like Google than one's own business) as well as technological (couldn't scale faster). However, Friendster is still alive and doing well, [71,72] especially in the Asia-Pacific market.

Ning: A Generic Social Site Hosting Platform

Ning is a community hosting platform that in 2008 had around 300,000–400,000 sites. Marc Andreessen, in an interview with Charlie Ross,[73] mentioned that they have about 20 million users in a million social networks and are adding 2 million users per month. The communities range from a site for supernatural believers (http://supernaturalnet.ning.com/) to Fort Worth public library staff to a movie community for movies with animated characters (http://my.spill.com/) to Information Zen (http://digitallandfill.ning.com/).

The value proposition of Ning is that it enables users to set up and manage a social networking community with capability to manage members, events, and groups, add real-time activity streams, and manage discussion boards. The article "Why Create a Social Network" (http://about.ning.com/why.php) lists some of the advantages, including "Interact with fans," "Exchange parenting tips," "Meet your neighbors," and "Connect with attendees." Ning has Facebook integration and also supports OpenSocial, so data integration with all the major social networking sites is possible. From a platform perspective, Ning has the Web Widget Framework with associated programming models in PHP and JavaScript.[74] The platform guidelines[75] are few and crisp.

Note: Our reviewer, Tom, has an interesting perspective on the future of social networking. In his opinion, "It might be worth making more clear that Ning is an interesting and different breed of cat. Unlike the others, there is no Ning social networking site. There are only branded sites of users. The only Ning UI is a small credit at the bottom of the site. The rest of the content is determined by users. The interesting question in progress here is whether social networking becomes about competing sites for social networking, or about independent choices linked via open protocols and links between sites. Or, put another way, is it winner-take-all and critical-mass-wins, as today with Facebook versus MySpace, or generic-build-your-brand social network sites like Ning + OpenSocial?"

Jive: An Enterprise Platform

Jive (www.jive.com) is an enterprise software company specializing in developing social software. It has two products: Clearspace for internal collaboration and Clearspace Community for external collaboration.

For internal collaboration, Clearspace keeps document repositories, conversations, connections between employees, projects, and blogs. I am sure in most of the organizations these artifacts are distributed in multiple places with no inference being made on the connections, be they social network or knowledge graph or threading or even material grouped by subjects or projects. In that respect Jive has a good product.

On the external domain, the Jive Clearspace community focuses on customer interactions, be they conversations or communications or participations. The capabilities include feedback loops for early customer engagement for R & D, technical support forms, and communities for marketing and sales.

Socialtext: A Hosted Enterprise Collaboration Tool

Socialtext (www.socialtext.com) has all the basic social media capabilities, such as social networking, personal home pages, wikis, and blogs. It also has a couple of innovative ideas such as distributed spreadsheets and social messaging. The idea of interlinked, distributed, and dynamic spreadsheets is interesting, but not surprising as Dan Bricklin, one of the developers of the first spreadsheet VisiCalc, is on the company's leadership team. The social messaging capability is also very useful for enterprises. It enables micro-sharing as you find in Twitter in an enterprise setting. The Socialtext platform can either be used as a hosted service or enterprises can deploy the capability as a hardware appliance inside their organizations. The SocialText platform has integration capabilities such as the OpenSocial interface, plugin architecture, and connectors for enterprise directories and other enterprise systems.

Awareness: An Enterprise Social Media and Web 2.0 Communities Platform

Very similar to Jive, Awareness (www.awarenessnetworks.com) specializes in developing software for internal and external community and social network capabilities for corporations. From an internal perspective, Awareness offers knowledge-sharing and collaboration, improved communication, and more important, capability to create a "corporate memory" of the various business related events, information exchanges and other activities that happens in an enterprise. I found the last one to be interesting and have a compelling value. On the externally facing aspects, the capabilities include interactions with customers for support, marketing, and sales. Awareness has a hybrid model—they can help corporations to build Web 2.0 communities as well as host them if needed.

Google: Social Network Interoperability Interfaces

Naturally any discussion will not be complete without touching upon Google's offering in the space. In many ways Google has lagged in the social networking space and even now does not have a comprehensive social networking offering.

Google has taken some leadership in interoperability and data availability between social sites. For example, it is one of the major players in the OpenSocial initiative. Google also is doing lots of other interesting work, such as a social graph in Google code[76] and the Google Friend Connect.[77,78]

Microsoft: Enterprise Content Management with Social Network Features

Microsoft is another company that does not have a major presence in the social networking space. Not to be outdone by competitors like Google, however, Microsoft invested around $250 million in Facebook, making the value of Facebook astronomical.[79]

Microsoft's SharePoint has been a very successful product that has found its way into corporations. The Microsoft SharePoint server is part of the Microsoft Office server suite and has a feature set that supports enterprise content management (which is what SharePoint does best), workflow, forms-based business processes, and business intelligence. Another offering—SharePoint Online—is a hosted version of SharePoint.

Microsoft is leveraging SharePoint to be an internal social network platform as well. Many companies have found success by building social networking features around SharePoint,[21] especially if they are a Microsoft shop and are using SharePoint for content management anyway. But it might not be a perfect solution and might be missing a few functionalities.[80] But Microsoft is a fast learner and will incorporate more and more features into SharePoint. For example, Microsoft will incorporate the search technologies from FAST, which it acquired in April 2008.[81]

A good source to get a first impression of social networking capabilities in SharePoint Server 07 is the white paper "Managing social networking with Microsoft Office Share-Point Server 2007".[82] Taking a quick look:

- From SharePoint's perspective, "Social networking as a concept involves the ability for a technology platform to provide enhanced information and interaction capabilities with regard to people and resources."

- From a corporate perspective, "The goal of a technology platform providing social networking is to enhance communication and collaboration and to increase productivity in day-to-day activities and projects."

- Productivity increase comes from the ability for information workers to "leverage existing organizational social relationships to quickly find resources and colleagues to assist in projects, (and to) help with identifying and unblocking daily work issues."

- Sharepoint follows the same path as other social networking platforms; the major element is the collection called Colleagues (the corporate version of friends in the consumer context), drawn off of and displayed in context of a profile.

- "My Site" is the canvas for users to keep all their social information, such as calendar, documents, links, and blogs.

- An advantage of SharePoint over similar products is the integration with Active Directory, which makes it easier to display more enterprise-level information and to infer relationships based on information from the Active Directory information.

- SharePoint has powerful search capabilities to search through the social attributes in the system and can be the basis for "colleague mining and assembly," as they call it.

As SharePoint is not a native social networking tool (like, for example, Ning), there are differences between creating a social networking site based on SharePoint, and one using the standard social networking platforms.[83] But in the end, a company has to look at the business value achieved by SharePoint, especially if it is leveraging SharePoint for content management and sharing.

IBM: Making Collaboration a Corporate Priority

Compared to Microsoft and Google, IBM has a very sensible and evolutionary offering in the social networking space based on extending their existing products suites as well as leveraging their breadth of application services and server technology. They have leveraged their Lotus Notes as well as same-time collaboration products. IBM also has lots of research happening in this space, and I found the SONAR (Social Networking Architecture) very interesting. It is "an API and architecture for retrieving and sharing social network data in an organization and aggregating it across applications."[84] It answers questions like "Who does a person communicate with most? Or "What are all the artifacts co-authored by two individuals?" Or "Who should I consult with regarding a certain topic?" This is where social networking software brings value into an organization. It is not that most of the information is not available; the information is available in multiple forms and there is no aggregator to enable the users to get the big picture and the social and knowledge relationships.

IBM's flagship products for enterprise social networking are Lotus Quickr, Lotus Connections, and IBM Mashup Center. Lotus Quickr (Figure 4-8) is more of a content- and file-sharing program with a content repository and templates.

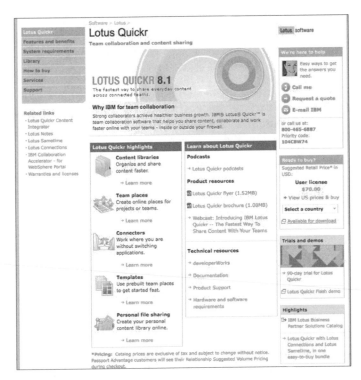

Figure 4-8 *IBM's Lotus Quickr.*

Lotus Connections (Figure 4-9) is more of a social networking product. An interesting observation is that many of the social networking features in their products came from internal IBM projects. For example, the internal project "Blue Pages" became the Profile in Notes Connections. Another internal project, "Dogear," became the book marking feature in Lotus Connections, and has 300,000 internal bookmarks.[85]

Lotus Connections has six main features:

- **Home Page:** The home page hosts five widgets and provides the single destination and a top-level structure.

- **Profiles:** This includes standard corporate attributes like name, organization, role, and so on. In that sense, the profile is the directory. It also has capability for tagging—which, when searched across, becomes the expertise location mechanism. Compared to the rich profiles in Facebook and MySpace, the Notes Connections profile is slightly anemic. But as a corporate artifact it needs to be more businesslike and one can use tags for adding one's likes and outside expertise and hobbies.

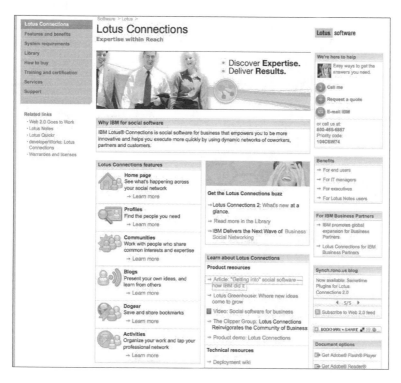

Figure 4-9 *IBM's Lotus Connections.*

- **Communities:** The Communities feature is more interesting. It has all the collaboration pieces such as blogs, activities, wikis, and integration with same-time and RSS feeds.

- **Blogs:** Connections has normal blog capabilities. Blogs can be associated with communities, thus giving them more context and relevance.

- **Dogear:** The Dogear feature is social bookmarking, an interesting feature. Naturally it is integrated with the other features. For example, one can share and discover bookmarks or one can have bookmarks under a community or an activity.

- **Activities:** The Activities feature is a way of organizing work for a specific project, including milestones, initiatives, meeting agendas, presentations, notes, and so on.

The Lotus Mashup Center (Figure 4-10) is positioned as a business mashup solution. It has capabilities such as easy aggregation of multiple business applications, the capability to create dynamic widgets, as well as the ability to publish and discover mashups and widgets.

Twitter: In a New Category by Itself—Microblogging

Saving the best for the last, this section covers Twitter and the domain of microblogging. For some, this epitomizes Web 2.0, and for others this is an example of how low Web 2.0 can go. Microblogging, with Twitter as the foremost example, is a great social

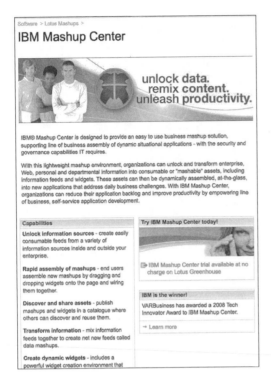

Figure 4-10   *IBM's Lotus Mashup Center.*

phenomenon that at times may be trivial but is certainly worth understanding and lever-aging from an enterprise perspective.

To understand Twitter one should read "Newbie's Guide To Twitter,"[87] which says "Twit-ter has not only tipped the tuna, but by some estimation, it has already jumped the shark." In essence, a Twitter is a short message (it allows only 140 characters) that one publishes. The subscription is known as following, where one can see the messages from others one is following. Naturally, the messages can be private or public. And Twitter works over IM and mobile phones. Even *The New York Times* is twittering [http://twitter.com/nytimes]!

Twitter is very useful, for example if a set of friends wants to organize a quick meeting in a pub or restaurant. It is also effective in quick communication with others and has be-come a medium as a personal news-wire to share world events (good and bad). For exam-ple, Twitter was the first (in seconds) when an earthquake happened in L.A. recently.[88,89] Or you can follow interesting sites or newspapers or people.[90]

Note: How do we know Twitter has entered into the social consciousness? Two reasons: First, usernames have been targets of takedowns (i.e. deletion of the user name by the Twit-ter admins) more than once.[91] For example, users who used the name of the main charac-ters from the hit AMC TV series Mad Men were taken down.[92]

Second, there was a "Twitter Debate" between the 2008 presidential campaigns, hosted by the Personal Democracy Forum.[93,94] Remember, twitters are only 140 characters long, so the questions and answers needed to be short, quick, and to the point. A good parameter for political debates, don't you think? But it did last four days and is 25 pages long [http://search.twitter.com/search?q=%23pdfdebate], so might not be as succinct as you would expect.

Microblogging is becoming a big industry. In addition to Twitter, the leader, there are other companies such as Pownce, Jaiku, Kwippy, Ienti.ca, and Plurk offering different levels of microblogging. For example, Pownce might be more suited for business[95] or Plurk is better suited for interactive and more interpersonal conversation[96] (as opposed to Twitter, which is more of a collective conversation). Because of the multiple services, even aggregators such as Friendfeed are becoming players in this space.[97] There are also open initiatives such as OpenMicroBlogging that add standardization, via interoperable protocols, to this domain.

Twitter is slowly becoming a corporate messaging tool, primarily straddling the thin line separating the corporate and the public world. Naturally one should not, under any circumstances, put corporate information in one's messages. Jeremiah Owyang of Forrester has a good writeup on how to get started in Twitter.[98] I am collecting good tips for the Twitter newbie in my blog, as well.[99]

Twitter is not for everybody,[100] and it does get bogged down with trivial messages—maybe we really do not want a minute-by-minute commentary on what everyone is doing. But if you have lots of mobile minutes, TwitterFone will read Twitters for you.[101] Jacob Harris, who is behind the *NY Times Twitter*, has a good discussion on Twitter.[102] There are other folks who go from Twittering to Plurk-ing,[103] and then wonder why we have so many social networking avenues.

Finally, in the words of TechCrunch,[104] the two main reasons for success are short messages (as opposed to blogs that require lots of writing, which does intimidate lots of folks) and ensuring that the messages go to a well defined audience (which creates a "cohesion and a sense of utility among users of a service"). This brings us to the business use of Twitter: Businesses have noticed Twitter,[105] but are still evaluating how to leverage the medium.

Social Networking Standards and Interfaces

For a domain like social networking to be pervasive and adopted by all, interoperability, data portability, identity federation, federated authentication, standard interfaces, componentization, and extensibility are all essential. Of prime importance are the user experiences and the ease with which users can accomplish things not just at one site, but across different websites with which they interact (of course, while preserving privacy and security). As the OAuth documentation[106] declares, "Users don't care about protocols and standards—they care about better experience with enhanced privacy and security." So true! As is the case elsewhere in this book, we will keep the discussions at this level when looking into the specifications. For the moment our main focus is on what and not how.

Note: As I was preparing for this chapter, MySpace joined the OpenID coalition and added support for the OpenID identity platform. They will be issuers of OpenID identities, but it was not clear whether they would accept users from other OpenID sites like AOL, Yahoo!, Wordpress, and so on.[107] This was big news;[108,109] even the BBC covered it.[46] The main advantages are data portability and identity federation. The potential to share profiles (based on user-defined policies) across different websites such as Google, AOL, and MySpace is exciting and very useful. Naturally, MySpace, because it is still new to this eco system, has not reached that stage. So challenges still exist, even with the availability of open standards.

This section looks at some of the standards and initiatives that could, potentially, make aspects such as interoperability, portability, and security possible.

OpenSocial

OpenSocial is an open standard with a simple value proposition: common APIs for social applications across multiple websites.[110] It is developed as a public standard—anybody can get involved. Two good sites to explore before developing open social applications are the documentation[111] and the best practices for designing social apps.[19]

At a high level, OpenSocial is a set of APIs that can expose a social graph and as Nic Carr explains,[112] OpenSocial enables the integration of enterprise and social networks. Mark Andresseen[113] sees a lot of value in a container-API–based model and is of the opinion that the OpenSocial extends the Facebook platform approach. I think Marc's blog[113] would be of interest to readers of this chapter because of the earlier discussion of the Facebook platform. Now let us drill down into the world of OpenSocial APIs.

In essence, the OpenSocial Specification[114] defines a set of interfaces that a social website (container) implements so that developers can develop social applications either as widgets or as standalone applications. In case of widgets, the Google widgets specification[115] defines the widget interfaces and OpenSocial defines the social interfaces; for standalone applications OpenSocial defines a set of REST APIs as well as the JSON RPC.

Note: An open standardized interface across different social networks means that a widget written using the APIs will have different context at the times those APIs are running. For example, if you write a widget that lists your friends and the friends' interests using OpenSocial APIs, then when the widget runs in Ning, it will show your friends in a social site hosted in Ning. If you run the widget in Orkut it will show your friends in Orkut. If you run it in Hi5 you will see corresponding friends, and if you are nostalgic and run the widget in your old MySpace account, naturally you will see all your teenage friends!

And if an application uses the REST APIs, it can actually list all your friends in all the social networking sites on which you have an account. So while you want to keep your business acquaintances, you can also keep a tab on your MySpace friends, giving you all in the security of the corporation without leaving company walls—firewalls, I mean!

So from an enterprise perspective, the REST APIs give the business flexibility to interact with the social sites securely and compliant to regulations. The corporate information will not cross the company's boundaries while still leveraging the social network and other social interactions.

Let us take a quick look under the covers of the OpenSocial specification:

■   Like any other social network artifact, OpenSocial is centered around people, relationships (the social graph), activities, and views. It also provides capabilities for storing sessions (persistence) and tapping into application/widget lifecycle events (such as add/remove application, approve application, policy, invites, and so on).

■   Gadgets are not limited to resources in the server they are running. They can make requests to remote servers with appropriate security. For example, you might have a photo printing widget that needs to pick the images from another site where you normally store your pictures in a private area. In this case, you will use an OAuth token, which will enable the printing widget to get the pictures securely.

■   As widgets will be running in the context of a browser, OpenSocial has defined a set of JavaScript APIs, which a widget hosting site/container will support.

■   Lots of sites implement the OpenSocial container interfaces (such as Hi5, MySpace, orkut, Ning, Google and Plaxo; the list at http://code.google.com/apis/opensocial/gettingstarted.html is growing) and developers can interact with these sites using the OpenSocial APIs, either as widgets (JavaScript APIs) or as standalone applications (REST/JSON APIs).

■   As of writing this chapter (August 2008) the OpenSocial version is 0.8 and the mailing list is busy with discussions on 0.8.1. So there is still work to be done.

■   There is one public open source implementation: Apache Shindig. Shindig means party, and another site, Partuza (Spanish slang for party),[116] has examples and makes it easy for developers to get started in the OpenSocial world.

OpenSocial has lots of potential and the implications are huge. I think Dan Faber, Editor-in-Chief of *CNet*, has the right perspective. He says,[117] "It could become a kind of identity fabric for the Internet—with user profile data, relationships (social graph), and other items associated with an individual, group, or brand that is used as a basis for more friction-free interactions of all kinds."

OpenID

OpenID (http://openid.net/) addresses the problem of multiple usernames and passwords that one needs to have for different websites.[118] It is an open standard for authentication that different service providers can implement. Instead of having multiple identities, you will have one identity with an OpenID provider, and other websites will accept that identity instead of requiring you to have a separate account with its own username and password. AOL, Wordpress, Yahoo!, Blogger, and Orange-France Telecom[119] all are OpenID providers. Two great sources to learn about OpenID are OpenID for non-Super Users[120] and OpenID for Developers (http://openid.net/developers/). Without getting into too much technical detail, let us take a quick look at the OpenID authentication specification version 2.0.[121]

The key characteristics of OpenID are

- It is an open standard and relies on common web mechanisms such as HTTP, SSL, Diffie-Hellman Key exchange, and so on.

- It is decentralized; you can choose any provider and can move between providers. There is no big identity provider in the sky!

The overall protocol is very simple:

- First, a user establishes an account with an OpenID provider. As you saw earlier, you already might have an account if you are an AOL user or have a Wordpress account.

- When a user wants to access another website (relying party), instead of creating a new user account he uses the OpenID identity—for example, username.wordpress. com or openid.aol.com/screenname or blogname.blogspot.com or www.flickr.com/ photos/username.

- The relying party then applies logic to figure out which OpenID provider to call, calls that OpenID provider, and establishes a secure channel (association). Then it sends out an OpenID authentication request.

- The OpenID provider then authenticates the user (for example by displaying a user-name/password form) and then redirects the user with an authentication assertion with additional information embedded in the HTTPS message.

- The relying party (which if you remember is the website the user wanted to access) parses the authentication assertion and proceeds. For example, if the assertion says that the authentication failed, then the website does not allow access.

In short, a simple open specification based on common protocols is a good way to solve the identity problem. Of course, this is well and good in theory, but one has to balance this with the security policies (and practices) of an enterprise.

An important barrier is the fact that everyone wants to own a user and so are eager to be OpenID providers. But very few are willing to accept other companies' OpenID identities. The MySpace announcement [107](of using OpenID but only acting as a provider) illustrates this.

OpenID is a young specification, with extensions being developed, such as OpenID at-tribute exchange, Open data transfer protocol, and OpenID Provider Authentication Policy Extension. The policy extension specification is interesting because it enables

- A relying party to specify what policies to be applied for an authentication

- An OpenID provider to return what polices were indeed applied for an authentication

Policies are becoming an important part of authentication and authorization and could be the topic of their own book.

OAuth

OAuth (http://oauth.net/) is another interesting open standard. It allows one to have granular access control.[118] The example in the OAuth site talks about the valet key and the regular key for cars, highlighting the capability to limit access to certain functions using different keys or tokens. Another example is your public calendar: You need read and write access, but your friends and others need only read access. The access token defined by OAuth enables you to do this: You have a read-write token you use with the calendar website, while you give your friends a read token they use to view your calendar safely. A good example showing how to share photos using OAuth is at Beginner's Guide to OAuth—Part II [122].

Some good links include Developing OAuth clients in Ruby,[123] the OAuth specification,[124] Beginner's Guide[125] and "OpenID and OAuth, and Why Should We Care?"[126] Let us take a quick look at the OAuth specification:

- OAuth enables you to share online resources such as photos, calendar, and so on between sites or between users without making them public and without giving away your username and password.

- OAuth authenticates a consumer for access and nothing more—not even identity. For example, it knows, via a set of electronic tokens, that a person can read your calendar. It does not care nor has the capability to know who it is. But this is fine because the underlying assumption is that you are the one who has the tokens and you distribute the read only tokens responsibly. It is fine to publish a token to read your public calendar.

- OAuth is based on common protocols such as HTTP and digital signatures. It also has to answer questions on business models, web exchanges, and security, which need to be evaluated and tested by user companies.

Other Social Networking Standards

Although we cannot go in detail into all the relevant standards, there are a few notable evolving standards that will become part of the social networking neighborhood and bear mention:

- **Friend of a Friend Project:** The foaf project (http://www.foaf-project.org/) is an interesting foray into the semantic web of social networking. Basically it is an RDF vocabulary to describe oneself (for example name, home page, blog address, who one knows—via the element foaf:knows and so on) so that machines can read and understand.[127] Basically you create a foaf file about yourself and publish it.[128] You also need to have an autodiscovery link that the spiders, during their crawl, will find and add to repositories.

- **Xhtml Friends Network:** XFN (http://gmpg.org/xfn/) is a way of representing relationships using hyperlinks. It adds an `rel` tag and associated semantics.[129]

Challenges in the Social Networking Industry

There are multiple issues facing the industry as it matures, including relevance of applications, openness, data portability, security, world-wide acceptance, and localization. Let us look at a few of these growing pains.

Relevance and Nature

One obvious effect of the popularity of social networking is the existence of too many applications, many not well behaved and many not well thought out. Facebook, as a part of its new look in July 2008, has new rules[130] to curtail the "spaminess," including too many invitations and feeds. It is an interesting read—the rules include "A Feed story describing or triggered by the consumption of content must be a one-line story; applications cannot incentivize users (for example, offer points, virtual or real payments, or a ranking) to publish stories to Feed; Applications cannot require users to publish a story to Feed in order to interact with any portion of the application...." From a Web 2.0 perspective, the open versus controlled platform is playing out in other domains as well—for example, the Google Android phone versus Apple iPhone and their respective development strategies. Apple wants to tightly control which and how many apps run on iPhone, and can even remotely disable an application a user has loaded as well as remove an application from its store. Android, on the other hand, is more open.

Another obvious side-effect is an unmanageable number of friends.[131] In a casual site, this could be fine, but as a business tool, the list needs to be manageable to get any usefulness. And if one spends too much time churning through social sites (whether a corporate one or an external one), that is too much time lost from work. In fact, "Do you think it's OK to hang out on Facebook or MySpace during work hours? Should businesses block social networking sites from their employees?" asks a columnist for MSNBC.[132] I don't think there is a firm answer yet. The alternative, to having all your friends on one site, is having to redefine all your connections and re-invite everyone for each site that you are member of. It would be great to define your friends with persistent (not MySpace or Facebook) identities and have the same network on the different sites. Sites like TripIt.com are cool but not worth the pain of re-creating your social network. Also, the networks are all flat now: You just have your friends. What you really have are collections: co-workers, soccer team, family. What is needed are groups and collections in the abstract that could be used by all the sites.

Openness and Data Portability

Naturally, as a domain matures (or for a domain to mature) interoperability, data portability, and openness will become dominant.

At least for now, although we do not have a single interoperable standard, we do have many standards! Facebook connect[133,134] is one, MySpace's data portability[135] is another, and of course OpenSocial is the third.

Regarding Facebook Connect, Om Malik[136] says "In addition to offering a simple authentication method, FC allows granular social interactions to be embedded in non-Facebook services. If Facebook can work with its partners to build interesting use-case scenarios that go beyond simple sign-on, it is quite feasible that Facebook can out-execute Google, MySpace, and everyone else with its ID ambitions." Facebook Connect generated lots of press[137] and even Time asked, "Facebook: Movement or Business?"[138] Facebook Connect has four primary features:[139] trusted authentication, real identity, friends access, and dynamic privacy. The Facebook Connect blog [140] appeared only recently and is still in limited Beta.

MySpace kicked off its data portability [141,142] one day ahead of the Facebook Connect announcement. MySpace joined the data portability project and also announced data sharing partnerships with Yahoo!, eBay, and Twitter.

Maybe it is too late. Already startups are figuring out ways of getting data out. "Facebook's data has left the barn," cries *The Washington Post*.[143]

One small fine-print item to note is that the data portability initiatives form the social networking companies are not all open.[144] "MySpace and Facebook are working hard to figure out how to make 'their' open application 'the' open application."says a blog in WebGuild.[145] MySpace's OpenID announcement confirms that it wants to become an OpenID provider and not a consumer, thus forcing users to register with MySpace. One hopes that these policies will change in the due course of time and in response to pressure from the users who now have to have multiple OpenIDs.

Note: As the social network as a platform matures, other social (and political) aspects come into the picture, as one blogger discovered.[146] Causes is a site that focuses on charitable donations and lives in Facebook and MySpace as widget. Its patrons complained at the inclusion of Palestine but not Israel in one of the "country" drop-down menus. Actually, Causes was not making any political statement, but the list box was filled with information from a payment processor. Naturally the people who complained to the agency that has its donations page in Causes, which is a Facebook widget, do not understand any of the dependencies. They judge the site by what they see.

Open standards or not, a platform war is still going on,[147] and companies are trying to innovate on their products and services to capture the mindshare.

Another development in this area is social aggregation across sites; eWeek calls it Socialcast 2.0.[148] In fact, Mashable[149] shows you 20 ways to aggregate social profiles! This becomes more interesting when you consider that there is 40%–60% overlaps between members of different sites.[150]

Security and Privacy

Naturally security and privacy concerns have come to the forefront in the social networking domain. An example of the dual nature of social networks (security versus the ability to connect) can be observed in the military. Soldiers are banned[151] from joining and posting information to social networks, which of course is being resisted by the soldiers as the social networks help them to keep in touch with friends and family. In a recent Black Hat conference, researchers showed security vulnerabilities that range from adding and extending bogus friends to viruses that can be propagated via social networking sites.[152] Another type of worm gets in via the Wall feature in Facebook.[153] In December 2008, a new kind of worm (Net-Worm.Win32.Koobface.a) that spreads through My-Space and Facebook, appeared.[154,155] The Koobface Trojan creates a message that lures users into a video site, which then asks the user to update Flash Player. If the unsuspecting user gives permission, instead of the expected Fash update, a network worm is installed into the user's machine and turns the machine into a zombie that becomes part of a botnet.

In addition to computer-related security risks, there are also social aspects of security and privacy in social networks. In fact, New York state lawmakers are drafting laws to keep predators away from "spacebook," as they call it.[156] Even internationally, privacy issues are raising their ugly heads. For example, the Canadian Internet Policy and Public Interest Clinic (CIPPIC) filed a complaint,[157] asking the Privacy Commissioner of Canada to review 22 violations of Canadian privacy law, making Facebook "a minefield of privacy invasion."

One nice feature Facebook added[158] was the privacy controls based on friend-groups, which means one can have a friend-group called co-workers that exposes a different profile than, say, the one given to casual friends. This change was promoted by the change in demographics of the Facebook membership, from a private college network to a more business-oriented one.

Note: A new kind of banner ad, called social banners, has emerged.[159] Although they do not violate the privacy of the social networking sites, they analyze interactions with friends in a site and use algorithms like Friendsrank[160] to find "influentials" and then display social ads. For example, rather than display an ad for a movie, it will display a short list of your friends (which it gathered by looking at your interactions) and ask which of your friends you want to invite for that movie. This is certainly clever, but it fringes the boundaries of privacy, to say the least. Or maybe this becomes a norm and we wouldn't mind having our interactions mined. Some compare this to Facebook's Beacon, which shared information between sites (for example, if you bought a book your friend would see it in Amazon via feeds) that elicited a very bad reaction from users and was scaled down. There is also a class-action suit against Beacon, and many wonder whether actions such as these will make platforms relevant outside their context.[161]

Data Ownership

As more and more user-generated content is posted in the various social network sites, the social media industry faces a content ownership challenge. Questions like "Who has what rights to the data?" and "What happens to the data if a user closes an account?" are important. This issue is very important to enterprises as more and more user-generated content will be created in communities and other enterprise-level websites—both internal and external. The data ownership of externally facing sites is even more important.

It is instructive to look a little deeper into the data ownership issue Facebook is having as of February 2009. Facebook is having a tough time in answering data ownership questions. It all started when Facebook updated its privacy policies on Feb 4, 2009.[162] The new policy, among other things, deleted the Expire on Termination clause and effectively gave perpetual and irrevocable license to all the materials for Facebook to use. Blogger Chris Walters noticed the changes and his blog "Facebook's New Terms Of Service: 'We Can Do Anything We Want With Your Content. Forever'"[163] and started an avalanche of protest. Realizing that they had angered the user community and fearing a backlash and user revolt, Facebook backtracked[164] on their policy, started reassuring users that the new policy is not effective, and reverted to their old policy. They stated that the company "doesn't claim rights to any of your photos or other content. We need a license to help you share information with your friends, but we don't claim to own your information." And Mark Zuckerberg, the CEO of Facebook, appeared on TV as well as other media and placated users. He declared that the data belongs to users and offered all users participation in carving out a new data policy for Facebook. Users can review, comment, and vote on the policy that will become Facebook's data sharing doctrine.

On Feb 26, 2009, Facebook started a new polling campaign[165] to draft the new Terms Of Service (TOS), which includes two areas: "Facebook Principles"[166] and "Statement of rights and responsibilities."[167] They started two groups to discuss, comment on, and post ideas about two topics:

- Facebook Principles deals with the foundational guiding philosophy and values of Facebook and its community. The ten principles[168] range from "Freedom to share and connect" and "Ownership and control of information" to "One World."

- The Statement is more prescriptive, and after it is finalized will be the future Terms of Use, Developer Terms of Service, and the Facebook Advertising Terms and Conditions. The Statement will govern Facebook's relationship with users and others who interact with them. The three statements of rights[167] are crisp and clear, viz: "Forever won't work: Facebook's use of our content has to have clear limits," "Opt-in only: Facebook can't just change the terms whenever they want" and "Write it in English: No legalese (or Latin!) please."

This episode showed the power of the social networks over the industry as Mark eloquently pointed out: "The past week reminded us that users feel a real sense of ownership over Facebook itself, not just the information they share."[169] And the discussion is far from over, as *WSJ*, quoting Mark, points out: "We're at an interesting point in the development of the open online world, where these issues are being worked out."[170] The lesson for enterprises is to make sure they have sensible terms on privacy and data ownership, especially in a connected world. And understand that there is no perfect solution, but the trick is to respond faster to any complaints from the community and deal with them in an open manner.

Worldwide Acceptance and Localization

One important trend to note is that social networking is an international phenomenon and cultural relevance is very important, as shown in the comScore survey in June 2008.[171] "Facebook: No. 1 Globally," says *Business Week:* "The social network site has vaulted over rival MySpace in worldwide audience growth, thanks to tools that translate content into many languages."[172,173,174,175]

But there are challenges, such as in Japan. *Tech Crunch* reports[176] that in Japan MySpace is ranked 95 and Facebook does not even come into the top 100. Cultural differences and translation challenges are some of the barriers to entry in Japan.

Quoting the comScore report regarding Facebook, "By increasing the site's relevance to local markets through local language interface translation, the site is now competing strongly or even capturing the lead in several markets where it had a relatively minor presence just a year ago." The report shows Facebook has a year-over-year increase of 1055% in Latin America and 300%–500% increase in Europe, the Middle East/Africa, and Asia Pacific. Social networking is a world phenomenon and is here to stay!

In Short

Social networking is becoming a popular domain by itself; were it a country, Facebook's population would be ranked as the sixth most populous in the world, behind Brazil. The effectiveness of social networks has grown beyond the span of teenagers and schools and is now becoming a force in politics and the judicial system, as well as an employment tool. In politics, the presidential election of 2008 proved the power of social networks to successfully mobilize a volunteer force as well as elicit campaign contributions, "combining the best elements of mass communication with the best elements of interpersonal communication."[177] The "bottom-up, unruly approach that turns first-time voters into activists"[178] not only works in politics but also for enterprises. Companies such as SalesForce.com and Starbucks are leveraging social networking in the same way: to turn customers into enthusiasts who help the companies with new ideas. On the legal side, a court in Australia approved the use of Facebook to serve court documents electronically in a civil case when lawyers couldn't reach the defendants in their homes or via email.[179] Enterprises are also using social networks to learn about potential candidates. In fact, a survey by Career Builder[180] revealed that one in five employers use social networking sites to research potential employees. Companies such as Google are thinking of new ways of monetizing social networks. For example, Google is applying its page ranking, which worked well in its search engine, to social networks for influence-ranking based advertising.[181] For enterprises, the question is not whether to embrace social media but how to identify business uses and then successfully implement them.[182]

<monologue>

I always traversed the web the old fashioned way to find new content and updates viz. start the day with Slashdot, Digg, and the like, and then visit each website I am interested in via bookmarks. Of course, the old fashioned way takes too much time and leads to visiting websites even when there are no updates. There are too many interesting websites with lots of information—but there is not enough time to visit all of them and check if they have any new information. How do we track them all and know when they have new materials? To answer that I realized I needed to dig deeper into the world of RSS and Atom and include this chapter in a book about Web 2.0.

</monologue>

CHAPTER 5

Content Aggregation, Syndication, and Federation via RSS and Atom

This chapter is about information distribution, ranging from news feeds to sophisticated content management systems, and two popular technologies: RSS and Atom. RSS (Really Simple Syndication) is a popular mechanism for publishing and receiving content from regularly changing websites such as blogs and news sites.[1] For example, when a new blog is written on a website such as WordPress, an RSS entry is created at the website with information such as when it was published, the link, a description, and other details. Users who are interested in the blog can subscribe to the RSS feed via RSS readers. Live BookMarks in the Firefox browser is one example. An RSS reader periodically visits the site and picks any new material, or in the case of Live BookMark, it creates a headlines index (with information such as publication date and title) and then users can click to read new blogs. It pushes all the updates to which you subscribe, even if they come from several websites, to one place. This is really a better alternative than visiting all the blog sites in which one is interested and checking for new entries. RSS aggregators can publish updates from a set of websites that cater to subjects of interest, like cars or computers or a primary election. Atom is employed in more complex content exchanges and replication between content management systems. Both RSS and Atom are based on XML markup of the content with extra information; but Atom has more capabilities and it also has an exchange protocol based on HTTP to exchange content.

Information processing involves multiple levels of sophistication such as aggregation, syndication, and federation. Although these words are used in the old news world, in the context of the Internet they have a slightly different and expanded meanings:

- *Content Aggregation* is the process of collecting and presenting information from different sources.
  As an example, RSS readers usually are aggregators, but newer readers can perform higher forms of collection as well.

- *Syndication* is when information is categorized and normalized, in addition to being collected.
  Syndication is seen in lots of websites that give you price comparisons. These pricing websites spider the net to grab the prices for your item. Then they analyze the prices and give you a sorted list; some of them even offer price alerts. All this syndication is a higher form of information collection than simple content aggregation.

- In a *federated* world, the content will be semantically analyzed and even combined in different ways such as by date of publication by a narrow topic or by other ways that is relevant to a discussion or interest group or an event.

Usually federation is a manual process. One good federation site is ABC News' The Note,[2] as shown in Figure 5-1. It takes a current item, summarizes the buzz from various blogs in a cohesive form, sometimes quotes them, and always has the links. So in one place, you can get a good overview of the topic and can drill deeper into the various blogs and related news items. In true Web 2.0 fashion, the site has links for RSS, Digg, Facebook, and more, as shown in Figure 5-2.

Figure 5-1   *ABC News' The Note.*

Figure 5-2   *ABC News' The Note link bar.*

This chapter covers the business, technology, history, and future of two popular Web 2.0 mechanisms: RSS and Atom. As you will see, these technologies did not progress linearly.

For example, RSS 2.0 is not the next version of RSS 1.0 and RSS 1.0 is not the next version of RSS 0.92. However, users are finally converging to one or two major technologies (RSS 2.0 and Atom).

Business View of Information Distribution

From a business perspective, efficient, timely, and targeted information distribution is essential, irrespective of whether the information is for alerts, marketing, technical or governmental updates, or any other purpose. Even when information is targeted to interested parties, information overload is a major impediment against efficient information consumption. People are subjected to a lot of information and sometimes are unable to parse the relevant parts quickly. From a user perspective, the ability to find the right information and the ability to get new and updated information are always challenging. From an organization perspective, the ability to reach information seekers at the right time is always difficult. The topics of this chapter, RSS and Atom technologies, provide a substrate and capability for an effective information dissemination infrastructure with a good balance between pull (the ability for users to get information when they need it) and push (the ability for information providers to notify users when new content is available or existing content has changed). RSS and Atom technologies actually turn a push model into a pull model.

Note: An important characteristic that makes information overload more pronounced is the fact that interest in any particular category of information is often temporal, transitionary, and limited. When you are buying a car you want all the information and help available, but after you've made your purchase, you probably will not use those information sources again for a while. You've shifted to looking for the latest information on that gigantic HDTV you have been looking for. Moreover, many pieces of information are limited to niche groups. For example, the social networking community site Ning has more than 20,000 special-interest social groups.

The business value of RSS and Atom technologies is in the improved information access and distribution they provide, thereby increasing effectiveness and productivity. For example, by using RSS feeds, customers and employees can choose what they want to read and more importantly can change topics as they change roles. They need not comb websites and can categorize the feeds. Naturally they can stop anytime by unsubscribing to the feeds. Also there are mechanisms by which the subscribers can choose sections of a site or collection, perhaps to see the technology or sports sections of a newspaper, for example. For organizations publishing information, this makes targeting and information selection easier and more efficient. Companies can have RSS feeds for multiple constituents: one RSS feed for new products, one for new support information (for example new updates), and so on. Moreover, there are RSS readers for mobile devices and that is another targeted avenue—a dedicated mobile RSS feed with relevant information! Users use either dedicated RSS readers (programs that pull information in which they are interested) or the Live BookMark feature in Firefox browser that pulls just the date and headline.

For enterprises this is great. There is no unwanted push to hostile users or customers. Also, by providing an RSS/Atom publishing mechanism, they reach a targeted audience to whom they can send information when and where the audience wants it. In fact, the social networking sites use RSS to build user loyalty through targeted information distribution.[3]

Naturally there are some drawbacks. For example, although the information comes to you after you sign up, you still have to find the source in the first place. Users need to search for sites with the feeds they want and include them in their subscription. But this limitation can be mitigated. Corporations can host RSS feed sites for information that is of interest to their customers in a central place, accessible to all users in the corporate network. Then employees need to go to only one place to find the interesting and relevant RSS feeds. Of course, companies need a few dedicated people to spend time going through Internet sites, searching for relevant sites, and then adding them to the corporate syndicated RSS sites, as needed. An interesting blog to gauge the utility of RSS is "35 Ways You Can Use RSS Today."[4] It outlines how you can track cheap tickets, track your favorite sports teams, monitor airport delays, and even track the latest uses of RSS.

Note: Typically users leverage RSS capability of their favorite blog sites or news sites. In addition users can find RSS destinations in three main ways:

- Registries: RSS registries contain a list of RSS feeds, usually categorized by main subjects or topics. Syndic8.com is the most popular RSS registry. It has a massive list and is very extensive. In fact, the market share data of various RSS formats (in Figure 5-3, later in this chapter) was taken from this site. The site is vast, so we can be sure that it represents the actual market share of the various RSS formats!

- Simple syndicators: RSS syndication is one step up from registries in the sense that it maintains more categorization and relevance. RSS syndicators are not as extensive as registries such as Syndic8.com, but maintain relevant information for a specific set of domains. For example, there are science and technology RSS feeds by the U.S. government [5] and Technorati.[6] Naturally you should check out Technorati's web 2.0 feeds [7] and its list of the top 10 RSS syndication products of 2008.[8]

- Search interfaces for RSS feeds: Another mechanism is the specialized search engines that search only through RSS feeds. For example, Blogdigger has extensive features like RSS groups and blog search, all built on RSS and Atom syndication technologies. Technorati provides the Technorati blog search in its feeds.technorati.com/search/ URL. For example, there you can search for VoIP feeds through the URL feeds.technorati.com/search/voip. Bloglines, BlogPulse, and Feedster all search through RSS feeds. Search4RSS (http://www.search4rss.com/) even has a Firefox search add-in and has graduated to a search aggregator. In fact, Google bought FeedBurner for $100 million, which shows the value of an RSS feed and RSS search ecosystem.

There certainly is tremendous business value for enterprises to leverage the various publishing patterns for information dissemination across (and outside) the organization, using RSS and Atom technologies. In fact, the Atom protocol is moving into mainstream: Major content management systems have started supporting the Atom format.

Podcasts

Podcasts are another important development in the RSS world. A podcast is basically the publishing of information—discussions, talks, news, public policy, health information, and so on—in MP3 audio format. The name comes from the ever popular iPod (iPod broadcast), but you can subscribe to and view a podcast on any MP3 player or simply on your computer. The distribution of podcasts is through an RSS mechanism. RSS 2.0 has an `<enclosure>` tag for incorporating the pointer to the MP3 file URL. When a user clicks the tag (or the reader might separate the URL and show a clickable button that the user clicks), the MP3 file is downloaded in the appropriate player, which can then be played on the computer or synched to an MP3 player. Other popular mechanisms such as iTunes have added their own XML namespaces and tags for RSS 2.0. In short, one can leverage the RSS infrastructure to distribute podcasts, thus utilizing all its advantages, such as syndication, specialized search websites, and the fact that podcasts can be accessed via the mobile mechanisms that people are familiar with. There are lots of good tutorials on the web; for example the University of Washington [9] has a good podcast tutorial.

The broadcasting industry, especially radio stations, has embraced podcasting. Most of the major news stations have podcast support; NPR actually has a lot more than news in their NPR podcast directory at http://www.npr.org/rss/podcast/podcast_directory.php. On the aggregator side, PodcastAlley (http://www.podcastalley.com/) has a good podcast directory and other podcast-related information. Podcast Central (http://www.podcastcentral.com/Resource.html) is also a good source. On the search side, Yahoo Audio Search (http://audio.search.yahoo.com/audio) searches through podcasts, and Podscope (http://www.podscope.com/) is an interesting audio/video search engine. When the phenomenon of podcasts started, there were good reader/creators like RSSRadio (http://www.dorada.co.uk/) and BlogMatrix Sparks!. Nowadays there are lots of good programs, many, part of Windows and OS X.

The following sections summarize the different formats. In essence, RSS and Atom are content exchange formats (description and syndication), with XML that contains not only the information but also metadata that is accessible via programs. The difference between RSS and Atom is in the structure, the data, and the metadata they provide and the complexity of the formats. Of course, remember that one needs to make sure the complexity is appropriate to the domain. A simpler format such as RSS 2.0 is better suited for a news feed, whereas for complex content management systems, publishing through Atom would be more viable.

RSS

RSS has a slightly contentious past, with multiple formats and information architectures, and was known at various times as Rich Site Summary or RDF Site Summary or Really Simple Syndication.[10] RSS Specifications[11] has a detailed history of RSS. Figure 5-3 shows the evolution of the various RSS versions and their current market share. Over the years, RSS 2.0 has emerged as the most popular RSS standard.

Although this section does not dig too extensively into the history of RSS, it does provide some of the important aspects to give some perspective on the versions and the way

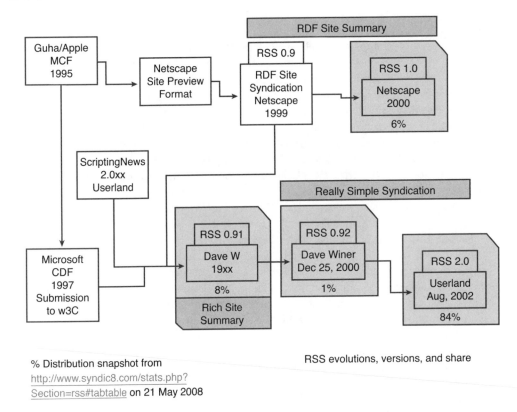

% Distribution snapshot from
http://www.syndic8.com/stats.php?
Section=rss#tabtable on 21 May 2008

Figure 5-3   *Evolution of RSS versions.*

they are structured. (Check out Wikipedia[12] for a more detailed history of syndication technologies.)

The precursor to RSS started from the Meta Content Format (MCF) by Dr. Guha[13] (when he was at Apple), as well as the Channel Definition Format (CDF) by Microsoft.[14] Guha later joined Netscape and started working on Resource Description Framework (RDF) with Tim Bray and others. RDF Site Summary, also known as RSS 0.9,[15] was born at Netscape as a channel description framework/content-gathering mechanism for their My Netscape Network (MNN) portal.

During the same time, Dave Winer at UserLand had a scheme called ScriptingNews.[16] RSS 0.91 (now called Rich Site Summary) was based on RSS 0.90, dropped the RDF pedigree, incorporated ScriptingNews, and was probably influenced by Microsoft's CDF as well.

The RDF strand continued to RSS 1.0, which added a few capabilities such as modules. RSS 1.0 came out December 6, 2000. As the XML Cover Pages points out, "Thus far, however, uptake for RSS 1.0 has been relatively limited, due to the difficulty in creating conforming documents in comparison to other syndication formats."[17] RSS 1.1 came out in 2005 and added some of the new features in RDF.

Dave Winer continued development of RSS 0.91 to 0.92 (which came out on Christmas day in 2000), and then through a brief lifespan as 0.93.[18] Finally, after development that took it to version 0.94, RSS 2.0 was released in September 2002. Extensibility was the major addition. Three things happened that solidified RSS 2.0:

- First, in July 2003, UserLand transferred ownership (of the RSS 2.0 specification) to the Berkman Center for Internet and Society at Harvard Law School.[19]

- Second, the usage license was changed to the Attribution-Share Alike 1.0 Generic license by Creative Commons.[20]

- Third, an independent advisory board[21] was created to guide the specification and adoption.

Thus, finally, RSS 2.0, now known as Really Simple Syndication, became a general property. It is now the most popular format of RSS and is widely used.

Note: As a footnote to the short history of the RSS, it is informative to read Dan Libby's e-mail to the rss-dev Yahoo group.[22]. There are lots of good workshops and other materials on the web, such as the workshop from Government Information Locator Service,[23] RSS tutorial for content publishers,[24] and w3cschools.com.[25]

Later this chapter, you can explore how the Atom format came into existence and the value of that format. For now, though, this section moves on to look at the salient characteristics of RSS 2.0.

RSS 2.0 Information Architecture

RSS is based on XML and the various elements manifest as XML tags. The sample from the RSS specification (http://cyber.law.harvard.edu/rss/examples/rss2sample.xml) is displayed in Example 5-1.

Example 5-1 *RSS sample*

```
<?xml version="1.0"?>
<rss version="2.0">
    <channel>
        <title>Liftoff News</title>
        <link>http://liftoff.msfc.nasa.gov/</link>
        <description>Liftoff to Space Exploration.</description>
        <language>en-us</language>
        <pubDate>Tue, 10 Jun 2003 04:00:00 GMT</pubDate>
        <lastBuildDate>Tue, 10 Jun 2003 09:41:01 GMT</lastBuildDate>
        <docs>http://blogs.law.harvard.edu/tech/rss</docs>
        <generator>Weblog Editor 2.0</generator>
        <managingEditor>editor@example.com</managingEditor>
        <webMaster>webmaster@example.com</webMaster>
        <item>
            <title>Star City</title>
            <link>http://liftoff.msfc.nasa.gov/news/2003/news-starcity.asp</link>
            <description>How do Americans get ready to work with Russians aboard
```

```
                the International Space Station? They take a crash course in culture,
                language and protocol at Russia's &lt;a
                href="http://howe.iki.rssi.ru/GCTC/gctc_e.htm"&gt;Star
                City&lt;/a&gt;.</description>
            <pubDate>Tue, 03 Jun 2003 09:39:21 GMT</pubDate>
            <guid>http://liftoff.msfc.nasa.gov/2003/06/03.html#item573</guid>
        </item>
        <item>
            <description>Sky watchers in Europe, Asia, and parts of Alaska and
                Canada will experience a &lt;a
                href="http://science.nasa.gov/headlines/y2003/30may_solareclipse.
                htm"&gt;partial eclipse of the Sun&lt;/a&gt; on Saturday, May 31st.
                </description>
            <pubDate>Fri, 30 May 2003 11:06:42 GMT</pubDate>
            <guid>http://liftoff.msfc.nasa.gov/2003/05/30.html#item572</guid>
        </item>
        <item>
            <title>The Engine That Does More</title>
            <link>http://liftoff.msfc.nasa.gov/news/2003/news-VASIMR.asp</link>
            <description>Before man travels to Mars, NASA hopes to design new
                engines that will let us fly through the Solar System more quickly.
                The proposed VASIMR engine would do that.</description>
            <pubDate>Tue, 27 May 2003 08:37:32 GMT</pubDate>
            <guid>http://liftoff.msfc.nasa.gov/2003/05/27.html#item571</guid>
        </item>
        <item>
            <title>Astronauts' Dirty Laundry</title>
            <link>http://liftoff.msfc.nasa.gov/news/2003/news-laundry.asp</link>
            <description>Compared to earlier spacecraft, the International Space
                Station has many luxuries, but laundry facilities are not one of them.
                Instead, astronauts have other options.</description>
            <pubDate>Tue, 20 May 2003 08:56:02 GMT</pubDate>
            <guid>http://liftoff.msfc.nasa.gov/2003/05/20.html#item570</guid>
        </item>
    </channel>
</rss>
```

The Firefox browser renders the sample in Example 5-1 as shown in Figure 5-4.

Example 5-1 shows how RSS adds metadata (information about the data) as XML tags. An RSS 2.0 feed is essentially a single <channel> element that has one or more <item> elements. The top level <rss> element should have the version attribute, which is "2.0" in this case. The <channel> should have a <title>, a <description>, and a <link> element. It also could have optional elements like <language>, <copyright>, <managing editor>, <publication date>, and <category>. As you can see, this enables an RSS reader to inspect an update or a new item and display the information to the user.

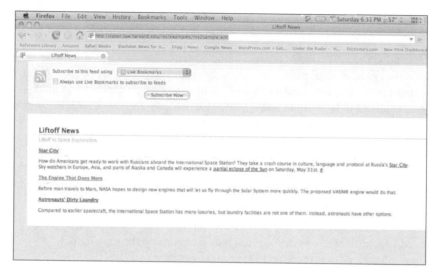

Figure 5-4 *RSS rendering in Firefox.*

The channel contains any number of `<item>` elements. An `<item>` element corresponds to an update or new entry or a story. As a historical anecdote, the 0.91 version by Netscape had a limitation of 15 items per channel, but the UserLand version didn't. It is interesting to note that RSS 2.0 is fully compatible with 0.91 and 0.92, so a valid RSS feed in 0.91 or 0.92 is valid in RSS 2.0 as well. A summary of the elements in various versions of RSS is at RSS Quick Summary.[26]

The item has information such as title, link, author, category, enclosure, and publication date. It is interesting to note that all the elements are optional, but an item without a link or a title is useless, for all practical purposes. The `<link>` element points to the actual blog entry. There can be many `<link>` elements that can point to pictures as well as multimedia content. In fact, in the case of podcasts, the link to the MP3 goes in the `<enclosure>` tag with URL, `type`, and `length` attributes.

The information model of RSS is very simple and straightforward. It is usually pull based, where a client/RSS reader pulls the information from a URL.

RSS 2.0 Modules

A discussion of RSS 2.0 would not be complete without mentioning extensibility through modules. A module is an XML fragment, embedded in an RSS 2.0 feed, which has elements based on its own namespace. (A namespace is a symbol for grouping elements in a particular extension to prevent name clashes that arise from two extensions using the same element name.) Naturally a module serves some purpose; it adds some information or metadata to the feed.

For example, the Creative Commons module[27] adds a `<license>` element (as a subelement of `<channel>`), where the publisher of the RSS feed can embed the type of license under which the feed can be used.

Another example is UserLand's blogchannel module,[28] which adds four elements (`<blogRoll>`, `<mySubscriptions>`, `<blink>`, and `<changes>`) related to blogs.

Another very good example is the MediaRSS module from Yahoo,[29] which adds elements that make syndication of multimedia more robust. It adds elements such as `<group>`, `<content>`, `<rating>`, and so on. The `<content>` element has about 14 attributes, ranging from `url` to `bitrate` to `samplingrate` to `medium`. As you can see, these elements make it possible to describe the various aspects of the content, which readers can use to optimize the user experience. (For example, RSS readers can select the right media depending on the capabilities of the device; they may even select based on contextual information like the battery life. The reader programs do this by interpreting the appropriate attributes in the `<content>` tag associated with each item.)

There are other domain-specific modules such as the trackback module,[30] which adds the trackback URL to an RSS feed, and the bittorrent module,[31] which provides the capability to add a bittorrent link to the `<enclosure>` element, and the icbm module,[32] which adds geo location (`longitude` and `latitude`) to an item or a channel.

How RSS Works

Now that you have seen the essentials, it is easy to see how RSS works. On the publishing side, a website publisher has different URLs, which contain information (such as news or support information or blog updates) in the RSS format. It usually publishes the various URLs in a registry. For example, the New York Times RSS feeds are at http://www.nytimes.com/rss, as shown in Figure 5-5. There you can see that the world business RSS feed is available at http://www.nytimes.com/services/xml/rss/nyt/WorldBusiness.xml.

Figure 5-5   *NYTimes RSS feed page.*

On the client side, the users use RSS readers, which can be either web based or desktop based. Users enter the URL from the registry site into the readers and from then on the readers ping the site for updates. In the Firefox browser, the Live BookMarks facility can be used to read RSS. Examples of popular readers[33,34] include NewzCrawler, FeedDemon and Awasu for Windows; NewsFire and NetNewsWire for Mac OS X; web/online readers such as Bloglines, Feedzilla, NewsGator, Microsoft Live, and My Yahoo! And finally, for Linux there is Straw, BottomFeeder, Liferea, and Syndigator. As you can see, there are lots of RSS readers to choose from.

RSS Readers for OS X and New Interfaces

As I was writing this chapter, there was a good discussion on internal Mac mailing list Atom readers as well as usage of RSS and news readers. (I thank the internal Mac-wiki and Mac-trolls participants for their observations and comments.)

The most common Mac reader is NetNewsWire,[35] also known as NNW. An interesting Mac Atom reader is Times.[36]. Although Times has a novel user interface (which looks like a newspaper with headlines and photos), the general consensus was that (at least as of early implementations) it suffers from crashes and little scalability.

I was following an internal discussion about RSS feeds, and from the various replies I was able to gather some of the normal RSS usage patterns of Cisco engineers:

- **Keep current with what is happening in the world:** For example, pull news from Wall Street Journal or New York Times, sorted by time, and read summary headlines in full screen mode; open any interesting ones or shoot to del.icio.us with a `toread` tag.

- **Track and read blogs:** Expand the groups and read the entries. (As these are selected blogs, there would be some utility in reading the whole thing anyway.)

- **Flag things to keep:** Flag items of interest and add them to snippets so that they are retained well past the feed life and are searchable. All other items will be discarded as per the feed life setting (usually 30 days).

RSS at CISCO

Cisco uses RSS as a publisher and as a consumer. As of early 2009, the RSS technology is in the beta stage of the vision-poc(proof of concept) -development-beta-release continuum. Figure 5-6 shows the Cisco Communications Center of Excellence (CCoE) site for RSS.

From Cisco's perspective, as a consumer of RSS feeds, the benefits of RSS include the following:

- RSS makes it easy to stay informed by automatically retrieving new content from the sites in which you are interested.

- RSS saves time by eliminating the need to visit the same sites frequently to stay up to date.

- RSS gives senders and receivers more control over communications. Content is delivered automatically—as soon as it's published.

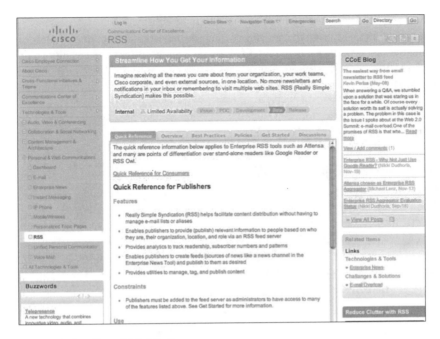

Figure 5-6   *Cisco RSS CCoE.*

- Receivers have the choice of which feeds they subscribe to. You can decide which content is most relevant and choose to subscribe to the information that matters to you.

- Managed RSS handles messages more intelligently than conventional e-mail. RSS messages are automatically organized into categories or folders that give every message delivered context and meaning.

- RSS makes it easy to scan through content quickly. You're presented with a headline and a short synopsis so you can decide whether it's worth diving into the full message.

Cisco RSS Publishing

Cisco's best practices, from a publisher's perspective, are listed in Table 5-1.

Table 5-1   *The Cisco RSS Publishing Best Practices*

Subject	Best Practice
Features	Helps facilitate content distribution without requiring anyone to manage e-mail lists or aliases.
	Enables publishers to provide (publish) relevant information to people based on who they are, their organization, location, and role via an RSS feed server.
	Provides analytics to track readership, subscriber numbers, and patterns.
	Enables publishers to create feeds (sources of news like a news channel in the Enterprise News Tool) and publish to them as desired.
	Provides utilities to manage, tag, and publish content.

Table 5-1 *The Cisco RSS Publishing Best Practices*

Subject	Best Practice
Constraints	Publishers must be added to the feed server as administrators to have access to many of the features listed.
Use	News and announcements
	New products or features
	Events and calendars
	Documents and resources
	Wikis, blogs, and discussion forums
	Podcasts and vodcasts

Cisco RSS Consumption

Internally Cisco uses the Attensa desktop reader for RSS. From a Cisco user's perspective, Cisco's best practices are listed in Table 5-2.

Table 5-2 *Cisco's RSS Consumption Best Practices*

Subject	Best Practice
Features	Really Simple Syndication (RSS) enables you to subscribe to content and receive automatic updates.
	Content typically includes headlines and links to full article. Examples are podcasts or MyNewsClips.
	Gives you control of how often to check for new content and how attachments are handled.
	Provides utilities to manage and tag subscriptions.
Constraints	Must be connected to Cisco's internal network to have access to internal content.
Use	News and announcements
	New products or features
	Events and calendars
	Documents and resources
	Wikis, blogs, and discussion forums
	Podcasts and vodcasts

Enterprise RSS Best Practices

Naturally there are lots of good RSS practices available on the web.[37,38,39,40,41] To get a feel for what kinds of RSS products and services enterprises might consider when they want to start RSS feeds (RSS Feed Servers and/or cloud managed platforms) or recommend

RSS readers for their employees, take a look at the offerings from companies like Attensa (http://www.attensa.com/), NewsGator (http://www.newsgator.com/), Moreover (http://w.moreover.com/), and NewsIsFree (http://www.newsisfree.com/). Yahoo Pipes for RSS mashups is an interesting offering. If you need good RSS buttons, Gtmcknight.com/buttons has some good ideas. Google.com/webmasters is a good source for ideas, especially for optimizing for search via meta description and meta keywords.

Cisco has a set of RSS tips and best practices that can be helpful for other organizations as well:

- Tip #1: RSS Feeds Versus E-mail
  E-mail is great for 1:1 conversations and responding to requests for information. The e-mail mentality is to clean your mailbox out so you are regarded as responsive and to avoid the dreaded "You're Over Your Rate Limit" notification.
  Feeds are filtered to your personal folder, so they don't count against your quota.
  Feeds are great for monitoring fluid events such as project updates, real time market status, competitive developments, and ongoing research. Think of feeds as sources of news.
  Feeds are categorized and automatically filtered to the appropriate folder. E-mails are not categorized; everything is dumped into your inbox.
  Feeds are searchable (archived) so the information is always available; E-mail is not. Within Outlook, your feeds are located in your Personal Folder. This makes it easier to differentiate between feeds and e-mail.

- Tip #2: Subscribing to Feeds
  Don't oversubscribe. Less is more.
  Limit yourself to what is relevant to you. If you're not currently reading "CNN Headlines," then don't subscribe to it when using RSS. Focus on what you care about.
  Preview the feed to judge the value of the feed before you subscribe.
  Start with no more than 5–7 feeds.
  Use keyword search to trim down the number of articles and feeds.

- Tip #3: The Secret to Speed Reading
  Approach feed reading the same way you read a newspaper or a magazine. Open the articles that are of interest to you and don't worry about the rest.
  Set up a specific time each day to scan your feeds. First thing in the morning is a good time to quickly see whether important developments need your attention.

- Tip #4: Don't Be Afraid to Delete
  Don't be afraid to delete or unsubscribe, and don't feel guilty about it.
  Give yourself permission to ignore things that don't look threatening or critical. It's okay to delete articles that aren't relevant. You can set a schedule for automatically deleting read and unread articles.
  Don't feel bad about unsubscribing to a feed. If you are not reading it, get rid of it. Remember, you can always subscribe to the feed at a later time.

- Tip #5: Subscribing to Feeds
  Organize your feeds based around projects you are working on, your job role, teams you are involved with, and keywords or topics relevant to you.

Make a "Must Read" personal folder for feeds you can't afford to miss.

Give your feeds meaningful titles. You can easily change the feed name to something that makes sense to your own organization or system.

Create folders based on reading necessity. For example: daily reads, weekly reads, monthly reads, and so on.

- Tip #6: Tips for Publishers

  Provide unique, meaningful, and descriptive names for feeds. Do not use acronyms.

  Pay attention to article titles. Provide unique but descriptive names so they catch the attention of readers.

  Always enter a short summary for the news article. The summary is what entices the user to click and read the entire article.

Atom

Now leave the world of simple formats and feature-rich readers for the world of content management and Atom. There are many reasons for the development of Atom. The IBM article "Use the Atom Format for Syndicating News and More"[42] talks about these reasons in the first couple of paragraphs. For various technical reasons, RSS 2.0 is static and occasionally limited, and a next version was warranted. Thus the Atom working group was born in the IETF standards body. Atom is now a set of breathing specifications with public consensus and extension specifications. Whereas RSS excels in simplicity and ad-hocness, Atom is more of a systemic, deliberate, and extensible style. Atom was developed by an IETF working group[43] and consists of two specifications: The Atom Syndication Format RFC 4287[44] and The Atom Publishing Protocol RFC 5023[45]. Atom is more complex than RSS, but for consumer programs it does not matter; nobody reads raw feeds anyway. In addition to publishing news, blogs, and the like, Atom has found its way in program-to-program communication, as in Google's data exchange and OpenSocial, for example. As far as enterprise use is concerned, Atom should be considered for content publishing and replication as well as for data interchange between systems. For normal blog and news feeds, RSS is still simpler and more efficient.

Note: Several excellent sites discuss Atom in detail. As an introduction, the overview article from at IBM's developerworks site [46] is a good read and [47] has a good comparison of Atom with RSS. Naturally one should follow with a read-through of the FrontPage[48] and then the IETF site.[43]

Table 5-3 lists the Atom RFCs and their capabilities.

Table 5-3 *Atom RFCs*

RFC	Description
The Atom Syndication Format—RFC 4827	This specification describes the format for syndication of web content such as blogs and news items. The information model is covered in the next section.

continues

Table 5-3   *Atom RFCs (continued)*

RFC	Description
The Atom Publishing Protocol—RFC 5023	This specification describes an application protocol for operations, publishing (create and delete), and editing collections, and using HTTP and XML 1.0. These collections, of course, are of the format defined in the Atom Syndication Format (RFC 4287). RFC 4287 defines the what and RFC 5023 defines how including the processing model.
Atom Threading Extensions—RFC 4685	This document defines an extension for expressing threaded discussions within the Atom Syndication Format (RFC 4287). For example, this document adds extension elements like <in-reply-to>, <replies>, <total>, <count>, and <updated>, which make it easy to publish threaded discussions, news items, blogs, and the like.
Atom License Extension—RFC 4946	Defines elements <license> and <rights> for describing licensing of a feed.
Feed Paging and archiving—RFC 5005	This document defines mechanisms for splitting a single item across multiple feeds.
Other drafts	A few more extensions are still working drafts. A current list can be found at http://www.intertwingly.net/wiki/pie/NonWorkingGroupDrafts.

Atom Information Architecture

Like RSS, Atom is also based on XML and the various elements manifest as XML tags. The sample from the Atom Syndication Format specification[49] is shown in Example 5-2.

Example 5-2   *Atom Sample*

```
<?xml version="1.0" encoding="utf-8"?>
  <feed xmlns="http://www.w3.org/2005/Atom">
    <title>Example Feed</title>
    <link href="http://example.org/"/>
    <updated>2003-12-13T18:30:02Z</updated>
    <author>
      <name>John Doe</name>
    </author>
    <id>urn:uuid:60a76c80-d399-11d9-b93C-0003939e0af6</id>
    <entry>
      <title>Atom-Powered Robots Run Amok</title>
      <link href="http://example.org/2003/12/13/atom03"/>
      <id>urn:uuid:1225c695-cfb8-4ebb-aaaa-80da344efa6a</id>
```

```
    <updated>2003-12-13T18:30:02Z</updated>
    <summary>Some text.</summary>
 </entry>    </feed>
```

As you can see, Atom is very similar to the RSS elements. RSS defines 30 elements, whereas Atom defines 21 elements. There is no top `<Atom>` element as there is an `<rss>` element, which means Atom can be embedded in other formats such as XMPP (Extensible Messaging and Presence Protocol). Atom defines a feed which consists of multiple entries. Elements such as `<title>`, `<link>`, `<author>`, and `<category>` are the same as RSS. `<description>` in RSS is known as `<subtitle>` in Atom. Because of the way Atom is specified, it has some good capabilities such as extensibility and the capability to add security by XML signature and XML encryption.

In Short

The industry has just started understanding the impact and usefulness of Atom and RSS. One just has to look at Google Data[50] (Gdata, as it is called), which uses Atom as its native format, to understand the interplay and applicability of RSS and Atom formats. GData also supports RSS; one can request RSS 2.0 too by using the `/alt=rss/` parameter.

Although Atom can be used for read and write, RSS can be used only for read operations because Atom has a separate publishing protocol capable of publishing as well as editing and updating.

Another indication of the popularity of these formats is the fact that all weblog platforms and blogging services, like WordPress, TypePad, and LiveJournal, generate RSS feeds. In the social networking field, RSS is used for news updates, changes to profiles, and the like.[3] Remember, liveliness is the major feature of a social network and RSS/Atom fits the bill for publishing changes.

Another interesting work in the RSS/Atom field is GeoRSS (http://georss.org/), which makes it possible to encode location information in RSS feeds. This adds another dimension (literally) and enhances the formats to be used in geo tagging. In short, the content aggregation and syndication made possible by Atom and RSS have lots of applicability—in both the enterprise world and the consumer world.

<monologue>

A recent study[1][2] found that approximately 40% of applications developed by Google are in beta stage. These are not just apps developed recently; some are apps developed *years* ago. There are concerns that Google might have redefined the term "beta."[3] You might wonder what exactly is happening and ask, "Why can't I get away with a prolonged beta status?" In his Web 2.0 Expo video on YouTube,[4] Eric Schmidt of Google mentions "double-secret-beta" status.

You might also have read about Google developing its own database file system[5] (called, what else, BigTable), scaling frameworks like MapReduce[6], and exotic names like Sawzall[7] and Hadoop. (Could Eeyore be far behind?) Amazon reportedly is using Erlang for its SimpleDB offering. 37Signals is talking about fast development based on Ruby on Rails. You might begin to wonder what is wrong with the relational database we love and cherish. And what about normal Java programs running on a cluster in your datacenter? Why are they putting precious stones on train tracks? You start wondering if the next big thing is De Beers taking over your computers for Ruby.

In my own case, I realized the potential of these architectures during my conversation in May 2008 with Don, our software SVP, when he mentioned REST (Representational State Transfer). (I never expected to have a RESTful conversation with a senior VP.) Seems he had discussions with John Chambers on REST. If REST had reached the high levels of Cisco it was time for me to include it in my book, at an appropriate business level.

</monologue>

CHAPTER 6

Web 2.0 Architecture Case Studies

A topic that is near and dear to enterprise management and analysts is the speed at which Web 2.0 applications change in terms of their features, or *feature velocity* as it is fondly referred to. Gone are the systemic, deliberate waterfall models with big project plans and multi-year development cycles. As another extreme, some websites update their underlying programs very frequently—sometimes four to five times a day. Because websites need to be accessible 24 hours a day, an enterprise must practice progressive, live infrastructure migration. Moreover, Web 2.0 applications need new tool sets. For example, traditional database and application architectures don't even have many of the capabilities that are essential to Web 2.0 applications, such as search, analytics, and inference engines. In Google's words[2], "...rather than the packaged, stagnant software of decades past, we're moving to a world of regular updates and constant feature refinement where applications live in the cloud." In addition, Web 2.0 ushers an era of mashups, Software as a Service (SaaS), and other inter-application practices that cross organizational boundaries, which need common and extensible interfaces for program-to-program communication.

In short, the development, maintenance, and upgrading of Web 2.0 applications need a different set of interfaces, tools, practices, and architectures. This chapter takes a quick look at this topic from two perspectives:

- An infrastructural and architectural perspective (with emphasis on scalability and distributability)

- A development methodologies/models and deployment practices point of view

These perspectives are interrelated, and thus there is no linear way through them. To match the pizzazz and capability of Web 2.0 CE (Consumer Edition), an enterprise needs to rely on particular architectures and infrastructures, and that necessitates a set of development and deployment methodologies. So let us start at some logical point and progress sideways. First we look at the architectures of some of the most successful web applications, such as Twitter, eBay, Amazon, and Google. Then the tour takes us to meet friendly stuffed baby elephants (Hadoop—a very popular framework for parallelism of data intensive processing) and Chubby distributed lock services. And remember Gall's law[8] of systematics:[9] "A complex system that works is invariably found to have evolved from a simple system that worked."

Web 2.0 Infrastructure Architecture: Scale, Concurrency, and Distributability

Web systems are massive, and that is reflected in their architectures and infrastructures. *Architecture* refers to the way various software components are combined together. *Infrastructure* refers to the actual computers and storage, as well as the network. There are multiple reasons for this. A large amount of data is created every day, and large numbers of users are interacting with the web at various levels—from users of information to its creators. In fact, everybody on the web is a creator; at a minimum they create analytics.

Keep the following points in mind while reading through this chapter:

- Although ordinary ERP (Enterprise Resource Planning) and other current average enterprise systems do not reflect the scale and diversity of web systems, in the future many systems that an enterprise practitioner develops and manages will.

- Of course, not all future web applications you develop will be as uniformly complex or approach the scale of a Google or an eBay. But the applications you design and develop should have some common aspects. For example, a short-lived business project (like a survey with a Ruby on Rails interface or a data conversion) might need a cloud infrastructure, an analytics project might need a Hadoop cluster, or a community around your offerings might need social networking and Twitter-like capability.

- In the Web 2.0 consumer world, applications can suddenly become popular and can test an infrastructure overnight. A mention in Slashdot or Digg (the so called Slashdott-ed/Digg effect) can skyrocket the number of hits on a site, which is good if it is built for handling the spike. So one needs to have positive self expectancy and plan for such spikes. Of course that does not mean you buy infrastructure for the peak loads; what it means is that you need to develop distributable scalable apps that can then leverage infrastructures such as cloud computing to accommodate the peak load.

- A funny thing happened during the microprocessor race to faster and faster clock speeds. Somewhere on the way, people stopped caring about the clock speed and started looking for overall system/application performance, and that led to a different disruptive solution: hyper-threading and now multi-core CPUs. As a result, HPC (high-performance computing), parallel programming, and parallel computing, which were once the realm of a few esoteric applications, are quickly becoming mainstream.[10] Until a couple of years ago, only applications such as Computational Fluid Dynamics, financial modeling, Life Sciences applications like genomics, and government and academia used parallel programming and high-performance computing. But the surge of web applications, especially in analytics as well as social applications, have necessitated the high-performance computing (and parallel computing) architectures and infrastructures for Web 2.0 applications. Future architectures will need to leverage this force, from moderately parallel systems to massively parallel systems, even in normal enterprise computing. With increased focus on virtualization and VDI (Virtual Desktop Infrastructure),[11,12] the same distributable requirements for cloud apps are increasingly applicable also to traditional laptops and desktops.

- Understanding the patterns and best practices of scaling and distribution architectures is important. Applying them to achieve business goals is the key. As HP's Tom Hogan pointed out[13], the ultimate goal is to deliver efficiency, increase speed and agility of business, mitigate risk (of not being able to deliver a capability when and where it is needed at the scale needed), and finally enable alignment and outcome-based deployment of resources. Although it is a mouthful, in the future customers and workforce will demand systems and interactions of Web 2.0 CE scale, and that is where an understanding of the best practices and patterns will help.

Petabyte-Scale Processing

One of the characteristics of many of the Web 2.0 applications is the massive amount of storage and the requirement for processing large amounts of data. The term used for describing this is *petabyte-scale processing*. Naturally the question comes up, what exactly is this petabyte and why is it important?

Wikipedia[14] defines a petabyte as 1000 terabytes (TB), and 1TB is 1000GB. Although corporate databases in the terabyte range are not the norm for basic ERP systems, customer data and other data warehouses can grow this big. For example E.Land group, a Korean retailer, has customer business warehouse databases of more than 6TB.

Beyond corporate databases, however, petabyte data is not that unusual in the web world. For example, Google is reported to be generating around 20 petabytes/day and the Internet Archive[15] is around 3 petabytes;[16] the data in the Library of Congress could be about 4–5 petabytes, and the Large Hadron Collider particle accelerator generates approximately 15 petabytes per year[17]. The Internet archives' Wayback Machine stores its massive data—85 billion web pages in 2 petabytes of data, growing at the rate of 20 terabytes per month—in a Petabox[18] (see Figure 6-1).

Although normal structured operational enterprise data does not need petabyte processing, analytics from the web, such as user data and preferences as shown by what users see and buy, as well as inferential data from various algorithmics like clustering, will require it. eBay generates a petabyte just from user activity logs. Also web analytics, log data, and the like are more unstructured than normal operational data and processing is involved even to extract pieces of data, which is where concepts such as MapReduce (covered later) come in.

Web 2.0 Infrastructure Architecture Case Studies

The best way to understand the challenges on Web 2.0 infrastructures is to look at companies such as Amazon, eBay, Google, and others. What are the massive systems that some of the companies face[19] and how do they manage the architectures, infrastructures, and development? It is interesting to see the different challenges they face and the innovative solutions they have developed to overcome them. One thing that is evident is that although they all have developed different unique solutions and there is no commonality in the implementations, we can learn a lot from the patterns they have followed—whether it is the BigTable datastore by Google or shard database by Flickr. Let us take a look.

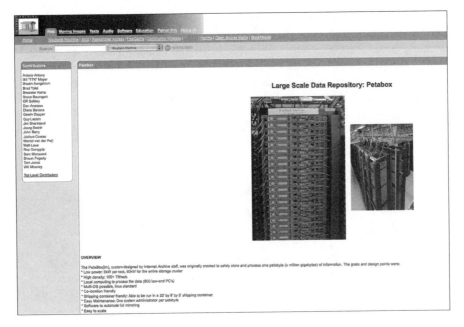

Figure 6-1 *Petabox for petabyte storage at Wayback Machine.*

eBay

eBay has both transactional as well as semi-structured data: transactional data for the buy/sell side, and semi-structured data about the goods, terms and conditions, pictures, and descriptions. Unlike Google, whose data is mostly search data, eBay has search as well as financial data at a very large scale. The various challenges and lessons eBay has learned from facing them[20,21] are very illuminating and typical of this megascale infrastructure:

- eBay has around 250 million users and it gets 25 billion page views a day.[22] They have anywhere from 10 to 12 million listings at any given time. Just imagine keeping track, maintaining photos and other details, searching across, and managing the commerce of 11 million items, all online, in real time.

- Their challenges are security, availability, massive scalability, feature velocity, and code maintainability. They have exceeded even the limits of compilers (for the number of methods per class).[21]

- One pattern they follow is horizontal scaling (that is, scaling out by adding more machines that run more software components, as opposed to scaling up where bigger machines are employed to run fewer software components) and functional decomposition (that is, creating larger systems out of smaller software components instead of one large computer program) of the program code for deployment flexibility. This way they can install pieces of functionality (as code components) without affecting other parts of the web application.

- Another effective pattern is the segmentation of data by function and usage patterns/characteristics. For example, they separate the user database (which needs random access) from the item database (which has search) while keeping the transaction database (which requires security as well as strict financial compliance) on different database servers. This way, they can optimize the different datasets for the function they perform and achieve appropriate database scalability. eBay has around 1000 functional logical databases in about 400 database servers!

- One way they achieve domain data segmentations is by the separation of non-transactional data from transactional flows.

- Data segmentation also helps mitigate business loss due to outage.

- eBay keeps business logic out of the database tier to accelerate database operations as well as maintain data integrity. This pattern can be seen in very high-scale environments; usually in enterprises quite a bit of business logic ends up in stored procedures. The reason for moving work out of databases is that at the highest volumes of transactions, the database becomes the bottleneck and it is easier to scale application functions than databases.

- eBay employs asynchronous integration (that is, systems communicate with each other, exchanging data without expecting instant feedback) which enables scaling at the application tier.

- eBay uses virtualization to eliminate physical dependencies and increase deployment flexibilities.

- eBay has a unique search engine, called Voyager, which maintains an in-memory index with parallelized query mechanisms.

- Even their code rollout is challenging and requires a custom tool called Turbo Roller.

YouTube

YouTube is another extreme from a data storage perspective. YouTube hosts lots of unstructured data in the form of pictures and video, but very few transactions. Their challenge is the massive amounts of data, around 80 million videos[23] (500 years of viewing), taking up more than 600 terabytes of storage.[24] If the storage and the daily uploads of 150,000 videos are not challenging enough, YouTube also has to put up with around 200 million viewers every day. Moreover, YouTube is adding new services such as video download,[25] which demonstrates how flexible in their infrastructure they have to be to offer new services. Their practices[26] are representative of web applications that require high-bandwidth network as well as a massive distributed store and search:

- Caching and content delivery networking are the main two practices.

- Fast front-end servers and search come next.

- For serving videos, they go for network designs that have simple network paths and use commodity servers and manage them through common tools.

- One interesting observation is that YouTube has very little custom development, as opposed to eBay and Amazon where the infrastructure is handcrafted.

Amazon

Amazon, like eBay, is interesting because it has transactional as well as unstructured data. Of all the infrastructures, most probably, Amazon has the most matured setup. It spans multiple types of domains. In fact, Amazon is so successful with its infrastructure that it offers the infrastructure as a cloud computing space for others to base their systems on. We can learn lots of best practices and architecture patterns from Amazon:

- As High Schalability[27] says, "Amazon grew from a tiny online bookstore to one of the largest stores on earth. They did it while pioneering new and interesting ways to rate, review, and recommend products."

- They have just started offering their second-generation infrastructure internally and as cloud for Amazon web services.[28]

- Werner Vogels, Amazon's CTO, has a good blog and a recent entry[29] talks about, among other things, Amazon's basic philosophy and how the company learned its lessons. Amazon considers itself an efficient and frugal company and Werner talks about the "efficiency principles" they are learning from the retail business, which they consider to be their core competence. It is their belief that in that margins in retail business are very low, they are able to translate the required efficiency into their compute infrastructure as well. Werner writes, "At Amazon we have a long history of implementing our services in a highly efficient manner. Whether these are our infrastructure services or our high-level e-commerce services, frugality is essential in our retail business." And "...having a low cost infrastructure is only the starting point of being as efficient as possible. You need to make sure that your applications will make use of the infrastructure in an adaptive and scalable manner to achieve a high degree of efficiency."

- Amazon is a big believer of services. In fact, building a book's page could require as many as 150 services. They use some SOAP protocol-based services, but the majority are REST based.

- As is customary with mega-scale systems, Amazon uses technologies as they see best fit rather than using any set of technologies exclusively across all applications. This best-of-breed concept enables them to deploy a variety of technologies and leverage them effectively.

- They have their own gossip-based protocols for availability, redundancy, and process monitoring. This is interesting because usually people do not develop new infrastructure protocols.

- They have an interesting team-building concept called a "two-pizza team." When faced with a problem, they form a team small enough to be fed by two pizzas and the team solves the problem. Their motto is to percolate decisions to the lowest level possible. Although this creates a good problem-solving team and excellent results, it also produces duplicity—multiple teams could be solving similar problems with different approaches.

- Another interesting business approach is the "working backwards from press release" practice. That is, they view the opportunity from a user perspective, look at the features as if they were being written for a press release, and then decide if it is worth doing. This enables a user-first attitude, rather than a technology approach where engineers implement their favorite features just because they are interesting from an engineering perspective.

- The CAP theory (that systems can have at most two of the three properties, Consistency, Availability, and tolerance to network Partitions) is another good insight that Amazon uses when thinking about massively distributed systems.

- They value innovation, closeness, and understanding the customer as well as the power of engineers working on pet projects that turn into high-value features. The Amazon Prime service (where for a fixed fee all your shipments are sent by high-priority shipping) actually rose out of a pet project from a developer. The Amazon Prime Service is a very popular feature and it also generates revenue for Amazon.

- Amazon considers their infrastructure as a competitive advantage and manages the development (of applications and the infrastructure) that way. The emergence of cloud computing and Amazon as the pioneer in that space proves the point.

Google

Naturally no discussion would be complete without a look at Google. Google, with more than a trillion pages and a vast array of products, is the final word on massive infrastructures and scalability. Covered in more detail later, Google has developed technologies for file systems (GFS, or Google File System), parallel processing (MapReduce), distributed lock management (Chubby), and even their own network switches. Google, realizing that normal relational databases do not fit their data access needs, developed their own data storage and retrieval techniques—GFS and the BigTable. They also developed a mechanism for massive parallel processing framework. It is called MapReduce, and it enables engineers to develop new services without worrying about scalability and infrastructure distribution. Google has a huge talent pool and can afford to solve the compute challenges they face by developing their own technologies. Although not all enterprises can match Google's resources, enterprises can benefit from Google's technologies such as MapReduce and BigTable. Moreover, enterprises can learn from Google's best practices, many of which will work not only at Google's scale but also at the scale required by average enterprises. Consider the following practices and technology developments:

- The key insights from Google[30] are simplicity, infrastructure as a competitive advantage, studying and implementing current thinking at a greater scale, developing scalable infrastructure components engineers can work on, and relying on parallelism based on small-sized compute tasks.

- Goggle manages a trillion unique web pages and has a total of around 500,000 servers in different data centers. It uses commodity hardware and has created an infrastructure that achieves high availability even when based on hardware components that fail. They achieve the availability though redundancy, parallelism, software algorithmics as well as a few proprietary hardware and network components. It is rumored that Google have their own routers, load balancers, and other infrastructure devices.

- Google looks at the stack as consisting of three layers: products, distributed infrastructure, and the computing platforms.
  - The products are the business layer, such as search, ads, mail, and cloud service offerings.
  - The distributed infrastructure layer gives Google its competitive advantage, and it grew out of innovation on existing technologies or the invention of new ones. The Google File System and the MapReduce systems fall into this category. It is likely that many more technological innovations we haven't seen are already in their infrastructure. A rule of thumb is that usually when Google talks about an innovative technology, they have been working on it for a year or two and it's almost certain that it is already in production. That way they still maintain the technological lead.
  - The computing platforms layer, in Google's mind, includes commodities and is positioned that way. For example, it is anecdotal that Google uses bare motherboards and attaches a bunch of them to racks using Velcro. When one board fails, it is not replaced at all. The replacement is done at the rack level, when more than 50% of the boards in a rack fail. Of course when you have more than a half-billion servers, there is no way they can be monitored and replaced on an individual basis.

- Although they have temporarily developed working solutions for the problem of distributed computing by using GFS, MapReduce, and the like, they are working on the bigger challenge of distribution across datacenters. It is relatively easier to have distributed data inside one datacenter, but providing data distribution over datacenters across the globe while assuring sub-second response time is a hard problem to solve. Most probably Google has multiple solutions to this problem that are already in place.

Network Law, Economies of Scale, Algorithmics, and Monopolies

While I was writing this chapter, an interesting blog exchange between Nicholas Carr and Tim O'Reilly caught my attention.[31,32,33,34] The discussions hovered around commoditization and competitive advantage, which is of interest to us in this chapter. Is technology and business model the competitive advantage, or is it just scale and network effect? By network effect,[35] they referred to the property where a particular device or program becomes more useful as more people use it. Consider, for example fax machines: If just one person has a fax machine, it is not worth much because that person cannot send anything to anybody; but as more and more people start installing fax machines, every fax machine can reach more people and thus each fax becomes more useful. In addition, as each fax machine comes into the fax network, it adds value to all the other fax machines. That is the network effect.

Tim[31] is of the opinion that although commoditization will occur at the cloud and other Internet platform levels, it is the network effect that will differentiate platforms, say between Microsoft, Google, Amazon, and Oracle. He calls them "new rules of competitive advantage" and defines them as "the design of systems that harness network effects to get better the more people use them."

Nick[32] is not convinced. Citing Google and iTunes, Nick argues that the reasons for success are harnessing collective intelligence (Google), or in iTunes' case "superior product and software design, superb marketing and branding, smart partnerships, and proprietary file standards that tend to lock in users." Nick says, "Although the cloud may explain Web 2.0, Web 2.0 doesn't explain the cloud," meaning technology and business models, along with scale, succeed. Well designed apps over scalable algorithmics still rule.

Which, of course, elicited a response from Tim,[33] saying there is more than one layer of network effects. The obvious first-order network effect—as in phone and fax network, where each person joining the network adds exponential value directly—is apparent. But Web 2.0 adds a second-order effect, where algorithmics such as PageRank and recommendation systems infer hidden relationships even when people do not formally "join" a network. Nick responded[34] by agreeing that, "Success in a capital-intensive utility industry often hinges on maximizing usage in order to utilize your capital equipment as productively as possible; seeking high margins, by keeping prices high, can actually be self-defeating in that it can constrain usage and lead to suboptimal capacity utilization." But one path to differentiating is "creating a good, useful, distinctive software tool"—be it an infrastructure or an innovative architecture or a new web application—which is the focus of this chapter.

Twitter

Twitter is interesting for a couple of reasons. First, it belongs to a category that is very important for enterprises, but hasn't been leveraged to the full extent. Enterprises are yet to leverage the idea of building a community around various aspects of their products and the various stages of development, such as research and development, beta, introduction, and continued enhancement. Second, Twitter uses Ruby on Rails as its technology stack, which is very interesting because usually, for scale, organizations develop their own technology stack layer over commodity software. Another interesting point is that there are well published Twitter outages[36] and their scaling problems are public and written about. But remember that Twitter's load can be very spikey, which makes it a difficult architecture to maintain. Also it seems bots go in and add everybody to one's friends, creating havoc with the system. Let us see how Twitter develops its infrastructure:[37]

- Twitter, so far, has been a small operation with limited resources. They have around 200 Rails instances over eight Sun servers. They use a Ruby on Rails framework (and some Erlang—one of my favorite languages) to support over a million users. The number of Twitter users is a secret but estimates put it at around a million.[38]

- Their scale has an interesting temporal characteristic: Recent posts become very popular (for example during Steve Jobs' speech), and so caching would help achieve high performance. They use the memcached software a lot.

- Although some are of the opinion that Twitter's choice of Ruby on Rails is hurting their scalability, Twitter is of the opinion that performance comes from application design rather than from the language substrate and framework. The concept that a scalable language is better than a faster language[39] is an interesting view, and explains why, of late, more and more web applications are written in scripting languages.

- It is rumored that Twitter APIs (Application Program Interfaces) generate 10 times more hits than actual live users; but the other side is that the APIs enable others to build different ecosystems and thus increase Twitter's popularity. This is one lesson enterprises can learn: Develop community mechanisms and have APIs others can leverage to create vertical community-based applications.

Flickr

With more than 2 billion photos[40] and associated tags, Flickr has to manage a billion scale infrastructures. Although many enterprises might not reach this scale, the Flickr architecture and lessons learned are applicable to corporate sites with lots of participatory materials—especially multimedia. Flicker's lessons learned on web application scaling[41,42] are very informative:

- They have realized that scalability is not about raw performance numbers or technologies, but is about data growth and the capability to handle higher traffic while not losing the system's maintainability.

- Flickr believes in open source software and uses the LAMP (Linux-Apache-MSQL-PHP) stack and the open source Squid software for caching.

- Managing sessions has been one of their challenges, and they employ cached sessions by using memcached software.

- Because storing data is one of their key challenges, they have developed their own file system called the Flicker File System.

Note: An especially interesting best practice from Flickr's lessons learned is the use of shard databases. Shard, a short name shared nothing,[43] involves horizontal partitioning[44] and distributing processing of data so that there is no sharing. This design achieves almost infinite scaling because one can add elements, be they application servers or database partitions, without affecting other parts of the system. In the case of Flickr,[45] they have billions of queries per day, and a shard architecture (Flickr calls it Federation) enables them to scale to that level. In the case of Flickr, shard architecture enables them to eliminate SPOF (single point of failure) as well as handle the traffic. Flickr has database servers that are row partitions, and assigns new users randomly to a database, thus avoiding bottlenecks in one database. The assignment is not static; they periodically access the load characteristics and migrate users to different shards (resource leveling). But without a single database, the challenge is to know now where a user is. Their solution is to have cached lookup table, a high-level diagram of which is shown in Figure 6-2.
For reliability and availability, a multi-master replication scheme is used. The shard servers are kept at less than 50% load so that if one fails another can still manage the load. This also helps them handle peak loads.

Technologies for Scalable Architectures

The three vectors—technologies, interfaces and interface programming styles (like REST), and development methodologies—need to be addressed simultaneously to develop and deploy Web 2.0 scale applications. To put them in perspective, Ray Ozzie, in his keynote at Microsoft PDC 2008,[46] characterized the "high-scale Internet infrastructure" as a new Web Tier, along with the Desktop Tier (scope of a single machine) and the Enterprise Systems

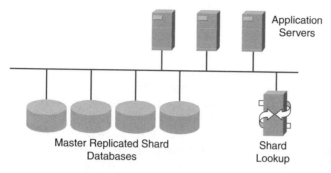

Figure 6-2   *Shard database block diagram.*

Tier (scope of the enterprise). This new Web Tier, with a scope spanning the internet, has a multitude of challenges such as meeting customer expectation of interactive, participatory web systems; operating across peaks and valleys; addressing continuity issues; and finally considering loosely coupled architecture, data replication strategies, and data partition strategies. In many Web 2.0 applications, the data is not necessarily relational, there are needs for executing simple but repeating operations on large-scale data, and the results need to be aggregated in a very timely fashion. This means traditional relational databases are not the best choice to act as datastores for a class of Web 2.0 applications.

The challenge facing the development of Web 2.0 applications is that it requires a fundamental shift (evolutionary, but still a shift) to match the feature velocity with appropriate development methodology. Moreover, the use of the right frameworks that match the scalability requirements of respective web applications is essential—a framework that works well for a search application is not effective for an e-commerce application.

Now it's time to quickly look into a few of these "scalable" technologies and their positioning.

Massive Scalability

This book has covered scalability in many ways, so let's take a moment to define it clearly. For a definition, I quote Amazon's Werner Vogles:[47] "A service is said to be scalable if when we increase the resources in a system, it results in increased performance in a manner proportional to resources added. Increasing performance in general means serving more units of work, but it can also be to handle larger units of work, such as when datasets grow." And "...an always-on service is said to be scalable if adding resources to facilitate redundancy does not result in a loss of performance."

Another view on scalability comes from Dr. Roy Fielding's dissertation thesis[48] where he talks about anarchic scalability. He says that "most software systems are created with the implicit assumption that the entire system is under the control of one entity....Such an assumption cannot be safely made when the system runs openly on the Internet. Anarchic scalability refers to the need for architectural elements to continue operating when they are subjected to an unanticipated load, or when given malformed or maliciously constructed data, since they may be communicating with elements outside their organizational control. The architecture must be amenable to mechanisms that enhance visibility and scalability."

Another aspect of scalability is the partitioning perspective of vertical scalability versus horizontal scalability.

- Vertical scalability is the capability to handle more, bigger, and varied problems by employing larger and faster computers. For example, the capability to handle bigger computations with more steps or more compute intensive algorithms falls in this class.
- Horizontal scalability is a different beast altogether. It focuses on the capability to handle more work or more data. Although faster and bigger computers would definitely help, they are not that efficient or effective. Naturally, for a quick turnaround one will buy bigger machines and scale that way, but eventually the applications need to be re-architected for horizontal scalability. The solution is to have lots of cheaper computers and/or horizontal data partitioning. Of course, then the problem moves into the distribution, management, and other tasks to keep all the numerous computers working together. Web 2.0 systems usually fall under this category.

Case for MapReduce and Its Cousin Hadoop

Although PageRank might be the best technology from Google, MapReduce would rank the highest in terms of the most widely used technology. PageRank is Google's method of ranking web pages based on relevance, and MapReduce is the framework for parallel processing. Both technologies have direct business relevance and are the best of their classes—maybe even the only ones in their classes.

The original MapReduce paper[49] was published in 2004 and the Internet was never the same again. MapReduce and its open source implementation Hadoop have become a major cottage industry. Companies from Ning and Facebook to fortune 500 companies use Hadoop for various applications. MapReduce is data parallelism; if you have to run a well defined small task over a large amount of data (that is, distributed repetitive processing of a massive data set), MapReduce is the scheme for you. MapReduce (and the open source Hadoop) has found applications in web indexing, analyzing web user logs, web session analytics, statistical analysis for recommendation systems, classification based on probabilistic algorithms such as Bayes classifiers and bioinformatics. For example, as CNet reports,[50] "MapReduce can find how many times a particular word appears in Google's search index; a list of the web pages on which a word appears; and the list of all websites that link to a particular website." And if you remember that Google has indexed more than 1 trillion web pages, this is not a task for the meek. But looking deeper, one realizes that the code required for the job is not that big (maybe 200–300 lines), but the quantity of data is huge. It is reported that Google runs around 100,000 MapReduce jobs per day on 500 servers, and each job takes about 10 minutes to complete.[50]

Outside Google, Apache Hadoop is an open source implementation of the MapReduce framework and has found a range of applications[51] from Amazon to Yahoo and Zvents. The applications spectrum is wide, including building a product search index (A9), Clickstream Analytics (Ad Network), machine learning from web analytic logs and other databases (Facebook, FOX media), large-scale image conversions by *The New York Times*,[52] and machine learning based on Bayesian classifiers (Zvents).

Why Hadoop?

Hadoop was started under the leadership of Doug Cutting at Apache foundation. Doug now works for Yahoo! Where did he get the name? According to Doug,[53] it is "the name my kid gave a stuffed yellow elephant. Short, relatively easy to spell and pronounce, meaningless, and not used elsewhere: Those are my naming criteria. Kids are good at generating such. Googol is a kid's term."

Yahoo has around 17,000 machines (in clusters of 2000 or fewer)[54] running Hadoop jobs. An interesting use case from Rackspace[55] shows the power of frameworks such as Hadoop for the right application. Rackspace is a hosting company that has a lot of servers, and the logs generated just from the mail servers are huge—about 10 billion events! They tried plain text file processing and then moved on to database processing and finally are using a Hadoop system to process the mail event logs.[56]

Scalable Interfaces

Usually enterprise systems are based on very deterministic protocols that are either proprietary or based on RPC (Remote Procedure Call) mechanisms such as CORBA (Common Object Requesting Broker Architecture) or Java RMI (Remote Method Invocation). The Microsoft world moved from OLE (Object Linking and Embedding) to COM to .NET technologies, whereas Oracle ERP apps and the SAP suite have their own internal proprietary protocols. Even when the protocols are exposed, they are exposed at the API level (like Java Message Service, or JMS) which means there is no interoperability between two vendors—you cannot add to a JMS queue from an IBM installation (say, WebSphere) and be able to read that message from a BEA installation (say, Weblogic). The reason is that although the APIs (such as put a message, get a message) at the language binding are standardized (the JMS specification), the binary representation on the wire is not. This will be analogous to plugging a 110V appliance into a 220V socket with the right pin adaptors but without a voltage convertor! Moreover, current enterprise systems are usually written in a single language or a small subset of languages. In short, developing scalable interfaces across multiple languages, systems, and applications is a challenge.

But the Web 2.0 world is different, with applications and mashups created from very dissimilar systems developed by an array of languages, including scripting. This flexible mish-mash can be achieved only through the use of open wire formats and evolvable microformats and "sloppily" constructed protocols. The "sloppiness" gives the rubber-like flexibility for mashups and other combinations. Currently the popular Web 2.0 formats are REST, JSON, XMPP/Jabber, and Microformats such as Atom.

REST

Representational State Transfer (REST) was formalized by Dr. Roy Fielding in his dissertation work.[48] Roy's work came up during the discussion about scalability. REST is a set of architectural principles or an architectural style that helps us to design scalable networked applications. The essence of REST is that resources have well defined permanent representations, which will be used to carry out operations (such as show, create, update, add, and delete) on these resources. For example, a web page is a resource with an HTML representation, or a photo is a resource with a JPEG representation. And a URL such as http://www.google.com is the handle for a resource.

Another REST principle is that resources must be linked together based on well known standards[57]. For example, a blog link would be http://doubleclix.wordpress.com/2008/10/27/microsofts-azure/, or a photo link would be http://flickr.com/photos/tags/penguin. The blog link is a specific resource, whereas the photo link is a list of resources. As you can see, the representation is very clear; it can be embedded anywhere and it can pass through all the devices such as firewalls and proxies without any problems.

The other options to REST are remote procedure calls or message oriented middleware where the operation, object, and other parameters are embedded in a big message. But that programmatic call cannot be embedded easily in web pages and cannot be parsed easily by devices such as firewalls and load balancers. That is why the Internet is made of web pages addressed via URLs and linked via URLs. A lot has been written and passionate debates have occurred (and still occur) on what is a RESTful architecture and what its merits are. Suffice to say, when you design interfaces to your systems, make them RESTful.

Web 2.0 Development and Deployment

Although you can implement new, interesting, and useful Web 2.0 technologies, technologies by themselves are not enough. You need to consider development and deployment practices as well, especially practices that match the feature velocity of web systems. For example, *Computerworld* reported that on June 16, 2008, Flickr deployed the "latest update to the photo-sharing website...with nine changes made by three of its developers.[58] The "deployment" was the 36th new release in a week where 627 changes were made by 21 developers. In fact, Flickr publishes developer blogs on the various development activities.[59] While this is not the norm, web applications do need a weekly or bi-weekly releases. For enterprises that are used to releases every few months, multi-releases per week is a big challenge. The good news is that enterprises can learn from the experiences of web applications like Flickr. The *Computerworld* article lists a few good lessons learned:

- Break the barrier between developers and end users, and involve users in quality assurance processes.

- Keep it simple.

- Use scripting languages.

- Release early and often.

- Let the users, not the developers, determine new features.

Another interesting and very insightful resource is *Getting Real* from 37signals.[60] I urge anyone involved with management, analysis, or development roles to read that book. They evangelize an iterative, user-centric development model that focuses on building less (one-downing rather than one-upping). In a world of feature creep and projects funded based on the number of features, this advice is very interesting. For Web 2.0 systems, fewer features and addressing a specific set of users is the key. Applications will be developed faster, and their smaller size make them easier to test, resulting in fewer bugs and easier interaction for users. Another important result of this development philosophy is that because of the focus on fewer features, the team has to prioritize and select the most important features to implement. For example, the folks at 37signals, while developing their project management software Basecamp, realized that project management is not about charts, graphs, reports, or stats. They realized that project management is not even a tool to broadcast schedules, but is about a shared plan with a focus on all project members taking ownership and responsibility. With this insight they were able to reduce the functionality to a core set, and they developed the software that implemented these capabilities very well. I am sure, from our daily experience with various websites, all of us realize that well developed software, with few features, is a joy to use.

From a development methodology perspective, agile development and Scrum methods are best suited for Web 2.0 applications. On the testing side, test-driven development and A/B testing methods should be employed.

Although development with fast feature velocity is a challenge, deploying and maintaining a running system under this level of fluidity is almost impossible. No wonder Google tries to keep its systems in a perpetual beta state. Google's response to the question (as to why more than 40% of its products are in beta) is very reveling about the nature of a web application. Google says that their applications "...have very high internal metrics...before coming out of beta....We believe beta has a different meaning when applied to applications on the web, where people expect continual improvements in a product."[2] They continue on the deployment of web apps: "On the web, you don't have to wait for the next version to be on the shelf or an update to become available. Improvements are rolled out as they're developed." Although all enterprise software cannot be in perpetual beta mode, there are things one can do to match the development practices with the feature velocity required from a web app. In fact, maybe there are some apps you can keep in beta state for a long time. Even *The New York Times* has a permanent prototype site to show off new user interfaces and "projects that aren't quite ready for prime time."[61]

Another aspect of deployment is that most web software and systems cannot be shut down for any period of time, so making continual incremental upgrades on a partitioned running system is a necessity.

In Short

Web 2.0 systems call for newer, nimble architectures and agile development processes. All the major Web 2.0 companies are following these newer practices and patterns on architecture and infrastructure. Enterprise systems, although most of them will not face the scale an Amazon or eBay or Google faces, will still encounter scalability and distributability issues. I end this chapter with two points of view.

First, Dr. Vishal Sikka[13] of SAP, spoke eloquently about timeless software that needs to be "delivered over containers that span multiple generations of technologies; minimizing the cost and maximizing the ease of its construction, deployment, and life-cycle management; in a landscape that is permanently heterogeneous." That is a challenge all enterprises will face, though perhaps not at the same scale as what SAP faces. The practices, architectures, and development models still apply.

Finally, I leave this chapter quoting an excellent article by Clay Shirky. Clay writes, "Evolvable systems—those that proceed not under the sole direction of one centralized design authority but by being adapted and extended in a thousand small ways in a thousand places at once—have three main characteristics that are germane to their eventual victories over strong, centrally designed protocols:

"First, only solutions that produce partial results when partially implemented can succeed. The network is littered with ideas that would have worked had everybody adopted them. Evolvable systems begin partially working right away and then grow, rather than needing to be perfected and frozen. Think VMS versus Unix, cc:Mail versus RFC-822, Token Ring versus Ethernet.

"Second, what is, is wrong. Because evolvable systems have always been adapted to earlier conditions and are always being further adapted to present conditions, they are always behind the times. No evolving protocol is ever perfectly in sync with the challenges it faces.

"And finally, Orgel's Rule, named for the evolutionary biologist Leslie Orgel—'Evolution is cleverer than you are.' As with the list of the web's obvious deficiencies above, it is easy to point out what is wrong with any evolvable system at any point in its life. No one seeing Lotus Notes and the NCSA server side-by-side in 1994 could doubt that Lotus had the superior technology; ditto ActiveX versus Java or Marimba versus HTTP. However, the ability to understand what is missing at any given moment does not mean that one person or a small central group can design a better system in the long haul."[62]

In his view, weak, relatively uncoordinated, imperfectly implemented protocols will succeed, HTTP/HTML being the prime example.

<monologue>

There is something about version numbers. They are significant in one way but on the other hand, they tend to trivialize and preempt fundamental innovations. Before we can even comprehend Web 2.0, Web 3.0 is on us and people are talking about Web 4.0. The conventional wisdom is that Semantic Web definitely is part of Web 3.0. Even the New York Times says so, in an article titled "Entrepreneurs See a Web Guided by Common Sense." [1] I tend to think that the web is moving toward the next generation in multiple ways: by embedding meaning as context (Semantic Web), by adding location as context (geoWeb) as well as by making tremendous progress in inferenceability, recommendations, and other collective intelligence. So think of the next version as any anonymous version indicator—maybe it is Web 3.0, maybe it is Web NG, maybe it is just "the web." Don't worry about version numbers but look at features that provide business benefits and start double-clicking.

</monologue>

Tending to Web 3.0: The Semantic Web

The evolution of the web from first generation (Web 1.0) to second generation (Web 2.0) was apparent in two major transition points: from static to dynamic, from publishing to participatory. The next level of innovation, from the second generation to the third, will be a transition from linked documents to linked data and will be focused around context. It is important to look at context as multi-dimensional and view context as spanning a wide variety of business forms. Context ranges from location (where you are and how things are arranged in a spatial world) to inferences based on activities of an individual and then extends to collective inferences based on what a set of individuals do (or do not do!). Context is also a property of data—the forms data can take, the relationships and constraints of those forms, as well as the codification of the information about any dataset (called *metadata*).

The business applications of capabilities derived from context are wide ranging from employing the inferences and insights to predict, recommend, show, sell and add features to existing products, to developing new products that cater to new population demographics based on the insights gained from data relationships. The business value of context and inference is tremendous, and the technologies that can get us there are just being developed. All in all, an exciting future awaits—both in the business of technology and in the technology behind the business.

This chapter touches upon the core of the next generation web: the Semantic Web. As usual, it discusses the underlying technologies quite a bit, but keeps the business values in the forefront. So no ontology listings, no schemas, no RDF listings (well, maybe a couple of simple ones), no deep discussions on modified temporal Bayesian or kernel-based support vector machines and classifiers, but a little bit of everything.

A Business Definition of the Semantic Web

Sir Tim Berners-Lee in his seminal article "Semantic Web Road map" [2] talks about Semantic Web as an architectural plan. Of course, Semantic Web has matured to a set of technologies and business practices since then. The essence of Semantic Web is the new perspective it brings. Currently the web is mostly made of content that is viewed in human-readable form, but the Semantic Web enables information in machine-understandable form. Note it is not just readable but understandable. This means the information on the web should also capture metadata and relationships, and then arbitrary programs can crawl through information repositories—small and big—and make inferences and find relevant answers.

In short, the Semantic Web is an information representation technology that enables machines to interpret data. For example, "<h1>The Hitchhiker's Guide to Web 2.0</h1>" is a markup. It tells the browser to render the text in big heading style. But it doesn't tell anything about the nature of the text at all. But "<BookTitle>The Hitchhiker's Guide to Web 2.0</BookTitle>" tells a lot about the text. Now we can tell a web crawler to look for a BookTitle containing "Web 2.0" to search for all Web 2.0 books. Actually Semantic Web covers much more than information tagging:

- It can represent relationships between pieces of information (using Resource Description Framework, or RDF, covered later). For example, a book should have one title, many authors, and a publisher.

- It can define domain vocabularies (called ontologies). For example, the title of a book will be marked up with the <BookTitle> </BookTitle> tags.

- It can infer connections based on deductive reasoning over these representation forms.

The World Wide Web Consortium (W3C) has a very simple definition of Semantic Web [3] "The Semantic Web is a web of data.... It is about common formats for integration and combination of data drawn from diverse sources.... It is also about language for recording how the data relates to real world objects." W3C is investing significant resources in developing Semantic Web,[3] the chief among the contributions being the Resource Description Framework (RDF) specifications for the representation of metadata, the Web Ontology Language (OWL) Specification for vocabularies and relationships, and the SPARQL Query Language for RDF.

It is also important to know what Semantic Web is not. Sir Tim Berners-Lee has a good write-up about it, [4] which says that Semantic Web is neither an artificial intelligence system nor is it a system with arbitrary complexity nor is it a proof system. From the collective experience of the industry so far, we also know that Semantic Web is not all encompassing and that it is an evolution. The web is not going to magically transform into the Semantic Web, but small parts of it will—the parts that will make business sense and add value to users.

It is very relevant to quote the epilogue paragraph "Engines of the Future"[2] where Tim says "Though there will still not be a machine which can guarantee to answer arbitrary questions, the power to answer real questions which are the stuff of our daily lives and especially of commerce may be quite remarkable." Don't look for Semantic Web to solve exotic problems, but to apply it to normal business systems.

A Business View of the Semantic Web

From a business perspective, the Semantic Web is an emerging area; it has lots of promise but it also needs judicious adoption. An article in the *Computer* magazine, titled "Web 3.0: Chicken Farms on the Semantic Web" [5], points out the chicken-and-egg problems the Semantic Web faces as it matures from academia to commercial business applications. The major challenge is the availability of data in the form that the semantic technologies require to make sense of it. In that sense, there might never be a single Semantic Web. Peter Rip [6] in his blog aptly says "There will never be 'A' Semantic Web and it will not replace the world wide web. There will be many Semantic Webs...Semantic Web is a richer, more structured way of sharing and communicating when a community develops its own vocabulary." The IEEE Computer society article summarizes, "It is an exciting time for those of us who have been evangelists, early adopters, and language designers for Semantic Web technology. What we see in Web 3.0 is the Semantic Web community moving from arguing over chickens and eggs to creating its first real chicken farms...."

I think that the quotes (from Peter as well as from the *Computer* magazine) crystallize the right business approach for this domain: If you see value, apply the Semantic Web technologies to an appropriate subset of data, website, or business process and proceed from there. Do not expect or strive for an all-encompassing Semantic Web implementation. As Peter Rip says, [6], [7], "...meaning is contextual, not universal.... There will be many Semantic Webs, all of which are ways to organize the information available on the World Wide Web.... The migration to Semantic Web technologies is really about evolution." This is relevant because this frames your thinking to look for smaller "chunks" of mixed data and inference around which you can build an interesting application.

For example, if you have an idea to combine product and customer information for the Small and Medium Business (SMB) market, you should think of encoding just that data into RDF and develop an SMB vocabulary using OWL, without waiting for all your company data to be RDF.

Or maybe you have an idea to infer module-defect relationships by looking into the support data and the product component list for the enterprise market. Remember, sometimes the second- or third-order relationships (those you find by digging into not only first-level links but into deeper associations) show insights that are not readily apparent.

An interesting article in *Scientific American* [8] says that a variety of applications "are emerging, from Vodafone Live!'s mobile phone service (a multimedia portal for accessing ring tones, games, and mobile applications) to Boeing's system for coordinating the work of vendors. Scientific researchers are developing some of the most advanced applications, including a system that pinpoints genetic causes of heart disease and another system that reveals the early stages of influenza outbreaks." In the public health reporting domain, Texas Health Science Center at Houston uses Semantic Web technologies to better detect, analyze, and respond to emerging public health problems. The system, called SAPPHIRE (Situational Awareness and Preparedness for Public Health Incidences using Reasoning Engines) gets details of emergency room cases every 10 minutes. The system performs various functions including classification of unexplained illnesses reporting an outbreak on influenza, in addition to keeping a single view of the current health conditions in the area. Readwrite web, [9] looking at "What's Next After Web 2.0," says intelligent web with smarter data gathering across unstructured data would be one key innovation. And the Houston healthcare application proves that point.

A quote from Nova Spivack [10] amplifies another aspect of the Semantic Web accurately "...the Semantic Web is a technology that's...a means to an end, not an end in itself." Semantic Web does not demo very well, neither can we see it, but it is best viewed through the applications that use it. So look for business apps that require inferred connections based on a field of expertise and associated vocabulary and you have found an application for Semantic Web.

ReadWriteWeb's Alex Iskod [11] and Richard MacManus [12] are of the opinion that although the classic way of annotating all web data—with Semantic Web mechanisms and then leveraging them for business—achieves maximum value, it might not be the most practical way [13]. They advocate an emerging trend of pragmatic consumer-centric applications based on applying simple vertical annotation and vocabulary over existing information—a good business strategy. Citing the example of Spock (see Figure 7-1), a people search engine that crawls the web for people and attributes (such as birthdays and addresses) and creates an information base, Alex notes [14] that Spock understands relationships and so it not only finds people but also infers relationships between people (for example, wife, daughter, successor, and vice president) and displays related people along with the search result, and that a best practice is to build adaptors to various forms of data (such as email, web/HTML, database) and add the heuristics and inferenceability to the adaptors.

An interesting report [15] on the impact of Semantic Web on UK higher education summarizes that "...the Semantic Web is most likely to make an impact: information management, digital libraries, virtual communities, and e-learning...." The Semantic Web based annotations enabled automatic processing and the digital libraries were made possible by better classification schemes as well as the capability to share these schemes across other libraries and information repositories. Looking at the future, they predict that "...in the future the Semantic Web may not even be noticeable. The tools of the Semantic Web will be integrated into Virtual Learning Environments and Virtual Research Environments on our desktops, as well as in browsers and search engines."

Another developing area for Semantic Web is the mobile space. A few new startups (for example, Siri, [16] which aims at applying Semantic Web ideas to intelligent interfaces, especially interactive paradigms to information from mobile phones) and ideas [17] are being developed.

Figure 7-1 *Spock.com, showing inferred relationship between people.*

Semantic Web—Agonies and Ecstasies   Two interesting applications applying Semantic Web principles, Powerset (for searching) and Twine (for information organization), [10] show that the journey in the Semantic Web land can be very challenging, and sometimes one has to try a few times to get to the right problems that capture the imagination of the users.

Powerset applies natural language processing to search. [18] Rather than index unstructured information, it extracts key concepts and semantic constructs and uses them to build relationship trees. Powerset's first attempt was to develop a contextual search of Wikipedia content. The comparisons [19] did not fare well, and there were even questions about applying the semantic technologies to search [20]. Comparing the results for questions like "Who invented dental floss?" "What is the capital of France?" and "Where is Paris?" while informal and not thoroughly scientific, there was not that much difference between the results from Google and Powerset, even after accounting for the fact that Google's search is much wider than Powerset's. The conclusion was that we can get good enough answers on natural language queries from Google, and the right task for Semantic Web technologies is to answer queries that require inference and optimization over data from multiple sources (from structured databases to unstructured web [20])—for example answers to questions like "What is the best vocation for me now?" or "Which senator took money from foreign entity?"

As our reviewer Tom points out this is the difference between intelligent parsing (don't change the content, but be smarter about it) versus intelligent content (explicit markup of content to enable search and other apps to be more effective). In the Wikipedia search case, Powerset is not actually adding any semantic-web style metadata to Wikipedia but applying general "intelligence" to generic text data.

Powerset was acquired by Microsoft in July 2008 [21]. The initial reaction was mixed, [22] and the thought was that Microsoft would incorporate the semantic technologies as implemented by Powerset not only into Windows Live Search but also into advertisements—a natural extension of the inference technologies. As expected, in September 2008 Microsoft integrated the Powerset technologies into Live Search and it shows improvement. The quote was "...Live Search, which is far behind Google in terms of market share, needs exactly these kinds of features to make its search more relevant" [23]—a validation of applying Semantic Web technologies at the right level to the right problem at the right time.

Twine is another interesting example: "part bookmarking tool, part social network, and part recommendation engine, helping users collect, manage, and share online information related to any area of interest," [10] and that complicates the value proposition. It is very difficult to explain Twine; it is to be experienced. Although Twine can be used for sharing bookmarks and other pieces of information around particular interests, [24] be they classical music or beer or the financial crisis, the power comes from the discoverability of related pieces of information powered by semantic technologies. In fact, the topic "Web 3.0—Semantic Web" [25] has around 2500 items and about 4900 members who are interested in this topic. (Assuming 10% of those will buy this book, we are looking at a readership of around 500! Well, I am digressing. Back to the main feature.) Twine did go through growing pains with regard to market position and feature set, [26] but finally launched 1.0 as an "interest network" [27].

The lesson to be learned from these two companies is that although there is a wide spectrum of problems to be solved and business advantages to be gained employing the semantic technologies, the selection of the right domain to which to apply semantic technologies and the nature of the resultant application is very important. Another lesson is that the UI—the interaction layer—is very important [20]. You cannot bring out the complexity to the user; you need to mask the inner workings and show a UI that makes it easy for users to get what they are looking for.

Some of the enterprise applications of Semantic Web include research, intelligent inference on customer data, online intelligent agent-based systems for travel, and web analytics for up-selling, cross-selling, and recommendations.

An interesting article from IBM [28] talks about the various aspects of planning a semantic website. The best practices include evaluating your data in the context of existing ontologies, choosing a Semantic URI (Uniform Resource Identifier) scheme, and taking advantage of existing semantic add tools. I believe the tip about leveraging existing ontologies is very important, as it saves lot of effort in structuring the data, as well as it helps in discovery and interoperability. Moreover, maintaining an ontology scheme on your own is a little involved.

Semantic Web Origins—From Aristotle to W3C

Tim Berners-Lee's article in *Scientific American* [29] lays out a clear vision for the Semantic Web. From Tim's perspective, "...the Semantic Web will bring structure to the meaningful content of web pages, creating an environment where software agents roaming from page to page can readily carry out sophisticated tasks for users" and "...the Semantic Web is not a separate web but an extension of the current one, in which information is given well-defined meaning, better enabling computers and people to work in cooperation...."

In Clay Shiky's words, [30] "...the Semantic Web is a machine for creating syllogisms; syllogism being a form of logic, first described by Aristotle, where '...certain things being stated, something other than what is stated follows of necessity from their being so.'"

Over the years, a fair number of documents, specifications, and primers have been developed for the Semantic Web. The "Semantic Web Roadmap"² and "What Semantic Web Is Not"⁴ clearly articulated the vision. The Semantic Web work started at the W3C, [3] and has resulted in around 10 main specifications and related supporting documents. The chief among these are covered in Table 7-1.

Table 7-1   *Semantic Web Activities and Specifications*

Activity	Description
Resource Description Framework(RDF)	Consists of a set of six specifications that describe how to represent information about stuff in the Internet.
Gleaning Resource Descriptions from Dialects of Languages (GRDDL)	Consists of a set of specifications to extract RDF data from XML and XHTML pages. This is very useful to create RDF from other formats automatically and aids in developing RDF more quickly and easily.
SPARQL Query Language for RDF	Consists of three specifications that describe how queries can be written, how the queries can be transmitted over the web, and the format for returning the query results.
Web Ontology Language (OWL)	A set of six specifications that describe how to represent terms and relationships (vocabulary) in RDF. It is especially useful for processing by programs.
RDFa in XHTML: Syntax and Processing	A set of specifications that specifies how RDF attributes can be added to XHTML pages. This is interesting because you can add Semantic Web capabilities, selectively to web pages without a lot of changes and work.

Inner Workings of Semantic Web Technologies

As Alex comments in ReadWriteWeb [31], consumers don't care about math or the architecture behind OWL or RDF; they would prefer natural intelligence rather than artificial intelligence; and the less they hear about semantics the better. They care about getting things done, finding the right information, utility, fun, and value. But that does not mean, as designers and business people, we shouldn't dig deeper into these. In fact, the contrary is true: designers and business people need to understand the technologies and their relevance and leverage their complexity to develop simple "magical" applications.

Semantic Web is a collection of technologies and practices that implement the "web of data" as opposed to the "web of links" we are used to. The current Internet, its markup languages and protocol, are best suited for a link-based presentation mode. Semantic Web works alongside the current web and adds annotation, an ontology and categorization (taxonomy), and reasoning to the data. Figure 7-2 shows the W3C Semantic Web Technology layer diagram.

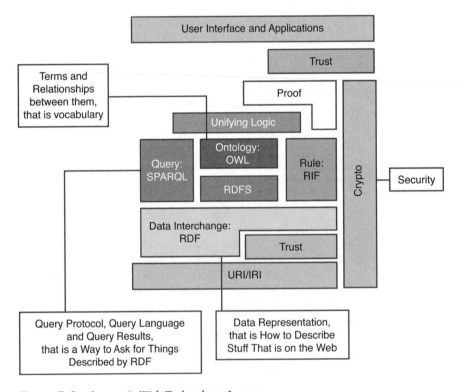

Figure 7-2 *Semantic Web Technology Layers.*

The following sections go through the relevant areas of Figure 7-2 without getting into excessive details.

Resource Description Framework

The Resource Description Framework (RDF) is the foundation for the Semantic Web. As the name implies, RDF is the language of Semantic Web. The RDF consists of six specifications:

- **RDF Primer:** An introduction to RDF [32]

- **RDF Concepts:** Defines the abstract syntax as well as discusses design goals, key concepts, and data types [33]

- **RDF/XML syntax:** Defines the RDF grammar in XML, mappings, and data models [34]

- **RDF Semantics:** Processing rules, inference mechanisms, and so forth [35]

- **RDF Vocabulary:** Language for defining vocabulary, similar to OWL [36]

- **RDF Test Cases:** Pointers and description of machine-readable test cases and results [37]

As you can see, the documents do a thorough job from concepts to the specifications to test cases to test implementations of the RDF domain.

The key concept of RDF is that it is a uniform mechanism to describe web resources and that it is not the resources themselves. In many cases, the resources might not be accessed at all, but the information about them and the relationships between them are enough to do the required processing and arrive at the results. The advantage of RDF is thatafter there is a uniform way of describing the various pieces that make up the web (or parts of the web), programs can then use this information to make various decisions and inferences to get things done—for example, create a vacation plan, make a table of contents, comb through product catalogues, find out relationships between various people, or create appointments based on calendars from multiple people and so forth. The best ways to understand RDF is through a set of examples, and so without further delay let us examine two examples (from the RDF Primer [32]) to get a feel for RDF.

The RDF model is very simple; it consists of a subject (or a resource), a predicate (or a property), and an object (or value). These three together are called a *triple* or a *statement*. In simple terms, a resource has a property that has a value. Figure 7-3 shows this relationship graphically (actually a directed graph!).

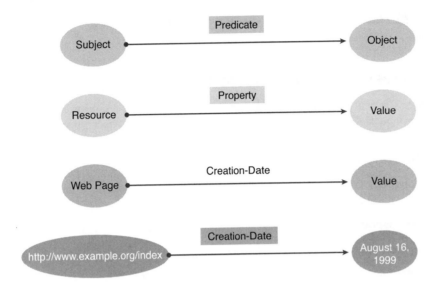

Figure 7-3   *RDF model.*

Now move one step deeper. In reality, the model in Figure 7-3 is conceptual. RDF captures the model in text, using the eXtensible Markup Language (XML). The RDF code for Figure 7-3 would be as follows:

```
<?xml version="1.0"?>
<rdf:RDF xmlns:rdf=http://www.w3.org/1999/02/22-rdf-syntax-ns#
           xmlns:exterms="http://www.example.org/terms/">
  <rdf:Description rdf:about="http://www.example.org/index.html">
      <exterms:creation-date>August 16, 1999</exterms:creation-date>
  </rdf:Description>
</rdf:RDF>
```

Looking a little into the code, `http://www.example.org/terms/` is a place where the terms for this RDF are defined. The `rdf:Description` is a placeholder to talk about the subject `rdf:about` (`http://www.example.org/index.html` is the subject/resource in this case), `creation-date` is the property or predicate, and `August 16, 1999` is the value or object.

Although Figure 7-3 shows a simple example, usually RDFs are very deep and nested to deal with scenarios such as information about a person with multiple addresses, phone numbers, email addresses and contact preferences. But still the basic triple syntax model is maintained. For example, if you were to add language and creator properties and associated values to Figure 7-3, the object graph would look like Figure 7-4. The graph now has one resource, three properties, and three values.

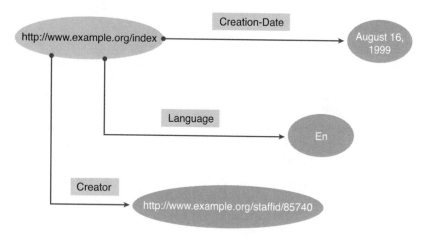

Figure 7-4   *RDF model with multiple properties.*

The RDF for Figure 7-4 is now

```
<?xml version="1.0"?>
<rdf:RDF xmlns:rdf="http://www.w3.org/1999/02/22-rdf-syntax-ns#
              xmlns:dc="http://purl.org/dc/elements/1.1/"
              xmlns:exterms="http://www.example.org/terms/">
    <rdf:Description rdf:about="http://www.example.org/index.html">
        <exterms:creation-date>August 16, 1999</exterms:creation-date>
        <dc:language>en</dc:language>
        <dc:creator rdf:resource="http://www.example.org/staffid/85740"/>
    </rdf:Description>
</rdf:RDF>
```

The RDF code now is more clear as to which is the resource (`http://www.example.org/index.html`) that has three properties: `creation-date`, `language`, and `creator`. Note that the language and creator are already defined in a different place (`http://purl.org/dc/elements/1.1/`) than the `http://www.example.org/terms/`. This is good because common terms such as `language` and `creator`, which is already defined, are being reused. And finally you can see how the three values (`August 16, 1999`, `en`, and `http://www.example.org/staffid/85740`) are encoded with the right predicates.

In short, RDF provides a language syntax to describe web resources in XML so that applications can read, understand, and reason about these resources, be they persons, catalogues, web pages, or room vacancies in hotels.

Web Ontology Language

The Web Ontology Language (OWL) is another core part of Semantic Web because there is no guarantee that all similar things will be described in the same way unless they all use a common vocabulary. For example, if different catalogues in different websites use different names for price, for example `<Price>`, `<ProdPrice>`, and `<PP>`, there is no way a program can comb through them and find the right price element. This is where OWL comes in the picture. Using OWL, the industry or a set of vendors (or even a few customers) or a research organization (or just an open source initiative) can work together to define a vocabulary for product catalogues.

OWL, in addition to enabling uniformity of vocabulary, also facilitates the capture relationships between the terms, such as rules like "Sales Price cannot be greater than List Price" or "Item should have at least one part number." These relationships when captured and employed widely would achieve better data integrity, especially essential to describe the products across the various websites. The uniformity and the integrity would make search and aggregation of products much easier, efficiently achieving increased scalability, interoperability, flexibility, extensibility, and ease of programming!

In short, OWL defines ways of defining terms, their relationships with each other, and their usage in the context of a domain. The OWL vocabulary would then be used in the RDF statements. Remember the `http://www.example.org/terms/` for RDF in Figure 7-3 and the `http://purl.org/dc/elements/1.1/` in Figure 7-4? These could be OWL vocabulary—in fact, the `http://purl.org/dc/elements/1.1/` is defined as part of the Dublin Core Metadata Initiative. That is why we are reusing the `language` and `creator` from there rather than inventing our own.

OWL specifications consist of six documents:

- OWL Web Ontology Language Overview [38]

- OWL Web Ontology Language Use Cases and Requirements [39]

- OWL Web Ontology Language Guide [40]

- OWL Web Ontology Language Reference [40]

- OWL Web Ontology Language Semantics and Abstract Syntax [42]

- OWL Web Ontology Language Test Cases [43]

OWL not only specifies a method to define elements of a vocabulary but also relationships (such as cardinality, equality, property restrictions, versioning, and annotations) between the elements. The thoroughness and the breadth of the capabilities means a full-fledged OWL definition would be exhaustive. The good news is that the standard developers have designed in flexibility. There are three OWL levels:

- OWL Lite

- OWL DL

- OWL Full

I like this a lot because this scheme reduces the barrier to start and use OWL. The OWL Lite supports classification hierarchy and simple constraints, which would be sufficient for most applications. But, as you start using OWL and Semantic Web in your applications and need more sophisticated language semantics, you can move up to OWL DL (which has additional constructs like class expressions, set operators, and so on. OWL DL has more "expressiveness, computational completeness (all conclusions are guaranteed to be computable) and decidability (all computations will finish in finite time)"[40]. OWL Full has more capabilities, which are more for theoreticians, for now. You will know when you need OWL Full and that most probably would be because of complex domains that require lots of rules, relationships, and restriction clauses.

Without going into too much detail, now take a quick look at an OWL-based vocabulary. The wine example [44] from the OWL guide [40] is an appropriate one as it will also give you context when you read through the guide. Figure 7-5 shows a graphical depiction of the vocabulary.

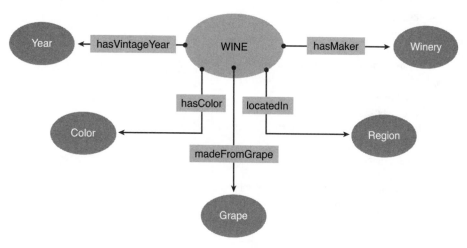

Figure 7-5 *Vocabulary graphic for the wine example.*

Wine vocabulary in OWL, snippets of which follow, is not that hard to comprehend. It is a very logical way of building the structure in XML, with appropriate definitions, relationships, and restrictions in place. For example wine has a property called `locatedIn`, which will have one value of type `region`. Wine also has properties like `hasColor`, `madeFromGrape`, `hasMaker`, and so forth. The following are snippets of the wine vocabulary in OWL, enough to define Merlot wine (the full wine vocabulary in OWL is many pages long):

```
<owl:Ontology rdf:about="">
    <rdfs:comment>An example OWL ontology</rdfs:comment>
    <owl:priorVersion>
      <owl:Ontology rdf:about="http://www.example.org/wine-020303"/>
    </owl:priorVersion>
    <owl:imports rdf:resource=
```

```
➡ "http://www.w3.org/2002/03owlt/miscellaneous/consistent002"/>
    <rdfs:comment>Derived from the DAML Wine ontology at
      http://ontolingua.stanford.edu/doc/chimaera/ontologies/wines.daml
      Substantially changed, in particular the Region based relations.
    </rdfs:comment>
    <rdfs:label>Wine Ontology</rdfs:label>
  </owl:Ontology>

  <owl:Class rdf:ID="Wine">
    <rdfs:subClassOf rdf:resource="&food;PotableLiquid" />
    <rdfs:subClassOf>
      <owl:Restriction>
        <owl:onProperty rdf:resource="#hasMaker" />
 <owl:cardinality rdf:datatype="&xsd;nonNegativeInteger">1</owl:cardinality>
      </owl:Restriction>
    </rdfs:subClassOf>
    <rdfs:subClassOf>
      <owl:Restriction>
        <owl:onProperty rdf:resource="#hasMaker" />
 <owl:allValuesFrom rdf:resource="#Winery" />
      </owl:Restriction>
    </rdfs:subClassOf>
    <rdfs:subClassOf>
      <owl:Restriction>
        <owl:onProperty rdf:resource="#madeFromGrape" />
 <owl:minCardinality rdf:datatype=
➡ "&xsd;nonNegativeInteger">1</owl:minCardinality>
      </owl:Restriction>
    </rdfs:subClassOf>
    <rdfs:subClassOf>
      <owl:Restriction>
        <owl:onProperty rdf:resource="#hasColor" />
        <owl:cardinality rdf:datatype=
➡ "&xsd;nonNegativeInteger">1</owl:cardinality>
      </owl:Restriction>
    </rdfs:subClassOf>
    <rdfs:subClassOf>
      <owl:Restriction>
        <owl:onProperty rdf:resource="#locatedIn"/>
        <owl:someValuesFrom rdf:resource="&vin;Region"/>
      </owl:Restriction>
    </rdfs:subClassOf>
    <rdfs:label xml:lang="en">wine</rdfs:label>
    <rdfs:label xml:lang="fr">vin</rdfs:label>
  </owl:Class>
    <owl:Class rdf:ID="Vintage">
      <rdfs:subClassOf>
```

```
    <owl:Restriction>
      <owl:onProperty rdf:resource="#hasVintageYear"/>
      <owl:cardinality
rdf:datatype="&xsd;nonNegativeInteger">1</owl:cardinality>
    </owl:Restriction>
  </rdfs:subClassOf>
</owl:Class>
```

Now that we have defined wine with a set of properties, let us define Merlot as red color, made from Merlot grapes, and so forth:

```
<owl:Class rdf:ID="Merlot">
  <rdfs:subClassOf>
    <owl:Restriction>
      <owl:onProperty rdf:resource="#hasColor" />
      <owl:hasValue rdf:resource="#Red" />
    </owl:Restriction>
  </rdfs:subClassOf>
  <owl:intersectionOf rdf:parseType="Collection">
    <owl:Class rdf:about="#Wine" />
    <owl:Restriction>
      <owl:onProperty rdf:resource="#madeFromGrape" />
      <owl:hasValue rdf:resource="#MerlotGrape" />
    </owl:Restriction>
    <owl:Restriction>
      <owl:onProperty rdf:resource="#madeFromGrape" />
      <owl:maxCardinality rdf:datatype=
➡"&xsd;nonNegativeInteger">1</owl:maxCardinality>
    </owl:Restriction>
  </owl:intersectionOf>
</owl:Class>
```

As you can see, OWL is not that hard and is flexible, and at the same time has capabilities to capture constrainers and relationships.

SPARQL

You have diligently captured the relationships and constraints in a set of OWL vocabulary and you have then used them in describing your data in RDF. What would you do with your RDF repository? How can you get inferences out of your hard work? That is where SPARQL comes in.

SPARQL, which stands for SPARQL Protocol and RDF Query Language, [45], [46] is a mechanism for querying data in RDF format. Somewhat analogous to the relational database query system SQL (Structured Query Language), SPARQL includes a protocol for remote querying (SPARQL Protocol for RDF—SPROT [47]), a language for writing the query (SPARQL Query Language for RDF-SPARQL [48]), and a format for returning the results (SPARQL Query Results XML Format—RESULTS [49]). The advantage of a standardized query mechanism over RDF repositories is that now you can develop a business application that can query across different semantic websites that have data in RDF format. Without a set of query standards, each website might write its own mechanisms and this will not scale, especially when you have to query across different websites or when you want to aggregate results from different websites. Navigating across different result sets and different query languages will greatly complicate the systems over the Semantic Web technologies.

The use cases and requirements [50] over which SPARQL was developed is an interesting read. The uses cases range a wide spectrum of uses, such as finding email from a Friend Of A Friend (FOAF) address book, finding parts (for supply chain applications), monitoring news, avoiding traffic jams, exploring neighborhoods (tourism), browsing patient records (healthcare), and building tables of contents (publishing).

Enterprise Applications of the Semantic Web

So far I have hinted at various ideas on enterprise applications, and this section detailing some of the real-world application ideas might be helpful to many readers. It so happened that I had attended the 2008 Semantic Technology Conference [51] and there were a few good sessions relevant to enterprise applications. This section presents a summary of my findings (and a little research) on enterprise applications from the conference.

Social Media, Education, and the Semantic Web

There is tremendous amount of data created in wikis such as Wikipedia, blogs such as WordPress, social networks such as Facebook and MySpace, photo publishing sites such as Flickr, video sharing sites such as YouTube, folksonomies, and social bookmarks. There are no semantics connecting these data and most of the data is still on unconnected islands. Of course, there is not going to be a Semantic Web that connects all of them. The industry is slowly recognizing this opportunity and there are domain-specific initiatives to add semantics and metadata.

For example DBpedia [52] is an effort to extract structured information from Wikipedia and enables one to ask sophisticated queries over the extracted data.

Another interesting work is OpenSocial for social networks. We look deep into OpenSocial in Chapter 4, "Social Networking." As our reviewer Tom points out, OpenSocial can be considered a domain-specific Semantic Web. Although it doesn't have OWL vocabularies, it has a schema and is applying the principles of Semantic Web. FOAF (Friends Of A Friend) is another project [53] that has a unified vocabulary [54] that can be used for publishing information about people.

An important application of the various forms of media available in the web is in education. Lots of information is available from many places, but those place do not have any commonality, which makes it is very difficult to query intelligently and efficiently through them to find relevant information, such as to create a lesson plan. One has to do lots of searches, then parse thru thousands of search results to decide which ones are relevant (say for a sixth grade cell project), then link the relevant parts of information into a coherent lesson plan. I am part of an effort, Lessonopoly [55], which is a part of the Silicon Valley Education Foundation, to develop a semantic search over various instructional media available. The aim of the effort is not just to search, which might not require all the power of Semantic Web, but to help teachers to collaboratively create lesson plans. The aim is to add two features:

- The capability to meaningfully stitch a fabric (of lessons, in this case) from a vast sea of materials which differ in content grade, content relevance, granularity, and format diversity

- The capability to perform semantic searches on the federated content with contextual attributes meaningful to teachers [56]

Semantically interlinked online communities (SIOC) is an interesting project [57] that provides a semantic framework to connect blogs, boards, and other forms of online communities. The SIOC Ontology [58] is an OWL vocabulary representing elements (like usergroup, user, forum, and so forth). This enables distributed conversations across different forums, import/export of content and summaries, as well as publishing and subscription of multiple distributed communities.

This might be of good use to an enterprise that wants to harness the power of multiple forms of distributed communities for support, product development, or just product forums. Also, if you are able to capture the communities by RDF then you can use SPARQL for interesting queries over the information.

Semantic Web SaaS Platform

Talis [59] is an interesting hosted Semantic Web application platform. Their services range from content store (which supports RDF content, query and search) and directory services to transaction gateways and most importantly integration, all employing the Semantic Web technologies. I categorize the services offerings as a Semantic Web infrastructure, because it enables an organization to build applications.

The interesting thing about Talis is that it provides not only tools for Semantic Web, but it also provides an opportunity for Semantic Web as Software As A Service(SaaS). You can use them as your hosting infrastructure. This gives you an opportunity to try out projects without a huge outlay in infrastructure and resources. As and when the projects become viable, you can make a formal proposal for a full-fledged internal project. Of course, as always, be careful about hosting any business critical data outside the company, and do not start a project without formal internal approvals from IT, security operations, and finance.

Semantic Web Support in Databases

Oracle database has good support for Semantic Web from generation of ontologies, to RDF store, to SPARQL queries. It also has analytics tools for link analysis, statistical analysis, pattern discovery, and so forth. Their presentation in the conference mentioned a few good applications leveraging the Semantic Web capabilities of the Oracle database:

- Life Sciences/bio informatics application by pharmaceuticals is an interesting application. They apply Oracle's semantic technologies for data integration of internal (from data warehousing) and external datasets (gene ontology, for example)

- The bio-surveillance application for inferring epidemics based on RDF/OWL data from hospitals in Houston, which I had mentioned earlier in this chapter, is built using Oracle database features.

Other Enterprise Applications

Some other enterprise applications include

- Companies such as GE are employing Semantic Technology for a variety of applications, from expert systems to adaptive work-center environments. GE even has gone as far as developing their own Semantic Language layer (Semantic Application Design Language SADL) and integrating it to the Eclipse development environment.

- Yahoo is using RDF and related Semantic Web technologies to integrate content (documents, multimedia, stock data, sports statistics, and semi-structured data like playlists, reviews, and comments) between its media websites such as U.S. Finance, U.S. Health, U.S. TV, U.S. Movies, CA Travel, Latin America Sports, and U.S. Finance. The business goals include capabilities to share and enrich content between sites (to provide value-added services), as well as discovering and updating changing content seamlessly between sites that have different data stores and representations.

- A host of applications, ranging from geospatial/sensor networks to media tagging to trip advisors to contextual advertising to knowledge extraction to eGovernment and federal government applications, apply the semantic technologies. The Semantic Web technologies are well suited for knowledge representation, maintenance, and extraction applications, especially if the inference also involves integration of data from outside the enterprise.

In Short

Semantic Web is an emerging trend that can enrich the intelligent, automated processing of web information. The semantic technologies are mature—RDF, OWL, and SPARQL being the major areas for definition, vocabulary, and query respectively. There are also advanced capabilities such as formal logic, agent technologies, and reasoning that I didn't cover in this chapter. Semantic Web technologies cannot be implemented in a fortnight, encompassing all the web data in an enterprise. The best advice is to apply the Semantic Web to a subset of data and business functions as it makes business sense.

<monologue>

Let me start with a story about the infrastructure of Internet retail sales. You see, the sales are very seasonal—a good majority of the sales happen between Thanksgiving and Christmas. And any delay in processing during that time is lost sales (and word gets around, which then reduces the customers coming to the site), so companies have to provision for the peak sales period and make sure that not even a single sales transaction is delayed because of performance. This is fine and good, but what happens to all the extra capacity that is sitting idle during the rest of the year? Well, one company in the Pacific Northwest came up with a brilliant idea: Why not set up infrastructure features so that others can use the idle capacity and then charge them for usage? It worked, in fact, very well. Who would have guessed that an effort by an Internet bookseller to sell extra capacity would turn into a phenomenon that has potentially very deep and long-lasting influence in the computing infrastructure as a whole? That is the rags-to-riches story of cloud computing! As one economist puts it,[1] "In the beginning computers were human. Then they took the shape of metal boxes, filling entire rooms before becoming ever smaller and more widespread. Now they are evaporating altogether and becoming accessible from anywhere." Read on for a quick glimpse into the murky world of evaporating-fuzzy-elastic computing infrastructures.

</monologue>

CHAPTER 8

Cloud Computing

When we originally proposed this book, we didn't even have a chapter on cloud computing in the list of topics. But as we were finalizing the book, things started moving fast in this space and cloud computing has becoming a major force. We believe that cloud computing is a fundamental infrastructure of Web 2.0. It enables and is enhanced by the Web 2.0 paradigms.

This chapter begins with a quick look at the business and technological relevance of cloud computing, moves on to cover the patterns and business value, and finally looks at offerings in this space. The chapter finishes with a look at some of the considerations for adopting the cloud computing model into enterprises.

It is also interesting to note that at the time of writing this chapter, some people feel that cloud computing is an imprecise term and needs focus.[2]

A good summary of cloud computing is James Governor's "15 Ways to Tell It's Not Cloud Computing."[3] The salient points are that there is no hardware or even knowledge of hardware, no big specification documents, and most importantly a pay-as-you-go structure.

Another blog[4] talks about cooler data centers, gaps in server farms, recurring credit charges to Amazon, and passwords masquerading as 64-bit hex access keys.

While the definition of cloud computing is not exactly as scientific as the blogs want it to be, as you will see, different types of clouds have different characteristics.

Unfortunately, topics such as SaaS, grids, parallel computing, and virtualization overlap with cloud computing, confusing any attempt to define it. So although this chapter focuses on cloud computing, it also compares and contrasts the adjacent domains.

Cloud Computing and Its Relevance

One might ask what, exactly, cloud computing is. The best definition I found that succinctly defines the domain of cloud computing is from Forrester: "A cloud is a pool of scalable, abstracted infrastructure that hosts end-use applications, billed by consumption."[5,6] In short, a cloud is a bunch of infrastructure—servers, network, and storage—hosted somewhere to be leased or used as necessary. It can be internal to a company (the so-called "private" cloud) or hosted on the internet as a "public" cloud. I tend to believe that the public-private difference is a spatial one: If the cloud is on your side of the firewall it is private and if it is on the other side, it is public. Just because we call it "public" does not mean all data is open. Public clouds can be as safe as private clouds. Whether an application goes into a private or public cloud is determined by policies, compliance, and regulations relevant to an organization, as well as the visibility and control requirements of an enterprise matched against the capabilities provided by a "public" cloud provider.

In some sense, cloud computing is a natural progression of grid computing and virtualization. It is also an artifact of advances in security, in the web, as well as in application development methods and models. But what makes a cloud a cloud are two important characteristics: elasticity and multi-tenancy.

- Elasticity is the capability to expand and contract computing resources as needed. It is this property that enables the cloud consumers to use as little as needed during slow times but expand quickly and use more resources during peak times. This gives enterprises an infrastructure that is flexible and agile. This is why cloud computing is also loosely known as "utility computing," a term that explains more accurately what it is all about.
  An offshoot of the elasticity is that consumers pay for only the resources they use, which is a change from the traditional provision-all-you-need method.
  Pay-as-you-go works equally well in private and public clouds. In the private scenario, payment is some sort of internal charge back, whereas in the public scenario you actually pay to the cloud provider.

- Multi-tenancy is the other aspect of cloud computing. Even if one has the ability to scale up and down to the requirements of the applications, it is of no use if the spare capacity cannot be used by other applications or customers. Multi-tenancy is the ability for different application to share the infrastructure—securely as well as isolated from each other.
  - Multi-tenancy in a private cloud setting involves other applications from the same company but from different organizations. Perhaps HR, e-commerce, and financial departments share an infrastructure.
  - In a multi-tenant public cloud environment, the infrastructure is shared by other customers' applications.

When one talks about a cloud infrastructure, one also needs to be cognizant of the two constituents: cloud providers and cloud consumers. There is no dichotomy, but there are differences in the interests of the two groups:

- Cloud providers, in general, have big data centers and lots and lots of computers and network gear. As Jeff Bezos calls it, they "handle the muck for you."[7] Providers look for capabilities such as security, role-based access control, capability to move virtual machine instances and associated network posture (firewall, load balancing, and so on), raw performance, and well toned control and management planes (with robust interfaces/APIs that cover all the facets of management and control).

- The cloud consumer's focus is on visibility and control of how computing resources are selected and employed for them, as well as blueprints and application architectures that help them to leverage a cloud infrastructure. Security, compliance, service level agreements, and handling of outages are all topics near and dear to cloud consumers.

How important is cloud computing to enterprises? According to Gartner,[8] the top two strategic technologies that will have significant impact on enterprises in the next three years are virtualization and cloud computing. In fact, they predict that 80% of Fortune 1000 companies will be using some form of cloud computing by 2012.

The next point to consider is the migration pattern: Who will embrace the cloud, when, and why. From what I see in the field, the enterprise migration into clouds will be in four stages:

- **Stage 1:** Service providers will build a few big clouds and a set of easy, new, ad-hoc applications will move to the cloud.
Startups will embrace cloud computing because it allows them to expand without huge cash outlays for computing infrastructure. There are also ad-hoc enterprise applications like short-lived surveys or document conversion projects, or enterprise analysis applications like clinical trial or financial modeling, which are well suited for initial cloud infrastructure exploration.
This is the stage in which the industry is as of January 2009.

- **Stage 2:** A class of enterprise apps that are inherently stand-alone will move into the cloud infrastructure. Enterprises will start building internal clouds ("private" clouds) as well as start experimenting with external clouds ("public" clouds).
At this stage, apps that are loosely coupled—in terms of security, integration as well as data requirements—would move to the cloud infrastructure. Also compute-intensive analysis applications would move into the cloud infrastructure. Again, nobody is going to simply migrate existing running apps into a cloud infrastructure that easily; there is no incentive.

- **Stage 3:** This is the refresh cycle time, when IT infrastructure expansion and/or replacement of older technologies projects are initiated. At this stage, enterprises have already done some cloud projects and are more comfortable with the notion of a cloud infrastructure and so some parts of mission-critical apps inside enterprises could move to a cloud infrastructure—internal or external. The applications that fall under the SaaS category—that is, whole functionality like that of CRM—are the best candidates. At this stage, I do not think enterprises are ready to refactor parts of application or systems into a cloud infrastructure.

- **Stage 4:** In this stage clouds have become prelavant, and there is no way companies are going to tool new datacenters that do not follow the cloud architecture, so applications of all sizes will start moving into a cloud infrastructure.

Note: Interestingly enough, Gartner recently came out with a press release depicting three phases of evolution for the cloud computing market[9]. Gartner, in their typical way, have a new name for cloud computing: service enabled application platforms (SEAPs). In their view, although cloud computing is exciting, it will take many years (seven to be exact) before it becomes a mainstream IT technology and business practice. The Gartner analysts characterize the three phases as

1. Pioneers & Trailblazers (2007-2011)—Tactical projects will be deployed over mainly proprietary cloud platforms focusing on technical innovation.

2. Market Consolidation (2010-2013)—Cloud infrastructure will become attractive to a broader user base, leading to long-term systemic cloud projects.

3. Mainstream and commoditization (2012-2015 and beyond—Different cloud platforms will take interoperability seriously and also the user base will embrace cloud computing as a normal IT infrastructure.

Although I do question the time horizon, the stages as described by Gartner seems right. In fact, it almost corresponds to the four-stage cloud migration I came up with prior to this. Of course, time will tell.

Cloud Computing Eco System

The big picture of cloud computing has more than one dimension. When you dive deeper into this domain, you might realize that the concept is not new at all. From Semantec offering virus signature updates, to the caching service by Alamai, to the mapping services by Navtec and Teleatlas, these all could fall into the "cloud" category somehow or other. In fact, even Quicken online is a specialized vertical cloud computing service.

But cloud computing as it is applied to IT infrastructure has a definite set of layers. Let us first define the cloud computing stack—the layers and their essential characteristics. Figure 8-1 shows the stack graphically. The stack is explained in more detail shortly. (Table 8-1, later, has the major companies and their offerings in the space.)

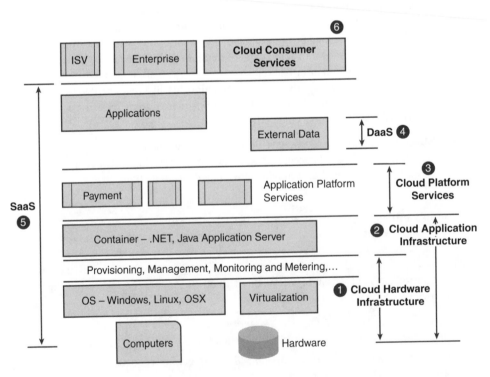

Figure 8-1   *Cloud computing stack.*

As is the case with many new technologies, the terms and definitions are neither uniform nor unique. Some folks talk about utility computing as the infrastructure part while defining cloud computing as an architecture encompassing not only the bare metal, but also the provisioning/monitoring/metering services as well as some part of the application stack. The layers and their definitions in Figure 8-1 are systemic and have conceptual and business value. An enterprise cannot enter into cloud computing without a good understanding of the layers and a view of where their cloud computing strategy fits. One should evaluate the cloud computing strategy from two dimensions: temporal (that is, short, medium and long term) as well as the strategic, tactical, and operational dimensions of an IT vision. An organization can use cloud infrastructure for ad hoc applications and for short-term operational scaling. But the real business benefits come from strategic use of cloud computing as a part of the long-term plan.

The following is a detailed explanation of the layers in Figure 8-1:

1. **Cloud Hardware Infrastructure or Compute Platform as a Service (PaaS):**
   This is the most basic form of Cloud Computing—raw processing power, storage, and/or database capacity in the cloud. Elastic Compute Cloud (EC2), popularized by Amazon and similar services by other companies, is a prime example of this category. This is pure hardware or a slice of hardware in the cloud. *Wired*[10] calls it hardware as a service (HaaS).

   The basic value propositions are a reduced data center footprint as well as ad-hoc scalability. This chapter covers the value propositions later. One can get as many "computers" as needed in the cloud. A "computer" is roughly a virtual machine with a specific processor capability, memory, and some storage space. Usually one can also specify the operating system image to be booted on the VM (Amazon calls it AMI—Amazon Machine Image), thus making the VM suitable for specific tasks such as those of a database server or a web server. The price is based on time, usually per hour. Usually vendors have their own UI and semantics for provisioning. This category also includes storage offerings[11]—you get infinite storage in cloud, which is reliable and fault-tolerant, as well as database capacity in the cloud.

2. **Cloud Application Infrastructure:** In this case, not only the computing platform (including the OS) but also application platforms such as application servers, e-commerce, servers, and so on are provided as a part of the service. Although the J2EE based Java application servers are more prevalent, Microsoft's .NET platform is also popular. The Windows Azure offering from Microsoft not only provides the .NET platform but also more functionalities such as SQL server and message queuing. One can look at this as an infinite Java Server farm or a .NET farm. Sun's project Caroline falls under this category, and so does Google's App Engine. Both provide containers for writing cloud applications, and the infrastructure takes care of the scaling.

3. **Cloud Platform Services:** This is a more specific case of the Cloud Application Infrastructure. In this case, it is still a platform, but geared toward a specific vertical slice of application functionality such as payment, sales, social networking, and so on. This is different from SaaS (layer 5) in the sense that the service is part of an application, but not the application itself. Many times the Cloud platform service (such as payment) is common to many different types of applications. Also the Cloud Platform Services face the IT side, whereas SaaS faces the actual users of an enterprise.

The Cloud Platform Services are not limited to e-commerce; they even extend to development environment that enables an organization to collaboratively develop, deploy, and monitor on a Cloud Hardware Infrastructure. An excellent example is the offerings from BungeeConnect (Bungeeconnect.com). Another example is Rightscale, which provides automated management, prepackaged components (such as auto scaling, virtual clusters and batch processing), as well as support, as a layer above cloud infrastructures like Amazon EC2 and others. Rightscale layers on additional capabilities to move up the value chain.

4. **Cloud Data Services or Data as a Service (DaaS):** For example, postcodeanywhere.com provides capability for worldwide address capture, geocoding, bank account validation, and similar services, all at the data layer, supporting other business functions. Amazon datasets[12] is another interesting offering. They host a centralized repository of public data sets like the U.S. Census database, 3D chemical structure database, and even human genome annotations!
Another offering, the IronCloud from strikeiron.com, provides an extensive set of data as managed infrastructure.
Although traditional DaaS was mostly based on bulk-load, newer data clouds are based on APIs and interfaces. With the advent of mashups, many times the data is in the form of a map or in JavaScript libraries similar to GUI primitives. As a result, businesses need to reevaluate their external data sources and how to interact with them from a cloud perspective. Many times, a cloud-based dynamic API interface that gives the liveliness of data would be more suited for today's web-based applications.

5. **Software as a Service (SaaS) or Cloud Enterprise Services:** As opposed to infrastructure where one has to deploy applications, many clouds such as salesforce.com actually host an application that is used by enterprises. This is the concept of an application platform as a service. This is commonly known as the more popular category SaaS or more precisely Managed Services Provider.
The major difference between SaaS and other forms of clouds is that SaaS is an application in the cloud, whereas the other forms provide only the infrastructure in the cloud or the "cloud" itself. The advantage here is that a particular vertical function is handled in the cloud. Otherwise companies will have to use a cloud hardware infrastructure or a cloud application infrastructure and then deploy their own apps, such as Oracle or Siebel or others. A good example is Ning, which helps people to host social networking sites. Another example is the mapping, Geographic Information System(GIS), and other services offered by companies like TeleAtlas. The APIs over Amazon cloud falls in this category. Akamai is in this category.

6. **Cloud Consumer Services:** The consumer services are another type of cloud. We all have been using this for some time—Quicken online tax preparation, even Facebook and MySpace belong to this category. Another very common consumer cloud are blog engines like Wordpress. Spring note and 43Folders belong to this category. Even iTunes belongs here.

Another dimension is the subscribers to these cloud based systems—consumers, enterprises, and Independent Software Vendors (ISVs):

■   Consumers are the end users, and usually the functionalities are things that make life easier for them.

- In the case of enterprises, the functionalities are enterprise-level tasks such as managing customers, managing events, billing, payment, and so on.

- ISVs constitute an interesting vector because they span the enterprise and consumer space. A cloud infrastructure enables them to build platforms for either enterprises or for consumers. For example, the Flicker backend is Amazon web services. Sometimes the lines blur. For example, Starbucks uses salesforce.com to build the online community "My Starbucks Idea"[13]

Figure 8-1 gives a layered view of the Cloud Computing Stack, but other views look at the cloud stack as a set of services—for example, The New York Times article "What Cloud Computing Really Means."[14] In his blog[15][16], Abhijit Dubey of McKinsey & Company talks about delivery platform, development platform, and application-led platforms. Marc Andreessen[17], in his blog, talks about three kinds of platforms one meets on the Internet: access API, plug-in API, and runtime environment. The six-layer stack presented in Figure 8-1 is a superset and can accommodate the different views. For example, the cloud hardware infrastructure and cloud software infrastructure combined are the same as the delivery platform concept; SaaS, of course, is Marc's runtime environment. Marc also combines development and delivery into one.

Note: A (discussion on cloud computing would not be complete without mentioning grids, parallel computing, and high-performance computing (HPC). In the early 1980s, HPC and parallel computing were applied by enterprises and research institutions to solve computationally intensive problems, and in the 1990s the domain of HPC evolved into grids. Grids focus on solving massive problems by breaking them into smaller tasks and distributing the tasks to different computers, be they inside an enterprise or be they distributed over the Internet. Grids are about distributed processing, either task parallelism or data parallelism—that is, breaking a problem into small tasks and running them in parallel (task parallelism) or running the same task on as many data sets as possible and then coordinating the results (data parallelism). Scientific problems such as weather predictions or DNA analysis, financial modeling, and other analyses of large data sets and similar problems are all good candidates for a grid. In comparison, cloud computing is general purpose and actually started from the grid-like problem sets.

For example, when the National Archives opened up 11,046 pages of Hillary Clinton's schedules on March 19, 2008, in the middle of a hotly contested U.S. presidential primary between her and Barack Obama, time was of the essence to analyze the material, and a resourceful newspaper turned to Amazon's Elastic Cloud to get massive computing power for a short period of time. It is rumored that they spent around $250 to analyze the material, in multiple runs, and were able to get to the street with an analysis earlier than other papers.

The New York Times has used the Amazon cloud for data analysis.[18][19]

Although both these examples show how a combination of cloud computing and grids can essentially achieve competitive advantage, cloud computing is more than a specialized grid infrastructure;[20] it is evolving into the infrastructure for startups with its own programming model as well as fine-grained authentication and authorization models. The grid market is evolving on its own under the leadership of The Open Grid Forum. I still have fond memories of participation under the Global Grid Forum (GGF)[21] umbrella and the meetings in Chicago and Tokyo.

Cloud and grid are about location independence (that is, where the actual computing happens), locality (executing code where data is), as well as mobility (of code and data). Moreover, both have on-demand characteristics, that is, computing resources can expand (within limits, of course) and more importantly, shrink (but less so in the world of grids and more so in the cloud world).[20] One difference is that grids are about maximizing the resources (that is, run in as manyinstances as possible), whereas clouds focus on acquiring just enough resources to perform a computing function, at any point in time, and then releasing excess resources—a just-in-time philosophy.

Cloud Computing Business Value

Naturally no technology can become an industry without a big business value proposition. The old adage of "better, cheaper, faster" applies here, too. *The New York Times*[14] summarizes the business value of cloud computing as "a way to increase capacity or add capabilities on the fly without investing in new infrastructure, training new personnel, or licensing new software." The domain is still in a very nascent stage and has lots of evolving to do.

The current value propositions for (and some arguments against) cloud computing are numerous:

■ One major category of applications that are ready for cloud computing includes data-intensive applications. Ad hoc, short-lived, temporary, or intensive applications and similar domains are best suited for a cloud computing infrastructure, because of factors like utilization, efficiency, and quick availability of vast computing resources that are essential for these applications.

■ In a business sense, cost effectiveness and the ability to scale as needed (which translates to flexibility) are the major value propositions. Cloud infrastructures enable a business to do on-the-fly, on-demand provisioning and hence offer just-in-time scalability.
An example is a French TV Channel that shifted to cloud computing for convertion of streaming videos. They can use a cloud to convert videos as they come in, scaling proportionally to the demand.

■ The financial characteristics, such as pay-as-you-go, no initial commitment or fees, and no long-term commitment, make a cloud infrastructure very attractive to CFOs. A cloud infrastructure reduces the permanent footprint of an organization's datacenter. Not only do the cloud infrastructures reduce initial investment, but they also turn capital expenditures into operational expenditures, which also means that you can scale down as needed. One still has to store the data; you can keep your data in the storage cloud and fire up a processing cloud as required.

- Another business advantage of the "variablize fixed expenses" characteristic is that it reduces risk in high-uncertainty or volatile market conditions, which allows executives to green-light some projects that otherwise would not have been approved.

- Another big advantage, especially for startups and small businesses, is that they can focus more on their core business and leave the hassles (of running a datacenter) to the cloud provider. (Bezos depicts the hassles as "muck.")

- Although there is a definite value proposition around cloud computing, enterprises have not adopted all forms of cloud computing, especially replacing their infrastructure with clouds.[22] The SaaS form of cloud, as well as consumer services, are the ones currently taking off.

- One area where cloud infrastructure is popular is in the startup space.[23] In the old world (or pre-cloud era), new companies had to estimate computing capacity, add some factor (maybe 10 times), and buy sufficient equipment.
  Although this method was fine for client server and other traditional models, the web-based applications do not fit this paradigm. With the web-based apps, they change rapidly and new apps come up within days, if not hours. Another factor is that the scaling of these web apps cannot be predicted—web apps are not deterministic and do not follow the normal curve; they are scale-free apps. For example, Animoto, an application in Facebook, went from 25,000 users to 250,000 users in three days[24,25]. They used Amazon's infrastructure through Rightscale and went from 40 instances to 4000 instances. This is the power of scale-free apps, and a traditional infrastructure cannot scale this way on short notice.

- Another area where the cloud infrastructure is well suited is for seasonal apps. These apps remain idle for a large part of the year and suddenly become a bottleneck. Examples include tax processing, quarter-end/year-end processing, e-commerce sites during the holiday season, or even when a site suddenly becomes popular, for example hit by an entry in the popular content sharing website dig.com or Slashdot-ted (i.e. become popular in the new site Slashdot.org). It is interesting to note that the Amazon AWS originated from their own infrastructure, which exhibits seasonal peaks.

Note: The discussion on business value would not be complete without a reference to Nicholas Carr[26] and his book "The Big Switch—Rewiring the World, from Edison to Google." I have a review of the book in my blog.[27]

In the book, Nic draws parallels between the electric utility industry and cloud computing. He does an excellent job in "weaving history, economics, and technology in an engaging way." "Utility computing is a new and disruptive force, but it's not without precedents," he says. According to Nic, the parallels between the development of the power grid and the emergence of cloud computing are uncanny. In the beginning, electricity was not available everywhere because there was no standard way of distribution. As a result, factories either had elaborate mechanical chain and pulley systems to run various machines or had to have big generators. In short, they either had efficient mechanical systems or needed to be in the business of power generation, which is not their core business. Nic compares the current state of IT systems to the state of electric power at this era.

In the power generation domain, as soon as standards and interoperability norms were established, power grids were developed and electric power became a utility. Big central power generation plants began appearing and then factories could get cheap power via connecting to the power grid. As a result, factories were able to convert the chain and pulley systems to very efficient electric-motor based shop floors. In a similar way, when cloud computing becomes pervasive and as easy to use and accessible as any utility, companies can simplify their computing infrastructures and focus more on their core business, just as factories with pulleys and chains transformed to ones with motors driven by electric power available as a utility.

Nic's comparison of current IT infrastructure to elaborate chains and pulleys system is not far off from current reality. Visit your datacenter and you can see the "hopeless confusion." Granted, what you see, in a datacenter, is rows of computer racks, but you just have to see a management console or deployment process through development-stage-production or look at an apps dependency diagram (if the IT folks have one) to understand the complexities. The parallel is exact, though perhaps more complex because in the world of pulleys and chains you can physically see them and if something is broken, it is visible. In the IT world, one often has to go thru myriad log files and a long process of debugging before one can even grasp what went wrong. In the end, a cold reboot might be the only solution, before anyone really gets to the root cause of a problem.

The core of Nic's argument in this book as well as in Does IT Matter? is that all datacenters use "similar software, running on similar hardware and employing similar kinds of workers." He goes on to say that IT is a commodity, and in this book he talks about computing power as being generated centrally and distributed like electric power. He is right. What cloud computing also does (which Nic touches upon lightly) is that it frees companies to focus on their core competence—that is, its business systems—and frees them from the "digital millwork." IT is a necessary component but not sufficient for a competitive advantage. And that might be the chief enabler from a cloud computing view.

Nic correctly defines cloud computing as a GPT (General Purpose Technology) with all the agonies (no standards, no broad distribution) and the ecstasies (can be applied broadly, offer huge economies of scale, can do innovative things) of being a GPT. That, in short, defines the current state of cloud computing.

Finally, the stories Nic tells are very relevant and contextual. He talks about how one early industry—distribution of ice harvested from huge stored sheets of lake ice—just melted away when faced with the advent of electric cooling. What industry will melt away because of the cloud computing?

Cloud Computing Offerings from Major Vendors

Naturally this section is outdated as soon as it is written. But it still provides a snapshot of the offerings and gives an idea about the capabilities. And by looking at what the companies are offering, one can get an idea of what is possible. The industry is in a nascent stage and so the offerings are diverse as well as not well coordinated. The leader, definitely, is

Amazon, which has mostly cohesive—occasionally bordering eccentric (for example the Mechanical Turk)—offerings. Because of this, Amazon also has captured the mindshare of Web 2.0 startups as well as developers. By some estimates they gross $500 million on their Amazon Web Services (AWS) business. Microsoft is not far behind. In an interesting article titled "Five Companies Shaping Cloud Computing"[28] James Maguire looks at Microsoft, Amazon, SalesForce, Google, and IBM as the contenders in the cloud space. The article observes that Microsoft is the current visionary, even though their Azure platform still is a work in progress.

Let us look at some of the companies in this space. Table 8-1 shows some of the major offerings in the backdrop of the categorization scheme presented earlier and then the offerings from major vendors are described in the following section.

Table 8-1   *Cloud Computing Vendor Space*

	Cloud H/W Infrastructure	Cloud Application Infrastructure	Cloud Platform Services	Cloud Data Services	SaaS	Cloud Consumer Services
Service Provider/ ISV	Amazon EC2 Rackspace mosso	Google App Engine Sun Project Caroline Microsoft Azure Salesforce Apex	Amazon payment services			
Enterprise	Amazon EC2 Rackspace mosso	Akamai Microsoft Azure Salesforce Apex	Amazon payment services		Salesforce CRM Netsuite Oracle On-demand Google Apps	
Consumer	Amazon EC2 Rackspace mosso	Google App Engine Microsoft Azure		TeleAtlas, NavTeq, Google Maps	Google Apps	Quicken Microsoft Live Mesh

Amazon

Amazon Web Services (AWS), while most probably not the first, is the industry standard in terms of a cloud computing offering. While talking at a session just before JavaOne 2008, Sun's CEO Jonathan Schwartz said "Amazon knocked the ball out of the park,"[29] and promptly announced Sun's cloud computing initiatives the next day.[30] That says it all. Table 8-2 lists Amazon's offerings and the business relevance of the components of the AWS. Naturally Amazon will add more services. Refer to http://aws.amazon.com for the latest list of AWS.

Table 8-2 *Amazon Cloud Offering*

Service	Functionality
Cloud Infrastructure	
EC2 (Elastic Compute Cloud)	The EC2 offering is the classical compute power—the ability to get one or more servers in minutes.
SimpleDB	As the name implies, storage that resembles a spreadsheet—columns with headings and data as rows. Can query based on simple primitives.
S3 (Simple Storage Service)	The S3, by design, has very simple storage semantics—objects have keys and are stored in buckets. The operations supported are write, read, delete, and list based on a key.
CloudFront	The CloudFront is an interesting service. It provides content delivery services like edge caching, increasing performance of websites.
SQS (Simple Queue Service)	The SQS is a web-scale messaging infrastructure where one can store messages between distributed components. Usually enterprises use IBM's MQ or TIBCO for their message infrastructure. This is required to create full business processing systems from various components.
Cloud Platform Services	
FPS (Flexible Payment Service)	FPS enables a business to have a robust consumer payment infrastructure, including credit card processing, micro-payments, payment aggregation, and recurring payments. This is definitely a very useful service for small businesses, especially if their services are based on the AWS infrastructure. A secure payment infrastructure is very difficult for small businesses to develop by themselves.
Amazon DevPay	The DevPay is the payment infrastructure for developers. It enables developers to set up a pay-as-you-go system for the programs they develop—basically a payment system for the SaaS.

Table 8-2 *Amazon Cloud Offering*

Service	Functionality
Amazon Mechanical Turk	Among all the AWS components, this is an interesting one. This enables one to define work and then farm it out to humans! Humans as a Service! Jobs such as translation, transcription, and data cleanup fit this category. It's interesting to read the history on Mechanical Turk.
Alexa Web Search	The search as a service. This enables one to have a search capability in a website or incorporate search as part of an application; may be even specialized search or value-added services on the top of a basic web search.
Alexa Web information Service	This is an interesting service. It gives out traffic data (with history going back five years), link structure, and other information about various websites. This service would be useful to create directories and then rank them based on popularity and other metrics.
Alexa Top Sites	This is an extension of the Web Information Service. It lists the top-ranked sites.
Alexa Site Thumbnail	The Site Thumbnail gives access to the thumbnail image of any URL.
Cloud Enterprise Services	
FWS (Fulfillment Web Service)	This is actually the a complete goods-selling service, both inbound and outbound. Inbound, a business can use Amazon's warehouses to store inventory, and outbound Amazon ships purchases to customers. Naturally Amazon's e-commerce infrastructure is used to sell goods.
AAWS (Amazon Associates Web Service)	This is the web service interface to Amazon's product data that can be incorporated into the Amazon Associates' websites. The actual buying happens at the Amazon site, but the associates' websites get a referral fee.

The most interesting Amazon Web Services, from an enterprise perspective, are the Cloud Infrastructure—the EC2, S3, CloudFront, and SimpleDB. For small businesses, payment services, fulfillment services, and even the site information would be of interest.

The Amazon offerings are based on the value proposition that they are simple, scale well (web-scale), and more importantly have zero upfront cost. Naturally, the services work together well and so it makes sense to use them with each other. For example, data could be stored in S3 with pointers in the simpleDB, all processed by EC2 instances and cached across the globe via CloudFront.

One of the important aspects of the cloud infrastructure is the pricing structure, which is very competitive, especially at this early stage of this industry. Table 8-3 lists the representative prices for the cloud infrastructure offerings from Amazon.

Table 8-3 *Amazon Web Services Price Structure*

Service	Price
EC2	Currently EC2 is priced per instance hour.
	A small-instance, single-Core/1.7GB memory/160GB disk/32-bit platform costs $0.10/hr for Linux and $0.125/hr for Windows.
	A large-instance, dual-Core/7.5GB memory/850GB disk/64-bit platform costs $0.40/hr for Linux and $0.50/hr for Windows.
	An extra-large–instance, quad-Core/15GB memory/1690GB disk/64-bit platform costs $0.80/hr for Linux and $1.00/hr for Windows.
	In addition, there are also data transfer charges.
SimpleDB	$0.14/machine hour consumed.
	$0.10/GB data in and $0.17 to $0.10/GB data out.
	$0.25/GB per month for data storage after 1GB.
CloudFront	$0.170/GB (U.S., Europe edges), $0.210/GB (Hong Kong edge), $0.221/GB (Japan edge), first 10TB/month data transfer out.
	$0.120/GB (U.S., Europe edges), $0.160/GB (Hong Kong edge), $0.168/GB (Japan edge), next 40TB/month data transfer out.
	CloudFront follows a progressive decreasing charge, based on increments of 100TB and then 250GB monthly transfers.
S3	$0.15/GB per month for data storage for the first 50GB and then a tiered model for every 50GB, then 400GB, and then 500GB.
	$0.10/GB data in and $0.17 to $0.10/GB data out.
	$0.01 per 1,000 writes and $0.01 per 10,000 reads.
	For Europe the storage is $0.180, other charges are same as the United States.
SQS	$0.01 per 10,000 requests.
	$0.10/GB data in and $0.17–$0.10/GB data out with a tiered system for higher transfers.

As is the case with any eco systems, there are lots of third-party vendors offering various services on the top of the Amazon cloud infrastructure. As of early 2009, there are around 100 companies offering various business solutions and more than 150 consumer offerings. In addition, there are companies specializing in developer tools.

Google

Next to Amazon, the Google App Engine[31] has the potential to be an industry mover. As of early 2009, Google's offering was still a little anemic. Google's aim is to provide "an environment to help web-based applications get off the ground quickly and grow easily."[23] Google claims that App Engine users have the same infrastructure Google uses. "Run your web applications on Google's infrastructure" is their tag line. This offering fits the cloud application category; Google provides the hardware infrastructure as well as the application container. As of early 2009, Google provides a python runtime virtual machine container, which means the applications need to be written exclusively in Python. The App Engine not only provides the container but also a good set of capabilities for a distributed data store with transaction semantics, integration with Google accounts for user authentication, authorization and management, as well as functionalities such as URL fetch and web app framework. What is interesting about services like URL fetch is that it uses Google's mechanisms to access external web pages and so can be very fast.

Microsoft

Although Amazon defined cloud computing and has a comprehensive offering, Microsoft is catching up quickly, very quickly. Because Microsoft has products spanning enterprise as well as consumer market, their cloud offering also reflects this duality. In the consumer space Microsoft has Live Mesh and in the enterprise space Microsoft offers Windows Azure.

Live Mesh

Microsoft Live Mesh was launched as an invitation-only, community technology preview (CTP)[32][33] in May 2008. This is a well thought-out comprehensive offering, and adds another dimension to cloud computing: the consumer cloud and connected desktop. The basic notion is to connect desktop, online storage, and devices in a mesh and then leverage the ubiquitous aspects of the mesh. In the Live Mesh world, the mesh connectivity extends from one's devices and storage to the devices and storage of a community. This offering falls under the Cloud Platform Services, extending to consumers and ISVs rather than enterprises. Their tag line[34] is "With Live Mesh, you can spend less time managing devices and data and more time connecting with family and friends or collaborating with colleagues." In "Ten Things to Know About Microsoft Live Mesh"[35], blogger Mary Jo Foley is of the opinion that Live Mesh is definitely a consumer play for Microsoft and that it has good architectural underpinnings that enable third-party developers to develop innovative services.

Azure

At the Los Angeles Professional Developer's Conference (PDC) in October 2008, Microsoft finally announced its foray into the cloud infrastructure.[36][37] The most interesting fact is that it is not a cloud OS, but the cloud itself. This means that for the first time, Microsoft is in the infrastructure, service provider business. Microsoft characterizes cloud computing as the fifth generation of computing: monolithic (1970s), client/server (1980s), web (1990s), service-oriented architecture (SOA) (now), and finally services (2009+). At least during the PDC they were not embracing the term "cloud" but are calling Azure "services exposed via web protocols."

Before taking a quick look at the technical aspects of the Azure platform, it is instructional and illuminating to look at Microsoft's business view of the cloud computing domain. The first half day at the PDC was spent on the business aspects. Some observations:

- Although some companies have the resources required for the operational discipline to run a global infrastructure, most find it a disproportionate burden. This is the first and foremost value proposition of a cloud infrastructure—similar to the "handling of muck" analogy by Amazon's Jeff Bezos.

- Major business challenges to be solved by cloud computing include meeting customer expectation of interactive, participatory web systems; operating across peaks and valleys (elastic infrastructure); solving continuity issues; and finally achieving a refined architecture (loosely coupled architecture, data replication strategies, and data partition strategies).

- Miscoroft's Chief Software Architect Ray Ozzie calls clouds "overdraft protection for your website," an interesting analogy.

- Microsoft sees current applications as having an enterprise scope, and whereas cloud expands the scope to the Internet; cloud is the externalization of enterprise IT systems. This "high-scale Internet infrastructure" is a new tier that spans the web and has different characteristics than the Desktop Tier (which has the scope of a single machine) and Enterprise Systems (which has the scope of the enterprise).

- In the current cloud computing platforms, the roles of software developer and operations are intertwined, but in reality they should be separate.

Microsoft's technical perspective of a cloud is very simple: "A set of connected servers on which to install and run services and store and retrieve data." Their offerings reflect that view of the world. Windows Azure is a comprehensive platform consisting of

- A hosting environment within which to deploy your services (you define the rules and provide your code; the platform takes care of the rest!) for a spectrum of users, from hobbyists to enterprise developers.

- A hosting environment that provides computers, the load balancers, the firewalls, and all the rest of the computer infrastructure.

- Automated service management (abstracts hardware, load balancing, and a host of other similar functions, based on the service model you create, which has things like service topology, size, health constraints, and so on).

- Scalable storage.

- A rich developer experience. This is where Microsoft has leverage: Azure fits seamlessly into their development environment. You can write your usual code, test it in their cloud simulation environment, debug the code, and then deploy it to the cloud. So current development skills are fully transferable! The deployment is so easy "even a CEO or a VP can do it!", as mentioned during a talk at the Microsoft PDC.

- A services layer with .NET services (service bus, access control and work flow services).

- Cloud platform services such as SQL services, SharePoint services, and SaaS services like CRM.

As of January 2009, Windows Azure is at the stage of Community Technology Preview. As Dan Faber puts it,[38] although we will see large-scale deployments in Windows Azure, only around 2010 and beyond would it be a mature platform to be reckoned with.

IBM

IBM naturally is adding the cloud feature set to its portfolio.[39, 40] As of early 2009, it is less ambitious and not heavily advertised. Most probably they are evaluating the market and are forming a strategy. Currently they have two offerings:

- One offering is the cloud storage service aimed at medium businesses and branded for remote data protection. They also have offerings in the realm of hosted email services.

- IBM also has the Blue Cloud initiative[41] with Google, currently offered for universities and other academic institutions. This offering is mostly in the form of a grid and comes from their high-performance on-demand computing division.

Sun

Until recently, Sun had two main initiatives:[42] their network.com and Project Caroline. At the JavaOne 2008 conference, Sun announced that its Open Solaris and MySQL will be available as part of the Amazon EC2.

Sun's network.com is a mature application execution platform based on the top of its N1 grid engine. To Sun's credit, they had this infrastructure long before cloud computing was in vogue. But the offering looked more like a grid than a traditional cloud infrastructure.

Project Caroline, an open source project from Sun's research organization, is a good hosting platform for a cloud infrastructure. It has programmatic interfaces to virtualize instances and provision, monitor, and manage instances as well as file systems and network resources. Naturally the underlying containers are Java virtual machines. This is a decent offering in the cloud application platform category. That is, the hardware infrastructure capability as well as application containers are available. Naturally there should be cloud providers who will host the platform so that developers can use the platform; currently only one instance is available,[43] which is more a research effort than a commercial offering.

As of January 2009, Sun has been more active in the cloud computing space. They acquired Q-layer, a company that offers products to simplify cloud management and provisioning. It is expected that Sun will make an announcement in March 2009 at the CommunityOne conference.

Other Companies

In addition to the traditional big names, there are other companies—both established and startups—offering different cloud infrastructures ranging from storage to processing to data services. A good list is available at IBM.[44] Table 8-4 lists some of the companies and their offerings.

Table 8-4 *Cloud Offering Spectrum*

Company	Offering
3Tera (www.3tera.com)	3Terra is an archetypical cloud company offering hosting solutions, SaaS platforms, a cloudware architecture, and everything in between.
EMC	EMC has storage solutions and backup solutions addressing individuals and small businesses. They are working toward cloud enterprise services, partnering with ERP vendors such as SAP and others
Dell	Dell actually sells to the clouds crowd under the trade name DCS (Dell Cloud Computing Solutions).[45, 46] It emphasizes analysis, ordering, project management, and data center scaling support. Their architectures (called hyperscale data centers) span from gaming to HPCC to simulation systems to Web 2.0 hosing. For now they do not have any hosting and operation of clouds, which makes sense in that Dell manufactures computers and do not want to compete with their customers.
Rackspace Mosso (www.mosso.com)	Rackspace is a traditional managed hosting company, which is slowly moving into the cloud space as well. The offering by Mosso, a startup funded by Rackspace, offers cloud hosting as well as storage hosting (CloudFS) on the top of Rackspace infrastructure.
Rightscale	Rightscale is an example of an application infrastructure layer over different cloud hardware infrastructures. They provide systems management, prepackaged components, and support for cloud infrastructures. Their value proposition is this layer, which makes deployment and management easier over multiple cloud hardware infrastructure providers.

Enterprise Adoption of Cloud Computing

The cloud computing industry is in the gold rush stage: very young, many ideas, not well defined, not enough general consensus, and lots of companies. For startups and small businesses, cloud computing is the right infrastructure, especially if they are using Web

2.0 applications such as social networking. It is interesting to note that outsourced cloud computing is not an option for the largest scale. For example, Facebook is borrowing $100 million to buy servers.[47] It is reported that Google has around a million servers and is adding 500,000 per year, and Microsoft is adding 200,000 servers.

Note: At the Web 2.0 Expo West 2008 at the San Francisco Mascone West it was fascinating to see the beginning of a disruptive technology maturing into an industry. Lots of companies, big and small, offered different aspects of cloud computing. Many are concentrating on the infrastructure (even just storage), whereas others offer mashup, social networking, and similar hosted cloud platforms, and still others offer a software layer over others' cloud infrastructure. There were some cool technologies as well.[48] SocialMix is a super mashup of social networking sites. Octopz is an "online collaboration software for architectural engineers and industrial designers, allowing them to communicate via text, VOIP, and webcam while working on three-dimensional models and schematics on their PCs from any location."[48] OpenCircle is a private meeting room for small businesses. Spigit is an enterprise-grade lightweight business intelligence engine for social networks. Vyew is a web-based collaboration and conferencing platform with whiteboard and annotation capabilities.

Some elements that are missing (other than a uniform vocabulary) include standardization. Every organization has its own GUI interfaces and also programmatic interfaces. Other challenges include enterprise integration capabilities, specifications and enforcement of Service Level Agreements (SLA) as well as platform stability. Of course, many of the companies will be bought out and many will merge and, in the end, the industry will stabilize.

For enterprises, there is definite value in adopting the cloud computing paradigm. Because of the nature of the current state of the industry, it is better to start slow and follow the adoption curve. Along with that, an understanding of the nature of cloud computing that a company can leverage, based on its IT maturity and business landscape, is essential. Mapping the IT systems to a layered stack diagram like that shown previously in Figure 8-1 would help. Most probably, the first steps would be scaling processing power, storage, backup, and even messaging and database clouds.

In an interesting article, "Is Cloud Right for You?"[49] Joe Weinman observes that highly interactive applications that have dispersed users with variable and unpredictable demand characteristics that cannot be shaped are the best candidates for a cloud infrastructure.

The following are some points to keep in mind as an enterprise moves to a Cloud Infrastructure:

- Integration is essential: Enterprises cannot move all applications to a cloud infrastructure in one step. This means that mechanisms to integrate data as well as functionalities inside and outside the cloud are necessary. Currently such mechanisms need to be developed in-house. And there is no interoperability anywhere in the cloud computing space, so there is no real way of moving processing or storage between different cloud providers.

- Infrastructure Security will be a major consideration: As always, when an infrastructure is outside an enterprise, one has to pay more attention to security. On the other hand, using the cloud from well established players has the advantage of a secure infrastructure.

- Don't forget Application-level security: In addition to the platform security, there are also other dimensions at the user level, including authentication, authorization, and uniform policy mediation.

- The ability to achieve compliance to regulations are indispensable: This is an important aspect because internal IT infrastructures, over the years, have built in various regulatory compliance primitives. When, suddenly some of the processing moves to an external or public cloud, the compliance policies need to move as well. For example, government regulations state that government processing needs to happen inside the United States and if a virtualized cloud environment "automagically" moves some government computing to a datacenter outside the country, the CIO of the government agency consuming the service is liable for legal proceedings! Declarative policies, visibility, and control are essential for computer processing that is under regulatory compliance requirements.

- Exceptions rule: A cloud application is not a traditional client-server application, and the applications need to accommodate multiple failure paths. In this respect, web-based apps would be better candidates than fat client apps.

- Outages do happen: Even the Amazon EC2 and S3 had a well-published outage. "Amazon Web Services Goes Down, Takes Many Startup Sites With It"[50] and "Amazon Explains Its S3 Outage"[51] are worth reading. So performance management as well as supporting Service-Level Agreements are challenging. In fact, Amazon Web Services introduced SLAs only recently.

- Deployment, monitoring, and management capabilities are still very primitive: There is no interoperability between clouds from different vendors and one has to pay attention to SLA policies. Moving apps from dev/stage/prod infrastructures needs to be done via proprietary GUIs or APIs.

- Align business strategy and consider application characteristics: As in any other technology, aligning business requirements and IT infrastructure, considering scaling requirements in the new Web 2.0 era, and achieving agility by a Cloud computing paradigm are essential. One characteristic that might not have been considered in the IT strategy is the application characteristic: Certain apps are well suited to leveraging cloud computing.

- Note whether your business strategy includes scale-free apps: If you have applications that have larger peak loads, seasonal apps with dynamic workloads, and ad-hoc apps, and you are balancing asset optimization against agility, cloud computing is the answer. In short, IT based on a cloud computing model can provide strategic advantage, especially in terms of agility, provided the technology is properly deployed and managed effectively.

In Short

The next phase of the Internet is cloud computing, where computing tasks will be assigned to a cloud—a combination of online resources including connections, software, services, and servers accessed over a network.[52] We will no longer care where our data is physically stored or where servers are physically located; we will use them (and pay for them) only when we need them. Cloud computing provides enterprises with a flexible and agile infrastructure (through elasticity), economies of scale (through multi-tenancy), and simplicity (via cloud providers), so that enterprises can focus on their core business as well as the application development to support their business. The maintenance of an IT infrastructure is outsourced. The domain is at its infancy stage; offerings from various companies are maturing and the classes of applications migrating to cloud computing are still developing. Of late, the terms "unified data center" and "unified cloud computing" have become popular to denote a cohesive approach to cloud infrastructures as well as interoperable cloud instances. In the words of Cisco CTO Ms. Padmasree Warrior, "Just as the Internet grew out of a collection of networks that learned how to communicate with each other, clouds will know how to interoperate and provide services to each other so applications can be run."

<monologue>

Mobile devices with web access extend the ubiquity of the Internet, offering anywhere, anytime access to information. This makes it possible to share information with colleagues and friends through photo and video media, as well as by voice. Consumers can quickly capture photos and videos with cameras embedded in their mobile devices and share them with relatives and friend via email or post them to MySpace or YouTube.

The power of this new, faster, richer, Mobile Web connectedness is evident from the impact the Mobile Web has brought to bear during recent disasters. During these events, Mobile Web users kept the world informed through user-generated content: breaking news and actual first-hand photos and videos from the scene. Web 2.0 and mobility and the connectedness they enable offer each enterprise the opportunity to transform and accelerate business processes and achieve employee productivity gains as well.

</monologue>

Web 2.0 and Mobility

Access the web over a wireless network via a mobile device such as a handheld computer, personal digital assistant (PDA), or browser-enabled smartphone, and you're on the Mobile Web.[1] It's important because if analysts' predictions are correct, the Mobile Web will experience phenomenal growth and forever change the way the world does business. So this chapter

- Briefly describes the evolution of Mobile Web technology

- Examines the generations of mobile phone services

- Touches on a number of mobile devices—the very first as well as the very latest—and key features such as voice recognition and position location

- Identifies some of the platforms used for developing Mobile Web applications

- Provides examples of the types of Mobile Web applications and services available today

- Describes how mobile devices are used in social networking

- Identifies Cisco's efforts to create Mobile Web applications

- Discusses some of the mobile information services being used by Cisco Sales

- Identifies the impact these applications are having on these business users

More importantly, the chapter provides insight into the business value of the Mobile Web.

Mobility provides an opportunity for enterprises to transform and accelerate business processes and increase employee productivity, particularly in a Web 2.0 world. Many enterprises such as Cisco have built out their mobile infrastructure and deployed mobile devices to their employees, particularly in sales and support. As enterprises develop new or modify existing applications, both internally and externally facing, they are doing so with web access—particularly Mobile Web access—in mind to take full advantage of Mobile Web technology.

Mobility, for example, provides immediate access to information and data enriched with context such as geoposition. Equipment location can be plotted on a map on a company website, a "webmap." With a web-enabled mobile device, a service technician can be notified immediately of an equipment failure, find the location on the webmap, find, connect, and share photos and videos of malfunctioning equipment with colleagues for a collaborative diagnosis, or research potential, innovative, user-generated content: problems and solutions shared on the web.

With access to the appropriate enterprise applications and websites, the technician can quickly and easily connect to order a part or loaner equipment, update the trouble ticket, and notify a customer that the problem is being solved. That's the power of the Mobile Web. As Mobile Web technology evolves, organizations need to understand and foster its application to fully realize the business transformation, process acceleration, and employee and customer connectedness it enables.

Evolution of Mobile Web Technology

This section provides a brief overview of the evolution of Mobile Web technology, outlining the generations of mobile technology. The section goes on to explore several types of mobile devices, the first and the very latest. Included is a discussion of some key features available on mobile devices today: voice recognition and position location. This will serve as a foundation for your exploration of Mobile Web applications and websites available today.

Generations of Mobile Phone Technology

AT&T introduced Mobile Telephone Service (MTS) in the United States in 1946. Weighing 76 lbs., the first mobile phone worked like a walkie-talkie, with one person speaking at a time and a push-to-talk button on the handset controlling the direction of the call.[2] Communications researchers came up with the idea of dividing large mobile telephone service areas into smaller "cells," enabling service providers to reuse radio frequencies within each cell and thereby increase the number of calls that could be handled by each cell.

In 1947, after AT&T first proposed the idea, the Federal Communication Commission limited the number of radio frequencies for mobile telephones. This continued until 1968, when AT&T proposed, and the FCC approved, a cellular system of small, low-powered cell towers. Each "cell" covered a smaller area and calls passed from tower to tower as the phone moved past them.[3]

Mobile phone (also known as wireless telephone) technology is usually divided into generations. The first mobile phone service, described previously, began after World War II. Commonly referred to as 0G, it preceded cellular phone service, offered only a few channels, and required an operator's help to place a call. The first generation of wireless cellular communication technology, called Analog Mobile Phone Service (AMPS) is known as 1G. Introduced in 1981, it enabled users to place calls without an operator and used analog radio signals to pass calls between cells.[4]

Second-generation technology (2G) introduced digital cellular in 1991, enabling data services, including the ability to send and receive pictures and video.[5] Digital also enabled access to webpages written in Wireless Markup Language (WML) via a browser, based on Wireless Application Protocol (WAP).[6] Currently, the most popular standard for digital services, Global System for Mobile Communication (GSM), got its start in Europe, where it was originally called Groupe Spécial Mobile. GSM introduced an alternative to voice calls: short alphanumeric text messaging via a protocol called Short Message Service (SMS).[7]

Subsequent generations offer even more data services. Enhanced Data Rates for GSM Evolution (EDGE), for example, is a mobile phone technology deployed in North America and often referred to as 2.75G. It enables faster data transmission on top of GSM.[8] Third-generation technology (3G), introduced in 2001, offers wide-area wireless voice and video telephony, as well as broadband wireless data access, and is faster than EDGE. 3G networks should not be confused with short-range wireless data networks, which are based on the IEEE 802.11 standard and commonly known as Wi-Fi or wireless local area network (WLAN).[9] Newer mobile devices can often connect to the web via one or more of these networks for data access.

Many newer devices can connect to other devices, such as headsets, via Bluetooth, a wireless protocol that enables data exchange over short distance.[10] In addition, satellite phones can connect to orbiting satellites and are often used in remote areas without access to terrestrial networks and cell towers.[11] Finally, 4G, or fourth generation, is expected to provide faster, higher-quality services, including Internet Protocol (IP)-based voice, data, and multimedia. This will require complete replacement of existing networks and, as Table 9-1 indicates, will probably occur around 2012-15.[12]

Table 9-1 *Generations of Mobile Technology*

Generation	Key Features	Date Available
0G	Pre-cellular service Required operator to place calls	1947
1G	Analog cellular service No operator required to place calls	1981
2G	Digital cellular service Text messaging via SMS Pictures Video Web access	1991
3G	Digital cellular service supporting voice and video telephony Broadband wireless data High-speed Internet access	2001
4G	Digital cellular, Internet Protocol (IP)–based voice and data Streamed multimedia	2012-15

Now take a brief look at various types of mobile devices designed to take advantage of these services.

Mobile Devices

Mobile devices have changed significantly since April 1973, when Dr. Martin Cooper placed the first public call on a 30-ounce portable, brick-shaped cellular phone, shown in Figure 9-1.[13]

Figure 9-1   *Martin Cooper uses first portable cellular phone.[13]*

In the beginning, cell phones were used primarily to make calls, and personal digital assistants (PDA) were developed as handheld devices to store memos, addresses, and phone numbers. In 1983 Casio introduced the first PDA, the PF-3000, shown in Figure 9-2.

Subsequent PDAs, like the Pilot 5000 introduced by Palm in 1998, provided a touch-sensitive screen and the capability to synchronize calendar and contacts with the user's personal computer.[15] As cell phone designers added features found on PDAs, the smartphone was born.[16] Figure 9-3 shows Simon, the first smartphone, a touch-sensitive device developed by IBM and sold in 1994.[17] Nokia introduced one of the world's best-selling smartphones, the 9000 Communicator shown in Figure 9-4, in 1996.[18]

Today, many mobile devices have a number of features, including an operating system, enabling them to run applications like small computers. Most are pocket-sized, have a miniature QWERTY keyboard to facilitate text messaging, and use a color display screen. Many devices, as noted previously, can connect to the web for data access via one or more of the cellular or wireless networks.

Some devices use voice recognition technology, location-based services, and device synchronization to increase ease of use.[20] Cameras are a popular feature for capturing

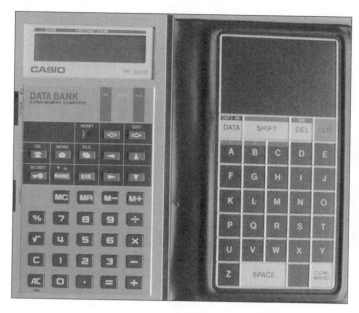

Figure 9-2   *Casio PF-3000, the first personal digital assistant (PDA).[14]*

Figure 9-3   *Simon, the first smartphone, developed by IBM.[17]*

Figure 9-4   *Nokia 9000 Communicator.[19]*

photos and videos on the go and sending them to family and friends or uploading them to the web. At the start of 2008, Nokia held 40% of the world's mobile phone market, shipping more devices in the last quarter of 2007 than the next three largest vendors, Samsung, Motorola, and Sony Ericsson, combined.[21] Figure 9-5 shows the Nokia E90 Communicator, one of the most popular Nokia devices in 2007.[22]

Figure 9-5   *Nokia E90 Communicator.[23]*

Figure 9-6 displays the BlackBerry Storm, the newest device from Research in Motion (RIM), released in November 2008.[24] The BlackBerry has been a popular business device and the Storm offers features sure to please business users, including the ability to open and edit Microsoft Word documents and Excel spreadsheets and view PowerPoint presentations.[25] But RIM hopes the Storm will be popular with consumers as well, thanks to its touchscreen and multimedia capabilities.[26] The Storm offers a clickable touchscreen and virtual mouse pointer that enable the user to point, cut, and copy screen text, two features not found on Apple's popular iPhone.[27]

Figure 9-6   *BlackBerry Storm.[28]*

Apple's iPhone was first introduced at the Macworld Expo in January 2007. It was billed as three devices combined in one: an iPod with a widescreen, a radically new mobile phone, and a groundbreaking web communications device. The iPhone not only changed the way people used their mobile phones, but also the mobile phone industry itself. Apple introduced iPhone 2.0 software in March 2008, enabling users to connect to corporate servers and to download third-party applications available for purchase at its App Store.

As the first widescreen iPod with video capabilities, the iPhone's bright widescreen display enables the user to view multimedia, such as photos, music videos, TV, and movies. The Multi-Touch screen enables flipping through photos and music collection album covers with the flick of a finger, and a user can easily purchase and download new music from Apple's iTunes Wi-Fi Store. The iPhone's Safari browser supports variants of Hypertext Markup Language (HTML) found on the desktop web, so specialized Mobile Web pages are not required.

The iPhone's built-in accelerometer senses whether or not the device is held vertically or horizontally and rotates the image to fill the screen. The user is able to zoom images in and out by moving thumb and index finger closer together or farther apart to pinch or stretch them. Running on the EDGE network, the iPhone offers conference calling and SMS, but more importantly it provides a web browser enabling the user to display and navigate complete web pages.[29] In July 2008, Apple released the iPhone 3G, pictured in Figure 9-7, offering faster data speeds via the 3G network and built-in Global Positioning System (GPS).[30]

Figure 9-7   *Apple iPhone 3G.[31]*

For quick reference, some key features of the iPhone, Nokia E90 Communicator, and BlackBerry Storm are listed in Table 9-2.

Table 9-2   *Key Features of Newest Mobile Devices Providing Web Access*

Device	Key Features
Nokia E90 Communicator	High-speed mobile broadband
	Conference calling
	Image and video cameras
	Music and media players
	Large color displays[32]
BlackBerry Storm	Mobile streaming
	Conference calling
	Multimedia
	Camera and video recording
	Touch screen navigation[33]
Apple iPhone	Wireless 3G
	Desktop-class web browser
	iPod music and video player
	Camera and video recording
	Wide, touchscreen display[34]

Many of the newer mobile devices described here offer easier and improved access to web-based data services. Many devices, like the iPhone, operate in both portrait and landscape modes. The user is able to change orientation as the device is running to obtain the best web content view.[35] This new capability completely shatters many of the limitations of what web content can be effectively rendered.

The iPhone is truly revolutionary because most previous mobile devices had much smaller and less "viewable" screens, and significantly less capable web browsers. But in addition to the unique capabilities and services Apple has to offer, companies like AT&T are looking to develop even more devices to enable users to easily access the web-based data services anytime, anywhere via their network.

Imagine a device enabling the concerned owner to track a lost pet via the Internet, provided Fido is wearing a web-enabled dog collar. Or consider the new parent able to snap photos and send them immediately to a web-enabled photo frame for Grandma to enjoy. Devices for web-enabled, in-car entertainment are another example, where backseat drivers could download and view movies purchased from iTunes while on the go.

Industry analysts predict the market for such devices will grow faster than that for mobile phones, as almost nine out of ten people already have cell phones.[36] Two key features of newer Mobile Web devices worth mentioning here, because of the number of applications and Mobile Web services they enable, are voice recognition and position location.

Voice Recognition and Position Location Technology

Voice recognition technology, improved in recent years thanks to better microphones, faster processors, and more effective software algorithms, is now able to recognize speech with nearly 100% accuracy. Described as mobile's newest killer application, voice recognition actually got its start in 1952 when Bell Labs developed a crude system able to recognize numbers spoken over a phone. Today's systems have evolved, after much experimentation, to a point where they can recognize countless dialects, accents, and speech patterns.

Some voice systems are sophisticated enough to identify context, recognizing whether or not the command "traffic" refers to road conditions, an old Steve Winwood tune, or a Michal Douglas film. Today's systems are so advanced that they can teach themselves, analyzing billions of phrases to improve speech pattern recognition. Voice technology enables mobile devices to respond to voice commands not only for dialing, but also for website navigation.[37] Voice may also play an important role in the area of device security, for example, in that it offers a way to authenticate user access to sensitive corporate information via mobile device.

Position location technology has also advanced in the last decade. Cell signals are used to locate and identify the position of a mobile device outside a user's home network, enabling "roaming," a term typically associated with GSM networks.[38] Any newer mobile devices, such as the iPhone 3G, are capable of registering via the GPS satellite navigation system developed by the U.S. Department of Defense. Figure 9-8 provides a diagram of how a mobile device, tracked by a GPS satellite, is associated with a particular cell tower, enabling an emergency system operator to obtain the device location from a location server.[39]

GPS supports the capability to physically locate a mobile device by its geographic coordinates with remarkable accuracy.[40] These technologies also enable Mobile Web applications to provide location-based services. These can help find a missing dog, as in the earlier example, or offer directions to the nearest restaurant, based on device location.

Another factor prompting the growth of position location services in the United States was the FCC mandate known as E911. The FCC required U.S. carriers, by 2001, to enable mobile phones to process emergency calls so that emergency services could locate the caller's geographic location within 100 meters.[41] The next section provides a brief introduction to platforms used to develop applications for mobile devices to take advantage of features such as these.

Developing Applications for Mobile Devices

Each mobile device has a mobile operating system (MOS), like a computer operating system, which serves as a platform on which other software programs run. The MOS enables features installed by the manufacturer to function properly and determines which third-party applications will run on the device. Symbian, the most popular MOS for smartphones, is used in mobile devices running on 2.5 or 3G networks.[42] Symbian-based devices are manufactured by Nokia, Samsung, and Sony Ericcson, for example.[43] Table

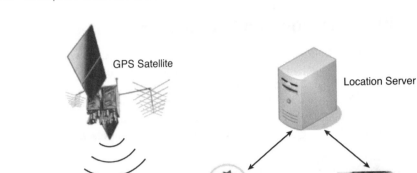

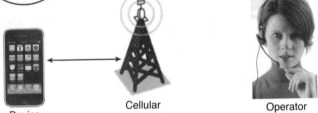

Figure 9-8   *How GPS locates a mobile device.[39]*

9-3 lists Symbian and other popular MOS and their market share in the third quarter of 2008.

Table 9-3   *Mobile Operating Systems (MOS)[44]*

Mobile Operating System	Market Share (Q3 2008)
Symbian OS	46.6%
Apple iPhone OS	17.3%
Research in Motion (RIM) Blackberry OS	15.2%
Microsoft Windows Mobile OS	13.6%
Linux and others	7.3%

Applications for mobile devices, like computer applications, are built using development platforms or environments specifically suited for the target MOS on which the application will be running. The Symbian Developer Network, for example, offers information on how to use a number of development tools, such as Java and C++, to build applications to run on smartphones with the Symbian MOS.[45] Binary Runtime Environment for Wireless (BREW) is an application development platform for mobile devices leveraging Qualcomm's mobile technology. Resulting applications require Qualcomm certification prior to release.[46]

Sun and Google offer popular mobile application development tools. Sun Microsystem's Java Platform Micro Edition, Java ME (formerly known as J2ME), for example, provides a subset of Java for application development on smaller, micro devices including mobile phones.[47] Google Android is a development platform that enables developers to write Java code that can control a mobile device and take better advantage of newer device features and technologies such as voice recognition and position location.[48]

Eclipse, a universal development toolkit, is also gaining traction as a mobile application development tool.[49] Motorola and Nokia, for example, are working to form an Eclipse Mobile Industry Working Group to define a common mobile application development kit (MADK) based on open standards to make Mobile Web applications and services easier to develop.[50] Finally, AJAX (Asynchronous JavaScript and XML) is a web development technology used to create interactive web applications, gaining popularity on the Mobile Web.[51]

Mobile Web Applications and Websites

Today's Mobile Web delivers information content, such as news, weather, and sports, and enables transactional services, such as messaging and online stock trading via Mobile Web applications and specially designed mobile websites. Much of the Mobile Web consists of lightweight pages developed specifically to deliver content to a mobile device. As mentioned previously, many mobile devices use a WAP browser to render content developed in WML, a specialized markup language that enables content to fit on the smaller device's screen.

The WAP Forum, founded in 1997, worked to bring wireless technologies together through a standard protocol. The Forum released the WAP 1.0 standard in 1998, followed by several subsequent releases. WAP 2.0, based on an abbreviated version of Extensible Hypertext Markup Language (XHTML) was released in 2002, the same year the WAP Forum and other wireless industry forums were consolidated into the Open Mobile Alliance (OMA). OMA is the organization responsible for developing interoperable standards for future mobile or wireless data services used to deliver content to mobile devices.[6] The next section focuses on the Mobile Web applications or webapps these standards enable.

Mobile Webapps

Web applications, or webapps, are developed in a browser-supported language such as HTML or Java, accessed on the web, and executed via a web browser.[52] Webapps reside on a server, are meant for use by humans, and leverage web pages as the presentation layer. Webapps often leverage underlying web services, which also reside on a server but are meant to interact with other programs. In simple terms, web services provide data to webapps, which are accessed via websites.[53] Mobile webapps are designed to be accessed and executed by the browser on a mobile device.

There have already been more than 500 million downloads from Apple's App Store, mentioned previously, which contains over 15,000 applications designed for use on the iPhone and iTouch mobile devices.[54] Users can browse all eleven categories of iPhone webapps or search by category.[55] To show the diversity of applications currently available, five of the most popular applications (as of the date of publication) listed in each category in the App Store library appear, with a brief description of their features, in Table 9-4.

Table 9-4 *Top 5 Most Popular iPhone Applications Listed on Apple's App Store*

Category	Application (Brief description of features)
Calculate	Arithmetic Problems (Train your brain to solve)
	Temperature Converter Calculator (Convert temp)
	WW (Weight Watchers points calculator)
	iCalc—Tip Calculator (Easily calculate tips)
	Federal Tax Calculator (2009 Tax estimate)[56]
Entertainment	Sundance Film Festival 2009 (Stay up to date)
	Are you compatible? Take the (Love) test
	Spreety TV iPhone (Watch top TV shows online)
	RiddlerX (Random riddles test your brain)
	Star104 Internet Radio Tuner (Music on the go)[57]
Games	Minicube (2×2×2 Rubik's Cube)
	Spellgaze (Battle opponents in gem-matching game)
	iMystical Mind Reader (Reads your mind)
	KingdomGame (Strategy game versus multiple players)
	iSpot the Difference (Photo hunt game)[58]
News	BBC (British Broadcasting Corp. news channel)
	iNews (iPhone news and more)
	Wii Headline News and Information (Wii game info)
	AP Mobile News Network (Associated Press news)
	Google Trends + Twitter (What's being said)[59]
Productivity	Free 2009 Calendar Wallpaper (iPhone Lock screen)
	x|Grapher (Financial market visualization tool)
	IBM Lotus iNotes (web email, collaborative tools)
	Intelesure (Telemarketing, direct mail solutions)
	Photoshop Pro Mobile Edition (Photoshop news)[60]

(*continues*)

Table 9-4   *Top 5 Most Popular iPhone Applications Listed on Apple's App Store (continued)*

Category	Application (Brief description of features)
Search Tools	easyTouch Dictionary (Dictionary webapp)
	Song Hog (Song lyric search engine)
	Home Plan Finder (Find plans from top designer)
	Googlie > Search Google Quickly (Faster search)
	Walmart.com .97 cent shipping deals (Bargains)[61]
Social Networking	Facebook (Optimized for iPhone and iPod Touch)
	eBuddy Lite Messenger (Free, easy-to-use chat)
	Send sms messages (Send free sms messages)
	IM+ for Skype (Voice and text other Skype users)
	Touch2TXT (Send SMS from iPod Touch world-wide)[62]
Sports	LiveScore (Live soccer scores from LiveScore.com)
	MLB (Major League Baseball news from Peter Gammons)
	BBC Sport Scotland (BBC Sport Scotland news)
	NFL (National Football League news from Adam Schefter)
	Online Bike Repair Manual (Mobile Bike Magazine)[63]
Travel	Pocket Norwich (Mobile guide to city of Norwich)
	TubeJP: London Tube Journey Planner (Tube map)
	Le Franco—Thai (Translate French words to Thai)
	Auto Reviews Mobile (Latest new auto reviews)
	Mobile Map Me (See where friends are on a map)[64]
Utilities	TokTok Translator (Translate words and phrases)
	MailCheck (Verify email address)
	Daily Free Stuff (Free stuff in one place)
	WeightDate Weight Tracker (Track loss/gain goals)
	Tonomemo (Handwritten memo in Japanese)[65]
Weather	Moon Phases (Countdown to next moon phases)
	EarthWinds (Shows current world image from above)
	USA Weather: Animated (Animated US weather maps)
	Weather (Current weather for city or ZIP code)
	WeatherBug (Live local weather around the world)[66]

As mentioned previously, iPhone users can download these and other webapps, many of which are free, from the App Store.[67] Apple Developer Connection helps users create their own webapps.[68] And developers can submit new webapps for consideration to be added to the App Store by completing a submission form online.[69] A number of sites deliver services designed specifically for mobile devices. Several are examined in the next section.

Web Portals and Wireless Application Service Providers

There are many examples of companies that added a site customized for mobile device access to their existing web presence: Amazon.com for online shopping, Ameritrade for online trading, BusinessWeek online for news and information, FedEx and UPS for package shipping, Moviefone for theater showtimes, IBM for corporate information, even the Board of Governors of the Federal Reserve, to name a few. But, perhaps even more interesting are those sites that aggregate a number of services in one site, called web portals, those companies that offer services for a fee, as service providers, and the ways social networking sites are taking advantage of mobile devices.

Web portals, such as Yahoo!, offer aggregated services including email, maps, news, photo-sharing, and search to mobile users via sites specifically designed for mobile device users. Figure 9-9 shows the Yahoo! mobile website.

Figure 9-9   *Yahoo! mobile website.[70]*

Yahoo! Mobile offers users the ability to search their site by speaking commands and is one example of how popular sites are leveraging voice recognition technology mentioned earlier to aid users in site navigation. Yahoo! oneSearch is designed to enable mobile users to search for stocks, news, sports, restaurants, movie info, and more by leveraging a system that learns and gets better the more you use it.[71]

Yahoo! Go version 2 enables users to leverage their mobile device's GPS system to get search results for restaurants, movies, directions, weather, and so on based on their location.[72] As voice and position location technologies continue to develop and perhaps learn from and interact with each other, a simple voice command, "sushi at 6," into your mobile device may enable it to select your favorite sushi restaurant, check on table availability, make a reservation, check traffic patterns, provide the best driving route, and suggest taking your umbrella based on the weather forecast.

Mobile Web portals are changing our ability to access information. Many companies and organizations have developed web portals, designed specifically for mobile devices, to provide their customers with access to services and information, wherever and whenever they need it. Many state and local agencies have established Mobile Web portals in addition to their regular websites. Michigan's state government, for example, launched mobile.mi.gov, shown in Figure 9-10, which offers anytime, anywhere access to agency services and information to millions of the state's mobile device users.[73]

Figure 9-10 *Michigan State Government's mobile webite.[74]*

Another example is the mobile website for the U.S. Air Force official air demonstration team, the Thunderbirds, usaftbirds.mobi, shown in Figure 9-11. The site offers information on team members, schedule, squadron history, and rich media, such as videos and ringtones. Designed by ESREVNI, a Las Vegas-based company, the site won first place in Netbiscuits Developer Challenge, recently announced at Yankee Group's Mobile InternetWorld. The challenge offered developers an opportunity to leverage Netbiscuit's development platform, which enables content to be written once and rendered correctly on all mobile phones, regardless of carrier.[75]

Figure 9-11   *United States Air Force Thunderbirds site.[76]*

Application service providers now offer many of their hosted services, such as user support and system monitoring, for example, to customers through a variety of mobile devices. These Wireless Application Service Providers (WASPs), as they are called, provide web-based access to applications and services, often at lower cost than on-premise services.[77] Three examples of WASPs and the service they provide are listed in Table 9-5.

Table 9-5   *Examples of Wireless Application Service Providers (WASPs)[78]*

Company	Service(s)
Air2Web	Mobile marketing campaigns direct to customers:
	Promote brands and products
	Provide additional product information
	Enable transactions via mobile device[79]

MobileAware	Mobile data services for banking, facilities management, manufacturing, transportation, utilities, and so on:
	Mobile customer self-service
	Mobile employee self-service
	Mobile service delivery[80]
ViryaNet	Mobile field services for utilities, retail, and so on:
	Call logging and real-time reports from the field
	Technician scheduling and dispatch
	Equipment warranty and parts inventory tracking[81]

The complexity of Mobile Web technologies and devices in the hands of their customers and employees can be quite challenging to some organizations with little experience in this area. These organizations can benefit from a WASP's expertise to extend their business processes to mobile device users and begin leveraging the power of the Mobile Web.[82]

Mobile Social Networking

Mobile social networking, like social networking, is about reaching out to individuals with like interests, creating profiles, making friends, participating in discussion forums and chat rooms. It's about sharing information, photos, and videos via blogs, and forming virtual communities. But in the case of mobile social networking, one or more members connect to others via a mobile device.

Mobile social networking is prevalent in Europe and countries in the Far East, like Japan, Korea, and China, with better mobile networks and less expensive pricing for data services. Web-based social networking services, such as Facebook and MySpace, are adding features for Mobile Web users.[83] Key features of these and new social networking services, such as Dodgeball, JuiceCaster, Loopt, Mig33, Mobikade, Mobimii, and MocoSpace, are listed in Table 9-6.

Table 9-6 *Mobile Social Networks[84]*

Network	Feature(s)
Dodgeball	Available in 22 cities across the United States.
	Alerts user of friends and other members located within a nearby radius so they can connect[85]
Facebook	Facebook Mobile Web: Site designed for a mobile browser[86]
	Facebook Mobile Uploads: Enables mobile users to upload photos and notes to Facebook
	Facebook Mobile Texts: Enables users to view profiles and send text messages to members[87]

(continues)

Table 9-6 *Mobile Social Networks[84] (continued)*

Network	Feature(s)
JuiceCaster	Enables instant messaging
	Provides discussion forums
	Upload photos and videos
	Mobile Video Search (MVS)[88,89]
Loopt	Alerts user when friends are nearby
	Shares user location with approved contacts
	Provides info on locations recommended by friends[90]
Mig33	Available worldwide
	Manage user profile
	Integrates with instant messaging: AIM, Yahoo!, Google Talk
	Upload photos
	Enables VOIP calling[91]
Mobikade	Provides free mobile games
	Supports microblogging
	Upload photos
	Offers free SMS[92,93]
Mobimii	Manage user profile
	Upload photos, videos, and tones
	Provides chatrooms
	Access mobimailbox
	View information about friends[94]
MocoSpace	Upload photos, videos
	Supports chat and microblogging[95]
MySpace	MySpace Mobile: site designed for mobile browsers[96]
	View profiles
	Send and receive text messages
	Browse photos[97]

Facebook's mobile features work well on the iPhone and there's even a Facebook application that works on BlackBerry smartphones. Facebook's mobile site (m.facebook.com), shown in Figure 9-12, is designed for mobile browsers.

There were 14 million mobile social networkers in 2007. That number is expected to increase to nearly 600 million by 2012, when revenue from user-generated content, mobile social networking, and related content services is expected to reach $6 billion.[84] JuiceCaster (www.juicecaster.com), whose site is shown in Figure 9-13, is working in

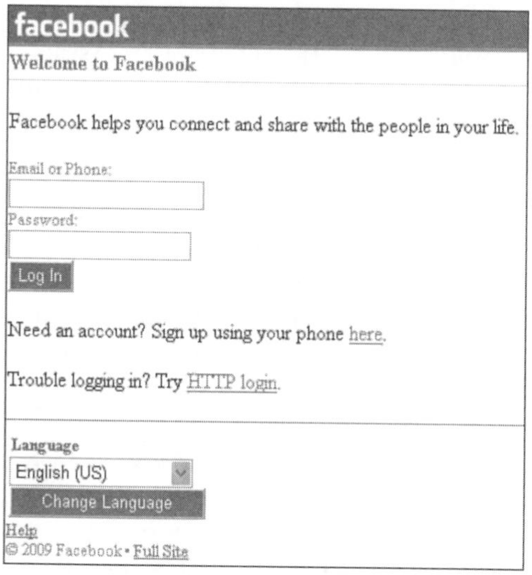

facebook

Welcome to Facebook

Facebook helps you connect and share with the people in your life.

Email or Phone:

Password:

Log In

Need an account? Sign up using your phone here.

Trouble logging in? Try HTTP login.

Language

English (US)

Change Language

Help
© 2009 Facebook • Full Site

Figure 9-12   *Facebook's Mobile webite.[86]*

partnership with mobile phone service providers to build its community.[83] JuiceCaster offers Mobile Video Search (MVS), the first service to enable users to search, access, and view video content on mobile devices.

Figure 9-13   *JuiceCaster's mobile social networking website.[83]*

Vogue magazine recently announced it plans to deliver SHOPVOGUE.TV on-demand mobile videos via JuiceCaster's MVS technology.[98] JuiceCaster users can publish photos and videos from their mobile phones to the popular photo and video storage site, Photobucket, in real time. The Flutter application enables iPhone users on JuiceCaster to send unlimited picture messages, with a link to the user's location pinned on Google Maps, to iPhones and many other mobile devices.[99] Users connect via their mobile browsers to the JuiceCaster network to take advantage of features such as MVS.

As mobile social networking evolves, it will have interesting social and business implications, particularly when member information is combined with location and presence. Imagine walking into a bar or a meeting and being able to browse and sort through photos and profile information about people around you, who are also in your network, to identify shared interest or intent.[100] Cisco is working to develop products to enable customers to leverage the new features mobility has to offer.

Mobile Web at Cisco

Cisco has long been a company that prides itself on its ability to run its business on the web. As new hires are brought on board, they are told that if they need information "it's on the web." Cisco has also been one of the leading global companies with a web presence, providing access to product information and an e-commerce engine for online product ordering.

It was only natural for Cisco to recognize the opportunity and the necessity to extend its brand and demonstrate its mobile leadership. It was also an important part of the Cisco strategy to increase customer intimacy by expanding and repurposing existing online product information services to mobile devices. As a result, Cisco created a Cisco.com mobile website offering a number of key features, including text messaging services.[101,102]

Cisco had first seen the advantage of making basic corporate information, such as news and directory, available to its employees via its intranet, then on the mobile intranet site. But more importantly, Cisco recognized the value of providing anytime, anywhere access to a number of mobile information services to its Sales organization, adding Sales services to the mobile intranet site as well. This section covers details concerning these key examples of the Mobile Web at Cisco.

Cisco.com Mobile

Cisco recognized that the growth of the mobile device market to billions of users and the evolution of mobile technology enabling high-speed wireless data would lead to customer demand for content optimized for mobile access. In 2006, Cisco began working to develop the Cisco.com mobile website. The current site, http://www.cisco.com/web/mobile/, is shown in Figure 9-14.[103] The site was designed to optimize Cisco.com content for mobile access and take advantage of mobile device functionality.

The Cisco.com Mobile website consists of

- Cisco logo
- Promotional landing area: Announcement of The Connected Life, Cisco's latest marketing campaign at The Mobile World Congress 2009

Figure 9-14   *Cisco's mobile website.[103]*

- Search bar: Searches Cisco.com

- The Human Network: Cisco marketing campaign material [1]

- New Products: Photos, videos, simple data sheets, contact links, and phone numbers for assistance [2]

- Technical Support: Click-to-dial support numbers, security advisories [3]

- Solutions: Marketing content for small business, consumer, service provider and mobility [4]

- Events: Dates and locations for Cisco Live, Virtual Cisco C-Scape, Consumer Electronics 2009, and so on [5]

- News: Headlines linked to articles on Cisco in the news [6]

- Select a Country: Content tailored (and translated) for China, France, Germany, India, Italy, Norway, Sweden, U.K., and Worldwide (which links back to the Cisco.com mobile site)[102,103] [7]

Cisco also offers information services via SMS.

Cisco Text Messaging Services

Customers, partners, and employees have the ability to stay current on Cisco news stories, product updates, security advisories, and more in the form of Cisco text messaging subscription via SMS. Users simply send a text message containing the code for the topic of interest followed by a space, followed by the word "digest" to start subscription or "stop" to stop it, to the appropriate phone number for their geographic location.

Cisco text messaging service topic codes are

- "pr" for press releases

- "fs" for feature stories

- "fn" for field notices

- "sa" for security alerts

- "sn" for security news

- "sr" for security responses

- "mobility" for news on Cisco's mobile solutions

The phone number 24726 is for subscribers in the United States and Canada, and phone number 44779780164 is for other countries, listed on Cisco's text messaging subscription page (http://www.cisco.com/web/mobile/sms.html). A user in Canada could subscribe to Cisco security alerts, for example, by sending the message "sa digest" to phone number 24726.[104] Cisco offers a number of mobile services to its employees, as you will see in the next section.

Cisco Mobile Intranet Services

Cisco's Mobility Solutions team deployed 10,000 Palm Treo 650's between September 2005 and April 2006. The team, working with 135 carriers in 89 countries worldwide, supports 26,454 mobile device users, of which 13,528 are in sales.[105] Devices currently supported include smartphones from Blackberry, Motorola, Nokia, and Samsung.[106] The team also supports Cisco's mobile services, known as Cisco Pocket Office (CPO), which enables employees to send and receive email, called Mobile Mail, and calendar messages real time.[107]

Additional services are available to employees via Cisco's intranet site, known as Cisco Employee Connection (CEC), and on Cisco's mobile intranet site, CEC Mobile, as well.[108] Because more than half of Cisco's Mobile Mail users are in sales, several sales-specific services are also available. Figure 9-15 provides a list and brief description of services provided to Cisco mobile device users via CEC Mobile.[109]

The Cisco mobile intranet site provides the following services. First are those at the top of the site:

- Directory: An abbreviated form of Cisco's employee directory, providing employee photo, reports and reporting chain, and contact information, including click-to-dial

- Select News: A variety of news channels, including global news and content for specific Cisco theatre locations

- GTRC Case Lookup: Look-up support cases logged with Cisco Global Technical Response Center

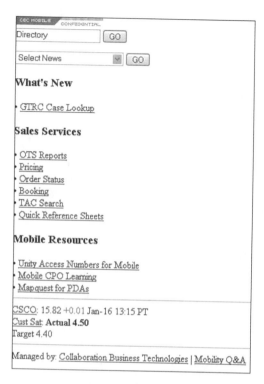

Figure 9-15   *Cisco's mobile intranet site.[108]*

Next are sales-specific services, also known as Mobile Sales Information Services (MSIS):

- OTS Reports: On the spot reports of bookings updated every 10 minutes, available to key executives

- Pricing: Search for price by product description, number, or family

- Order Status: Check order status by sales order number, purchase order number, or Internet Commerce Network (ICN) number

- Booking: Access product and service booking information, based on sales hierarchy assignment

- TAC Search: View status and history of Technical Assistance Center (TAC) service request

Next are mobile resources:

- Unity Access Numbers for Mobile: Click-to-dial numbers for Unity voicemail numbers, organized by theatre

- Mobile CPO Learning: Cisco Pocket Office (CPO) usage guides for key devices supported by the Cisco Mobility Solutions team

- MapQuest for PDAs: Link to the MapQuest Maps site

The bottom of the site provides the following:

- CSCO: The latest Cisco stock price

- Cust Sat: Actual and target customer satisfaction scores

- Collaborative Business Technologies: Feedback form

- Mobility Q&A: Answers to FAQs, support phone numbers

It is interesting to note that Mobile Web services, such as these, can play an important role in an enterprise's overall business capability delivery strategy. During a server upgrade in mid-2008, for example, Cisco's employee directory service went down. Cisco was able to leverage its mobile directory service as a temporary measure while service was restored. The next section defines the sales-specific services.

Cisco Mobile Sales Information Services

Mobile access is particularly important to the sales organization because most sales account managers and systems engineers spend a good deal of their time in the field with customers, often away from their computers. As previously mentioned, more than half of Cisco's mobile device users are in sales. Many find mobile access to sales-specific services, known as Mobile Sales Information Services (MSIS), increases their productivity, enabling anytime, anywhere access to information and services needed to do their jobs.

For two years, from mid-2006, a small team supported Cisco's MSIS, as a part of the Worldwide Sales Processes and Systems (WWSPS) organization. The team tested new devices and delivered the On the Spot (Bookings) Reports service at the end of 2007 to key executives, including CEO John Chambers. The remaining MSIS, deployed for more than three years, provide business value to Cisco sales employees and their customers.

Analysis of results of a survey of leading MSIS users, conducted mid-2006, indicates anytime, anywhere access to information

- Provides competitive advantage

- Accelerates response to customer questions

- Increases customer confidence

- Drives higher customer satisfaction

- Improves work/life balance

- Reduces follow-up time and evening workload[110]

From an internal Mobile Web application perspective, however, only a single application, the MSIS OTS (Bookings) application, has been added to the portfolio in more than three years. This is clearly an area where more could be done because there are many opportunities to enable business capabilities as mobile services worth exploring. These include mobile alerts, offering immediate click-to-resolve access to the underlying applications and systems, and streamlining and accelerating workflow.

Many day-to-day services could become accessible via the Mobile Web, including travel itinerary information, mileage and expense tracking, approvals for deals, travel, even paid time off (PTO) for vacation. As the directory service outage example mentioned previously indicates, mobile services can deliver business-critical capabilities. Finally, and perhaps most importantly, these Mobile Web services can become building blocks to develop and enable new services, combined and configured in ways we've only begun to scratch the surface of.

Take a moment now to learn about Cisco's Mobile Web strategy.

Cisco's Mobile Web Strategy

Mobile devices, and the Mobile Web applications they enable users to access, have been a key focus of this chapter. They are the piece of the puzzle that employees, partners, and customers touch—the visible component of the overall technology and infrastructure stack. Managing devices for an enterprise the size of Cisco is a complicated task.

Since 2005, Cisco's Mobility Solutions team has focused on device management for the global organization. The Mobility Solutions team works through implementation details, partnering with other Cisco teams, such as WWSPS mentioned previously, to make the tough calls on architectural and policy issues. Cisco Mobility Solutions is chartered to

- Test and evaluate new devices to ensure features such as sound quality, battery life, and so on meet user needs

- Work through device management issues, such as re-provisioning and recycling

- Partner with carriers to establish mobile services in every country where Cisco operates

- Negotiate volume discounts and cost-effective data plans, establishing creative approaches, such as minute "pooling" to reduce expenses

- Ensure Mobile Mail and other applications are provisioned and sustained, in partnership with Cisco's IT Infrastructure team

Perhaps the most important aspect of the Mobility Solutions team's job is working with Cisco Information Security to ensure global network security and data privacy policies are enforced.[111]

The Cisco product portfolio contains a number of mobility solutions designed to enable real-time collaboration across the enterprise. The goal is to provide a set of tools and capabilities that create a consistent user experience across devices, including mobile devices. Cisco Unified Mobile Communicator (CUMC), for example, is a software application that extends enterprise communications applications and services to mobile phones and smartphones.

The CUMC application enables users to

- Access company and personal directories

- View contact busy or available status

- Send secure text messages to colleagues, even when they are busy

- Receive and play back office voicemail on a mobile device

- Display a list of messages and select ones for playback

- Conference and collaborate via Cisco Unified MeetingPlace, a Cisco web-based meeting solution

CUMC also enables users to view call history on their mobile device for any of their phones.[112]

Cisco is focused on providing the best possible communication experience, seamlessly bridging handoff between networks and devices. Imagine being on a call in your office, picking up your cell phone, and continuing the conversation as you walk to a video-enabled conference room, where the call moves seamlessly to the conference room videophone or TelePresence unit, "dusting" the call between devices with a finger-flick.[113]

The Cisco WebEx Meeting Center iPhone application, available on the iPhone App Store, recently won the Macworld Expo Best of Show 2009 award. The Cisco WebEx Meeting Center product makes it possible for employees and customers around the world to collaborate, sharing documents and presentations. WebEx Connect Meeting Center for the iPhone provides a number of exciting capabilities.

With the Cisco WebEx Meeting Center application for the iPhone, users can

- Start or join a WebEx Meeting from an iPhone

- See a list of participants

- Pass the "ball" to another presenter

- Start a text chat with one or all participants

- Participate in the audio portion or join the presentation[114]

This author is lucky enough to be using the Cisco WebEx Meeting Center iPhone app every day, and loves it. The best part is that it is just one of the cool Mobile Web products Cisco has in the works and there are more to come.

Despite the global economic downturn causing lower mobile web service forecasts, Mobile Web growth is expected to continue. Decreased consumer spending, volatility of global currency, and the dwindling of available credit have caused device manufacturer Nokia to predict that device sales will decrease by 5% or more year-over-year in 2009. Nokia has also reduced its forecast for the portion of mobile services focused on text messaging, maps, gaming, music, and multi-media. Nokia's prior Mobile Web service revenue forecast of approximately $125 billion in 2010 has been reduced to $50 billion in 2011. However, this still represents a huge opportunity for companies like Cisco developing mobile applications and services for their employees, customers, and partners.[115]

In Short

Like the web, the Mobile Web continues to evolve. This chapter described that evolution, outlining the generations of mobile phone technology: 0G, 1G, 2G, 3G, and 4G. It also touched briefly on how mobile devices have changed, from Simon, the very first mobile smartphone, to Apple's iPhone 3G, one of the very latest. Several technologies, from voice recognition to position—or GPS—location have also significantly changed the services that mobile devices are able to provide to their users. Mobile application development platforms enable mobile device applications to take advantage of these device features.

Many companies and organizations have augmented their traditional websites with ones capable of providing services to a variety of mobile devices. The chapter explored web applications or webapps, providing examples of many available for the iPhone, and the notion of web portals, aggregating mobile device services such as news, sports, weather, restaurants, maps, and so on. Coverage of one example, Yahoo!'s mobile portal, explained how Yahoo! is leveraging both voice and GPS to improve services to their customers. Mobile social networking sites, such as Facebook Mobile Web and JuiceCaster, are truly changing the way people communicate and share information, photos, and videos on their mobile devices and on the web.

The final focus was on Cisco, and what Cisco has done to build out its Mobile Web presence. Cisco is clearly leader in the Mobile Web space, with its customer-facing Cisco.com and employee-facing CEC Mobile sites. The company certainly has one of the largest global workforces leveraging mobility, particularly its mobile sales force. The chapter identified the Mobile Web services Cisco currently offers to its own internal employees, particularly sales, and identified some of the business value of the Mobile Web. Finally, the chapter also provided a peek at Cisco's Mobile Web strategy and its award-winning WebEx Meeting Center application for the iPhone.

The power of the Mobile Web is evident when you consider examples like the "macaca moment," when an unfortunate remark by former Sen. George Allen (R-Va.) was captured on video, posted on the web, and cost him his reelection.[116] The Mobile Web offers business value, providing anytime, anywhere access to information that can increase productivity and streamline and accelerate processes. Like Cisco, Web 2.0 and mobility Cisco's company vision is "Changing The Way We Work, Live, Play, and Learn[SM]." This certainly applies to Web 2.0 and mobility at Cisco as well.

<monologue>

Cisco, a company that prides itself on its ability to anticipate and prepare for market transitions, is taking steps to evolve into the next generation company—Cisco 3.0, reinventing itself around Web 2.0 and then taking the lessons learned to its customers. A world leader in networking for the Internet, Cisco now leads the business revolution caused by the move to the Internet. The company is evolving organizationally to distribute decision-making, innovate faster, bring products to market sooner, and capitalize on market transitions, such as ubiquitous video and visual networking.

Cisco is using Web 2.0 technologies—such as Cisco TelePresence, Cisco WebEx, and Unified Communications—to enable collaboration between employees, partners, and customers, yielding increased productivity and deeper relationships. Leveraging other Web 2.0 technologies, such as blogs and wikis, and new business models, such as social networking and folksonomies, the company is increasing peer-to-peer collaboration and ideation and transforming key business processes. Cisco is sharing case studies showcasing its own business process transformations with partners and customers, evolving its leadership consultancy.

</monologue>

CHAPTER 10

Web 2.0 @ Cisco: The Evolution

This chapter offers a case study of Web 2.0 adoption at Cisco, detailing the evolutionary changes the introduction of Web 2.0 technology and tools is having on the company. Although Chapter 2, "User Generated Content Wikis, Blogs, Communities, Collaboration, and Collaborative Technologies," provides a more in-depth overview of each of these technologies, the following sections

- Provide a brief introduction to what Web 2.0 means at Cisco

- Examine how Cisco's Intranet Strategy Group vision enabled Web 2.0 technology adoption across the company

- Explain how Cisco's Web 2.0 technology vision has evolved

- Offer practical advice from Cisco's lessons learned

- Provide examples of how each technology is being used internally with employees and externally with partners and customers

- Underscore the organizational and process transformations underway

- Highlight the business value achieved

- Describe the groups currently leading Cisco's adoption of Web 2.0 technology

- Outline Cisco's internal website, which provides Cisco employees with the information they need to effectively use Web 2.0 technologies

- Showcase Web 2.0 technology adoption metrics

- Describe the Communication and Collaboration Board now leading this effort

Cisco's evolutionary approach to Web 2.0 technology and tool adoption serves as a model for other companies, yielding practical advice and examples for others to follow. So, let's begin with a closer look at what Web 2.0 means at Cisco.

As Figure 10-1 indicates, as a worldwide leader in networking, Cisco played a key role in the first phase of the Internet, Web 1.0. Cisco products power the network:

- Providing the pipes connecting people with personal computers (PCs) to the web, getting people online

- Transporting data around the globe

- Enabling email, instant messaging, e-commerce and other web-based applications

Figure 10-1 *Cisco Systems: Worldwide leader in networking for the Internet.[1]*

As Chapter 1, "An Introduction to Web 2.0," mentioned, the term "Web 2.0" was defined in Tim O'Reilly's pioneering article "What is Web 2.0," published in 2005.[2] According to O'Reilly, Web 2.0 is the business revolution in the computer industry. The revolution was caused by the move to the Internet as a platform, and an attempt to understand the rules for success on that new platform.[3]

This chapter describes how Cisco is taking evolutionary steps to lead the Web 2.0 business revolution internally and with its partners and customers to show them how to use the web and Web 2.0 tools effectively. O'Reilly also touts a fundamental Web 2.0 principle, "The Web as [the] Platform," which aligns with Cisco's strategy as well. In Web 2.0, Cisco networks serve as the platform that transports data, voice, and video beyond PCs to Internet telephones, cell phones, PDAs, iPods, video game consoles, and televisions.

John Chambers, Cisco's chairman and chief executive officer, has long held a vision of the intelligent network serving as a platform for pervasive and ubiquitous communications for users at home and at work, providing access to people, information, and applications regardless of location, access method, or device. The quote from Chambers, shown in Figure 10-2, describes this evolution as a key element of Cisco's strategy, a story based on market transitions, or change, and its effect on Cisco customers.

Cisco recognizes that the network is at the center of a number of market transitions as it evolves from the pipes or plumbing, connecting the Internet, to the platform enabling people to share and experience life via social networking and Web 2.0. Cisco prepares 3–5 years in advance of a major transition. It does so by listening to customers, taking risks, innovating and investing, so that it can capitalize on the transition when it is realized in the market.

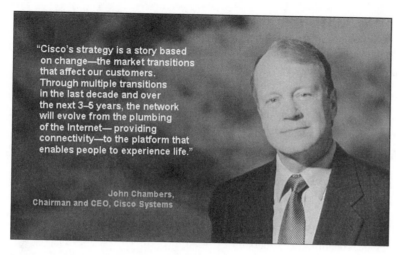

"Cisco's strategy is a story based on change—the market transitions that affect our customers. Through multiple transitions in the last decade and over the next 3–5 years, the network will evolve from the plumbing of the Internet— providing connectivity—to the platform that enables people to experience life."

John Chambers,
Chairman and CEO, Cisco Systems

Figure 10-2 *Cisco's corporate story.[4]*

Chambers believes the changes that affect Cisco's customers most define Cisco's competitive opportunities, saying, "By the time our competitors recognize the transition, it's too late to catch up." Cisco's ability to anticipate and prepare for market transitions is critical to Cisco's success and the success of its customers. The Internet isn't a network of computers; it's a network of billions of people worldwide. Cisco calls this the Human Network.[4]

The forward-looking strategy for Cisco is enabling the company to unleash the power of "human network effect" both inside and outside the company. In the midst of a spiraling economy, Cisco has $26 billion in cash and two dozen products in development. Many of the 26 new market adjacencies for Cisco will produce revenue within three to four years; perhaps 25% of its revenue within five years. Approximately 75% of the revenue for Cisco comes from the pipes that keep the data moving across the web: routers, switches, and advanced technologies. Cisco anticipates a market transition caused by the hunger for video, which will lead to company spending on network and infrastructure upgrades that, by 2013, are expected to reach $50 billion.

Internally, the company has begun to reorganize. Cisco is moving from an organization with one or two primary products where all decisions came from 10 people at the top, to one with its leadership and decision-making spread across the organization. Now a network of cross-functional, interdepartmental councils and boards, working groups consisting of 500 top executives, from Cisco's global, international workforce are responsible for one another's success, innovate much faster, and launch new businesses together.

Cisco is now bringing resources together to bring more of its growing portfolio of products to market sooner, especially to new markets. For instance,

- **StadiumVision:** A board of 15 people built this new Cisco product that enables sports venue owners and stadium operators to push video, digital content, and targeted advertisements to fans during sporting events, then collaborated with sales and marketing to sell it. **Result:** A multimillion-dollar business deal with the Arizona Cardinals, Dallas Cowboys, and New York Yankees developed in less than four months.

- **MediaNet:** A council-developed strategy for a prototype of this new Cisco network platform, designed to carry rich media, such as high-quality video, securely to any screen, including TVs, PCs, and mobile devices. **Result:** Prototype developed in four months, product available in twelve.

This new distributed leadership structure and resulting faster product innovation and delivery ensures Cisco products are positioned to gain market share.

Cisco is transforming itself from a being a technology company to a leadership consultancy to other businesses as well. Having tried this new model first itself, Cisco has begun sharing case studies and best practices with customers from emerging markets such as China, Russia, Mexico, and Brazil and with other large corporations, such as Proctor & Gamble, AT&T, and General Electric, all wanting to learn from Cisco's experience. Analysts predict that the collaboration marketplace could be a $34 billion opportunity.[5] Cisco wants to be the name that comes to mind when companies think about collaboration technologies and collaborative leadership.

Cisco is leading the effort to drive greater communication and collaboration between people, evolving the network with its own products and other Web 2.0 technologies and breaking down barriers between the company and its partners. For example, Cisco is using collaboration technologies such as Cisco TelePresence, Cisco WebEx, and Unified Communications, described in Chapter 2. By incorporating these collaboration technologies into its core business processes, Cisco is transforming those processes.

Cisco is fundamentally changing the way employees, customers, and partners work together. These efforts are yielding increased productivity and deeper relationships, balancing innovation with operational excellence.[6] Cisco is leveraging new Web 2.0 technologies, such as wikis and blogs, and new business models, such as social networking and folksonomies, to increase peer-to-peer collaboration and innovation.[7]

Cisco is making the next-generation workforce experience, mentioned briefly in Chapter 1, a reality by enabling users to

- Connect to access the right people, content, and other resources, anytime, anywhere they're required

- Communicate with greater efficiency and overall effectiveness

- Collaborate with others, both inside and outside the company

- Learn from other members of the human network

But take a step back to learn how these evolutionary Web 2.0 technology changes started.

Intranet Strategy Group

Cisco has been recognized as an industry leader for its customer- and employee-facing websites almost since their inception. In December 1996, *CommunicationsWeek* announced that Cisco's customer-facing e-commerce site, Cisco Connection Online (CCO), at http://www.cisco.com, had achieved $75 million in sales since its launch five months earlier. The article heralded the fact that Cisco was predicting $1 billion in sales by fiscal year end.[8]

Eighteen months later, CIO Communications selected Cisco's intranet as a winner of its "WebMaster 50/50 Award" in the Intranet category. The award focused on selecting 50 exemplary Internet sites and 50 intranets for excellence in execution, innovative use of technologies, and demonstrated benefits from over 700 applicants.[9] The Intranet Strategy Group, part of the Employee Commitment team in Cisco's Human Resources organization, was responsible for developing Cisco's intranet, Cisco Employee Connection (CEC).

In March 2005, the Nielson Norman Group, a user-experience research group, recognized Cisco's Intranet Strategy Group in its "Intranet Design Annual 2005: The Year's Ten Best Intranets." Cisco and nine others were chosen, in part, for providing productivity tools for their employees. This media recognition helped to establish Cisco as a clear leader in both the Internet and intranet domains.

The Cisco Intranet Group realized the value of community, establishing its own internally-focused Intranet Excellence Award, a precursor to the current Collaboration Across Cisco Award. According to then Group leader, Matthew Burns, the award recognizes those not just implementing standards, but working with their team and others to add new capabilities that others can leverage.[10] In the months that followed, many internal Cisco teams received the Intranet Excellence Award, not only for working collaboratively and sharing best practices, but for helping to extend the intranet community within their respective organizations—in essence social networking had begun!

It was a natural extension of the Intranet Strategy Group's charter, recognizing a need for collaborative tools to enable employee productivity, to begin exploring Web 2.0 technologies. Early explorations, for example, focused on blogs, discussion forums, and wikis. The team's Web 2.0 vision of an integrated Web 2.0 *Enterprise* Experience was presented by Burns at Intranet Week 2007 and is shown in Figure 10-3.

To realize the integrated Web 2.0 *Enterprise* Experience vision, Web 2.0 technologies were seamlessly incorporated as elements of Cisco's intranet page design templates. Other enterprise services and tools, such as Cisco's new Facebook-style internal employee directory service, Directory 3.0; Cisco's version of Wikipedia, called Ciscopedia; collaborative communities; and video assets collected in a home-grown YouTube-like tool called C-Vision were incorporated as well. The Intranet Strategy Group began systematically piloting and testing each Web 2.0 technology, establishing a vision for how it would evolve and integrate with other technologies, services and tools.

The following sections outline Cisco's exploration and the evolution of several of these key Web 2.0 technologies.

Web 2.0 *Enterprise* Experience

Integrated *Enterprise* Experience

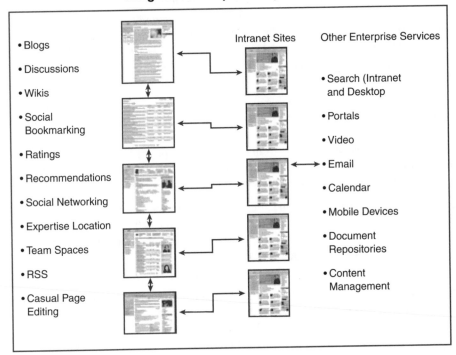

- Blogs
- Discussions
- Wikis
- Social Bookmarking
- Ratings
- Recommendations
- Social Networking
- Expertise Location
- Team Spaces
- RSS
- Casual Page Editing

Intranet Sites

Other Enterprise Services

- Search (Intranet and Desktop
- Portals
- Video
- Email
- Calendar
- Mobile Devices
- Document Repositories
- Content Management

Figure 10-3 *Cisco's Web 2.0 Enterprise Experience.[11]*

Blogs

The Intranet Strategy Group began a blog (short for "web log") pilot. This effort was designed to enable employees to publish comments, opinions, and other information on work-related topics. In preparation for the rollout, the group envisioned three different types of blogs: employee, concept, and group blogs.[11]

This vision has evolved slightly to the current blog types listed on the CCoE site:

- **Personal Blog:** Enable employees to publish a personal journal on work-related topics.

- **Project/Team Blog (Concept Blog):** Enable project/teams to communicate, connected to project/team documents and data.

- **Executive Blog:** Enable organization/enterprise executives to communicate less formally and enable employees to comment.

Personal blogs are designed to be integrated with the Cisco employee directory, providing an opportunity for an individual to present thoughts, offer opinions on work-related topics, and add another dimension to a personal profile. Michael Beesley, director of engineering in Cisco's edge-routing business unit, has one of the most popular personal blogs, writing about such topics as "ASR Completes Security Testing."[5] Cisco employees are required, however, to post non-work-related topics on blogs outside the intranet.

Cisco is working to enable blogs focused on specific topics or concepts and others targeted at specific communities or groups. Concept blogs will be integrated with specific intranet site pages, offering content from experts, news, and/or project updates. Group blogs will be integrated with specific communities of interest. The latest vision for internal blogs also includes expert and news blogs.[12]

Cisco has a number of popular Executive or C-level blogs. One is Chambers' "On My Mind" blog, shown in Figure 10-4. It has been one of the most popular blogs at Cisco, with nearly 100,000 hits from its inception in June 2007 to the end of January 2009.[13] Note that the blog provides a video and an opportunity to subscribe via RSS feed.

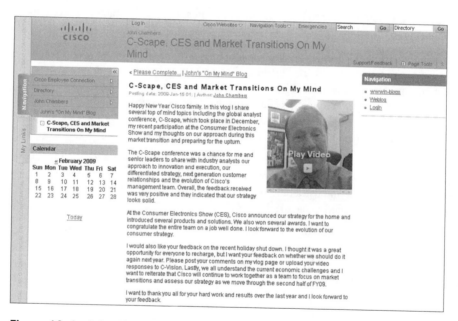

Figure 10-4 *John Chambers' "On My Mind" blog, posted 15 January 2009.[14]*

Jere King, vice president of marketing, is another example. Her blog has been second to that of Chambers in terms of comments since its inception.[14] King is using her blog to drive communication, feedback, and productivity forward. She has taken it upon herself to act as a change agent in her organization and has a few tips on what makes her blog so successful:

- **Consistency:** Publish a new blog entry on the same day, every week, say Friday.

- **Call to Action:** Every blog entry should have a specific call to comment—something to focus that week's conversation, a reason to interact.

- **Promotion:** Promote each new blog entry, again on the same day every week, via an email newsletter to the team. In addition, post it as the "Top of Mind" feature on Cisco's marketing homepage.

- **Quick Response:** Check the blog every day and immediately respond to comments. Email other team members when something is relevant to their area, or they would be a good person to comment back and continue the conversation.

- **Changing Behaviors:** Use every opportunity to push the blog—even putting off live discussions in meetings if there is a virtual discussion on that topic already in the blog.

- **Be a Story Teller:** Capture and keep the reader's attention by telling a story.

- **Create an Online Watering Hole:** Get people to gather, discuss, share ideas—think water cooler!

- **Make It Worthwhile:** Have passion, be engaged, and have something to say.[15]

These tips have enabled King to become one of the most popular bloggers at Cisco and her model is emulated by many.

According to Deanna Govoni, program manager for Cisco's blog initiative, each blog basically serves as a website maintained by an author, or group of authors, containing news and/or commentary on specific subject matter, delivered in a professional manner. As a means of one-to-many communication, authors drive the conversation and create and post topics. Their purpose could be to showcase thought leadership, engage others in communication, and receive feedback.

Cisco's initial blog pilot led to a development of a number of guidelines and best practices posted on the Communications Center of Excellence (CCoE) site. Govoni encourages Cisco bloggers to create and use a blog based on the outcome they're looking for. For example, users are encouraged to blog if they

- Want to engage a community on a specific topic

- Have identified a target audience and objective

- Have something interesting to say

- Have passion surrounding a chosen topic

- Have knowledge to share with others

- Want to gather feedback and start a conversation

- Want to network with peers

- Want to stop spamming colleagues

Cisco wants users to leverage blogs to start conversations and improve communications.

To help ensure Cisco bloggers are successful, Govoni and her team have identified several guidelines on when *not* to use a blog. Users are discouraged from using a blog if they:

- Don't have enough resources or content to maintain

- Are unable to respond to comments

- Don't have a clear topic

- Are simply regurgitating news

- Are looking to foster a fully interactive discussion (use a discussion forum here instead)

Because one purpose of a blog is to start a conversation and get feedback, Govoni has also identified a number of blogging best practices:

- Update blog frequently, at least once a week.

- Be transparent.

- Respond to comments quickly to keep listeners engaged.

- Ensure blog does not interfere with primary employment responsibilities.

Most successful bloggers would agree that these best practices ring true. Finally, Govoni also has a number of guidelines on increasing blog traffic:

- Be entertaining, and show your personality/video/photos.

- Locate relevant blogs in your niche and engage in the conversation.

- Promote your blog.

- Collaborate with your peers.

- Participate in other blogs.

- Use trackbacks (links within blogs) to connect to other blogs to keep traffic flowing.

- Keep your blog current.

One other suggestion is to end each blog with a question, such as "What do you think?" to start the conversation. [16]

CCO, the Cisco external site mentioned previously, has evolved into much more than an e-commerce site. Known as Cisco.com, the site offers information on solutions, products and services, ordering, support, training and events. Cisco.com is also home to Partner Central, an area focused on Cisco's partner community described in Chapter 11, "Cisco's Approach to Sales 2.0".[17]

The Cisco.com site contains a fairly hip consumer section. This section provides helpful consumer-focused blog posts and twitters in an area called DigItALL Consumer. Its "Digital Crib," section enables video blogger Meghan Asher, video artist Lincoln Schatz, and NBA player and Houston Rockets forward Shane Battier to share videos on their digital lifestyles.[5]

Cisco has also enabled several external business blogs, available at http://blogs.cisco.com. These blogs are used to

- Provide insights and opinions from Cisco leaders and corporate representatives to showcase thought leadership.

- Provide product information and updates and solicit valuable feedback from the blogosphere, including customers, partners, and competitors.

- Enable event reporting and create event logs.

Be sure to note "More Cisco Talk" at the bottom of the column on the left side.[12][18]

As a company, Cisco has begun realizing the business value of this new medium, leveraging blogs strategically to reach customers and influence the marketplace. In 2007, Mark Chandler, SVP, Legal Services and General Counsel, worked with Cisco's public relations team to reach out to the public via Cisco's corporate blog. This occurred during a trademark case concerning the iPhone, and led to Chandler winning PR News' Legal PR Award 2008 for Best Spokesperson.[19]

In 2008, Cisco's Data Center team used Cisco's corporate blog to engage in a heated debate with Dell over data center storage networking protocols. According to Data Center Knowledge (http://www.DataCenterKnowledge.com), the discussion provided an overview of the competition between several technologies and showcased the way Cisco and Dell are using blogs to advocate next-generation technologies they support.[20] The Data Center team has also successfully leveraged blogs to help launch a new product.

Members of Cisco's Data Center team leveraged both intranet and the Internet blogs to increase awareness of the Data Center 3.0 product. The Data Center 3.0 Blog initiative

- Was used to help launch the new Data Center 3.0 product.

- Engaged tier 1 and 2 bloggers on the Internet.

- Built and nurtured relationships.

- Transferred knowledge and passion about technology on blogs focused on data centers (topics and concepts).

- Offered editorial content and influenced opinions.

- Engaged in conversations with top data center experts (groups and communities).

- Provided opportunity to enter data center communities the team was not previously part of.

- Became as influential as the data center-focused press and business analysts.

- Provided lower-cost marketing approach.

Moreover, it provided a key learning opportunity for the team to understand the power of leveraging this new medium as a way of marketing their product.[21]

Prior to the Cisco Live 2008 event, Cisco worked to build community and create buzz in Twitter, an externally hosted micro-blogging tool. Participants Twittered throughout the event, using it as a business communication tool. This experience enabled them to capture some of Twitter's key features:

- Provides a fun tool to help users network.

- Enables users to follow peers/friends to keep up to date.

- Limits "Tweet" to a 140-character message (mini RSS feed).

- Users can monitor conversations and build relationships.

- Has low cost and high impact.

Twitter provided another medium for reaching the public and established a number of Twitter-based Cisco communities of "twitterers" and their followers.[16] Finally, Cisco blog comments have been integrated with discussion forums, so that comments on a blog can be maintained as an ongoing discussion, as needed.

Discussion Forums

To achieve its integrated Web 2.0 *Enterprise* Experience, Cisco's Intranet Strategy Group also launched an initial discussion forum pilot. They began to enable employees to share thoughts and ideas and start threaded conversations, to discuss topics, and to ask questions and get answers from the Cisco community. The group envisioned several ways Cisco employees could use discussion forums including as a means of exchanging ideas on designated topics, and as a way to facilitate information exchange within a team or group.

The group realized that discussion topics of common interest could be registered on an enterprise site, enabling experts to share knowledge on a particular subject. The main idea was to foster and chronicle fully interactive conversations between individuals, subject matter experts, groups, and teams. Although blogs were identified as the means of one person posting their ideas and getting feedback, employees were encouraged to use discussion forums to enable multiple people to participate in the conversation.

The Intranet Strategy Group identified several integration points for discussion forums: integration with intranet site content, with community context, and as a connection from blog comments.[11] Cisco users are able to navigate through the hierarchy of discussion areas, selecting from among the various discussion topics. Like blogs, discussion forums are RSS-enabled, so users can subscribe to get updates on their favorite topics. Also, forums enable users to click on the name of the forum poster, which links to a page showing that person's activity in the forum space and, eventually, a link to his or her Cisco Directory information page.

Each organization has appointed a point of contact or team to manage forums within their organization.[22] At the end of January 2009 there were more than a hundred open group discussion forums, and the top five forums with the most threads were Wikis, Blogs (Internal), Discussion Forums, General Discussions, and Collaboration Learning.[23] And that doesn't include discussion forums enabled through collaboration community tools that have evaluated or deployed.

Cisco's discussion forum pilot led to the establishment of a few basic guidelines provided by Molly Barry, web program/project manager for Cisco's discussion forum initiative, also highlighted on the CCoE site. Barry suggests discussion forums

- Should be used to foster and chronicle fully interactive conversations.

- Occur between individuals, subject matter experts, groups, and teams working together and/or needing information, answers, or solutions that can be added to and referenced anytime.

- Enable gathering of feedback and multiple opinions.

- Establish a venue for community-driven support as well as Q&A.

According to Barry, discussion forum usage at Cisco also led to a few guidelines on when to use them. For example, users should use a discussion forum when they

- Intend to foster or display a dialogue between individuals, groups, and teams.

- Can provide support for questions and answers as a reference to an audience.

And, of course, the pilot also helped identify a few guidelines on when not to use them, such as when users

- Don't desire or need to start a full conversation.

- Are unable to regularly monitor the forum and respond to messages posted there.[24]

Discussion forums launched enterprise-wide in March 2008.

One particularly interesting example of a successful discussion forum at Cisco is the one built by Cisco's green-minded employees. Cisco's EcoBoard, established in October 2006, developed the vision and strategy to enable the company to be more "green" through its operations, products, and architecture solutions for its customers.[25] In an effort to augment traditional forms of communication, email, news stories, and so on, Kenis Dunne, executive communication manager, launched the "Let's Talk" discussion forum, shown in Figure 10-5. Note the video feature contained in the forum page.

Dunne started a number of discussion forum threads on the site to facilitate conversations on Cisco's green initiative and topics such as telecommuting and water bottles. Key takeaways, according to Dunne, include the following:

- Leverage a logical framework to guide the pattern of discussion threads.

- Mirror content employees begin seeing elsewhere.

- Partner with subject matter experts to enhance content.

- The best enabler for success is a community already interested in your body of work.

- Look viral, but act strategic.

- Watch each thread, let software prompt you with updates.

- The goal is to be effective and accurate and avoid miscommunication.

- Use as an additional communication channel to augment news.

- Push to eliminate email while extending access to the full story.

- Promote awareness via voicemail and executive champions.

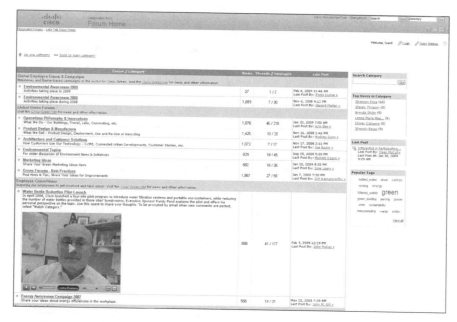

Figure 10-5 *Cisco's green "Let's Talk" discussion forum.[26]*

- Forums provide more in-depth, effective commentary on a topic than a survey.

- Forums give employees a place to have their voices heard.

The forum is also associated with Cisco's internal employee website as a means to keep employees current on this popular environmental initiative.[27]

Cisco has established a number of internal discussion forums focused on providing technical support to employees. Maya Winthrop, for example, is listed as Cisco's top discussion forum contributor. With nearly 450 posts, Winthrop moderates a cross-functional CCoE technologies and tools forum, answering user questions on WebEx Connect, the iPhone, and so on.[28]

Cisco IT is currently leveraging a discussion forum to support rolling out WebEx Connect across the company. The forum contains threads focused on service alerts, frequently asked questions (FAQs), support, suggested enhancements, and so on.[29] User feedback gained from these threads provides the product support team with insight into performance issues and training needs, but more importantly user requests for enhancements and new features help shape product support and development.

In addition, Cisco's WebEx Connect user community can not only provide ideas for new features and help prioritize them, but also support one another or develop solutions and share them with the community. Recently, new WebEx Connect users identified a need to invite entire groups to join a Connect team space, using a Cisco Mailer alias list as the source of names in the group. Because the capability was not on the product delivery roadmap, members of the Connect user community devised steps to enable the capability, which was turned into the Cisco Mailer BulkInvite Widget made available soon afterward.[30]

Cisco is also using discussion forums to support customers and partners. At Linksys, for example, voluntary discussion forums with customers and partners, in the form of message boards, have been in use for some time. The reasons are simple: Forums engage customers, and engaged customers stay customers and spend more. Customers use forums to find answers, to connect with others, and to make a contribution.

Customers engaged in discussions remain on the company website 50% longer, and the customers who most frequently post comments on discussion forums actually spend more. According to the 90-9-1 rule, 90% of customers browse and look at discussion forums, but may never post; 9% participate; 1% will post most of the content. That 1% is considered the super user, the person that raises a hand and contributes.

The importance of recognizing contribution to discussion forums cannot be overstated, as even just one super user can save the company huge amounts in support costs. At Cisco's Linksys and other companies, support forums are being used in lieu of phone support to help reduces costs. Live customer support, for example, costs 87% more per transaction than forums and other self-service options.

Another advantage to discussion forums, besides costs, is the quantity and quality of the content itself. The tribal knowledge that customers, partners, product teams, sales, support, services, and marketing personnel accumulate through discussion on a particular question or problem can be provided in a self-service mode. It can also serve as a knowledge base for new hires and phone support teams.[31]

Implemented successfully, discussion forums can add huge value to the business, particularly if the quality level of the content is closely guarded and exceptional behavior is applauded. Forums require ongoing management, promotion, and strong signposting to drive traffic to them. They also require the proper structure and atmosphere to remain healthy, that is, to engage users and keep them coming back.

In a healthy community there will be at least 5–10 posts per day. This significantly reduces back-and-forth email traffic as the conversation takes place via the forum. In some Cisco forums, a hundred or more daily posts may occur, as engineers around the globe often contribute to technical forums, again reducing Cisco email traffic.

Cisco learned the value of enabling external customers and partners to participate in customer service–focused community forums on Christmas Eve 2006, when an earthquake that hit the South Pacific brought down its Linksys contact centers. The holidays are a busy time for the centers as consumers who buy Linksys products as presents reach out with questions. Instead, customers turned to a forum, enabled through Lithium Technologies' online community–based CRM solution, for support and customers began helping customers.

The online community enabled super users, many of whom were non-employees, to share their knowledge, answering questions about Linksys products, providing live, peer-based support throughout the holiday rush. The community response even enabled Linksys to discontinue customer support via email, reducing support costs. By mid-2008 the Linksys community forum had 100,000 registered users and more than 7 million views. This story was broadly communicated, which in itself proved rewarding to those who took part.[32] Now let's turn our attention to wikis.

Wikis

One of the most widely adopted Web 2.0 technologies at Cisco has been the wiki platform, enabling Cisco employees and teams to publish pages of web content, which others can edit and to which they can contribute. The Intranet Strategy Group identified a number of potential uses for wikis at Cisco, such as project and team collaboration and ideation, or the generation of ideas. As they rolled out the wiki pilot, they identified a need to develop templates to help teams develop wiki sites faster and to create consistency across various sites.

The Internet Strategy Group identified the importance of tool usability and ease of navigation, both in the tool used to create the wiki sites and within the sites themselves. The group also identified the need for integration with team spaces, Cisco's document repositories, and other services.[11] Figure 10-6, for example, shows a wiki page meant to serve as an information source for the Manager Portal project. It provides a description of the project, a list of team members (linked to Cisco Directory), weekly project updates, and links to release status documentation, enabling the team to stay aligned and better manage the portal development project.

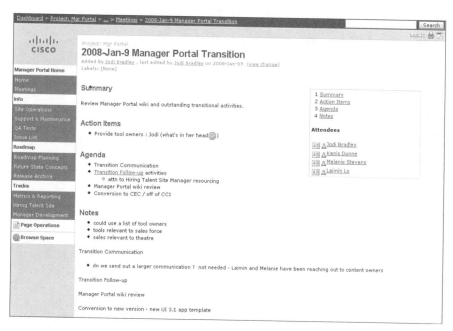

Figure 10-6   *Manager portal wiki.[33]*

The Cisco Customer Advocacy Remote Operations Services (ROS) team built a network operations–related knowledge base on a wiki-like framework, called a twiki. In 2006, solutions architect Craig Tobias came up with the idea of creating wiki pages, like file drawers, on every topic he could think of related to the complex task of proactively monitoring, managing, and securing complex network infrastructures. Tobias pulled together the team of individuals responsible for supporting this area within Cisco and asked them to leverage their knowledge and experience to add content to each topic.

The ROS wiki allowed the team to contribute content directly through their browsers, enabling multiple people to contribute content to a single document. It also facilitated continuous improvement of the content, enabling the team to refine each document over time, based on peer review. According to Tobias, wikis

- Are a key part of a larger community platform.

- Focus on consolidating fact-based information.

- Enable users to contribute via their browsers.

- Facilitate multiple people contributing to a single document, refining its content over time.

- Embody the practice of peer review.

Tobias and his team developed well over a hundred pages of content, a knowledge base that saves customers and employees countless hours of network diagnosis and problem-solving.

Tobias also has a number of wiki best practices and lessons learned, as follows:

- **Information Architecture:** Start with a solid framework.

- **Branding:** Give your wiki an identity.

- **Navigation:** Make your site easy to navigate.

- **Images:** A picture is worth a thousand words.

- **Open:** Be open; lock as little down as possible.

- **Purpose:** Clearly state what you're trying to do.

- **Support:** Support users so they'll contribute.

- **Training:** Provide user training.

- **Drive Adoption:** The more users contribute, the better your content.

The ROS wiki has been so successful and well-received that customers often subscribe to Cisco's ROS just to gain access to the knowledge base.[34] Now let's turn our attention to another use case, an example of wiki-driven collaboration and innovation.

In August 2006, the Emerging Markets Technology Group (EMTG) set up a wiki as a collaborative platform, called I-Zone. The site was designed to enable the entire company to submit and brainstorm on ideas for new businesses. The I-Zone initiative, led by Guido Jouret, vice president and chief technology officer in EMTG, has enabled Cisco to benefit from ideas from anywhere in the company, leveraging collaboration to drive new growth markets.[7]

Since its inception, the I-Zone team has reviewed hundreds of ideas and the process has already yielded success. In 2007, the I-Zone wiki led to the incubation of four new Cisco business units. In 2008, ideas captured through I-Zone led to the start of one additional business unit each quarter.

I-Zone has provided an open forum where ideas for new products, as well as new ways to use existing Cisco products, can be posted and others can comment or pose questions on the ideas. In this way, average ideas can trigger collaboration that yields idea improvement or an even better idea. Ideas are also kept on file for consideration at a later date because timing often plays a part in whether an idea should move forward, and today's good idea might look even better tomorrow.

The team has recently moved I-Zone to a leading innovation social networking platform, Brightidea. The new platform enables employees to post their ideas, vote on and browse for ideas, and get the latest information on idea submissions. Now the I-Zone wiki legacy lives on in another Cisco organization.[35]

In November 2007, a group within Customer Advocacy (CA) decided to leverage a wiki platform to enable CA employees to collaborate more effectively. The initiative, led by Patrick Tam, operations manager in CA's Office of Strategy and Planning (U.S.), is known as CA Collaboratory, as shown in Figure 10-7.

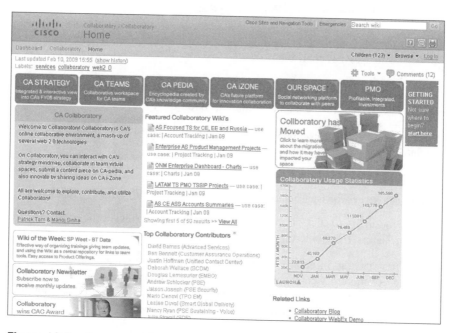

Figure 10-7 *Customer Advocacy's Collaboratory wiki site.[36]*

Collaboratory consists of a number of wiki-based components:

- **CA Strategy:** An interactive and integrated view of CA's FY08 strategy.

- **CA Teams:** A set of collaborative workspaces for CA teams organized by theaters, functions, and governance councils.

- **CA-pedia:** An encyclopedia of CA-related content and knowledge, built by the community.

- **CA I-Zone:** A future platform for CA collaboration on innovative ideas (similar to EMTG's I-Zone).

- **Our Space:** A social networking platform for peer-to-peer collaboration within the organization.

- **(Services) PMO:** A comprehensive view of CA's FY09 initiative investment portfolio.

The site also features a Wiki of the Week and a top contributors list, related links, and Collaboratory usage statistics. As Figure 10-8 shows, Collaboratory has grown from 22,000 plus users, just after its launch in November 2007, to well over 165,000 users at the end of 2008, one reason the site has moved to its own, dedicated server.[36]

According to Tam, key Collaboratory facts include:

- Serves as Customer Advocacy's internal Web 2.0 platform.

- Developed to present CA strategy in a multi-dimensional way.

- Centralizes information about CA via CA-pedia.

- Provides directory of 70+ CA teams.

- 10% of CA employees contribute.

- Had 26,000 hits within first two months.

The CA Strategy wiki, shown in Figure 10-8, is used to

- Communicate the organization's complex, multi-dimensional FY10 Strategy Architecture.

- Support fiscal year planning.

- Enable employees to visualize how their initiatives connect to other CA initiatives.

- Provide the ability to click on an initiative and drill down to review initiative objectives, challenges, risks, milestones, and financials.

Within two months of its inception, more than 50 global CA teams had built workspaces as part of the Collaboratory community, sharing information on initiatives, projects, and team knowledge through a wiki-based knowledge base called CA-pedia. In June 2008, Collaboratory won the coveted Collaboration Across Cisco Award, mentioned earlier in the chapter.[38]

There are several other Cisco examples of wikis being leveraged as a community support platform. For instance, Cisco IT supports Windows-based PCs as official desktop hardware, so Mac users have established their own Mac-Wiki support community, Mac Trolls. The site provides a wealth of useful information, enabling new Mac users to become productive more quickly and offering experienced users the opportunity to learn and share their knowledge and innovative ideas as well. Mac-Wiki won the Collaboration Across

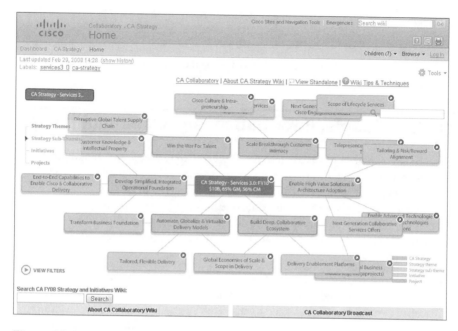

Figure 10-8 *Customer Advocacy's strategy wiki site.[37]*

Cisco Award in January 2008, acknowledging over 100 key contributors and distilled content from more than 40,000 emails at the time.[39]

Another example is the recently launched WebEx Connect Community wiki, providing links to

- Best practices

- Clearinghouse for submitting Connect feature enhancements

- FAQs

- Getting started information

- Metrics reports on Connect adoption and usage

- Program team and key stakeholders

- Program tracks and status updates (metrics, performance testing)

- Related blogs and initiatives across Cisco

- Service alerts and resolutions

- Support and learning resources

- Tips and tricks

- Use cases

- Widget approval and governance

■ Widgets

Developed through a collaborative partnership between the Connect IT team, the US-Canada Collaboration team, and others, the wiki-based community site offers support to WebEx Connect users across the company.[40]

Connecting People, Information, and Communities

An important component of Cisco's Intranet Strategy Group vision was recognition of a need to improve employee access to people, information, and communities, which led to Cisco's Directory 3.0, Ciscopedia, and Communities initiatives. In 2006, Cisco's Directory provided contact details, such as photo, title, organization, phone, email, and address for the global workforce, totaling more than 50,000. The organization realized the need to make it easier to search through this content, to find the right person to answer a question or assist on a project.

The Directory team studied a number of possible approaches to connecting people and the decision was made to add an Expertise section to existing Directory entries. This new release, called Directory 3.0, is designed to enable connections between people, groups, and information to facilitate teamwork, collaboration, and networking across the company. The Facebook-style pages enable employees to easily find the right person to answer a question, provide a product demo to a customer, or make a conference presentation, anywhere, anytime, in any language. The first Directory 3.0 employee profile prototype is shown in Figure 10-9.

The Intranet Strategy Group developed mock-ups and held focus groups across the organization to obtain feedback on the new design and then began to implement it. Numerous additional changes were made to the user interface before Phase 1 of Directory 3.0 was rolled out in March 2008. Phase 1 adds an "Expertise" section designed to enable the workforce to enter keywords or phrases identifying business or technical knowledge so that a search of Directory 3.0 will enable users to quickly find people with the required expertise.

Directory 3.0 Phase 2, launched at the end of January 2009, offers new features and functionality, as well as improved performance and scalability, providing a powerful foundation that enables individual, information, and community connections. Directory 3.0 now offers enhanced search, enabling users to take advantage of the expertise section enabled in Phase 1. Users can search for and find people within the company based on keywords they've entered in the expertise section of their directory profile.

The keywords entered in the Directory expertise section are linked to topical information defining those terms in Ciscopedia, Cisco's version of Wikipedia.[41] Where CA-pedia, mentioned previously, focuses on topics related to the CA organization, Ciscopedia focuses on topics of interest to the broader company. When the beta version of Ciscopedia launched at the end of January 2009, it contained over 540 Sales and marketing-related terms merged into Ciscopedia from Salespedia, a Sales collaboration tool described in Chapter 11. As a result, Salespedia is currently the most popular tag in Ciscopedia, followed by acronym and internetworking terms.[42]

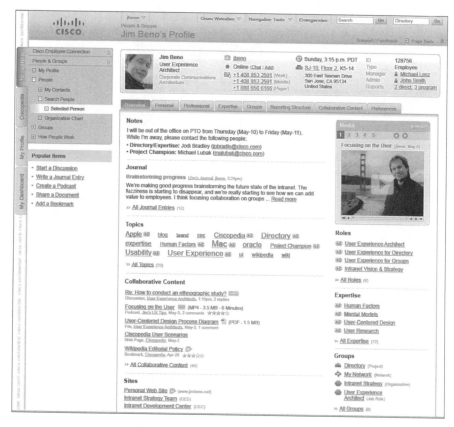

Figure 10-9   *Employee profile prototype for Directory 3.0.[11]*

The idea of Ciscopedia came about as Jim Beno, a user experience architect on the Intranet Strategy Group team at the time, began doing research on how experts felt about identifying their expertise in Directory 3.0. Jim discovered that many experts were concerned about being flooded by requests for basic information and preferred to write a summary on the topic of their expertise, providing links to key resources. The Strategy Group vision of Ciscopedia, an open encyclopedia like Wikipedia, where everyone at Cisco contributes to the content, was born![43]

According to Ciscopedia project manager, Nikki Dudhoria, Ciscopedia is

- An online, wiki-based, topical information hub

- A place for employees to share expertise

- Information aggregated from multiple sources

- Owned and governed by the entire Cisco community

Figure 10-10 provides an example of a Ciscopedia prototype page, developed by Beno on the topic of user centered design.

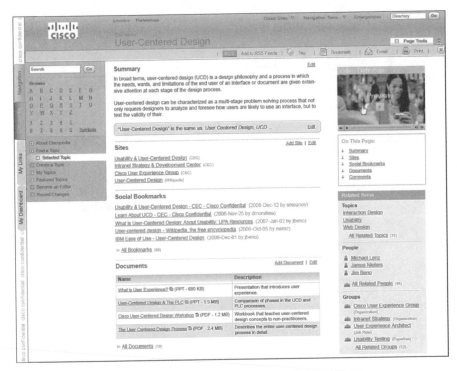

Figure 10-10 *Ciscopedia prototype page on user-centered design.[11]*

Like this example, each Ciscopedia topical entry is meant to

- Educate users.

- Share associated resources.

- Serve as a "hub," aggregating related information.

- Enable users to easily navigate to other relevant sources of information on the Cisco intranet.

Figure 10-11 illustrates the types of information aggregated into Ciscopedia topic pages.

In 2006, research analysts from Butler Group, an IT research and analysis company based in the U.K, reported that company productivity can be reduced by up to 10% as employees waste time searching—or searching ineffectively—for information.[45] When fully realized, Ciscopedia will provide a searchable, centralized location for employee-authored content and knowledge-sharing by subject matter experts. Ciscopedia will enable users to quickly and easily find information aggregated from other sources, including blog entries, discussion forum threads, websites, bookmarks, and documents, increasing overall employee productivity.[46]

The Intranet Strategy Group vision also identified communities as a key piece of Cisco's Web 2.0 strategy, enabling employees to collaborate with others who have similar expertise

The Ciscopedia difference - aggregation and connections

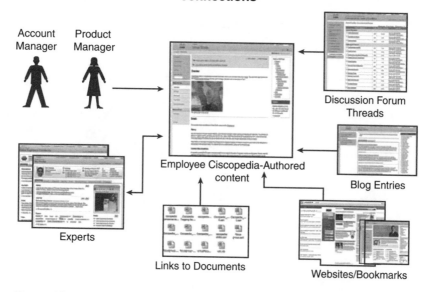

Account Manager   Product Manager

Discussion Forum Threads

Employee Ciscopedia-Authored content

Blog Entries

Experts

Links to Documents

Websites/Bookmarks

Figure 10-11   *Ciscopedia topical information hub of employee-authored content.[44]*

and interests. Figure 10-12 shows a prototype for a community page focused on Cisco's Commerce Business Transformation Office. The community page contains information specifically designed to meet the interests and information needs of its members.

A key piece of Cisco's Web 2.0 strategy is enabling more effective connections and capabilities based on the interrelationships between people, information, and communities. As mentioned earlier, Cisco Directory pages currently contain information about people and their expertise. These people-specific pages will evolve to link to their blog entries, rich media, such as videos and podcasts they've created, their interests and expertise, the communities they're part of, their recent bookmarks, and other recent activities, such as discussion forum posts, presentations, etc. Directory pages will also contain embedded Unified Communications capabilities, described in Chapter 2, such as presence indicators, click-to-dial, click-to-chat, and so on, enabling the ability to connect and communicate with people in real-time.

Ciscopedia pages contain topical information, including an overview of the topic, function-specific content from sales and engineering, for example, and associated documents and tags. These information-specific pages will evolve to link to people who are experts in the topic, as well as related rich media, such as recent videos and podcasts. Ciscopedia pages will also link to other resources that are topic-related, including recent discussion forum and blog activities, links to associated communities, related content in WebEx Connect team spaces, and so on.

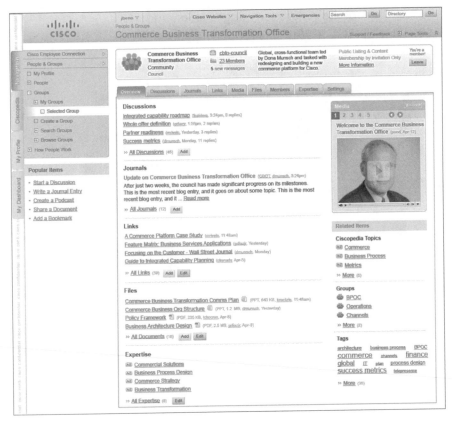

Figure 10-12 *Community prototype page for Commerce Business Transformation Office.[11]*

Community pages, which are currently under development, will also help tie together related content distributed in other Web 2.0 technologies and tools. Community pages will contain an overview of the community; provide the ability to access community members and content in real-time; and to subscribe to community updates created and delivered via store-and-forward mechanisms, email, or Really Simple Syndication (RSS). Community pages will also list top contributors and offer links to community related content, including rich media, such as video and podcasts, a community calendar, activities of community members, as well as associated documents, tags, projects, communities, and WebEx Connect team spaces.

One key advantage of stratifying content along the lines of people, information, and communities is that it can be leveraged multiple times through cross-references. Rather than creating duplicative and redundant content, aggregated and consolidated information sources can scale to serve as a reference to multiple interests. For example, an information page on Unified Communication (UC) will be updated and referred to by experts in the UC space. That same page can also be updated and referenced by sales and engineering communities focused on UC.

At the heart of this integrated workforce experience vision is the My Cisco view, which essentially renders the information related to me. It provides news and information in a single portal, including my profile, colleagues, communities, WebEx spaces, RSS feeds, messages, meetings, tasks, tags, and so on. The My Cisco view also enables contextual relational navigation, which means that from My View, I can click on and navigate to any of my related people, information, communities, and all the rich media they contain, including video."

Video

The beginning of this chapter identified Cisco's anticipation of a market transition caused by the hunger for access to video leading to network-related spending expected to reach $50 billion by 2013.[5] Video plays an important role in Cisco's Web 2.0 strategy, as well, leading to the development of its own YouTube behind the firewall, enabling employees to share information in the form of videos and photos. C-Vision is a video wiki, which enables Cisco employees to publish informal and engaging video messages in much the same way YouTube is used on the Internet.

The C-Vision portal, shown in Figure 10-13, is designed for internal Cisco use only.

The portal also offers a number of features to make video sharing easier. For example, C-Vision

Figure 10-13   *C-Vision Portal.[47]*

- Enables employees to publish informal and engaging video messages captured via desktop web camera.

- Upload and download audio, video, and photos.

- Play back videos in full-screen mode.

- Tag, rate, and comment on videos.

- Create albums or favorites.

- Build groups and communities with similar interests.[47]

The Cisco video-sharing portal has become widely used, attracting over 47,000 unique viewers and a total of over 2,100 videos and over 400 photos uploaded and published in 2009.[48] Most of the video content, consists of short product reports, updates from engineering, and ideas from sales. This content has been created by employees recording video via their desktop camera and uploading it to the site with a few mouse clicks.

C-Vision provides another avenue for information sharing and idea exchange, another water cooler to facilitate the connection and communication among Cisco employees. In the process of piloting the series of Web 2.0 technologies and tools outlined here, Cisco recognized the need to establish a program dedicated to communication, collaboration, and Web 2.0 to help manage the explosion of Web 2.0 technology adoption, to ensure scalability and reduce the threat of network overload. Let's now turn our attention to learn more about that program.

Communications Center of Excellence (CCoE)

In 2007, the foundational efforts of the Intranet Strategy Group described in the chapter led to the establishment of the Communications Center of Excellence (CCoE). According to Burns, the cross-functional CCoE initiative was chartered to bring together the resources of the community to provide guidance on the right tools to use to solve specific communications needs. The scope of these communications needs included everything from email to web to rich media.

The underlying CCoE value proposition focused on consolidation and alignment of ongoing Web 2.0 activities, which led to its formation. For example, CCoE

- Helps drive an enterprise collaboration framework, using collaborative tools.

- Harnesses energy (and funding!) to create better, broader capabilities, which can be leveraged by all.

- Avoids spending additional resources and funding on siloed, often redundant activities.

The value of consolidating efforts to drive adoption of collaborative tools more holistically across the company was soon realized as teams began to contribute resources and content toward the effort.

The original CCoE website, shown in Figure 10-14, was created to consolidate this enterprise Web 2.0 technology content in one location.

Figure 10-14   *Original Communications Center of Excellence website.[11]*

Some of the content Burns and team provided on the CCoE site include

- Web 2.0 technology pages, with info for getting started

- Technology roadmaps

- Communications challenges

- Solutions, best practices, and success stories

- Discussion forums

- News blog and project update blog

- One-minute video overviews

- Process and policies[11]

Since that time, Cisco's Web 2.0 initiative has gone through an organizational change, resulting in the establishment of the groups currently leading Cisco's adoption of Web 2.0 technology, introduced in Chapter 1:

- **Corporate Communications Architecture (CCA)**, the business organization led by Jim Grubb, vice president of corporate communications, which evolved from the original Intranet Strategy Group, is focused on communication with internal employees as well as external audiences and includes Executive Technical Marketing, Collaboration Business Services, and Collaboration Business Technologies. The fact that the Corporate Communications team is also focused on rich media, such as video, synergizes and accelerates the incorporation of rich media into the people, information, community, and My Cisco pages, which comprise Cisco's integrated workforce experience.

- **Communications & Collaboration IT (CCIT)**, the IT organization led by Sheila Jordan, vice president of information technology, communications, and collaboration technology, is building the architecture to enable key business processes including communication, collaboration, delivery of employee services, innovation, and management.[50]

- **Communications & Collaboration Delivery Team (CCDT)**, the team formed out of these two organizations, is now leading the Web 2.0 technology delivery effort.

These teams now partner to build out the latest version of the CCoE site, shown in Figure 10-15. Today, CCoE provides employees with the information they need to effectively use Web 2.0 technologies to get engaged and increase both internal and external collaboration across the company. For example, the CCoE site provides

- **Vision, Strategy and Initiatives**, providing information on plans for the future and strategic imperatives designed to achieve that vision.

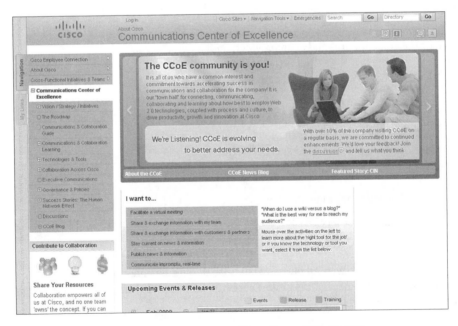

Figure 10-15   *Communications Center of Excellence (CCoE).[51]*

- **Technology Roadmap**, laying out plans for Cisco, Web 2.0, personalization technologies, and related applications and services for the fiscal year.

- **Communications & Collaboration Guide**, tools and quick reference guides designed to help employees understand how and when to use each technology.

- **Communications & Collaboration Learning**, providing information on training series and other learning materials.

- **Technologies & Tools**, offering information on each of the various Web 2.0 technologies and tools, including availability, quick reference info, overview, and related discussions.

- **Collaboration Across Cisco**, showcasing and rewarding initiatives that implement Web 2.0 technologies to enable collaboration with employees, customers, and partners in an exceptional way.

- **Executive Communications**, offering tools and templates to enable more consistent, effective executive communications.

- **Governance and Policies**, providing links to the Cisco Code of Business Conduct and Social Networking Handbook, which provides policies, procedures, guidelines, and best practices in employee Web 2.0 technology use.

- **Success Stories**, focused on bringing stories on the Human Network Effect to light.

- **Discussions**, providing a list of discussion forums, organized by categories: General, Executive, Communications & Collaboration Guide, or Technologies & Tools, and ranked by views.

- **CCoE Blog**, where team members share thoughts and news on Web 2.0 technology rollouts affecting the company.[51]

Table 10-1 shows how Cisco's Web 2.0 technology adoption and usage exploded during 2008, thanks to CCoE guidance and support. Wiki pages, for example, have grown five-fold in the last year, to eight times the number of pages of two years ago. TelePresence meetings have doubled in the last year, five times the number of two years ago. And there are now 31 times the number of WebEx Connect users than a year ago.

Table 10-1   *Cisco's Web 2.0 Technology Adoption Metrics[52]*

Technology	Adoption Metrics		Increase of bold metrics
Blogs	February 2008	January 2009	
Active Blogs	756	1,992	
Registered Bloggers	2,870	7,792	3X
Published Blog Entries	3,296	11,457	
Total Comments	2,588	8,827	

continues

Table 10-1 *Cisco's Web 2.0 Technology Adoption Metrics[52](continued)*

Technology	Adoption Metrics		Increase of bold metrics
Discussion Forums	January 2008	January 2009	
Categories	157	1,270	
Forums	312	2,847	
Threads	1,059	14,499	12X
Messages	3,058	44,297	
Registered Users	2,582	32,666	
Groups	41	137	
Wikis	January 2007	January 2009	
Accounts (15K Editors)		72,020	5X
Spaces (330/Quarter)		3,633	
Pages (18K/Quarter)	35,621	187,280	
C-Vision	January 2008	January 2009	
Video Publishers	130	2,108	16X
Photo Publishers	40	438	
Videos Uploaded	300	6,797	
Photos Published	100	3,475	23X
Unique Viewers	3,257	46,871	
TelePresence	January 2008	January 2009	2X
Meetings	90,000	215,833	
WebEx Connect	January 2008	January 2009	
Users	1,000	31,047	31X
Spaces	2,500	66,816	
Documents	2,000	238,310	
CCoE Website	January 2008	January 2009	
Unique Users	24,608	57,019	2X
Visits	26,868	63,935	
Hits	37,450	89,890	

In January 2009, the CCoE site had nearly 90,000 hits, more than double the number measured a year earlier. The most hit pages in January 2009: CCoE Home, WebEx, RSS Publishers, Directory, and Blogs.[23] The next step in our ongoing metrics gathering process will be to identify and measure the business impact of these technologies: reduced search time, improved access to information, reduced email, faster and more effective decision-making, and increased ability to solve the more difficult problems, for Cisco and perhaps the world. In the words of vice president Jim Grubb, known as John Chamber's product "Demo Guy," "Collaboration this way helps a world community solve big problems."[5]

Communication and Collaboration Board

In keeping with the Cisco distributed leadership model, a cross-functional Communication and Collaboration (C&C) Board was established in late 2007. Its mission is to drive more effective communication and collaboration at Cisco through the innovative use of Web 2.0 technologies and tools. The Board, whose members are shown in Figure 10-16, is responsible for delivering the vision, policies, and strategy and defining the architectural framework.

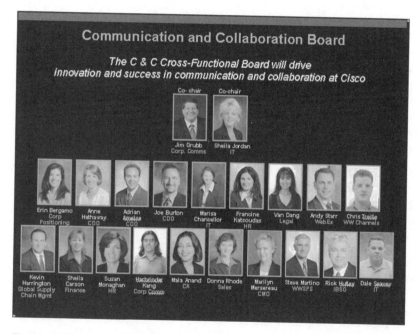

Figure 10-16 *Communication and Collaboration Board members.[53]*

The Board meets regularly to review Web 2.0 technology roadmaps presented by the collaboration delivery team. Board meetings also enable members to hear read-outs from its other subcommittees focused on areas such as technical integration, metrics and value proposition, governance and policies, communication, and organization adoption. Each cross-functional Board member works to foster more effective collaboration in his or her function.

C&C Board members also serve as the conduit for functional requirements to the Board and for collaboration communications from the Board to the functional organization—a true model of collaborative leadership in action! Many of the dramatic increases in Web 2.0 technology adoption have been a direct result of CCoE and C&C Board efforts to drive a collaboration framework based on Web 2.0 technologies and tools across the company. Now let's talk about the future of Web 2.0 at Cisco.

Cisco 3.0

Cisco is evolving into the next generation company—Cisco 3.0, re-inventing itself around Web 2.0 and then taking the lessons learned to its customers. The company is evolving organizationally to distribute decision-making, innovate faster, bring products to market sooner, and capitalize on market transitions, such as ubiquitous video and visual networking. Cisco's Linksys Wireless Home products, for example, enable consumers to easily manage music, photos, and video content stored in home devices and across the network.

Cisco is using Web 2.0 technologies such as Cisco TelePresence, Cisco WebEx, and Unified Communications to enable collaboration between employees, partners, and customers, yielding increased productivity and deeper relationships. Cisco's Q3 Company Meeting in February 2009 was held virtually over live video on Cisco TV, Cisco's internal video channel, from its campus in Bangalore, India, with employees around the globe watching on IPTV or taking part via TelePresence. CEO John Chambers uses TelePresence to meet with a dozen customers in Russia; meetings and travel that would have taken 96 hours now take 8 hours, enabling Chambers to meet with twice as many customers and cut his travel schedule in half.

TelePresence is greener, faster, and cheaper than air travel and enables employees, family and friends to connect in new ways. In the future, consumers will leverage the visual networking capability of TelePresence, part of the media-enabled connected home, to interact with friends and family members across the country or around the globe—talking, sharing special events, or even watching sporting events together.[54] According to popular cartoonist, Scott Adams, even Dilbert uses TelePresence.[55]

Other Web 2.0 technologies, such as blogs and wikis, and new business models, such as social networking, folksonomies, and even virtual realities, are enabling the company to increase peer-to-peer collaboration and ideation, and to transform key business processes. The capability to connect people, information, and communities is leading to a more collaborative and connected company, where technologies such as discussion forums, wikis, and WebEx Connect are seeing explosive growth and adoption. Cisco is also leveraging new technologies to interact with its customers with evolutionary new approaches such as "Digital Cribs," mentioned earlier.

Cisco provides customers with insight into the key business trends, such as collaboration through the http://www.cisco.com/en/US/netsol/ns870/index.html link on its Cisco.com site, a part of its Five Ways to Thrive initiative described in Chapter 11. Cisco has even had a presence in the web-based virtual world, Second Life, since December 2006, offering a way for Cisco to interact with the public and broaden brand awareness in a virtual environment that is creative and fun.[56][57] Although recent news reports tout the end of

Second Life, it has afforded Cisco a set valuable learning experiences in this new medium, being leveraged by Cisco in other virtual environments.[58] Cisco's Partner Space, a Cisco-sponsored virtual community for example, is discussed in Chapter 11, which is focused on Cisco's approach to Sales 2.0.

Cisco's intranet evolution, depicted in Figure 10-17, is enabling an agile and collaborative workforce. Between 2002 and 2006, the focus was on a Unified Intranet, where employees and information are more and more connected. It began by establishing a consistent user interface, unifying navigation, integrating enterprise news, and streamlining intranet page development. This period enabled a more informed workforce, empowering corporate communications and increasing findability of content and enabling efficiency. Between 2006 and 2008, the focus was on Web 2.0 collaboration tools; the democratization of publishing; the establishment of multiple communication vehicles: blogs, discussion forums, and wikis; enabling communication and collaboration.

Cisco's Intranet Evolution

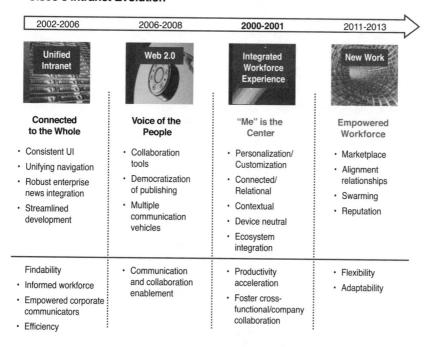

Enabling an Agile and Collaborative Workforce

Figure 10-17   *Cisco's Intranet Evolution.*

The current intranet evolution focus, on the Integrated Workforce Experience, began in 2008 and is expected to continue into 2011. With "me" in the center, personalization and customization are key, as are the connected and relational nature of workforce experience components: people, information and communities, their contextual elements, and the importance of device neutrality. Ecosystem partners and customers are being integrated, productivity is being accelerated, and cross-functional/cross-company collaboration is fostered as a key part of resulting business process transformation.

Between 2011 and 2012, Cisco's intranet evolution will focus on New Work. In this phase, employees will be able to find projects and initiatives they wpuld like to work on advertised in a marketplace, swarming to participate in activities with other members of the community. Alignment and relationships will be critical to success as will digital reputation, established by what employees say and do via collaborative technologies and tools. Flexibility and adaptability will also be important elements of the empowered workforce, as communities and teams will self-organize around the work effort.

In Short

This chapter began by briefly explaining why Web 2.0 and the "Web as a Platform" concept resonated so well with Cisco, the "Network as a Platform" company. Then it examined how the Intranet Strategy Group helped drive collaborative technology adoption across the company. It explored Cisco adoption of several technologies: blogs, discussion forums, and wikis, providing examples of each. It outlined some of the basic details of these implementations and shared guidelines and tips, drawn from some of the most successful implementations, Jere King's blog and Collaboratory, for example.

Next, the chapter described some of the services and tools Cisco developed using these technologies as a part of the Intranet Strategy Group vision: Directory 3.0 and C-Vision. It provided snapshots and details about these tools to provide insight into how Web 2.0 technologies and services continue to evolve and provide value to the business. As the statistics shown in the chapter indicate, these technologies and tools have been hugely successful and have enabled the organization to identify expertise and begin forming communities of interest.

Finally, the chapter identified a few of the organizational changes that have occurred as Cisco continues to place an emphasis on the importance of Web 2.0 technologies and tools in our efforts to transform the company into a more collaborative organization. The CCoE and C&C Board have begun to drive a more cohesive architectural framework for collaboration across the company. They have also consolidated many of the fragmented and sometimes redundant efforts, as teams now collaborate on collaborative initiatives.

So, what's ahead for FY09 and beyond? Much can be said for the work that's already gone into the evolution of Web 2.0 technology and tools at Cisco, but there is still much more work ahead. The goal is to continue driving productivity, growth, and innovation, leveraging Web 2.0 technologies such as Directory 3.0 and Ciscopedia, for example.

Web 2.0 technologies enable Cisco to connect to the right people, resources, and information at the right time, but also to drive a more integrated workforce experience. As Cisco continues to become more adept as a company in the use of Web 2.0 technologies, it leverages its power to communicate more effectively and efficiently and to collaborate both internally and externally with employees, customers, and partners. But above all, Cisco continues to change the way people "live, work, play, and learn,"[SM] with the "Network as the Platform."

<monologue>

Cisco Sales is using the company's own Web 2.0 technologies such as Cisco TelePresence, Cisco WebEx, and Unified Communications as a key part of company's Web 2.0 evolution. This approach enables Sales to be early adopters of Cisco technology, to pilot and use the technology from day to day in their workflow so they become thoroughly familiar with the products they sell to Cisco customers. It also enables Sales to collaborate more effectively with Sales team members, partners, and customers, improving communication and establishing deeper relationships.

Sales teams are also leading Cisco adoption and use of other Web 2.0 technologies, such as blogs and wikis, and new business models, such as social networking and folksonomies, even the Mobile Web. In doing so, Sales is increasing peer-to-peer collaboration and innovation and transforming key selling processes. Cisco Sales is developing and sharing case studies showcasing these selling process transformations with partners and customers, increasing Cisco's leadership consultancy.

</monologue>

Cisco's Approach to Sales 2.0

This chapter provides a case study of the Cisco approach to Sales 2.0, explaining how Web 2.0 is transforming the way Cisco sells to its customers. This chapter

- Explains how Web 2.0 changes the selling process, describes Sales 2.0, and identifies key differences between Sales 1.0 and Sales 2.0.

- Outlines how Cisco Sales' explorations of Web 2.0 technologies, Connected Communities, Finding Expertise, and Web 2.0 Explorers, helped shape the vision and lay the foundation for this fundamental change in Cisco's selling processes.

- Describes initiatives in the U.S.-Canada Theater driving collaboration technology adoption across Sales.

- Provides examples of Cisco's Sales 2.0 best practices and the business impact and results identified so far.

The Cisco approach to Sales 2.0 is characterized by highly collaborative interactions between employees, partners, and customers. These interactions are enabled by Cisco's own Web 2.0 collaboration technologies, Cisco TelePresence, Cisco WebEx, and Unified Communications, as well as other Web 2.0 technologies and tools. The ongoing selling process transformations that Web 2.0 technology has enabled in Cisco Sales serves as a model for the rest of the company and other enterprises to follow.

Web 2.0 Changes Sales Processes

Web 2.0 is changing both the sales process and the buying processes. Customers use web-based search engines such as Google to find information about products and services and are, therefore, becoming much more educated consumers. Customers who have used e-commerce sites such as Amazon.com expect one-stop shopping and faster delivery. Customers using these sites can choose to reveal information about themselves or remain anonymous, whereas sellers must reveal more product information than ever before in order to remain competitive.

Company marketing and selling processes are also changing in Sales 2.0 in ways intended to match new customer buying behaviors and expectations. Annual technology trade shows, for example, are giving way to collaborative spaces where virtual trade shows are "always on." Partners can promote their products in virtual booths and collaborate with other partners. This section focuses on how Web 2.0 is changing key aspects of the selling process.

Sales 2.0

As enterprise Sales teams adapt their processes to embrace Web 2.0 and web-based communication, traditional Sales is changing, particularly in high-tech companies such as Cisco. This new selling approach, called Sales 2.0, fosters collaboration and information-sharing with customers to increase customer intimacy and loyalty. It supports collaboration and co-creation with selling partners, thereby improving Sales strategy.

Sales 2.0 uses Web 2.0 tools, such as instant messaging, web conferencing, and social networking, to increase Sales productivity and close significantly more deals. This approach leverages the skills of the next generation of sales professionals and enables seasoned professionals to engage as well. All this benefits both the customer and the bottom line.

Sellers are adopting Web 2.0 technologies to increase their social networks, build stronger relationships, and work more efficiently to sell more products. Networking and relationship-building play key roles in successful selling. Social networking enables sellers, customers, and partners to connect and extend their reach exponentially, for mutual benefit. Web 2.0 technologies make it possible to quickly find the right person through this extended, global network to connect, engage, share information, and collaborate immediately on a deal.

Where Sales 1.0 focused on selling products in volume, for example, Sales 2.0 focuses on customers, and how to enable them to more effectively manage their businesses. In Sales 2.0, teams are engaging in web-based collaborations with more customers and partners per day, instead of accumulating frequent flyer miles or spending hours on the road. These and other differences between Sales 1.0 and 2.0 enabled by Web 2.0 technologies and tools are highlighted in Table 11-1.

Table 11-1 *How Web 2.0 Changes Key Aspects of the Selling Process [1]*

Aspect	Sales 1.0	Sales 2.0
Focus	Sell products	Help customers make the right buying decisions
Leads	Prospect lists	Connected, global social network/ community
Pipeline	Volume	Velocity
Product Information	You control what customers know	Customers educate themselves via the web
Travel	Frequent flyer miles	Web-based collaborations

Sales 2.0 technologies accelerate the selling process by facilitating the buyer's decision-making process and improving the quality of the interaction. Company websites provide interactive, user-friendly interfaces, focused on customer needs and preferences. Effective sites are designed to attract and engage the customer 24×7, whenever they want or need information. Companies are beginning to enable customers and partners to join and

participate in communities to share knowledge and experiences, improving the quality of the customer experience, as many consumer-based social networking sites, such as MySpace and Facebook, have done.[1]

Collaborative technologies enable Sales to become more efficient, often reducing travel time and expense. Web conferencing, for example, enables Sales to meet directly with customers and partners and engage the right subject matter experts all at the same time. These interactions, through technologies such as Cisco TelePresence, are as effective as meeting face-to-face. The real advantage of these technologies is that they enable more interactions per day, and more engagements per subject matter expert, because no travel time is required, adding huge savings to the bottom line. The next section shifts to discuss how Web 2.0 is changing Sales at Cisco.

Cisco Sales Explores Web 2.0

Many groups within the Cisco Sales organization are working to explore the possibility, recognize the opportunity, and realize the potential of Web 2.0 to deliver business value to Sales. The largest Theater Sales team, United States and Canada (U.S.-Canada), and the Sales IT support team, Worldwide Sales Processes and Systems (WWSPS), have collaborated on many of these efforts. Both teams play key roles, leading or sponsoring Web 2.0 initiatives that deliver business value to Sales and, more important, the broader population at Cisco as well.

U.S.-Canada Sales and WWSPS drove much of the early exploration of Web 2.0 technology in Sales, recognizing that collaborative technology could drive Sales productivity. In March 2006, as early Web 2.0 explorations began at Cisco, Rob Lloyd, senior vice president of U.S.-Canada sales operations, commissioned WWSPS to explore Web 2.0 technology in support of the Theater. WWSPS began by partnering with Cisco's Intranet Strategy team, described in Chapter 10, "Web 2.0 @ Cisco: The Evolution."

During the discovery process, several compelling Sales requirements surfaced, including the need to

- Organize into communities of practice based on an account, campaign, vertical, theater, technology, and so on, creating an initiative titled Connected Communities.

- Find the right person or content required to prepare a presentation, answer a question, or provide support to a customer, launching an effort called Finding Expertise.

- Identify the importance of the Mobile Web to Sales, developing new capabilities such as the new Mobile On the Spot (Bookings) Report.

- Share information, presentations, news, and events on rapidly evolving collaborative technologies, fostering a community known as the Web 2.0 Explorers.

- Investigate technologies such as mashups as a way to accelerate capability delivery, through a mashup proof of concept (PoC), demonstrating the feasibility and business value of the technology.

- Develop a taxonomy of Sales-related abbreviations, acronyms, and terms called Salespedia.

- Align WebEx Connect–related efforts across Sales and provide a vision of a Sales desktop based on Connect, establishing a WebEx Connect initiative for Sales.

- Contribute ideas on new products, services, and process changes, gathered from Sales practices and suggested by customers, starting a program called iFeedback.

The next sections provide a brief look at each of these early explorations.

Connected Communities

In early 2006, U.S.-Canada Sales and WWSPS realized the need to enable teams to organize into forums or groups, and took the lead to support development and deployment of community sites for many Sales teams. By August 2006, the U.S.-Canada Theater and WWSPS had established several of these wiki-based forums and collaboration portals, called Connected Communities. As the business value of more effective knowledge-sharing became evident, many segments and verticals developed web-based communities of practice.

One early example, specifically targeted at Sales team members selling Service Oriented Network Architecture (SONA) solutions and services, was announced in August 2006. The initial wiki-based SONA Portal was developed to consolidate SONA sales material in one site, providing quick access to content designed to meet the customers' needs and interest level. The SONA Connected Community was designed to help accelerate understanding and usability of these SONA messages.

The SONA Community enabled Sales teams to interact via discussion forums, owned and managed by the SONA team, and provided an encyclopedia archive of SONA-related topics. It also provided a calendar of SONA events, linked to Cisco's calendar solution, to increase awareness of SONA community events. The SONA Portal has evolved into the Enterprise & Mid-Market Solutions Marketing Enterprise Architecture website, shown in Figure 11-1. Like its predecessor, this new SONA portal provides educational and architecture-selling resources, connecting the Sales team to information.[3]

The business value of Connected Communities is that they foster increased collaboration and knowledge-sharing. They support the exchange of best practices, business and technology expertise, and lessons learned among Sales teams. Connected community sites enable account teams and entire Sales organizations to work more closely and interactively with one another. They also improve productivity because all relevant communication and content can be encapsulated within the persistent context of the community effort or work, and experts within the community can weigh in to help guide and often times accelerate the community effort.

Finding Expertise

By mid-2006, Cisco's Directory provided contact details, such as photo, title, organization, phone, email, and address. Many employees expressed the need to search through Directory content to find the right person to answer a question or assist on a project. The Internet Strategy group, part of the Employee Commitment team in Cisco's Human Resources organization, was responsible for managing the Directory application.

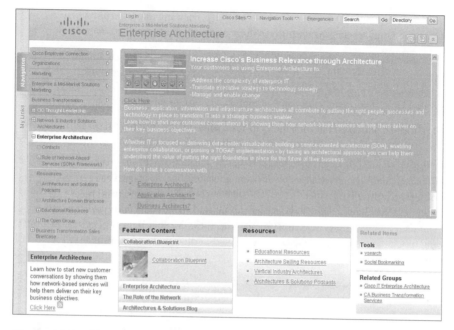

Figure 11-1   *Cisco's Service Oriented Network Architecture (SONA) Portal.[3]*

The group realized that searching for the right person within the global workforce of more than fifty thousand often either took too long or proved unsuccessful, so they decided to add an Expertise section to existing Directory entries. U.S.-Canada Sales and WWSPS, realizing the business value of sales employees being able to find the right expertise quickly, supported the effort. They partnered with the Cisco Directory team, providing requirements and resources to support and accelerate delivery of a Finding Expertise capability in Directory 3.0. This latest Directory release, described in more detail in Chapter 10, was announced at the end of January 2009.

The business value of the Directory Expertise section is that it enables everyone across the company—employees, contractors, and vendors—to input their roles, subject matter expertise, and interests in their profiles.[2] As soon as that task is complete, Sales users will be able to search Directory 3.0 and find expertise. This real-time access and capability to bring expertise and support in at appropriate times in the Sales cycle, without having to know the expert personally or by name, will result in higher productivity and shorter Sales cycle time, as you will see from other examples later in the chapter. This ability to reach experts is enhanced even further via mobility.

Mobile Sales 2.0

As Chapter 9, "Web 2.0 and Mobility," identified, mobile access to information is an issue of particular importance to the Sales organization. Most sales account managers and systems engineers spend a good deal of their time in the field with customers, often away from their computers. More than half of Cisco's mobile device users are in Sales. Many find mobile access to sales-specific services, known as Mobile Sales Information Services (MSIS), in true Sales 2.0 fashion, increases their productivity, enabling anytime, anywhere access to information and services needed to do their jobs.[4]

For the past two years, a small team within WWSPS supported MSIS, testing new devices, working through Sales billing and other issues, in partnership with members of the U.S.-Canada Sales team and others.[5] During that time, many opportunities to enable business capabilities as mobile services worth exploring were identified. These include mobile alerts, offering immediate click-to-resolve access to the underlying applications and systems, streamlining, and accelerating workflow.[6]

Many day-to-day services of particular interest to Sales could be accessible via the Mobile Web, including travel itinerary information, mileage and expense tracking, approvals for deals, travel, even Paid Time Off (PTO) for vacation. As the Directory service outage example mentioned in Chapter 9 indicates, mobile services can deliver business-critical capabilities. Finally, and perhaps most important, these Mobile Web services can become building blocks to develop and enable new services, combined and configured in ways we've only begun to scratch the surface of.

The On the Spot (Bookings) Reports service delivered at the end of 2007 to key executives, including CEO John Chambers, is described in Chapter 9. It is the sole new mobile service added to the MSIS portfolio in more than three years. Because MSIS provide clear business value, this is an area where more could be done to enable new Mobile Sales 2.0 capabilities offering additional value to Sales. Other opportunities to leverage Web 2.0 for business value were identified by a community known as the Explorers.

Web 2.0 Explorers

At the beginning of May 2007, WWSPS convened a meeting of Web 2.0 thought leaders from the U.S.-Canada team and other interested parties, calling this community forum the Web 2.0 Explorers. The group was formed to keep early technology exploration alive, until funding became available for additional sponsored initiatives. The Web 2.0 Explorers team met at least monthly for more than a year. The team grew from its inception, from a handful to well over sixty regular members from Sales, Customer Advocacy, Cisco Development Organization (CDO), and the Communications Center of Excellence (CCoE) initiatives.

Guest speakers at Explorers meetings shared information updates on collaborative technologies, such as WebEx Connect, and emerging Web 2.0 concepts, such as mashups. Explorers meetings provided a venue to collaborate with like-minded individuals on ways to foster Web 2.0 applications to drive innovation and business value in Sales and other organizations. Members took an active role in sharing information, presentations, news, and events on the Explorers community site, proudly displaying a compass as the site logo, as shown in Figure 11-2.[7]

The Explorers community provided business value previously mentioned for Connected Communities, Knowledge-Sharing. The Explorers community also offered additional value as it provided a forum to gather a set of collaboration capability requirements from members across the global Sales organization. These requirements also validated the many opportunities to enable business capabilities as mobile services worth exploring, mentioned in

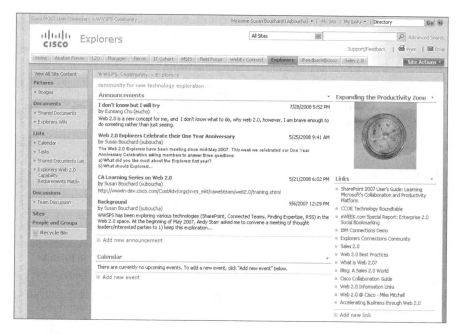

Figure 11-2   *Web 2.0 Explorers community site.[7]*

Chapter 9. These include mobile alerts, offering immediate click-to-resolve access to the underlying applications and systems, streamlining, and accelerating workflow.[8]

In addition, the Sales capability requirements gathered by members of the Explorers community helped shape the vision and establish the foundation for many Sales 2.0 initiatives, including the first Web 2.0 strategy and framework for the Worldwide Sales organization. The capabilities also served as the basis for an early conceptual vision of a Sales desktop, designed to fulfill the Sales requirements, built on Cisco's WebEx Connect collaborative platform. The community identified mashups as a potential enabler of many of these capabilities.

Mashups

In October 2007, the Web 2.0 Explorers team organized a Monster Mashup event, where team members viewed a demonstration of mashup capabilities. Mashup technology has been used within Sales for several years to aggregate links to selling content from product and marketing business unit sites into a Cisco tool called Sales Rack managed by WWSPS. As a result of the demo, the Explorers team sponsored a mashup technology proof of concept (PoC), gathering use cases from Explorers members.

The mashup PoC team developed an application for the Cisco Development Organization (CDO) team members to aggregate product quality data from multiple sources and present it in a comprehensive dashboard, as a set of dense charts with histories and drill-downs. The mashup provided a more holistic view of the product quality data and significantly reduced the time required for data gathering and aggregation.[9] The mashup PoC team also developed an application in partnership with WWSPS to screen scrape content from a web-based Sales Bookings application and reformat the content to fit on a mobile device in about three hours, offering significant value from a rapid prototyping, time-to-market delivery and cost savings perspective. Previous estimates to produce the capability via traditional development methods were at least three months.[10]

Results of the Explorers mashup PoC are compelling, from a business value standpoint. Mashups may prove extremely useful in developing business applications quickly and in creating new Mobile Sales 2.0 services to address the opportunities discussed in Chapter 9. The results of these technology explorations have been shared with Explorers team members, including Cisco's Mobility Solutions and members focused on Cisco's Communications Center of Excellence (CCoE) initiative. The lessons learned serve as a foundation for mashup technology exploration for CCoE and for Cisco, in general. The next initiative, Salespedia, serves as the foundation for another Cisco initiative, Ciscopedia.

Salespedia

> **Salespedia**, [Seylz-**pee**-dee-*uh*] -*noun* 1. a centralized list of Sales-related terms and abbreviations, 2. an index of knowledge/information of those engaged in Sales and Sales support.

Salespedia is an online collaborative encyclopedia developed by WWSPS to provide information in the Sales domain. It includes abbreviations, acronyms, and terms with definitions or descriptions. It also provides links to relevant websites and other content in one centralized, searchable location.

Salespedia establishes a collaborative platform for Sales knowledge, presented in one centralized location, and sets the stage for Sales knowledge-sharing. Combined with the Finding Expertise and Connected Communities efforts, Salespedia enables more powerful connections between people, communities, and information. It represents a significant step toward delivery of an Integrated Workforce Experience (IWE) for Sales.

Built on the Web 2.0 concept of user-generated content, Salespedia solicited information-sharing from Sales' subject matter experts. WWSPS team members and others have been encouraged to share and collaborate by adding relevant terms and definitions, contributing to the Sales knowledge base. Sales interns and new hires, in particular, have reported finding the acronyms and links to related information sources extremely useful as they join Cisco.

While developing Salespedia, WWSPS has been working closely with Ciscopedia, Cisco's version of Wikipedia, and Directory 3.0 Expertise initiatives described in Chapter 10. Salespedia provides the start of a consistent set of abbreviations, acronyms, and terms that can be leveraged in Sales' Directory Expertise sections. Salespedia also contains categories of Sales terms, such as roles, theaters, projects, and skills, to help drive consistency across Sales Directory Expertise entries and serve as a foundation for a Cisco Glossary.[11][12]

When the beta version of Ciscopedia launched at the end of January 2009, it contained over 540 Sales and marketing–related terms merged into Ciscopedia from Salespedia.

"Salespedia" is currently the most popular tag in Ciscopedia, followed by "acronym" and "internetworking terms."[13] After Salespedia's additional 500+ acronyms and abbreviations are merged into Ciscopedia the enterprise will have access to the entire Salespedia glossary. Another example of a Sales initiative providing leading practices for the entire company is the one focused on WebEx Connect.

WebEx Connect Initiative for Sales

WebEx, acquired by Cisco in 2007, offers WebEx Meeting Center meeting capabilities, outlined in Chapter 2, "User-Generated Content: Wikis, Blogs, Communities, Collaboration, and Collaborative Technologies." WebEx Connect, currently in beta release, offers a number of out-of-box capabilities: Instant Messenger, Chat, Contacts, Spaces, and Calendar. In early 2008, WWSPS established an initiative to assess the capabilities of WebEx Connect.

WWSPS worked to identify how WebEx Connect could be leveraged as a Sales collaboration platform to

- Increase customer intimacy and loyalty

- Drive deeper customer relationships

- Improve strategy through co-creation

- Develop more effective awareness of customer, industry, and technology trends through communities of practice

- Accelerate the buyer's decision process

The initiative helped align WebEx Connect–related efforts across Sales, providing an early conceptual vision of a Sales desktop, designed to fulfill the additional Sales requirements gathered from the Web 2.0 Explorers members, including

- Stock ticker

- Metrics dashboard

- Meetings, alerts, and news feeds

- A view of bookings from Sales' My Bookings Report (MBR)

- Return-on-investment (ROI) calculator

- Sales account information

These capabilities or features appear in the early vision of a Sales desktop, based on WebEx Connect, shown in Figure 11-3.[14]

The effort led to the creation of a list of out of the box WebEx Connect capabilities and widgets in development of primary importance to Sales.[15] Widgets are essentially portable chunks of application code that enable a capability, performing a service such as retrieving data. More important, it led to the development of a widget documentation pattern used to capture essential information about current and planned widgets in one location.[16]

Instant Messenger   Sales Desktop

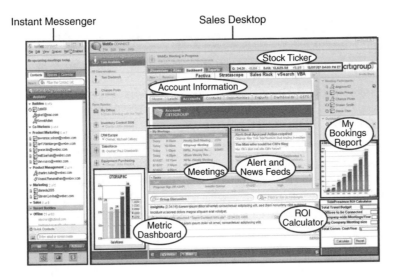

Figure 11-3 *Early conceptual vision of Sales desktop.[14]*

The business value of this initiative is that many of these capabilities were developed as widgets, thereby enabling a working conceptual model of the Sales desktop to be presented at the Global Sales Meeting in September 2008. The code underlying existing Mobile Sales Information Services, described in Chapter 9, was used to build several desktop widgets. Others were created by mashing up, or combining, back-end data services or developing new ones.

In addition, the WWSPS WebEx Connect team partnered with the U.S.-Canada team in 2008 to establish a WebEx Connect Early Adopters Program (EAP). The EAP was designed to help field sales teams learn to leverage WebEx Connect to collaborate more effectively with employees, partners, and customers. Guidelines, training material, best practices, and lessons learned through the EAP are being leveraged to support WebEx Connect adoption across the company through the company current EAP website, shown in Figure 11-4.

The site provides getting started information, service alerts, and links to enable users to contribute their ideas and learn more.[17] Now turn your attention to an initiative designed to broaden ideation across the Sales organization.

Sales Innovation via iFeedback

WWSPS partnered with the U.S.-Canada Theater team members, members of the I-Zone team, and others to collaborate on an initiative, called iFeedback, designed to gather and maximize the business value of innovative ideas of Cisco Sales employees. Like Cisco's current I-Zone initiative and Customer Advocacy's planned CA I-Zone initiative, described in Chapter 10, iFeedback is intended to act as an idea pipeline that moves ideas into action. Figure 11-5 provides a snapshot of an initial iFeedback Collaboration community site, where the innovation-focused Sales community can shares ideas when the initiative is launched.[18]

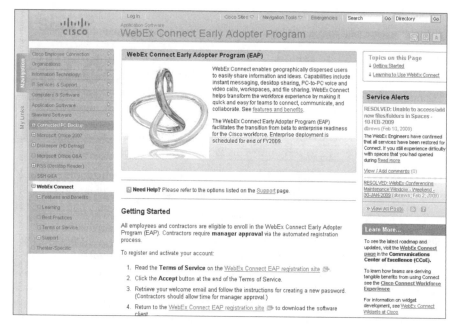

Figure 11-4   *WebEx Connect Early Adopter Program site.[17]*

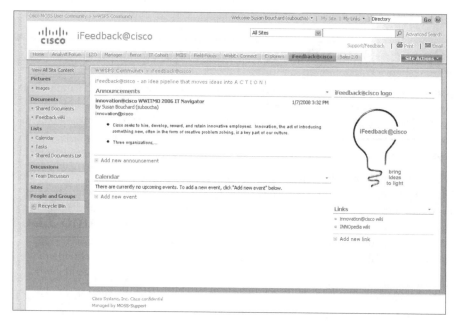

Figure 11-5   *Sales Innovation iFeedback Collaboration community site.[18]*

Key objectives of the proposed iFeedback initiative are

- Enable Sales to learn to leverage innovation to increase productivity, as many other companies are doing today.

- Accelerate the movement of ideas from the innovative source to subject matter experts (SMEs), who can review or test the ideas and turn them into action.

- Facilitate employees' use of collaborative software to brainstorm ideas to solve core problems, one at a time.

- Develop case studies and success stories that enable us to capture and reuse creative and innovative processes to solve problems for ourselves and our customers.

- Drive innovation to become so ingrained in Cisco culture (long term) that everyone is expected to submit ideas for innovations and improvements as part of any job.

As this list indicates, the iFeedback initiative is meant to transform Sales.

The business value of the iFeedback initiative is that it will provide an opportunity to tap into the tribal knowledge that Sales teams possess regarding Cisco customers, partners, products, and markets. Ideas contributed through iFeedback could be honed by the power of this collective intelligence. Very much a Sales 2.0 initiative, it could also help shape, in real-time, the overall Sales strategy. Imaginative Sales employees, partners, and customers could work together to solve core problems via collaborative brainstorming sessions, turning innovation into realization.[19]

Now turn your attention to several key collaboration initiatives currently underway in the U.S.-Canada Theater.

U.S.-Canada Sales Theater Initiatives

Cisco's U.S.-Canada Theater was launched in 2006 as part of a broader reorganization of the Worldwide Field Organization. The Theater was designed to maximize the synergies between the United States and Canada, both in terms of geographic proximity and market maturity, to best serve Cisco customers and accelerate growth. The Theater represents 53% of Cisco's total business, has over 5,000 employees, and 13,900 U.S. and Canada partners.[20]

The U.S.-Canada Theater, under Rob Lloyd's leadership, has sponsored many of Sales' Web 2.0 initiatives previously mentioned. These efforts have helped drive collaboration technology adoption across the Theater, enabling U.S.-Canada to become one of the leading organizations from a Sales 2.0 perspective. More important, however, U.S.-Canada Sales 2.0 initiatives provide best practices and lessons learned to the larger Cisco Sales community, the broader population at Cisco, and to customers and partners as well.

As the Theater home page shown in Figure 11-6 indicates, Collaboration is a key initiative as is Five to Thrive, an initiative described later in the chapter. The Theater is made up of a number of organizations, such as Sales Planning & Operations and Field Marketing. U.S.-Canada Field Marketing is led by Jere King, vice president of marketing, whose blog was mentioned in Chapter 10.

The Theater is also organized by market segments, such as Advanced Technologies, Canada, Public Sector, U.S. Commercial, U.S. Enterprise, and U.S. Service Provider, listed

Figure 11-6   *U.S.-Canada Sales Theater home page.[21]*

on the page under Segments. The site provides Theater employees a place to find Lloyd's key messages, including his blog, as well as a number of Hot Topics, Theater News, and Discussions. It is shown here to help frame how U.S.-Canada Theater organizations and initiatives described later in the chapter relate to one another.[21]

Sales Planning & Operations

Donna Rhode, vice president of Sales Planning & Operations (SPO), leverages the SPO homepage, shown in Figure 11-7, to provide access to her "On the SPOT" blog, news, and related items. Rhode, a member of Cisco's Communication and Collaboration (C&C) Board mentioned in Chapter 10, puts U.S.-Canada and SPO team efforts in perspective, saying, "By offering sales team members the tools to collaborate in today's business world, an organization enables both better workplace practice and improved service to customers and partners. A high degree of collaboration leads to an environment where salespeople can respond more quickly to their customers' needs due to the ability to connect with specialists and executives with short notice, spend more time off airplanes, and be able to interact and share ideas with a wide spectrum of individuals and cross-functional teams. Through collaboration, a sales team expands its strength to be greater than the sum of its parts. More insight, expertise, and best practices make the team stronger, thereby providing an important competitive edge."[22]

Under Rhode's leadership, the U.S.-Canada SPO organization develops tools to help Sales to understand how to use Web 2.0 technologies and leverage them in a Sales 2.0 way to increase collaboration, improve productivity, transform selling processes, and provide business value. Key SPO initiatives include

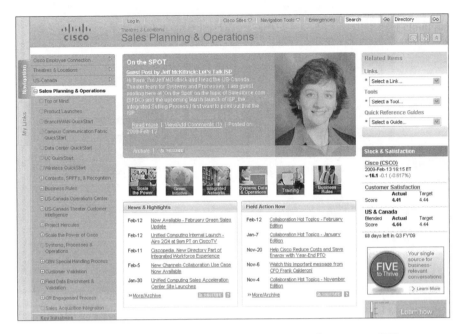

Figure 11-7   *U.S.-Canada Sales Planning & Operations home page.[23]*

- **Scale the Power,** a program focused on effective use of resources, such as video technology and telephony.

- **Administrator Training,** training content on topics such as virtual team meeting scheduling.

- **Collaboration Portal,** collaboration-related content aggregated in one location.

- **Collaboration Guide,** a comprehensive technology reference guide.

- **Collaboration Hot Topics,** key information and news headlines.

- **Collaboration Library,** a collection of papers and use cases showcasing business value of collaboration.

- **Collaboration Cockpit,** technology installation and adoption metrics.

- **Web 2.0 Committee,** a bi-weekly forum of Segment leaders working on key collaboration priorities for the Field.

- **Worldwide Sales Collaboration Board,** a monthly forum of global collaboration initiative leaders.

- **Five to Thrive,** a fast-tracked, cross-functional program designed to enable sales teams to help customers leverage Cisco solutions to succeed during the economic downturn.

The following sections provide more details about each of these initiatives.

Scale the Power

The Scale the Power (STP) initiative facilitates and positively impacts virtual interactions between Cisco customers, partners, and employees enabling them to leverage cutting-edge video, voice, and collaboration technologies and telephony tools. STP's goal was to

- Make the latest Unified Communications products available to the field.

- Install wireless area network (WAN) upgrades in all Field Sales Offices (FSOs).

- Video-enable all FSOs, via Cisco Unified Video Advantage—(CUVA) and Meeting-Place, to support virtual face-to-face meetings.

- Build out of large high-quality video conference rooms in FSOs.

- Roll out TelePresence for U.S.-Canada.

Figure 11-8 shows SPO's STP site, which provides collaboration technology–related news, success stories, tools, resources, related items, a learning center, and upcoming events.

Figure 11-8 *Sales Planning & Operations' Scale the Power site.[24]*

Thanks to the Scale the Power initiative, enhanced audio/video (EAV) rooms have been installed across the Theater. These conference, training, and demonstration rooms are equipped with advanced audio video systems and special room lighting and acoustics appropriately sized to support video teleconferencing activities. The goal of this Sales 2.0 initiative is to enable customers and partners to experience the same high-quality interaction they would experience visiting Cisco headquarters, in or near their everyday work locations.

As the list of STP's goal at the beginning of the section indicates, the initiative focused on deploying technologies to Field Sales Offices, putting collaborative tools in the hands of front-line, customer- and partner-facing teams. As a result, Sales teams can now conduct business virtually with partners, customers, and associates without traveling, which enables executives and subject matter experts (SMEs) to scale more effectively.[24]

Administrator Training

A key aspect of the Scale the Power initiative is focused on training key staff members: executive administrative assistants and field sales administrators (FSAs). Sales executives often rely on their administrative assistants, and Sales teams rely on their FSAs to schedule and support virtual meetings for their organizations. The U.S.-Canada Theater realized that providing a comprehensive training program to this group would enable them to be more effective, and would also help to increase adoption of collaborative and virtual meeting technologies across Sales.

The Collaboration Training for Cisco Administrators site offers a training program broken down into three modules:

- Key elements of a successful virtual meeting, offering an online video tutorial and overview presentation

- WebEx Meeting Center–focused training

- TelePresence overview

Assistants who have taken the training have a better understanding of the technology features and capabilities. They are also more likely to help others use the technology and make them aware of Sales 2.0 practices that can add value to virtual meetings and collaborative activities.[25]

Collaboration Portal

The U.S.-Canada Sales Collaboration Portal, shown in Figure 11-9, provides a "one stop shop" for all things Sales 2.0, making them more relevant and easily accessible to the field. The Collaboration Portal team works closely with groups focused on the CCoE initiative mentioned in Chapter 10 to share best practices and lessons learned. This is not a duplication of CCoE, the enterprise collaboration technology site, but provides a front door to CCoE for Sales.

Access to the Collaboration Portal and its content is open to all Cisco users, to encourage the broadest possible participation and content leverage. The Collaboration Portal provides links to Sales 2.0 Hot Topics, Sales Tools, Related Items, Collaboration Discussion, and more. It also provides access to the U.S.-Canada Collaboration Guide, Collaboration White Papers, Metrics, and an overview of the U.S.-Canada Web 2.0 Committee described later in the chapter.[26]

Collaboration Guide

The U.S.-Canada Theater established a Collaboration Guide to provide a brief overview of Cisco's collaboration technologies and tools, including the following:

Figure 11-9   *U.S.-Canada Sales Collaboration portal.[26]*

- **Collaboration Continuum:** Mapping audience interaction types to technology solutions

- **Collaboration Tools:** Blogs, Ciscopedia, Directory 3.0, and discussion forums, connecting people and information

- **Community Platforms:** Technologies enabling connected teams

- **Document Management:** Platforms helping users to share, store, and archive content more effectively

- **Video Creation and Publishing Tools:** Podcast, VoDcasts, CUVA, C-Vision, and vSearch, enhancing communication and increasing connectedness

- **Web 2.0 Quick Reference Guide:** Mapping Web 2.0 technology to intended audience and use case, describing the technology from the user point of view

- **Virtual Meetings:** Mapping meeting size and purpose to technology solutions

- **Virtual Meeting Platforms and Tools:** Enabling virtual face-to-face interactions

- **Virtual Meeting Quick Reference Guide:** Mapping technology/application to audience, experience, and type of virtual meeting

- **Glossary and Resources:** Buzzwords and related links

- **Technology Comparison Chart:** Technology features from a user perspective

The Collaboration Continuum shown in Figure 11-10 identifies technologies used for interpersonal, team, and community collaboration. It also provides technology recommendations based on the audience interaction types listed in Table 11-2.

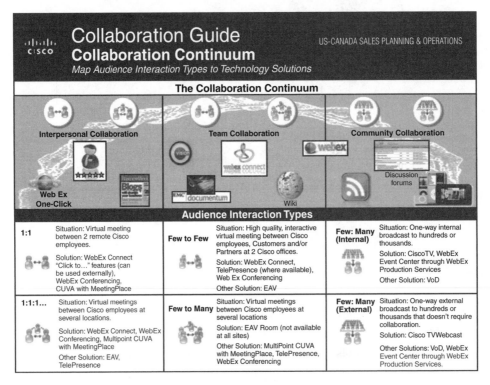

Figure 11-10   *U.S.-Canada Collaboration Guide Collaboration Continuum.[27]*

Table 11-2   *Collaboration Guide Collaboration Continuum Audience Interaction Types [27]*

Interaction	Situation	Solution
One to One	Virtual meeting between two remote Cisco employees	■ WebEx Connect "Click to..." features (can be used externally) ■ WebEx Conferencing ■ CUVA with MeetingPlace
Few to Few	High-quality, interactive virtual meeting between Cisco employees, Customers, and/or Partners at two Cisco offices	■ WebEx Connect ■ TelePresence (where available), WebEx Conferencing ■ EAV Room

Table 11-2 *Collaboration Guide Collaboration Continuum Audience Interaction Types*
[27]

Interaction	Situation	Solution
Few to Many (Internal)	One-way internal broadcast to hundreds or thousands	■ Cisco TV ■ WebEx Event Center through WebEx Production Services ■ VoD
Few to Many (External)	One-way external broadcast to hundreds or thousands, which doesn't require collaboration	■ CiscoTV Webcast ■ VoD ■ WebEx Event Center through WebEx Production Services
Many to Many	Virtual meetings between Cisco employees at several locations	■ WebEx Connect ■ WebEx Conferencing ■ Multipoint CUVA with MeetingPlace ■ EAV Room ■ TelePresence

The Collaboration Guide offers significant business value because it is designed to increase Sales productivity and save time. It offers pros, cons, best use, and getting started links for each technology. The Guide provides explanations of key concepts such as Really Simple Syndication (RSS), social tagging, and social networking tools. It also answers questions on the differences between these technologies.

The Collaboration Guide is designed to enable Sales 2.0 teams to leverage these tools to reduce travel expenses and be more connected. The Guide helps Sales teams to leverage collaboration and virtual meeting tools. It provides guidelines on when to use MeetingPlace, WebEx, and TelePresence to hold virtual meetings, and a (CUVA) camera to create a video on demand (VoD).

The Guide offers brief descriptions of types of virtual meetings: sales calls, briefings, seminars, and broadcasts, and recommends Cisco technology options for each. It also answers questions on the differences between meeting technologies and offers simple graphic examples of types of video interactions and provides technology solutions for each situation. The Guide provides ratings for the video quality, interactivity, and ease of setup for each virtual meeting technology and collaboration application.

Finally, the Collaboration Guide saves time by providing a robust set of definitions of collaboration buzzwords. It also provides a centralized source of links to related information. In a Sales 2.0 way, it provides access to key information to help Sales use collaboration tools and technologies to best support the customer. The CCoE site has incorporated the Collaboration Guide content for use across the broader enterprise.[27]

Collaboration Hot Topics

Sales teams often use newsletters to get the word out on Sales initiatives and new technologies. The U.S.-Canada team also recognized the value of communicating key collaboration hot topics to the field on a regular basis. As collaboration became such a buzzword at Cisco, the U.S.-Canada Theater jumped at the opportunity to put together a comprehensive monthly newsletter, called Collaboration Hot Topics, providing key information on collaboration tools, technologies, and best practices. Table 11-3 shows sample newsletter topics.

Table 11-3   *Sample Topics in Collaboration Hot Topics Newsletters [23]*

Date	Topics
December 2008	■ Updated Collaboration Guide Now Available ■ Check Out Collaboration Connection Radio ■ Add a Virtual Demo to Your Sales Strategy ■ Migrate Your Unified Communications Customers Today ■ Provide Greater Value for Customers with Interactive Technology Demos ■ Help Customers Experience the Cisco WebEx Connect Workforce ■ Empower Customers Through Collaboration Without Boundaries Session ■ Learn How to Enable the Enterprise with New Webcast Series ■ TelePresence Updates: ■ Learn More About Cisco TelePresence Solution Release 1.5 ■ Get Started Selling TelePresence Step-by-step ■ Continue the Momentum with Cisco TelePresence Proposal Central
January 2009	■ A Blueprint for Enterprise Collaboration ■ Cisco Unified Workspace Licensing Turns One Million! ■ NEW! Meetings in Motion on the iPhone 3G ■ TelePresence Updates: ■ Cisco TelePresence Executive Metrics Dashboard Now Live ■ Accelerate TelePresence Sales with Help from Cisco Executives ■ Cisco TelePresence Suites ■ AT&T Offers Multipoint, Intercompany Capabilities with Their TelePresence Solution

Table 11-3   *Sample Topics in Collaboration Hot Topics Newsletters [23]*

Date	Topics

February 2009	■ WebEx Connect Sales Training Modules Now Available
	■ New Channels Collaboration Use Case Now Available
	■ Partner-to-Partner Collaboration Fuels Profitable Growth
	■ New Directory Now Available, Salespedia Now Merged with Ciscopedia
	■ Live Daily Demo! Cisco WebEx Meeting Center on the iPhone
	■ Announcing the Cisco WebEx Connect Community Wiki
	■ CIO Insights on Collaboration
	■ Cisco on Cisco on Collaboration
	■ Cisco TV Updates
	   ■ TechWiseTV: Collaboration Without Boundaries
	   ■ CIT Workshop: Accelerating Learning 2.0 with Cisco WebEx
	   ■ BizWiseTV: The Collaboration Advantage
	■ TelePresence Updates
	   ■ Cisco TelePresence Meeting on Us: Schedule a Meeting on Us for Your Customer Today
	   ■ Cisco TelePresence University Connection

Each Collaboration Hot Topics newsletter provides insightful Sales 2.0–inspired content. Newsletters are thoughtfully crafted by the U.S.-Canada team to provide the field with the information they need to understand to leverage collaborative technology more effectively and become more productive. Newsletters usually include Web 2.0 concept definitions, introduce and provide status updates on collaborative technologies, announce collaboration initiatives, and share collaborative best practices drawn from the Sales community.

The February 2009 edition just listed in Table 11-3, for example, contains a number of news headlines linking to initiatives worth itemizing here, to help connect the dots:

■ **WebEx Connect Sales Training Modules Now Available** refers to a set of Flash training modules developed, as a part of the WebEx Connect Initiative for Sales mentioned earlier in the chapter, to help the Field understand how to best leverage Connect.

■ **New Channels Collaboration Use Case Now Available** creates awareness of the latest Channels-focused addition to the Collaboration Library described later in the chapter.

■ **Partner-to-Partner Collaboration Fuels Profitable Growth** showcases a recent Cisco study that revealed collaboration among Cisco partners generates 31% of

Channel revenue, a topic discussed later in this chapter, in the "Worldwide Channels" section.

- **New Directory Now Available, Salespedia Now Merged With Ciscopedia** highlights the connections between Cisco Directory 3.0 and Ciscopedia, both described in Chapter 10 and in Salespedia, mentioned earlier in the chapter.

- **Live Daily Demo! Cisco WebEx Meeting Center on the iPhone** showcases live demos of the award-winning mobile WebEx Meeting Center application available on the iPhone, described in Chapter 9.

- **Announcing the Cisco WebEx Connect Community Wiki** creates awareness of this community wiki effort highlighting WebEx Connect best practices, metrics, and capability development, described in Chapter 10.

The Collaboration Hot Topics newsletter provides a great example of how to effectively evangelize benefits of Web 2.0 and to drive its adoption. The newsletter was first delivered to the U.S.-Canada team via email, but has become so popular and widely acclaimed that it is now posted on Cisco's intranet, on both the Sales Planning & Operations home page and the Collaboration portal.[23]

Collaboration Library

The U.S.-Canada Theater has developed a collection of white papers and use cases focused on collaboration. For example:

- "The Next Revolution in Productivity and Innovation" demonstrates the power of collaboration at work, sharing the company's perspective on the collaboration revolution underway.

- "The Next Frontier in Collaboration: Improving Customer Intimacy and Enhancing Operational Efficiencies" describes the steps Cisco has taken to think beyond the norm about collaboration technologies and management practices and shares the business results.

- "The Next Frontier in Collaboration: Transforming How Cisco and Channel Partners Work Together" provides an overview of how Cisco and its channel partners work more effectively together and with end customers.

Collaboration white papers and use cases are developed quarterly, each with a different focus, creating a reference library of success stories for Sales teams to share with customers and partners.

The last entry in the list focuses on Channels, and is the latest addition to the collection. It provides more details on the business value of collaboration with channel partners and customers, as cited in the Nexus example showcased in Chapter 10. It is also cited in the Netera example described in the "Worldwide Channels" section later in this chapter, and mentioned briefly in Chapter 2. This new Channels collaboration use case is shown in Table 11-3, a sample topic from the February 2009 *Collaboration Hot Topics Newsletter*. The Newsletter provides a means of bringing Collaboration Library content to the Theater's attention.[28]

Collaboration Cockpit

The U.S.-Canada Collaboration Cockpit provides metrics on a number of key SPO initiatives and U.S.-Canada Theater technology adoption:

- Enhanced Audio Visual (EAV) rooms/sites enablement, through Scale the Power (STP) and non-STP installations

- Video site enablement schedule by location

- Number and location of TelePresence rooms enabled

- U.S.-Canada Theater website hits

- Donna Rhode's On the SPOT blog hits and comments

- Theater WebEx Connect usage, documents, and spaces

- Theater WebEx Connect training sessions

- C-Vision and Cisco TV views

Because metrics are an important part measuring the success of U.S.-Canada initiatives, they are reported weekly. Some of these metrics are gathered from website tracking tools. Others, such as the WebEx Connect user metrics shown in Table 11-4, are based on CCoE metrics, discussed in Chapter 10.[29]

Table 11-4 *U.S.-Canada Versus Cisco WebEx Connect User Metrics January 2009 [29][30]*

WebEx Connect	U.S.-Canada Theater	Cisco	U.S.-C as Percentage of Cisco Users
Users	4,395	31,047	14%

The SPO team continues to refine its metrics-gathering process to measure technology adoption for each segment. More important, however, the team is working to identify metrics to measure the business value of collaboration technology adoption. Based on some work being done by Cisco's Customer Value Chain Management (CVCM) initiative, focused on measuring the business value of collaboration, these metrics have begun to take shape as shown in Table 11-5.[31]

Table 11-5 *Collaboration Technology Business Value Metrics[31][32]*

Metric	Focus	Definition	Sample Measure(s)
Availability	Technology	How available the technology is for deployment or use (internally and externally)	- Time to download or use - Number of clicks to access technology

(continues)

Table 11-5 *Collaboration Technology Business Value Metrics[31][32] (continued)*

Metric	Focus	Definition	Sample Measure(s)
Awareness	People	How aware users are of the technology	■ Number of downloads ■ Number of upgrades
Application	Process	How much the technology is actually being used, even for experimentation	■ Number of functional uses ■ Number of mashups leveraging the technology
Adoption	Community	How much usage is growing; sets a stake in the ground as to where usage is and where it needs to be by a certain date	■ Number of executives proficient in the technology ■ Number of users taking technology training or certification
Acceleration	Transformation	How much the technology is changing the business and our customers' businesses (the domino effect)	■ Number of times technology is used with customers and partners ■ Number of best practices shared, indicating thought leadership

Metrics in this space might include such measures as time to access C-Vision Videos, percentage of employees using Directory 3.0 to find experts, percentage of time Ciscopedia yields needed information via search results, number of employee locator mashups, productive virtual meeting time, time-to-decision using WebEx polling function, number of TelePresence sessions with customers, number of presentations at external technology conferences or working groups, and so on.[32]

Web 2.0 Committee

The U.S.-Canada Web 2.0 Committee consists of account managers (AMs) and systems engineers (SEs) from across the Theater and a number of WWSPS team members. The Committee represents U.S.-Canada and feeds into the Worldwide Sates Collaboration Board (WWSCB) described in the next section. Members of the Web 2.0 Committee play key roles in U.S.-Canada collaborative programs. They are generally responsible for managing communication and often day-to-day support of most U.S.-Canada Web 2.0 initiatives and also serve as Sales 2.0 evangelists. Web 2.0 Committee members are expected to drive their team's engagement in and support of Sales 2.0 collaborative initiatives, such as Scale the Power and the WebEx Connect Early Adopters Program described earlier in this chapter.[33]

Worldwide Sales Collaboration Board

U.S.-Canada and WWSPS have partnered to establish a Worldwide Sales Collaboration Board (WWSCB) with senior, global representatives from Sales theaters and groups: Inside

Sales, Channels, Europe, Asia Pacific, and Sales partners, such as Customer Advocacy and Global Accounts, for example. The Board represents Worldwide Sales and feeds into the Communication and Collaboration Board, a group chartered to drive adoption of Web 2.0 collaborative technologies company-wide. Members of the Sales Collaboration Board, shown in Figure 11-11, are theater business representatives and governance owners.

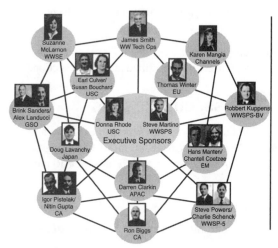

- Worldwide sales

- Feeds into Communication & Collaboration Board, a company-wide committee

- Theatre business representative

- Theatre governance owner

- Inventory holder of Theatre Web 2.0 activities

- Web 2.0 evangelist

Figure 11-11   *Worldwide Sales Collaboration Board.[34]*

Members of the WWSCB are aware of theater Web 2.0 activities and serve as Sales 2.0 evangelists. WWSCB members are expected to sponsor their theater or group's engagement in and support of Sales 2.0 collaboration initiatives.[35] The Board is currently sponsoring a sub-committee focused on defining work scenarios, where collaboration might accelerate decisions or enable business process transformation.

Now let's review how collaborative Web 2.0 technologies are enabling business process transformation in the U.S.-Canada Theater Advanced Technology Segment.

Advanced Technology

U.S.-Canada's Advanced Technologies (AT) organization was established in 2002 to focus on selling emerging technologies to customers in the region. The team has grown under the leadership of Carl Wiese, vice president of U.S.-Canada advanced technology sales, from a few to over 800 sales professionals. The $5 billion organization represents a third of U.S.-Canada Theater sales.

AT is a key part of Cisco's business, growing 137% in the past three years, accounting for 63% of the U.S.-Canada Theater's growth. The Advanced Technologies portfolio includes

- **Unified Communications:** Collaboration, voice, video, and mobile applications on both fixed and mobile networks

- **Data Center:** Data center switching, storage area networking, and application networking services

- **Contact Center:** Call routing and reporting as well as agent desktop capabilities

- **Wireless:** Wireless access points, local area network (LAN) controllers, and secure mobility services

- **Security:** Intrusion protection, firewalls, virtual private networks (VPN) security management, desktop security, email, and web security

The AT team, whose deep technical knowledge and strategic selling skills are among the best in the industry, is in the midst of a Sales 2.0 initiative, described in the next section.[35]

Specialist, Optimization, Access, and Results

In 2008, the U.S.-Canada Theater recognized that existing sales support headcount and sales processes would be unable to support Cisco's aggressive Advanced Technology (AT) sales efforts. As a result, the Specialist, Optimization, Access, and Results (SOAR) initiative was launched to

- Improve customer support and accelerate AT growth

- Drive adoption of Web 2.0 technologies and tools and virtualization to transform the selling process

- Increase depth and quality of specialist interactions

- Identify and leverage expertise of deeper sub-specialists through virtual interactions and tools

- Increase sales and specialist productivity, accessing virtual resources to provide rapid response

- Implement self-help tools to drive self-sufficiency and increase access to information[36]

The U.S.-Canada's SOAR team began working together with the same precision, dedication, discipline, and professionalism as Canada's Air Force Demonstration team, the Snowbirds, whose synchronized aerobatics is showcased on the SOAR Canada site.

SOAR's home page, shown in Figure 11-12, provides links to the SOAR Canada and SOAR Inside Sales sites as well as individual segment-specific sites, including SOAR U.S. Commercial, Enterprise, Public Sector, and Service Provider.

The site highlights SOAR news, features VoDs, and provides links to SOAR resources, including the Technology Solutions Network (TSN). SOAR leverages the global TSN as a collection of on-demand virtual specialists that make up SOAR's rapid response team.[37]

In addition to providing a single point of contact for quick access to technical resources to the SOAR team, TSN specialists support a wide range of technical pre-sales activities to support sales account teams:

- Bill of Materials (BOM) support

- Locating product or competitive product information

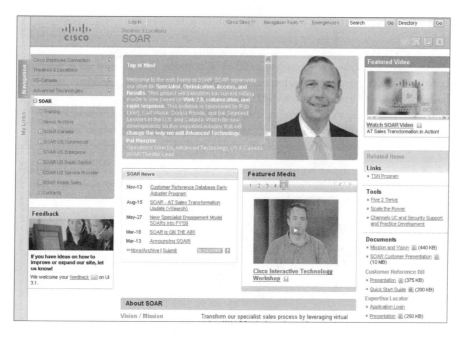

Figure 11-12   *Specialist, Optimization, Access, and Results home page.[37]*

- Finding, creating or validating presentations

- List pricing

- Request for Proposal (RFP)/Request for Information (RFI) assistance

TSN serves as an example of a Sales 2.0 program designed to transform and increase the number and quality of SE-to-customer interactions via real-time collaboration solutions, while reducing the time specialists spend traveling. The SOAR team also benefits from the TSN knowledge wiki, a self-service tool providing access to AT-related content, collaboratively developed and maintained by TSN specialists.[38][39]

The SOAR team also leverages content on the SE Connection Portal, which provides the SE community with a wealth of information on

- Customer support

- Product demonstration and testing

- Network design and modeling

- SE development, training, and leadership programs[40]

Many members of the SOAR team collaborate via SE Community wikis, among the first Connected Communities mentioned previously in the chapter.[41] Community wikis enable SEs to exchange information with product development teams on delivery schedules and features, significantly improving communication, reducing email traffic, and increasing productivity.

Many SEs on the SOAR team also share informational videos they have created themselves on an SE community-based video-sharing portal called vSearch. Figure 11-13 showcases the U.S.-Canada vSearch Spotlight page, accessible via the U.S.-Canada Collaboration Portal mentioned previously in this chapter. The Spotlight page showcases best practices used to build communities and helps users to learn how to find vSearch content.[42]

Figure 11-13   *U.S.-Canada vSearch Spotlight page.[42]*

Like C-Vision, mentioned in Chapter 10, vSearch provides a virtual water cooler for the SE community to share knowledge and information.

The SOAR initiative leverages TSN and SE Connection resources to enrich the customer experience, ensuring the right resources are available at the right time to support a sales opportunity anywhere in the world. The SOAR team has also contributed significantly to Sales' self-help tools mentioned earlier and others, including weekly virtual product demos and a customer reference database.

SOAR launched a series of high-level technology webinars called Virtual Demos, highlighted in the December 2008 Collaboration Hot Topics listed previously in Table 11-3. The demos, targeted at customers, provide live, high-quality, interactive technology demonstrations using Cisco's WebEx product. Sales teams can connect customers in any TelePresence location to Unified Communications, Security, and Data Center demonstrations provided by expert systems engineers located in Cisco's San Jose Executive Briefing Center from 6:00 a.m.–7:00 p.m. Pacific Time. These demos enable a Sates team to assess a prospect's interest in a more scalable way.

Table 11-6 presents some of the outstanding results in terms of business value metrics.

Table 11-6   *Specialist, Optimization, Access, and Results Business Value Metrics[43]*

Metric	Measure	Results
Customer Reach	Increase in external interactions (Percent)	39–51% Increase
Interaction Quality	Satisfaction rating (out of 5.0)	4.7–4.9 Rating
Time Saved	Time saved per week per specialist (Hours)	6–17 Hours Saved
Expenses Reduced	Decrease in travel and entertainment (T&E) expense (Percent)	52–63% Decrease
Bottom Line	Full-time equivalent (FTE) saved per virtual specialists (VS)	1 FTE / 5 VS

These SOAR metrics are based on a survey of support specialists conducted in March 2008 and year-over-year expense analysis in July 2008. SOAR is enabling Cisco to increase the number of external customer interactions specialists can have every week, in some cases by more than 50%. But equally important, SOAR is improving Cisco's ability to shorten the sales cycle, bringing in the right specialist at the right time—all while improving the quality of life and work-life balance for Cisco's sales professionals.[43]

In November 2008 Wiese announced Cisco's new Collaboration Connection interactive talk radio, which is another program designed to help Sales team members talk about collaboration with their customers, with maximum impact. Like Cisco TV, mentioned in Chapter 10, Collaboration Connection talk radio features a variety of conversations every month, including collaboration-focused interviews with key stakeholders from both inside and outside the company. Sales teams can contribute to the program by submitting comments and questions on specific content or suggestions on future topics.[44]

Now turn your attention to how Sales 2.0 is helping to enable a cross-functional collaborative initiative driving change both inside and outside the company.

Five to Thrive

In October 2008, the U.S.-Canada Theater launched a fast-tracked, cross-functional program, Called Five to Thrive, whose interally-focused website is shown in Figure 11-14.

The program had aggregated a wide array of content, such as presentations, VoDs, and other tools into a set of playbooks. Each playbook is designed to enable Sales teams to help customers keep pace with the rapidly changing business environment and succeed during the economic downturn, often by leveraging Cisco collaboration technology solutions.

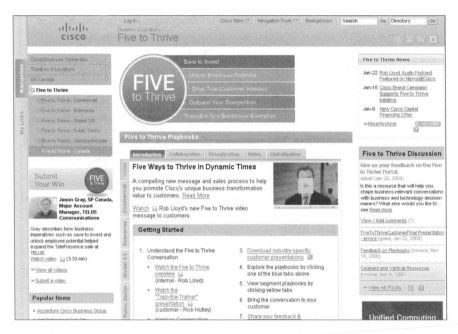

Figure 11-14   *U.S.-Canada Theater Five to Thrive site.[45]*

The Five to Thrive program focuses on five proven success strategies, or business imperatives, if you will:

- **Save to Invest**, by reducing costs to provide funding for investments in improvements that yield competitive advantage

- **Unlock Employee Potential**, by improving innovation and productivity to build an "anytime, anywhere" workforce

- **Drive True Customer Intimacy**, by including customers in business processes so processes truly meet customer needs

- **Outpace Your Competition**, using Web 2.0 collaboration technologies to yield new business models

- **Transition to a Borderless Enterprise**, increasing potential for success via collaboration with global ecosystem partners

The Five to Thrive program enables Sales to share Cisco's value proposition with global employees, customers, and business partners in meaningful ways, particularly during challenging economic times.[46]

Cisco believes that collaboration, virtualization, and video technologies can help customers succeed and is working to show them how by making this information available through the externally-focused Cisco.com site shown in Figure 11-15.

Table 11-7 consolidates content from the Cisco.com Thrive in Dynamic Times site, which consists of a collection of individual pages, each presenting one of the Five to Thrive strategies.

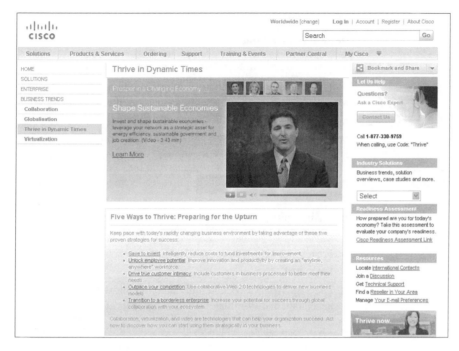

Figure 11-15   *Cisco.com Thrive in Dynamic Times site.[47]*

The Cisco.com Thrive in Dynamic Times strategy pages feature VoDs, articles, and stories from employees, customers, and partners sharing best practices and experiences, showcasing the practicality, business value, and return on investment (ROI) of the strategy at hand.[47] Readers are encouraged to visit the site often to learn more.

The cross-functionally driven Five to Thrive Program has been well received. It is helping drive conversations around business process transformation based on network-centric collaboration and virtualization technologies. Content from the building blocks for business-relevant conversations on how to Thrive in Dynamic Times are being rolled into Cisco's next marketing campaign, along with content from Cisco's worldwide Channels organization.[53] The global Channels organization is the next area of focus.

Worldwide Channels

Cisco's Worldwide Channels organization, led by Keith Goodwin, senior vice president of Worldwide Channels, is working with customers and partners to collaborate and grow the market together to achieve the Channels 3.0 vision. Because over 80% of Cisco's revenue flows through Channels, the indirect sales route-to-market plays a key role in Cisco's strategy, particularly in dynamic times such as these. Worldwide Channels' vision focuses on working with what Cisco considers the world's best partners to transform the customer experience. Its mission is to accelerate partner and customer success, creating capacity for growth.[54]

Table 11-7 *Cisco's Five to Thrive Business Strategies[47]*

Strategy	Recommendations
Save to Invest	■ Reduce travel costs by conducting meetings via technologies such as TelePresence and WebEx ■ Reduce real estate and energy costs by enabling a remote yet connected workforce ■ Use managed services to preserve capital and human resources ■ Centralize and consolidate IT infrastructure and resources[48]
Unlock Employee Potential	■ Adopt a structure of collaborative leadership and decision-making ■ Enable employees to work securely from anywhere, at any time ■ Foster innovation by promoting employee communication and participation ■ Leverage a pervasive and unified communications platform to accelerate decision-making and increase its effectiveness[49]
Drive True Customer Intimacy	■ Increase quality, timeliness, and frequency of interactions with customers ■ Support customers anywhere, anytime, by extending customer reach ■ Connect customers with the right expertise the first time to improve customer experience ■ Ensure innovation processes include partners[50]
Outpace Your Competition	■ Include partners and suppliers in your innovation processes to improve time to market ■ Prospect collaboratively to broaden sales and growth potential ■ Leverage current resources to enter new global markets ■ Uncover new revenue streams by unlocking new business models[51]
Transition to a Borderless Enterprise	■ Promote a culture focused on partnership and collaboration ■ Share capabilities throughout your company and the ecosystem via the cloud ■ Leverage global resources and talent to accelerate innovation and execution ■ Adopt a model of end-to-end governance[52]

Like U.S.-Canada's Five to Thrive program, Channels has a program, called Navigate to Accelerate, designed to help partners navigate the economic storm and accelerate as the market turns. The program focuses on Cisco providing partners with a compass to help them focus on their customer base, changing needs, managing finances, and the future. The program is intended to help partners make strategic investments in technology and partnerships that will enable them to prepare for the eventual upturn in the economy.[55]

Cisco, its channel partners, and its customers are learning to work together in new ways, using collaborative technologies such as Cisco TelePresence, WebEx, and Unified Communications, described in Chapter 2. The SOAR example described earlier in the chapter shows how these tools have enabled Cisco to more effectively meet customer needs for specialized expertise, nearly doubling customer interactions while reducing specialist travel. This virtual expert model is also being applied within Channels.

As Cisco's portfolio of products has grown, so has the complexity of selling to support those products. This has caused an increasing need for more effective and more innovative collaboration between Cisco and its partners, often yielding deeper partnerships between the two. Customers are often more global and increasingly demand deeper sub-specialist technical knowledge from Cisco and its Channel partners.

Cisco to Partner

As in the SOAR example, the Channels Virtual Expert Program is leveraging Cisco technologies such as TelePresence and WebEx to enable SEs to work more productively and effectively. SEs cover more partners virtually, resolving partner issues faster, reducing travel, and improving their own quality of life and work-life balance. Results of the program, showcasing the business value, are summarized in Table 11-8.

Table 11-8   *Channels Virtual Experts Program Business Results[56]*

Measure	Results
Increase in expert productivity (percent)	100%
Increase in partner-facing time (percent)	50–100% increase
Increase in sales (percent)	50% (based on example from one technology area)
Decrease in travel expenses	65% decrease
Channel partner satisfaction rating (out of 5.0)	4.43 (based on a 4.25 target)
Number of webcast views	7,000 (and growing)

One other advantage, particularly important as Cisco and its partners and customers focus on Green initiatives such as the one mentioned in Chapter 10, is that a reduction in travel of this magnitude also enables the company to decrease its carbon footprint. Partner issues that might have taken nearly a week to resolve, with back-and-forth communication and travel to a partner or customer site, can now be resolved in 10–15 minutes as virtual on-demand experts can be brought to bear quickly.

SEs are a key part of Cisco's efforts to educate partners and customers through virtual demos and webcasts focused on delivering information on Cisco products and technology services to audiences ranging from 150 to 400 remote participants. These demos can be replayed for review or shared with new employees. SEs are also becoming adept at using WebEx to remotely control a partner's computer, walking them through steps to resolve an issue. SEs often leverage partner resources as their hands and eyes to TeleWork, solving technical issues while providing partners with hands-on training sessions. Nexus, a Cisco channel partner mentioned in Chapter 2, is a great example of Partner to Customer Collaboration and its business value.

Partner to Partner

Cisco recently deployed Cisco Partner Space, shown in Figure 11-16, which is a virtual environment designed to facilitate three key collaboration models: Cisco to Partner, Partner to Customer, and Partner to Partner.

Figure 11-16   *Cisco Partner Space virtual tradeshow environment.[57]*

Partner Space provides partners the opportunity to share their products in virtual booths, taking part in a tradeshow that is always on. So far, with over 3,500 visitors each month and 400 partner booths, Partner Space enables partners to increase their visibility online, collaborate with others, and win more business.

Cisco's annual Partner Summit, formerly limited to 2,500 in-person attendees, expanded its reach, holding the first Virtual Partner Summit in Partner Space in 2008. 2,000 additional attendees were able to view live feeds from keynote speeches, theater sessions, and the show floor. The Unified Communications team increased its September 2008 summit attendance from 300 to more than 1,000 by enabling virtual participation.

Cisco's Wireless Partners Collaboration Workspace provides another example of a Channels-focused collaborative initiative that has successfully increased reach and streamlined communication between Cisco and its partners. Nearly 1,600 members, from 355 partners in 22 countries supporting wireless customers, leverage WebEx collaborative technology to share documents and participate in discussions. The Workspace also enables members to send each other event reminders and post news and announcements. A poll of partner members yielded positive ratings of either "very good" or "excellent" from 74% of those polled.

Partner to partner collaboration helps drive partner revenue by extending the partner's geographic reach. Collaborating with other partners also helps to expand a partner's portfolio of solutions and add to its competencies. Collaborative communities enable partners to find other partners to work with, expanding their reach. This is particularly important in a competitive environment where partnerships based only on prior relationships or word of mouth limits visibility and opportunity.

Cisco's research, summarized in Table 11-9, shows 31% of channel partner revenues, increasing rapidly by 15% per year, results from partner to partner collaboration. More than a thousand channel partners have created profiles in Partner Exchange, a profile search tool within Partner Space, enabling partners to search for partners by technology expertise, geographic location, or business focus.

Table 11-9   *Channels Partner to Partner Collaboration Business Results[56]*

Measure	Results
Resulting Partner revenue (percent)	31%
Growth in revenues (percent)	15% increase
Partners winning larger deals (percent)	78%
Partner Exchange profiles	1,000+ (and growing)

Some Cisco channel partners attribute an even larger increase in revenue to partner to partner collaboration.

Netera Networks(http://www.netera.networks.com), for example, has seen solid benefits from partner to partner collaboration, including a 38% increase in revenues and between $3–4 million in new pipeline revenue. Netera also reports benefits from improving internal collaboration, using Cisco WebEx technologies, to see a 20% productivity increase in their engineering pool, a 22% decrease in time-to-resolution on customer issues, and overall cost savings to their customers. With a 5.0 out of 5.0 customer satisfaction rating and an increase in employee satisfaction, Netera has seen significant business value from using collaborative technologies.

Cisco Partner Locator is another tool enabling more than 40,000 visitors per month to more easily connect with partners and other customers. Partner Locator enables customers to search for keywords and phrases and receive a list of partners that match customer needs in terms of technical, geographic, and skill perspective. Partner Locator has become Cisco's most utilized tool.

To more effectively transform its business processes and manage change, Cisco follows a methodical approach to

- **Build initiatives leveraging regular partner feedback**, engaging frequently to assess partner collaboration needs.

- **Provide a strong role model, reinforcing new methods**, leading by example, showcasing technology adoption and use.

- **Encourage early adoption and support grassroots efforts**, fostering employee innovation and showcasing partner technology champions.

- **Match organizational structure to new collaboration workflow**, enabling teams to organize in ways that support the program.

- **Measure performance and offer incentives to get results**, encouraging partner participation through discounts and program improvements that foster adoption and reward innovation.

Table 11-10 shows key benefits from improved collaboration.

Table 11-10   *Key Benefits from Improved Collaboration[56]*

Cisco	Channel partners	Customers
100% expert productivity increase	31% increase in revenue from partner-to-partner collaboration	Reduced time to issue resolution (from a few days to a few minutes)
65% decrease in travel costs	20% improvement in partner productivity (observed by one channel partner)	Improved quality of service from Cisco and partners
2–3 times extended reach to broader partner community	Enhanced partner satisfaction	Enhanced customer satisfaction from offerings and services provided
Increased sales (approximately 50% in one example)	$370K per year of travel avoidance (observed by one channel partner)	Greater connectivity with channel partner and Cisco
Increased employee satisfaction		

Table 11-10 *Key Benefits from Improved Collaboration[56]*

Cisco	Channel partners	Customers
Decreased carbon footprint		

As these examples show, Web 2.0 technologies increase collaboration; enhance productivity; decrease travel costs; improve employee, partner and customer satisfaction; and drive deeper relationships that generate more revenue. Web 2.0 collaborative technologies enable process transformation and yield significant business results.[56]

Marketing

I would be remiss not to mention that Marketing, led by Sue Bostrom, executive vice president and chief marketing officer, plays a key role in Sales 2.0 and in the success of Cisco sales team efforts. Cisco has marketing teams focused on consumer, corporate, enterprise, and mid-market solutions, globalization, service provider, small business, strategic, and worldwide field marketing. The organization is responsible for product marketing campaigns and annual events, such as Cisco Live 2008, mentioned in Chapter 10.[58]

Collaboration Consortium

One key Cisco initiative, the Collaboration Consortium, was launched by Cisco in July 2008. Cisco currently chairs the collaboration research initiative comprising 17 member organizations, spanning vertical markets in both public and private sectors, including 15 Cisco customers, Stanford University, Wharton Business School, and SBTadvisors (http://www.sbtadvisors.com/), a strategy and business transformation consulting firm acting in an advisory role. Cisco currently chairs the organization. Its primary objectives are

- Provide a forum enabling members to share best practices and lessons learned from collaboration efforts.

- Develop a Collaboration Framework to apply collaboration to business to transform business processes.

- Establish priorities focused on key areas such as vision and strategy, business models, culture, adoption and metrics.[59]

In Short

This chapter identified what Sales 2.0 is about and demonstrated its practical application in Cisco Sales. It described how Web 2.0 led to Sales 2.0, changing both the buying and the selling processes, as well as key aspects of Sales 2.0 selling. It went on to explain how early explorations of WWSPS and the U.S.-Canada Theater teams, such as Connected Communities, Finding Expertise and Web 2.0 Explorers, shaped the Sales 2.0 desktop vision.

The chapter touched on the importance of mobility to sales and showcased a number of U.S.-Canada Theater initiatives such as Scale the Power, the Collaboration Guide, and

SOAR, which are helping to drive collaboration technology adoption across Sales. Finally the chapter described the Five to Thrive initiative, showcasing, internally and externally, the business imperatives enabling business to thrive in dynamic times and the ways collaborative Channels initiatives such as Cisco Partner Space are yielding significant business value and results, for Cisco, its partners, and its customers.

The book introduced the reader to Web 2.0 from an enterprise perspective, highlighting the importance of user-generated content and showcasing ways the enterprise can best leverage technologies such as wikis, blogs, communities, and collaborative technologies. It provided insight into the fundamental practices and frameworks that comprise the rich portfolio of Web 2.0 technologies and tools. But perhaps more important from an enterprise perspective, the book outlined the Web 2.0 evolution at Cisco—how it has changed the organization, transforming and accelerating processes to increase productivity and deliver measurable business value, particularly in Sales.

There are "rinse and repeat patterns" provided here that will resonate, establishing a guideline or recipe to follow. However, there are still

- Bridges to build to enable communities to **connect**

- Panoramic pictures to aggregate and **communicate**

- Business processes to transform through new ways to **collaborate**

- Best practices to share and innovative lessons to **learn**

Web 2.0 enables the enterprise to extend its reach to connect, communicate, collaborate, and learn through the human network. We hope reading this book will provide a compass to lead you to explore the possibility, recognize the opportunity, and realize the potential of Web 2.0 to deliver business value to your enterprise. Safe journey!

References

Chapter 1

[1] The Facebooker who friended Obama http://www.nytimes.com/2008/07/07/technology/07hughes.html

[2] http://doubleclix.wordpress.com/2009/02/22/mark-andreessen-on-charlie-ross-innovation-silicon-valley-viral-platforms/

[3] Web Networking Photos Come Back to Bite Defendants http://abcnews.go.com/Technology/wireStory?id=5407999

[4] http://www.nytimes.com/2008/08/24/fashion/24blog.html?emc=eta1

[5] http://www.oreillynet.com/pub/a/oreilly/tim/news/2005/09/30/what-is-web-20.html

[6] http://battellemedia.com/archives/003243.php

[7] http://en.wikipedia.org/wiki/Web_2.0

[8] http://www.readwriteweb.com/about_readwriteweb.php

[9] http://www.readwriteweb.com/archives/on_web_30.php

[10] O'Reilly Radar–Web 2.0, Principles and Best Practices - http://www.oreilly.com/radar/web2report.csp

[11] https://www.gartner.com/it/content/502400/502437/wi_brochure.pdf

[12] http://www.msnbc.msn.com/id/24729135/

[13] http://news.slashdot.org/news/08/06/14/0248211.shtml

[14] http://news.slashdot.org/news/08/06/14/0248211.shtml

[15] http://www.hansardsociety.org.uk/

[16] http://tech.slashdot.org/tech/08/09/10/203233.shtml

[17] http://profy.com/2008/01/25/enterprise-20-top-5-corporate-challenges-for-2008-and-beyond/

[18] http://www.channelinsider.com/c/a/Commentary/Is-WEB-20-the-Future-for-the-Enterprise/?kc=EWKNLEDP042508C

[19] http://ideas.salesforce.com/popular/ideas_under_consideration

[20] http://www.eweek.com/c/a/Enterprise-Applications/Inside-Salesforce-Ideas/

[21] http://www.webware.com/html/ww/100/2008/winners.html

[22] http://blog.softwareabstractions.com/the_software_abstractions/2008/06/responding-to-d.html

[23] http://publishing2.com/2008/06/04/what-newspapers-still-dont-understand-about-the-web/

[24] http://www.slate.com/id/2207912

[25] http://thecaucus.blogs.nytimes.com/2008/09/26/live-blog-friday-night-fights/

[26] SMN: NPR adds social networking http://www.mercurynews.com/ci_10592733

[27] http://www.npr.org/api/index

[28] http://crave.cnet.co.uk/software/0,39029471,49299033-1,00.htm

[29] http://seoblog.databanq.com/what-is-web-30/

[30] http://www.slideshare.net/mstrickland/the-evolution-of-web-30?src=embed

[31] http://www.slideshare.net/ricmac/web-technology-trends-for-2008-and-beyond?src=related_normal&rel=370508

[32] http://www.forbes.com/2008/08/20/google-yahoo-microsoft-ent-tech-cx_ml_0820wheregoweb.html

[33] http://www.readwriteweb.com/archives/why_gen_y_is_going_to_change_the_web.php

[34] http://www.readwriteweb.com/archives/too_many_choices_too_much_content.php

[35] Attack of the twitter clones http://www.twittown.com/blogs/misc-thoughts/attack-twitter-clones

[36] http://news.cnet.com/8301-17939_109-10006185-2.html

[37] http://tech.slashdot.org/tech/08/09/05/2246259.shtml

[38] http://e-vangelie.blogspot.com/2008/08/gartners-emerging-technologies-hype.html

[39] Where the web is weak http://www.forbes.com/technology/2008/05/14/web-hacking-google-tech-security08-cx_ag_0514webhack.html

[40] http://youtube.com/watch?v=T0QJmmdw3b0

[41] http://www.yourdonreport.com/index.php/web-20-resources/

[42] http://msdn.microsoft.com/en-us/library/bb735306.aspx

[43] http://svefoundation.org/programs/center_innovation.asp

[44] http://lessonopoly.org/svef/

[45] http://googleblog.blogspot.com/2008/07/we-knew-web-was-big.html

[46] http://www.openajax.org/index.php

[47] Track rumored Starbucks closing http://seattletimes.nwsource.com/flatpages/businesstechnology/locationsofstarbucksstoresclosingacrossthenation.html

[48] http://en.wikipedia.org/wiki/The_Long_Tail

[49] http://www.longtail.com/the_long_tail/

[50] The Long Tail: Wired http://www.wired.com/wired/archive/12.10/tail.html

[51] http://news.google.com/?ncl=1249938201&hl=en&topic=t

[52] http://www.fastcompany.com/magazine/131/revolution-in-san-jose.html?page=0%2C0

[53] http://news.google.com/?ncl=1249938201&hl=en&topic=t

[54] http://www.webex.com/enterprise/cisco-webex-connect.html

[55] http://itunes.apple.com/WebObjects/MZStore.woa/wa/viewSoftware?id=305923566&mt=8

[56] http://www.nytimes.com/2007/10/26/opinion/26brooks.html

[57] http://www.pcworld.com/businesscenter/article/151323/how_businesses_can_benefit_from_social_networking.html

http://asert.arbornetworks.com/2008/06/the-tiger-effect/

Blog: Cloud Computing & Grids http://doubleclix.wordpress.com/2008/08/03/cloud-computing-and-grids/

Blog: Cloud Computing, Grids and Paczkis - Part Deux http://doubleclix.wordpress.com/2008/09/23/cloud-computing-grids-and-paczkis-part-deux/

http://www.salesforce.com/products/ideas/

http://mystarbucksidea.force.com/apex/ideaHome

What is Web 2.0? Ideas, technologies and implications http://www.scribd.com/doc/8516/what-is-web-2-020Jisc?ga_related_doc=1

Chapter 2

[1] *Benchmark 2008: Everyone Goes Online, But Gen Yers Are The Early Adopters*, C. Golvin, R. Fiorentino, M. de Lussanet, D. Wilkos, http://www.forrester.com/Research/Document/Excerpt/0,7211,44132,00.html

[2] *Benchmark 2008: Forecast Growth Of Devices And Access In The US*, C. Golvin, M. de Lussanet, R. Fiorentino, D. Wilkos, http://www.forrester.com/Research/Document/Excerpt/0,7211,44133,00.html

[3] *Benchmark 2008: Mobile Is Everywhere*, C. Golvin, M. de Lussanet, R. Fiorentino, D. Wilkos, http://www.forrester.com/Research/Document/Excerpt/0,7211,44130,00.html

[4] *Global Enterprise Web 2.0 Market Forecast*: 2007 To 2013, G. Young, et al, http://www.forrester.com/Research/Document/Excerpt/0,7211,43850,00.html

[5] *Personal web page*, http://en.wikipedia.org/wiki/Personal_web_page

[6] *AOL*, http://en.wikipedia.org/wiki/Aol

[7] *GeoCities*, http://en.wikipedia.org/wiki/GeoCities

[8] *2008 International Internet Trends Study*, www.optenet.com/mailing/pdfs/TrendReport.pdf

[9] *User Generated Content*, http://en.wikipedia.org/wiki/User-generated_content

[10] *User Generated Content: Is it Good for You?*, D. Waisberg, http://emetrics.org/2007/washingtondc/track_web20_measurement.php#usergenerated

[11] *Web Design Site*, J. Kaminski, http://www.bellaonline.com/articles/art1678.asp

[12] *Trust in Advertising a Global Neilsen Report October 2007*, www.nielsen.com/solutions/TrustinAdvertisingOct07.pdf

[13] *Google Answers: Amazon's recommendations systems*, http://answers.google.com/answers/threadview/id/29373.html

[14] *Social media*, http://en.wikipedia.org/wiki/Social_media

[15] *Blogs*, http://en.wikipedia.org/wiki/Blog

[16] *Don Dodge on the Next Big Thing*, http://dondodge.typepad.com/the_next_big_thing/2006/02/blog_vs_web_sit.html

[17] *Trackback*, http://en.wikipedia.org/wiki/Trackbacks

[18] Video blogging, http://en.wikipedia.org/wiki/Video_blog

[19] *Reuters extends relationship with Nokia through mobile ad network*, O. Luft, http://www.journalism.co.uk/2/articles/530925.php

[20] *Weblog software*, http://en.wikipedia.org/wiki/Blog_publishing_system

[21] *Blogger (service)*, http://en.wikipedia.org/wiki/Blogger_(service)

[22] *Blogger*, http://www.blogger.com

[23] *ExpressionEngine*, http://en.wikipedia.org/wiki/Expression_Engine

[24] *ExpressionEngine*, http://expressionengine.com

[25] *Movable Type*, http://en.wikipedia.org/wiki/Movable_Type

[26] *Movable Type,* http://movabletype.com

[27] *TypePad*, http://en.wikipedia.org/wiki/Typepad

[28] *TypePad*, http://www.typepad.com

[29] *Wordpress*, http://en.wikipedia.org/wiki/Wordpress

[30] *Wordpress,* http://wordpress.com

[31] *Blogging For Dummies*®, S. Gardner, S. Birley, http://cisco.safaribooksonline.com/9780470230176/c04

[32] *Blogs turn 10—who's the father?* D. McCullagh and A. Broache, http://news.cnet.com/2100-1025_3-6168681.html

[33] Blogger Marc Orchant suffers massive heart attack..., http://www.disruptiveconversations.com/2007/12/blogger-marc-or.html

[34] *Some Brand-Name Bloggers Say Stress of Posting Is a Hazard to Their Health*, D. Frost, http://www.nytimes.com/2008/01/07/technology/07blogger.html?_r=1&oref=slogin

[35] *The 'Fake' Steve Jobs Is Giving Up Parody Blog*, http://www.nytimes.com/2008/07/10/technology/10blog.html?ref=business

[36] *Sweden's most popular professional blogger quits*, http://www.kullin.net/2007/10/swedens-most-popular-professional.html

[37] *FAQs,* http://www.blogpulse.com/about.html

[38] *Blogpulse, http://www.blogpulse.com*

[39] *Google Trends*, http://en.wikipedia.org/wiki/Google_trends

[40] *Google Trends*, http://www.google.com/trends

[41] *Technorati Support*, http://support.technorati.com/support/siteguide/channels

[42] *Technorati*, http://www.technorati.com

[43] Technorati State of the Blogosphere 2008 Report, http://technorati.com/blogging/state-of-the-blogosphere/

[44] *2008 Blogging Report*, G. Ness, http://www.sundog.net/index.php/sunblog/entry/2008-blogging-report

[45] *What's Hot, What's Not?* Google Trends vs. Technorati Charts vs. BlogPulse, A. Agarwal, http://labnol.blogspot.com/2006/05/whats-hot-whats-not-google-trends-vs.html

[46] *Measuring the Brand Blog*, Z. Rogers, http://www.clickz.com/3460841

[47] *Robert* Scoble, http://en.wikipedia.org/wiki/Robert_Scoble

[48] *Does your blog affect your brand?*, S. Falkow http://falkow.blogsite.com/public/blog/81993

[49] *Wiki*, http://en.wikipedia.org/wiki/Wiki

[50] *What is Wiki?* http://wiki.org/wiki.cgi?WhatIsWiki

[51] *Comparison of wiki farms*, http://en.wikipedia.org/wiki/Wiki_farm

[52] *Clearspace*, http://en.wikipedia.org/wiki/Clearspace

[53] *Jive, http://www.jivesoftware.com/*

[54] *WikiMatrix*, http://www.wikimatrix.org/show/Clearspace

[55] *Confluence*, http://en.wikipedia.org/wiki/Confluence

[56] *Confluence*, http://www.atlassian.com/software/confluence/

[57] *DocuWiki*, http://en.wikipedia.org/wiki/DocuWiki

[58] *Google Sites, http://en.wikipedia.org/wiki/Google_Sites*

[59] *Google Sites, http://sites.google.com*

[60] *MediaWiki*, http://en.wikipedia.org/wiki/Mediawiki

[61] *PBwiki, http://en.wikipedia.org/wiki/Pbwiki*

[62] *PBwiki*, http://pbwiki.com/

[63] *Socialtext*, http://en.wikipedia.org/wiki/Socialtext

[64] *Socialtext*, http://www.socialtext.com/

[65] *TikiWiki*, http://en.wikipedia.org/wiki/Tikiwiki

[66] *Wetpaint*, http://en.wikipedia.org/wiki/Wetpaint

[67] *Wikia*, http://en.wikipedia.org/wiki/Wikia

[68] *Wikis for Dummies*, D. Woods, P. Thoeny, W. Cunningham, http://cisco.safaribooksonline.com/9780470043998/ch05

[69] *Wikipedia: About*, http://en.wikipedia.org/wiki/Wikipedia:About

[70] *Wikipedi*, http://www.wikipedia.org/

[71] *Socialtext: Products & Services: Wiki Workspaces*, http://www.socialtext.com/products/wiki.php

[72] *Socialtext Dashboard*, http://socialtext.blip.tv/#1312651

[73] *Socialtext: About Us*, http://www.socialtext.com/about/

[74] *Socialtext Delivers Business Value With Enhanced Wiki*, B. Mosher, http://www.cmswire.com/cms/enterprise-20/socialtext-delivers-business-value-with-enhanced-wiki-002553.php

[75] *Socialtext Dashboard*, http://socialtext.blip.tv/#254303

[76] *Wiki...wiki...wiki*, C. Tobias, CA Learning Series, July 2008

[77] *The Scout Report—September 17, 1999*, http://www.mail-archive.com/scout-report@hypatia.cs.wisc.edu/msg00038.html

[78] *itList*, http://www.itlist.com/

[79] *Reuters Livewire: Putting Your Bookmarks on the Web*, *http://www.backflip.com/company/press_livewire120899_out.ihtml*

[80] *Inside Social Bookmarking*, http://insidesocialbookmarking.com/

[81] *Delicious,* www.delicious.com

[82] *Social Bookmarking Tools* (I), D. Hammond et. al., http://www.dlib.org/dlib/april05/hammond/04hammond.html

[83] *Stumbleupon,* http://en.wikipedia.org/wiki/Stumbleupon

[84] *Ma.gnolia,* http://en.wikipedia.org/wiki/Ma.gnolia

[85] *Blue Dot*, http://en.wikipedia.org/wiki/Blue_dot

[86] *Diigo*, http://en.wikipedia.org/wiki/Diigo

[87] *Connectbeam*, http://www.connectbeam.com/

[88] *IBM Research Center Project: Dogear*, http://domino.watson.ibm.com/cambridge/research.nsf/0/1c181ee5fbcf59fb852570fc0052ad75

[89] *Furl,* http://www.furl.com/

[90] *Stumbleupon,* http://www.stumbleupon.com/

[91] *Faves,* http://faves.com/home

[92] *Social bookmarking: Pushing collaboration to the edge*, S. McGillicuddy, http://searchcio.techtarget.com/news/article/0,289142,sid182_gci1195182,00.html

[93] *Flickr,* http://en.wikipedia.org/wiki/Flickr

[94] Flickr of idea on a gaming project led to photo website, J, Graham, http://www.usatoday.com/tech/products/2006-02-27-flickr_x.htm

[95] *Flickr*, http://www.flickr.com

[96] *Flickr... 3 billion photos*, http://www.doeswhat.com/2008/11/06/flickr-3-billion-photos/

[97] *Facebook*, http://www.facebook.com/facebook

[98] *Facebook*, http://en.wikipedia.org/wiki/Facebook

[99] *Facebook* Press Room, http://www.facebook.com/press/info.php?statistics

[100] *YouTube*, http://en.wikipedia.org/wiki/Youtube

[101] *YouTube looks for the money clip*, Y. Yen, http://techland.blogs.fortune.cnn.com/2008/03/25/youtube-looks-for-the-money-clip/

[102] *YouTube Fact Sheet*, *http://www.youtube.com/t/fact_sheet*

[103] *YouTube*, http://www.youtube.com/

[104] *Folksonomies—Cooperative Classification and Communication Through Shared Metadata*, A. Mathes, http://www.adammathes.com/academic/computer-mediated-communication/folksonomies.html

[105] *Communities*, http://en.wikipedia.org/wiki/Communities

[106] *Virtual Communities*, http://en.wikipedia.org/wiki/Online_communities

[107] *The Human Network Effect*, http://www.cisco.com/web/about/humannetwork/index.html

[108] *Collaboration*, http://en.wikipedia.org/wiki/Collaboration

[109] The Wisdom of Crowds: Why the Many Are Smarter Than the Few and How Collective Wisdom Shapes Business, Economies, Societies and Nations, J. Surowiecki

[110] *The Next Frontier in Collaboration: Transforming how Cisco and Channel Partners work together—Cisco U.S. and Canada Channels—A case study.*

[111] *Unified Communications TelePresence*, http://wwwin.cisco.com/europe/tmo/uc/telepresence/

[112] http://wwwin-tools.cisco.com/sales/servlet/getDocument?message_id=493461&linkurl=/salesrack/products/ps7060&portalID=37609

[113] *WebEx Solution Overview*, http://wwwin.cisco.com/csg/docs/WebEx_Solution_Overview.ppt

[114] *WebEx Meeting Applications*, http://wwwin.cisco.com/csg/webex/

[115] *Technology Marketing Organisation Unified Communications*, http://wwwin.cisco.com/europe/tmo/uc/

[116] *NEW Storyboard 11_5_08 for T-Mobile v2.ppt*

[117] *The Business Value of Unified Communications*, J. Metzler, http://www.nexusis.com/resources/Business_Value_of_UC.pdf

[118] *The Next Frontier in Collaboration: Transforming How Cisco and Channel Partners Work*, http://sjc-fs2-web/wg-u/us-c_web/Published/us-canada/uscpo/docs/Channels_Collaboration_Case_Study.pdf

Chapter 3

[1] http://www.adobe.com/resources/business/rich_internet_apps/#open

[2] http://www.infoworld.com/article/09/01/13/02TC-toy-2009_1.html?source=NLC-DAILY&cgd=2009-01-13

[3] http://www.capzles.com/#/ff8fc5bc-de7c-40ee-bdbf-71ca61e120b3

[4] http://www.slideshare.net/pstahl/checking-the-feel-of-your-ui-with-an-interaction-audit/

[5] https://data.nasdaq.com/MR.aspx

[6] http://www.techradar.com/news/digital-home/home-networking/samsung-and-yahoo-unleash-internet-widgets-498107

[7] http://weblog.infoworld.com/fatalexception/archives/2008/12/are_operating_s.html?source=NLC-DAILY&cgd=2008-12-26

[8] http://en.wikipedia.org/wiki/Mashup_(web_application_hybrid)

[9] http://gmapsmania.googlepages.com/100thingstodowithgooglemapsmashups

[10] http://beermapping.com/maps/maps.php?m=pacific

[11] http://www.earthalbum.com/

[12] http://www.programmableweb.com/mashups

[13] http://www.readwriteweb.com/archives/mashup_business.php

[14] http://www.webmonkey.com/blog/How_HTML_5_Is_Already_Changing_the_Web

[15] http://www.infoworld.com/article/08/06/23/eich-javascript-interview_1.html

[16] http://www.adobe.com/products/air/

[17] http://silverlight.net/

[18] http://en.wikipedia.org/wiki/XMLHttpRequest

[19] http://www.openajax.org/index.php

[20] http://tools.ietf.org/html/rfc4627

[21] http://dojotoolkit.org/

[22] http://widgets.yahoo.com/

[23] http://desktop.google.com/plugins/

[24] https://www.adaptivepath.com/ideas/essays/archives/000385.php

[25] http://en.wikipedia.org/wiki/Ajax

[26] http://www.google.com/googlebooks/chrome/small_00.html

[27] http://webkit.org/blog/214/introducing-squirrelfish-extreme/

[28] http://apple.slashdot.org/apple/08/09/19/2315247.shtml

[29] http://www.satine.org/archives/2008/09/19/squirrelfish-extreme-fastest-javascript-engine-yet/

[30] http://technorati.com/posts/p1hnKCNLV7bAGXnqvTsMPBBwjsnuhXFG6o8FCaU%2Bb28%3D

[31] http://summerofjsc.blogspot.com/2008/09/squirrelfish-extreme-has-landed.html

[32] http://www.openajax.org/runtime/wiki/Summary_Report

[33] http://www.rubyonrails.org/

[34] http://wiki.rubyonrails.org/rails/pages/RealWorldUsagePage1

[35] http://www.infoworld.com/article/09/01/12/02NF-ruby-on-rails-merb_1.html

Ajax: The Definitive Guide, Anthony T. Holdener III, O'Reilly Media, Inc., 2008

Dojo: The Definitive Guide, Matthew A. Russell, O'Reilly Media, Inc., 2008

Chapter 4

[1] http://www.time.com/time/politics/article/0,8599,1811857,00.html

[2] http://venturebeat.com/2009/02/02/stanford-class-to-help-parents-be-better-facebook-friends-with-their-kids/

[3] Forbes Five Social Networking Sites Of The Wealthy
http://www.forbes.com/2008/05/02/social-networks-vip-tech-personal-cx_nr_0502style_slide_5.html?thisSpeed=15000

[4] http://regulargeek.com/2008/06/18/quick-guide-to-social-media/

[5] http://regulargeek.com/2008/06/24/required-reading-in-social-media/

[6] Facebook influencing datacenter architectures http://www.gridtoday.com/grid/2448510.html

[7] How Social Networks May Kill Search as We Know It http://tech.slashdot.org/tech/08/04/16/1833256.shtml

[8] How Social Networking Saved New Orleans
http://www.networkworld.com/news/2008/062708-new-orleans.html?ts

[9] Top 10 Takeaways From Graphing Social West http://www.digitalpodcast.com/podcastnews/tag/gspwest08/

[10] http://www.informationweek.com/news/personal_tech/music/showArticle.jhtml?articleID=207600014&subSection=All+Stories

[11] http://www.washingtonpost.com/wp-dyn/content/article/2008/05/25/AR2008052501779.html

[12] http://timespeople.nytimes.com/packages/html/timespeople/faq/#1

[13] Business Benefits: IBM http://www-01.ibm.com/software/lotus/news/social_software.html#benefits

[14] http://www.information-age.com/magazine/april-2008/features/319126/social-networking-within-the-enterprise.thtml

[15] IBM and employee-centered social media http://www.webguild.org/presentations/ibmsocialmedia.pdf

[16] http://online.wsj.com/article/SB123273549517510905.html?mod=todays_us_marketplace

[17] Gartner Analysts Decry Facebook, Twitter Bans at Work http://www.eweek.com/c/a/Messaging-and-Collaboration/Gartner-Analysts-Decry-Facebook-Twitter-Bans-at-Work/?kc=EWKNLCSM081208STR1

[18] http://gigaom.com/2008/03/13/aol-buys-bebo-time-warner-still-schizophrenic/

[19] Social Design Best Practices http://code.google.com/apis/opensocial/articles/best-prac.html

[20] http://developers.facebook.com/get_started.php?tab=principles

[21] Firm builds a social network with SharePoint, NewsGator RSS http://www.networkworld.com/news/2008/080108-firm-builds-a-social-network.html

[22] http://www.crunchbase.com/company/facebook

[23] http://en.wikipedia.org/wiki/Facebook

[24]http://www.facebook.com/press/releases.php?p=3102

[25] http://www.facebook.com/press/info.php?statistics

[26] http://developers.facebook.com/news.php?blog=1&story=134

[27] http://wiki.developers.facebook.com/index.php/Facebook_Developer_Garage

[28] http://wiki.developers.facebook.com/index.php/Garage_Guide

[29] http://wiki.developers.facebook.com/index.php/Garage_Ninjas

[30] http://radar.oreilly.com/2007/10/good-news-bad-news-about-faceb.html

[31] http://www.techcrunch.com/2008/07/25/facebooks-iphone-app-has-1-million-users/

[32] http://www.gamespot.com/news/6194976.html

[33] http://games.slashdot.org/games/08/07/24/2128238.shtml

[34] http://techland.blogs.fortune.cnn.com/2008/01/11/will-someone-please-start-a-facebook-group-to-save-scrabulous/

[35] http://bits.blogs.nytimes.com/2008/07/29/facebook-shuts-down-scrabulous/?ref=technology

[36] http://www.crn.com/software/209900944

[37] http://arstechnica.com/news.ars/post/20080826-facebook-yanks-international-access-to-scrabulous.html

[38] http://www.washingtonpost.com/wp-dyn/content/article/2008/08/01/AR2008080103131.html?sub=AR

[39] http://www.facebook.com/apps/application.php?id=2552096927

[40] http://www.mercurynews.com/ci_9977659

[41] http://wiki.developers.facebook.com/index.php/Photo_uploads

[42] http://wiki.developers.facebook.com/index.php/API

[43] http://wiki.developers.facebook.com/index.php/Events.get

[44] http://wiki.developers.facebook.com/index.php/Friends.areFriends

[45] http://wiki.developers.facebook.com/index.php/Friends.get

[46] http://www.informationweek.com/news/internet/social_network/showArticle.jhtml?articleID=209601047

[47] http://wiki.developers.facebook.com/index.php/FBMLspec

[48] http://developers.facebook.com/anatomy.php

[49] http://developers.facebook.com/tools.php?fbml

[50] http://www.facebook.com/developers/message.php

[51] http://www.linkedin.com/static?key=company_info

[52] http://www.techcrunch.com/2008/03/20/linkedin-now-for-companies-2/

[53] http://blog.linkedin.com/blog/2008/08/introducing-the.html

[54] http://www.techcrunch.com/2009/01/22/facebook-now-nearly-twice-the-size-of-myspace-worldwide/

[55] http://bradgreenspan.com/?p=21

[56] http://freemyspace.com/?q=node/13

[57] Wikipedia MySpace http://en.wikipedia.org/wiki/MySpace

[58] http://www.newscorp.com/news/news_251.html

[59] http://www.comscore.com/press/release.asp?press=2396

[60] http://uk.reuters.com/article/technologyNews/idUKN1335759220080614

[61] http://arstechnica.com/news.ars/post/20080613-myspace-eying-facebook-in-rearview-mirror-with-big-redesign.html

[62] http://developer.myspace.com/community/

[63] http://developer.myspace.com/community/myspace/opensocial.aspx

[64] http://developer.myspace.com/community/myspace/anatomyOfAnApp.aspx

[65] MySpace REST API http://developer.myspace.com/community/RestfulAPIs/resources.aspx

[66] MySpace Data Availability http://developer.myspace.com/community/myspace/dataavailability.aspx

[67] MySpace Application Guidelines http://developer.myspace.com/community/myspace/applicationguidelines.aspx

[68] MySpace data Availability Guidelines http://developer.myspace.com/community/myspace/da2.aspx

[69] MySpace application takedown process http://developer.myspace.com/Community/blogs/devteam/archive/2008/08/21/when-good-apps-go-bad.aspx

[70] Wallflower at the Web Party
http://www.nytimes.com/2006/10/15/business/yourmoney/15friend.html?oref=slogin

[71] http://www.gmanews.tv/story/104375/Friendster-to-introduce-text-alerts-in-Asia-RP

[72] http://www.gmanews.tv/story/104375/Friendster-to-introduce-text-alerts-in-Asia-RP

[73] http://doubleclix.wordpress.com/2009/02/22/mark-andreessen-on-charlie-ross-innovation-silicon-valley-viral-platforms/

[74] http://developer.ning.com/notes/Ning_Architecture_Basics

[75] Ning Platform Guidelines http://developer.ning.com/notes/Guidelines_for_Developing_on_the_Ning_Platform

[76] http://code.google.com/apis/socialgraph/

[77] http://news.cnet.com/8301-13953_3-9941039-80.html

[78] http://www.google.com/friendconnect/home/moreinfo

[79] http://www.businessweek.com/technology/content/oct2007/tc20071024_654439.htm?chan=top+news_top+news+index_top+story

[80] http://mikeg.typepad.com/perceptions/2007/10/social-networki.html

[81] http://www.internetnews.com/webcontent/article.php/3753626/Search+Social+Networking+Key+in+SharePoint.htm

[82] White paper: Managing social networking with Microsoft Office SharePoint Server 2007 http://technet.microsoft.com/en-us/library/cc262436.aspx

[83] http://wsuelearner.wordpress.com/2008/04/21/can-microsoft-sharepoint-support-social-networking/

[84] http://www.haifa.ibm.com/projects/imt/sonar/index.shtml

[85] http://www-01.ibm.com/software/lotus/news/social_software.html

[86] NYTimes Hail to the twitterer http://www.nytimes.com/2008/08/03/weekinreview/03leibovich.html

[87] Newbie's guide to Twitter http://news.cnet.com/8301-17939_109-9697867-2.html?tag=nwb.sidebar

[88] http://latimesblogs.latimes.com/technology/2008/07/quake-has-every.html

[89] Twitter earthquake http://blog.twitter.com/2008/07/twitter-as-news-wire.html

[90] What's your favorite Twitter feed to follow (and why)? http://www.37signals.com/svn/posts/1110-whats-your-favorite-twitter-feed-to-follow-and-why

[91] http://news.cnet.com/8301-17939_109-10026135-2.html?tag=mncol;posts

[92] http://venturebeat.com/2008/08/25/twitter-blacklists-mad-men-characters-some-of-them/

[93] NPR Podcast Twitter Debate http://www.npr.org/templates/story/story.php?storyId=91779992

[94] http://www.techpresident.com/blog/entry/26569/breaking_pdf2008_hosts_obama_mccain_twitter_debate

[95] http://en.wikipedia.org/wiki/Pownce

[96] http://www.insidecrm.com/features/plurk-071008/

[97] http://news.cnet.com/8301-17939_109-10006185-2.html?tag=nl.e776

[98] http://www.web-strategist.com/blog/2009/02/08/for-the-professional-how-to-get-started-on-twitter/

[99] http://doubleclix.wordpress.com/2009/02/22/twitter-tips/

[100] The Truth (and lies) About Using Twitter http://etech.eweek.com/content/web_technology/the_truth_and_lies_about_using_twitter.html?kc=EWKNLCSM081208STR2

[101] TwitterFone http://news.cnet.com/8301-17939_109-10010652-2.html?tag=nl.e776

[102] http://www.nimblecode.com/articles/2008/05/27/explaining-twitter

[103] O'Brien: More social-networking tools than anyone needs http://www.mercurynews.com/ci_9548959

[104] Why Twitter Hasn't Failed: The Power Of Audience http://www.techcrunch.com/2008/08/10/why-twitter-hasnt-failed-the-power-of-audience/

[105] http://www.cio.com/article/print/420763

[106] Getting Started - Part I http://oauth.net/documentation/getting-started

[107] http://www.washingtonpost.com/wp-dyn/content/article/2008/07/21/AR2008072101453.html

[108] http://www.businessweek.com/ap/financialnews/D9233U7G0.htm

[109] http://www.pcworld.com/businesscenter/article/148751/
myspace_eases_data_portability_policies_adopts_openid.html

[110] http://code.google.com/apis/opensocial/

[111] OpenSocial API documentation http://code.google.com/apis/opensocial/docs/index.
html

[112] Nic Carr on Open Social http://www.roughtype.com/archives/2007/10/
opensocial_and.php

[113] Marc Andreessen on OpenSocial http://blog.pmarca.com/2007/10/open-social-a-n.
html

[114] Open Social Specification http://code.google.com/apis/opensocial/docs/0.8/spec.
html

[115] Google Gadgets Specification http://code.google.com/apis/gadgets/docs/spec.html

[116] http://opensocialapis.blogspot.com/2008/08/lets-get-this-partuza-started.html

[117] http://blogs.zdnet.com/BTL/?p=6813

[118] http://mashable.com/2008/07/28/openid-and-oauth/

[119] http://www.orange.fr/bin/frame.cgi?u=http%3A//openid.orange.fr/

[120] http://www.intertwingly.net/blog/2007/01/03/OpenID-for-non-SuperUsers

[121] http://openid.net/specs/openid-authentication-2_0.html

[122] Beginner's Guide to OAuth – Part II - http://www.hueniverse.com/hueniverse/2007/
10/beginners-gui-1.html

[123] http://stakeventures.com/articles/2008/02/23/developing-oauth-clients-in-ruby

[124] http://oauth.net/core/1.0/

[125] http://www.hueniverse.com/hueniverse/2007/10/beginners-gui-1.html

[126] http://mashable.com/2008/07/28/openid-and-oauth/

[127] http://www.xml.com/pub/a/2004/02/04/foaf.html

[128] http://wiki.foaf-project.org/FAQ

[129] http://gmpg.org/xfn/intro

[130] http://facereviews.com/2008/07/22/facebook-new-rules-less-virality/

[131] http://www.washingtonpost.com/wp-dyn/content/article/2007/08/24/
AR2007082400481_pf.html

[132] http://www.msnbc.msn.com/id/24529992/

[133] http://news.cnet.com/8301-17939_109-9998117-2.html?tag=nl.e776

[134] Announcing Facebook Connect
http://developers.facebook.com/news.php?blog=1&story=108

[135] http://www.techcrunch.com/2008/06/26/myspace-opens-up-the-data-pipe-with-launch-of-data-availability/

[136] Why Facebook Connect Matters & Why It Will Win http://gigaom.com/2008/07/23/facebook-connect/

[137] http://news.google.com/?ncl=1229280989&hl=en&topic=t

[138] http://www.time.com/time/business/article/0,8599,1826081,00.html?imw=Y

[139] http://www.techcrunch.com/2008/05/09/facebook-responds-to-myspace-with-face-book-connect/

[140] http://developers.facebook.com/news.php?blog=1&story=151

[141] http://www.techcrunch.com/2008/05/08/myspace-embraces-data-portability-partners-with-yahoo-ebay-and-twitter/

[142] http://news.cnet.com/8301-17939_109-9939286-2.html?tag=nl.e776

[143] Facebook's data has left the barn http://www.washingtonpost.com/wp-dyn/content/article/2008/05/18/AR2008051800093.html

[144] http://www.businessweek.com/technology/content/may2008/tc20080515_372632.htm

[145] http://www.webguild.org/2008/05/facebooks-facebook-connect.php

[146] The Trojan Social Open-Source Drop-Down http://blogs.eweek.com/epiphanies/content/machinations/the_trojan_social_opensource_dropdown.html

[147] Time: Who Will Rule the New Internet? http://www.time.com/time/business/article/0,8599,1811814,00.html

[148] new technologies aggregation socialcast http://www.eweek.com/c/a/Enterprise-Apps/Enterprise-20-Technologies-Worth-Watching/7/

[149] 20 Ways To Aggregate Your Social Networking Profiles http://mashable.com/2007/07/17/social-network-aggregators/

[150] Membership overlaps http://www.thebizofcoding.com/2007/12/2008_killer_app_category_tools.html

[151] http://www.telegraph.co.uk/scienceandtechnology/technology/facebook/4636962/Soldiers-banned-from-MySpace-and-Facebook.html

[152] http://www.eweek.com/c/a/Security/Security-Researchers-Outline-Security-Risks-of-Social-Networking-Sites-at-Black-Hat/?kc=EWKNLCSM081208STR3

[153] Facebook gets malware alert http://ct.cnet-ssa.cnet.com/clicks?t=70673035-ac1c726a577fecb4a820726b38919eae-bf&brand=CNET-SSA&s=5

[154] http://www.kaspersky.com/news?id=207575670

[155] http://www.readwriteweb.com/archives/the_facebook_virus_spreads_no_social_network_is_safe.php#more

[156] Keeping Predators Away From 'Spacebook'
http://cityroom.blogs.nytimes.com/2008/01/29/keeping-predators-away-from-space-book/?hp

[157] http://arstechnica.com/news.ars/post/20080530-canadian-group-files-complaint-over-facebook-privacy.html

[158] http://www.techcrunch.com/2008/03/18/facebook-to-launch-new-privacy-controls-confirms-chat-is-coming/

[159] http://theharmonyguy.com/2008/06/20/more-advertising-issues-on-facebook/

[160] http://news.cnet.com/8301-10784_3-9974220-7.html

[161] http://blog.socialmedia.com/make-fast-join-the-facebook-class-action-lawsuit/

[162] http://www.pcworld.com/article/159703/facebook_privacy_change_sparks_federal_complaint.html?tk=rel_news

[163] http://consumerist.com/5150175/facebooks-new-terms-of-service-we-can-do-anything-we-want-with-your-content-forever

[164] http://www.mercurynews.com/ci_11738546

[165] http://www.pcworld.com/article/160358/rewriting_facebooks_terms_of_service.html

[166] http://www.facebook.com/group.php?gid=54964476066

[167] http://www.facebook.com/group.php?gid=67758697570

[168] http://www.readwriteweb.com/archives/cartoon_twitter_evidence.php

[169] http://www.mercurynews.com/ci_11798886

[170] http://blogs.wsj.com/digits/2009/02/17/zuckerberg-on-privacy-this-is-just-the-beginning/

[171] http://www.comscore.com/press/release.asp?press=2396

[172] Facebook: No. 1 Globally
http://www.businessweek.com/technology/content/aug2008/tc20080812_853725.htm?chan=technology_technology+index+page_top+stories

[173] http://news.google.com/?ncl=1236257424&hl=en&topic=t

[174] http://www.technewsworld.com/story/Facebook-Stands-Atop-Social-Networking-World-64154.html?welcome=1218681026

[175] http://www.crn.com/software/210003629

[176] http://www.techcrunch.com/2008/08/03/taking-social-networks-abroad-why-myspace-and-facebook-are-failing-in-japan/

[177] http://www.chron.com/disp/story.mpl/front/6095469.html

[178] http://www.cnn.com/2008/POLITICS/11/07/sanchez.technology/

[179] http://arstechnica.com/tech-policy/news/2008/12/facebook-profile-used-to-serve-legal-docs-in-australian-case.ars

[180] http://www.careerbuilder.com/share/aboutus/pressreleasesdetail.aspx?id=pr459&sd=9%2F10%2F2008&ed=12%2F31%2F2008&siteid=cbpr&sc_cmp1=cb_pr459_&cbRecursionCnt=1&cbsid=7091f0351d2c4773bbfef3fe48c968f1-289172962-JH-5

[181] http://www.businessweek.com/magazine/content/08_40/b4102050681705.htm?chan=top+news_top+news+index+-+temp_technology

[182] http://technology.inc.com/managing/articles/200901/leary.html?partner=rss-alert

http://blog.wired.com/27bstroke6/2008/09/researchers-use.html

http://www.techradar.com/news/internet/web/top-15-things-you-should-never-do-on-facebook-470875

http://www.eweek.com/c/a/Messaging-and-Collaboration/Should-Facebook-Be-Banned-from-Work/

http://www.webguild.org/2008/11/motrin-ad-campaign-a-social-media-case-study.php

http://www.readwriteweb.com/archives/10_ways_social_media_will_change_in_2009.php

http://www.cnn.com/2009/TECH/02/04/facebook.anniversary/index.html

http://blogs.zdnet.com/BTL/?p=12041

http://www.140characters.com/2009/01/30/how-twitter-was-born/

http://news.cnet.com/8301-17939_109-10156481-2.html

http://news.cnet.com/8301-13577_3-10160850-36.html?tag=newsEditorsPicksArea.0

http://www.pcworld.com/article/159560/social_network_hazards.html

http://www.thestandard.com/news/2009/02/16/facebook-claims-permanent-rights-user-content

http://tech.slashdot.org/article.pl?sid=09/02/17/2213251

http://blogs.zdnet.com/Howlett/?p=666

http://www.theonion.com/content/news/myspace_outage_leaves_millions

10 Things that would be nice to know before starting a Facebook application http://padrenel.blogs.experienceproject.com/3459.html

http://www.hi5networks.com/press.html

http://catbird.tumblr.com/post/35429148

http://www.readwriteweb.com/archives/facebook_hits_100_million_user.php

http://www.networkworld.com/news/2008/062708-new-orleans.html?ts

http://www.techcrunch.com/2008/01/26/facebook-apps-on-any-website-clever-move/

The Facebook Application Platform by Tim O'Reilly; O'Reilly Radar Team

http://news.bbc.co.uk/2/hi/technology/7521002.stm

http://www.channelinsider.com/c/a/Messaging-and-Collaboration/How-VARs-Can-and-Are-Leveraging-Web-20-and-Social-Networking-for-Business/?kc=EWKNLEDP042408A

http://www.nytimes.com/2008/07/07/technology/07hughes.html

Web Networking Photos Come Back to Bite Defendants
http://abcnews.go.com/Technology/wireStory?id=5407999

http://wiki.developers.facebook.com/index.php/Main_Page

Chapter 5

[1] http://www.whatisrss.com/

[2] http://abcnews.go.com/Politics/TheNote/

[3] Slideshare RSS & Atom in Social Web, Slide 26 http://www.slideshare.net/hchen1/rss-and-atom-in-the-social-web

[4] 35 Ways you can use RSS today http://www.micropersuasion.com/2006/06/35_ways_you_can.html

[5] http://www.usa.gov/Topics/Reference_Shelf/Libraries/RSS_Library/Science.shtml

[6] http://feeds.technorati.com/blogs/directory/

[7] http://feeds.technorati.com/blogs/directory/technology/web-2.0

[8] http://www.readwriteweb.com/archives/top_10_rsssyndication_products_of_2008.php

[9] Podcasting Tutorial http://catalyst.washington.edu/help/web/podcasting/index.html

[10] RSS Specifications History et al http://www.rss-specifications.com/history-rss.htm

[11] http://www.rss-specifications.com/history-rss.htm

[12] http://en.wikipedia.org/wiki/History_of_web_syndication_technology

[13] Dr. Guha's contributions to RSS—A must read http://wp.netscape.com/columns/techvision/innovators_rg.html

[14] Microsoft's CDF submission to W3C http://www.w3.org/Submission/1997/2/, http://www.w3.org/TR/NOTE-CDFsubmit.html

[15] RSS 0.9 details cached http://www.purplepages.ie/RSS/netscape/rss0.90.html

[16] ScriptingNews 2.0b1 http://my.userland.com/stories/storyReader$11

[17] RSS 1.1 http://xml.coverpages.org/ni2005-01-18-a.html

[18] http://backend.userland.com/rss093

[19] http://cyber.law.harvard.edu/rss/announceRss2.html

[20] http://creativecommons.org/licenses/by-sa/1.0/

[21] http://www.rssboard.org/

[22] http://tech.groups.yahoo.com/group/rss-dev/message/239

[23] RSS workshop http://www.rssgov.com/rssworkshop.html

[24] RSS tutorial for web masters http://www.mnot.net/rss/tutorial/

[25] http://www.w3schools.com/rss/default.asp

[26] RSS Quick Summary http://www.intertwingly.net/slides/2003/rssQuickSummary.html

[27] http://cyber.law.harvard.edu/rss/creativeCommonsRssModule.html#license

[28] http://backend.userland.com/blogChannelModule

[29] http://search.yahoo.com/mrss

[30] http://madskills.com/public/xml/rss/module/trackback/

[31] http://www.reallysimplesyndication.com/bitTorrentRssModule

[32] http://postneo.com/icbm/

[33] BBC http://news.bbc.co.uk/1/hi/help/3223484.stm

[34] http://www.rss-specifications.com/rss-reader-linux.htm

[35] www.newsgator.com

[36] http://www.acrylicapps.com/times/

[37] RSS best practices http://www.rssboard.org/rss-profile

[38] http://www.johnpanzer.com/RSSAtomFeedsBestPractices/

[39] MS blog http://blogs.msdn.com/rssteam/default.aspx

[40] Guidelines and good practices http://www.ariadne.ac.uk/issue35/miller/

[41] Article on RSS feed quality
http://webservices.xml.com/pub/a/ws/2002/11/19/rssfeedquality.html?page=2

[42] Thinking XML: Use the Atom format for syndicating news and more http://www.
ibm.com/developerworks/xml/library/x-think24.html

[43] IETF Working Group Atom Publishing Format and Protocol (atompub) http://www.
ietf.org/html.charters/OLD/atompub-charter.html

[44] Atom Syndication format rfc4287 http://www.ietf.org/rfc/rfc4287

[45] Atom Publishing protocol rfc 5023 http://www.rfc-editor.org/rfc/rfc5023.txt

[46] An overview of the Atom 1.0 Syndication Format http://www-128.ibm.com/
developerworks/xml/library/x-atom10.html

[47] http://intertwingly.net/wiki/pie/Rss20AndAtom10Compared

[48] An excellent site to start reading about Atom http://www.intertwingly.net/wiki/pie/FrontPage

[49] (http://www.ietf.org/rfc/rfc4287)

[50] http://code.google.com/apis/gdata/reference.html

Comparison of RSS 2.0 and Atom 1.0 http://www.intertwingly.net/wiki/pie/Rss20AndAtom10Compared

RSS 1.0 Specification http://web.resource.org/rss/1.0/spec

RSS 0.91 specification http://backend.userland.com/rss091, also at http://www.scripting.com/netscapeDocs/RSS%200_91%20Spec,%20revision%203.html

RSS 0.92 specification http://backend.userland.com/rss092

Web 2.0 Mashups and Niche Aggregators, By Martin Kelley http://www.oreilly.com/catalog/9780596514006/

Content Syndication with RSS, by Ben Hammersley

Secrets of RSS By Steven Holzner

Developing Feeds with RSS and Atom by Ben Hammersley

How to Build an RSS 2.0 Feed by Mark Woodman

How to get most out of technorati RSS feeds http://www.micropersuasion.com/2006/10/how_to_get_the_.html

Weather RSS feeds

Directory of rss weather feed from all over the world rssweather.com

Weather Channel rss subscription http://www.weather.com/weather/rss/subscription

Weatherunderground http://www.wunderground.com/ also has RSS feeds

Balkanizing RSS http://blogs.zdnet.com/Hinchcliffe/?p=16

Programming PHP4, java with JAXP or Rome http://www.xml.com/pub/a/2006/02/22/rome-parse-publish-rss-atom-feeds-java.html

RSS feed Validators—to make sure your feeds are properly formatted

W3C Validator http://validator.w3.org/feed/

http://feedvalidator.org/

Google news RSS http://news.google.com/?output=rss

Radio Userland http://radio.userland.com/

RSS 2.0 specification http://www.rssboard.org/rss-specification

Chapter 6

[1] http://royal.pingdom.com/2008/09/24/why-is-almost-half-of-google-in-beta/

[2] http://www.networkworld.com/community/node/33131

[3] http://tech.slashdot.org/tech/08/09/25/1235216.shtml

[4] Interview with Eric Schmidt at Web 2.0 Expo 2007
http://www.youtube.com/watch?v=dxzDU3tTzGA

[5] http://labs.google.com/papers/bigtable.html

[6] http://labs.google.com/papers/mapreduce.html

[7] http://research.google.com/archive/sawzall.html

[8] http://en.wikipedia.org/wiki/Gall%27s_law

[9] http://www.amazon.com/exec/obidos/tg/detail/-/0961825170/

[10] http://doubleclix.wordpress.com/2006/10/01/book-review-multi-core-programming-increasing-performance-through-software-multi-threading/

[11] http://www.vmware.com/vmworldnews/vdi.html

[12] http://www.brianmadden.com/blogs/brianmadden/archive/2007/03/14/when-to-use-vdi-when-to-use-server-based-computing-and-how-the-citrix-ardence-dynamic-desktop-fits-into-all-this.aspx

[13] http://doubleclix.wordpress.com/2008/10/21/what-is-cloud-computing-and-do-i-need-to-be-scared/

[14] http://en.wikipedia.org/wiki/Petabyte

[15] http://www.archive.org/index.php

[16] http://www.archive.org/web/petabox.php

[17] http://en.wikipedia.org/wiki/Large_Hadron_Collider

[18] http://www.archive.org/web/petabox.php

[19] http://highscalability.com/links/weblink/24

[20] http://www.infoq.com/articles/ebay-scalability-best-practices

[21] http://www.addsimplicity.com/downloads/eBaySDForum2006-11-29.pdf

[22] http://www.techcrunch.com/2008/08/20/ebay-the-doldrum-years/

[23] http://ksudigg.wetpaint.com/page/YouTube+Statistics?t=anon

[24] http://digital-orb.com/ytsc.html

[25] http://tech.yahoo.com/news/afp/20090213/tc_afp/usitinternetfilmtelevisionyoutube-google_20090213031339

[26] http://highscalability.com/youtube-architecture

[27] http://highscalability.com/amazon-architecture

[28] http://aws.amazon.com/contact-us/new-features-for-amazon-ec2/

[29] http://www.allthingsdistributed.com/2008/10/using_the_cloud_to_build_highl.html

[30] http://highscalability.com/google-architecture

[31] Web 2.0 and Cloud Computing by Tim O'Reilly http://radar.oreilly.com/2008/10/web-20-and-cloud-computing.html

[32] What Tim O'Reilly gets wrong about the cloud http://www.roughtype.com/archives/2008/10/what_tim_oreill.php

[33] http://radar.oreilly.com/2008/10/network-effects-in-data.html http://radar.oreilly.com/2008/10/network-effects-in-data.html

[34] Further musings on the network effect and the cloud http://www.roughtype.com/archives/2008/10/further_thought.php

[35] http://en.wikipedia.org/wiki/Network_effect

[36] http://www.techcrunch.com/2008/01/15/twitter-fails-macworld-keynote-test/

[37] http://highscalability.com/scaling-twitter-making-twitter-10000-percent-faster

[38] http://twitterfacts.blogspot.com/2008/01/number-of-twitter-users.html

[39] http://smoothspan.wordpress.com/2007/09/14/twitter-scaling-story-mirrors-the-multicore-language-timetable/

[40] http://highscalability.com/flickr-architecture

[41] http://www.slideshare.net/iamcal/moving-pictures-web-20-expo-nyc-presentation/

[42] http://www.slideshare.net/iamcal/scalable-web-architectures-common-patterns-and-approaches-web-20-expo-nyc-presentation/

[43] http://en.wikipedia.org/wiki/Shared_nothing_architecture

[44] http://en.wikipedia.org/wiki/Shard_(database_architecture)

[45] http://www.scribd.com/doc/2592098/DVPmysqlucFederation-at-Flickr-Doing-Billions-of-Queries-Per-Day

[46] http://doubleclix.wordpress.com/2008/10/27/microsofts-azure/

[47] http://www.allthingsdistributed.com/2006/03/a_word_on_scalability.html

[48] http://www.ics.uci.edu/~fielding/pubs/dissertation/top.htm

[49] Google Research Publication : MapReduce: Simplified Data Processing on Large Clusters http://labs.google.com/papers/mapreduce.html

[50] http://news.cnet.com/8301-10784_3-9955184-7.html

[51] http://wiki.apache.org/hadoop/PoweredBy

[52] http://open.blogs.nytimes.com/2007/11/01/self-service-prorated-super-computing-fun/

[53] http://weblogs.java.net/blog/tomwhite/archive/2006/02/hadoop.html

[54] http://wiki.apache.org/hadoop-data/attachments/HadoopPresentations/attachments/HadoopEBIG-Oct2008.pdf

[55] http://highscalability.com/how-rackspace-now-uses-mapreduce-and-hadoop-query-terabytes-data

[56] http://blog.racklabs.com/?p=66

[57] http://www.infoq.com/articles/rest-introduction

[58] http://www.computerworld.com/action/article.do?command=viewArticleBasic&articleId=9110219

[59] http://code.flickr.com/

[60] http://gettingreal.37signals.com/

[61] http://firstlook.blogs.nytimes.com/prototypes/

[62] http://www.shirky.com/writings/evolve.html

Hadoop: Wikipedia http://en.wikipedia.org/wiki/Hadoop

Smart Web App Development by Roger Smith, InformationWeek, April 11,2008

http://blogs.zdnet.com/BTL/?p=10433

http://highscalability.com/eve-online-architecture

http://highscalability.com/outside-scales-engine-yard-and-moving-php-ruby-rails

http://www.techcrunch.com/2008/03/12/youtube-the-platform/

http://www.computerworld.com/action/article.do?command=viewArticleBasic&articleId=9127985&intsrc=hm_list

Chapter 7

[1] http://www.nytimes.com/2006/11/12/business/12web.html?_r=2&hp&ex=1163394000&en=a34a6306f48166fb&ei=5094&partner=homepage&oref=slogin&oref=slogin

[2] http://www.w3.org/DesignIssues/Semantic.html

[3] http://www.w3.org/2001/sw/

[4] http://www.w3.org/DesignIssues/RDFnot.html

[5] http://www.computer.org/portal/site/computer/index.jsp?pageID=computer_level1_article&TheCat=1075&path=computer/homepage/0108&file=webtech.xml&xsl=article.xsl

[6] http://earlystagevc.typepad.com/earlystagevc/2006/06/i_wish_i_said_t.html

[7] http://www.mkbergman.com/?p=284

[8] http://thefigtrees.net/lee/sw/sciam/semantic-web-in-action#single-page

[9] http://www.readwriteweb.com/archives/whats_next_after_web_20.php

[10] http://www.technologyreview.com/web/21583/page1/

[11] http://www.readwriteweb.com/archives/the_top-down_semantic_web.php

[12] http://www.readwriteweb.com/archives/10_semantic_apps_to_watch.php

[13] http://www.readwriteweb.com/archives/semantic_web_difficulties_with_classic_approach.php

[14] http://www.readwriteweb.com/archives/spock_vertical_search_done_right.php

[15] http://www.jisc.ac.uk/whatwedo/services/techwatch/reports/horizonscanning/hs0502

[16] http://www.readwriteweb.com/archives/semantic_stealth_startup_siric.php

[17] http://tomgruber.org/writing/semtech08.pdf

[18] http://www.readwriteweb.com/archives/does_microsoft_powerset_beat_google.php

[19] http://www.readwriteweb.com/archives/powerset_vs_google.php

[20] http://www.readwriteweb.com/archives/semantic_search_the_myth_and_reality.php

[21] http://www.readwriteweb.com/archives/microsoft_acquires_powerset.php

[22] http://www.readwriteweb.com/archives/does_microsoft_powerset_beat_google.php

[23] http://www.readwriteweb.com/archives/live_search_powerset_integrati.php

[24] http://www.twine.com/about

[25] http://www.twine.com/twine/1w3b23v2-6j0/web-3-0-semantic-web

[26] http://www.readwriteweb.com/archives/twine_disappoints.php

[27] http://www.readwriteweb.com/archives/twine_public_launch.php

[28] http://www.ibm.com/developerworks/xml/library/x-plansemantic/index.html?ca=drs-

[29] http://www.sciam.com/article.cfm?id=the-semantic-web

[30] http://www.shirky.com/writings/semantic_syllogism.html

[31] http://www.readwriteweb.com/archives/semantic_web_what_is_the_killer_app.php

[32] RDF Primer—W3C Recommendation http://www.w3.org/TR/rdf-primer/

[33] Resource Description Framework (RDF): Concepts and Abstract Syntax http://www.w3.org/TR/rdf-concepts/

[34] RDF/XML Syntax Specification http://www.w3.org/TR/rdf-syntax-grammar/

[35] RDF Semantics http://www.w3.org/TR/rdf-mt/

[36] RDF Vocabulary Description Language 1.0: RDF Schema http://www.w3.org/TR/rdf-schema/

[37] RDF Test Cases http://www.w3.org/TR/rdf-testcases/

[38] OWL Web Ontology Language Overview http://www.w3.org/TR/owl-features/

[39] OWL Web Ontology Language Use Cases and Requirements http://www.w3.org/TR/webont-req/

[40] OWL Web Ontology Language Guide http://www.w3.org/TR/owl-guide/

[41] OWL Web Ontology Language Reference http://www.w3.org/TR/owl-ref/

[42] OWL Web Ontology Language Semantics and Abstract Syntax http://www.w3.org/TR/owl-semantics/

[43] OWL Web Ontology Language Test Cases http://www.w3.org/TR/owl-test/

[44] http://www.w3.org/TR/owl-test/misc-000-guide#misc-000-guide

[45] http://en.wikipedia.org/wiki/SPARQL

[46] http://thefigtrees.net/lee/sw/sparql-faq#what-is

[47] http://www.w3.org/TR/rdf-sparql-protocol/

[48] http://www.w3.org/TR/rdf-sparql-query/

[49] http://www.w3.org/TR/rdf-sparql-XMLres/

[50] RDF Data Access Use Cases and Requirements http://www.w3.org/TR/rdf-dawg-uc/

[51] http://semantic-conference.com/

[52] http://dbpedia.org/About

[53] http://www.foaf-project.org/

[54] FOAF Vocabulary Specification http://xmlns.com/foaf/spec/

[55] www.lessonopoly.org

[56] http://doubleclix.wordpress.com/2007/09/14/publishing-search-fulfilment-and-conversation-as-four-pillars-of-any-software-system/

[57] http://sioc-project.org/

[58] http://rdfs.org/sioc/spec/

[59] http://www.talis.com/

The GeoSpatial Web, Arno Scharl & Klaus Tochtermann (Eds), Springer

http://ftp.informatik.rwth-aachen.de/Publications/CEUR-WS/Vol-426/

http://www.readwriteweb.com/archives/10_future_web_trends.php

Semantic Web Patterns: A Guide to Semantic Technologies http://www.readwriteweb.com/archives/semantic_web_patterns.php

SPARQL Design http://sparql.sourceforge.net/design-spec/design.html

SPARQL FAQ http://thefigtrees.net/lee/sw/sparql-faq#tutorials

Chapter 8

[1] http://www.economist.com/specialreports/displaystory.cfm?story_id=12411882

[2] Cloud Computing: Eyes on the Skies http://www.businessweek.com/print/magazine/content/08_18/b4082059989191.htm##

[3] http://www.redmonk.com/jgovernor/2008/03/13/15-ways-to-tell-its-not-cloud-computing/?

[4] http://cloudsecurity.org/2008/04/25/12-signs-that-your-company-is-already-in-the-cloud/?

[5] http://doubleclix.wordpress.com/2008/10/04/clouds-ready-to-chuck-training-wheels-a-view-from-users-vendors-and-vcs/

[6] http://neotactics.com/blog/technology/challenges-for-cloud-computing

[7] http://www.10gen.com/assets/10gen_New_Cloud_Computing_Company_Unveils_Limited_Alpha_(Apr_15_2008).pdf

[8] http://blogs.zdnet.com/BTL/?p=10441

[9] http://www.gartner.com/it/page.jsp?id=871113

[10] http://www.wired.com/techbiz/it/magazine/16-05/mf_amazon?currentPage=all

[11] Cloud Storage Alternatives http://webworkerdaily.com/2008/05/07/three-cloud-storage-alternatives/

[12] http://www.earthtimes.org/articles/show/amazon-web-services-launches-ldquopublic,643947.shtml

[13] http://mystarbucksidea.force.com/home/home.jsp

[14] What cloud computing really means http://www.nytimes.com/idg/IDG_002570DE00740E180025742400363509.html?ref=technology

[15] Winning the SaaS Platform Wars http://www.sandhill.com/opinion/editorial.php?id=188

[16] http://mckinsey.com/clientservice/hightech/pdfs/Emerging_Platform_Wars.pdf

[17] http://blog.pmarca.com/2007/09/the-three-kinds.html

[18] http://open.nytimes.com/2007/11/01/self-service-prorated-super-computing-fun/

[19] http://www.johnmwillis.com/amazon/the-night-the-nyt-used-hadoop-and-ec2-to-convert-4tbs/

[20] http://doubleclix.wordpress.com/2008/08/03/cloud-computing-and-grids/

[21] http://en.wikipedia.org/wiki/Global_Grid_Forum

[22] Cloud and utility http://gh-linux.blogspot.com/2008/03/is-cloud-computing-nothing-but-utilty.html

[23] Cheap infrastructure http://www.technologyreview.com/Biztech/20663/

[24] http://blog.rightscale.com/2008/04/23/animoto-facebook-scale-up/?

[25] http://www.omnisio.com/v/9ceYTUGdjh9/jeff-bezos-on-animoto

[26] Nicholas Carr http://www.roughtype.com/archives/2007/12/the_technoutili.php

[27] http://doubleclix.wordpress.com/2008/07/26/book-review-nicholas-carr-the-big-switch-rewiring-the-world-from-edison-to-google/

[28] http://itmanagement.earthweb.com/features/article.php/3798591/Five-Companies-Shaping-Cloud-Computing-Who-Wins.htm

[29] http://gigaom.com/2008/05/04/sun-amazon-web-services/

[30] http://www.sun.com/aboutsun/pr/2008-05/sunflash.20080505.3.xml

[31] Google AppEngine http://code.google.com/appengine/

[32] Microsoft Live mesh https://www.mesh.com/Welcome/Welcome.aspx

[33] Information Week http://www.informationweek.com/news/internet/web2.0/showArticle.jhtml?articleID=207401672

[34] https://www.mesh.com/Welcome/LearnMore.aspx

[35] http://blogs.zdnet.com/microsoft/?p=1355

[36] http://news.cnet.com/microsoft-launches-windows-azure/

[37] http://doubleclix.wordpress.com/2008/10/27/microsofts-azure/

[38] http://news.cnet.com/8301-10805_3-10139597-75.html

[39] http://www.eweek.com/c/a/Enterprise-Apps/IBM-Floats-into-The-Cloud-With-Caution/?kc=EWKNLBOE050308STR5

[40] Blue Cloud http://www-03.ibm.com/press/us/en/pressrelease/22613.wss

[41] http://www.eweek.com/c/a/Infrastructure/IBM-to-Deliver-Computing-Power-Under-Blue-Cloud/

[42] Sun's cloud offering http://www.datacenterknowledge.com/archives/2008/Feb/19/sun_preps_cloud_platform_to_vie_with_amazon.html

[43] http://research.sun.com/spotlight/2008/2008-04-09_caroline.html

[44] Cloud vendors http://www.johnmwillis.com/cloud-computing/cloud-vendors-a-to-z-revised/

[45] http://www.dell.com/cloudcomputing/

[46] http://direct2dell.com/cloudcomputing/default.aspx

[47] http://venturebeat.com/2008/05/09/facebook-borrows-100m-to-build-out-its-infra-structure/

[48] http://www.eweek.com/c/a/Messaging-and-Collaboration/Coolest-Technologies-Demoed-at-Web-20/?kc=EWKNLEDP050208A

[49] http://gigaom.com/2008/08/13/is-the-cloud-right-for-you-ask-yourself-these-5-questions/

[50] http://www.techcrunch.com/2008/02/15/amazon-web-services-goes-down-takes-many-startup-sites-with-it/

[51] http://blogs.zdnet.com/BTL/?p=8010

[52] http://wwwin.cisco.com/data-shared/cec/rendered_news/html/channels/1/5/204337.shtml

http://arstechnica.com/software/news/2009/01/google-to-enlist-army-of-saas-resellers-for-google-apps.ars

http://news.google.com/?ncl=1292618689&hl=en&topic=t

http://www.nytimes.com/2008/05/25/technology/25proto.html?_r=3&ref=business&oref=slogin&oref=slogin

http://www.economist.com/business/PrinterFriendly.cfm?story_id=11413148

http://gigaom.com/2008/07/01/10-reasons-enterprises-arent-ready-to-trust-the-cloud/

http://gigaom.com/2008/02/28/how-cloud-utility-computing-are-different/

http://www.nytimes.com/idg/IDG_002570DE00740E180025742400363509.html?ref=technology

http://www.techcrunch.com/2008/04/21/who-are-the-biggest-users-of-amazon-web-services-its-not-startups/

[http://mitworld.mit.edu/video/417

Amazon Web Services http://aws.amazon.com/

http://www.johnmwillis.com/category/amazon/

http://en.wikipedia.org/wiki/Cloud_computing

Book: Programming Amazon Web Services http://www.oreilly.com/catalog/9780596515812/

http://www.datacenterknowledge.com/archives/2008/Apr/17/new_cloud_platforms_pro-liferating.html

Computing in the cloud workshop at Princeton http://citp.princeton.edu/cloud-workshop/

http://www.readwriteweb.com/archives/ibm_unveils_blue_cloud_what_da.php

http://www.informationweek.com/news/internet/web2.0/showArticle.jhtml?articleID=207401733

Resources http://groups.google.ca/group/cloud-computing/web/cloud-computing-blogs-resources

http://blogs.sun.com/innovation/date/20080312

http://wikis.sun.com/display/shoal/Shoal+Home

http://www.andykessler.com/andy_kessler/2008/05/wsj-the-war-for.html

http://www.infoworld.com/article/09/02/03/Sun_to_take_to_the_cloud_1.html?source=NLC-TB&cgd=2009-02-03

Chapter 9

[1] *Mobile Web*, http://en.wikipedia.org/wiki/Mobile_Web

[2] *The timeline of mobile phones*, http://www.phonehistory.co.uk/mobile-phones-time-line.html

[3] *Selling the Cell Phone, Part 1: History of Cellular Phones*, M. Bellis, http://inventors.about.com/library/weekly/aa070899.htm

[4] *1G, 2G, 3G, 4G*, J. Shepler, http://searchmobilecomputing.techtarget.com/generic/0,295582,sid40_gci1078079,00.html

[5] *2G*, http://en.wikipedia.org/wiki/2G

[6] *Wireless Application Protocol*, http://en.wikipedia.org/wiki/Wireless_Application_Protocol

[7] *GSM*, http://en.wikipedia.org/wiki/GSM

[8] *iPhone Q&A*, http://www.everyipod.com/iphone-faq/iphone-edge-3g-support-difference-between-edge-and-3g-mvno.html

[9] *3G*, http://en.wikipedia.org/wiki/3G

[10] *Bluetooth*, http://en.wikipedia.org/wiki/Bluetooth

[11] *Satellite Phone*, http://en.wikipedia.org/wiki/Satellite_phone

[12] *4G*, http://en.wikipedia.org/wiki/4G

[13] *Martin Cooper—History of Cell Phone*, http://inventors.about.com/cs/inventorsalphabet/a/martin_cooper.htm

[14] *casio pf-3000*, http://www.voidware.com/calcs/pf3000.htm

[15] *Personal digital assistant*, http://en.wikipedia.org/wiki/Personal_digital_assistant

[16] *What Makes a Smartphone Smart?* L. Cassavoy, http://smartphones.about.com/od/smartphonebasics/a/what_is_smart.htm

[17] *Pocket Computing*, http://cdecas.free.fr/computers/pocket/simon.php

[18] *Smartphone*, http://en.wikipedia.org/wiki/Smartphone

[19] *Nokia 9000-additional pictures,* http://mobile.softpedia.com/phonePictures/8

[20] *Mobile device*, http://en.wikipedia.org/wiki/Mobile_device

[21] *IDC Finds Slower Growth in the Mobile Phone Market in 2007 While Samsung Captures the Number Two Position For the Year,* http://www.idc.com/getdoc.jsp;jsessionid=LTQOIV4H4ODDCCQJAFICFFAKBEAUMI WD?containerId=prUS21053908

[22] *Most popular Nokia mobile phones for Q4 2007*, http://ukphonenews.co.uk/most-popular-nokia-mobile-phones-for-q4-2007/

[23] http://www.nokiausa.com/find-products/phones/nokia-e90-communicator/specifications Note: Click on Display

[24] *BlackBerry Storm review: Inelegant touch screen doesn't live up to the hype*, J. Rauschert, http://www.mlive.com/flintjournal/index.ssf/2008/11/blackberry_storm.html

[25] *BlackBerry® Storm™ smartphone in detail*, http://blackberry.vodafone.co.uk/storm/specifications/

[26] *Verizon officially debuts RIM BlackBerry Storm*, http://news.cnet.com/verizon-officially-debuts-rim-blackberry-storm/

[27] *BlackBerry Storm: Can it beat the iPhone?* http://www.telegraph.co.uk/finance/yourbusiness/businesstechnology/3248117/BlackBerry-Storm-Can-it-beat-the-iPhone.html

[28] http://www.blackberry.com/blackberrystorm/

[29] *The iPhone PocketGuide, Third Edition*, C. Breen, http://cisco.safaribooksonline.com/9780321603982/ch01

[30] *iPhone vs iPhone 3G*, http://www.techwarelabs.com/reviews/phones/iPhone-vs-iPhone3G/

[31] http://www.apple.com/iphone/gallery/#image3

[32] *Nokia E90 Communicator*, http://www.nokiausa.com/A4486902

[33] *BlackBerry Storm Features*, http://www.blackberry.com/blackberrystorm/features.shtml

[34] *iPhone3G*, http://www.apple.com/iphone/features/

[35] *Microsoft® Mobile Development Handbook*, A. Wigley et. al., http://cisco.safari-booksonline.com/9780735623583

[36] *AT&T Wants More Web-Enabled Devices*, L. Holson, http://bits.blogs.nytimes.com/2008/10/17/att-wants-more-web-enabled-devices/

[37] *Now You're Talking*, J. Borzo, http://money.cnn.com/magazines/business2/business2_archive/2007/02/01/8398978/index.htm

[38] *Roaming*, http://en.wikipedia.org/wiki/Roaming

[39] http://www.nmci.ca/index_files/gps_diagram.htm

[40] *What is GPS?* http://www8.garmin.com/aboutGPS/

[41] *E911,* http://www.webopedia.com/TERM/E/E911.html

[42] *Introduction to Mobile Devices*, http://www.webopedia.com/quick_ref/mobile_OS.asp

[43] *Mobile operating system*, http://en.wikipedia.org/wiki/Mobile_operating_system

[44] *Global smart phone shipments rise 28%*, http://www.canalys.com/pr/2008/r2008112.htm

[45] *Symbian Developer Network*, http://developer.symbian.com/main/index.jsp

[46] *Binary Runtime Environment for Wireless,* http://en.wikipedia.org/wiki/BREW

[47] *Java Platform*, Micro Edition,

[48] *Android* (operating system), http://en.wikipedia.org/wiki/Google_Android

[49] *Eclipse*, http://www.eclipse.org/org/

http://en.wikipedia.org/wiki/Java_Platform,_Micro_Edition

[50] *Defining an industry standard for mobile application development platform,* http://ianskerrett.wordpress.com/2008/11/12/defining-an-industry-standard-for-mobile-application-development-platform/

[51] *Ajax (programming)*, http://en.wikipedia.org/wiki/AJAX

[52] *Web application*, http://en.wikipedia.org/wiki/Web_applications

[53] *Dev Shed Lounge*, http://forums.devshed.com/dev-shed-lounge-26/web-application-vs-web-service-63625.html

[54] http://www.apple.com/

[55] *Web apps*, http://www.apple.com/webapps/whatarewebapps.html

[56] *Calculate: Most popular*, http://www.apple.com/webapps/calculate/index_top.html

[57] *Entertainment: Most popular*, http://www.apple.com/webapps/entertainment/index_top.html

[58] *Games: Most popular*, http://www.apple.com/webapps/games/index_top.html

[59] *News: Most popular*, http://www.apple.com/webapps/news/index_top.html

[60] *Productivity: Most popular*, http://www.apple.com/webapps/productivity/index_top.html

[61] *Search Tools: Most popular*, http://www.apple.com/webapps/searchtools/index_top.html

[62] *Social Networking: Most popular*, http://www.apple.com/webapps/socialnetworking/index_top.html

[63] *Sports: Most popular*, http://www.apple.com/webapps/sports/index_top.html

[64] *Travel: Most popular*, http://www.apple.com/webapps/travel/index_top.html

[65] *Utilities: Most popular*, http://www.apple.com/webapps/utilities/index_top.html

[66] *Weather: Most popular*, http://www.apple.com/webapps/weather/index_top.html

[67] *App Store*, http://www.apple.com/iphone/features/appstore.html

[68] *WebApps Dev Center,* http://developer.apple.com/webapps/

[69] *iPhone Web Application Submission*, https://daw.apple.com/cgi-bin/WebObjects/DSAuthWeb.woa/wa/login?appIdKey=D534F5C413E680ACBC861EE8025883117C9705F90893AF782751628F0291F620&path=/iphone/index.php

[70] *Yahoo! Mobile*, http://mobile.yahoo.com/

[71] *The simplest way to get answers: just ask,* http://mobile.yahoo.com/onesearch/voice

[72] *Review: Yahoo Go Version 2—Including GPS Support*, http://www.berryreview.com/2007/06/27/review-yahoo-go-version-2-including-gps-support/

[73] *Michigan Launches Mobile Web Portal*, http://www.govtech.com/gt/articles/98747

[74] http://www.michigan.gov/

[75] *Netbiscuits Announces Winners to Mobile Web Developer Challenge at Yankee Group's Mobile Internet World*, http://www.marketwatch.com/news/story/Netbiscuits-Announces-Winners-Mobile-Web/story.aspx?guid=%7B9467EBB5-D5BC-4ABD-8280-7B857DB7314C%7D

[76] http://usaftbirds.mobi/

[77] *Wireless application service provider,* http://searchmobilecomputing.techtarget.com/sDefinition/0,,sid40_gci342916,00.html

[78] *Wireless Network Services and Application Providers*, http://www.mobileinfo.com/links/wrls_net_services/W-ASPs.htm

[79] *Industry Solutions,* http://www.air2web.com/solutions.html

[80] *Solutions*, http://www.mobileaware.com/solutions.jsp

[81] *Solutions Overview*, http://www.viryanet.com/solutions/overview/

[82] *Industry Analysts,* http://www.mobileaware.com/testimonials.jsp

[83] Mobile social network, http://en.wikipedia.org/wiki/Mobile_social_network

[84] *The Truth About Profiting from Social Networking*, P. Rutledge, http://cisco.safaribooksonline.com/9780768684438/ch47

[85] http://www.dodgeball.com/

[86] http://m.facebook.com/

[87] *Mobile*, http://www.facebook.com/help.php?page=432

[88] http://www.juicecaster.com/

[89] *JuiceCaster*, http://en.wikipedia.org/wiki/JuiceCaster

[90] http://www.loopt.com/

[91] http://www.mig33.com/

[92] http://www2.mkade.com/

[93] *Mobikade*, http://en.wikipedia.org/wiki/Mobikade

[94] http://www.mobimii.com/

[95] http://www.mocospace.com/

[96] m.myspace.com

[97] http://www.myspace.com/index.cfm?fuseaction=mobile

[98] VOGUE Magazine Mobilizes Fashion Videos Using JuiceCaster's Mobile Video Search, http://www.reuters.com/article/pressRelease/idUS140433+22-Jan-2008+BW20080122

[99] Flutter: Unlimited Picture Messages on the iPhone, http://www.juicecaster.com/flutter/

[100] *I Saw The Future of Social Networking The Other Day,* M. Arrington, http://www.techcrunch.com/2008/04/09/i-saw-the-future-of-social-networking-the-other-day/

[101] *Cisco Mobile Web*, S. Lau, *http://zed.cisco.com/confluence/display/MKTGWEB/Cisco+Mobile+Web*

[102] *Cisco Mobile Web*, S. Lau, http://zed.cisco.com/confluence/download/attachments/110314/MobilityMarketingOverview12Jun06+v2.ppt?version=1

[103] http://www.cisco.com/web/mobile/index.html

[104] *CISCO Text Messaging Subscription (SMS)*, http://www.cisco.com/web/mobile/sms.html

[105] *Email re: Cisco Mobile Usage*, F. Murphy, 1/21/09

[106] *Smartphone Project*, http://wikicentral.cisco.com/confluence/display/PROJECT/Smartphone+Project

[107] Check Your Email and Calendar Anywhere, Anytime, http://wwwin.cisco.com/data-shared/cec/rendered_news/html/channels/1/8/102811.shtml

[108] *Mobile CEC Services*, http://wwwin.cisco.com/webdev/mobile/services.shtml

[109] http://wwwin.cisco.com/cec/mobile/

[110] Mobile Sales Information Services Executive Briefing Center Preso for Pfizer, S. Bouchard, Nov 2007.

[111] *Mobile Phones*, http://wwwin.cisco.com/it/services/mobilephones/index.shtml

[112] *Cisco Unified Mobile Communicator (CUMC) 3.1*, http://wwwin.cisco.com/it/new/cumc.shtml

[113] *Cisco to Combine Google's Android*, UC and Enterprise 2.0, D. Greenfield, http://blogs.zdnet.com/Greenfield/?p=182

[114] *MacWorld Kudos to the Cisco WebEx Team*, http://blogs.cisco.com/webexperience/comments/macworld_kudos_to_the_cisco_webex_team/

[115] *Nokia cuts mobile web services forecast*, http://www.fiercemobilecontent.com/story/nokia-cuts-mobile-web-services-forecast/2008-12-05

[116] *GOP issues rules to avoid Macaca moments*, C. Budoff, http://www.politico.com/news/stories/0607/4483.html

Chapter 10

[1] *History and Culture*, http://wwwin-tools.cisco.com/exec/comm/etl/tools/page/cbook#a=0

[2] *What is Web 2.0*, T. O'Reilly, http://www.oreillynet.com/pub/a/oreilly/tim/news/2005/09/30/what-is-web-20.html, September 2005

[3] *Web 2.0 Compact Definition: Trying Again*, T. O'Reilly, http://radar.oreilly.com/archives/2006/12/web-20-compact-definition-tryi.html, December 2006

[4] *Cisco Corporate Story*, http://wwwin-tools.cisco.com/exec/comm/etl/tools/page/cbook#a=0

[5] *How Cisco's CEO John Chambers is Turning the Tech Giant Socialist*, E. McGirt, http://www.fastcompany.com/magazine/131/revolution-in-san-jose.html

[6] *The Next Frontier in Collaboration: Transforming How Cisco and Channel Partners Work*, http://sjc-fs2-web/wg-u/us-c_web/Published/us-canada/uscpo/docs/Channels_Collaboration_Case_Study.pdf

[7] *CBTV: Web 2.0*, http://wwwin-tools.cisco.com/exec/comm/etl/tools/siena/media/video/2007/dr-144/CBTV_Web_2_0.mp4

[8] *Cisco's $1 Billion Web Site*, J. Frook, CommunicationsWeek, http://www.commweek.com

[9] *Letter from CIO Communications, In. to Matthew Burns, Content Program Manager, Cisco Systems Inc, 7 May 1997*

[10] *Cisco Employee Connection Among World's Best Intranets*, http://wwwin.cisco.com/data-shared/cec/rendered_news/html/channels/1/5/101010.shtml

[11] *Web 2.0 Enterprise Experience, M. Burns, 4ᵗʰ Intranet Week—Driving Intranet Success and Value with New Technologies and Innovative Strategies*, http://workspace/Livelink/livelink.exe?func=ll&objId=25464530&objAction=Open

[12] *Blogs,* http://wwwin.cisco.com/cisco/ccoe/technologies/blogs.shtml

[13] *Email from S. Canny dated 2 February 2008 Subject: wwwin-blogs-metrics.xls*

[14] *C-Scape, CES and Market Transitions On My Mind,* http://wwwin-blogs.cisco.com/chambers/entry/c_scape_ces_and_market

[15] *It's Showtime for Blogs,* J. King, Worldwide Sales Collaboration Board, February 2008

[16] *Blogs,* D. Bell, CA Learning Series, http://wwwin.cisco.com/CustAdv/orgs/svcs_mkt/cawebteam/web2.0/ppt/blogs.ppt, July 2008

[17] *Cisco.com,* http://www.cisco.com

[18] *Forum Home,* D. Govoni, http://wwwin-forums.cisco.com/thread.jspa?threadID=10612&tstart=0

[19] *PR News' Legal PR Awards 2008,* http://www.prnewsonline.com/awards/legal/winners_2008.html

[20] *Cisco, Dell Blogs Feud over FCoE vs. iSCSI,* R. Miller, http://www.datacenterknowledge.com/archives/2008/04/14/cisco-dell-blogs-feud-over-fcoe-vs-iscsi/

[21] *Blogs,* A. Piese, CA Learning Series, http://wwwin.cisco.com/CustAdv/orgs/svcs_mkt/cawebteam/web2.0/ppt/blogs.ppt, July 2008

[22] *Discussion Forums,* http://wwwin.cisco.com/cisco/ccoe/technologies/collabsocial_discussionforums.shtml

[23] *Email from L. Dixon dated 1 February 2009 Subject: CCoE Monthly Statistics*

[24] *Discussion Forums,* M. Barry, CA Learning Series, http://wwwin.cisco.com/CustAdv/orgs/svcs_mkt/cawebteam/web2.0/ppt/forums.ppt, July 2008

[25] *Cisco Green Governance,* http://wwwin.cisco.com/cisco/green/governance

[26] *Discussion Forums > Let's Talk Cisco Green,* http://wwwin-forums.cisco.com/category.jspa?categoryID=11

[27] *Discussion Forums,* K. Denis, CA Learning Series, http://wwwin.cisco.com/CustAdv/orgs/svcs_mkt/cawebteam/web2.0/ppt/forums.ppt, July 2008

[28] *Discussion Forums,* http://wwwin-forums.cisco.com/index.jspa?categoryID=1

[29] *Discussion Forums > WebEx Connect,* http://wwwin-forums.cisco.com/category.jspa?categoryID=292

[30] *Discussion Forums > WebEx Connect > Cisco Mailer BulkInvite Widget,* http://wwwin-forums.cisco.com/thread.jspa?threadID=14165&tstart=0

[31] *Discussion Forums, K. Orton, CA Learning Series,* http://wwwin.cisco.com/CustAdv/orgs/svcs_mkt/cawebteam/web2.0/ppt/forums.ppt, July 2008

[32] *Linksys Gets Shaken, a Community Is Stirred: How Lithium Technologies' online community-based CRM solution saved Christmas,* L. McKay, http://www.destinationcrm.com/Articles/Columns-Departments/REAL-ROI/Linksys-Gets-Shaken,-a-Community-Is-Stirred-49190.aspx

[33] *Dashboard > Project: Mgr Portal*, http://zed.cisco.com/confluence/display/PRTL/2008-Jan-9+Manager+Portal+Transition

[34] *Wiki...wiki...wiki*, C. Tobias, CA Learning Series, http://wwwin.cisco.com/CustAdv/orgs/svcs_mkt/cawebteam/web2.0/ppt/wiki.ppt, July 2008

[35] *i-zone*, https://na5.brightidea.com/ct/c_es.bix?a=OD619

[36] *Collaboratory*, http://collaboratory.cisco.com/confluence/display/CAWIKI/Home

[37] *Collaboratory*: CA Strategy Home, http://collaboratory.cisco.com/confluence/display/CASTR/Home

[38] *Wiki...wiki...wiki*, P. Tam, CA Learning Series, http://wwwin.cisco.com/CustAdv/orgs/svcs_mkt/cawebteam/web2.0/ppt/wiki.ppt, July 2008

[39] *Collaborate Across Cisco Award for Mac-Wiki*, P. Chou, http://wwwin-blogs.cisco.com/pchiou/entry/collaborate_across_cisco_award_for

[40] *WebEx Connect Community*, http://wikicentral.cisco.com/confluence/display/GENERAL/WebEx+Connect+Community

[41] *People (Directory) Help New Features*, http://wwwin.cisco.com/dir/help/features.shtml

[42] *Collaboration Tools: Ciscopedia*, http://ciscopedia.cisco.com/display/cpda/Ciscopedia

[43] *Relational Navigation, Directory 3.0 & Ciscopedia*, J. Beno, http://wwwin-blogs.cisco.com/jbeno/entry/relational_navigation_directory_3_0, September 2007

[44] *Ciscopedia, CApedia, & Salespedia*, N. Dudhorria, CA Learning Series, http://wwwin.cisco.com/CustAdv/orgs/svcs_mkt/cawebteam/web2.0/ppt/ciscopedia.ppt, July 2008

[45] *Time spent searching cuts into company productivity*, D. Dubie, http://www.networkworld.com/news/2006/102006-search-cuts-productivity.html

[46] *Cisco Employee Connection C-Vision*, http://wwwin-cvision.cisco.com/

[47] *Video Sharing (C-Vision)*, http://wwwin.cisco.com/cisco/ccoe/technologies/cvision.shtml

[48] *Email from L. Dixon dated 4 February 2009 Subject: CBS Utilization Summary January 2009*

[49] *Corporate Communications Architecture*, http://wwwin.cisco.com/corpcom/arch/index.shtml

[50] *Communication and Collaboration IT*, http://wwwin.cisco.com/it/ccit/

[51] *Communications Center of Excellence*, http://wwwin.cisco.com/cisco/ccoe/

[52] *C&C Utilization Metrics > Chambers Collaboration Reports > 2009_Jan_COLLAB*, http://team.cisco.com/sites/ccoe/metrics/Chambers%20Monthly%20Collab%20Reports/2009_Jan_COLLAB.ppt

[53] *C&C Board Members 13 October 2008*, WebEx Connect > Files > CC Board of Directors

[54] *Cisco Company Meeting*, *12 February 2009*, http://wwwin.cisco.com/corpcom/arch/ciscotv/index.shtml

[55] *Strip for Feb 22, 2009*, http://www.dilbert.com/strips/comic/2009-02-22/

[56] *Second Life*, http://zed.cisco.com/confluence/display/LLSL/Second+Life+at+Cisco

[57] *New Media: Second Life*, http://wwwin.cisco.com/corpcom/newmedia/second_life.shtml

[58] *The End of Second Life*, O. Thomas, http://valleywag.gawker.com/5158190/the-end-of-second-life

[59] *Email from J. Grobb dated 12 March 2009 Subject: None Attachment: Internet Evolution.pptx*

Chapter 11

[1] *Sales 2.0 FOR DUMMIES—Sales 2.0 Conference Special Edition*, Thompson, D. & Kao, L. (2008) Hoboken, NJ: Wiley Publishing, Inc.

[2] *Connecting People, Communities, and Information*, http://wwwin.cisco.com/data-shared/cec/rendered_news/html/channels/1/8/204871.shtml

[3] *Enterprise & Mid-Market Solutions Marketing Enterprise Architecture*, http://wwwin.cisco.com/enterprise/sona/

[4] *Mobile Sales Information Services Executive Briefing Center Preso for Pfizer*, S. Bouchard, Nov 2007.

[5] *WWSPS Community > MSIS > Mobility for Sales > Mobility for Sales Partnership*, http://team.cisco.com/sites/WWSPS/msis/Mobility%20for%20Sales/Mobility%20for%20Sales%20Partnership.aspx

[6] *Mobile Sales Information Services Opportunity Roadmap*, http://team.cisco.com/sites/WWSPS/msis/Shared%20Documents/MSIS%20Opportunity%20Roadmap.ppt

[7] *WWSPS Community > Explorers*, http://team.cisco.com/sites/WWSPS/explorers/default.aspx

[8] *WWSPS Community > Explorer > Capability Requirements*, http://team.cisco.com/sites/WWSPS/webexconnect/Lists/Web%2020WebEx%20Connect%20Capability%20Requirements1/AllItems.aspx

[9] *Introduction to Mashups and Use Case Templates*, S. Bouchard, N. Trevino and M. Hosseini, http://workspace/Livelink/livelink.exe?func=ll&objId=28339469&objAction=Open

[10] *WWSPS Community > MSIS > Mobility for Sales > Mobile MBR L1*, http://team.cisco.com/sites/WWSPS/msis/Mobility%20for%20Sales/Mobile%20MBR%20L1.aspx

[11] *WWSPS Community > Sales 2.0 > Salespedia Overview > Home*, http://team.cisco.com/sites/WWSPS/Sales20/Salespedia%20Wiki/Home.aspx

[12] *WWSPS Community > Sales 2.0 > Salespedia*, http://team.cisco.com/sites/WWSPS/Sales20/Lists/Salespedia/AllItems.aspx

[13] *Collaboration Tools: Ciscopedia*, http://ciscopedia.cisco.com/display/cpda/Ciscopedia

[14] *Cisco WebEx Connect Vision Widget Roadmap*, http://workspace/Livelink/livelink.exe?func=ll&objId=28936737&objAction=Open

[15] *WWSPS Community > WebEx Connect > WebEx Connect Capability Inventory*, http://team.cisco.com/sites/WWSPS/webexconnect/Lists/WebEx%20Connect%20Capability%20Inventory/AllItems.aspx

[16] *WWSPS Community > WebEx Connect > WebEx Connect Widget Documentation*, http://team.cisco.com/sites/WWSPS/webexconnect/Lists/WebEx%20Connext%20Widget%20Documentation/AllItems.aspx

[17] *WebEx Connect Early Adopter Program*, http://wwwin.cisco.com/it/services/webexconnect/index.shtml

[18] *iFeedback@Cisco*, http://team.cisco.com/sites/WWSPS/iFeedback/default.aspx

[19] innovation@cisco overview, http://ework.cisco.com/Livelink/livelink.exe?func=ll&objId=16298976&objAction=Open

[20] *About U.S.-Canada, http://wwwin.cisco.com/us-canada/about.shtml*

[21] *U.S.-Canada*, http://wwwin.cisco.com/us-canada/

[22] *Email from D. Rhode dated 29 June 2008 Subject: Quote*

[23] *Sales Planning & Operations*, http://wwwin.cisco.com/us-canada/uscpo/

[24] *Scale the Power*, http://wwwin.cisco.com/us-canada/uscpo/stp/

[25] *Collaboration Training for Cisco Administrators,* http://wwwin.cisco.com/us-canada/uscpo/stp/collabTraining.shtml

[26] *Collaboration*, http://wwwin.cisco.com/us-canada/uscpo/collaboration/

[27] *Collaboration Guide*, http://wwwin.cisco.com/us-canada/uscpo/docs/CollaborationGuide.ppt

[28] *Collaboration White Papers and Use Cases*, http://wwwin.cisco.com/us-canada/uscpo/collaboration/salestools.shtml

[29] *Email from E. Culver dated 13 February 2009 Subject: Collaboration Cockpit*

[30] *C&C Utilization Metrics > Chambers Collaboration Reports > 2009_Jan_COLLAB*, http://team.cisco.com/sites/ccoe/metrics/Chambers%20Monthly%20Collab%20Reports/2009_Jan_COLLAB.ppt

[31] *Customer Value Chain Management (CVCM) stAr Framework*, presented at CCoE Business Solutions Consortium, 19 Feb 2009

[32] *U.S.-Canada Collaboration Metrics*, S. Bouchard, 19 Feb 2009, http://sjc-fs2-web/wg-u/us-c_web/Published/us-canada/uscpo/collaboration/USCanadaCollaborationMetrics.ppt

[33] *U.S.-Canada Web 2.0 Committee January 2009*, http://sjc-fs2-web/wg-u/us-c_web/Published/us-canada/uscpo/collaboration/USC_Web_20_Committee.ppt

[34] *Email from C. Schenck dated 4 February 2009 Subject: WWSCB Members*

[35] *About AT*, http://wwwin.cisco.com/us-canada/at/about.shtml

[36] *SOAR Mission-Vision*, http://wwwin.cisco.com/us-canada/at/docs/soar/mission-vision.ppt

[37] *SOAR, http://wwwin.cisco.com/us-canada/at/soar/*

[38] *Technology Solutions Network*, http://wwwin.cisco.com/WWSales/wwops/techops/tsn/

[39] *Technology Solutions Network (TSN Overview)*, http://gsops-wiki.cisco.com/confluence/download/attachments/2785292/TSN_Overview.ppt

[40] *SE Connection*, http://wwwin.cisco.com/WWSales/wwops/techops/

[41] *Email from S. Bouchard dated 29 August 2006 Subject: Connected Communities Background*

[42] *vSearch Spotlight*, http://wwwin.cisco.com/us-canada/uscpo/stp/vSearch.shtml

[43] *Fidelity Canada* SOAR Program Overview, P. Romzek, M. LaManna, E. Renfer, http://wwwin.cisco.com/us-canada/at/soar/docs/livelink/FidelityCanada.ppt

[44] *Collaboration Connection Radio*, http://wwwin.cisco.com/voice/news/executives/collaboration_connection/index.shtml

[45] *Five to Thrive*, http://wwwin.cisco.com/us-canada/five2thrive/

[46] *Introducing the Five to Thrive Program*, D. Rhode, http://wwwin-blogs.cisco.com/drhode/entry/introducing_the_five_to_thrive

[47] *Thrive in Dynamic Times*, http://www.cisco.com/en/US/netsol/ns917/index.html

[48] *Save to Invest, http://www.cisco.com/en/US/netsol/ns918/index.html*

[49] *Unlock Employee Potential*, http://www.cisco.com/en/US/netsol/ns919/index.html

[50] *Drive True Customer Intimacy*, http://www.cisco.com/en/US/netsol/ns920/index.html

[51] *Outpace Your Competition*, http://www.cisco.com/en/US/netsol/ns922/index.html

[52] *Transition to a Borderless Enterprise*, http://www.cisco.com/en/US/netsol/ns921/index.html

[53] *Continued Evolution of the Human Network Effect*, http://wwwin.cisco.com/data-shared/cec/rendered_news/html/channels/1/7/202469.shtml

[54] *Channels 3.0*, http://wwwin.cisco.com/wwchannels/channels3.0/

[55] Navigate to Accelerate, E. Peres, http://wwwin.cisco.com/wwchannels/download/ent/n2a_field_training.ppt

[56] *The Next Frontier in Collaboration: Transforming How Cisco and Channel Partners Work*, http://sjc-fs2-web/wg-u/us-c_web/Published/us-canada/uscpo/docs/Channels_Collaboration_Case_Study.pdf

[57] *Cisco Partner Space*, http://www.ciscopartnerspace.com

[58] *Marketing*, http://wwwin.cisco.com/marketing/

[59] *Collaboration Consortium Achieving Value from Collaboration*, http://wwwin-blogs.cisco.com/cisco-ccoe/entry/collaboration_consortium_achieving_value_from

Index

Numbers

2G technology, 204

3G technology, 205

3Tera, cloud computing services, 198

4G technology, 205

37signals, *Getting Real*, 156

2008 presidential election, Web 2.0 impact on, 5

A

A-Space, 11

administrator training for U.S.-Canada Sales team, 282

adoption of Web 2.0 at Cisco, 24, 234

internal Web 2.0 leveraging, 27-29

Intranet Strategy Group, 235

through blogs, 236-241

through CCoE, 258-261

through discussion forums, 241-244

through video, 255-256

through wikis, 245-250

Web 2.0-centric products, 25-26

adoption of Web 2.0 EE (Enterprise Edition), challenges to, 16

aggregation, content aggregation, 125

AIR, 82

Air2Web, 218

Ajax, 83-87

Amazon, infrastructure/architecture case study, 148-149

anarchic scalability, 153

Anderson, Chris, 23

Andreessen, Marc, 4, 19, 106, 114, 187

Apache Hadoop, 154-155

Apache Shindig, 115

APIs

Facebook architecture components, 101

OpenSocial, 114-115

App Engine (Google), 195

Apple iPhone, 209-210

applications, 214

applications

Facebook applications, 98-99

application building blocks, 100-101

essential elements of, 103-104

for mobile devices, 211-213

webapps, 213-216

architectural models as Web 2.0 meme, 19-20

architecture, 144

scalable technologies, 152-153

architecture/infrastructure case studies

Amazon, 148-149

eBay, 146-147

Flickr, 152

Google, 149-151

Twitter, 151-152

YouTube, 147

AT (Advanced Technologies) organization, 291-292

AT&T
MTS, 204

Atom, 125-126, 128
business value of, 127
elements, 141
information architecture, 140
readers, Times, 135
RFCs, 139

Attensa, 138

Awareness, 108

AWS (Amazon Web Services), cloud computing, 192-194

Azure, 195-197

B

Barry, Molly, 241

Basecamp, 157

Battier, Shane, 239

Beesley, Michael, 237

Beno, Jim, 251

Berners-Lee, Tim, 161-162, 167

best practices for RSS, 138-139

Bezos, Jeff, 196

BigTable, 149

BlackBerry Storm, 208

Blogger, 38

BlogMatrix Sparks!, 129

BlogPulse, 43

blogs, 37-38, 42-45
buzz-tracking services, 45
Cisco's adoption of Web 2.0, 236-241
microblogging, 113
software, 38
vlogs, 38

blogsphere, definitions of Web 2.0 in, 5

Blue Shirt Nation, 94

Bluetooth, 205

Bostrum, Sue, 303

Bray, Tim, 130

Bricklin, Dan, 107

broadcasting industry, adoption of podcasting, 129

BungeeConnect, 186

Burns, Matthew, 235

business aspects of Web 2.0, 6
newspaper industry, impact on, 10
radio industry, impact on, 11
Salesforce IdeaExchange, 7
myStarbucks Idea, 8-10

business definition of Semantic Web, 161-162

business value
of cloud computing, 188-190
of social networking, customer interaction, 93

Butler Group, 252

buzz-tracking services, 45

C

C&C (Communication and Collaboration) Board, 261

C-Vision, 255-256

CA Collaboratory, 247

CAP theory, 149

Carr, Nicholas, 114, 150-151, 189-190

case studies, architecture/infrastructure
  Amazon, 148-149
  eBay, 146-147
  Flickr, 152
  Google, 149-151
  Twitter, 151-152
  YouTube, 147

Causes, 119

CCA (Corporate Communications Architecture), 258

CCDT (Communications & Collaboration Delivery Team), 258

CCIT (Communications & Collaboration IT), 258

CCoE (Cisco Communications Center of Excellence), 27, 135
  Cisco's adoption of Web 2.0, 258-261

CDF (Channel Definition Format), 130

CEC (Cisco Employee Connection), 224, 235

CEC Mobile, 224

challenges to Web 2.0 EE adoption, 16

Chambers, John, 142, 232, 262, 272

characteristics
  of MDP, 105-106
  of social applications, 94-95
  of Web 2.0, 16-18
    architectural models, 19-20
    cloud computing, 19
    data, 21
    long tail, 23
    mashups, 22
    mobility, 24
    RIA, 18
    scale-free nature, 23
    social networks, 19
    user-generated content, 18
    web-centric development, 19-20

Christie, Blair, 27

Circle of Friends, 98

Cisco Intranet Group, 235

Cisco mobile intranet services, 224-226

Cisco Mobility Solutions, 227

Cisco MSIS, 226-227

Cisco Partner Locator, 302

Cisco RSS Publishing Best Practices, 136-137

Cisco TelePresence, 65-66

Cisco text messaging services, 223

Cisco to partner collaboration, 299-300

Cisco UC (Unified Communications), 69-73

Cisco WebEx Meeting Center, 228

Cisco's adoption of Web 2.0, 24
  internal Web 2.0 leveraging, 27-29
  through blogs, 236-241
  through CCoE, 258-261
  through discussion forums, 241-244
  through video, 255-256
  through wikis, 245-250
  Web 2.0-centric products, 25-26

Cisco's Mobile Web strategy, 227-228

Cisco.com mobile website, 222

Ciscopedia, 250-252

CiteUlike, 57

Clearspace, 47, 107

client-side processing (RIAs), 81

Clinton, Hillary, 187

cloud application infrastructure, 185

cloud computing, 181

  as Web 2.0 meme, 19

  business value of, 188-190

  characteristics of, 182, 186

  consumers, 182

  enterprise adoption of, 198-200

  enterprise migration into, 183-184

  hardware infrastructure, 185

  layers, 185-187

  providers, 182

  vendors, 191, 198

    Amazon, 192-194

    Google, 195

    IBM, 197

    Microsoft, 195-197

  versus grids, 187-188

Cloud Data Services, 186

Cloud Platform Services, 185

collaboration

  as UGC, 65

    Cisco TelePresence, 65-66

    Unified Communications, 69-73

    WebEx, 67-69

  Cisco to partner collaboration, 299-300

  partner to partner collaboration, 300-303

Collaboration Cockpit, 289-290

Collaboration Consortium initiative, 303

Collaboration Continuum, 283

Collaboration Guide, 282, 285

Collaboration Hot Topics Newsletter, 286-288

Collaboration Library, 288

Collaboration Portal, 282

collaboration technologies, 234

  use of by Sales 2.0, 269

    Connected Communities, 270

    Finding Expertise, 270-271

    iFeedback, 276, 278

    mashups, 273

    Mobile Sales 2.0, 271-272

    Salespedia, 274-275

    Web 2.0 Explorers community site, 272-273

    WebEx Connect initiative, 275-276

communities as UGC, 63-64

Communities initiative, 253

comparing

  Sales 1.0 and Sales 2.0, 268

  Web 2.0 CE and Web 2.0 EE, 14-16

component tags (FBML), 103

confluence, 47

Connectbeam, 58

Connected Communities, 269-270

Connotea, 57

content aggregation, 125

control tags (FBML), 103

Cooper, Dr. Martin, 206

CPO (Cisco Pocket Office), 224

CUMA (Cisco Unified Mobile Communicator), 227

Cunningham, Ward, 46

customer interaction as benefit from social networking, 93

Cutting, Doug, 155

CVCM (Customer Value Chain Management) initiative, 289

D

DaaS (data as a service), 186

data as Web 2.0 meme, 21

Data Center 3.0 Blog initiative, 240

data ownership issues for social networking sites, 120-121

data parallelism, 154, 187

data portability of social networking sites, 118-119

database support for Semantic Web, 178

DCS (Dell Computing Solutions), 198

defining Web 2.0 from blogsphere, 5

Delicious, 56

Dell, cloud computing services, 198

deployment/development best practices, 156-157

design tags (FBML), 102

development of RSS, 130-131

development/deployment best practices, 156-157

DigItALL Consumer, 239

Diigo, 58

Directory 3.0, 250

disadvantages of RSS, 128

discussion forums, Cisco's adoption of Web 2.0, 241-244

DocuWiki, 47

Dodgeball, 219

Dogear, 58

Dogster, 92

Dojo, 83

Dougherty, Dale, 5

Dubey, Abhijit, 187

Dudhoria, Nikki, 251

Dunne, Kenis, 242

E

eBay, infrastructure/architecture case study, 146-147

EC2 (Elastic Compute Cloud), 185

Eclipse, 213

EDGE (Enhanced Data Rates for GSM Evolution), 205

education applications (Semantic Web), 176-177

elasticity, 182

enterprise adoption of cloud computing, 198-200

enterprise applications of Semantic Web, 176-178

enterprise migration into cloud computing, 183-184

enterprise RSS best practices, 137

ERP (Enterprise Resource Planning) systems, 144-145

evolution

of Mobile Web technology, 204

  mobile devices, 206-213

  mobile phone technology, 204-205

  mobile social networking, 219-220

  position recognition technology, 211

  voice recognition, 211

  web portals, 216-219

  webapps, 213-216

evolution of UGC

  blogs, 37-38, 42-45

  collaboration, 65-73

  communities, 63-64

  folksonomies, 60

  personal webpages, 35-37

  photos, 60, 63

  social bookmarking, 54-56, 60

  videos, 62-63

  wikis, 46, 50-54

of Web 2.0, 230

  Web 3.0, 262-263

Explorers community site, 272-273

Explorers mashup PoC, 274

ExpressionEngine, 38

F

f8, 97

Faber, Dan, 115, 197

Faceboogle, 91

Facebook, 60, 96, 219

   applications, 98-104

   architecture, 99-101

   data ownership issues, 121

   development platform, 96

   Hackathon, 97

Faves, 58

FBJS (Facebook JavaSCript), 100, 103

FBML (Facebook Markup Language),
   100

   Facebook architecture components, 102

feature velocity, 143

   development/deployment best practices,
   156-157

federation, 125

Fielding, Dr. Roy, 153

   REST, 155-156

Finding Expertise, 269-271

FireFox, Live Bookmarks facility, 135

Five to Thrive program, 278, 295-297

Flickr, 60, 63

   infrastructure/architecture case study,
   152

   website updates and development, 156

FOAF (Friends Of A Friend) project,
   117, 176

folksonomies, 60

following, 112

Forrester Research, Web 2.0 trends,
   34-35

FQL (Facebook Query Language),
   Facebook architecture components,
   101

Friendster, 105-106

Furl, 57

future of Web 2.0 at Cisco, 262-263

G

gadgets, 84

Gall's law of systemantics, 143

Gartner Hype Cycle, 16

Gdata, 141

GeoCities, 35

Getting Real, 156

Goodwin, Keith, 297

Google

   cloud computing, 195

   gadgets, 84

   infrastructure/architecture case study,
   149-151

   MapReduce, 154-155

   social networking interoperability
   interfaces, 108

Google Chrome, 85

Google File System, 150

Google Sites, 47

Google Trends, 43

Governor, James, 181

Govoni, Deanna, 238

GRDDL (Gleaning Resource
   Descriptions from Dialects of
   Languages), 167

Greenspan, Brad, 105

grids, 187-188

Grubb, Jim, 258, 261

Gtmcknight.com, 138

Guha, Dr., 130

H

Haas (hardware as a service), 185

Hackathon, 97

Hadoop, 154-155

Hansard Society, 6

Harris, Jacob, 113

Hogan, Tom, 145

Honesty Box, 98

horizontal scalability, 146, 154

HPC (high-performance computing), 187

   mainstream adoption of, 144

HTML (HyperText Markup Language), 82

HTTP (HyperText Transfer Protocol), 82

   architectural constraints, 87-88

I

I-Zone, 246

IBM

   cloud computing, 197

   Lotus Connections, 110-111

   Lotus Mashup Center, 111

iFeedback, 270, 276-278

iLike, 98

impact of Web 2.0 on society, 4

importance of Web 2.0, 3

information architecture of Atom, 140

information distribution, 127

   Atom, 128

      elements, 141

      information architecture, 140

      RFCs, 139

   RSS, 129

      best practices, 138-139

      Cisco's uses of, 135-137

      client-side operation of, 135

      disadvantages of, 128

      enterprise best practices, 137

      information architecture, 131-133

      modules, 133-134

      podcasts, 129

      precursors of, 130-131

      publishing-side operation of, 134

      readers, 135

      uses of, 135

infrastructure/architecture case studies, 144

   Amazon, 148-149

   eBay, 146-147

   Flickr, 152

   Google, 149-151

   Twitter, 151-152

   YouTube, 147

initiatives for U.S.-Canada Sales theater, 278

   advanced technologies, 291-292

   Five to Thrive, 295-297

   SOAR team, 292-295

   SPO, 279

      administrator training, 282

      Collaboration Cockpit, 289-290

      Collaboration Guide, 282, 285

      Collaboration Hot Topics, 286-288

      Collaboration Library, 288

      Collaboration Portal, 282

      Scale the Power, 281-282

      Web 2.0 Committee, 290

      WWSCB, 290

Intellipedia, 11

interface scalability, 155-156

internal Web 2.0 leveraging by Cisco, 27-29

Intranet Strategy Group, 235

iPhone, 209-210

   applications, 214

Iskod, Alex, 164

ISVs (Independent Software Vendors), 187

J

Jacoby, Rebecca, 27
JavaScript, 82
Jive, 107
Jobs, Steve, 151
Jordan, Sheila, 258
Jouret, Guido, 246
JSON, 83
JuiceCaster, 220

K

Kapow, 273
Karnadikar, Nitin, 6
key RIA technologies, 82-84
    Ajax, 85-87
    HTTP, 87-88
    OpenAjax, 88
    RoR, 89
King, Jere, 237
Koobface Trojan, 120

L

layers of cloud computing, 185-187
Lessonopoly, 20, 177
leveraging UGC, costs of, 36
LinkedIn, 104
Linux, RSS readers, 135
Live Mesh, 195
Lloyd, Rob, 269, 278
long tail as Web 2.0 meme, 23
Loopt, 220
Lords of the Blog, 6
Lotus Connections, 110-111
Lotus Mashup Center, 111
Lyons, Daniel, 43

M

Ma.gnolia, 57
Mac OS X operating system, 135
Mac Trolls, 248
MacManus, Richard, 164
Maguire, James, 191
Malik, Om, 43, 119
MapReduce, 149-150, 154-155
marketing, Collaboration Consortium
    initiative, 303
mashups, 79
    as requirement for Sales 2.0, 273
    as Web 2.0 meme, 22
MCF (Meta Content Format), 130
McManus, Rich, 5
MDP (MySpace Developer Platform),
    characteristics of, 105-106
MediaNet, 234
MediaWiki, 47
memes of Web 2.0, 16-18
    architectural models, 19-20
    cloud computing, 19
    data, 21
    long tail, 23
    mashups, 22
    mobility, 24
    RIA, 18
    scale-free nature, 23
    social networks, 19
    user-generated content, 18
    web-centric development, 19-20
messages, following, 112
metadata, 161
    RSS, 132-133
microblogging, 111-113

Microsoft
  cloud computing
      Azure, 195-197
      Live Mesh, 195
  SharePoint, 108-109
Mig33, 220
migration of enterprises into cloud computing, 183-184
Mobikade, 220
Mobile On the Spot Report, 269
Mobile Sales 2.0, 271-272
Mobile Web technology
  Cisco mobile intranet services, 224-226
  Cisco MSIS, 226-227
  Cisco text messaging services, 223
  Cisco's Mobile Web strategy, 227-228
  Cisco.com mobile website, 222
  evolution of, 204-205
  mobile devices, 206-209
      applications, 211-213
      key features, 209-210
  mobile social networking, 219-220
  position recognition technology, 211
  voice recognition, 211
  web portals, 216-219
  webapps, 213-216
MobileAware, 219
mobility, 34
  as Web 2.0 meme, 24
Mobimii, 220
MocoSpace, 220
modules (RSS), 133-134
MOS (mobile operating systems), 211
Movable Type, 38
MSIS (Mobile Sales Information Services), 225-227, 271-272
MTS (Mobile Telephone Service), 204

multi-tenancy, 182
MVC (Model-View-Controller) pattern, 89
MVS (Mobile Video Search), 221
MySpace, 105, 220
  data portability, 119
  MDP, characteristics of, 105-106

N

Navigate to Accelerate, 299
the network effect, 150
The New York Times, TimesPeople, 92
NewsGator, 138
NewsIsFree, 138
newspaper industry, Web 2.0 impact on, 10
Nielson Norman Group, 235
Ning, 106-107, 127
NNW (NetNewsWire), 135
NPR, adoption of podcasting, 129

O

O'Reilly, Tim, 18, 150-151, 232
OAuth, 117
Obama, Barack, 187
OMA (Open Mobile Alliance), 213
open standards for social networking sites, 119
OpenAjax, 83, 88
OpenCircle, 199
OpenID, 113-117
OpenSocial, 94, 114-115, 176
Oracle databases, Semantic Web support, 178
Orchant, Marc, 43
origins of Semantic Web, 167
OWL (Web Ontology Language), 167, 172-175

Owyang, Jeremiah, 113

Ozzie, Ray, 152, 196

P

PaaS (platform as a service), 185

Palm Pilot 5000, 206

Partner Locator, 302

partner to partner collaboration, 300-303

PBWiki, 47

PDAs, 206

personal blogs, 237

personal webpages, 35-37

petabyte-scale processing, 145

photos as UGC, 60-63

platform components (Facebook)

APIs, 101

FBML, 102

FQL, 101

Podcast Central, 129

PodcastAlley, 129

podcasting, 129

Podscope, 129

position recognition technology, 211

Powerset, 165-166

Pownce, 113

presidential election of 2008, impact of Web 2.0 on, 5

price structure of AWS, 194

privacy concerns for social networking sites, 119-120

Project Caroline, 197

public clouds, 181

pull, 127

push, 127

Q-R

RackSpace, 155

cloud computing services, 198

radio industry, Web 2.0 impact on, 11

RDF (Resource Description Framework), 167, 171

specifications, 169-170

triples, 169

RDF Site Summary, 130

readers (RSS), 135

registries (RSS), 128

REST (Representational State Transfer), 142, 155-156

RFCs (requests for comments), Atom-related, 139

Rhode, Donna, 279

RIA (Rich Internet Applications), 77, 80

as Web 2.0 meme, 18

client-side processing, 81

key technologies, 82-84

Ajax, 85-88

OpenAjax, 88

RoR, 89

mashups, 79

server-side processing, 81

Rightscale, 186

cloud computing services, 198

Rip, Peter, 163

RoR (Ruby on Rails), 83, 89

ROS (Remote Operating System) wiki, 54

Ross, Charlie, 106

RSS (Real Simple Syndication), 125

best practices, 138-139

business value of, 127

client-side operation of, 135

disadvantages of, 128

enterprise best practices, 137

information architecture, 131-133

modules, 133-134

podcasts, 129

precursors of, 130-131

publishing-side operation of, 134

readers, 135

registries, 128

uses for, 135-137

RSSRadio, 129

S

SaaS (Software as a Service), 143, 177, 186

Sales 1.0, versus Sales 2.0, 268

Sales 2.0, 267-268

marketing, Collaboration Consortium initiative, 303

U.S.-Canada Sales team

SPO, 279

theater initiatives, 278-297

use of collaborative technologies, 269

versus Sales 1.0, 268

Web 2.0 technology requirements

Connected Communities, 270

Finding Expertise, 270-271

iFeedback, 276, 278

mashups, 273

Mobile Sales 2.0, 271-272

Salespedia, 274-275

Web 2.0 Explorers community site, 272-273

WebEx Connect initiative, 275-276

Web technology requirements, 269

Worldwide Channels, 297-299

Cisco to partner collaboration, 299-300

partner to partner collaboration, 300-303

WWSPS, 269

Sales Rack, 273

Salesforce IdeaExchange, 7

myStarbuck Idea, 8-10

Salespedia, 269, 274-275

sanitation tags (FMBL), 102

SAPPHIRE (Situational Awareness and Preparedness for Public Health Incidences using Reasoning Engines), 164

scalability, interface scalability, 155-156

scalable architecture technologies, 152-143

scale-free nature of Web 2.0 applications, 23

Schmidt, Eric, 16, 19, 142

Scientific American, 163

Scoble, Robert, 46

Scobliezer, 46

Scrabulous, 98

ScriptingNews, 130

SEAPs (software enabled application computing), 183

security concerns for social networking sites, 119-120

Semantic Web, 163-166

business definition of, 161-162

database support, 178

education applications, 176-177

enterprise applications, 178

mobile space, 164

origins of, 167

OWL, 172-175

RDF, 169-171

SaaS platform, 177

social media applications, 176-177

SPARQL, 175

server-side processing (RIAs), 81

shard databases, 152

SharePoint, 108-109

SharePoint Online, 108

Shiky, Clay, 167

Silicon Valley Education Foundation, Lessonopoly, 20

Silverlight, 83

Simpy, 57

SIOC (semantically interlinked online communities), 177

SOAR (Specialist, Optimization, Access, and Results) team, 292-295

social applications, 94

social aspects of Web 2.0, 5-6

social banners, 120

social bookmarking, 54-56, 60

social data tags (FBML), 102

social media applications (Semantic Web), 176-177

social networking, 90

    applications, abundance of, 118

    as business tool, 118

    as Web 2.0 meme, 19

    Awareness, 108

    Blue Shirt Nation, 94

    business value of, customer interaction, 93

    data ownership issues, 120-121

    data portability, 118-119

    Dogster, 92

    Faceboogle, 91

    Facebook, 96

        applications, 98-99, 103-104

        architecture, 99-102

        development platform, 96

        Hackathon, 97

    Friendster, 105-106

Google, 108

IBM

    Lotus Connections, 110-111

    Lotus Mashup Center, 111

Jive, 107

LinkedIn, 104

Microsoft SharePoint, 108-109

mobile social networking, 219-220

MySpace, 105-106

Ning, 106-107

open standards, 119

OpenID, 113

security concerns, 119-120

social applications, 94-95

Socialtext, 107

standards

    foaf project, 117

    OAuth, 117

    OpenID, 115-117

    OpenSocial, 114-115

    XFN, 117

TimesPeople, 92

Twitter, 111-113

viral nature of, 92

worldwide acceptance of, 121

SocialCalendar, 99

SocialMix, 199

Socialtext, 47, 52-54, 107

SONA (Service Oriented Network Architecture), 270

SPARQL, 167, 175

SPO (Sales Planning & Operations), 279

    administrator training, 282

    Collaboration Cockpit, 289-290

    Collaboration Guide, 282, 285

    Collaboration Hot Topics, 286-288

    Collaboration Library, 288

Collaboration Portal, 282

Scale the Power initiative, 281-282

Web 2.0 Committee, 290

WWSCB, 290

SquirrelFish Extreme JavaScript engine, 85

StadiumVision, 233

standards for social networking

FOAF project, 117

OAuth, 117

OpenID, 115-117

OpenSocial, 114-115

XFN, 117

Starbucks, myStarbucks Idea, 8-10

STP (Scale the Power) initiative, 281-282

Stumbleupon, 57

Sun Microsystems, cloud computing, 197

Superwall, 98

syndication, 125

T

tags (FBML), 102

Talis, 177

Tam, Patrick, 247

task parallelism, 187

TB (terabyte), 145

technologies for scalable architectures, 152-153

Technorati, 43, 128

TelePresence, 65, 262

text messaging, Cisco text messaging services, 223

The Big Switch: Rewiring the World, From Edison to Google, 189-190

TikiWiki CMS/Groupware, 50

Times, 135

TimesPeople, 92

Tobias, Craig, 245

training, for U.S.-Canada Sales team administrators, 282

triples, 169

TSN (Technology Solutions Network), 292

tutorials for podcasts, 129

Twine, 165-166

Twitter, 111-113

following, 112

infrastructure/architecture case study, 151-152

microblogging, 113

"two-pizza teams", 148

TypePad, 38

U

U.S.-Canada Sales team, 269

theater initiatives, 278

advanced technologies, 291-292

Five to Thrive, 295-297

SOAR team, 292-295

SPO, 279-282, 285-290

Web 2.0 technology requirements, 269

Connected Communities, 270

Finding Expertise, 270-271

iFeedback, 276, 278

mashups, 273

Mobile Sales 2.0, 271-272

Salespedia, 274-275

Web 2.0 Explorers community site, 272-273

WebEx Connect intiative, 275-276

UGC

blogs, 37-38, 42-43, 45

collaboration, 65

Cisco TelePresence, 65-66

Unified Communications, 69-73

WebEx, 67-69

communities, 63-64

folksonomies, 60

personal webpages, 35-37

photos, 60, 63

social bookmarking, 54-56, 60

videos, 62-63

wikis, 46, 50-54

UM (unified messaging), 71

Unified Communications, 69, 71-73

user-generated content as Web 2.0 meme, 18

V

vendors of cloud computing, 191, 198

Amazon, 192-194

Google, 195

IBM, 197

Microsoft

Azure, 195-197

Live Mesh, 195

Sun, 197

versions of the web, 11

Web 1.0, 13

Web 1.5, 13

Web 2.0, 13

Web 3.0, 14

vertical scalability, 154

video, Cisco's adoption of Web 2.0, 255-256

videos as UGC, 62-63

viral nature of social networking, 92

Virtual Demos, 294

ViryaNet, 219

vlogs, 38

Vogels, Werner, 148, 153

voice recognition technology, 211

vSearch, 294

Vyew, 199

W

Walters, Chris, 121

WAP Forum, 213

WASPs (Wireless Application Service Providers), 218

Wayback Machine, petabyte-scale processing, 145

Web 1.0, 13

Web 1.5, 13

Web 2.0, 13

adoption of at Cisco, 234

Intranet Strategy Group, 235

through blogs, 236-241

through CCoE, 258-261

through discussion forums, 241-244

through video, 255-256

through wikis, 245-250

impact on society, 4

Web 2.0 CE (Consumer Edition), 143

versus Web 2.0 EE, 14-15

Web 2.0 Committee, 290

Web 2.0 EE (Enterprise Edition)

adoption challenges, 16

versus Web 2.0 CE, 14-15

Web 2.0 Explorers, 269, 272-273

Web 2.0 meme map, 17

Web 3.0, 11, 14, 160-263

web portals, 216-219

web-centric development as Web 2.0 meme, 19-20

webapps, 213-216

WebEx, 67-69

Webex Connect, 26

as requirement for Sales 2.0, 275-276

Wetpaint, 50

white papers, Collaboration Library, 288

widgets, 84

wiki farms, 47

Wikia, 50

wikis, 46, 50-54

   Cisco's adoption of Web 2.0, 245-250

   Connected Communities, 270

   key features, 50

Winer, Dave, 130

"wisdom of the crowds", 65

Woods, Tiger, 22

WordPress, 38

Wordscraper, 98

worldwide acceptance of social networking, 121

Worldwide Channels, 297-299

   Cisco to partner collaboration, 299-300

   partner to partner collaboration, 300-303

WWSCB (Worldwide Sales Collaboration Board), 290

WWSPS (Worldwide Sales Processes and Systems), 269

   Web 2.0 technology requirements

      Connected Communities, 270

      Finding Expertise, 270-271

      iFeedback, 276-278

      mashups, 273

      Mobile Sales 2.0, 271-272

      Salespedia, 274-275

      Web 2.0 Explorers community site, 272-273

      WebEx Connect initiative, 275-276

X-Y-Z

XFN (XHTML Friends Network), 117

XHTML, 83

XML

   Atom elements, 141

   RSS metadata, 132-133

XMLHttpRequest, 83

Yahoo Audio Search, adoption of podcasts, 129

Yahoo! Pipes, 138

Yahoo! widgets, 84

Yahoo! Go version 2, 217

Yahoo! Mobile, 216

Yourdon, Ed, 17

YouTube, 62-63

   infrastructure/architecture case study, 147

Zuckerberg, Mark, 96, 121

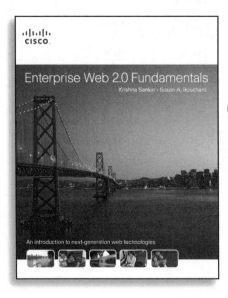

FREE Online Edition

Your purchase of **Enterprise Web 2.0 Fundamentals** includes access to a free online edition for 45 days through the Safari Books Online subscription service. Nearly every Cisco Press book is available online through Safari Books Online, along with more than 5,000 other technical books and videos from publishers such as Addison-Wesley Professional, Exam Cram, IBM Press, O'Reilly, Prentice Hall, Que, and Sams.

SAFARI BOOKS ONLINE allows you to search for a specific answer, cut and paste code, download chapters, and stay current with emerging technologies.

Activate your FREE Online Edition at www.informit.com/safarifree

> **STEP 1:** Enter the coupon code: ZAGYZAA.

> **STEP 2:** New Safari users, complete the brief registration form.
> Safari subscribers, just log in.

If you have difficulty registering on Safari or accessing the online edition, please e-mail customer-service@safaribooksonline.com